JOHN WILLIS

SCREEN WORLD

1987

Volume 38

CROWN PUBLISHERS, INC.

NEW YORK

Copyright © 1987 by John Willis. All rights reserved. Manufactured in U.S.A.
Library of Congress Card No. 50-3023
ISBN 0-517-56615-X

1964

1967

in "A Walk With Love and Death"
1969

Director of "The Bible"
1970

as Noah in "The Bible"
1970

in "Chinatown"
1974

1982

in "Observations under the Volcano"
1984

Directing "Prizzi's Honor"
1985

2

TO

JOHN HUSTON

one of our most creative, masterful, and respected craftsmen, who has left his signature on a great and rich diversity of memorable films filled with realistic details as an actor, director, and writer.

MARLEE MATLIN AND WILLIAM HURT
in "Children of a Lesser God"
© *Paramount Pictures*

4

CONTENTS

EDITOR: JOHN WILLIS

Assistant Editors: Stanley Reeves, Walter Willison

Staff: Joe Baltake, Marco Starr Boyajian, William Camp, Mark Cohen, Mark Gladstone,
Miles Kreuger, Giovanni Romero, John Sala, Van Williams
Designer: Peggy Goddard

Acknowledgments: This volume would not be possible without the cooperation of Ian Abrams, Stacy Adams, Marlene Adelstein, Gary Aldeman, Tom Allen, Jane Alsobrook, Eden Ashley, David Badagliacca, Fred Baker, Nina Baron, David Bass, Karen Basto, Mike Berman, Jim Bertges, Marion Billings, Seymour Borde, Michael Brady, Joseph Brenner, Susan Brockman, Michael Broidy, Donette Brown, Don Buckley, Ken Burns, John Calhoun, Fabiano Canosa, Philip Castanza, Helen Cavanaugh, Howard Cherman, Phyllis Ciccone, Anne Cochran, Ben Commack, Robert Conkling, Bill Connelly, Karen Cooper, Gary Croudus, Lynne Dahlgren, Alberta D'Angelo, James Darbinian, Ira Deutchman, Donna Dickman, Anne Dillon, Michael Donnelly, Bob Dorfman, Dennis Dorph, Betty Einbinder, Allison Enelio, Catherine Ericson, Steve Fagan, Suzanne Fedak, Al Finley, Mary Lou Finnin, Elliott Fishoff, Rodman Flender, Peter Flynn, Dom Frascella, Renee Furst, Glennis Gold, Ted Goldberg, Thomas Grane, Joseph Green, Loritta Green, Christina Haller, Lisa Halliday, Mark Halpern, Allison Hanau, Peter Haas, Richard Hassanein, Ted Hatfield, Stan Hayes, Amy Heller, Gary Hertz, Lauren Hyman, Lloyd Ibert, Sam Irvin, Jeffrey Jacobs, Michael Jeck, Jim Jeneji, Terry Johnson, Stephen Jones, Andy Kaplan, Mike Kaplan, Steve Kasloff, Helen Kavanaugh, Michael Kelly, Bill Kenly, Ken Kenyon, Thomas Keough, Allison Kossow, Don Krim, Richard Kronberg, Jack Kurnes, Ann Lander, Maryanne Lataif, Lori Long, Wynn Lowenthal, Peter Lowry, Arlene Ludwig, Jeff Mackler, Steve Mackler, Cathy Magill, Howard Mahler, Craig Marks, Barbara Marshall, Ed Martin, Jane Martin, Pricilla McDonald, Jeff McKay, Blanca Merced, Lou Morino, Paul Mowry, Robert Newcombe, Bill O'Connell, Ivy Orfa, Kevan Olesen, Sue Oscar, Cynthia Parsons, Chris Paton, Janet Perlberg, John Pierson, Jim Poling, Gerald Rappoport, Jackie Rayanal, David Restivo, David Rice, Ruth Robbins, Reid Rosefelt, Melisa Rosen, Richard Rosenberg, Kelly Ross, Mary Runsen, Ed Russell, Cindy Ryfle, Suzanne Salter, Carl Samrock, Jeff Saxon, Les Schecter, Barbara Schwei, George Schrul, Russell Schwartz, Mike Scrimenti, Eve Segal, Ron Sherwin, Jacqueline Sigmund, Marcia Silen, Michael Silverman, Bill Slobodian, Stephen Soba, Fran Speelman, Barbara Sperry, Alicia Springer, John Springer, Anne Marie Stein, Larry Steinfeld, Moira Stokes, Stuart Strutin, Ken Stutz, Sarah Talbot, John Tilley, Maureen Tolsdorf, Bruce Trinz, Mary Vole, Debbie von Aherns, Marc Weiss, Cara White, David Whitten, Christopher Wood, David Wright, Jane Wright, Stuart Zakim, Michael Zuker

1. Tom Cruise

2. Eddie Murphy

3. Paul Hogan

4. Rodney Dangerfield

5. Bette Midler

6. Sylvester Stallone

7. Clint Eastwood

8. Whoopi Goldberg

9. Kathleen Turner

10. Paul Newman

11. Michael J. Fox

12. Sigourney Weaver

13. Robert Redford

14. Ralph Macchio

15. Chevy Chase

16. Jane Fonda

TOP BOXOFFICE STARS OF 1986
(Tabulated by Quigley Publications)

17. Matthew Broderick   18. Michael Douglas   19. Harrison Ford   20. Woody Allen

1986 RELEASES

January 1 through December 31, 1986

21. Rob Lowe   22. Leonard Nimoy   23. William Shatner   24. Meryl Streep

25. William Hurt   Madonna   Tom Hanks   Goldie Hawn

THE BEST OF TIMES

(UNIVERSAL) Producer, Gordon Carroll; Director, Roger Spottiswode; Screenplay, Ron Shelton; Photography, Charles F. Wheeler; Designer, Anthony Brockliss; Editor, Garth Craven; Costumes, Patricia Norris; Music, Arthur B. Rubinstein; Production Manager, Joel Glickman; Assistant Directors, James Robert Dyer, Harry V. Bring; Associate Producer, Fredda Weiss; Visual Consultant, David Nichols; Sound, Kirk Francis, Hudson Marquez; Production Coordinator, Fran Roy; Costume Supervisors, Ellis Cohen, Nancy McArdle; Costumer, Dan Bronson; Orchestration, Mark Hoder; Choreographer, Linda Hart; Songs by various artists; Presented by Kings Road Entertainment; Technicolor; Panavision; Rated PG13; 105 minutes; January release

CAST

Jack Dundee	Robin Williams
Reno Hightower	Kurt Russell
Gigi Hightower	Pamela Reed
Elly Dundee	Holly Palance
The Colonel	Donald Moffat
Darla	Margaret Whitton
Charlie	M. Emmet Walsh
Eddie	Donovan Scott
Schutte	R. G. Armstrong
Mac	Dub Taylor
Arturo	Carl Ballantine
Rosie	Kathleen Freeman
Chico	Tony Plana
Teddy	Kirk Cameron
Jaki	Robyn Lively
Carlos	Eloy Casados
Olin	Jeff Doucette
Marcy	Anne Haney
Luther Jackson	Bill Overton
Mando	Peter Van Norden
Ronny	Patrick Brennan
Johnny "O"	Jeff Severson
Dickie Larue	Hap Lawrence
Bam Bam	Nick Shields
Old Man Lester	Hugh Stanger
Felipe	Wayne Montanio
"Iron Jaws"	"Iron Jaws" Wilson
Mrs. Jackson	Brenda Huggins
Michelle	Hilary Davis
Blade	Michael Rich

and William Schilling, Hugh Gillin, Jake Dengel, Linda Hart, Marie Cain, Peggy Moyer, Norm Schachter, Christopher Mankiewicz, J. P. Bumstead, Robert Dickman, Jim Giovanni, Steve Shargo, Darryl B. Smith, Wayne Adderson, Raymond W. Clanton, Fred A. Nelson, Vister Hayes, Michelle Guastello, Cathy Cheryl Davis, Susan Signorelli, Philipe Gerard, Christopher Cory, and Buck

Right: Holly Palance, Robin Williams
Top: Kurt Russell, Robin Williams
Pamela Reed © Universal

Robin Williams, Kurt Russell

Margaret Whitton, Robin Williams

BLACK MOON RISING

(NEW WORLD) Producers, Joel B. Michaels, Douglas Curtiss; Director, Harley Cokliss; Screenplay, John Carpenter, Desmond Nakano, William Gray; Story, John Carpenter; Photography, Misha Suslov; Designer, Bryan Ryman; Editor, Todd Ramsay; Music, Lalo Schifrin; Costumes, Jack Buehler; Production Manager, George W. Perkins; Assistant Directors, Betsy Magruder, Rip Murray, Josh King; Visual Effects, Max W. Anderson; Production Coordinator, Coni Lancaster; Sound, Jonathan Stein, Steve Nelson; Stunts, Bud Davis; Special Effects, Larry Cavanaugh, Bruce Steinheimer, Al Bartoli, Casey Cavanaugh; Assistant Art Director, Miles Ciletti; Set Decorator, Aleka Corwin; Special Effects Props/Electronics, Brent Scrivner; Special Visual Effects, Cinemotion Pictures Inc./Jonathan Seay, David Stump; Color; Rated R; 100 minutes; January release

CAST

Quint	Tommy Lee Jones
Nina	Linda Hamilton
Ryland	Robert Vaughn
Earl Windom	Richard Jaeckel
Ringer	Lee Ving
Johnson	Bubba Smith
Billy Lyons	Dan Shor
Tyke Thayden	William Sanderson
Iron John	Keenan Wynn
Luis	Nick Cassavetes
Frenchie	Don Opper
Reynoso	William Marquez
Boy in Grocery Store	David Pressman
The Mover	Stanley DeSantis
Mr. Melato	Richard Angarola
Mr. Emilio	Edward Parone
Windbreaker Man	Bill Moody
Maintenance Man	Al White
Ryland's Receptionist	Lana Lancaster
Maitre D'	Dalton Cathey
Waiter	Townsend Coleman
Foreman	Dave Adams
Officer	Rudy Daniels
Mechanic's	E. J. Castillo, Peterson Banks
Technician's	Frank Dent, Steve Fifield
Ringer's Men	Carl Ciarfalio, Don Pulford
Man in Cul-De-Sac	Vincent Pandoliano
Watchman	David Donham
Casino Security	Doug McHugh, Eric Trules
Redhead	Lisa London

and Greg Gault, Debbie Evans, Pete Antico, Michael Haynes, Dennis R. Scott, Bud Ekins, Polly Burson, Chuck Hart, Carey Loftin, Gary Davis, Beau Gibson, J. N. Roberts, Randy Hall

**Right: Tommy Lee Jones, and
Top with Keenan Wynn** © *New World*

**Richard Jaeckel, Tommy Lee Jones,
Don Opper**

**Bill Moody, Linda Hamilton,
Bubba Smith**

DOWN AND OUT IN BEVERLY HILLS

(TOUCHSTONE) Producer/Director, Paul Mazursky; Screenplay, Paul Mazursky, Leon Capetans; Based upon the play *Boudu Sauve Des Eaux* by Rene Fauchois; Co-Producer/Designer, Pato Guzman; Photography, Donald McAlpine; Editor, Richard Halsey; Costumes, Albert Wolsky; Music, Andy Summers; Associate Producer, Geoffrey Taylor; Production Manager, John Broderick; Assistant Directors, Peter Bogart, Eric Jewett, Jodi Ehrlich; Art Director, Todd Hallowell; Set Decorator, Jane Bogart; Sound, Jim Webb, Crew Chamberlain, William Stevenson, Carl Mahakian; Production Coordinator, Kool Lusby; Hair, Renate Leuschner-Pless; Assistant Editor, Frank E. Jimenez; Special Effects, Ken Speed; Choreographer, Bob Banas; Presented in association with Silver Screen Partners II; Color; Panavision; Dolby Stereo; Rated R; 97 minutes; January release

CAST

Jerry Baskin	Nick Nolte
Dave Whiteman	Richard Dreyfuss
Barbara Whiteman	Bette Midler
Orvis Goodnight	Little Richard
Jenny Whiteman	Tracy Nelson
Carmen	Elizabeth Pena
Max Whiteman	Evan Richards
Matisse	Mike
Dr. Von Zimmer	Donald F. Muhich
Sidney Waxman	Paul Mazursky
Pearl Waxman	Valerie Curtin
Mel Whiteman	Jack Bruskoff
Sadie Whiteman	Geraldine Dreyfuss
Lou Waltzberg	Barry Primus
Sheila Waltzberg	Irene Tsu
Nagamichi	Michael Yama
Ranbir	Ranbir Bahi
Al	Felton Perry
Tom Tom	Eloy Casados
Ed	Michael Greene
Patrick	Ken Koch
Dorothy	Dorothy Tristan
Yamato	Raymond Lee
Roxanne	Sue Kiel
Lance	Jason Williams
Geraldo	Darryl Henriques
Nigel	Nick Ullett
Cop	Michael Blue
Caterer	Allan Malamud
Caterer's Assistant	Salvatore Espinoza
Maurice	Michael Voletti
Barry	Sandy Ignon
Sandra Goodnight	Margrit Ramme
Translator	Pearl Huang
Minister Chan	Yung Sun
Dr. Toni Grant	Herself

and Carolyn Allport, Reza Bashar, Joseph Makkar, Betsy Mazursky, Donald V. Allen, Neil Cunningham, Bobby Good, Eugene Choy, Mae Koh-Ruden, George Sasaki, Leland Sun, Andre Philippe, Lew Hopson, Carlton Cuse, Bill Cross, Alexis Arquette

Left: Bette Midler Above: Nick Nolte
Top: Nick Nolte © *Touchstone*

Right: Richard Dreyfuss, Nick Nolte

Richard Dreyfuss, Nick Nolte

**Margrit Ramme, Little Richard, Bette Midler,
Richard Dreyfuss (also above)
Top: Little Richard**

**Richard Dreyfuss, Tracy Nelson
Above: Mike as Matisse
Top: Bette Midler**

11

POWER

(20th CENTURY-FOX) Producers, Reene Schisgal, Mark Tarlov; Director, Sidney Lumet; Screenplay, David Himmelstein; Associate Producers, Wolfgang Glattes, Kenneth Utt; Photography, Andrzej Bartkowiak; Designer, Peter Larkin; Costumes, Anna Hill Johnstone; Editor, Andrew Mondshein; Music, Cy Coleman; Production Manager, Kenneth Utt; Assistant Directors, Wolfgang Glattes, Anthony Gittelson; Sound, Chris Newman; Art Director, William Barclay; Set, Thomas C. Tonery, Kenneth Kammerer; Production Coordinator, Grace Blake; Orchestrations, Sonny Kompanek; Video Segments Producer, Lynn M. Klugman; Technicolor; Panavision; Rated R; 111 minutes; January release

Kate Capshaw   **Denzel Washington**

CAST

Pete St. John .... Richard Gere
Ellen Freeman .... Julie Christie
Wilfred Buckley .... Gene Hackman
Sydney Betterman .... Kate Capshaw
Arnold Billings .... Denzel Washington
Senator Sam Hastings .... E. G. Marshall
Claire Hastings .... Beatrice Straight
Wallace Furman .... Fritz Weaver
Governor Andrea Stannard .... Michael Learned
Jerome Cade .... J. T. Walsh
Irene Furman .... E. Katherine Kerr
Lucille DeWitt .... Polly Rowles
Phillip Aarons .... Matt Salinger
Sheikh .... Tom Mardirosian
Roberto Cepeda .... Omar Torres
Interpreter .... Ricardo Gallarzo
Helen .... Jessica James
Frank McKusker .... Glenn Kezer
David Garber .... Douglas Newell
Ralph Andropwicz .... Scott Harlan
Wilson Jacobs .... Nick Flynn
Charles Whiting .... Ed VanNuys
Leonard Thompson .... Noel Harrison
The Voice .... Jackson Beck
and Leila Danette, Kevin Hagen, Timothy Jecko, Margaret Barker, D. B. Sweeney, Linda DeNiro, Lynn Klugman, John Robert Evans, Elizabeth Kendrick, Jim Hartz, Roger Grimsby, Margaret Hall, Brad Holbrook, Donna Hanover, Frank Casey, Kristi Witker, Marvin Scott, Daryl Edwards, Martha Pinson, Jack Zahniser, Burke Pearson, Janet Sarno, Robert Fieldsteel, Gregory Wagrowski, Ron Stein, Robert Kruger

Right: Gene Hackman, Richard Gere
© *Lorimar*

Richard Gere, Julie Christie

PRETTY IN PINK

(PARAMOUNT) Producer, Laren Shuler; Director, Howard Deutch; Screenplay, John Hughes; Executive Producers, John Hughes, Michael Chinich; Photography, Tak Fujimoto; Designer, John W. Corso; Editor, Richard Marks; Costumes, Marilyn Vance; Music, Michael Gore; Music Supervision, David Anderle; Associate Producer, Jane Vickerilla; Production Manager, Arne Schmidt; Assistant Directors, Stephen Lim, Carol L. Green; Production Associates, Karen Kovacevich, Elena Spiotta; Associate Editor, Jane Schwartz Jaffe; Sets, Louis M. Mann; Sound, C. Darin Knight; Orchestrations, L. Leon Pendarvis; Choreographer, Kenny Ortega; Special Effects, John Frazier; Songs by various artists; Soundtrack album on A&M Records; Technicolor; Panavision-Dolby Stereo; Rated PG-13; 96 minutes; January release

CAST

Andie	Molly Ringwald
Jack	Harry Dean Stanton
Duckie	Jon Cryer
Iona	Anne Potts
Steff	James Spader
Blane	Andrew McCarthy
Donnelly	Jim Haynie
Jena	Alexa Kenin
Benny	Kate Vernon
Bouncer	Andrew "Dice" Clay
Kate	Emily Longstreth
English Teacher	Margaret Colin
Terrence	Jamie Anders
Girl Friend/Gym Class	Gina Gershon
Sales Girl	Bader Howar
Boy in record store	Christian Jacobs
Benny's Mom	Audre Johnston
Girl at party	Melanie Manos
Mrs. Dietz	Maggie Roswell
Simon	Dweezil Zappa
The Rave-Ups	Jimmer Podrasky, Tommy Blatnik, Timothy J., Terry Wilson
Talk Back	Bruno, Jeffrey Hollie, Kevin Ricard, David Sutton, Kevin Williams, Rock Deadrick
Girl at prom	Karen Laine
Duckette	Kristy Swanson
Kevin	Kevin D. Lindsay

Right: Jon Cryer, Annie Potts, Molly Ringwald © *Paramount*

Andrew McCarthy, Molly Ringwald

James Spader, Molly Ringwald

Dweezil Zappa, Alexa Kenin, Molly Ringwald

Molly Ringwald, Harry Dean Stanton

13

THE ADVENTURES OF MARK TWAIN

(ATLANTIC) Producer/Director, Will Vinton; Executive Producer, Hugh Tirrell; Associate Producer/Screenplay, Susan Shadburne; Music, Billy Scream; Character Designer, Barry Bruce; Set Design, Joan C. Gratz, Don Merkt; Clayanimators, Barry Bruce, William L. Fiesterman, Tom Gasek, Mark Gustafson, Craig Bartlett, Bruce McKean; Production Supervisor/General Manager, David Altschul; Production Coordinator, Patricia von Hinckeldey; Editors, Kelley Baker, Michael Gall, Will Vinton, Ed Ghis, Skeets McGrew; Sound, Andy Wiskes, Gary McRobert, Kelley Baker; Song, Billy Scream, Susan Shadburne; Vocals, Craig Carothers; Creative Consultant, Walter Murch; In Claymation; Color; Rated G; 90 minutes; January release

VOICE CAST

Mark Twain	James Whitmore
Tom Sawyer	Chris Ritchie
Huck Finn	Gary Krug
Becky Thatcher	Michele Mariana
Adam	John Morrison
Eve	Carol Edelman
Jim Smiley/Newspaper Boy	Dallas McKennon
The Stranger	Herb Smith
Aunt Polly	Marley Stone
The Mysterious Stranger	Michele Mariana, Wilbur Vincent
Capt. Stormfield	Wally Newman
Three-Headed Alien	Tim Conner
St. Peter	Todd Tolces
The Indexivator	Billy Scream
Dan'l Webster	Wilf Innton
Homer	Tom Gasek
Injun Joe	Compton Downs
God	Billy Victor

Mark Twain with the voice of James Whitmore

Rutger Hauer, C. Thomas Howell

THE HITCHER

(TRI-STAR) Producers, David Bombyk, Kip Ohman; Director, Robert Harmon; Screenplay, Eric Red; Executive Producers, Edward S. Feldman, Charles R. Meeker; Photography, John Seale; Designer, Dennis Gassner; Editor, Frank J. Urioste; Co-Producer/Production Manager, Paul Lewis; Music, Mark Isham; Assistant Directors, Craig Beaudine, Leigh Webb; Sound, Art Names, Warren Hamilton, Jr.; Special Effects, Art Brewer; Sound Effects, Mark Mangini, Stephen Flick; Song, Mickey Jones; Presented by HBO Pictures in Association with Silver Screen Partners; Metrocolor; Panavision; Dolby Stereo; Rated R; 97 minutes; February release

CAST

John Ryder	Rutger Hauer
Jim Halsey	C. Thomas Howell
Nash	Jennifer Jason Leigh
Capt. Esteridge	Jeffrey DeMunn
Sgt. Starr	John Hackson
Trooper Donner	Billy Greenbush
Trooper Prestone	Jack Thibeau
Interrogation Sergeant	Armin Shimerman
Trooper Dodge	Eugene Davis
Trooper Hapscomb	Jon Van Ness
Trooper Hancock	Henry Darrow
Trooper Conners	Tony Epper
Proprietor	Tom Spratley
Construction Man	Colin Cambel

Left Center: Rutger Hauer, C. Thomas Howell
© *Tri-Star*

WILDCATS

(WARNER BROS.) Producer, Anthea Sylbert; Director, Michael Ritchie; Screenplay, Ezra Sacks; Photography, Donald E. Thorin; Designer, Boris Leven; Editor, Richard A. Harris; Music, Hawk Wolinski, James Newton Howard; Associate Producer/Production Manager, Gordon A. Webb; Assistant Directors, Tom Mack, Emmitt-Leon O'Neil; Sound, Ronald A. Jacobs, Jim Alexander; Marching Band Music, Phil Marshall; Ms. Hawn's Costumes, Wayne A. Finkelman; Costumes, Eddie Marks; Choreography, Joel Hall, Paula Tracy Smuin; Special Effects, Cliff Wenger; Songs by various artists; A Hawn/Sylbert Production; Technicolor; Panavision; Dolby Stereo; Rated R; 107 minutes; February release

CAST

Molly	Goldie Hawn
Verna	Swoosie Kurtz
Alice	Robyn Lively
Marian	Brandy Gold
Frank	James Keach
Stephanie	Jan Hooks
Darwell	Bruce McGill
Edwards	Nipsy Russell
Bird	Mykel T. Williamson
Finch	Tab Thacker
Trumaine	Wesley Snipes
Cerulo	Nick Corri
Krushinski	Woody Harrelson
Marvel	Willie J. Walton
Peanut	Rodney Hill
Central Player	Lindsey Orr
Alonzo	Albert Michel
Translator	Eddie Frescas
Coes	M. Emmet Walsh
Marva	Ellia English
Jeannie	Jenny Havens
Mr. Remo	Tony Salome
Principal Walker	George Wyner
Doctor	Noel De Souza
Mrs. Chatham	Ann Doran
Mrs. Connoly	Gloria Stuart
Angelique	Pilar Delano
Mayhew	Bruce French

and Royce Wallace, Hakeem, Lee Weaver, L. L. Cool J., Vincent Isaac, Stan Foster, Dap "Sugar" Willie, Chino "Fats" Williams, John Vargas, David Kanakes, David Nieker, Tom E. Willman, Gwen McGee, Tan'ya Harris, Deborah Webber, Gary Austin, Richard B. Brown, Sylvester Blaylock, Steven L. Carlson

Left: Goldie Hawn, Mykel T. Williamson
(also at top) © *Warner Bros.*

Robin Lively, Brandy Gold,
Goldie Hawn

Goldie Hawn

HANNAH AND HER SISTERS

(ORION) Producer, Robert Greenhut; Director, Screenplay, Wood Allen; Executive Producers, Jack Rollins, Charles H. Joffe; Photography, Carlo Di Palma; Designer, Stuart Wurtzel; Costumes, Jeffr Kurland; Editor, Susan E. Morse; Associate Producer, Gail Sicil Production Manager, Ezra Swerdlow; Assistant Directors, Thom Reilly, Ken Ornstein; Production Coordinator, Helen Robin; Soun Les Lazarowitz, Tod Maitland, Lee Dichter; Songs by various artist Technicolor; Panavision; Rated PG-13; 107 minutes; February releas

CAST

Mickey	Woody Alle
Elliot	Michael Cain
Hannah	Mia Farro
April	Carrie Fish
Lee	Barbara Hersh
Hannah's Father	Lloyd Nola
Hannah's Mother	Maureen O'Sulliva
Dusty	Daniel Ster
Frederick	Max von Sydo
Holly	Dianne Wie
Paul	Lewis Blac
Mary	Julia Louis-Dreyf
Larry	Christian Clemensc
Gail	Julie Kavn
Ed Smythe	J. T. Wals
Writer	John Turtur
Ron	Rusty Mage
Hannah's Twins	Allen Decheser, Artie Deches
Dr. Abel	Ira Wheel
Dr. Wilkes	Richard Jenki
Brunch Guest	Tracy Kenne
Dr. Grey	Fred Melame
Dr. Smith	Benno Schmi
Carol	Joanna Gleasc
Manon Lescaut	Maria Chia
Dr. Brooks	Stephen Defluit
Rock Band	The 39 Step
Himself	Bobby Sho

and Rob Scott, Beverly Peer, Daisy Previn, Moses Farrow, Paul Bate Carrotte, Mary Pappas, Bernie Leighton, Ken Costigan, Helen Mille Leo Postrel, Susan Gordon-Clark, William Sturgis, Daniel Habe Verna O. Hobson, John Doumanian, Fletcher Previn, Irwin Tener baum, Amy Greenhill, Dickson Shaw, Marje Sheridan, Iva Kronenfeld

Left Center: Barbara Hershey, Max von Sydow, Daniel Stern, Michael Caine Top: Woody Allen © Orion

1986 Academy Awards For Best Original Screenplay, Best Supporting Actress (Dianne Wiest), Best Supporting Actor (Michael Caine)

Mia Farrow, Michael Caine

Sam Waterston, Carrie Fisher

Lloyd Nolan, Maureen O'Sullivan with children
Top: Mia Farrow, Barbara Hershey, Dianne Wiest

(Pictured on Book Jacket)

9½ WEEKS

(MGM/UA) Producers, Antony Rufus Isaacs, Zalman King; Director, Adrian Lyne; Screenplay, Patricia Knop, Zalman King, Sarah Kernochan; Based on the novel by Elizabeth McNeill; Executive Producers, Keith Barish, Frank Konigsberg; Photography, Peter Biziou; Designer, Ken Davis; Editors, Tom Rolf, Caroline Biggerstaff; Costumes, Bobbie Read; Music, Jack Nitzsche, Michael Hoenig; Music Supervision, Becky Mancuso; Production Executive, Robert E. Relyea; Co-Executive Producer, Richard Northcott; Production Manager, Roger Paradiso; Assistant Directors, Benjy Rosenberg, Kyle McCarthy; Associate Producers, Steven D. Reuther, Stephen J. Ross; Art Director, Linda Conaway-Parsloe; Set Decorator, Christian Kelly; Sound, Bill Daly; Assistant Costume Designer, Aude Bronson-Howard; Special Effects, Dan Kirshoff; Music Coordinators, Gaylon J. Horton, Elliot Lurie, Judy Ross; Presented by Producers Sales Organization and Sidney Kimmel; from Jonesfilm; Songs by various artists; Original Soundtrack on Capitol; Dolby Stereo; Panavision; Technicolor; Rated R; 113 minutes; February release

CAST

John	Mickey Rourke
Elizabeth	Kim Basinger
Molly	Margaret Whitton
Harvey	David Margulies
Thea	Christine Baranski
Sue	Karen Young
Ted	William De Acutis
Farnsworth	Dwight Weist
Sinclair, the Critic	Roderick Cook
Gallery Client	Victor Truro
Bedding Saleswoman	Justine Johnston
Whore	Cintia Cruz
Chinatown Butcher	Kim Chan
Angry Chinatown Customer	Lee Lai Sing
Chinatown Shopper	Rudolph Willrich
Flea Market Shawl Seller	Helen Hanft
Flea Market Chicken Seller	Michael P. Moran
Flower Delivery Boy	Raynor Scheine
Bruce	Olek Krupa
Michael	Michael Margotta
Riding Crop Salesman	Peter Pagan
Italian Singer	Terri Perri
Soap Opera Woman	Kim Michel
Soap Opera Man	Jeff Severson
Clothing Saleswoman	Corvova Choy Lee
John's Secretary	Ellen Barber
Jewelry Saleswoman	Ethel Ayler
Perfume Lady	Elizabeth Senn

and Julian Beck, John P. Connolly, Cassandra Danz, Beata Jachulski, Charles Malota, Daniel E. Amrich, Salvatore Sciangula, Dan Lauria, Corey Parker, Joe Maruzzo, Tom Traino, Gittan Goding, David M. Everard, Luther Rucker, Joey Silvera, Petina Cole, Mary Clayton, Kim Isaacson, Sarah Kernochan, David Tabor, Sandy Alexander, Leslie Arnett, Peter Bucossi, Sandy Richman, Webster Whinery

Top Right: Kim Basinger, Mickey Rourke (also below) © MGM/UA Entertainment

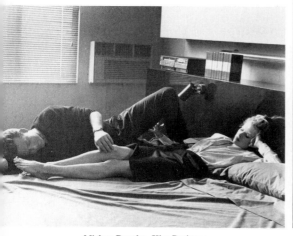

Mickey Rourke, Kim Basinger

Mickey Rourke, Kim Basinger

THE DELTA FORCE

(CANNON GROUP) Producers, Menahem Golan, Yoram Globus; Director, Menahem Golan; Screenplay, James Bruner, Menahem Golan; Music, Alan Silvestri; Associate Producer, Rony Yacov; Production Supervisor, Itzhak Kol; Photography, David Gurfinkel; Editor, Alain Jakubowicz; Designer, Lucisano Spadoni; Special Effects, John Gant; Stunts, Don Pike; Costumes, Tami Mor; Production Manager, Dov Maoz; Assistant Directors, Tony Brandt, Mike Katzin, Michal Engel, Haim Rinsky; Sound, Eli Yarkoni, Yosi Yarkoni; Soundtrack on Enigma Records and Cassettes in the U.S.A.; Color; Rated R; 126 minutes; February release

CAST

Major Scott McCoy	Chuck Norris
Col. Nick Alexander	Lee Marvin
Ben Kaplan	Martin Balsam
Harry Goldman	Joey Bishop
Abdul	Robert Forster
Sylvia Goldman	Lainie Kazan
Father O'Malley	George Kennedy
Ingrid	Hanna Schygulla
Debra Levine	Susan Strasberg
Capt. Campbell	Bo Svenson
Gen. Woodbridge	Robert Vaughn
Edie Kaplan	Shelley Winters
Pete Peterson	William Wallace
Tom Hale	Charles Floye
Bobby	Steve James
Sister Mary	Kim Delaney
Dr. Jack	Gerry Weinstock
Dave Hoskins	Marvin Freedman
Jim Montgomery	Bob Levit
Tina	Chelli Goldberg
Lesley	Chris Ellia
Robert Levine	Jerry Lazarus
Ellen Levine	Natalie Roth
Ted Bilicki	Jerry Hyman
Rosalee Bilicki	Gael Lehrer
Jay Bilicki	Hank Leininger
Ed	Howard Jackson
Andy	Eric Norris
Sister Ann	Zipora Peled
Mike Fraser	Aaron Kaplan
Sally Fraser	Caroline Langford
David Rosovsky	Yehuda Efroni
Mustafa	David Menahem
Father Nicholas	Shai K. Ophir
Jaffar	Avi Lozaiah
George Berri	Uri Gavriel
Peter	Panos Nicolaou

and Elki Jacobs, Menahem Eini, Assaf Dayan, Jack Cohen, Adiv Gahshan, Haim Sirafi, Mosco Alkalai, Larry Price, Susan Ophir, Jack Messinger, Janet Harshman, Ezra Kafri, Danny Friedman, Richard Salano, Andy Shulman, Joe Sapel, Richard Peterson, Eugene Klein, Albert Amar, Ben Ami Shmueli, Moti Shirin, Itzik Aloni, Boaz Ofri, Albert Iluz, Osnat Vishinski, David Leshnik

Right Center: Lee Marvin (R) Above: David Menahem, Hanna Schygulla Top: Chuck Norris
© *Cannon*

Robert Forster

Martin Balsam, Shelley Winters

F/X

(ORION) Producers, Dodi Fayed, Jack Wiener; Director, Robert Mandel; Screenplay, Robert T. Megginson, Gregory Fleeman; Executive Producer, Michael Peyser; Photography, Miroslav Ondricek; Editor, Terry Rawlings; Designer, Mel Bourne; Costumes, Julie Weiss; Music, Bill Conti; Production Managers, Jon Landau, Thomas A. Razzano; Assistant Directors, Thomas Reilly, Ken Ornstein; Special Effects Consultant, John Stears; Special Make-up, Carl Fullerton; Sound, Jim Shields, Les Lazarowitz, Frank J. Graziadei; Songs by various artists; Technicolor; Panavision; Rated R; 107 minutes; February release

CAST

Rollie Tyler	Bryan Brown
Leo McCarthy	Brian Dennehy
Ellen	Diane Venora
Lipton	Cliff DeYoung
Col. Mason	Mason Adams
Nicholas DeFranco	Jerry Orbach
Mickey	Joe Grifasi
Andy	Martha Gehman
Capt. Wallenger	Roscoe Orman
Lt. Murdoch	Trey Wilson
Varrick	Tom Noonan
Gallagher	Paul D'Amato
Marisa Velez	Jossie deGusman
Whitemore	Jean De Baer
Miss Joyce Lehman	M'el Dowd
Adams	Tim Gallin
Sgt. Littauer	Patrick Stack
The Director	John Doumanian
Charlie	Ray Iannicelli
Ballistics Expert	Edward Crowley
Reporter 1	Gibby Brand
Car Pound Attendant	Jim Elliott
Mitchell	Christopher Curry
McCoy	James Lovelett
Capt. Tolosa	George Kodisch
Captain Watts	Jim Cordes

and Richard Hayes, Christopher McHale, James Pickens Jr., Michael Fischetti, Angela Bassett, Yolanda Lloyd, Marvin Beck, John McLoughlin, Jim Babchak, Bernie Friedman, Drummond Erskine, Joseph Petangelo, Gerald Campbell

Left: Bryan Brown, Cliff De Young
Top: Bryan Brown, Diane Venora
© Orion/S. Karin Epstein

Brian Dennehy, Trey Wilson

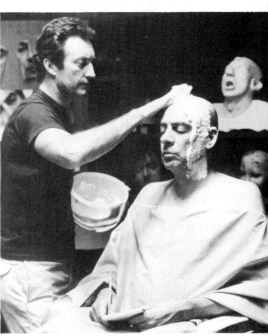

Bryan Brown, Jerry Orbach

SALVADOR

(HEMDALE FILM CORP.) Producers, Gerald Green, Oliver Stone; Director, Oliver Stone; Executive Producers, John Daly, Derek Gibson; Screenplay, Oliver Stone, Richard Boyle; Associate Producers, Bob Morones, Brad H. Aronson; Editor, Claire Simpson; Photography, Robert Richardson; Music, Georges Delerue; Designer, Bruno Rubeo; Production Executive, Brad H. Aronson; Production Supervisor, Michael Bennett; Assistant Director, Ramon Mendez: Costumes, Kathryn Greko Morrison; Music Supervisor, Bud Carr; Special Effects, Yves DeBono; Casting Bob "Blackie" Morones; Stunts, Bill Catching; Sound, David Lewis Yewdall; Color; Rated R; 123 minutes; March release

CAST

Richard Boyle	James Woods
Dr. Rock	James Belushi
Ambassador Thomas Kelly	Michael Murphy
John Cassady	John Savage
Maria	Elepedia Carrillo
Major Max	Tony Plana
Jack Morgan	Colby Chester
Cathy Moore	Cynthia Gibb
Col. Hyde	Will MacMillian
Pauline Axelrod	Valerie Wildman
Archbishop Romero	Jose Carlos Ruiz
Col. Julio Figueroa	Jorge Luke
Army Lieutenant	Juan Fernandez
Human Rights Leader	Salvador Sanchez
Assistant Human Rights Leader	Rosario Zuniga
Maria's Brother	Martin Fuentes
Australian Reporter	Gary Farr
French Reporter	Gilles Milinaire
Major Max Assistant	Ramon Menendez
Roberto	John Doe
Boyle's Wife	Maria Rubell
Sister Stan	Danna Hansen

and Leticia Valenzuela, Roberto Sosa Jr., Daria Okugawa, Sue Ann McKean, Joshua Gallegos, Sigridur Gudmunds, Erica Carlson, Kara Glover, Ma Del, Arturo Bonilla, Miguel Ehrenberg, Sean Stone, Tyrone Jones

Top: James Belushi, James Woods,
John Savage © *Cinema*

Elpedia Carrillo, James Woods,
James Belushi

POLICE ACADEMY 3: BACK IN TRAINING

(**WARNER BROS.**) Producer, Paul Maslansky; Director, Jerry Paris; Based on characters created by Neal Israel & Pat Proft; Screenplay, Gene Quintano; Photography, Robert Saad; Designer, Trevor Williams; Editor, Bud Molin; Music, Robert Folk; Casting, Fern Champion, Pamela Basker; Associate Producer, Donald West; Production Manager, Suzanne Lore; Assistant Directors, Michael Zenon, Rocco Gismondi, Bill Bannerman; Art Director, Rhiley Fuller; Set Decorator, Sean Kirby; Sound, Dale Johnston, David Lee; Musical Supervision, Tena Clark; Additional Orchestration, Don Davis; Production Coordinator, Alexandra Raffe; Costumes, Aleida MacDonald; Stunts, Alan Oliney; Special Effects, Cliff Wenger, Eric Roberts; Songs, Tena Clark, Tony Warren, Andy Hernandez, Lorenzo Pryor, Lauren Wood, Rick Chudacoff; A Police Academy Productions Presentation; Technicolor; Panavision; Rated PG; 90 minutes; March release

CAST

Sgt. Mahoney	Steve Guttenberg
Sgt. Hightower	Bubba Smith
Sgt. Tackleberry	David Graf
Sgt. Jones	Michael Winslow
Sgt. Hooks	Marion Ramsey
Lt. Callahan	Leslie Easterbrook
Commandant Mauser	Art Metrano
Cadet Sweetchuck	Tim Kazurinsky
Cadet Zed	Bobcat Goldthwait
Commandant Lassard	George Gaynes
Cadet Adams	Shawn Weatherly
Sgt. Copeland	Scott Thomson
Sgt. Blanks	Brant Van Hoffman
Sgt. Fackler	Bruce Mahler
Governor Neilson	Ed Nelson
Cadet Fackler	Debralee Scott
Lt. Proctor	Lance Kinsey
Cadet Nogata	Brian Tochi
Cadet Kirkland	Andrew Paris
Chief Hurst	George R. Robertson
The Hooker	Georgina Spelvin
Cadet Hedges	David Huband
Cadet Baxter #1	R. Christopher Thomas
Cadet Baxter #2	David Elliott
Mr. Kirkland	Arthur Batanides
Mr. Bellows	Jack Creley
Ms. Tyler	Rita Tuckett
Mr. Delaney	Chas Lawther
Ms. Click	Lyn Jackson
Mrs. Hurst	Mary Ann Coles

and Sam Stone, Grant Cowan, Bruce Pirie, Doug Lennox, Teddy Abner, Susan DeRyck, Marcia Watkins, Pam Hyatt, Fran Gebhard, Les Nirenberg, Gloria Summers, Fred Livingstone, Gladys O'Connor, Elias Zarou, Gary Flanagan, Pierre Berube, Peter Colvey, Alex Pauljuk, Anton Tyukodi

Right Center: Steve Guttenberg, Georgina Spelvin, Shawn Weatherly Above: Lance Kinsey, Art Metrano Top: Brian Tochi, Michael Winslow © *Warner Bros.*

Shawn Weatherly, Steve Guttenberg

George Gaynes

22

JUST BETWEEN FRIENDS

(ORION) Producers, Edward Teets, Allan Burns; Director/Screenplay, Allan Burns; Photography, Jordan Cronenweth; Designer, Sydney Z. Litwack; Editor, Ann Goursaud; Associate Producer, James H. Rascoe; Casting, Geri Windsor, Eugene Blythe; Music, Patrick Williams, Earl Klugh; Production Manager, Edward Teets; Assistant Directors, Patrick Crowley, Hans Beimler, Carey Dietrich; Set Decorators, Bruce Weintraub, Chris Butler; Costumes, Cynthia Bales; Sound, Kirk Francis; Production Coordinator, Patt McCurdy; Set Designer, Joseph Lucky; Special Effects, Eric Rylander; Production Executives, Ted Rich, Bernie Oseransky; Soundtrack on Warner Bros. Records; An MTM Enterprises Production; DeLuxe Color; Panavision; Rated PG-13; 120 minutes; March release

CAST

Holly Davis	Mary Tyler Moore
Karen	Julie Payne
Judy	Beverly Sanders
Helga	Salome Jens
Chip Davis	Ted Danson
Charlie	Read Morgan
Sandy Dunlap	Christine Lahti
Harry Crandall	Sam Waterston
Kim Davis	Susan Rinell
Jeff Davis	Timothy Gibbs
Carla	Diane Stilwell
Bill	James MacKrell
Stage Manager	Chet Collins
Sportscaster	Castulo Guerra
George Margolin	Mark Blum
Mr. Hasegawa	Robert Kino
Ruth Chadwick	Jane Greer
Bob Chadwick	George D. Wallace
Andrea	Andra Akers
Bill	Robert Rothwell
Janet	Darwyn Carson
Heather	Brigitte & Tiffany Desper
Herself	Dorothy Francis
Marci	Jeannie Elias

and Terri Hanauer, Helene Winston, Gary Riley, Leda Siskind, Joshua Harris, Lisle Wilson, John Terry Bell, Lewis Arquette, Suzanne Wishner, Christina Kokubo, Leslie Ann Rieder

Right: Christine Lahti, also at top with Mary Tyler Moore
© Orion/Fred Sabine

Timothy Gibbs, Mary Tyler Moore, Susan Rinell

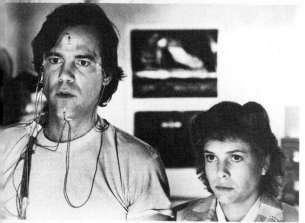

DREAM LOVER

(MGM/UA) Producers, Alan J. Pakula, Jon Boorstin; Director, Alan J. Pakula; Screenplay, Jon Boorstin; Photography, Sven Nykvist; Designer, George Jenkins; Editors, Trudy Ship, Angelo Corrao; Music, Michael Small; Costumes, Marit Allen; Art Director, John J. Moore; Scientific Consultant, Mark R. Rosekind; Executive Producer/ Production Manager, William C. Gerrity; Associate Producer, Susan Solt; Production Coordinator, Juliette Steyning-Brown; Assistant Directors, David Tringham, Michael Stevenson, Ken Shane, Alex Hapsas, Joseph Ray; Sound, Chris Newman; Orchestrations, Christopher Dedrick; Technicolor; Dolby Stereo; Filmed in Lightflex; Rated R; 104 minutes; March release.

CAST

Kathy Gardner	Kristy McNichol
Michael Hansen	Ben Masters
Ben Gardner	Paul Shenar
Kevin McCann	Justin Deas
Martin	John McMartin
Claire	Gayle Hunnicutt
Danny	Joseph Culp
Billy	Matthew Penn
Shep	Paul West
Vaughn Capisi	Matthew Long
Dr. James	Jon Polito
Nurse Jennifer	Ellen Parker
Policewoman	Lynn Webster
Hotel Manager	Brenda Cowling
Man at Hilton Hotel	Charles West
Ben's Secretary	Lesa Lockford
Policeman	Dennis Creaghan

and Dolores Sutton, Denise Stephenson, Helen Caldwell, Mike Potter, Stuart St. Paul.

Left: Joseph Culp, Kristy McNichol
Top: Ben Masters, Kristy McNichol
© *MGM/UA Entertainment*

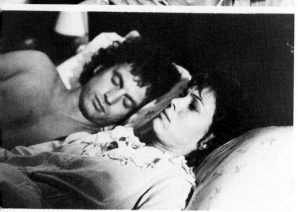

Justin Deas, Kristy McNichol
Above: Paul Shenar

Ben Masters, Kristy McNichol
Above: Justin Deas, Kristy McNichol

Alex McArthur, Patricia Charbonneau
Top: Patricia Charbonneau, Audra Lindley
Top Right: Helen Shaver, Alex McArthur
Below: Patricia Charbonneau, Andra Akers

DESERT HEARTS

(SAMUEL GOLDWYN) Producer/Director, Donna Deitch; Screenplay, Natalie Cooper; Based on the novel *Desert of the Heart* by Jane Rule; Designer, Jeannine Oppewall; Photography, Robert Elswit; Editor, Robert Estrin; A Desert Hearts Production; Technicolor; Rated R; 93 minutes; March release (No other technical credits supplied)

CAST

Vivian Bell	Helen Shaver
Cay Rivvers	Patricia Charbonneau
Frances Parker	Audra Lindley
Silver	Andra Akers
Gwen	Gwen Welles
Darell	Dean Butler
Art Warner	James Staley
Lucille	Katie La Bourdette
Walter	Alex McArthur
Joe Lorenzo	Anthony Ponzini
Pat	Denise Crosby
Buck	Tyler Tyhurst

© *Samuel Goldwyn*

Helen Shaver, Patricia Charbonneau

THE MONEY PIT

(UNIVERSAL) Producers, Frank Marshall, Kathleen Kennedy, Art Levinson; Director, Richard Benjamin; Screenplay, David Giler; Executive Producers, Steven Spielberg, David Giler; Photography, Gordon Willis; Designer, Patricia Von Brandenstein; Costumes, Ruth Morley; Music, Michel Colombier; Editor, Jacqueline Cambas; Production Manager, Art Levinson; Assistant Directors, Michael Haley, Ellen Rauch, James Skotchdopole; Art Director, Steve Graham; Special Effects, Michael Wood; Sound, Charles L. Campbell, Louis L. Edemann, Nat Boxer, Steve Scanlon, Andy McKee; Songs by various artists; Color by Du Art; Panavision; Dolby Stereo; Rated PG; 91 minutes; March release

CAST

Walter Fielding	Tom Hanks
Anna Crowley	Shelley Long
Max Beissart	Alexander Godunov
Estelle	Maureen Stapleton
Art Shirk	Joe Mantegna
Curly	Philip Bosco
Jack Schnittman	Josh Mostel
Shatov	Yakov Smirnoff
Brad Shirk	Carmine Caridi
Ethan	Brian Backer
Benny	Billy Lombardo
Marika	Mia Dillon
Carlos	Jon van Dreelen
Walter Fielding, Sr	Douglass Watson
Paramedic	Susan Browning
Benny's Mom	Mary Louise Wilson

and Lucille Dobrin, Tetchie Agbayani, Scott Turchin, Radu Gavor, Grisha Dimant, Lutz Rath, Joey Balin, Wendell Pierce, Henry Baker, Irving Metzman, Frank Maraden, Mike Russo, Joe Ponazecki, Michael Hyde, Mike Starr, Frankie Faison, Jake Steinfeld, Matthew Cowles, Nestor Serrano, Michael Jeter, Afremo Omilami, Bruno Iannone, Ron Foster, Alan Altshuld, Tzi Ma, Cindy Brooks, Leslie West, "The Fabulous Heavyweights," Tom Filiault, Doug Plavin, Chris Tuttle, Ed Vadas, "White Lion", Robey, Richard Ziker, Scott Wilder

Right: Tom Hanks, Philip Bosco
Top: Shelley Long, Tom Hanks
© *Universal*

Shelley Long, Tom Hanks, and above with Maureen Stapleton

Shelley Long, Alexander Godunov

ECHO PARK

(ATLANTIC) Producer, Walter Shenson; Director, Robert Dornhelm; Screenplay, Michael Ventura; Photography, Karl Kofler; Editor, Ingrid Kooler; Music, David Rickets; Soundtrack on A & M Records; In color; Rated R; 93 minutes; April release.

CAST

May	Susan Dey
Jonathan	Thomas Hulce
August	Michael Bowen
Henry	Christopher Walker
Gloria	Shirley Jo Feeney
August's Father	Heinrich Schweiger
Hugo	John Paragon
Sid	Richard Marin
Cheri	Cassandra Peterson

(No photos available)

Right: Rosanna Arquette, Alexandra Paul
Below: Andy Garcia, Alexandra Paul,
Jeff Bridges Top: Bridges, Arquette

EIGHT MILLION WAYS TO DIE

(TRI-STAR) Producer, Steve Roth; Director, Hal Ashby; Screenplay, Oliver Stone, David Lee Henry; Based on books by Lawrence Block; Photography, Stephen H. Burum; Designer, Michael Haller; Editors, Robert Lawrence, Stuart Pappe; Co-Producer, Charles Mulvehill; Music, James Newton Howard; Costumes, Gloria Gresham; Casting, Lynn Stalmaster; Production Manager, Charles Mulvehill; Assistant Directors, Andy Stone, Robert Engelman; Art Director, Mark W. Mansbridge; Set Decorators, Barbara Krieger, John Thomas Walker; Sound, Walter Gest, Jeff Wexler, Don Coufal, Jim Stuebe; Special Effects, Phil Corey, Tom Ward; Stunts, Bobby Bass; Special Effects, John Hughes, Mike Edmonson; Technicolor; Rated R; 115 minutes; April release

CAST

Scudder	Jeff Bridges
Sarah	Rosanna Arquette
Sunny	Alexandra Paul
Chance	Randy Brooks
Angel	Andy Garcia
Linda Scudder	Lisa Sloan
Laurie	Christa Denton
Quintero	Vance Valencia
Hector Lopez	Wilfredo Hernandez
Hector's Wife	Luisa Leschin
Durkin	Vyto Ruginis
Homicide Detective	Chip Arnold
Deputy D. A.	James Avery
Slim	Gene Ross
Nose Guard	Tom "Tiny" Lister, Jr.
Victor Padillo	Robb Madrid
Jamie Rodriguez	Roberto Jimenez
Buster	Loyd Catlett

and Jack Younger, ZoAnne LeRoy, Abigail Shelton, Don Edmonds, Phil Peters, Elva Garcia, Michael Galindo, Pete Galindo, Miriam Schubach, Lois Gerace, Jay Ingram, Sue Rihr, William Marquez, Fred Asparagus, Regan Newman, Richard A. Michels, Arie Gedis, Rosalind Ingledew, Arthur Ervin, Frank Dent, Henry Lewis, Victor Rivers, Danny De LaPaz, Oliver "Ollie" Farley, Gilbert D. Darra, Art Fransen

© *Tri-Star Pictures*

Randy Brooks, Andy Garcia

WITNESS TO APARTHEID

(DEVELOPING NEWS) Producer/Director, Sharon I. Sopher; Co-producer/Co-director, Kevin Harris; Written by Sharon I. Sopher, Peter Kinoy; Editor, Laurence Solomon; Associate Producer, Peter Kinoy; Photography, Peter Tischhauser; Sound, Steven Musgrave; Researcher, Peter Davis; Sound, Ehud Tomalak; Art Director, Beverly Littlewood; Not rated; 56 minutes; April release. A documentary about apartheid in South Africa.

Top Right: Bishop Desmond Tutu, and below with Sharon Sopher
Afrapix Photos

MURPHY'S LAW

(CANNON GROUP) Producer, Pancho Kohner; Director, J. Lee Thompson; Screenplay/Associate Producer, Gail Morgan Hickman; Executive Producers, Menahem Golan, Yoram Globus; Co-Producer, Bill Ireland; Photography, Alex Phillips; Music composed and performed by Marc Donahue, Valentine McCallum; Editor, Peter Lee Thompson, Charles Simmons; Designer, William Cruise; Production Executive, Jeffrey Silver; Production Manager, George Van Noy; Assistant Directors, Steve Lazarus, Robert C. Ortwin, Jr.; Costumes, Shelley Komarov; Sound, Craig Felburg; Special Effects, Pioneer Fx; Songs by various artists; Color; Rated R; 100 minutes; April release

CAST

Jack Murphy	Charles Bronson
Arabella McGee	Kathleen Wilhoite
Joan Freeman	Carrie Snodgress
Art Penney	Robert F. Lyons
Frank Vincenzo	Richard Romanus
Jan	Angel Tompkins
Ben Wilcove	Bill Henderson
Ed Reineke	James Luisi
Lt. Nachman	Clifford A. Pellow
Dr. Lovell	Janet MacLachman
Cameron	Lawrence Tierney
Judge Kellerman	Jerome Thor
Dave Manzarek	Mischa Hausserman
Reese	Cal Haynes
Santana	Hans Howes
Carl	Joseph Spallina Roman
Tony Vincenzo	Chris De Rose
Kelly	Frank Annese
Hog	Paul McCallum
Sonny	Dennis Hayden
Max	Tony Montero
Jack	David Hayman
Blonde	Lisa Vice
Mrs. Vincenzo	Janet Rotblatt

and Greg Finley, Jerry Lazarus, Robert Axelrod, John Hawker, Bert Williams, Daniel Halleck, Randall Carver, Gerald Berns, Don L. Brodie, Graham Timbes, David K. Johnston, Paul McCauley, Brooks Wachtel, Richard Hochberg, John F. McCarthy, Leigh Lombardi, Charlie Brewer, Charles A. Nero, Wheeler Henderson, Frank Bove, Chris Stanley, Linda Harwood, Nancie Clark

Right: Kathleen Wilhoite, Charles Bronson, Cal Haynes, Hans Howes Top: Charles Bronson, Kathleen Wilhoite © Cannon

Carrie Snodgress

Charles Bronson

29

DESERT BLOOM

(COLUMBIA) Producer, Michael Hausman; Director/Screenplay, Eugene Corr; Story, Linda Remy, Eugene Corr; Executive Producer, Richard Fischoff; Photography, Reynaldo Villalobos; Music, Brad Fiedel, Michael Melvoin; Art Director, Lawrence Miller; Editors, David Garfield, John Currin, Cari Coughlin; Costumes, Hilary Rosenfeld; Casting, Deborah Lucchesi; Music Supervisor, Bones Howe; Associate Producer, Linda Remy; Production Manager, Lee R. Mayes; Assistant Directors, Michael Hausman, Ned Dowd; Set Decorator, Bob Zilliox; Sound, Michael Evje; "*Mockin' Bird Hill*," Vaughn Horton; From Columbia-Delphi IV Productions; A Carson Productions Group, Ltd. Production in Association with the Sundance Institute; Metrocolor; Panavision; Rated PG; 106 minutes; April release

CAST

Rose	Annabeth Gish
Jack	Jon Voight
Lily	JoBeth Williams
Starr	Ellen Barkin
Robin	Jay D. Underwood
Dee Ann	Desiree Joseph
Barbara Jo	Dusty Balcerzak
Mr. Mosol	Allen Garfield
Shelly	Tressi Loria
Meryl	Laura Rasmussen
Colonel	William Lang
Driver	Jim McCarthy
Mrs. Muratore	Ann Risley
Mr. Brandal	Rick Scheiffer
R.C. Volunteer	Irene Goodnight
R.C. Nurse	Eugenia Moran
Nurse	Danica Remy
Texan	Bruce Wineinger
Publicist	Armen Dirtadian
Ava	Molly Fontaine
Radio Clerk	Al Petito
Photographer	Randy Harris
Delivery Boy	Chris Corr
Tour Guide	Fred C. Smith
Nick	Steven Mastroieni

and Bob Gish, Onna Young, Jesse Sloan, Kiysha Doty, Todd Barish, Sherry Allen, Doris Berman, Reynaldo Villalobos Jr., Judith Gish, Mike Stein, Ray LeFre, Tamara Cooley, Patty Harbor, Johnny L. Watkins, Mark Jenkins

**Left: Jon Voight, JoBeth Williams
Top: Ellen Barkin, Annabeth Gish, Desiree
Joseph, JoBeth Williams, Dusty Balcerzak,
John Voight © *Columbia***

Ellen Barkin, JoBeth Williams

Annabeth Gish, Jay Underwood

VIOLETS ARE BLUE

(COLUMBIA) Producer, Marykay Powell; Director, Jack Fisk; Screenplay, Naomi Foner; Executive Producer, Roger M. Rothstein; Photography, Ralf Bode; Designer, Peter Jamison; Editor, Edward Warschilka; Costumes, Joe I. Tompkins; Casting, Pat McCorkle; Song, "One Day," Patrick Williams, Will Jennings; Vocals, Laura Branigan; Music, Patrick Williams; Production Manager, Roger M. Rothstein; Assistant Directors, Jim Van Wyck, Aldric La-Auli Porter; Art Director, Bo Welch; Set Decorator, Jane Bogart; Sound, Jim Alexander; Special Effects, Ken Speed; From Columbia-Delphi IV Productions/Rastar; Metrocolor; Panavision; Rated PG-13; 90 minutes; April release

CAST

Gussie Sawyer	Sissy Spacek
Henry Squires	Kevin Kline
Ruth Squires	Bonnie Bedelia
Ralph Sawyer	John Kellogg
Addy Squires	Jim Standiford
Ethel Sawyer	Augusta Dabney
Sara Mae	Kate McGregor-Stewart
George	Adrian Sparks
Sally	Annalee Jefferies
Tony	Mike Starr
Squid	Brian Sargis
Bryant	Keith Sargis
Ben	Michael Mack
Erin	Erin Malooly
Kathleen	Megan Malooly
Girl's Mother	Kathleen Fannon
Lloyd Lynch	Doug Roberts

Top: Bonnie Bedelia, Kevin Kline Below: Kline,
Sissy Spacek (also Right) Top Right:
Bedelia, Spacek © Columbia

Kevin Kline, Sissy Spacek

ON THE EDGE

(SKOURAS) Producers, Jeffrey Hayes, Rob Nilsson; Director/ Screenplay, Rob Nilsson; Story, Rob Nilsson, Roy Kissin; Associate Producer, Roy Kissin; Executive Producers, John Dern, Jr., Peter Roth, John H. Stout, Stephen L. Wald; Music, Herb Pilhofer; Photography, Stefan Czapsky; Editors, Rich Harkness, Bert Lovitt; Camera, Stephen Lighthill; Color; Rated PG-13; 91 minutes; May release (No other credits submitted)

CAST

Wes Holman	Bruce Dern
Elmo Glidden	John Marley
Flash	Bill Bailey
Owen Riley	Jim Haynie
Ellie	Jean Shelton
Tomaso	Frank Triest
Johnny	John Tidwell
Walt	Walt Stack
Marcie	Marcie Stack
Pill	Leona Harris
Larry	Lawrence Menkin
Bartender	Bill Ackridge
Cindy Paine	Jennifer Biddulph
Jenna Mervin	Donna Andrews
Marianna Knutson	Barbara Magid
Daryl Beard	Don Pickett
Garry Bjorklund	Garry Bjorklund
Matt Singleton	Bill Sevald
Ray Lopes	Roy Kissin
Adam Wilkes	Keith Hastings
Harrison	Scott Harrison
Pendergast	Chris Johnson

and Nancy Fish, Elizabeth Zeier, Luigi Alfano, Bill Luft, Chuck Lempert, Fred Bushardt, Ron Bickerstaff, Mike Cerre, Marty Liquori, Jeannine Yeomans, Tom Nettles, Henry D. Moore, Jr., Peter Roth, Chuck Crawford, Robindira Howell, Ray Goman, Will Prater, Barry Spitz, Bill Jelliffe, James Harrison, Jim Sparkman, Michael Kissin, Robert Elross, Roland Betts, Jerry Hauke, Dan Leegant, Ron Angier

Top: Bruce Dern also Right (center)
© *Skouras*

32

Bill Bailey, Bruce Dern

BIG TROUBLE

(COLUMBIA) Director, John Cassavetes; Screenplay, Warren Bogle; Photography, Bill Butler; Designer, Gene Callahan; Editors, Donn Cambern, Ralph Winters; Costumes, Joe I. Tompkins; Casting, Mike Fenton, Jane Feinberg, Judy Taylor; Music, Bill Conti; Production Manager, Howard Pine; Assistant Directors, Duncan Henderson, Chris Ryan; Set Decorator, Lee Poll; Sound, Martin Bolger; Art Director, Pete Smith; Set Designer, Joseph Hubbard; Stunts, Gray Johnson; Production Coordinator, Jeannie Jeha; Columbia-Delphi III Production; Songs by various artists; Metrocolor; Panavision; Rated R; 93 minutes; May release

CAST

Steve Rickey	Peter Falk
Leonard Hoffman	Alan Arkin
Blanche Rickey	Beverly D'Angelo
O'Mara	Charles Durning
Noozel	Paul Dooley
Winslow	Robert Stack
Arlene Hoffman	Valerie Curtin
Dr. Lopez	Richard Libertini
Peter Hoffman	Steve Alterman
Michael Hoffman	Jerry Pavlon
Joshua Hoffman	Paul LaGreca
Detective Murphy	John Finnegan
Police Captain	Karl Lukas
Gail	Maryedith Burrell
Doris	Edith Fields
Jack	Warren Munson
Mrs. Winslow	Rosemarie Stack
Helen	Barbara Tarbuck
Mr. Williams	Al White
Porter	Theodore Wilson
Wanda	Gloria Gifford
Gaetano Lopez	Gaetano Lisi
Flavio Lopez	Chester Grimes
Whitlow Keppler	Lenny Geer

and Herb Armstrong, Jaime Sanchez, Irene Olga Lopez, Daphne Eckler, Carol Reinhard, Conroy Gedeon, Melvin Jones, Luis Contreras, John M. Kochian, Jr., Domingo Ambriz, John Bianchini, Nafa Rasho, Roger Ito, Perry Fluker, Lynn Ready, Steven Lambert, Yukio G. Collins, Howard Clapp, Jeff Howard, Leland Sun, Albert Leong, Danny Lew, Michaelani, Dennis Phung, Walter Soo Hoo, Richard Walter, Joseph G. Medalis

Right: Peter Falk, Beverly D'Angelo, Alan Arkin Top: Charles Durning, D'Angelo, Richard Libertini (with hat), Falk, Arkin, Valerie Curtin © *Columbia*

Peter Falk, Alan Arkin

Peter Falk, Beverly D'Angelo

TOP GUN

(PARAMOUNT) Producers, Don Simpson, Jerry Bruckheimer; Director, Tony Scott; Screenplay, Jim Cash, Jack Epps, Jr.; Executive Producer/Production Manager, Bill Badalato; Photography, Jeffrey Kimball; Designer, John F. DeCuir, Jr.; Editors, Billy Weber, Chris Lebenzon; Music, Harold Faltermeyer; Associate Producer, Warren Skaaren; Assistant Directors, Daniel P. Kilsrud, Sharon Mann, Patrick Cosgrove; Special Photographic Effects, Gary Gutierrez; Set Decorator, Robert R. Benton; Special Effects, Allen Hall; Sound, William B. Kaplan; Men's Costumes, James W. Tyson; Women's Costumes, Bobbie Read; Special Sound Effects, John Paul Fasal; Stunts, R. A. Rondell; Special Visual Effects, USFX/Colossal Pictures; Songs by Giorgio Moroder, Tom Whitlock, and various other artists; Soundtrack on Columbia; Dolby Stereo; Metrocolor; Panavision Widescreen; Rated PG; 109 minutes; May release

CAST

Maverick	Tom Cruise
Charlie	Kelly McGillis
Ice	Val Kilmer
Goose	Anthony Edwards
Viper	Tom Skerritt
Jester	Michael Ironside
Cougar	John Stockwell
Wolfman	Barry Tubb
Slider	Rick Rossovich
Merlin	Tim Robbins
Sundown	Clarence Gilyard, Jr.
Hollywood	Whip Hubley
Stinger	James Tolkan
Carole	Meg Ryan
Chipper	Adrian Pasdar
Lt. Davis	Randall Brady
Air Boss Johnson	Duke Stroud
Sprawl	Brian Sheehan
Inquiry Commander	Ron Clark
Bartender	Frank Pesce
Perry Siedenthal	Pete Pettigrew
Radio Operator	Troy Hunter
Mrs. Metcalf	Linda Rae Jurgens
Admiral T. J. Cassidy	Himself

and R. A. Rondell, Gary Epper, Randy Peters, Steve Holladay, Donna Keegan

Left Center: Tom Cruise (Right)
Top: Val Kilmer, Tom Cruise
© *Paramount*

Tom Cruise (R)

1986 Academy Award For Best Original Song (Take My Breath Away)

Kelly McGillis, Tom Cruise, and at top

SHORT CIRCUIT

(TRI-STAR) Producers, David Foster, Lawrence Turman; Director, John Badham; Screenplay, S. S. Wilson, Brent Maddock; Photography, Nick McLean; Art Director, Dianne Wager; Editor, Frank Morriss; Music, David Shire; Executive Producers, Mark Damon, John Hyde; Co-producer, Dennis Jones; Supervising Producer, Gregg Champion; Associate Producers, Gary Foster, Dana Satler; Casting, Mike Fenton, Jane Feinberg, Judy Taylor; Production Manager, Steve H. Perry; Assistant Directors, Jerry Ziesmer, Bryan Denegal; Visual Consultant, Philip Harrison; Robots, Syd Mead, Eric Allard; Assistant Art Director, Donald B. Woodruff; Set Decorator, Garrett Lewis; Sound, Willie D. Burton; Special Electrical Effects, Bob Jason, Larry "Big Mo" Keys, Walter Nichols; Robot Voices Synthesizer, Frank Serafine; Production Coordinator, Cliff Hill; Dolby Stereo; Metrocolor; Panavision; Rated PG; 99 minutes; May release

CAST

Stephanie Speck	Ally Sheedy
Newton Crosby	Steve Guttenberg
Ben Jabituya	Fisher Stevens
Howard Marner	Austin Pendleton
Skroeder	G. W. Bailey
Frank	Brian McNamara
Voice of Number Five	Tim Blaney
Duke	Marvin McIntyre
Otis	John Garber
Mrs. Cepeda	Penny Santon
General Washburne	Vernon Weddle
Senator Mills	Barbara Tarbuck
Marner's Aide	Tom Lawrence
Norman	Fred Slyter
Zack	Billy Ray Sharkey
Reporters	Robert Krantz, Jan Speck
Barmaid	Marguerite Happy
Farmer	Howard Krick
Farmer's Wife	Marjorie Huehes
Gate Guard	Herb Smith

and Jack Thompson, William Striglos, Mary Reckley Lisa McLean, Eleanor C. Heutschy, Walter Scott, James W. Gavin, Karl Wickman

Ally Sheedy, Steve Guttenberg, and Top with Fisher Stevens © *Tri-Star*

A GREAT WALL

(ORION CLASSICS) Producer, Shirley Sun; Director, Peter Wang; Screenplay, Peter Wang, Shirley Sun; Photography, Peter Stein, Robert Primes; Editor, Grahame Weinbren; Music, David Liang, Ge Ganru; Designer, Wing Lee; Art Directors, Cheung Ming Ming, Feng Yuan; Costumes, Calvin Tsao; Assistant Director, Li-Shin Yu; Production Managers, Du Qinying, Lisa Hsia; Executive Producers, Wu Yangchian, Zhu Youjun, E. N. Wen; Presented by W & S Productions and Nanhai Film Company; The first American film made in China; English and Mandarin with subtitles; Color; Rated PG; 100 minutes; May release

CAST

Leo Fang	Peter Wang
Grace Fang	Sharon Iwai
Paul Fang	Kelvin Han Yee
Lili Chao	Li Quinqin
Mr. Chao	Hu Xiaoguang
Mrs. Chao	Shen Guanglan
Liu Yida	Wang Xiao
Yu	Xiu Jian
Jan	Ran Zhijuan
Old Liu	Han Tan
Linda	Jeannette Pavini
Neil Mahoney	Howard Frieberg
Mr. Wilson	Bill Neilson
Kathy	Teresa Roberts

© *Orion*

Li Qinquin, Wang Xiso
Above: Peter Wang, Hu Xiaoguang

COBRA

(WARNER BROS.) Producers, Menahem Golan, Yoram Globus; Director, George P. Cosmatos; Screenplay, Sylvester Stallone; Based on the novel "*Fair Game*" by Paula Gosling; Executive Producer, James D. Brubaker; Photography, Ric Waite; Designer, Bill Kenney; Editors, Don Zimmerman, James Symons; Associate Producer, Tony Munafo; Costumes, Tom Bronson; Music, Sylvester Levay; Casting, Joy Todd; Production Manager, Mary Eilts; Assistant Directors, Duncan Henderson, Janet Knutsen, Eric Jewett; Stunts, Terry Leonard; Art Directors, William Skinner, Adrian H. Gorton; Assistant Art Directors, Cathryn Langs, Gayle Simon; Set Designer, David Klassen; Set Decorator, Robert Gould; Sound, Michael Evje; Special Effects, Philip Cory; A Cannon Group, Inc. Production; Eagle Stereo; Panavision; Technicolor; Rated R; 87 minutes; May release

CAST

Marion Cobretti	Sylvester Stallone
Ingrid	Brigitte Nielsen
Gonzales	Reni Santoni
Detective Monte	Andrew Robinson
Night Slasher	Brian Thompson
Cho	John Herzfeld
Nancy Stalk	Lee Garlington
Captain Sears	Art LaFleur
Supermarket Killer	Marco Rodriguez
Security Guard	Ross St. Phillip
Chief Halliwell	Val Avery
Dan	David Rasche
Low Rider	John Hauk
Prodski	Nick Angotti
Waitress	Nina Axelrod
Dr. Demopoulos	Harry B. Demopoulos
Commissioner Reddesdale	Bert Williams

and Joe Bonny, Bradley Bovee, Kevin Breslin, Roger Aaron Brown, John Cahill, Malik Carter, Louise Caire Clark, Christine Craft, Gregory Norman Cruz, Deborah Dalton, Scott Dockstader, Laura Drake, Ken Hill, Arthur Kassell, Karen Kondazian, Fred Lucky, Robert Martini, Joe Masino, Jr., Dorothy Meyer, Paul Monte, Joe Stone, Jim Wilkey, Leslie Morris, Clare Nono, Steve Lentz, Glenda Wina, Michael Bershad, Joe Fowler, Bradley Bovee, Dave Darling, Mark DeAlessandro, Scott Dockstader, Richard Epper, Corey Eubanks, Debbie Evans, Joe Finnegan, Terry Jackson, John Michael Johnson, Tracy Lyn Keehn, Paul Lane, Lane Leavitt, Mike McGaughy, Gary McLarty, Branscombe Richmond, Kerry Rossall, Mike Runyard, Ben Scott, Mike Tillman

© *Warner Bros.*

Sylvester Stallone, Brigitte Nielsen
Top Right: Sylvester Stallone

Sylvester Stallone

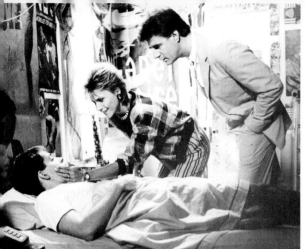

FERRIS BUELLER'S DAY OFF

(ORION) Producers, John Hughes, Tom Jacobson; Director/Screenplay, John Hughes; Executive Producer, Michael Chinich; Photography, Tak Fujimoto; Designer, John W. Corso; Editor, Paul Hirsch; Costumes, Marilyn Vance; Casting, Janet Hirshenson, Jane Jenkins; Music, Ira Newborn; Music Supervisor, Tarquin Gotch; Associate Producer, Jane Vickerilla; Production Manager, Arne Schmidt; Assistant Directors, Stephen Lim, Ken Collins; Stunts, Bennie Dobbins; Choreography, Kenny Ortega; Set Decorator, Jennifer Polito; Sound, James Alexander; Set Designer, Louis Mann; Special Effects, John Frazier; Assistant Choreographer, Wilbert Bradley; Orchestrations, Alf Clausen, Don Nemitz; Songs by various artists; Dolby Stereo; Metrocolor; Panavision; Rated PG-13; May release

CAST

Ferris Bueller	Matthew Broderick
Cameron Frye	Alan Ruck
Sloane Peterson	Mia Sara
Ed Rooney	Jeffrey Jones
Jeanie Bueller	Jennifer Grey
Katie Bueller	Cindy Pickett
Tom Bueller	Lyman Ward
School Secretary	Edie McClurg
Boy in police station	Charlie Sheen
Economics Teacher	Ben Stein
English Teacher	Del Close
Florence Sparrow	Virginia Capers
Garage Attendant	Richard Edson
Attendant's Co-Pilot	Larry Flash Jenkins
Chez Quis Maitre'D	Jonathan Schmock
Men's Room Attendant	Tom Spratley
Businessman	Dave Silvestri
Girl in Pizza Joint	Debra Montague
Pizza Man	Joey Viera
Flower Deliveryman	Louis Anderson
Singing Nurse	Stephanie Blake
Balloon Man	Robert McKibbon
Pumpkin Head	Paul Manzanero
Girl on Trampoline	Miranda Whittle
Police Officer	Robert Kim
Gym Teacher	Edward LeBeau
Bus Driver	Dee Dee Rescher

and Kristy Swanson, Lisa Bellard, Max Perlich, T. Scott Coffey, Eric Saiet, Jason Alderman, Joey Garfield, Kristin Graziano, Bridget McCarthy, Anne Ryan, Eric Edidin, Brendan Babar, Tiffany Chance, Dick Sollenberger, Bob Parkinson, Richard Rohrbough, Polly Noonan

**Top Left: Matthew Broderick, Cindy Pickett,
Lyman Ward Below: Matthew Broderick,
Jeffrey Jones © *Paramount***

Matthew Broderick

Mia Sara, Alan Ruck,
Matthew Broderick

Matthew Broderick, Mia Sara, also Top Left with Alan Ruck and children Below: Alan Ruck, Matthew Broderick, Mia Sara (also Right) Above: Jennifer Grey, Charlie Sheen

POLTERGEIST II:
The Other Side

(MGM) Producer/Screenplay, Mark Victor, Michael Grais; Director, Brian Gibson; Executive Producer, Freddie Fields; Photography, Andrew Laszlo; Designer, Ted Haworth; Editor, Thom Noble; Visual Effects, Richard Edlund; Music, Jerry Goldsmith; Associate Producer, Lynn Arost; Production Manager, Tom Joyner; Assistant Directors, William S. Beasley, Regina Gordon; Paranormal Research, Terri Barrile; Paranormal Phenomena Advisor, Kevin Ryerson; Psychic Adviser, Jill Cook; Conceptual Artist, H. R. Giger; Set Designers, Roy Barnes, Greg Papalia; Assistant Art Director, William J. Durrell, Jr.; Costumes, April Ferry, Mort Schwartz, Michele Neely; Special Effects, Michael Lantieri, Clay Pinney, Doug DeGrazzie, Bill Aldridge, Albert Delgado; Orchestrations, Arthur Morton; Special Sound Effects Designer, Frank Serafine; Creatures, Steve Johnson, Randall William Cook; Panavision; Metrocolor; Dolby Stereo; Rated PG-13; 92 minutes; May release

CAST

Diane Freeling	JoBeth Williams
Steve Freeling	Craig T. Nelson
Carol Ann Freeling	Heather O'Rourke
Robbie Freeling	Oliver Robins
Tangina Barrons	Zelda Rubinstein
Taylor	Will Sampson
Kane	Julian Beck
Gramma Jess	Geraldine Fitzgerald
Old Indian	John P. Whitecloud
Vomit Creature	Noble Craig
Daughter	Susan Peretz
Mother	Helen Boll
Young Jess	Kelly Jean Peters
Young Diane	Jaclyn Bernstein

and Robert Lesser, Jamie Abbott, Ann Louise Bardach, Syd Beard, David Beaman, Hayley Taylor-Block, Pamela Gordon, Chelsea Hertford, Whitby Hertford, Rocky Krakoff, Carrie Lorraine, Kathy Wagner, Bill Schroeder, Dana Dru Evenson, Denise Feir, Deidre Flynn, Jerry Gatlin, Brooke Hudson, Vickie Miller, Deep Roy, Desiree Szabo, George P. Wilbur

**Top: Zelda Rubinstein, JoBeth Williams,
Heather O'Rourke, Oliver Robins, Craig T.
Nelson © MGM Entertainment**

Will Sampson, Heather O'Rourke
Above: Zelda Rubinstein, JoBeth Williams

SWEET LIBERTY

(**UNIVERSAL**) Producer, Martin Bregman; Director/Screenplay, Alan Alda; Executive Producer, Louis A. Stroller; Photography, Frank Tidy; Designer, Ben Edwards; Costumes, Jane Greenwood; Editor, Michael Economou; Music, Bruce Broughton; Associate Producers/Production Manager, Judith Stevens; Associate Producer, Michael Economou; Assistant Directors, Yudi Bennett, Mark McGann; Sound, Bill Virney, Al Mian, Jeff Haas; Art Director, Christopher Nowak; Special Effects, Eddie Brohan, Candy Flanagan; Song, Howie Rice, Allan Rich, Patti La Belle; Color; Panavision; Rated PG; 107 minutes; May release

CAST

Michael Burgess	Alan Alda
Elliott James	Michael Caine
Faith Healy	Michelle Pfeiffer
Stanley Gould	Bob Hoskins
Gretchen Carlsen	Lise Hilboldt
Cecelia Burgess	Lillian Gish
Bo Hodges	Saul Rubinek
Leslie	Lois Chiles
Grace	Linda Thorson
Nurse	Diane Agostini
Film Crew Member	Antony Alda
Male Student	Alvin Alexis
Running Boy	Christopher Bregman
Hank	Leo Burmester
Asst. Camera	Cynthia Burr
Eagleton	Timothy Carhart
Gov. Swayze	Bryan Clark
Female Student	Bonnie Deroski
Lopert	Frank Ferrara
Frank Stirling	Michael Flanagan
Jesse	Dann Florek
Camera Operator	David Gideon
TV Interviewer	Katherine Gowan
2nd FX Man	Terry Hinz
Teamster	John Leonidas
Cinematographer	Christopher Loomis
1st FX Man	Kevin McClarnon
Floyd	John C. McGinley
Teamster #2	William Parry
Mrs. Delvechio	Polly Rowles
Soundman	Fred Sanders
Pilot	Robert Schenkkan
Edson	Larry Shue
Hotel Clerk	Steven Stahl
Claire	Lynne Thigpen
Johnny Delvechio	Richard Whiting
Publicist	Robert Zaren

Right: Michelle Pfeiffer, Alan Alda
Top: Michael Caine, Lois Chiles
© *Universal*

Lillian Gish

Lise Hilboldt, Alan Alda

BACK TO SCHOOL

(ORION) Producer, Chuck Russell; Director, Alan Metter; Screenplay, Steven Kampmann, Will Porter, Peter Torokvei, Harold Ramis; Story, Rodney Dangerfield, Greg Fields, Dennis Snee; Executive Producers, Estelle Endler, Michael Endler, Harold Ramis; Photography, Thomas E. Ackerman; Designer, David L. Snyder; Editor, David Rawlins; Casting, Caro Jones, Melissa Skoff; Music, Danny Elfman; Production Manager, Chuck Russell; Assistant Directors, Robert P. Cohen, Steve Cohen, Dustin Bernard; Costumes, Durinda Wood; Production Coordinator, Mary McLaglen; Music Supervisor, Linda Goldner Perry; Sound, William Nelson; Assistant Art Director, Marjorie Stone McShirley; Set Decorator, Linda DeScenna; Set Designer, Edmund Silkaitis; Special Effects, Michael Lantieri, Timothy J. Moran; Conductor, Lennie Niehaus; DeLuxe Color; Panavision; Rated PG-13; 96 minutes; June release

CAST

Thornton Melon	Rodney Dangerfield
Diane	Sally Kellerman
Lou	Burt Young
Jason Melon	Keith Gordon
Derek	Robert Downey, Jr.
Philip Barbay	Paxton Whitehead
Valerie	Terry Farrell
Coach Turnbull	M. Emmet Walsh
Vanessa	Adrienne Barbeau
Chas	William Zabka
Dean Martin	Ned Beatty
Dr. Barazini	Severn Darden
Professor Terguson	Sam Kinison
Giorgio	Robert Picardo
As Himself	Kurt Vonnegut, Jr.
Marge	Edie McClurg
Tony Meloni	Boris Aplon
Agnes	Nora Boland
Lisa	Lisa Denton
Young Thornton	Jason Hervey
Mrs. Stuyvesant	Beth Peters
Petey	Brad Zutaut

and Sarah Abrell, Dana Allison, Kimberlin Brown, Bob Drew, Holly Hayes, Leslie Huntly, James Ingersoll, Michael McGrady, Santos Morales, Phil Rubenstein, Timothy Stack, Steve Sweeney, Stacey Toten, John Young, Josh Saylor, William Grauer, Kristen Aldrich, Beck LeBeau, Tricia Hill, Jill D. Merin, John James, Eric Alver, Theresa Lyons, Dallas Winkler, Lisa LeCover, Kimberlee Carlson

Left: Rodney Dangerfield, Keith Gordon Above: Randi Randolph, Dangerfield, Stacey Toten, Cindy Brooks Top: Caitland McLean, Dangerfield
© *Orion/Joyce Rudolph*

Sally Kellerman, Rodney Dangerfield

Rodney Dangerfield

LABYRINTH

(TRI-STAR) Producer, Eric Rattray; Director, Jim Henson; Executive Producer, George Lucas; Executive Supervising Producer, David Lazer; Screenplay, Terry Jones; Story, Denise Lee, Jim Henson; Special Effects, George Gibbs; Designer, Elliot Scott; Editor, John Grover; Photography, Alex Thompson; Conceptual Design, Brian Froud; Music, Trevor Jones; Songs, David Bowie; Director of Choreography/Puppet Movement, Cherly McFadden; Choreographer, Charles Augins; Crystal Ball Manipulation, Michael Moschen; Puppeteer Coordinator, Brian Henson; Assistant Coordinator, Kevin Clash; Associate Producer, Martin Baker; Assistant Director, Ken Baker; Production Supervisor, Douglas Twiddy; Sound, Peter Sutton; Art Directors, Roger Cain, Peter Howitt, Michael White, Terry Ackland-Snow; Costumes, Brian Froud, Ellis Flyte; Creature Design, Brian Froud; Soundtrack Album on EMI AMERICA Records; Dolby Stereo; Color; Rated PG; 101 minutes; June release

CAST

Jareth	David Bowie
Sarah	Jennifer Connelly
Toby	Toby Froud
Stepmother	Shelley Thompson
Father	Christopher Malcolm
Fairy	Natalie Finland
Hoggle	Shari Weiser, Brian Henson
Ludo	Ron Mueck, Rob Mills
Didymus	Dave Goelz, David Barclay, David Shaughnessy
The Worm	Karen Prell, Timothy Bateson
The Wiseman	Frank Oz, Michael Hordern
The Hat	Dave Goelz, David Shaughnessy
The Junk Lady	Karen Prell, Denise Bryer

and Steve Whitmire, Kevin Clash, Anthony Asbury, David Healy, Robert Beatty, Toby Philpott, Ian Thom, Charles Augins, Sherry Amott, Danny John-Jules, Cheryl Henson, Kevin Bradshaw, Alistair Fullarton, Rollin Krewson, Richard Bodkin, Percy Edwards, Michael Attweel, Sean Barrett, John Bluthel, Anthony Jackson, Douglas Blackwell, Peter Marinter, Kerry Shale

Top Left: David Bowie
© *Tri-Star*

David Bowie, Jennifer Connelly

Jennifer Connelly

43

THE KARATE KID PART II

(COLUMBIA) Producer, Jerry Weintraub; Director, John G. Avildsen; Screenplay, Robert Mark Kamen; Executive Producer, R. J. Louis; Photography, James Crabe; Designer, William J. Cassidy; Editors, David Garfield, Jane Kurson, John G. Avildsen; Music, Bill Conti; Costumes, Mary Malin; Casting, Caro Jones; Associate Producer, William J. Cassidy, Karen Trudy Rosenfelt, Susan E. Ekins; Based on characters created by Robert Mark Kamen; Production Manager, Howard Pine; Assistant Directors, Clifford C. Coleman, Dennis MaGuire, Christine Larson; Production Coordinator, Jeannie Jeha; Art Director, William F. Matthews; Martial Arts Choreographer, Pat E. Johnson; Sound, William J. Randall; Set Decorator, Lee Poll; Set Designer, Jim Teegarden; Special Effects, Dennis Dion, Walter Dion, Paul Haines, Al Wininger; Orchestrations, Jack Eskew; Choreographers, Paul DeRolf, Nobuko Miyamoto, Jose DeVega, Randall Sabusawa; "The Glory of Love" Theme, Peter Cetera, David Foster; Songs by various artists; Soundtrack on United Artists Records; Dolby Stereo; DeLuxe Color; Rated PG-13; 113 minutes; June release

CAST

Miyagi	Noriyuki "Pat" Morita
Daniel	Ralph Macchio
Kreese	Martin Kove
Johnny	William Zabka
Dutch	Chad McQueen
Jimmy	Tony O'Dell
Bobby	Ron Thomas
Tommy	Rob Garrison
Chozen	Yuji Okumoto
Toshio	Joey Miyashima
Sato	Danny Kamekona
Kumiko	Tamlyn Tomita
Yukie	Nobu McCarthy
Miyagi's Father	Charlie Tanimoto
Ichiro	Arsenio "Sonny" Trinidad
Taro	Marc Hayashi
Kumiko's Street Friend	Natalie N. Hashimoto
Sato's Houseman	Wes Chong

and Pat E. Johnson, Bruce Malmuth, Eddie Smith, Garth Johnson, Brett Johnson, Will Hunt, Evan Malmuth, Lee Arnone, Sarah Kendall, Raymond Ma, George O'Hanlon, Jr., Tsuruko Ohye, Robert Fernandez, Diana Mar, Bradd Wong, Clarence Gilyard, Jr., Michael Morgan, Jack Eiseman, Jeffrey Rogers, Aaron Seville, Traci Toguchi

Top: Noriyuki "Pat" Morita, Ralph Macchio
© Columbia

Ralph Macchio, Noriyuki Morita

Ralph Macchio, Tamlyn Tomita (also Top)
Above: Noriyuki "Pat" Morita, Martin Kove

Noriyuki "Pat" Morita, Ralph Macchio
Top: Ralph Macchio, Yuji Okumoto

RUNNING SCARED

(MGM) Producers, David Foster, Lawrence Turman; Director/ Photography/Executive Producer, Peter Hyams; Screenplay, Gary DeVore, Jimmy Huston; Story, Gary DeVore; Designer, Albert Brenner; Editor, James Mitchell; Associate Producer, Jonathan A. Zimbert; Music, Rod Temperton; Music Supervisor, Dick Rudolph; Production Manager, Jack Terry; Assistant Directors, Jim Van Wyck, Deborah Dell'Amico, Aldric La'Auli Porter; Set Decorator, George P. Gaines; Sound, Gene Cantamessa; Special Effects, Henry E. Millar, Dave Blitstein, Doug Hubbard; Musical Arrangers, Larry Williams, James Flamberg, Wells Christie, Jerry Hey, Randy Kerber, Udi Harpaz; Songs by various artists; Panavision; Metrocolor; Dolby Stereo; Rated R; 107 minutes; June release

CAST

Ray Hughes	Gregory Hines
Danny Costanzo	Billy Crystal
Frank	Steven Bauer
Anna Costanzo	Darlanne Fluegel
Snake	Joe Pantoliano
Captain Logan	Dan Hedaya
Tony	Jonathan Gries
Maryann	Tracy Reed
Julio Gonzales	Jimmy Smits
Vinnie	John DiSanti
Ace	Larry Hankin
Women's Room Lawyer	Don Calfa
Subpoena Lawyer	Robert Lesser
Apartment Manager	Betty Carvalho
Thug	Louis Perez
Paging Officer	Ron Cummins
Nude Woman	Natividad Rios Kearsley
Evidence Officer	John LaMotta
Desk Officer	Richard Kuss
Property Officer	Jeff Silverman
Apartment Manager's Son	Dax Brooks
Tatoo Customer	Jaime Alba
Julie	Meg Register
Lunch Girl	Debbie Johnson
Bank Manager	Fred Buch
Sgt. Garcia	Ricardo Guiterrez
Juan	Frankie Davila
Adam Robertson	Ernest Perry, Jr.
Aunt Sophie	Etel Billig
Funeral Priest	James Noah
Father Gibson	Bob Zrna
Sister Rebecca	Deanna Dunagan

and Joe Guastaferro, Mike Bacarella, Johnny O'Donnell, Richard Wharton, Tony Zurita, Jr., Saralynne Crittenden, Jim Ortlieb, Julian Pena, Alex Leonard Jenkins, William Lozada, Irma O'Quendo, Charles D. Scholvin, Joel Becker, Greg W. Elam, Rick Sawaya, Cliff Cudney, Kay H. Whipple

Top Right: Billy Crystal, Gregory Hines
(also below)
© *MGM Entertainment*

**Billy Crystal, Gregory Hines,
Joe Pantoliano**

Darlanne Fluegel, Billy Crystal

SPACECAMP

20th CENTURY-FOX) Producers, Patrick Bailey, Walter Coblenz; Director, Harry Winer; Screenplay, W. W. Wicket, Casey T. Mitchell; Story, Patrick Bailey, Larry B. Williams; Executive Producer, Leonard Goldberg; Photography, William Fraker; Designer, Richard MacDonald; Editors, John W. Wheeler, Timothy Board; Music, John Williams; Costumes, Patricia Norris; Associate Producer, David Salven; Executive in Charge of Production, Herb Jellinek; Production Manager, David Salven; Assistant Directors, James B. Simons, Tena Psyche Yatroussis; Production Supervisor, Wendy Bailey; Production Executive, Leonard S. Smith, Jr.; Art Directors, Richard J. Lawrence, Leon Harris; Set Decorator, Richard C. Goddard; Sound, David MacMillan; Special Effects, Chuck Gaspar; Robot Design, Mark Stetson; Special Sound Effects, Ed Bannon, Bruce Glover; Presented by ABC Motion Pictures; Songs by various artists; Original Soundtrack on RCA; Panavision; MGM Color; Dolby Stereo; Rated PG; 112 minutes; June release

CAST

Andie	Kate Capshaw
Kathryn	Lea Thompson
Tish	Kelly Preston
Rudy	Larry B. Scott
Max	Leaf Phoenix
Kevin	Tate Donovan
Zach	Tom Skerritt
Brennan	Barry Primus
Launch Director	Terry O'Quinn
Banning	Mitchell Anderson
Gardener	T. Scott Coffey
NASA #1	Daryl Roach
NASA #2	Peter Scranton
Boy on rooftop	Rocky Krakoff
Young Andie	Hollye Rebecca Suggs
NASA #3	Terry White
Senior Counselor	Susan Becton
Rudy's Father	D. Ben Casey
Girl	Kathy Hanson
Tom the Technician	Ron Harris
Hideo Takamini	Scott Holcomb
Counselor #2	Kevin Gage
Rudy's Brother	Saundra McGuire
Kathryn's Father	Bill Phillips
Bully in dorm	Jon Steigman
Rudy's Brother	Adrian Wells
Special Vocal Effects	Frank Welker

Right: Leaf Phoenix, Lea Thompson, Kate Capshaw, Larry B. Scott, Kelly Preston Above: Kate Capshaw, Leaf Phoenix Top: Kate Capshaw, Lea Thompson, Leaf Phoenix, Larry B. Scott, Tate Donovan
© *ABC Motion Pictures*

Kelly Preston, Larry B. Scott, Lea Thompson, Kate Capshaw

Lea Thompson, Larry B. Scott, Tate Donovan

RUTHLESS PEOPLE

(BUENA VISTA) Producer, Michael Peyser; Directors, Jim Abrahams, David Zucker, Jerry Zucker; Screenplay, Dale Launer; Executive Producers, Richard Wagner, JoAnna Lancaster, Walter Yetnikoff; Photography, Jan DeBont; Art Director, Donald Woodruff; Editors, Arthur Schmidt, Gib Jaffe; Production Manager, Jeffrey Cherno; Assistant Directors, Bill Beasley, Bruce Humphrey, Dannielle Weiss; Costumes, Rosanna Norton; Visual Consultant, Lilly Kilvert; Music, Michel Colombier; Animation Sequence Producer, Sally Cruikshank; Musical Supervision, Tommy Mottola; Production Coordinator, Karen Penhale; Sound, Thomas D. Causey; Special Effects, John Frazier, Rocky A. Gehr; Produced in association with Silver Screen Partners II; Presented by Touchstone; Dolby Stereo; Soundtrack on Epic; Color by DeLuxe; Rated R; 93 minutes; June release

CAST

Sam Stone	Danny DeVito
Barbara Stone	Bette Midler
Ken Kessler	Judge Reinhold
Sandy Kessler	Helen Slate
Carol	Anita Morris
Earl	Bill Pullman
Police Commissioner	William G. Schilling
Lt. Bender	Art Evans
Lt. Walters	Clarence Felder
Bedroom Killer	J. E. Freeman
Stereo Customer	Gary Riley
Loan Officer	Phyllis Applegate
Hooker in car	Jeannine Bisignano
Technician	J. P. Bumstead
"Little Equipment" Ernie	John Cutler
Redheaded Cop	Jim Doughan
Cop at jail	Christopher J. Keene
Coroner	Henry Noguchi
Secretary to Chief of Police	Janet Rotblatt
The Mugger	Frank Silvera
Candy	Susan Marie Snyder
Cop with killer photo	Arnold Turner
Sam's Attorney	Bob Tzudiker
Cop #2	Charles A. Vanega
Social Worker	Louise Yaffe
Judge	Charlotte Zucker
Waiter	Arturo Bonilla
Newscasters	Rick DeReyes, Mie Hunt, Ron Tan
Aerobic Instructors	Beth R. Johnson, Susan Stadner, Richard Wilson
Model	Twyla S. Littleton
Elderly Woman	Mary Elizabeth Thompson

Top Left: Danny DeVito
Below: Bette Midler
© *Touchstone*

Judge Reinhold, Danny DeVito

Bill Pullman

Bette Midler, Judge Reinhold, Helen Slater
Above: Anita Morris Top: Judge Reinhold

Danny DeVito Above: Bette Midler
Top: Judge Reinhold, Helen Slater

RAW DEAL

(DE LAURENTIIS ENTERTAINMENT GROUP) Producer, Martha Schumacher; Director, John Irvin; Story, Luciano Vincenzoni, Sergio Donati; Screenplay, Gary M. DeVore, Norman Wexler; Music, Cinemascore; Costumes, Clifford Capone; Designer, Giorgio Postiglione; Editor, Anne V. Coates; Photography, Production Executive, Lucio Trentini; Production Manager, Fred Caruso; Assistant Directors, Henry Bronchtrin, Bruce Moriarty; Stunts, Glenn Randall; Production Coordinator, Angela Heald; Sound, David Hildyard; Art Director, Maher Ahmad; Special Effects, Joe Lombardi; Special Make Up Effects, Dean Gates; Songs by various artists; Technicolor; Dolby Stereo; Rated R; 97 minutes; June release

CAST

Kaminski	Arnold Schwarzenegger
Monique	Kathryn Harrold
Patrovita	Sam Wanamaker
Rocca	Paul Shenar
Max	Robert Davi
Baker	Ed Lauter
Shannon	Darren McGavin
Baxter	Joe Regalbuto
Marcellino	Mordecai Lawner
Lamanski	Steven Hill
Amy Kaminski	Blanche Baker
Lamanski's Girl	Robey
Dangerous Man	Victor Argo
Killer's	George Wilbur, Denver Mattson
Trager	John Malloy
Sergeant	Lorenzo Clemons
Dingo	Dick Durock
Spike	Frank Ferrara
Jesus	Thomas Rosales
Carson	Jack Hallett
Man in Tux	Leon Rippy
Rice	Jay Butler
Fake State Trooper	Norman Maxwell
Rudy	Tony DiBenedetto
Metzger	Tom Hull
Saleswoman	Mary Canon
Blair	Steve Holt

and Gary Houston, Gregory Noonan, Cedric Guthrie, Gary Olsen, Brooks Gardner, Pat Miller, Jery Hewitt, James Eric, Ralph Foody, Howard Elfman, John Hately, Joel Kramer, Jeff Ramsay, Bill McIntosh, Ted Grossman, Kent Hays, Greg Walker, Cliff Happy, Mike Adams, Dean Smith, Alex Ross, Socorro Santiago, Richard McGough, Sharon Rice, R. Pickett Bugg, John Clark, Scott Blount, Phil Adams, Chuck Hart, Larry Hold, Ken Sprunt

Right: Arnold Schwarzenegger
© *DeLaurentiis Entertainment Group*

Arnold Schwarzenegger

Arnold Schwarzenegger, Kathryn Harrold

LEGAL EAGLES

(UNIVERSAL) Producer, Director, Ivan Reitman; Screenplay, Jim Cash, Jack Epps, Jr.; Story, Ivan Reitman, Jim Cash, Jack Epps, Jr.; Executive Producers, Joe Medjuck, Michael C. Gross; Photography, Laszlo Kovacs; Design, John DeCuir; Editors, Sheldon Kahn, Pem Herring, William Gordean; Music, Elmer Bernstein; Associate Producers, Sheldon Kahn, Arnold Glimcher; Costumes, Albert Wolsky, Bernie Pollack, Alison "Gail" Bixby; Production Manager, John G. Wilson; Assistant Directors, Peter Giuliano, Sarah M. Brim, Katterlie Frauenfelder, Rodney A. Hooks; Set Designers, Peter J. Kelly, Carlos Cerrada, Steve Sardanis; Special Effects, Thomas Fisher, Bill Shirmer, Ted Coplen, Jay King; Sound, Jim Webb, Crew Chamberlain, William F. Ferson; Songs by Rod Stewart, Mike Chapin, Holly Knight, Gene Black, Daryl Hannah, Michael Monteleone, The Rascals, Steppenwolf; Visual Effects, Boss Film Corporation, Richard Edlund; Art Coordinator, Anna Reinhardt; Color; 116 minutes; Rated PG; June release

CAST

Tom Logan	Robert Redford
Laura Kelly	Debra Winger
Chelsea Deardon	Daryl Hannah
Cavanaugh	Brian Dennehy
Victor Taft	Terence Stamp
Bower	Steven Hill
Blanchard	David Clennon
Forrester	John McMartin
Jennifer Logan	Jennie Dundas
Judge Dawkins	Roscoe Lee Browne
Carol Freeman	Christine Baranski
Barbara	Sara Botsford
Marchek	David Hart
Sebastian Deardon	James Hurdle
Hit Man	Gary Klar
Clerk	Christian Clemenson
Judge #1	Bart Burns
Reporter	Bruce French
Doreen	Lynn Hamilton
Taxi Driver	Paul Jabara
Short Lady	Chevi Colton

and Annie Abbott, Kristine Sutherland, Everett Quinton, Peter Boyden, Thomas Barbour, Mary Alison Griffin, Vincent Gustaferro, Burke Byrnes, Ken Kliban, Debra Stricklin, Ron Foster, Rudy Willrich, Robert Benedetti, Grant Heslov, Robert Curtis Brown, Brian Doyle-Murray, Shannon Wilcox, Charles Brown, Kevin Hagan, Jay Thomas, Alex Nevil, Lou Cutell, Olivia Ward, Duitch Helmer, John Marion, Barbara Pallenberg, Gabrielle DeCuir, Liz Sheridan, Michael Anthony, Danny Aiello III

Right: Daryl Hannah, Debra Winger
Above: Jennie Dundas, Robert Redford
Top: Daryl Hannah, Debra Winger,
Robert Redford © *Universal*

Robert Redford, Debra Winger

Debra Winger, Robert Redford

51

THE MANHATTAN PROJECT

(20th CENTURY-FOX) Producers, Jennifer Ogden, Marshall Brickman; Director, Marshall Brickman; Screenplay, Marshall Brickman, Thomas Baum; Photography, Billy Williams; Designer, Philip Rosenberg; Costumes, Shay Cunliffe; Editor, Nina Feinberg; Music, Philippe Sarde; Associate Producer, Roger Paradiso; Production Managers, Jennifer Ogden, Roger Paradiso; Assistant Directors, Ron Bozman, Kyle McCarthy; Special Visual Effects/Technological Design Supervision, Bran Ferren; Orchestrations, Bill Byers; Sound, Les Lazarowitz; Art Director, Robert Guerra; Assistant Costume Designer, Holly Hynes; Special Effects, Connie Brink; A Gladden Entertainment Corporation Presentation; Technicolor; Dolby Stereo; 120 minutes; Rated PG-13; June release

CAST

John Mathewson	John Lithgow
Government	Richard Council
Government Aide	Robert Schenkkan
General	Paul Austin
Scientists	Adrian Sparks, Curt Dempster
Lab Assistant	Bran Ferren
Paul Stephens	Christopher Collet
Elizabeth Stephens	Jill Eikenberry
Jenny Anderman	Cynthia Nixon
Science Teacher	Greg Edelman
Roland	Abe Unger
Max	Robert Leonard
Tennis	David Quinn
Craig	Geoffrey Nauffts
Emma	Katherine Hiler
Terry	Trey Cummins
Local FBI	Steve Borton, Harlan Cary Poe
Jenny's parents	Ned Schmidtke, Sarah Burke
Jenny's brother	Allan & Arthur DeCheser
Lt. Col. Conroy	John Mahoney
Conroy's Lieutenant	Fred G. Smith
Eccles	John David Cullum
Moore	Manny Jacobs
Price	Charlie Fields
Saito	Eric Hsiao
Halley's Comet Kid	Trevor Bolling
Laser Efficiency Kid	Richard Cardona
Flirting Kids	Heather Dominic, Bruce Smolanoff
Registrar	Joan Kendall
Cabbie	John Doumanian
Injection Doctor	Tom Tarpey
FBI	Alec Massey, Edward D. Murphy, Dee Ann McDavid

and Joan Harris, Kerry Donovan, Ken Chapin, Peter McRobbie, Warren Keith, Bruce Chapshaw, Stephen Markle, Al Cerullo, Rocjard Kemloms, Sully Boyar, Timothy Carhart, Fred Melamed, Warren Manzi, Michael Terezco, Frank Ferrara, Jimmy Ray Weeks, William Weslow, Dan E. Butler, Steve Zettler, Richard Caselnova, Michael C. Russo, Roy Farfel

Left: Jill Eikenberry, John Lithgow Top: (C) Christopher Collet, John Mahoney, John Lithgow Below: Christopher Collet, Cynthia Nixon
© Gladden Entertainment Group

AMERICAN ANTHEM

(COLUMBIA) Producer, Robert Schaffel, Doug Chapin; Executive Producer, Freddie Fields; Director, Albert Magnoli; Screenplay, Evan Archerd, Jeff Benjamin; Story, Evan Archerd, Jeff Benjamin, Susan Williams; Photography, Donald E. Thorin; Editor, James Oliver; Music, Alan Silvestri; Designer, Ward Preston; Set Decorators, Chris Westlund, JoAnn Chorney; Sound, Chuck Wilborn; Costumes, Jodie Tillen; Assistant Director, Jerry Ballew; Technical Adviser, Kathy Johnson; Casting, Barbara Miller, Irene Mariano, Darlene Wyatt; Dolby Stereo; MGM Color; Rated PG-13; 100 minutes; July release

CAST

Steve Tevere	Mitch Gaylord
Julie Lloyd	Janet Jones
Linda Tevere	Michelle Phillips
Mikey Tevere	R. J. Williams
Coach Soranhoff	Michael Pataki
Danielle	Patrice Donnelly
Kirk Baker	Stacey Maloney
Becky	Maria Anz
Arthur	Andrew White

(No photos available)

Christopher Collet, John Lithgow

OUT OF BOUNDS

(COLUMBIA) Producers, Charles Fries, Mike Rosenfeld; Director, Richard Tuggle; Screenplay, Tony Kayden; Executive Producers, John Tarnoff, Ray Hartwick; Photography, Bruce Surtees; Designer, Norman Newberry; Editors, Kent Beyda, Larry Bock; Casting, Janet Hirshenson, Jane Jenkins; Music, Stewart Copeland; Music Supervisor, John David Kalodner; Production Manager, Ray Hartwick; Assistant Directors, Bill Scott, Robert Engleman; Costumes, Donna Linson; Set Decorator, Cloudia; Sound, James Tannenbaum; Set Designer, Joseph Pacelli, Jr.; Special Effects, Alan Hall, Lou Cooper, Albert Delgado; Production Coordinator, Shari Leibowitz; Stunts, M. James Arnett; Songs by various artists; Soundtrack on I.R.S. Records; Dolby Stereo; Columbia-Delphi V Productions; DeLuxe Color; Panavision; Rated R; 93 minutes; July release

CAST

Daryl Cage	Anthony Michael Hall
Dizz	Jenny Wright
Roy Gaddis	Jeff Kober
Lt. Delgado	Glynn Turman
Hurley	Raymond J. Barry
Murano	Pepe Serna
Crystal	Michelle Little
Marshall	Jerry Levine
Lemar	Ji-Tu Cumbuka
Tommy Cage	Kevin McCorkle
Chris Cage	Linda Shayne
Mrs. Cage	Maggie Gwinn
Mr. Cage	Ted Gehring
Gil	Meatloaf
Biker	Allan Graf
Martha	Jennifer Balgobin
News Vendor	Kevin Breslin
Police Captain	Murray Lebowitz
Newscasters	Peggy Jo Abraham, Bill Press
Neighbor	Bill Lane
Trucker Cowboy	Dick Ziker
Bus Driver	Bennie Moore
Barney the dog	Popeye

and Dan Lewk, John Vickery, Tony Acierto, David Chung, Tony Kayden, John Tarnoff, Scott Edmund Lane, Stephanie Gregg, Lloyd Nelson, Ollie Lake, James Espinoza, Barbara Lee Soltani, Jefery Smith

Anthony Michael Hall, Glynn Turman
Top: Jenny Hall, Anthony Michael Hall
© Columbia

STAND BY ME

(COLUMBIA) Producers, Andrew Scheinman, Bruce A. Evans, Raynold Gideon; Director, Rob Reiner; Screenplay, Raynold Gideon, Bruce A. Evans; Based on novella "The Body" by Stephen King; Photography, Thomas Del Ruth; Designer, Dennis Washington; Editor, Robert Leighton; Music, Jack Nitzsche; Casting, Jane Jenkins, Janet Hirshenson; Production Manager, Steve Nicolaides; Assistant Directors, Irby Smith, Jim Behnke, Carol Bonnefil; Production Supervisor, Jeff Stott; Costumes, Sue Moore; Set Designer, Richard MacKenzie; Set Decorator, Richard D. Kent; Sound, Bob Eber; Stunts, Rick Barker; Music Supervisor, Celest Ray; Special Effects, Richard L. Thompson, Henry Millar; "Stand by Me", B. E. King, J. Leiber, M. Stoller; Songs by various artists; An Act III Production; Technicolor; Panavision; Rated R; 87 minutes; July release

CAST

Gordie Lechance	Wil Wheaton
Chris Chambers	River Phoenix
Teddy Duchamp	Corey Feldman
Vern Tessio	Jerry O'Connell
The Writer	Richard Dreyfuss
Ace Merrill	Kiefer Sutherland
Billy Tessio	Casey Siemaszko
Charlie Hogan	Gary Riley
Eyeball Chambers	Bradley Gregg
Vince Desjardins	Jason Oliver
Mr. Lachance	Marshall Bell
Mrs. Lachance	Frances Lee McCain
Mr. Quidacioluo	Bruce Kirby
Milo Pressman	William Bronder
Mayor Grundy	Scott Beach
Denny Lachance	John Cusack
Bob Cormier	Matt Williams
Lardass Hogan	Andy Lindberg
Bill Travis	Dick Durock
Donnelley Twins	Kenneth Hodges, John Hodges
Moke	Korey Scott Pollard
Jack Mudgett	Rick Elliott
Ray Brower	Kent Lutrell
Gordon's Son	Chance Quinn

and Madeleine Swift, Popeye, Geanette Bobst, Art Burke, O. B. Babbs, Charlie Owens, Susan Thorpe, Jason Naylor

Wil Wheaton, River Phoenix, Jerry
O'Connell, Corey Feldman
Above: River Phoenix, Kiefer Sutherland

© Columbia

NOTHING IN COMMON

(TRI-STAR) Producer, Alexandra Rose; Director, Garry Marshall; Screenplay, Rick Podell, Michael Preminger; Photography, John A. Alonzo; Designer, Charles Rosen; Editor, Glenn Farr; Executive Producer, Roger M. Rothstein; Costumes, Rosanna Norton; Music, Patrick Leonard; Associate Producer, Nick Abdo; Casting, Jane Alderman, Shelley Andreas; Music Supervision, Danny Bramson; Production Manager, Roger M. Rothstein; Assistant Directors, Katy Emde, Alan B. Curtiss; Sound, Bruce Bisenz; Set Decorator, Jane Bogart; Set Designers, William L. Skinner, Roland E. Hill, Jr.; Production Coordinator, Katharine Ann Curtiss; Special Effects, William Grant Burdette, Jr.; Choreography, Shirley Kirkes; Songs, Patrick Leonard, Christopher Cross, Jon Bettis, Tom Bailey, Alannah Currie, James P. Dunne, and various artists; Soundtrack on Arista; Metrocolor; Panavision; Rated PG; 118 minutes; July release

CAST

David Basner	Tom Hanks
Max Basner	Jackie Gleason
Lorraine Basner	Eva Marie Saint
Charlie Gargas	Hector Elizondo
Andrew Woolridge	Barry Corbin
Donna Mildred Martin	Bess Armstrong
Cheryl Ann Wayne	Sela Ward
Shelley the stewardess	Cindy Harrell
Roger the commercial director	John Kapelos
David's Secretary	Carol Messing
Ted Geller	Bill Applebaum
Mishi	Mona Lynden
Cameron	Anthony Starke
Rick	Julio Alonso
Dale	Jane Morris
Brian	Dan Castellaneta
Eric	Mike Hagerty
Lewis	Jeff Michalski
Receptionist	Toni Hudson
Gene	Bruce A. Young
Mitchell	Ben Rawnsley
Louise Pelham	Lynda Goodfriend
Robert	Mark Von Holstein
Ed Bedsole	Ron Dean
Lucille	Elma Veronda Jackson
Jo-Jo	Noelle Bou-Sliman
Max's Doctor	Jack Larson

and Vicki Lucachick, Kathi Marshall, Scott Marshall, Kim Genelle, Andrew Paris, Steve Assad, Vincent Guastaferro, John Antony, Lucinda Crosby, Andra Akers, Tracy Reiner, Harvey Keenan, Sam Denoff, John Yune, Lorna Thayer, Meg Wyllie, Bobbie Jo Burke, Shirley Kirkes, Maxine Dunn, David Hall, Bo Sabato, Leslie Alcott, Anthony W. Marshall, Paul Zimmerman, Harry Gelt, Julie Paris, Jeris Poindexter, Anne Rasmussen, Jason Alderman, Michael I. Gold, Steve Restivo, Susan Cotton, Thomas Smrt, Frank Campanella, Melvin E. Pape, Lou Evans, Corey McKinney, Conrad Janis and The Unlisted Jazz Band

Left: Tom Hanks, Eva Marie Saint
Top: Jackie Gleason, Tom Hanks
Below: Tom Hanks, Barry Corbin, Sela Ward
© *Tri-Star*

Tom Hanks, Bess Armstrong

Tom Hanks, Hector Elizondo

ABOUT LAST NIGHT . . .

(TRI-STAR) Producers, Jason Brett, Stuart Oken; Director, Edward Zwick; Screenplay, Tim Kazurinsky, Denise DeClue; Based on play "*Sexual Perversity in Chicago*" by David Mamet; Photography, Andrew Dintenfass; Designer, Ida Random; Editor, Harry Keramidas; Executive Producer, Arnold Stiefel; Costumes, Deborah L. Scott; Music, Miles Goodman; Music Supervision, Bones Howe; Associate Producer/Production Manager, E. Darrell Hallenbeck; Casting, Gail Eisenstadt; Assistant Directors, Allan Wertheim, Donald Eaton; Assistant Art Director, William Elliott; Set Designer, Beverli Eagan; Set Decorator, Chris Butler; Special Effects, Darrell Pritchett; Sound, Jacques Nosco; Songs by various artists; Soundtrack on EMI America Records and XDR Cassettes; Dolby Stereo; Metrocolor; Panavision; Rated R; 113 minutes; July release

CAST

Danny	Rob Lowe
Debbie	Demi Moore
Bernie	Jim Belushi
Joan	Elizabeth Perkins
Mr. Favio	George DiCenzo
Mother Malone	Michael Alldredge
Steve Carlson	Robin Thomas
Alex	Donna Gibbons
Pat	Megan Mullally
Leslie	Patricia Duff
Mrs. Lyons	Rosana DeSoto
Carrie	Sachi Parker
Gary	Robert Neches
Gus	Joe Greco
Carmen	Ada Maris
Crystal	Rebeca Arthur
Colin	Tim Kazurinsky
Ira	Kevin Bourland
Man in Joan's apartment	Dean Bastounes
Madge	Charlotte Maier
Gloria	Marjorie Bransfield
Girl at bar	Kimberley Pistone
Lisa	Lindy Huddleson
Ruthie	Dawn Arnemann

and Raffi DiBlasio, Sheenika Smith, Heath Wagerman, Brie O'Banion, Catherine Keener, Steven Eckholdt, Robert B. Durkin, Ray Wohl

Top: Elizabeth Perkins, Rob Lowe, Demi Moore, Jim Belushi © *Tri-Star*

Demi Moore, Elizabeth Perkins

55

VAMP

(NEW WORLD) Producer, Donald P. Borchers; Director/Screenplay, Richard Wenk; Story, Donald P. Borchers, Richard Wenk; Music, Jonathan Elias; Special Make-Up Effects, Greg Cannom; Associate Producer, Susan Gelb; Sound, Gregg Barbanell, Mark Ulano, Costumes, Betty Pecha Madden; Designer, Alan Roderick-Jones; Jan Brodin; Photography, Elliot Davis; Editor, Marc Grossman; Production Manager, Mario Davis; Assistant Directors, Matia Karrell, Betsy Pollock, Benita Allen, Whitney Hunter, Grant Gilmore; Production Coordinator, Lisa Hollingshead; Associate Editor, Joe Woo, Jr.; Dialogue Director, Gordon Hunt; Production Consultant, Bob Manning; Art Directors, Carol Clements, Philip Aja; Special Effects, Image Engineering, Inc., Peter Chesney, Jarn Heil, Tom Chesney, Chris Chesney, Joseph Viskocil; Orchestrations, Jonathan Elias, Douglas Hall; Synthesizer Realization, Jonathan Elias, Paul Seymour; Special Visual Effects, Apogee, Inc.; Songs by various artists; Presented in association with Balcor Films Investors; Metrocolor; Rated R; 93 minutes; July release

CAST

Keith	Chris Makepeace
Vic	Sandy Baron
A. J.	Robert Rusler
Amaretto	Dedee Pfeiffer
Duncan	Gedde Watanabe
Katrina	Grace Jones
Snow	Billy Drago
Vlad	Brad Logan
Cimmaron	Lisa Lyon
Fraternity Leader	Jim Boyle
Students	Larry Spinak, Eric Welch, Stuart Rogers
Sock Salesman	Gary Swailes
Coffee Shop Proprietor	Ray Ballard
Maven	Paunita Nichols
Dragon Girl	Trudel Williams
Hard Hat	Marlon McGann
Shorty	Thomas Bellin
Pool Player	Bryan McGuire
Seko	Leila Hee Olsen
Jett	Hilary Carlip
Dominique	Francine Swift
Candi	Tricia Brown

and Noami Shohan, Janeen Davis, Ytossie Patterson, Tanya Papanicolas, Robin Kaufman, Hy Pike, Pops, Bob Schott, Adam Barth, Bill Morphew, Simmy Bow, Roger Hampton, Andy Rivas, Julius LeFlore, Greg Lewis, Dar Robinson, Russell Clark, Dar Robinson

Top Right: Chris Makepeace, Dedee Pfeiffer
© *New World Pictures*

Grace Jones, Robert Rusler

UNDER THE CHERRY MOON

(WARNER BROS.) Producers, Robert Cavallo, Joseph Ruffalo, Steven Fargnoli; Director, Prince; Screenplay, Becky Johnston; Music/Songs, Prince and The Revolution, John L. Nelson; Music, Clare Fischer; Associate Producer/Production Supervisor, Graham Cottle; Photography, Michael Ballhaus; Editor, Eve Gardos; Designer, Richard Sylbert; Costumes, Marie France; Creative Consultant, Mary Lambert; Casting, Jose Villaverde; Production Manager, Bernard Mazauric; Assistant Directors, Michel Cheyko, Marc Jeny, Michel Ferry; Art Director, Damien Lafranchi; Set Decorator, Ian Whittaker; Sound, Daniel Brisseau; Makeup, Robyn Lynch; Special Effects, Maurice Zisswiller; Dolby Stereo; Technicolor; Rated PG-13; 98 minutes; July release

CAST

Christopher Tracy	Prince
Tricky	Jerome Benton
Mary Sharon	Kristin Scott Thomas
Mr. Sharon	Steven Berkoff
Katy	Emmanuelle Sallet
Mrs. Sharon	Alexandra Stewart
Mrs. Wellington	Francesca Annis
The Girlfriends	Pamela Ludwig, Barbara Stall, Karen Geerlings
The Jaded Three	Victor Spinetti, Myriam Tadesse, Moune De Vivier
Young Boy at party	Amoury Desjardins
Young Girl at party	Garance Tosello
Eddy	Sylvain Levignac
Lou	Guy Cuevas
Larry	Patrice Mellenec
Mary's Minder	Azouz Saieb
Sharon's Butler	Jean Allaz
Sharon's Maid	Rosette Taubert
Mary's Chauffeur	John Rico
Maitre D'	Maurice Lenorman
Police Inspector	Sam Karmann
Mrs. Wellington's Butler	John Cooper
Champagne Lady	Jobby Valente
The Dancer	Alexa Fioroni

and Veronique Denoyel, Lydie Diakhate, Patricia Poulain, Catherine Allard, Nicky South, Christine Christen-Giguet, Beatrice Berthet, Nicolas Monard, Michael Kotzritzki, Claude Copola, Monica Quigley, Giselle Finazzo

Prince

PSYCO III

(**UNIVERSAL**) Producer, Hilton A. Green; Director, Anthony Perkins; Screenplay, Charles Edward Pogue; Based on characters created by Robert Bloch; Associate Producer/Production Manager, Donald E. Zepfel; Photography, Bruce Surtees; Designer, Henry Bumstead; Editor, David Blewitt; Music, Carter Burwell; Assistant Directors, Gary Daigler, Katterli Frauenfelder; Costumes, Peter V. Saldutti, Marla Denise Schlom; Special Effects, Karl G. Miller, Louis R. Cooper, Dan Lester; Sound, John Stacy, Jim Thompson; Special Visual Effects, Syd Dutton, Bill Taylor; Special Makeup, Michael Westmore; Songs, Carter Burwell, Steve Bray, Stanton-Miranda, David Sanborn; Color; Panavision; Dolby Stereo; Rated R; 93 minutes; July release

CAST

Norman Bates	Anthony Perkins
Maureen	Diana Scarwid
Duane	Jeff Fahey
Tracy	Roberta Maxwell
Sheriff Hunt	Hugh Gillin
Myrna	Lee Garlington
Statler	Robert Alan Browne
Father Brian	Gary Bayer
Sister Margaret	Patience Cleveland
Red	Juliette Cummins
Deputy Leo	Steve Guevara
Ruthie	Kay Heberle
Kyle	Donovan Scott
Sister Catherine	Karen Hensel
Lou	Jack Murdock
Patsy	Katt Shea Ruben
Harvey Leach	Hugo L. Stanger
Belltower Nun	Lisa Ives
Bartender	Angele Ritter
Nun	Diane Rodriguez

**Right: Anthony Perkins Top: Roberta
Maxwell, Anthony Perkins**
© *Universal*

**Hugh Gillin, Anthony Perkins, Diana
Scarwid Above: Jeff Fahey, Diana Scarwid**

Diana Scarwid, Anthony Perkins

MAXIMUM OVERDRIVE

(DE LAURENTIIS ENTERTAINMENT GROUP) Executive Producers, Mel Pearl, Don Levin; Producer, Martha Schumacher; Director/Screenplay, Stephen King; Photography, Armando Nannuzzi; Music, AC/DC; Designer, Giorgio Postiglione; Editor, Evan Lottman; Costumes, Clifford Capone; Production Manager, Marilyn Stonehouse; Assistant Directors, Tony Lucibello, Elizabeth Scherberger; Production Coordinator, Angela Heald; Sound, Ed White, Greg Sheldon; Set Designer, Hilton Rosemarin; Special Effects Makeup, Dean Gates, Special Effects, Steven Galich; Translation, Roberto Croci/Mara Trovato; Special Visual Effects, Barry Nolan; Digital Sound, Chris Hyams-Hart; Songs by various artists; Co-Producer, Milton Subotsky; Technicolor; Dolby Stereo; Rated R; 97 minutes; July release

CAST

Bill Robinson	Emilio Estevez
Hendershot	Pat Hingle
Brett	Laura Harrington
Connie	Yeardley Smith
Curt	John Short
Wanda June	Ellen McElduff
Duncan	J. C. Quinn
Camp Loman	Christopher Murney
Deke	Holter Graham
Handy	Frankie Faison
Joe	Pat Miller
Max	Jack Canon
Steve	Barry Bell
Frank	John Brasington
Andy	J. Don Ferguson
Brad	Leon Rippy
Barry	Bob Gooden
Rolf	R. Pickett Bugg
Videoplayer	Giancarlo Esposito
2nd Man	Martin Tucker
2nd Woman	Marla Maples
Bridgemaster	Ned Austin
Helper	Richard Chapman, Jr.
Coach	Bob Gunter
Umpire	Bill Huggins

Left: An Evil Truck
Top: Emilio Estevez
© *DeLaurentiis*

Pat Hingle, Emilio Estevez, Laura Harrington, Pat Miller

HEARTBURN

(PARAMOUNT) Producers, Mike Nichols, Robert Greenhut; Director, Mike Nichols; Screenplay, Nora Ephron, from her novel; Photography, Nestor Almendros; Designer, Tony Walton; Costumes, Ann Roth; Editor, Sam O'Steen; Music, Carly Simon; Associate Producer, Joel Tuber; Production Manager, Ezra Swerdlow; Assistant Directors, Joel Tuber, David Dreyfuss, Timothy M. Bourne; Art Director, John Kasarda; Set Decorator, Susan Bode; Sound, James Sabat; Assistant Costume Designer, Gary Jones; Music Producers, Russ Kunkel, Bill Payne, George Massenburg; Songs by various artists; Technicolor; Panavision; Rated R; 108 minutes; July release

CAST

Rachel	Meryl Streep
Mark	Jack Nicholson
Richard	Jeff Daniels
Vera	Maureen Stapleton
Julie	Stockard Channing
Arthur	Richard Masur
Betty	Catherine O'Hara
Harry	Steven Hill
Dmitri	Milos Forman
Annie	Natalie Stern
Thelma Rice	Karen Akers
Juanita	Aida Linares
Della	Anna Maria Horsford
Detective O'Brien	Ron McLarty
Dr. Appel	Kenneth Welsh
Subway Thief	Kevin Spacey
Eve	Mercedes Ruehl
Diana	Joanna Gleason
Dan	R. S. Thomas
Ellis	Jack Gilpin
Sidney	Christian Clemenson
British Moderator	John Wood
Jeweler	Sidney Armus
Contractor Laszlo	Yakov Smirnoff
Judith	Caroline Aaron
Hairdresser	Lela Ivey
Hairdresser's Friend	Tracey Jackson
Rachel's Sister	Libby Titus
Hospital Receptionist	Angela Pietropinto
Wedding Speaker	Dana Ivey
Jonathan Rice	John Rothman
Anesthetist	Elijah Lindsay
Butcher	Jack Neam
Arthur & Julie's Daughter	Kimi Parks
Judge	Salem Ludwig

and Cynthia O'Neal, Susan Forristal, Patricia Falkenhain, Margaret Thomson, Charles Denney, Gregg Almquist, Garrison Lane, Ryan Hilliard, Dana Streep, Mary Streep, Cyrilla Dorn, May Pang, Michael Regan, Ari M. Roussimoff, Luther Rucker

Top: Jack Nicholson, Meryl Streep
Right: Jack Nicholson, Meryl Streep
Below: Meryl Streep, Maureen Stapleton,
Christian Clemenson, Rich Thomas, Mercedes Ruehl
Right Center: Jack Nicholson, Meryl Streep,
Karen Akers, John Rothman, Catherine O'Hara
© *Paramount/Brian Hamill*

Susan Forristal, Meryl Streep, Jeff Daniels

THE GREAT MOUSE DETECTIVE

(BUENA VISTA) Producer, Burny Mattinson; Directors, John Musker, Ron Clements, Dave Michener, Burny Mattinson; Music, Henry Mancini; Story Adaptation, Pete Young, Vance Gerry, Steve Hulett, Ron Clements, John Musker, Bruce M. Morris, Matthew O'Callaghan, Burny Mattinson, Dave Michener, Melvin Shaw; Based on book *Basil of Baker Street* by Eve Titus; Supervising Animators, Mark Henn, Glen Keane, Robert Minkoff, Hendel Butoy; Consultant, Eric Larson; Art Director, Guy Vasilovich; Production Executives, Edward Hansen, Peter Schneider; Production Manager, Don Hahn; Editors, Roy M. Brewer, Jr., James Melton; Assistant Directors, Timothy J. O'Donnell, Mark A. Hester; Special Photographic Effects, Philip L. Meador; Production Coordinators, Dennis Edwards, Joseph Morris, Ron Rocha; Presented by Walt Disney Pictures; Animated; Color by DeLuxe; Dolby Stereo; Soundtrack on Buena Vista; Rated G; 80 minutes; July release

CAST (VOICES)

Professor Ratigan	Vincent Price
Basil	Barrie Ingham
Dawson	Val Bettin
Olivia	Susanne Pollatschek
Fidget	Candy Candido
Mrs. Judson	Diana Chesney
The Mouse Queen	Eve Brenner
Flaversham	Alan Young
Sherlock Holmes	Basil Rathbone
Watson	Laurie Main
Lady Mouse	Shani Wallis
Bar Maid	Ellen Fitzhugh
Citizen	Walker Edmiston
Bartholomew	Barrie Ingham
Thug Guards	Wayne Allwine, Val Bettin, Tony Anselmo, Walker Edmiston

**Dawson and Basil
in "The Great Mouse Detective"**

HAUNTED HONEYMOON

(ORION) Producer, Susan Ruskin; Director, Gene Wilder; Screenplay, Gene Wilder, Terence Marsh; Photography, Fred Schuler; Designer, Terence Marsh; Editor, Christopher Greenbury; Music, John Morris; Costumes, Ruth Myers; Special Effects, John Stears, Ian Scoones, John Markwell, John Hatt, Les Dear; Associate Producers, Basil Rayburn, Emile Buyse; Set Decorator, Michael Seirton; Art Director, Alan Tomkins; Production Supervisor, Basil Rayburn; Assistant Directors, Roy Button, Patrick Kinney; Sound, Simon Kaye, Tommy Staples; Orchestrator, Jack Hayes; Choreography, Graciela Daniele; Songs by various artists; Color; Rated PG; 83 minutes; July release

CAST

Larry Abbot	Gene Wilder
Vickie Pearle	Gilda Radner
Aunt Kate	Dom DeLuise
Charles	Jonathan Pryce
Dr. Paul Abbot	Paul L. Smith
Francis, Sr.	Peter Vaughan
Pfister	Bryan Pringle
Francis, Jr.	Roger Ashton-Griffiths
Montego	Jim Carter
Sylvia	Eve Ferret
Nora Abbot	Julann Griffin
Susan	Jo Ross
Rachel	Ann Way
Werewolf	Will Keaton
Producer	Don Fellows
Sponsor	Lou Hirsch
Announcer	Christopher Muncke
The Host	Bill Bailey
P.R. Man	David Healy
Eddy—SFX Man	Howard Swinson
Engineer	Edward Wiley
Production Assistant	Andrea Browne
Radio Actor #1	Matt Zimmerman
Larry's Mother	Sally Osborn
Little Larry	Alastair Haley
Toby the Dog	Scampi
Conductor	Andy Ross

**Gene Wilder, Gilda Radner and
Above: with Dom DeLuise**

FLIGHT OF THE NAVIGATOR

(**BUENA VISTA**) Producers, Robby Wald, Dimitri Villard; Director, Rindal Kleiser; Screenplay, Michael Burton, Matt MacManus; Based on a story by Mark H. Baker; Executive Producers, Jonathan Sanger, Mark Damon, John Hyde; Photography, James Glennon; Designer, William J. Creber; Editor, Jeff Gourson; Co-Producer, David Joseph; Music, Alan Silvestri; Co-Executive Producer, Malcolm Harding; Production Manager, Malcolm Harding; Assistant Directors, Peter Bogart, Randall Badger, Terry Miller, Jr.; Visual Effects, Peter Donen; Art Director, Michael Novotny; Max and the Creatures Performed by Tony Urbano, Tim Blaney; Sound, Robert Wald; Sound, Emil Razpopov, Dessie Markovsky; Costumes, Mary Lou Byrd; Special Effects, Jack Bennett, John Boisseau, Bruce Hannover; Production Coordinator, Bridget Murphy; Presented by Walt Disney Pictures; Color; Dolby Stereo; Rated PG; 90 minutes; July release

CAST

David Freeman	Joey Cramer
Helen Freeman	Veronica Cartwright
Bill Freeman	Cliff DeYoung
Carolyn McAdams	Sarah Jessica Parker
Jeff (16 years)	Matt Adler
Dr. Faraday	Howard Hesseman
Max	Paul Mall
Troy	Robert Small
Jeff (8 years)	Albie Whitaker
Dr. Carr	Jonathan Sanger
Mrs. Howard	Iris Acker
Mr. Howard	Richard Liberty
Detective Banks	Raymond Forchion
Woman Officer	Cynthia Caquelin
Night Guard Brayton	Ted Bartsch
Female Technician	Gizelle Elliot
Observation Guard	Tony Tracy
NASA Officer	Philip Hoelcher
Lieutenant King	Chase Randolph
Gas Station Attendant	Rusty Pouch
Tourist Man	Robert Goodman
Tourist Child	Ryan Murray
Jennifer Bradley	Keri Rogers
Kid in Mustang	Kenny Davis
Bixby	Bruce Laks

and Brigid Cleary, Michael Strano, Parris Buckner, Robyn Peterson, Julio Mechoso, Butch Raymond, Bob Strickland, Michael Brockman, Louis Cutolo, Debbie Casperson, John Archie, Tony Calvino, Peter Lundquist, Jill Beach, Courtney Brown, Kevin McCoy, Arnie Ross, Fritz Braumer.

Right: Joey Cramer in spacecraft
Top: Jonathan Sanger, Veronica Cartwright, Cliff DeYoung
© *PSO Presentations*

Joey Cramer with Max

Howard Hesseman

ALIENS

(20th CENTURY-FOX) Producer, Gale Anne Hurd; Director Screenplay, James Cameron; Story, James Cameron, David Giler, Walter Hill; Based on characters created by Dan O'Bannon, Ronald Shusett; Photography, Adrian Biddle; Designer, Peter Lamont; Editor, Ray Lovejoy; Music, James Horner; Executive Producers, Gordon Carroll, David Giler, Walter Hill; Alien Effects, Stan Winston; Certain Special Visual Effects, The L. A. Effects Group, Inc.; Visual Effects, Robert Skotak, Dennis Skotak, Brian Johnson; Alien Design, H. R. Giger; Conceptual Designer, Ron Cobb; Conceptual Artist, Syd Mead; Special Effects, John Richardson; Costumes, Emma Porteous; Production Supervisor, Hugh Harlow; Production Managers, Mo Coppitters, Gil Whelan; Assistant Directors, Derek Cracknell, Melvin Lind; Sound, Roy Charman; Video Effects, Richard Hewitt; Art Directors, Terence Ackland-Snow, Bert Davey, Fred Hole, Michael Lamont, Ken Court; Set, Crispian Sallis; Orchestrator, Greig McRitchie; A Brandywine Production; Color by Eastman Kodak; Dolby Stereo; Rated R; 137 minutes; July release

CAST

Ripley	Sigourney Weaver
Newt	Carrie Henn
Corporal Hicks	Michael Biehn
Burke	Paul Reiser
Bishop	Lance Henriksen
Private Hudson	Bill Paxton
Lieutenant Gorman	William Hope
Private Vasquez	Jenette Goldstein
Sergeant Apone	Al Matthews
Private Drake	Mark Rolston
Private Frost	Ricco Ross
Corporal Ferro	Colette Hiller
Private Spunkmeyer	Daniel Kash
Corporal Dietrich	Cynthia Scott
Private Crowe	Tip Tipping
Private Wierzbowski	Trevor Steedman
Van Leuwen	Paul Maxwell
ECA Rep	Valerie Colgan
Insurance Man	Alan Polonsky
Med Tech	Alibe Parsons
Doctor	Blain Fairman
Cocooned Woman	Barbara Coles
Alien Warrior	Carl Toop
Power Loader Operator	John Lees

and Louise Head, Kiran Shah, Paul Weston, Chris Webb, Malcolm Weaver, Sean McCabe, Steve Dent, Sue Crosland, Stuart St. Paul, Jazzer Jeyes, Bill Weston, Stuart Fell, Jason White, Simon Crane, Eddie Powell, Eleanor Bertram

Top Left: Sigourney Weaver and Marines
Below: Michael Biehn
© *20th Century Fox*

1986 Academy Awards For Best Visual Effects, Best Sound Effects Editing

Sigourney Weaver, Carrie Henn

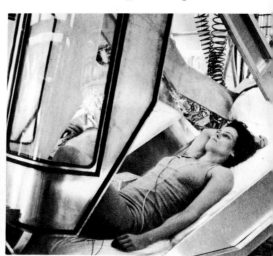

Sigourney Weaver

62

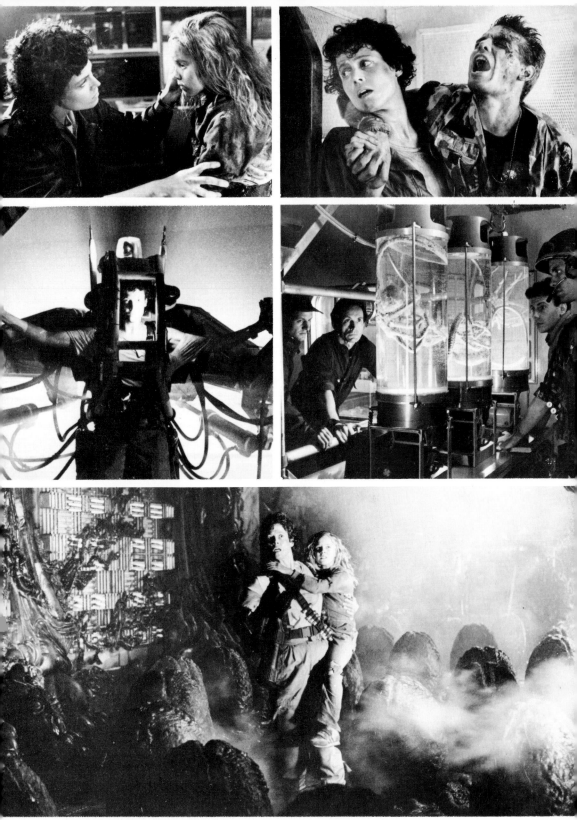

Sigourney Weaver, Carrie Henn also Top Left Below: Sigourney Weaver Top Right: Sigourney Weaver, Michael Biehn Below: William Hope, Lance Henriksen, Paul Reiser, Michael Biehn

BIG TROUBLE IN LITTLE CHINA

(20th CENTURY-FOX) Producer, Larry J. Franco; Director, Joh
Carpenter; Screenplay, Gary Goldman, David Z. Weinstein; Adapta
tion, W. D. Richter; Executive Producers, Paul Monash, Keith Baris
Photography, Dean Cundey; Designer, John J. Lloyd; Editor, Mar
Warner, Steve Mirkovich, Edward A. Warschilka; Visual Effects
Richard Edlund; Costumes, April Ferry; Associate Producers, Jim Lau
James Lew; Music, John Carpenter in association with Alan Howart
Production Manager, James Herbert; Assistant Directors, Larry Frar
co, Matt Earl Beesley; Art Director, Les Gobruegge; Set Director
George R. "Bob" Nelson; Sound, Thomas Causey; Special Effects
Joseph Unsinn, Stanley Amborn, James Fredburg; Martial Ar
Choreographer, James Lew; Production Coordinator, Mary Sutto
Hallmann; Set Designers, Craig Edgar, Steve Schwartz; Sound Effects
William Hartman, Anthony R. Milch; Title Song, John Carpenter/"Th
Coupe De Villes"; Original Soundtrack on Enigma Records; Par
avision; Color by DeLuxe; Rated PG-13; 100 minutes; July release

CAST

Jack Burton	Kurt Russe
Gracie Law	Kim Cattra
Wang Chi	Dennis Du
Lo Pan	James Hon
Egg Shen	Victor Won
Margo	Kate Burto
Eddie Lee	Donald L
Thunder	Carter Won
Rain	Peter Kwon
Lightning	James Pa
Miao Yin	Suzee Pa
Uncle Chu	Chao Li Ch
Needles	Jeff Imada
Joe Lucky	Rummel Mo
One Ear	Craig N
White Tiger	June Kin
Mrs. O'Toole	Noel Toy
Chinese Girl in White Tiger	Jade G
Pinstripe Lawyer	Jerry Hardin
Chang Sing 1 thru 6	James Lew, Jim Lau
	Ken Endoso, Stuart Quan
	Gary Toy, George Cheung
Wounded Chang Sing	Jimmy Jue
Sewer Monster	Noble Craig
Chinese Guard	Danny Kwan
Tara	Min Luong
Chinese Gambler	Paul Lee

and Al Leong, Gerald Okamura, Willie Wong, Eric Lee, Yukio G
Collins, Bill M. Ryusaki, Brian Imada, Nathan Jung, Daniel Inosanto,
Vernon Rieta, Daniel Wong, Daniel Eric Lee, Lia Chang, Dian Tanaka,
Donna L. Noguschi, Shinko Isobe

Suzee Pai, Peter Kwong, Kim Cattrall
Above: Dennis Dun, Kurt Russell, Victor Wong

64

THE FLY

(20th CENTURY-FOX) Producer, Stuart Cornfeld; Director, David Cronenberg; Screenplay, Charles Edward Pogue, David Cronenberg; From the story by George Langelaan; Photography, Mark Irwin; Designer, Carol Spier; Editor, Ronald Sanders; Music, Howard Shore; Co-Producers, Marc-Ami Boyman, Kip Ohman; The Fly Created/Designed by Chris Walas, Inc.; Production Manager, David Coatsworth; Assistant Directors, John Board, Kim Winther, Patricia Rozema, Thomas P. Quinn; Production Coordinator, Debbie Cooke; Visual Consultant, Harold Michaelson; Art Director, Rolf Harvey; Set, Elinor Rose Galbraith, James McAteer; Costumes, Denise Cronenberg; Additional Photography, Kenneth Post, Robin Miller; Sound, Bryan Day, Michael Lacroix; Sound Effects, Jane Tattersall; Special Effects, Louis Craig, Ted Ross; Computer/Video Effects, Lee Wilson; Orchestrations, Homer Dennison; Opticals, Dreamquest; A Brooksfilm Production; Color by DeLuxe; Dolby Stereo; Rated R; 95 minutes; August release

CAST

Seth Brundle	Jeff Goldblum
Veronica Quaife	Geena Davis
Stathis Borans	John Getz
Tawny	Joy Boushel
Dr. Cheevers	Les Carlson
Marky	George Chubalo
2nd Man in Bar	Michael Copeman
Gynecologist	David Cronenberg
Nurse	Carol Lazare
Clerk	Shawn Hewitt
Brundle Stunt Double	Brent Meyers
Gymnastic Doubles	Doron Kernerman, Romuald Vervin

Right: Jeff Goldblum
© 20th Century Fox/Attila Dory

1986 Academy Award For Best Makeup

Geena Davis, Jeff Goldblum

PARTING GLANCES

(CINECOM) Producers, Yoram Mandel, Arthur Silverman; Director/Screenplay, Bill Sherwood; Executive Producer, Paul A. Kaplan; Associate Producers, Nancy Greenstein, Victoria Westhead; Photography, Jacek Laskus; Casting, Daniel Haughey; Designer, John Loggia; Art Directors, Daniel Haughey, Mark Sweeney; Costumes, Sylvia Heisel; Film/Sound/Music Editor, Bill Sherwood; Production Manager, Victoria Westhead; Assistant Directors, Yoram Mandel, Tony Jacobs; Production Coordinators, Nancy Greenstein, Deborah Rosenberg; Sound, Scott Breindel; A Rondo Productions Film; Color; Not Rated; 90 minutes; February release

CAST

Michael	Richard Ganoung
Robert	John Bolger
Nick	Steve Buscemi
Peter	Adam Nathan
Joan	Kathy Kinney
Cecil	Patrick Tull
Betty	Yolande Bavan
Douglas	Richard Wall
Douglas' Sidekick	Jim Selfe
Sarah	Kristin Moneagle
Dave	John Siemens
Sam	Bob Kohrherr
Klaus	Theodore Ganger
Liselotte	Nada
Ex-Seminarian	Patrick Ragland
Ricky	Cam Brainard
Commendatore (ghost)	Daniel Haughey
Chris (little girl)	Sylwia Hartowicz
Chris's Mother	Hanna Hartowicz
Cab Driver	Nicholas Hill

Right: Steve Buscemi
Top: Yolande Bavan, Richard Ganoung
© *Cinecom*

Richard Ganoung, Adam Nathan

SHE'S GOTTA HAVE IT

(ISLAND PICTURES) Producer, Shelton J. Lee; Director/
Screenplay/Editor, Spike Lee; Photography, Ernest Dickerson; Music,
Bill Lee; Associate Producer, Pamm Jackson; Designer, Wynn
Thomas; Art Director, Ron Paley; Production Supervisor, Monty Ross;
Sound, Steve Ning, Carol Everson, Paul Holtzman; Costumes, John
Michael Reefer; Vocals, Ronnie Dyson; Color; Rated R; 100 minutes;
August release

CAST

Nola Darling	Tracy Camila Johns
Jamie Overstreet	Tommy Redmond Hicks
Greer Childs	John Canada Terrell
Mars Blackmon	Spike Lee
Opal Gilstrap	Raye Dowell
Clorinda Bradford	Joie Lee
Dr. Jamison	Epatha Merkinson
Sonny Darling	Bill Lee
Ava	Cheryl Burr
Noble	Aaron Dugger
Keva	Stephanie Covington
Shawn	Renata Cobbs
Toby	Cheryl Singleton
Dog 1	Monty Ross
Dog 2	Lewis Jordan
Dog 3	Erick Dellums
Dog 4	Reggie Hudlin
Dog 5	Eric Payne
Dog 6	Marcus Turner
Dog 7	Gerard Brown
Dog 8	Ernest Dickerson
Dog 9	Eric Wilkins
Dog 10	Fab Five Freddy Braithwaite
Dog 11	Scott Sillers
Dog 12	Geoffrey Garfield
Receptionist	Kathy Banks
Soundman	Steve Nicks
Female Walk On	Pamm Jackson

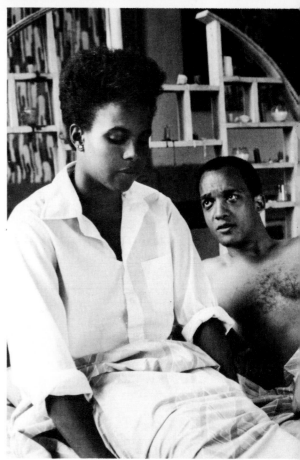

Right: Tracy Camila Johns, Tommy Redmond Hicks
© *Island Pictures*

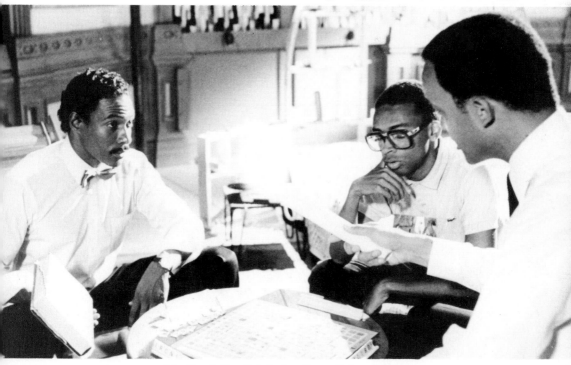

John Canada Terrell, Spike Lee, Tommy Redmond Hicks

EXTREMITIES

(ATLANTIC) Producer, Burt Sugarman; Director, Robert M. Young; Photography, Curtis Clark; Screenplay, William Mastrosimone; Music, J. A. C. Redford; Editor, Arthur Coburn; Designer, Chester Kac zenski; Executive Producers, Thomas Coleman, Michael Rosenblat Line Producer, George W. Perkins; Line Producer/Production Mana ger, Scott Rosenfelt; Assistant Directors, Sharon Mann, Victoria F Rhodes; Music Supervisor, Steve Tyrell; Sound, Jan Brodin; Stunts Jeannie Epper; Production Coordinator, Patricia Bischetti; Costumes Linda Bass; Consultant, Kathy O'Rear; Color; Rated R; 91 minutes August release

CAST

Marjorie	Farrah Fawce
Joe	James Russ
Terry	Diana Scarwi
Patricia	Alfre Woodar
Officer Sudow	Sandy Marti
Officer #1	Eddie Vele
Officer #2	Tom Evere
Woman on phone	Donna Lynn Leav
Mother at Police Station	Enid Ker

Top Left: Alfre Woodard, Farrah Fawcett
Below: Farrah Fawcett, James Russo
© *Atlantic Entertainment Group*

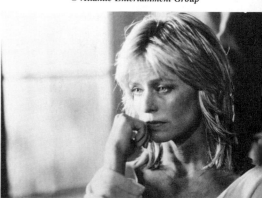

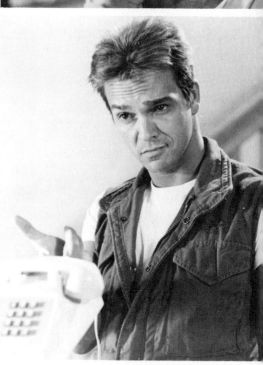

Diana Scarwid

James Russo
Above: Farrah Fawcett

68

BLUE VELVET

(DE LAURENTIIS ENTERTAINMENT GROUP) Executive Producer, Richard Roth; Director/Screenplay, David Lynch; Photography, Frederick Elmes; Designer, Patricia Norris; Editor, Duwayne Dunham; Sound, Alan Splet; Music, Angelo Badalamenti; Assistant Directors, Ellen Rauch, Ian Woolf; Sound, Ann Kroeber; Sound Effects, Richard Hyams; Special Effects Make-up, Dean Jones; Special Effects, Greg Hull, George Hill; Production Supervisor, Gail M. Kearns; Songs by various artists; Soundtrack on Varese Sarabande Records; Dolby Stereo; Rated R; 120 minutes; September release

CAST

Jeffrey Beaumont	Kyle MacLachlan
Dorothy Vallens	Isabella Rossellini
Frank Booth	Dennis Hopper
Sandy Williams	Laura Dern
Mrs. Williams	Hope Lange
Ben	Dean Stockwell
Detective Williams	George Dickerson
Mrs. Beaumont	Priscilla Pointer
Aunt Barbara	Frances Bay
Mr. Beaumont	Jack Harvey
Mike	Ken Stovitz
Raymond	Brad Dourif
Paul	Jack Nance
Hunter	J. Michael Hunter
Don Vallens	Dick Green
Yellow Man	Fred Pickler
Dr. Gynde	Philip Markert
Double Ed	Leonard Watkins
Double Ed	Moses Gibson
Nurse Cindy	Selden Smith
Coroner	Peter Carew
Little Donny	Jon Jon Snipes
Piano Player	Andy Badale
Master of Ceremonies	Jean Pierre Viale
Desk Sergeant	Donald Moore
Party Girls	A. Michelle Depland, Michelle Sasser, Katie Reid

Top Left: Isabella Rossellini
© DeLaurentiis

Kyle MacLachlan, Dennis Hopper

THE LIGHTSHIP

(CASTLE HILL) Producers, Moritz Borman, Bill Benenson; Executive Producer, Rainer Soehnlein; Director, Jerzy Skolimowski; Screenplay, William Mai, David Taylor; Based on the book by Siegfried Lenz; Photography, Charly Steinberger; Editor, Barry Vince; Music, Stanley Myers; A CBS Production; Color; Rated PG-13; 95 minutes; September release

CAST

Caspary	Robert Duvall
Captain Miller	Klaus Maria Brandauer
Eddie	Arliss Howard
Gene	William Forsythe
Alex	Michael Lyndon
Coop	Tom Bower
Stump	Robert Costanzo
Nate	Badja Djola
Thorne	Tim Phillips

Top: Klaus Maria Brandauer
Below: Klaus Maria Brandauer, Michael Lyndon
© CBS Productions

Klaus Maria Brandauer, Robert Duvall
Top: Robert Duvall, Arliss Howard

BLAKE EDWARDS' THAT'S LIFE!

(COLUMBIA) Producer, Tony Adams; Director, Blake Edwards; Screenplay, Milton Wexler, Blake Edwards; Music, Henry Mancini; Song: "Life in a Looking Glass," Henry Mancini, Leslie Bricusse; Vocals, Tony Bennett; Photography, Anthony Richmond; Editor, Lee Rhoads; Executive Producer, Jonathan D. Krane; Associate Producers, Trish Caroselli, Connie McCauley; Production Manager/Assistant Director, Alan Levine; Assistant Director, K. C. Colwell; Costumes, Tracy Tynan; Music Supervision, Al Bunetta, Tom Bocci; Production Coordinator, Carrie Dieterich; Sound, Don Summer; Set Decorator, Tony Marando; Songs by various artists; Paradise Cove-Ubilam Production; DeLuxe Color; Panavision; Rated PG-13; 102 minutes; September release

CAST

Harvey Fairchild	Jack Lemmon
Gillian Fairchild	Julie Andrews
Holly Parrish	Sally Kellerman
Father Baragone	Robert Loggia
Megan Fairchild Bartlet	Jennifer Edwards
Steve Larwin	Rob Knepper
Larry Bartlet	Matt Lattanzi
Josh Fairchild	Chris Lemmon
Janice Kern	Cynthia Sikes
Fanny Ward	Dana Sparks
Kate Fairchild	Emma Walton
Madame Carrie	Felicia Farr
Corey	Theodore Wilson
Andre	Nicky Blair
Dr. Keith Romanis	Jordan Christopher
Belmont	Biff Elliot
Phil Carlson	Hal Riddle
Harold	Harold Harris
Jesse Grant	Jess G. Henecke
Lisa	Lisa Kingston
Dr. Gerald Spelner	Dr. Charles Schneider
Chutney	Chutney Walton
Honey	Honey Edwards

and Sherry P. Sievert, Joe Lopes, James Umphlett, Frann Bradford, Ken Gehrig, Donna McMullen, Scott L. McKenna, Cora Bryant, Robin Foster, Eddie Vail, Deborah Figuly, Larry Holt, Gene Hartline, Ernie Anderson, Harry Birrell

Right: Dana Sparks, Matt Lattanzi
Above: Felicia Farr Top: Robert
Loggia, Jack Lemmon
© Columbia

Jack Lemmon (C) and clockwise from top:
Chris Lemmon, Emma Walton, Julie Andrews,
Jennifer Edwards

Sally Kellerman, Jack Lemmon

71

PEGGY SUE GOT MARRIED

(TRI-STAR) Producer, Paul R. Gurian; Director, Francis Coppola; Screenplay, Jerry Leichtling, Arlene Sarner; Photography, Jordan Cronenweth; Designer, Dean Tavoularis; Editor, Barry Malkin; Executive Producer/Production Manager, Barrie M. Osborne; Costumes, Theadora Van Runkle; Music, John Barry; Casting, Pennie duPont; Assistant Directors, Douglas Claybourne, Mark A. Radcliffe, Carey Dietrich; Art Director, Alex Tavoularis; Assistant Art Director, James Murakami; Set Decorator, Marvin March; Sound, Richard Bryce Goodman; Special Effects, Larry Cavanaugh; Production Coordinator, Lisbeth Wynn-Owen; Choreography, Toni Basil; Staging, Chrissy Bocchino; From Rastar; Songs by various artists; DeLuxe Color; Panavision; Rated PG-13; 105 minutes; September release

CAST

Peggy Sue	Kathleen Turner
Charlie Bodell	Nicolas Cage
Richard Norvik	Barry Miller
Carol Heath	Catherine Hicks
Maddy Nagle	Joan Allen
Michael Fitzsimmons	Kevin J. O'Connor
Walter Getz	Jim Carrey
Delores Dodge	Lisa Jane Persky
Rosalie Testa	Lucinda Jenney
Arthur Nagle	Wil Shriner
Evelyn Kelcher	Barbara Harris
Jack Kelcher	Don Murray
Nancy Kelcher	Sofia Coppola
Elizabeth Alvorg	Maureen O'Sullivan
Barney Alvorg	Leon Ames
Scott Bodell	Randy Bourne
Beth Bodell	Helen Hunt
Doug Snell	Don Stark
Mr. Snelgrove	Ken Grantham
Janet	Ginger Taylor
Sharon	Sigrid Wurschmidt
Terry	Glenn Withrow
Leon	Harry Basil
Leo	John Carradine
Lisa	Sachi Parker
Sandy	Vivien Straus
Mr. Gilford	Morgan Upton
Dr. Daly	Lewis Leibovich

and Bill Bonham, Joe Lerer, Barbara Oliver, Lawrence Menkin, Dan Suhart, Leslie Hilsinger, Al Nalbandian, Dan Leegant, Ron Cook, Mary Leichtling, Steve Holladay

Right: Kathleen Turner, Joan Allen, Catherine Hicks Above: Kathleen Turner, Nicolas Cage Top: Kathleen Turner, Barry Miller
© *Tri-Star*

Kathleen Turner, Don Murray, Barbara Harris

Barry Miller, Kathleen Turner

THE NAME OF THE ROSE

(20th CENTURY-FOX) Producer, Bernd Eichinger; Director, Jean-Jacques Annaud; Screenplay, Andrew Birkin, Gerard Brach, Howard Franklin, Alain Godard; A Palimpsest of Umberto Eco's novel; Photography, Tonino Delli Colli; Designer, Dante Ferretti; Editor, Jane Seitz; Music, James Horner; Costumes, Gabriella Pescucci; Production Executive, Anna Gross; Executive Producers, Thomas Schuehly, Jake Eberts; Co-Producers, Franco Cristaldi, Alexandre Mnouchkine; Associate Producers, Pierre Hebey, Herman Weigel; Production Supervisor, Gerald Morin; Assistant to the Director/Continuity/Storyboard, Laurence Duval-Annaud; Assistant Directors, Gianni Arduini, Victor Tourjansky, Knut Winkler, Margot Rothkirch; Special Effects, Adriano Pischiutta, Giancarlo Mancini; Sound, Frank Jahn; Art Directors, Giorgio Giovannini, Rainer Schaper; A Bernd Eichinger/Bernd Schaefers Production; Dolby Stereo; Rated R; 130 minutes; September release

CAST

William of Baskerville	Sean Connery
Bernardo Gui	F. Murray Abraham
Adso of Melk	Christian Slater
Severinus	Elya Baskin
Jorge de Burgos	Feodor Chaliapin, Jr.
Ubertino de Casale	William Hickey
The Abbot	Michael Lonsdale
Salvatore	Ron Perlman
Malachia	Volker Prechtel
Remigio de Varagine	Helmust Qualtinger
The Girl	Valentina Vargas
Berengar	Michael Habeck
Venantius	Urs Althaus
Michele da Censena	Leopoldo Trieste
Jerome of Kaffa	Franco Valobra
Hugh of Newcastle	Vernon Dobtcheff
Pietro d'Assisi	Donal O'Brian
Cuthbert of Winchester	Andrew Birkin
Cardinal Bertrand	Lucien Bodard
Jean d'Anneaux	Peter Berling
Bishop of Alborea	Pete Lancaster
Jorge's Novice	Mark Bellinghaus
Adelmo	Lars Bodin-Jorgensen
Nero	Peter Welz
Executioner	Alberto Capone
The Voice of Adso as an Old Man	Dwight Weist

and Franco Adducci, Niko Brucher, Aristide Caporali, Fabio Carfora Peter Cloes, Mario Diano, Fabrizio Fontana, Rolando Fucili, Valerio Isidori, Luigi Leone, Armando Marra, Maurizio Mauri, Ludger Pistor, Francesco Scali, Maria Tedeschi, Andrea Tilli, Ennio Lollainni, Emil Feist, Francesco Maselli, Renato Nebolini, Antonio Cetta, Franco Covielleo, Daniele Ferretti, Sabatino Gennardo, Luciano Invidia, Mauro Leoni, Massimiliano Scarpa, Umberto Zuanelli, David Furtwaengler, Patrick Kreuzer, Kim Rossi Stuart, Franco Diogene, Giodana Falzoni, Eckehard Koch, Gina Poli, Gianni Rizzo, Lothar Schonbrodt, Vittorio Zarfati, Carlo Bianchino, Eugenio Bonardi, Pietro Ceccarelli, Franco Marino, Hans Schoedel.

Top Right: Sean Connery, F. Murray Abraham
Below: F. Murray Abraham
© 20th Century Fox/Mario Tursi

Christian Slater, Sean Connery

Sean Connery

CHILDREN OF A LESSER GOD

(PARAMOUNT) Producers, Burt Sugarman, Patrick Palmer; Director, Randa Haines; Screenplay, Hesper Anderson, Mark Medoff; Based on the stage play by Mark Medoff; Photography, John Seale; Designer, Gene Callahan; Editor, Lisa Fruchtman; Music, Michael Convertino; Associate Producer, Candace Koethe; Production Manager, Stephane Reichel; Assistant Directors, Jim Kaufman, Kim Winther; Production Associate, Robin Chaykin; Art Director, Barbra Matis; Set Decorator, Rose Marie McSherry; Special Actor's Consultant, James Carrington; Choreography, Dan Siretta, Nikki Sahagen; Costumers, Fabienne April, Arthur Rowsell; Assistant Costumer, Mario Davignon; Sound, Richard Lightstone; Special Effects, Neil Trifunovich, Ron Thiessen; Orchestrations, Chris Boardman, Shirley Walker; Production Coordinator, Eve Cantor; Sign Language Instructors, Mary Beth Miller, Alan R. Barwiolek; Songs by various artists; Metrocolor; Panavision; Rated R; September release

CAST

James	William Hurt
Sarah	Marlee Matlin
Mrs. Norman	Piper Laurie
Dr. Curtis Franklin	Philip Bosco
Lydia	Allison Gompf
Johnny	John F. Cleary
Glen	Philip Holmes
Cheryl	Georgia Ann Cline
Danny	William D. Byrd
Tony	Frank Carter, Jr.
William	John Limnidis
Orin	Bob Hiltermann
Mary Lee Ochs	E. Katherine Kerr
Alan Jones	John Basinger
Tom Schuyler	Barry Magnani
Marian Loesser	Linda Bove
Martha Franklin	Ann Hanson
Mr. Harrison	James H. Carrington
Glen's Father	Max Brown
Glen's Mother	Maria Cellario
Glen's Brother	Jon-Paul Dougherty
Sarah's Friends	Linda Swim, Lois Clowater
Waiter	Allan R. Francis
Cafeteria Cook	Richard Kendall
Ricky	Christopher Shay

and Laraine Isa, Nanci Kendall, Marie Brazil, Charlene Legere, Pat Vaughan, Margaret Amy Moar, Leigh French, Archie Hauh, III, Jack Blessing, Nicholas Guest, Gig Vorgan, Lynne Marie Stewart

1986 Academy Award For Best Actress (Marlee Matlin)

Piper Laurie, Marlee Matlin
Above: Marlee Matlin, Linda Bove

Top: William Hurt (center)
Below Left: William Hurt, Marlee Matlin
© *Paramount/Takashi Seida*

Philip Holmes, William Byrd, Frank Carter,
Jr., Georgia Ann Cline, Allison Gompf
Above and Top: William Hurt, Marlee Matlin

William Hurt, and Top with
Philip Bosco

75

DOWN BY LAW

(ISLAND PICTURES) Producer, Alan Kleinberg; Director/Screenplay, Jim Jarmusch; Photography, Robby Muller; Music, John Lurie; Editor, Melody London; Songs, Tom Waits, Naomi Neville; Vocals, Tom Waits, Irma Thomas; Co-Producers, Tom Rothman, Jim Stark; Executive Producers, Otto Grokenberger, Cary Brokaw, Russell Schwartz; Production Manager, Rudd Simmons; Production Coordinator, Kathie Hersch; Assistant Directors, Claire Denis, Guido Chiesa; Sound, Drew Kunin; Costumes, Carol Wood; A Black Snake/Grokenberger Film Production; Color; Rated R; 107 minutes; September release

CAST

Zack	Tom Waits
Jack	John Lurie
Roberto	Roberto Benigni
Nicoletta	Nicoletta Braschi
Laurette	Ellen Barkin
Bobbie	Billie Neal
Gig	Rockets Redglare
Preston	Vernel Bagneris
Julie	Timothea
L. C.	L. C. Drane
Detective Mandino	Joy Houck, Jr.
Young Girl	Carrie Lindsoe
Detective's	Ralph Joseph, Richard Boes
Cajun Detective	Dave Petitjean
Uniformed Cop	Adam Cohen
Corpse	Alan Kleinberg
Prisoner	Archie Sampier
Guards	David Dahlgren, Alex Miller, Elliot Keener, Jay Hilliard

Right: John Laurie, Tom Waits, Roberto Benigni (also Top)
© *Black Snake Inc.*

Tom Waits, Ellen Barkin

Roberto Benigni, Nicoletta Braschi

THE MEN'S CLUB

(ATLANTIC) Producer, Howard Gottfried; Director, Peter Medak; Screenplay, Leonard Michaels; Executive Producers, Thomas Coleman, Michael Rosenblatt, John Harada; Associate Producer, Jimsie Eason; Production Advisor, Hamilton Ho; Photography, John Fleckenstein; Music, Lee Holdridge; Editors, Cynthia Scheider, David Dresher, Bill Butler; Designer, Ken Davis; Production Manager/Production Executive, Roger "Biff" Johnson, Jr.; Assistant Directors, Roger Joseph Pugliese, Sunny Zimmerman; Costumes, Marianna Elliot, Peter Mitchell; Choreographer, Lester Wilson; Production Consultant, Howard Alper; Art Director, Laurence Bennett; Sound, Jim Tannenbaum, Leo Chaloukian; Production Coordinator, David Darmour; Stunts, Jay Jones; Special Effects, Frank Inez; Songs by various artists; Color; Rated R; 100 minutes; September release

CAST

Phillip	David Dukes
Kramer	Richard Jordan
Solly Berliner	Harvey Keitel
Harold Canterbury	Frank Langella
Cavanaugh	Roy Scheider
Paul	Craig Wasson
Terry	Treat Williams
Nancy	Stockard Channing
Felicia	Gina Gallegos
Hannah	Cindy Pickett
Redhead	Gwen Welles
Lake	Penny Baker
Stella	Rebeccah Bush
Stacey	Claudia Cron
Page	Ann Dusenberry
Allison	Marilyn Jones
Billy	Manette LaChance
Teensy	Jennifer Jason Leigh
Jo	Ann Wedgeworth
Waitress	Alurie Ambert
Nurse	Joan Foley
Phoebe	Kelly Haverur

Top: David Dukes, Frank Langella, Treat Williams, Roy Scheider, Harvey Keitel, Craig Wasson, Richard Jordan Below: Marilyn Jones, Keitel Right: Ann Wedgeworth
© Atlantic Entertainment

Craig Wasson, Rebeccah Bush
Above: Jennifer Jason Leigh

77

'NIGHT, MOTHER

(UNIVERSAL) Producer, Aaron Spelling, Alan Greisman; Director, Tom Moore; Screenplay, Marsha Norman; Based on the play by Marsha Norman; Executive Producers, Dann Byck, David Lancaster; Photography, Stephen M. Katz; Designer, Jack De Govia; Editor, Suzanne Pettit; Music, David Shire; Associate Producers, Cheryl Downey, Wallace Worsley; Production Manager, Wallace Worsley; Assistant Directors, Cheryl Downey, Patrick Regan; Set Decorator, Bonnie Dermer; Costumes, Bob Blackman; Assistant Art Director, John R. Jensen; Set Designer, Beverli Eagan; Make-Up, Brenda Todd; Assistant Costume Designer, Camille Argus; Sound, John Stacy, Bruce Smith; Color; Rated PG-13; 96 minutes; September release.

CAST

Jessie Cates	Sissy Spacek
Thelma Cates	Anne Bancroft
Dawson Cates	Ed Berke
Loretta Cates	Carol Robbins
Melodie Cates	Jennifer Roosendah
Kenny Cates	Michael Kenworthy
Agnes Fletcher	Sari Walke

Top: Anne Bancroft, Sissy Spacek
© *Universal*

Anne Bancroft, Sissy Spacek

OTELLO

(CANNON GROUP, INC.) Producers, Menahem Golan, Yoram Globus; Director, Franco Zeffirelli; Executive Producer, John Thompson; Associate Producer, Fulvio Lucisano; Photography, Ennio Guarnieri; Production Supervisors, Mike Hartman, Roberto Giussani; Editors, Peter Taylor, Franca Silvi; Costumes, Anna Anni, Maurizio Millenotti; Art Direction, Gianni Quaranta; Music, Giuseppe Verdi; Libretto, Arrigo Boito; Music Producer/Conductor, Lorin Maazel; Orchestra/Chorus, Teatro alla Scala; Chorus Master, Giulio Bertola; Production Managers, Cosimo Barbara, Lanfranco Diotallevi, Antonio Gabrielli, Sergio Giussani; Assistant Directors, Pippo Pisciotto, Lorenzo Mariani, Massimo Luconi, Luciano Bacchielli; Sound, Roberto Edwin Forrest; Assistant Art Director, Luigi Silvio Marchione; Set Decorators, Bruno Carlino, Stefano Paltrinieri; Assistant Costume Designers, Enrico Serafini, Anna Biagiotti, Alfonsina Lettieri; Dolby Stereo, Federico Savini; Special Effects, Giovanni Corridori; Cinecitta Color; Italian with subtitles; Rated PG; 122 minutes; September release

CAST

Otello	Placido Domingo
Desdemona	Katia Ricciarelli
Iago	Justino Diaz
Emilia	Petra Malakova
Cassio	Urbano Barberini
Lodovico	Massimo Foschi
Montano	Edwin Francis
Roderigo	Sergio Nicolai
Brabanzio	Remo Remotti
Doge	Antonio Pierfederici

The Voices of Cassio, Lodovico, Roderigo, Montano, and Araldo are sung by Ezio DiCesare, John Macurdy, Constantin Zaharia, Edward Toumajin, Giannicola Pigliucci.

Left: Katia Ricciarelli, Urbano Barberini
Top: Justino Diaz, Placido Domingo, Katia
Ricciarelli © *Cannon*

Placido Domingo, Katia Ricciarelli
Above: Placido Domingo, Justino Diaz

Placido Domingo

Dee Wallace, Cloris Leachman
Right: Ron Kuhlman, Cloris Leachman

SHADOW PLAY

(NEW WORLD) Producers, Dan Biggs, Susan Shadburne, Will Vinton; Director/Screenplay, Susan Shadburne; Photography, Ron Orieux; Editor, Kenji Yamamoto; Art Director, Steve Karatzas; Music/Song, John Newton; Vocals, Taber Shadburne; Production Manager, Don Zavin; Assistant Directors, Norman Bonney, Barbara Andersen, Ryan Holznagel; Sound, Glenn Micallef; Assistant Art Director, Paul Raubertas; Special Visual Effects, Will Vinton Productions, Inc./Bruce McKean; Presented with Millennium Pictures; Color; Rated R; 101 minutes; September release

CAST

Morgan Hanna	Dee Wallace-Stone
Millie Crown	Cloris Leachman
John Crown	Ron Kuhlman
Jeremy Crown	Barry Laws
Bette Mertz	Delia Salvi
Zelda	Susan Dixon
Byron Byron	Al Strobel
Archie	Glen Baggerly
Sarah	Juleen Murray
Lois	Michele Mariana
Conroy	Bob Griggs
Sophie	Marjorie Card Hughes
Dr. Feldman	Richard Wiltshire
Marty	George Stokes
Girl in the lighthouse	Myra Chamberlin
Tony	Steven Rock-Savage

© New World

Cloris Leachman, Dee Wallace

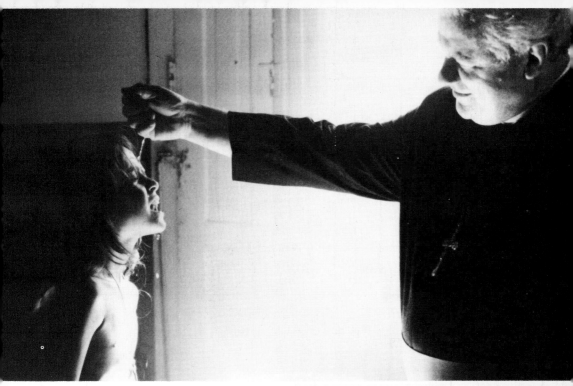

Alessandro Rabelo, Charles Durning
Right: Alessandro Rabelo, Ajay Naidu

WHERE THE RIVER RUNS BLACK

(MGM) Producers, Joe Roth, Harry Ufland; Director, Christopher Cain; Screenplay, Peter Silverman, Neal Jimenez; Based on the book *Lazaro* by David Kendall; Co-Producer, Dan Farrell; Executive Producer, James G. Robinson; Photography, Juan Ruiz-Anchia; Designer, Marcos Flaksman; Music, James Horner; Editor, Richard Chew; Associate Producer/Assistant Director, James Ragan; Line Producers, Flavio R. Tambellini, Bruno Barreto; Production Manager, Angelo Gastal; Assistant Directors, Aluisio Branches, Bia Castro; Technical Coordinator, William Edwards; Production Coordinator, Joao Alfredo Viegas; Dolphin Trainers, Kathy Krieger, Scott Amsel; Amazon Animal Effects, Donald Pennington; Art Director, Paulo Flaksman; Set Dresser, Alexandre Meyer; Special Effects, Edu Paungarten; Sound, Romeu Quinto, Andy Wiskes; Dolby Stereo; Color; Rated PG; 100 minutes; September release.

CAST

Father O'Reilly	Charles Durning
Lazaro	Alessandro Rabelo
Segundo	Ajay Naidu
Eagle Woman	Divana Brandao
Father Mahoney	Peter Horton
Orlando Santos	Castulo Guerra
Mother Marta	Conchata Ferrell
Sister Ana	Dana Delany
Raimundo	Chico Diaz
Lazaro at age four	Marcelo Rabelo
Francisco	Ariel Coelho
Jose	Paulo Sergio Oliveira
Brother Carlos	Mario Borges
Luis	Francois Thijm
Priest in confessional	Geraldo Salles
Caimanero	Sandro Soviatt
Vaika Man	Raimundo Carvalho
Ice Cream Vendor	Jose Ricardo Matos
Floyd Jenkins	David C. Russel
Miner in truck	Telmo Maia
Man Getting Shoeshine	Paulo Quindere

Divana Brandao, Marcelo Rabelo

LET'S GET HARRY

(TRI-STAR) Producers, Daniel H. Blatt, Robert Singer; Directo
Alan Smithee; Screenplay, Charles Robert Carner; Story, Mark Fe
berg, Samuel Fuller; Photography, James A.' Contner; Art Directo
Mort Rabinowitz; Editors, Ralph E. Winters, Rick R. Sparr, Rob
Hyams; Music, Brad Fiedel; Associate Producer, David Shamroy Ha
burger; Casting, Judith Holstra, Marcia Ross; Production Manag
David S. Hamburger; Assistant Directors, Benjamin Rosenberg, J
Behnke, Tony Perez; Set Designer, Mark Fabus; Sound, Don Johns
Special Effects, Eddie Surkin, W. Kimball Englehart; Costumes, Gil
Texter; Associate Producer, Mark Feldberg; Production Coordinat
Patt McCurdy; "One Endless Circle," Timothy B. Schmit, Ed Sanfo
From Tri-Star-Delphi IV and V Productions; Dolby Stereo; Metrocol
Panavision; Rated R; 100 minutes; October release

CAST

Jack	Gary Bus
Theresa	Cecile Call
Veronica	Elpidia Carri
Walt Clayton	Matt Cla
Pablo	Rodolfo De Alexand
Shrike	Robert Duva
Dwarf	Javier Estra
Spence	Glenn Fr
Ambassador Douglas	Bruce Gr
Dean Reilly	Jerry Hard
Harry	Mark Harme
Mr. Burck, Sr.	Ben Johns
Al King	James Kea
Pinilla	Pierrino Mascari
Jack's Girlfriend	Diane Peters
Carlos Ochobar	Guillermo Ri
Kurt Klein	Rick Rossovi
Corey	Michael Schoeffli
Alphonso	Gregory Sier
Mickey	Jon Van Ne
Pachowski	Tom Wils

and Fidel Abrego, Jere Burns, Terry Camilleri, Salvador Godine
David Hess, Jonathan Kano, Guillermo LaGunes, Alfredo Ramire
Robert Singer, J. W. Smith, Cesar Sobrevals, John Wesley, Jor
Zepeda

**Top: Rick Rossovich, Glenn Frey, Michael
Schoeffling, Mark Harmon, Tom Wilson**
© *Tri-Star*

**Mark Harmon
Top: Robert Duvall**

82

SOMETHING WILD

(ORION) Producers, Jonathan Demme, Kenneth Utt; Director, Jonathan Demme; Screenplay, E. Max Frye; Photography, Tak Fujimoto; Editor, Craig McKay; Designer, Norma Moriceau; Executive Producer, Edward Saxon; Music, John Cale, Laurie Anderson; Song, David Byrne; Associate Producers, Bill Miller, Ron Bozman; Production Manager, Kenneth Utt; Assistant Directors, Ron Bozman, Kyle McCarthy; Associate Editor, Camilla Toniolo; Sound, Les Lazarowitz, Frank Graziadei; Art Director, Steve Lineweaver; Costumes, Eugenie Bafaloukas; Stunts, John Robotham; Songs by various artists; Presented by Religioso Primitiva; Soundtrack on MCA; Dolby Stereo; Rated R; 116 minutes; October release

CAST

Charles Driggs	Jeff Daniels
Audrey Hankel	Melanie Griffith
Counter Man	George Schwartz
Frenchy	Leib Lensky
The Country Squire	Tracey Walter
Country Squire Bulldog	Maggie T.
Charlie's Secretary	Patricia Falkenhain
Graves' Secretary	Sandy McLeod
Richard Graves	Robert Ridgely
TV Newscaster	Buzz Kilman
"Dad"	Kenneth Utt
"Rose"	Adelle Lutz
Irate Chef	Charles Napier
Motel Philosopher	Jim Roche
Motorcycle Cop	John Sayles
Used Car Guy	John Waters
Hitchhiking Cowboy	The Texas Kid
Hitchhiking Kids	Byron D. Hutcherson, Eleana Hutcherson
Guitar Player	Thomas Cavano
Junk Store Gals	Dorothy Demme, Emma Byrne
"Peaches"	Dana Preu
Max the Dog	Himself
Donna Penski	Mary Ardella Drew
James Williams	Joseph Lee Davis
Kevin Stroup	Edward Saxon
The Willies	The Feelies
Stylish Reunion Couple	James Hurd, Joanna Kitchen-Hurd
Larry Dillman	Jack Gilpin
Peggy Dillman	Su Tissue
Guido Paonessa	Gary Goetzman
Irene	Margaret Colin
Ray Sinclair	Ray Liotta
Chloe	Chloe Amateau
Robbery Victim	Dung Chau

and "The Crew," Steve Scales, John Montgomery, Kristin Olsen, Heather Shaw, Vic Blair, D. Stanton Miranda, Ding-a-Ling, Johnny Marrs, Gil Lazier, Anna Levine, Sister Carol East, George Henry Wyche, Jr., Marilee K. Smith, Jeffrey R. Rioux, Jeff Herig, Debbi Ellis, John Robotham, George Marshall Ruge, Billy Anagnos

Melanie Griffith, Jeff Daniels (also Top Right)
Right Center: Ray Liotta, Melanie Griffith

HOOSIERS

(ORION) Producers, Carter DeHaven, Angelo Pizzo; Director, David Anspaugh; Screenplay, Angelo Pizzo; Executive Producers, John Daly, Derek Gibson; Photography, Fred Murphy; Designer, David Nichols; Editor, C. Timothy O'Meara; Music, Jerry Goldsmith; Associate Producer/Production Manager, Graham Henderson; Assistant Directors, Herb Adelman, Harvey Waldman, Larry M. Davis; Costumes, Jane Anderson; Production Coordinator, Karen Altman Morgenstern; Music Supervisor, Budd Carr; Orchestrations, Arthur Morton; Art Director, David Lubin; Stunts, Ernie Orsatti; Songs by various artists; Presented with Hemdale Film Corporation; CFI Color; Rated PG; 114 minutes; October release

CAST

Coach Norman Dale	Gene Hackman
Myra Fleener	Barbara Hershey
Shooter	Dennis Hopper
Cletus	Sheb Wooley
Opal Fleener	Fern Persons
George	Chelcie Ross
Rollin	Robert Swan
Rooster	Michael O'Guinne
Reverend Doty	Wil Dewitt
Sheriff Finley	John Robert Thompson
Preacher Purl	Michael Sassone
Millie	Gloria Dorson
Mayor Carl	Mike Dalzell
Junior	Calvert L. Welker
J. June	Eric Gilliom
Referees-Oolitic	Robert Boyle, Jerry D. Petro
Referee-Cedar Knob	Sam Smiley
Coach-Cedar Knob	Tom McConnell
"Gorilla" Player-Cedar Knob	Dennis Farkas
Referee-Verdi	Tim Fogarty
Referee-Logootee	Don Stratigos
Referee-Dugger	Ken Strunk
Referees-Terhune	Jerry D. Larrison, Thomas W. Marshall
Coach's-Jasper	Gary Long, C. W. Mundy
Player-Jasper	Jeff Moster
Doc Buggins	Ralph H. Shively
Reporters	Rich Komenich, Scott Miley, Robert Sutton
Coach-State	Ray Crowe
Official-Finals	Ray Craft
P.A. Announcer-Finals	Tom Carnegie
Radio Announcer-Finals	Hillard Gates
Hickory Cheerleaders	Laura Robling, Nancy Harris, Libbey Schenck

and "The Hickory Huskers": Brad Boyle (Whit), Steve Hollar (Rade), Brad Long (Buddy), David Neidorf (Everett), Kent Poole (Merle), Wade Schenck (Ollie), Scott Summers (Strap), Maris Valainis (Jimmy)

Right: Robert Swan, Dennis Hopper, Gene Hackman
Top: Barbara Hershey, Gene Hackman
© *Orion/Morgan Renard*

Gene Hackman (Coach)

Steve Hollar, Kent Poole, Gene Hackman,
Scott Summers, Brad Boyle, Wade Schenck

TRUE STORIES

(WARNER BROS.) Executive Producer, Edward R. Pressman; Producer, Gary Kurfirst; Director, David Byrne; Screenplay, Stephen Tobolowsky, Beth Henley, David Byrne; Co-Producer, Karen Murphy; Photography, Ed Lachman; Music, Talking Heads; Editor, Caroline Biggerstaff; Designer, Barbara Ling; Sound, Leslie Shatz; Casting, Victoria Thomas; Production Associate, Christina Patoski; Associate Producers, Neal Weisman, Michael Flynn; Production Executive, Allan Nicholls; Costumes, Elizabeth McBride; Fashion Show Designer, Adelle Lutz; Set Decorator, Susan Beeson; Assistant Set Decorator, Jeanette Scott; Assistant Designer, John T. Hagen-Brenner; Assistant Costume Designer, Rudy Dillon; Orchestrations, Dick Bright; Songs, Talking Heads, Meredith Monk, David Byrne, Terry Allen, Carl Finch, Steve Jordan, Zuzuca; The Talking Heads album "*True Stories*" and Soundtrack album "*Sounds from True Stories*" on Sire/Warner Bros. Records; Dolby Stereo; Color; Rated PG; 111 minutes; October release

CAST

Louis Fyne	John Goodman
Kay Culver	Annie McEnroe
The Lying Woman	Jo Harvey Allen
Earl Culver	Spalding Gray
The Cute Woman	Alix Elias
Mr. Tucker	Roebuck "Pops" Staples
Ramon	Humberto "Tito" Larriva
The Preacher	John Ingle
The Computer Guy	Matthew Posey
Narrated by	David Byrne
The Lazy Woman	Swoosie Kurtz
Linda Culver	Amy Buffington
Larry Culver	Richard Dowlearn
The Little Girl on the road	Capucine DeWulf

and Cynthia Gould, Kelly Wright, Hinpheth Siharath, Phyllis Wallace, Linda McCauley, The McCauley Kids, Marion Henley, Huey P. Meaux, James Jackson, Angus G. Wynne III, Cora Cardona, Andrew Barach, Gregory Gunter, Ric Spiegel, Tom Denolf, Ed Geldart, Bale Allen, Liz Moore, The Bert Cross Choir, Frank Smith, L. T. Felty, David Averett, Hey Now Kids, The St. Thomas Aquinas School Choir, John Pritchett, Steve Jordan, Rio Jordan, Christopher Johnson, R. L. Anderson, Norman Seaton, Charles Connour, Randy Erwin, Tyler Junior College Apache Belles, Heather Hanks, Chris Douridas, Steve Jordan, Los Vampiros, Otis Gray, Edward Kwan, Dallas Boy Scout Troop #872, Garland Blue Star Line Dancers, Sumter Bruton, Art Guinn, Bob Lukeman, Scott Jenkins

Top: David Byrne Right: Spalding Gray,
Annie McEnroe Below: Swoosie Kurtz
© *Warner Bros.*

Jo Harvey Allen

85

SOUL MAN

(NEW WORLD) Producer, Steve Tisch; Director, Steve Miner; Screenplay, Carol Black; Co-Producers, Carol Black, Neal Marlens; Line Producer, Donna Smith; Photography, Jeffrey Jur; Editor, David Finfer; Music, Tom Scott; Associate Producers, Bernhard Goldmann, Stephen Vaughan; Production Manager, Donna Smith; Music Supervisor, David Anderle; Assistant Directors, Betsy Magruder, Josh King, Stuart Hagen; Art Directors, Don Diers, John Rienhart; Set Designer, Larry Fulton; Costumes, Sharon Simonaire; Assistant Costumer, Sara Markowitz; Sound, Donald Summer; Production Coordinator, Kool Lusby; Special Effects, Roger George; Stunts, Chris Howell; Presented in association with Balcor Film Investors; Panavision; Technicolor; Dolby; Rated PG-13; 101 minutes; October release

CAST

Mark Watson	C. Thomas Howell
Gordon Bloomfeld	Arye Gross
Sarah Walker	Rae Dawn Chong
Professor Banks	James Earl Jones
Whitney Dunbar	Melora Hardin
Mr. Dunbar	Leslie Nielsen
Bill Watson	James B. Sikking
Dr. Aronson	Max Wright
Ray McGrady	Jeff Altman
George Walker	Jonathan "Fudge" Leonard
Brad Small	Mark Neely
Leon	Wolfe Perry
Zendel	Laurel Green
Bruce Wizansky	Jerry Pavlon
Barky Brewer	Wally Ward
Officer Schkolnick	Paul O'Brien
Ernie	Dave Reynolds
D. J.	Freddie Dawson
Booey Fraser	Eric Schiff
Frank	Ron Reagan
Man in Cell	M. C. Gainey
Mr. Walker	Felix Nelson
Mrs. Walker	Betty Cole
Mr. Whicher	Donald Hotton
Mrs. Dunbar	Ann Walker
Bundy Dunbar	Bo Mancuso
Mrs. Sherwood	Linda Hoy
Bouchard Man	Robert Burleigh
Andrew	Jonathan Wise
Mrs. Watson	Marie Cheatham
Lisa Stimson	Julia Louis-Dreyfus
Seth	John David Bland
Girl	Amy Stock

Left: C. Thomas Howell, Rae Dawn Chong
Above: Arye Gross, James Earl Jones
Top: C. Thomas Howell, Arye Gross
© New World

Dave Reynolds, Ron Reagan

Arye Gross, James B. Sikking,
Marie Cheatham

TOUGH GUYS

(TOUCHSTONE) Producer, Joe Wizan; Director, Jeff Kanew; Screenplay, James Orr, Jim Cruickshank; Co-Producers, Jana Sue Memel, Richard Hashimoto; Photography, King Baggot; Designer, Todd Hallowell; Editor, Kaja Fehr; Music, James Newton Howard; Consultant, Issur Danielovitch; Production Manager, Penelope L. Foster; Assistant Directors, Ed Milkovich, Christopher Griffin; Set Decorator, Jeff Haley; Sound, C. Darin Knight, Tom C. McCarthy; Costumes, Erica Phillips; Special Effects, Chuck Gaspar, Joe D. Day, Stan Parks; Scenic Artist, Albert N. Gaynor; "They Don't Make Them Like They Used To" by Burt Bacharach, Carole Bayer Sager, Kenny Rogers; Songs by various artists; Color by De Luxe; Panavision; Dolby Stereo; Rated PG; 102 minutes; October release.

CAST

Harry Doyle	Burt Lancaster
Archie Long	Kirk Douglas
Deke Yablonski	Charles Durning
Belle	Alexis Smith
Richie Evans	Dana Carvey
Skye Foster	Darlanne Fluegel
Leon B. Little	Eli Wallach
Vince	Monty Ash
Philly	Billy Barty
Schultz	Simmy Bow
Gladys Ripps	Darlene Conley
Jimmy Ellis	Nathan Davis
Man in Gay Bar	Matthew Faison
Gang Leader	Corkey Ford
Federale Captain	Rick Garcia
Richie's Boss	Graham Jarvis
Train Engineer	Doyle L. McCormack
Syms	Bob Maxwell
Derek	Steven Memel
Female Officer	Jeanne Mori
Yogurt Boy	Scott Nemes
Hotel Clerk	Ernie Sabella
Sandy	Hilary Shepard
Howard	Jake Steinfeld
Jarvis	Charles Sweigart
Restaurant Hostess	Eleanor Zee
Gang Members	Darryl Shelly, Kenny Ransom, Joe Seely
Newscaster	Michele Marsh

and Ron Ryan, Ruth De Sosa, John Mariano, Larry Mintz, Dick Hancock, John Demy, Grant Aleksander, Michael F. Kelly, Jeffrey Lynn Johnson, Hugo Stanger, Jimmy Lennon, Philip Culotta, Donald Thompson, Lisa Pescia, Jeff Levine, Seth Kaufman, Todd Hallowell, Steven Greenstein, Thomas F. MaGuire, Ellen Albertini Dow, Scanlon Gail, James Clark, Skip Stellrecht, David Michael O'Neill, James Deeth, Harry Hauss, Denver Mattson, Flea, Anthony Kiedis, Cliff Martinez, Hillel Slovak

Left: Charles Durning, Burt Lancaster
Above: Kirk Douglas, Burt Lancaster (R)
Top: Kirk Douglas, Burt Lancaster
© *Touchstone/Christine Loss*

Kirk Douglas, Darlanne Fluegel

Burt Lancaster, Alexis Smith

JUMPIN' JACK FLASH

(20th CENTURY-FOX) Producers, Lawrence Gordon, Joel Silver; Director, Penny Marshall; Screenplay, David H. Foanzoni, J. W. Melville, Patricia Irving, Christopher Thompson; Story, David H. Franzoni; Photography, Matthew F. Leonetti; Designer, Robert Boyle; Editor, Mark Goldblatt; Assistant Producers, Richard Marks, George Bowers, Elaine K. Thompson; Music, Thomas Newman; Costumes, Susan Becker; Production Manager, Arthur Seidel; Assistant Directors, Beau E. L. Marks, K. C. Colwell, Michael Katleman; Art Director, Frank Richwood; Set Designers, Henry Alberti, Richard McKenzie, Richard Pitman; Sound, Jerry Jost; Special Effects, Thomas Ryba; Stunts, Bennie E. Dobbins; Orchestrations, James Campbell, Armin Steiner; Computer Effects, Steve Brumette; Songs by various artists; Dolby Stereo; Soundtrack on Mercury Records; Color by DeLuxe; Rated R; 100 minutes; October release

CAST

Terry Doolittle	Whoopi Goldberg
Marty Phillips	Stephen Collins
Jeremy Talbot	John Wood
Cynthia	Carol Kane
Liz Carlson	Annie Potts
Mr. Page	Peter Michael Goetz
Archer Lincoln	Roscoe Lee Browne
Lady Sarah Billings	Sara Botsford
Mark Van Meter	Jeroen Krabbe
Carl	Vyto Ruginis
Jack	Jonathan Pryce
Hunter	Tony Hendra
Doug	Jon Lovitz
Fred	Phil E. Hartman
Karen	Lynne Marie Stewart
Jackie	Ren Woods
Page's Secretary	Tracy Reiner
Larry (The Heavyset Guard)	Chino Fats Williams
Sperry Repairman	Jim Belushi
Lord Malcolm Billings	Paxton Whitehead
Gillian	June Chadwick
Fiona	Tracey Ullman
African Embassy Guest	Jeffrey Joseph
French Embassy Guest	Caroline Ducroco
Receptionist at Elizabeth Arden	Julie Payne
Karen at Elizabeth Arden	Deanna Oliver
Earl the guard	Carl LaBove
Pedicurist at Elizabeth Arden	Donna Ponterotto
Night Guard at bank	Matt Landers
Harry Carlson, Jr.	Benji Gregory
Kristi Carlson	Kellie Martin
Superintendent	Edouardo DeSoto
Detective	Garry K. Marshall

and James Sheridan, Charles Dumas, James Edgcomb, Gerry Connell, Miguel A. Nunez, Jr., Jose Santana, Bob Ernst, Kim Chan, Anthony Hamilton, Heide Lund, Kenneth Danzinger, Eric Harrison, Teagan Clive, Tom McDermott, Mark Rowen, J. Christopher Ross, Hilaury Stern, George Jenesky

Right: Vyto Ruginis, John Wood, Tony Hendra **Top:** Peter Michael Goetz, Jon Lovitz, Whoopi Goldberg, Stephen Collins **Below:** Whoopi Goldberg, Jeroen Krabbe © *20th Century-Fox*

Whoopi Goldberg

Whoopi Goldberg, Carol Kane

THE BOY WHO COULD FLY

(LORIMAR) Producer, Gary Adelson; Director/Screenplay, Nick Castle; Associate Producer, Brian Frankish; Co-producer, Richard Vane; Casting, Barbara Miller; Music, Bruce Broughton; Visual Effects, Richard Edlund; Editor, Patrick Kennedy; Designer, Jim Bissell; Photography, Steven Poster, Adam Holender; Production Manager, Warren Carr; Assistant Directors, Michael Steele, Patrice Leung; Production Associate, Karen Siegel; Production Coordinators, Patti Allen, Mary Mason; Art Director, Graeme Murray; Costumes, Trish Keaton; Set Decorators, Kimberley Richardson, Anne Marie Corbett; Set Designer, Jim Teegarden; Sound, Rob Young; Flying Effects, Bob Harmon, Reg Smith, John Thomas; Special Effects, John Thomas, Bill Orr; Stunts, John Scott, Betty Thomas; Orchestrations, Mark C. McKenzie; Songs, Stephen Bishop, Bruce Broughton, Nick Castle; Dolby Stereo; DeLuxe Color; Rated PG; 114 minutes; November release

CAST

Milly	Lucy Deakins
Eric	Jay Underwood
Charlene	Bonnie Bedelia
Louis	Fred Savage
Mrs. Sherman	Colleen Dewhurst
Uncle Hugo	Fred Gwynne
Geneva	Mindy Cohn
Mrs. D'Gregario	Hanet MacLachlan
Mona	Jennifer Michas
Erin	Michelle Bardeaux
Colette	Aura Pithart
Joe	Cam Bancroft
Gary	Jason Priestly
Sonny	Chris Arnold
Bad Boy	Sean Kelso
Female Administrator	Meredith B. Woodward
Attendant's	Raimund Stamm, Dan Zale
Dad	Dwight Koss
Tour Guide	Janes McLarty
Institute Receptionist	Betty Phillips
Mr. Brandt	Terry D. Mulligan
Ms. O'Neil	Tannis Rae
Dr. Nelson	Tom Heaton
Mrs. Betuel	Angela Gann
Officer	Scott Irvine
Dr. Karen Siegel	Karen Siegel
The Coupe de Villes	John Carpenter, Nick Castle, Tommy Wallace
Guest Coupe	Warren Carr
"Max"	"Jake"

and special thanks to Louise Fletcher

**Right: Fred Savage, Lucy Deakins, Mindy Cohn
Colleen Dewhurst Above: Lucy Deakins Top:
(L) Bonnie Bedelia, Lucy Deakins, Fred Savage
(R)Lucy Deakins, Fred Gwynne
© *Lorimar***

Lucy Deakins, Jay Underwood

Jay Underwood, Lucy Deakins

89

STAR TREK IV: THE VOYAGE HOME

(PARAMOUNT) Producer, Harve Bennett; Director, Leonard Nimoy; Story, Leonard Nimoy, Harve Bennett; Screenplay, Steve Meerson, Peter Krikes, Harve Bennett, Nicholas Meyer; Based on Star Trek created by Gene Rodenberry; Executive Producer, Ralph Winter; Photography, Donald Peterman; Designer, Jack T. Collis; Music, Leonard Rosenman; Executive Consultant, Gene Roddenberry; Production Manager, Mel Efros; Assistant Directors, Patrick Kehoe, Douglas E. Wise, Frank Capra III; Visual Effects, Ken Ralston; Associate Producers, Brooke Breton, Kirk Thatcher; Sound, Gene S. Cantamessa; Special Effects, Michael Lanteri, Clay Pinney, Brian Tipton, Don Elliott, Robert Spurlock, Tim Moran; Costumes, Robert Fletcher; Art Directors, Joe Aubel, Pete Smith; Set Designers, Dan Gluck, James Bayliss, Richard Berger; Sound Effects, Mark Mangini; Special Sound Effects, John Pospisil, Alan Howarth, George Budd; Additional Music, Leonard Rosenman and The Yellowjackets; Orchestrations, Ralph Ferraro; Production Coordinator, Gina Neilson; Effects Photography, Don Dow; Creature Creation, Richard Snell Designs, Dale Brady, Craig Caton, Allen Feuerstein, Shannon Shea, Brian Wade, Nancy Nimoy; Star Trek TV Theme, Alexander Courage; Songs, Craig Huxley, Kirk Thatcher; Dolby Stereo; Soundtrack on MCA; Technicolor; Panavision; Rated PG; 119 minutes; November release

CAST

Kirk	William Shatner
Spock	Leonard Nimoy
McCoy	DeForest Kelley
Scotty	James Doohan
Sulu	George Takei
Chekov	Walter Koenig
Uhura	Michelle Nichols
Amanda	Jane Wyatt
Gillian	Catherine Hicks
Sarek	Mark Lenard
Lt. Saavik	Robin Curtis
Federation Council President	Robert Ellenstein
Klingon Ambassador	John Schuck
Admiral Cartwright	Brock Peters
Starfleet Communications Officer	Michael Snyder
Starfleet Display Officer	Michael Berryman
Saratoga Science Officer	Mike Brislane
Commander Rand	Grace Lee Whitney
Alien Communications Officer	Jane Wiedlin
Starship Captain	Vijay Amritraj
Commander Chapel	Majel Barrett
Saratoga Helmsman	Nick Ramus
Controller's	Thaddeus Golas, Martin Pistone
Bob Briggs	Scott DeVenney
Joe	Richard Harder
Nichols	Alex Henteloff
FBI Agent	Jeff Lester

and Viola Stimpson, Phil Rubenstein, John Miranda, Joe Knowland, Bob Sarlatte, Everett Lee, Tony Edwards, Eve Smith, Tom Mustin, Greg Karas, Raymond Singer, David Ellenstein, Judy Levitt, Teresa E. Victor, James Menges, Kirk Thatcher, Joe Lando, Newell Tarrant, Mike Timoney, Jeffrey Martin, Joseph Naradzay, Donald W. Zautcke, R. A. Rondell

Top Left: Leonard Nimoy, DeForest Kelley, George Takei, Nichelle Nichols, James Doohan, William Shatner Below: Shuttle, and Bird of Prey Ship
© *Paramount/Bruce Birmelin*

Mark Leonard, Jane Wyatt, Leonard Nimoy

DeForest Kelley, Walter Koenig, William Shatner,
Catherine Hicks Above: Kirk Thatcher, Leonard
Nimoy

Catherine Hicks, Leonard Nimoy, William Shatner
Above: Brock Peters, Robert Ellenstein (C)

52 PICK-UP

(CANNON) Producers, Menahem Golan, Yoram Globus; Director, John Frankenheimer; Screenplay, Elmore Leonard, John Steppling; Based on the novel by Elmore Leonard; Executive Producer, Henry T. Weinstein; Photography, Jost Vacano; Designer, Philip Harrison; Editor, Robert F. Shugrue; Costumes, Ray Summers; Music, Gary Chang; Production Manager, Jeffrey Silver; Assistant Directors, Bradley Gross, Jodi Ehrlich, Scott Cameron; Production Executive, Rony Yacov; Art Director, Russell Christian; Sound, Ed Novick; Scenic Artist, Bill Hall; Set, Max Whitehouse, Sarah Burdick, Hal Martin; Makeup/Special Effects, Dee Mansano; Production Coordinator, Caroline Baron; Special Effects, Eric Allard, Philip Bartko, Tom Mertz; Songs by various artists; TVC Color; Ultrastereo; Rated R; 114 minutes; November release

CAST

Harry Mitchell	Roy Scheider
Barbara Mitchell	Ann-Margret
Doreen	Vanity
Alan Raimy	John Glover
Leo Franks	Robert Trebor
Jim O'Boyle	Lonny Chapman
Cini	Kelly Preston
Mark Averson	Doug McClure
Bobby Shy	Clarence Williams III
Dan Lowenthal	Alex Henteloff
Counter Girl	Michelle Walker
Test Site Worker	Philip Bartko
Injured Driver	Robin Bronfman
O'Boyle's Wife	Debra Burger
Janet	Laisa Carrie
Drug Dealer	Blackie Dammett
Lisa	Barbara Ferris
Policeman	John Francis
James Boyer	Conroy Gedeon
Ed Salvan	Bill Gratton
Patron	Jai M. Jefferson
Lady in hall	Lenora Logan
Passer-By	Mark M. Mayuga
Grady	William J. Murphy
Tom	Anthony Palmer
Vendor	Frank Sivero

and Tom Byron, Harvey Cowen, Ron Jeremy Hyatt, Amber Lynn, Sharon Mitchell, Ines Ochoa, Allyson Palmeter, Katherine Poland, Debra Satell, Shirley Thompson, Amy White, Charles Bowden, Marc Castenada, Mike Caruso, Steven Clawson, Christopher Cory, Maurice Jenkins, John Kahnen, Bobby Ponce, Ray Vela, Lorrie Lovett, Sandra Perron, Barbara Summers, Arlin Miller, Ted Grossman

Right: John Glover, Clarence Williams III, Robert Trebor, Roy Scheider Top: Ann-Margret
© *Cannon*

Roy Scheider, Ann-Margret

Vanity, Kelly Preston

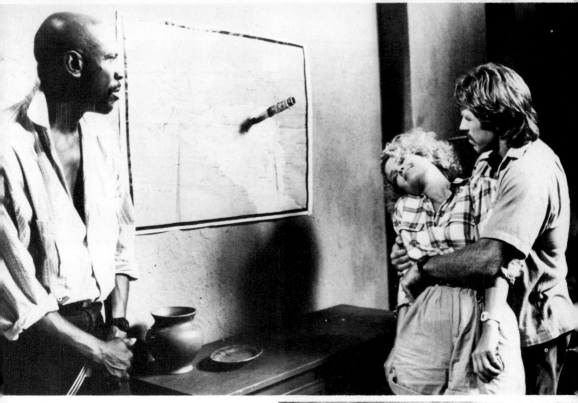

FIREWALKER

(CANNON) Producers, Menahem Golan, Yoram Globus; Director, J. Lee Thompson; Screenplay, Robert Gosnell; Story, Robert Gosnell, Jeffrey M. Rosenbaum, Norman Aladjem; Executive Producers, Norman Aladjem, Jeffrey M. Rosenbaum; Editor, Richard Marx; Designer, Jose Rodriguez Granada; Photography, Alex Phillips; Costumes, Poppy Cannon; Music, Gary Chang; Production Manager, Pablo Buelna; Assistant Directors, Russ Harling, Javier Carreno, Javier Chincilla, Guillermo Carreno; Production Executive, Rony Yacov; Associate Producer, Carlos Gil; Assistant Art Director, Fernando Martinez; Production Coordinator, Enid L. Kantor; Special Effects, Reyes Abades Tejedor, Sergio Jara, Manuel Cordero, Daniel Cordero; TVC Color; Ultrastereo; Rated PG; 104 minutes; November release

CAST

Max Donigan	Chuck Norris
Leo Porter	Lou Gossett
Patricia Goodwyn	Melody Anderson
Tall Eagle	Will Sampson
El Coyote	Sonny Landham
Corky Taylor	John Rhys-Davies
Boggs	Ian Abercrombie
The Chinaman	Richard Lee-Sung
The Indian Girl	Zaide S. Gutierrez
Willie	Alvaro Carcano
Tubbs	John Hazelwood
Co-pilot	Jose Escandon
Guerrilla Leader	Mario Arevalo
Tough Guerrilla	Juan Garcia Jaramillo
Big Man	Miguel Fuentes
Train Soldier #2	Julio Monje
Young Indian	Nicolas Jasso

and Aaron Norris, Bobby Angelle, Rick Avery, Clay Boss, Phil Chung, Bobby Cummins, Mike DeLuna, Jon Epstein, Dean Ferrandini, Andy Gil, Mike Johnson, Sonny Jones, Steve Lambert, Gary Pike, Rick Prieto, Branscom Richmond, Danny Rodgers, Robert Wall

**Top: Lou Gossett, Melody Anderson,
Chuck Norris**
© *Cannon*

Melody Anderson, Chuck Norris

HALF MOON STREET

(20th CENTURY-FOX) Producer, Geoffrey Reeve; Director, Bob Swaim; Executive Producers, Edward R. Pressman, David Korda; Associate Producer, John Davis; Music, Richard Harvey; Editor, Richard Marden; Costumes, Louise Frogley; Designer, Anthony Curtis; Photography, Peter Hannan; Screenplay, Bob Swaim, Edward Behr; Based on the novel *Doctor Slaughter* by Paul Theroux; Production Supervisor, Tom Sachs; Production Coordinator, Linda Rabin; Production Executive, Tom Reeve; Assistant Directors, Terry Madden, Lee Cleary; Art Director, Peter Williams; Sound, Robin Gregory; Special Effects, Arthur Beavis; Presented by RKO Pictures and Edward R. Pressman Film Corporation in association with Showtime/The Movie Channel Inc.; Technicolor; Rated R; 98 minutes; November release

CAST

Lauren Slaughter	Sigourney Weaver
Lord Bulbeck	Michael Caine
General Sir George Newhouse	Patrick Kavanagh
Lady Newhouse	Faith Kent
Lindsay Walker	Ram John Holder
Hugo Van Arkady	Keith Buckley
Mr. Van Arkady	Annie Hanson
Julian Shuttle	Patrick Newman
Captain Twilley	Niall O'Brien
Karim Hatami	Nadim Sawalha
Sonny	Vincent Lindon
Madame Cybele	Muriel Villiers
Tom Haldane	Michael Elwyn
Mrs. Haldane	Ninka Scott
Rex Lanham	Jasper Jacob
George Hardcastle	Donald Pickering
The Hon. Maura Hardcastle	Maria Aitken
Colonel Hassan Ali	Hossein Karimbeik
Mrs. Hassan Ali	Anita Edwards
Bill Rafferty	Angus MacInnes
Alan Platts-Williams	Rupert Vansittart
Sidney Platts-Williams	Anne Lambton
Dutch	Judy Liebert
Eddy Pressback	Mac MacDonald
Chinese Ambassador	Robert Lee
T.V. Newsreader	Andrew Seear
Van Arkady's Secretary	Janet McTeer
Barry Gingham	Timothy Peters

and John Sinclair, Eiji Kusuhara, Togo Igawa, Brian Hawksley, Dulice Liecier, Judy Maynard, Andy Lucas, Haluk Bilginer, Dave Duffy, Kevork Malikyan, Philip Whitchurch, Hugo De Vernier, Rosemary McHale, Carol Cleveland, Katharine Schofield, Siobhan Redmond, Claude Villers, Robert Guillermet, Joy Lemoine, Joe Powell

Top: Sigourney Weaver, and Right Center with Michael Caine
© *20th Century Fox/Keith Hamshere*

Michael Caine

JAMES CLAVELL'S TAI-PAN

(DE LAURENTIIS ENTERTAINMENT GROUP) Producer, Raffaella De Laurentiis; Director, Daryl Duke; Screenplay, John Briley, Stanley Mann; Based upon the novel by James Clavell; Associate Producer/Production Manager/Assistant Director, Jose Lopez Rodero; Editor, Antony Gibbs; Designer, Tony Masters; Photography, Jack Cardiff; Costumes, John Bloomfield; Music, Maurice Jarre; Production Executive, Charles Jennings; Stunts, Vic Armstrong; Special Visual Effects, Kit West; Art Directors, Benjamin Fernandez, Pierluigi Basile; Sound, Les Wiggins, Nelson Stoll, John Haptas; Production Supervisor, Bert Batt; Production Coordinator, Golda Offenheim; Special Effects, John Baker, Dino Galliano; Dolby Stereo; Soundtrack on Varese Sarabande Records; Technicolor; Rated R; 127 minutes; November release

CAST

Tai-Pan	Bryan Brown
May-May	Joan Chen
Brock	John Stanton
Culum	Tim Guinee
Gorth	Bill Leadbitter
Gordon	Russell Wong
Mary	Katy Behean
Tess	Kyra Sedgwick
Shevaun	Janine Turner
Quance	Norman Rodway
Orlov	John Bennett
Vargas	Derrick Branche
Jin Qua	Chang Cheng
Captain Glessing	Patrick Ryecart
Horatio	Nicholas Gecks
Mrs. Brock	Carol Gillies
Cooper	Michael C. Gwynne
Tillman	Bert Remsen
Mrs. Quance	Barbara Keogh
Ah Gip	Lisa Lu
Mrs. Fotheringill	Rosemarie Dunham
Zergeyev	Robert Easton
Lin	Zhang Jie
Nagrek	Rob Spendlove
Chen Sheng	Chen Shu
Kwang Kuo	Kwang Pan
Elderly Chinese Woman	Chan Lub Bun
Wung	Chan Koon Tai
Lin Din	Richard Foo
Executioner	Siu Kam
Doctor Gonzales	Job Stewart

and Jovita Adrineda, Patty Toy, Joycelyne Lew, Denise Kellogg, Charles Woods, Pat Gorman, Bob Appleby, Ian Sheridan, Mac Wheater, Leslie Peterkin, Vic Armstrong, Dickey Beer, Billy Horrigan, Bronco McLoughlin

Top Right: Bryan Brown, Joan Chen
Below: Bryan Brown
© *DeLaurentiis*

Joan Chen

Joan Chen

THE MOSQUITO COAST

(WARNER BROS.) Producer, Jerome Hellman; Director, Peter Weir; Screenplay, Paul Schrader; From the novel by Paul Theroux; Executive Producer, Saul Zaentz; Music, Maurice Jarre; Photography, John Seale; Editor, Thom Noble; Costumes, Gary Jones; Designer, John Stoddart; Casting, Dianne Crittenden; Associate Producer, Neville Thompson; Assistant Directors, Mark Egerton, Steve Andrews, Philip Patterson, Russ Kneeland, Mike Hammerman; Production Manager, Stewart Krohn; Production Coordinator, Judi Bunn; Assistant Costume Designer, Sue Gandy; Art Directors, John Wingrove, Brian Nickless; Special Effects, Larry Cavanaugh, Bruce Steinheimer; Sound, Chris Newman, Ken Weston, Richard Daniel, Alan Splett; Songs, Gary Johnson, Anthony Carter; Dolby Stereo; Soundtrack on Fantasy Records; Technicolor; Panavision; Rated PG; 117 minutes; November release

CAST

Allie Fox	Harrison Ford
Mother	Helen Mirren
Charlie	River Phoenix
Jerry	Jadrien Steele
April	Hilary Gordon
Clover	Rebecca Gordon
Clerk	Jason Alexander
Mr. Polski	Dick O'Neill
Mrs. Polski	Alice Sneed
Mr. Semper	Tiger Haynes
Captain Smalls	William Newman
Reverend Spellgood	Andre Gregory
Mrs. Spellgood	Melanie Boland
Emily Spellgood	Martha Plimpton
Convert 1	Raymond Clare
Man at bar	Emory King
Mr. Haddy	Conrad Roberts
Francis Lungley	Michael Rogers
Mr. Maywit	Tony Vega, Sr.
Mrs. Maywit	Aurora Clavel
Ma Kennywick	Butterfly McQueen
Bucky	Michael Opoku
Drainy	Aldolpho Salguero
Leon	Rafael Cho
Alice	Sofia Cho
Verny	Margarita Cho
Dixon	Wilfred Peters
Peaseee	Luis Palacio

and Juan Antonio Llanes, Abel Woodrich, Jorge Zepeda, Rich "Nubbs" Gowdy, Jack Dearlove, Isabel Goldberg

Right: Harrison Ford, Helen Mirren, and Top with River Phoenix, Hilary Gordon
© *Warner Bros.*

Harrison Ford, Conrad Roberts,
River Phoenix

Martha Plimpton, River Phoenix

NOBODY'S FOOL

(ISLAND PICTURES) Producers, James C. Katz, Jon S. Denny; Director, Evelyn Purcell; Screenplay, Beth Henley; Executive Producer, Cary Brokaw; Photography, Mikhail Suslov; Music, James Newton Howard; Editor, Dennis Virkler; Designer, Jackson DeGovia; Costumes, Ellen Mirojnick; Production Manager, Michael Fottrell; Assistant Directors, Marty Ewing, Denis Stewart; Production Liaison, Mel Klein; Art Director, John R. Jensen; Production Coordinator, Rebecca Greeley; Sound, James Tannenbaum; Stage Lighting Designer, Dan Dugan; Choreography, Bonnie Oda Homsey; Shakespearean Sequences Staging, Stephen Tobolowsky; Stunts, Michael Adams; Special Effects, The EFX Shop, Robert Stuard; Produced in association with Katz/Denny Productions; CFI Color; Panavision; Rated PG-13; 107 minutes; November release

CAST

Cassie	Rosanna Arquette
Riley	Eric Roberts
Pat	Mare Winningham
Billy	Jim Youngs
Pearl	Louise Fletcher
Shirley	Gwen Welles
Kirk	Stephen Tobolowsky
Nick	Charlie Barnett
Ralphy	J. J. Hardy
Frank	William Steis
Jane	Belita Moreno
Mr. Fry	Lewis Arquette
Bingo	Ronnie Claire Edwards
Linda	Ann Hearn
Winston	Scott Rosensweig
Prissy Lee	Cheli Chew
Mrs. Cain	Sheila Paige
Jennieva	Alma Beltran
Hank	Budge Threlkeld
Tracy	Lisa DeBennedetti
Barb	Wylie Small
Miss Francis	Natalie Golden
Fairy Dancers	Kristy Kennedy, Arwen Nichols
Madge	Loraine Wallace
Band Singer	Rod Hart
Bea Burger	Kay Pasa
Stuart Andrews	Brian Fitzgerald

and Mark Atkinson, Derek Barnes, John Hoover, Mark Sanders, Brian West, Jay Dusard, Christopher Michael Johnson, Diane Costa, Marsha Hicks, Walt Zandt, Kat, Barbara Brown, Bonnie Oda Homsey, Dean Ricca, Joe Clarke, Becky Bell Maxwell, Bruce Wright, Frederick Bailey, Melissa Grier, Kerrie Cullen, Paul E. Pinnt

Right: Rosanna Arquette, and Top with Eric Roberts © *Island Pictures*

Mare Winningham, Rosanna Arquette

Eric Roberts, Rosanna Arquette

NUTCRACKER

(ATLANTIC) Producers, Willard Carroll, Donald Kushner, Pete Locke, Thomas L. Wilhite; Director, Carroll Ballard; Executive Producers, Thomas Coleman, Michael Rosenblatt; Conceived by Ke Stowell, Maurice Sendak; From the story by E.T.A. Hoffmann; De signer/Costumes, Maurice Sendak; Choreographer/Original Production Staged and Choreographed by Kent Stowell; Music, Peter Ilyic Tchaikovsky; Music Performance, London Symphony Orchestra; Conductor, Sir Charles MacKerras; Photography, Stephen H. Burum; Editors, John Nutt, Michael Silvers; Production Manager/Assistant Director, Eugene Mazzola; Assistant Director, Jodi Ehrlich; Production Executive, Jonathan Debin; Production Supervisor, Sylvia White; Production Coordinator, Pat Chapman; Art Director, Peter Horne; Visual Adaptation, Henry Selick; Incidental Music, Mark Adler; Sound, Be Burtt; Narration Recording, Ward Botsford; Stage Manager, Rebecca Wakefield; Special Effects, Esquire Jauchem, Gregory Meeh; Color Soundtrack on TELARC: Rated G; 89 minutes; November release

CAST

Herr Drosselmeier	Hugh Bigne
Young Clara	Vanessa Shar
Dream Clara	Patricia Barke
Nutcracker	Wade Walthal
Frau Stahlbaum	Maia Rosa
Dr. Stahlbaum	Carey Homm
Grandparents	Benjamin & Beatrice Basse
Uncle	Gregory Drape
Ballerina Doll	Patricia Barke
Sword Dancer	Courtland Weave
Pas de Trois	Alejandra Bronfman, Kevin Kaiser Reid Olso
Fritz	Russell Burne
Nutcracker (Fight Scene)	Jacob Ric
Mouse Captain	Benjamin Houl
Mother Mouse	Deborah Inkste
Peacock	Maia Rosa
Chinese Tiger	Jeffrey N. Bulloc

and Martha Boyle, Dianne Brace, Elizabeth McCarthy, Laur Schwenk, Christian Cederlund, Gerard Ebitz, Sterling Kekoa, Jennife Homans, Ann Renhard, Lisa Stolzy, Whitney Onishi, Natalie Ryder Emerald Stacy, Cary Stidham, Elizabeth Parham, Vera Parham, Emil Penhollow, Gloria Riviera, Joseph Carver, Alex Gardner, Jason Taka maru, Andrew Wilson, Chaundra Bigney, Bridget Alsdorf, Tod Brown, Erik Cederlund, Margaret Farmer, Robert La Turner, Katrenn Marenych, Jeffrey Plourde, Christopher Smidt, Carolyn Stoklosa Anne Wescott, Marianne Chikos, Elizabeth Christianson, Lindsay Clothier, Sarah Frederick, Michele Blue, Sarah Coan, Rebecca Dunne Christa Halby, Heather Boe, Tracy Carboneau, Charina Dimaano Nicole Fiset, Joey-Lynn Mann, Erin Sokol, Hanna Burdge, Laar Estelle, Betsy Fenton, Gabrielle Gardner, Eugenia Georvasilis, Le Johnson, Christine Lebar, Catherine Mee Moen, Christina Nicolaidis Rebecca Osmon, Freedom Ozog, Amy Ritter, Noelle Schroeder Ashley Sherwood, Rana Standal, Nicole Wolgamott, Rebecca Brown Kippy Clark, Christine Elias, Christa Halby, Abby Hall, Heathe Hollenbeck, Jennifer Kader, Sun Lee, Mandi Lyons-Hansen, Michell McRae, Sara Pritchard, Jennifer Taylor, Kyoko Terada, Erica Fisch bach, Jeffrey Plourde, Rachel Harrison, Jennifer Owen, Jacob Rice Caaron Donaldson, Kara Chin, Jamie Geier, Mari London, Caroline Newman, Jenifer Peterson, Lucinda Hughey, Irene Damestoy, Susa Gladstone, Amy Greene, Stephanie Irwin, Kay Preston, Juli Tobiason, Heidi Vierthaler, Clara Wilson, Todd Brown, Jennifer Por ter, Angela Sterling, Tryon Woods, Carol Anderson, Irene Damestoy Laura Schwenk, Lisl Vaillant

Top Left: Vanessa Sharp, Hugh Bigney
© *Atlantic Entertainment Group*

Patricia Barker as adult Clara

BILLY GALVIN

(VESTRON) Producers, Sue Jett, Tony Mark; Director/Screenplay, John Gray; Photography, Eugene Shlugleit; Editor, Lou Kleinman; Designer, Shay Austin; Executive Producers, Stuart Benjamin, Howard L. Baldwin, William Minot, Lindsay Law; Production Manager, Eva Fyer; Art Director, Cecilia Rodarte; Costumes, Oleksa; Presented by American Playhouse in Association with Cinema Ventures I, Ltd, Robert A. Nowotny and Mark Clark; An Indian Neck-Mark Jett Production; Color; Rated PG; 94 minutes; November release

CAST

Jack Galvin	Karl Malden
Billy	Lenny Von Dohlen
Mae	Joyce Van Patten
Nora	Toni Kalem
Donny	Keith Szarabajka
George	Alan North
Nolan	Paul Guilfoyle
Kennedy	Barton Heyman
Margaret the Bingo Queen	Lynne Charnay
Diner Owner	Steve Sweeney
Nurse	Mary Ann Stackpole
Cop	David Brezniak
Waitress	Mara Clark
Lead Singer at the cemetery	Denis O'Gorman

and "Daybreak," Paul Cullen, Paul Tansino, John "Max" Maxner, Bob Daguardia, Robert Torres, Pedro Kuperman, Gary Littlejohn, John Michael Stewart

Left: Toni Kalem, Karl Malden
Top: Lenny Von Dohlen, Karl Malden
© Vestron/Nancy Howard

Toni Kalem, Lenny Von Dohlen
Above: Joyce Van Patten, Lenny Von Dohlen

Karl Malden

AN AMERICAN TAIL

(UNIVERSAL) Producers, Don Bluth, John Pomeroy, Gary Goldman; Director, Don Bluth; Screenplay, Judy Freudberg, Tony Geiss; Story, David Kirschner, Judy Freudberg, Tony Geiss; Created by David Kirschner; Executive Producers, Steven Spielberg, David Kirschner, Kathleen Kennedy, Frank Marshall; Music, James Horner; Songs, Cynthia Weil, James Horner, Barry Mann; Designer/Storyboard, Don Bluth; Production Managers, Fred Craig, Thad Weinlein; Associate Producers, Kate Barker, Deborah Jelin; Assistant Directors, G. Sue Shakespeare, David Steinberg; Layouts, Larry Leker, Mark Swan, Mark Swanson; Backgrounds, Don Moore, William Lorencz, Barry Atkinson, David Goetz, Richard Bentham; Directing Animators, John Pomeroy, Dan Kuenster, Linda Miller; Special Effects, Dorse A. Lanpher; Editor, Dan Molina; "Somewhere Out There" performed by Linda Ronstadt, James Ingram; Orchestrations, Greig McRitchie; Choreography, Estelle & Alfonso; Original Soundtrack on MCA; Dolby Stereo; Color by DeLuxe; Rated G; 80 minutes; November release.

CAST (VOICES)

Mama Mousekewitz .... Erica Yohn
Papa Mousekewitz .... Nehemiah Persoff
Tanya Mousekewitz .... Amy Green
Fievel Mousekewitz .... Phillip Glasser
Henri .... Christopher Plummer
Warren T. Rat .... John Finnegan
Digit .... Will Ryan
Moe .... Hal Smith
Tony Toponi .... Pat Musick
Bridget .... Cathianne Blore
Honest John .... Neil Ross
Gussie Mausheimer .... Madeline Kahn
Tiger .... Dom DeLuise

Top: Bridgit, Gussie, Fievel, Honest John
Below: Fievel, Tanya, Papa
© Universal

Toponi, Fievel Above: Papa, Fievel,
Tanya, Mama Top: Fievel

LITTLE SHOP OF HORRORS

(WARNER BROS.) Producer, David Geffen; Director, Frank Oz; Screenplay/Lyrics, Howard Ashman; Music, Alan Menken; Based on the musical stage play by Howard Ashman and Alan Menken; Music Producer, Bob Gaudio; Original Motion Picture Score, Miles Goodman; Photography, Robert Paynter; Designer, Roy Walker; Editor, John Jympson; Special Visual Effects, Bran Ferren; *Audrey II* Design/Creation, Lyle Conway; Costumes, Marit Allen; Production Supervisor, Eric Angelson; Line Producer, William S. Gilmore; Associate Producers, David Orton, Denis Holt; Choreographer, Pat Garrett; Orchestrations/Musical Supervision, Robby Merkin; Vocal Arranger, Robert Billig; Music Coordinator, Jim Henrikson; Music Arrangements/Adaptation, Robby Merkin, Bob Gaudio; Assistant Directors, Dusty Symonds, Gareth Tandy, Nick Heckstall-Smith; Production Manager, Donald Toms; Production Coordinator, Vicki Manning; Art Directors, Stephen Spence, John Fenner; Assistant Art Director, Jim Morahan; Sound, Peter Sutton; Assistant Costume Designer, William McPhail; Animatronics Coordinator, Barbara Griffiths; Animatronics Designers, Neal Scanlan, Christian Ostwald; Special Effects, Christine Overs, Tim Willis; Orchestrations, Thomas Pasatieri; Special Visual Effects, Associate & Ferren; Presented by The Geffen Company; Dolby Stereo; Soundtrack on Geffen Records; Technicolor; Panavision; Rated PG-13; 93 minutes; December release

CAST

Seymour Krelborn	Rick Moranis
Audrey	Ellen Greene
Mushnik	Vincent Gardenia
Orin Scrivello, D.D.S.	Steve Martin
Crystal	Tichina Arnold
Chiffon	Tisha Campbell
Ronette	Michelle Weeks
Patrick Martin	James Belushi
Wink Wilkinson	John Candy
First Customer	Christopher Guest
Arthur Denton	Bill Murray
Narrator	Stanley Jones
"Downtown" Old Woman	Bertice Reading
"Downtown" Bum's	Ed Wiley, Alan Tilvern, John Scott Martin
Chinese Florist	Vincent Wong
Doo Wop Street Singers	Mak Wilson, Danny Cunningham, Danny John-Jules, Gary Palmer, Paul Swaby
Second Customer	Mildred Shay
Third Customer	Melissa Wiltsie
Fourth Customer	Kevin Scott
Fifth Customer	Barbara Rosenblat
Radio Station Assistant	Adeen Fogle
Audrey & Seymour's Kids	Kelly Huntley, Paul Reynolds
Dental Nurse	Miriam Margolyes
Boy Patient	Abbie Dabner
Second Patient	Frank Dux
Patient on ceiling	Peter Whitman
Girl Patient	Heather Henson
Girl's Mother	Judith Morse
Agent	Bob Sherman
"Life" Magazine Lady	Doreen Hermitage
Her Assistant	Kerry Shale
Network Exec's	Robert Arden, Stephen Hoye, Bob Sessions
Television Reporter	Michael J. Shannon
The Voice of "Audrey II"	Levi Stubbs

Top Right: Michelle Weeks, Tisha Campbell, Tichina Arnold Below: Ellen Greene, Vincent Gardenia, Rick Moranis
© Geffen Films

Rick Moranis, Ellen Greene Above: Moranis, Steve Martin, Greene

BRIGHTON BEACH MEMOIRS

(UNIVERSAL) Producer, Ray Stark; Director, Gene Saks; Screenplay, Neil Simon; Based on the stage play by Neil Simon; Executive Producer, David Chasman; Photography, John Bailey; Editor, Carol Littleton; Designer, Stuart Wurtzel; Costumes, Joseph G. Aulisi; Associate Producer/Production Manager, Joseph M. Caracciolo; Music, Michael Small; Assistant Directors, Robert Girolami, Louis D'Esposito, James Skotchdopole, Jane Paul; Sound, Chris Newman; Art Director, Paul Eads; Assistant Art Directors, Tom Warren, Wynn Thomas, Mindy Roffman; Orchestrations, David Berger, Chris Dedrick, Sonny Kompanek, Bob Wilber; Songs by various artists; Panavision; Color; Rated PG-13; 108 minutes; December release

CAST

Kate	Blythe Danner
Jack	Bob Dishy
Stanley	Brian Drillinger
Laurie	Stacey Glick
Blanche	Judith Ivey
Eugene	Jonathan Silverman
Nora	Lisa Waltz
Mr. Greenblatt	Fyvush Finkel
Mrs. Laski	Kathleen Doyle
Andrew	Alan Weeks
Woman in street	Marilyn Cooper
Pool Players	Jason Alexander, Christian Baskous
Policemen	Brian Evers, Ed Deacy
Dance Teacher	Wanda Bimson
Stunt Driver	Edgard Mourino
Recruiting Sergeant	Richard Bright
Frank Murphy	James Handy
Mrs. Murphy	Bette Henritze
Mr. Stroheim	Steven Hill
Mr. Farber	David Margulies

Left: Bob Dishy, Blythe Danner
Top: Bob Dishy, Jonathan Silverman
© Universal

Stacey Glick, Brian Drillinger, Blythe Danner, Bob Dishy, Judith Ivey,
Lisa Waltz, Jonathan Silverman

Bob Dishy, Blythe Danner, Jonathan Silverman Top Left: Judith Ivey, James Handy Below:
Jonathan Silverman Top Right: Judith Ivey, Blythe Danner Below: Jonathan Silverman, Kathleen Doyle

NO MERCY

(TRI-STAR) Producer, D. Constantine Conte; Director, Richard Pearce; Screenplay/Co-Producer, Jim Carabatsos; Executive Producer, Michael Hausman; Photography, Michel Brault; Designer, Patrizia Von Brandenstein; Editors Jerry Greenberg, Bill Yahraus; Costumes, Hilary Rosenfeld; Music, Alan Silvestri; Casting, Howard Feuer; Production Manager, Lee R. Mayes; Assistant Directors, Ned Dowd, Cara Giallanza; Art Director, Doug Kraner; Set Decorators, Derek R. Hill, Gretchen Rau; Sound, John Pritchett; Special Effects, Joseph Digaetano, III, Larry Reid, Robert Hohman, Lou Carlucci; Stunts, Glenn H. Randall, Jr.; Music Supervision, Dick Rudolph; Songs, Michael McDonald, David Pack, Junior Walker, Mighty Joe Young; Dolby Stereo; Metrocolor; Panavision; Rated R; 107 minutes; December release

CAST

Eddie Jillette	Richard Gere
Michel Duval	Kim Basinger
Losado	Jeroen Krabbe
Captain Stemkowski	George Dzundza
Joe Collins	Gary Basaraba
Allan Deveneux	William Atherton
Paul Deveneux	Terry Kinney
Lt. Hall	Bruce McGill
Angles Ryan	Ray Sharkey
Alice Collins	Marita Geraghty
Cara	Aleta Mitchell
Quiet	Fred Gratton
Pinto	Dionisio
Benny Blue	Ray Brown
Old Asian Man	Kim Chan
Reblue	George Dickerson
Curtis	Raynor Scheine
Lawrence	Carl Gordon
Bernice	Victoria Edwards
Susan	Annalee Jefferies
Moon	Ed Nakamoto
Miles	John Snyder
Waitress	Caris Corfman
Blind Woman	Pearl Jones
Policeman	John Schluter
Driver	Mike Bacarella
Sgt. Savoy	Charles Dutton

and Harold Evans, Dave Petitjean, Stephen Payne, Leon Rippy, Bill Hart, Thomas Rosales, Jr., Randall Trepagnier, Khon Reid, Helen Yu-Shin McKay

Top Right: Richard Gere, Kim Basinger
© *Tri-Star*

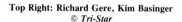

Richard Gere

Kim Basinger

104

HEARTBREAK RIDGE

(WARNER BROS) Producer/Director, Clint Eastwood; Screenplay, James Carabatsos; Executive Producer/Production Manager, Fritz Manes; Photography, Jack N. Green; Designer, Edward Carfagno; Editor, Joel Cox; Music, Lennie Niehaus; Assistant Directors, Paul Moen, L. Dean Jones, Jr., Michael Looney; Casting, Phyllis Huffman; Set Decorator, Robert Benton; Sound, William Nelson, Alan Murray, Robert Henderson; Stunts, Wayne Van Horn; Special Effects, Chuck Gaspar; Costume Supervision, Glenn Wright; Songs, Hal David, Paul Hampton, Sammy Fain, Paul Francis Webster, Clint Eastwood, Sammy Cahn, Mario Van Peebles, Desmond Nakano; In association with Jay Weston Productions; A Malpaso Production; Dolby Stereo; Panavision; Technicolor; Rated R; 128 minutes; December release

CAST

Highway	Clint Eastwood
Aggie	Marsha Mason
Major Powers	Everett McGill
Sgt. Webster	Moses Gunn
Little Mary	Eileen Heckart
Roy Jennings	Bo Svenson
Lieutenant Ring	Boyd Gaines
Stitch	Mario Van Peebles
Choozoo	Arlen Dean Snyder
Fragetti	Vincent Irizarry
Aponte	Ramon Franco
Profile	Tom Villard
Quinones	Mike Gomez
Colins	Rodney Hill
"Swede" Johanson	Peter Koch
Colonel Meyers	Richard Venture
Major Devin	Peter Jason
Quartermaster Sgt.	J. C. Quinn
Mrs. Aponte	Begona Plaza
Judge Zane	John Eames
Emcees	Thom Sharp, Jack Gallagher
Reese	John Hostetter
Sarita Dwayne	Holly Shelton-Foy

and Nicholas Worth, Timothy Fall, Jon Pennell, Trish Garland, Dutch Mann, Darwyn Swalve, Christopher Lee Michael, Alex. M. Bello, Steve Halsey, John Sasse, Rebecca Perle, Annie O'Donnell, Elizabeth Ruscio, Lloyd Nelson, Sgt. Maj. John H. Brewer, Michael Maurer, Tom Ellison

Top: Clint Eastwood, Moses Gunn
Right: Clint Eastwood, Mario Van Peebles
Below: 2nd Reconnaissance Platoon
© *Warner Bros.*

Marsha Mason, Clint Eastwood

CRIMES OF THE HEART

(DE LAURENTIIS) Producer, Freddie Fields; Director, Bruce Beresford; Screenplay, Beth Henley, based on her play; Photography, Dante Spinotti; Designer, Ken Adam; Editor, Ann Goursaud; Executive Producer, Burt Sugarman; Co-Producers, Arlyne Rothberg, Bill Gerber; Costumes, Albert Wolsky; Music, Georges Delerue; Associate Producer, P.K.Fields Zimmerman; Production Manager, Don Heitzer; Assistant Directors, Richard Luke Rothschild, Joel B. Segal; Production Supervisor, Lucio Trentini; Set Decorator, Garrett Lewis; Sound, Brue Bizenz; Art Director, Ferdinando Giovannoni; Hair/Makeup, J. Roy Helland, Kelvin Trahan, Marlies Vallant; Stunts, Debby Lynn Ross; Casting, Susan Bluestein; Songs, Mildred J. & Patty S. Hill, Jay Booker, Cole Porter, Dann Rogers, Don Huber, Jack Keller; Soundtrack on Varese Sarabande Records; Technicolor; Panavision; Rated PG-13; 105 minutes; December release

CAST

Lenny Magrath	Diane Keaton
Meg Magrath	Jessica Lange
Babe Magrath	Sissy Spacek
Doc Porter	Sam Shepard
Chick Boyle	Tess Harper
Barnette Lloyd	David Carpenter
Old Granddaddy	Hurd Hatfield
Zackery Botrelle	Beeson Carroll
Lucille Botrelle	Jean Willard
Uncle Watson	Tom Mason
Willie Jay	Gregory Travis
Annie May Jenkins	Annie McKnight
Little Lenny	Eleanor Eagle
Little Meg	Jessica Ezzell
Little Babe	Natalie Anderson
Zackery's Concubine	Connie Adams

**Top: Diane Keaton, Sissy Spacek,
Jessica Lange**
© *DeLaurentiis*

Diane Keaton, Sam Shepard

Jessica Lange, Sissy Spacek, Diane Keaton Top Left: Diane Keaton, Tess Harper
Below: Jessica Lange, Diane Keaton, Sissy Spacek Right: Jessica Lange, Sam Shepard

WISDOM

(20th CENTURY-FOX) Producer, Bernard Williams; Director/ Screenplay, Emilio Estevez; Executive Producer, Robert E. Wise; Editor, Michael Kahn; Photography, Adam Greenberg; Designer, Dennis Gassner; Music, Danny Elfman; Production Manager, Carl Olsen; Assistant Directors, Bernard Williams, Donald Eaton, Wendy Ikeguchi; Stunts, Bud Davis; Special Effects, Richard Helmer; Art Director, Dins Danielsen; Fashion Designer, Jonathan Kinsey; Production Coordinators, Karen Danweagle, Pamela Killebrew; Set Decorator, Richard Hoover; Visual Concepts, Mentor Huebner; Sound, Ed White; Music Arrangements/Programming, Steve Bartek; Songs by various artists; Presented by Gladden Entertainment; Color by DeLuxe; Dolby Stereo; Rated R; 108 minutes; December release

CAST

Karen Simmons	Demi Moore
John Wisdom	Emilio Estevez
Lloyd Wisdom	Tom Skerritt
Samantha Wisdom	Veronica Cartwright
Williamson	William Allen Young
Cooper	Richard Minchenberg
Motel Manager	Ernie Brown
Theo	Bill Henderson
Sheriff	Gene Ross
Jake Perry	Liam Sullivan
City Burger Manager	Charlie Sheen
Network Anchorman	Hal Fishman
Local Anchorman	Chuck Henry
Gun Salesman	Nick Shields
Loan Officer at bank #1	Barbara Stamm
Al Gomez	Santos Morales
Yuppie Employer	Gus Corrado
Katie	Golden Henning
Carol	Rene Sprattling
Nancy	Kate McKinnon
Matt	Tim Sapunor
Bob	Charlie Holliday

and Ron Presson, Estee Chandler, Jeff Boudov, Thomas Witt-Ellis, David DeFrancesca, Leon Corcos, Janet Rotblatt, Erika Lincoln, Sid Conrad, Henry Proach, Matt Robinson, Bob Devon Jones, Jimmy Walker Lane, Walter Edward Smith, John Deaderick, Beau Dare, Gil Parra, Jaime Namson

**Top: Emilio Estevez and below
with Demi Moore**
© *Gladden Entertainment/Michael Paris*

**Demi Moore, Emilio Estevez
(also Top)**

THREE AMIGOS

(ORION) Producers, Lorne Michaels, George Folsey Jr.; Executive Producer, Steve Martin; Director, John Landis; Screenplay, Steve Martin, Lorne Michaels, Randy Newman; Photography, Ronald W. Browne; Editor, Malcolm Campbell; Music, Elmer Bernstein; Songs, Randy Newman; Designer, Richard Sawyer; Set Decorator, Richard Goddard; Set Designers, Mark Faybus, Stan Tropp; Costumes, Deborah Nadoolman; Sound, William Kaplan; Assistant Director, David Sosna; Casting, Jackie Burch; Technicolor; Rated PG; 105 minutes; December release

CAST

Dusty Bottoms	Chevy Chase
Lucky Day	Steve Martin
Ned Nederlander	Martin Short
Carmen	Patrice Martinez
El Guapo	Alfonso Arau
Jefe	Tony Plana
Harry Flugelman	Joe Mantegna

(No photos available)

Right: Keenan Wynn, Ricky Paull Goldin
Top: Rosie Marcel, Keenan Wynn, Ricky Paull Goldin,
Kirbi the Tri-Lat, Sydney Penny
©*Taliafilm II*

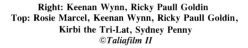

HYPER SAPIEN

(TRI-STAR) Producer, Jack Schwartzman; Executive Producer, Talia Shire; Director, Peter Hunt; Screenplay, Christopher Adcock, Christopher Blue, Marnie Paige; Story, Christopher Blue; Co-producer, Ariel Levy; Photography, John Coquillon; Music, Arthur B. Rubinstein; Production Manager, Eda Lishman; Assistant Directors, Barry Langley, Jerry Daly, Jay Coquillon; Costumes, Kathy Marshall; Art Director, Richard Hudolin; Set Decorator, Tedd Kuchera; Sound, Garrell Clark; Stunts, John Scott; Editor, Rick Benwick; Special Effects, David Harris, Brian Warner, Peter Davey; Orchestrations, Mark H. Hoder; Casting, Bette Chadwick; Color; Rated PG; 92 minutes; December release

CAST

Uncle Aric	Dennis Holahan
Robyn	Sydney Penny
Tavy	Rosie Marcel
Dirt McAlpin	Ricky Paull Goldin
Mrs. McAlpin	Hersha Parady
Cee Gee	Patricia Brookson
Mr. McAlpin	Peter Jason
Hyper Sapien Leader	Jeremy Wilkins
Teel	Him Gray
Voice of Kirbi, The Tri-Lat	Marilyn Schreffler
Grandpa McAlpin	Keenan Wynn
Lucy	Gladys Taylor
Lyth	Linda Elder
Patterson	Chuck Shamata
Dr. Tedra Rosen	Talia Shire
Television Host	Army Archerd
Riss	David Siversten
Senator Myrna King	Gail Strickland

and Clarice McCord, Bruce Miller, Barry Onody, Jamie Clarke, Jack Goth, Robert Christie, Rod Jarvis, Dan MacDonald, Rhiannon Owens, David Jacox, Christy Baker, David Lereaney, Michael Tait, Greg Solem, Gsena Hecht, Trevor Hayden, Maureen Thomas

Sydney Penny, Ricky Paull Goldin

KING KONG LIVES

(DE LAURENTIIS ENTERTAINMENT GROUP) Producer, Martha Schumacher; Director, John Guillermin; Screenplay, Ronald Shusett, Steven Pressfield; Based on the character *King Kong* created by Merian C. Cooper and Edgar Wallace Production Manager, Lucio Trentiti; Assistant Directors, Brian Cooke, Matt Earl Beesley, Bruce Moriarity; Executive Producer, Ronald Shusett; Music, John Scott; Editor, Malcolm Cooke; Photography, Alec Mills; Designer, Peter Murton; Creatures, Carlo Rambaldi; Special Visual Effects, Barry Nolan; Costumes, Clifford Capone; Art Directors, Fred Carter, Tony Reading, John Wood; Stunts, Bud Davis; Sound, David Stephenson; Special Effects, Joseph Mercurio; Special Effects Make-up, Dean Gates; Technicolor; Dolby Stereo; Rated PG-13; 105 minutes; December release

CAST

King Kong	Peter Elliot
Lady Kong	George Yiasomi
Hank Mitchell	Brian Kerwin
Amy Franklin	Linda Hamilton
Colonel Nevitt	John Ashton
Dr. Ingersoll	Peter Michael Goetz
Dr. Benson Hughes	Frank Maraden
Faculty Doctor #1	Alan Sader
Faculty Doctor #2	Lou Criscuolo
Crew Chief	Marc Clement
Surgeon #1	Natt Christian
Surgeon #2	Mac Pirkle
Journalist	Larry Sprinkle
TV Reporter	Rod Davis
Mazlansky	Robin Cahall
Security Chief	Don Law
Wrangler #1	Jack Maloney
Major Pete	Jimmie Ray Weeks
Radioman #1	Jeff Benninghofen
Sergeant	Jim Grimshaw
Captain #1	Bernard Additon
Captain #2	Michael McLendon
Boyfriend	Jimmy Wiggins
Girlfriend	Mary Swafford
Vance	Michael Forest
Mom #1	Dandy Stevenson
Mom #2	Lydia Smith

and Richard Rhodes, Larry Souder, Ted Prichard, Jayne Linday-Gray. Debbie McLeod, Elizabeth Hayes, David DeVries, Bonnie Cook, J. Michael Hunter, Leon Rippy, Wallace Merck, Dean Whitworth, Hershel Sparber, Hope Nunnery, Margaret Freeman, Winston Hemingway, Tom Parkhill, Buck Ford, Derek Pearson, Gary Kaikaka, Duke Ernsberger, Mike Starr, Shannon Rowell

Top Right: King Kong
© *DeLaurentiis Entertainment Group*

Linda Hamilton, Brian Kerwin

Lady Kong

THE MORNING AFTER

(20th CENTURY-FOX) Producer, Bruce Gilbert; Director, Sidney Lumet; Screenplay, James Hicks; Associate Producers, Wolfgang Glattes, Lois Bonfiglio; Executive Producer, Faye Schwab; Photography, Andrzej Bartkowiak; Designer, Albert Brenner; Costumes, Ann Roth; Editor, Joel Goodman; Music, Paul Chihara; Production Manager, C. Tad Devlin; Assistant Directors, Wolfgang Glattes, Aldric La'auli Porter, Brenda Kalosh; Sound, David Ronne, Robert Crosby; Art Director, Kandy Stern; Assistant Costume Designer, Neil Spisak; Special Effects, Tom Ward; Songs by various artists; Solo Saxophone, George Howard; From Lorimar Film Partners; Color by DeLuxe; Panavision; Rated R; 103 minutes; December release

CAST

Alex Sternbergen	Jane Fonda
Turner Kendall	Jeff Bridges
Joaquin Manero	Raul Julia
Isabel Harding	Diane Salinger
Sgt. Greenbaum	Richard Foronjy
Bobby Korshack	Geoffrey Scott
Frankie	James "Gypsy" Haake
Red	Kathleen Wilhoite
Hurley	Don Hood
Airline Clerk	Fran Bennett
Airline Supervisor	Michael Flanagan
Bartender	Bruce Vilanch
Mr. Harding	Michael Prince
Mrs. Harding	Frances Bergen
Driver	Jose Santana
Man	Bob Minor
Cabbie	George Fisher
Detective	Rick Rossovich
Secretary	Laurel Lyle
Woman on Mateo Street	Kathy Bates
Nurse	Anne Betancourt
Hairstylist #1	Patti Song
Salon Customer	Betty Lougaris
Detectives	Drew Berman, Sam Scarber, Michael Zand
Body Builder	Gladys Portugues
Miss Olympia	Corinna Everson

Right: Raul Julia, Diane Salinger
Top: Jane Fonda
© *Lorimar*

Jeff Bridges, Jane Fonda

Jeff Bridges, Jane Fonda

THE GOLDEN CHILD

(PARAMOUNT) Producers, Edward S. Feldman, Robert D. Wachs; Director, Michael Ritchie; Screenplay/Co-producer, Dennis Feldman; Executive Producers, Richard Tienken, Charles R. Meeker; Photography, Donald E. Thorin; Designer, J. Michael Riva; Editor, Richard A. Harris; Music, Michel Colombier; Associate Producer/Production Manager, Gordon A. Webb; Costumes, Wayne Finkelman; Assistant Directors, Tom Mack, Emmit-Leon O'Neill, W. Alexander Ellis; Visual Effects, Ken Ralston, Pamela Easley; Make-Up Design, Ken Chase; Art Director, Lynda Paradise; Set Decorator, Marvin March; Sound, Jim Alexander; Movement Adviser, Michael Smuin; Special Effects, Cliff Wenger, Danny Gill, Mark Noel, Eric Roberts, Gintar Repecka; Set Designers, Virginia Randolph, Judy Cammer; Stunts, Chuck Waters, Mickey Gilbert; Special Sound Effects, John Paul Fasal; Orchestrations, Michel Colombier, Robbie Buchanan; Demon Supervisor, Phil Tippett; Demon Designer, Randy Dutra; Co-produced by Industrial Light & Magic; Songs, John Barry, Ann Wilson, Nancy Wilson, Sue Ennis, Stephen Pearcy, Warren DeMartini, Juan Croucier, Irving Berlin; Dolby Stereo; Soundtrack on Capitol; Metrocolor; Panavision; Rated PG-13; 96 minutes; December release

CAST

Chandler Jarrell	Eddie Murphy
Sardo Numspa	Charles Dance
Kee Nang	Charlotte Lewis
The Old Man	Victor Wong
Til	Randall "Tex" Cobb
Doctor Hong	James Hong
Kala	Shakti
Yu	Tau Logo
Khan	Tiger Chung Lee
Fu	Pons Maar
Tommy Tong	Peter Kwong
Detective Boggs	Wally Taylor
Yellow Dragon	Eric Douglas
TV Host	Charles Levin
Friend at Pink's	Kenneth "Fruitty" Frith, Jr.
Herb Shop Clerk	Bennett Ohta
Old Chinese Woman	Kinko Tsubouchi
Jabbering Old Man	Govind Chipalu
Security Men	Chantara Nop, Phok Ok
Businessman/Customer	Bob Tzudiker
Russell	Cliffy MaGee
Waiter	Jeff Soo Hoo
Chicken Lady on plane	Bindra Joshi
Tortoise Lady	Judy Hudson
Buttonman	Ron Packham
Voice of Kala	Marilyn Schreffler
Voice of the Thing	Frank Welker
The Golden Child	J. L. Reate

Left: Eddie Murphy, Randall "Tex" Cobb
Above: Eddie Murphy, Eric Douglas
Top: Charlotte Lewis, Eddie Murphy
© *Paramount/Bruce Talamon*

Charles Dance, Eddie Murphy

Vince Deadrick, Sr., Eddie Murphy

Victor Wong, Eddie Murphy Above and
Top: Charlotte Lewis, Eddie Murphy

Eddie Murphy, J. L. Reate

Riley Steiner, Charles Homet
in "Beginners Luck"
© *New World*

Louise Smith in "Working Girls"
© *Miramax*

BEGINNERS LUCK (New World) Producer. Caroline Mouris; Director, Frank Mouris; Screenplay, Caroline and Frank Mouris; Editor, Ray Anne School; Photography, Ayne Coffey; Sound, Charlie Lew, Stewart Adam, Associate Editor, Mark Simon; Music, Richard Lavsky; Assistant Editors, Rena Schwarz, Cynthia Zeman; Presented by The Hot Talk Company; Color; Rated R; 85 minutes; January release. CAST: Sam Rush (Hunter), Riley Steiner (Tech), Charles Homet (Aris), Kate Talbot (Bethany), Mickey Beaman (Babs), Phil Kilbourne (Willem), Bobbie Steinbach (Courtney), Stephen Weagle (Don), Cynthia Weagle (Stella), Stephen Weagle (Ronnie), Cynthia Weagle (Bonnie), John Adair (Rev. Rice/Gas Attendant/Taxi Driver/Motel Manager), Rima Miller (Judith), John Eisner (Nathan)

WORKING GIRLS (Miramax) Producers, Lizzie Borden, Andi Gladstone; Direction/Story, Lizzie Borden; Screenplay, Lizzie Borden, Sandra Kay; Photography, Judy Irola; Designer, Kurt Ossenfort; Sound, J. T. Takagi; Music, David van Tieghem, Roma Baran; In color; Not rated; 90 minutes; January release. CAST: Louise Smith (Molly), Ellen McElduff (Lucy), Amanda Goodwin (Dawn), Marusia Zach (Gina), Janne Peters (April), Helen Nicholas (Mary)

FOREST OF BLISS (Film Forum) Producers, Robert Gardner, Akos Ostor; Director/Photography, Robert Gardner; Sound/Second Camera, Ned Johnston; Sound Editing, Michel Chalufour; Production Assistant, Maria Sendra; Produced for the Film Study Center, Harvard University; Documentary; Winner First Prize, 1986 USA Film Festival, Dallas; Color; Not Rated; 90 minutes; January release

HOUSE (New World) Producer, Sean S. Cunningham; Director, Steve Miner; Screenplay, Ethan Wiley; Story, Fred Dekker; Photography, Mac Ahlberg; Editor, Michael N. Knue; Designer, Gregg Fonseca; Costumes, Bernadette O'Brien; Music, Harry Manfredini; Associate Producer/Production Manager, Patrick Markey; Assistant Directors, H. Gordon Boos, David Householter, Heidi Gutman; Sound, Richard Lightstone; Art Director, John Reinhart; Creature Designs, Kirk Thatcher, James Cummins; Creature Effects, Backwood Film, James Cummins; Special Effects, Tassilo Baur, Joe Viskocil; Color; Rated R; 93 minutes; January release. CAST: William Katt (Roger Cobb), George Wendt (Harold Gorton), Richard Moll (Big Ben), Kay Lenz (Sandy), Mary Stavin (Tanya), Michael Ensign (Chet Parker), Erik Silver/Mark Silver (Jimmy), Susan French (Aunt Elizabeth), Alan Autry, Steven Williams (Cops), Jim Calvert (Grocery Boy), Jayson

Kane (Cheesy Stud), Billy Beck (Priest), Steve Susskind (Frank McGraw), Dwier Brown (Lieutenant), Joey Green (Fitzsimmons), Stephen Nichols (Scott), Robert Joseph (Robert), Peter Pitofsky (Witch), Elizabeth Barrington, Jerry Marin, Felix Silla (Little Critters), and Mindy Sterling, Bill McLean, John Young, Donald Willis, Ronn Carroll, Curt Wilmot, Ronn Wright, Renee Lillian

HAMBURGER: The Motion Picture (FM Entertainment) Producers, Edward S. Feldman, Charles R. Meeker; Director, Mike Marvin; Screenplay, Donald Ross; Photography, Karen Grossman; Art Director/Set Decorator, Maria Rebman Caso; Designer, George Costello; Music, Peter Bernstein; Editors, Steven Schoenberg, Ann E. Mills; Costumes, Shari Feldman; Co-Producers, Robert Lloyd Lewis, Donald Ross; Associate Producer, Jeffrey Sudzin; Assistant Directors, Mary Ellen Woods, Gregory Goodman, Katherine Carmichael; Special Effects, Roger George, Lise Romanoff; Songs by various artists; C.F.I. Color; Panavision; Rated R; 90 minutes; January release. CAST: Leigh McCloskey (Russell), Dick Butkus (Drootin), Randi Brooks (Mrs. Vunk), Chuck McCann (Dr. Mole), Jack Blessing (Nacio Herb Zipser), Charles Tyner (Lyman Vunk), Debra Blee (Mia Vunk), Sandy Hackett (Fred Domino), John Young (Prestopopnick), Chip McAllister (Magneto Jones), Barbara Whinnery (Sister Sara), Maria Richwine (Conchita), Karen Mayo-Chandler (Dr. Gotbottom), and Bob Hogan, Lillian Garrett, Robert Gray, Sarah Abrell, Peggy Rea, Bob Minor, Bob Drew, Lenore Woodward, Santos Morales, Frank Lugo, Rob Paulsen, Jim Jackman, Steve Conte, Jon Lovitz, Peter Georgilas, Cindy Adlesh, Nancy Omi, Linda Lutz, Justine Lenore, Lelund Sun, Gino Dentie, Tony Epper, Diane Kay Grant, Dutch Van Dalsem, Rent-A-Gang, Tony Brafa, Anthony Georgilas, Travis McKenna, Tom Tangen, Betsy Lynn Thompson, Carol Gwynn Thompson

THE CLAN OF THE CAVE BEAR (Warner Bros.) Producer, Gerald I. Isenberg; Director, Michael Chapman; Screenplay, John Sayles; Based on novel *The Clan of the Cave Bear* by Jean M. Auel; Photography, Jan De Bont; Designer, Anthony Masters; Editor, Wendy Greene Bricmont; Associate Producer, Richard Briggs; Co-Executive Producer, Sidney Kimmel; Co-Producer, Stan Rogow; Executive Producers, Jon Peters, Peter Guber, Mark Damon, John Hyde; Music, Alan Silvestri; Production Manager, Justis Greene; Assistant Directors, Jerry Grandey, Rob Cowan, Warren Carr, Alan Goluboff; Special Make-ups, Michael G. Westmore, Michele Burke; Clan Body Movement, Peter Elliot; Sound, Larry Sutton; Costumes, Kelly Kimball; A Jozak/

William Katt in "House"
© *New World*

"Forest of Bliss"
© *Robert Gardner/Jane Tuckerman*

114

"Hamburger"
© Busterberger

Jason Gedrick, Louis Gossett
in "Iron Eagle" © Tri-Star

Decade Production; Technicolor; Technovision; Dolby Stereo; Rated R; 100 minutes; January release. CAST: Daryl Hannah (Ayla), Pamela Reed (Iza), James Remar (Creb), Thomas G. Waites (Broud), John Doolittle (Brun), Curtis Armstrong (Goov), Martin Doule (Grod), Adel C. Hammoud (Vorn), Tony Montanaro (Zoug), Mike Muscat (Dorv), John Wardlow (Droog), Keith Wardlow (Crug), Karen Austin (Aba), Barbara Duncan (Uka), Gloria Lee (Oga), Janne Mortil (Ovra), Lycia Naff (Uba), Linda Quibell (Aga), Bernadette Sabath (Ebra), Penny Smith (Ika), Joey Cramer (Young Broud), Rory L. Crowley (Durc), Nicole Eggert (Middle Aula), Emma Floria (Young Ayla), Pierre Lamielle (Brac), Mary Reid (Ayla's Mother), Samantha Ostry (Young Uba), Shane Punt (Young Vorn), Christiane Boyce, Catherine Flather (Baby Durc), Natino Bellantoni (Gorn), Rick Valiquette (Voord), Alan Waltman (Norg), Paul Carafotes (Brug), Guila Chiesa, Shauna Fanara, Amy Cyr, Colin Doyle and Salome Jens (Narrator)

THE LONGSHOT (Orion) Producer, Lang Elliott; Director, Paul Bartel; Screenplay, Tim Conway; Executive Producer, Mike Nichols; Associate Producer, Tom Egan; Photography, Robby Muller; Costumes, Sandra Culotta; Design Consultant, Joseph M. Altadonna; Music, Charles Fox; Vocals, Irene Cara, "Ice T", Tim Conway; Editor, Alan Toomayan; Production Manager, Pat Kehoe; Assistant Directors, Michael Schroeder, Dennis White; Production Coordinator, Paula Benson-Himes; Sound, Jon Earl Stein; Assistant Design/Set Decorator, Bob Schulenberg; Songs, Gloria Sklerov, Lenny Macaluso, Tim Conway, Charles Fox; Color by DeLuxe; Rated PG-13; 89 minutes; January release. CAST: Tim Conway (Dooley), Jack Weston (Elton), Harvey Korman (Lou), Ted Wass (Stump). Pat Li (Ono), Garry Goodrow (Josh), Brad Trumbull (Track Cop), Dave Johnson (Track Announcer), Dick Enberg (Radio Announcer), Anne Meara (Madge), Frank Bonner (Realtor), Benny Baker (Mr. Hooper), Yvonne Del Walker (Mrs. Hooper), Ernie Anderson (Old Man), Jinaki (Toby), Anzio (Cashier), Jorge Cervera (Santiago), Stella Stevens (Nicki Dixon), Susan Tolsky (Dee), Ted Bolczak (Cab Driver), Brad Logan (Doorman), Stephen Ciotta (Lizard), George DiCenzo (DeFranco), Edie McClurg (Donna), Hank Rolike (Jelly), Jonathan Winters (Tyler), and Eddie Deezen, Gregory Wolf, Don Draper, Maria Korman, Mickey Elliott, Joseph Ruskin, Ollie the Fish, Kelly Conway, Virginia Vincent, James Bacon, Nick Dimitri, Buckley Norris, Pat Kehoe, Pat Studstill, Tom Finnegan

IRON EAGLE (Tri-Star) Producers, Ron Samuels, Joe Wizan; Director, Sidney J. Furie; Screenplay, Kevin Elders, Sidney J. Furie; Photography, Adam Greenberg; Designer, Robb Wilson King; Editor, George Grenville; Music, Basil Poledouris; Executive Producer, Kevin Elders; Associate Producer, Lou Lenart; Production Manager, Arthur C. Schaefer, Jr.; Assistant Directors, Alan C. Blomquist, Elie Cohn, Richard Graves; Sound, Keith Stafford, Bill Nelson; Special Effects, Ken Pepiot, Paul Stewart; Songs by various artists; Soundtrack Album on Capitol Records; Metrocolor; Dolby Stereo; Rated PG-13; 119 minutes; January release. CAST: Lou Gossett, Jr. (Chappy), Jason Gedrick (Doug), David Suchet (Minister of Defense), Tim Thomerson (Ted), Larry B. Scott (Reggie), Caroline Lagerfelt (Elizabeth), Jerry Levine (Tony), Robbie Rist (Milo), Michael Bowen (Knotcher), Bobby Jacoby (Matthew), Melora Hardin (Katie), David Greenlee (Kingsley), Michael Alldredge (Col. Blackburn), Tom Fridley (Brillo), Rob Garrison (Packer), Chino "Fats" Williams (Slappy), Jay Footlik (Thatcher), Jacque Lynn Colton (Hazel), Shawnee Smith (Joanie), Heather De Vore Haase (Tally), Kathy Wagner (Amy), Kevin King (Farnsworth), Will Jeffries (Smiley), David Ward (Lt. Col. Kerns), Terry Willis (Tally's Dad), F. William Parker (Kingsley's Dad), and Albert R. Schara, Christopher Bradley, Michael Kehoe, Steve Rabin, Kevin Elders, Terry Becker, Paul O'Brien Richards, Lance LeGault, Max Thayer, Debbie Bloch, Roger Nolan, Jerry Hyman, Uri Gabriel, David Menachem, Yossi Shiloah, Itzik Saydof, Arnon Zadok

BAD GIRLS DORMITORY (Films Around the World Inc.) Producer, Entertainment Concepts; Director/Screenplay, Tim Kincaid; Executive Producer, Cynthia DePaula; Photography, Arthur D. Marks; Music, Man Parrish; Eastmancolor; Rated R; 95 minutes; January release. CAST: Carey Zuris (Lori), Teresa Farley (Marina), Natalie O'Connell (Paige), Rick Gianasi (Don Beach), Marita (Miss Madison), Jennifer DeLora (Lisa), Donna Eskra (Rebel), Dan Barclay (Dr. DeMarco), Rebecca Rothbaum (Nurse Stevens), Rachel Hancock (Harper), Charmagne Eckert (Valeska)

Daryl Hannah in "Clan of the
Cave Bear" © Warner Bros./Jonesfilms

Tim Conway, Harvey Corman
in "The Longshot" © Orion/Gail Adler

Janette Boyd in "Stripper"
© *Embassy International*

Rob Lowe, Patrick Swayze
in "Youngblood" © *United Artists*

STRIPPER (20th) Producers, Jerome Gary, Geof Bartz, Melvyn J. Estrin; Director, Jerome Gary; Executive Producer, Arnon Milchan; Editors, Geof Bartz, Bob Eisenhardt, Lawrence Silk; Photography, Edward Lachman; Co-Producers, Tom Tyson, Michael Nolin; Music, Buffy Sainte-Marie, Jack Nitzsche; Production Executives, Joe Grace, Steve Hirsch; Production Manager, Diana Young; Associate Producers, Laura Bemis, Meir Teper; Assistant to Director, Noreen O'Reilly; Art Direction, Candy Pratts, Chuck Price, Laurie Post; Sound, Kirk Francis, Bernard Hayden; Treatment, Jerome Gary, Laurie Frank; Score, Anthony Marinelli, Brian Banks; An Embassy International Picture; Documentary; Color by DuArt; Rated R; 90 minutes; January release. CAST: Janette Boyd, Sara Costa, Kimberly Holcomb (Danyel), Loree Menton (Mouse), Lisa Suarez (Gio), Ellen Claire McSweeney (Inspiration Shakti Om), and Jackie Coleman, Jack Cooney, Dahlia, Debbie DeGoutiere, Fuchs, Ann Gordon, Sandi Hall, Leanne Hoskins, Debra Lynn, Sheri Partridge, Tarren Rae, Suzanne Primeaux, Jean Runnals, Shalina, Taffy, Darcey Taylor, Audrey Stonehouse, Ken Hemmerick, Bianca Boyd, Walter Cartier, Alan DeLong, Janice Harrington, John Landaker, Debra Woodson, Geof Bartz, Robert Colvin, Nicole DeBeers, Venus Delight, Legs Diamond, Laure Fay, Emily Foster, Kirk Francis, Charles Gaines, Daniel Harris, Joanne Hatch, Catherine Kent, Paul Kodalis, Jess and Dorothy Mack, Carol McManus, Ed Menken, Joy Michaels, Rick Overton, Eddie Pollock, Larry Runnals, Mitzi Wasyliw, Pat Alexander, Gloria Costa, Carol Cox, Crystal, Jamal Rofeh, Ronnie Spitz

YOUNGBLOOD (MGM/UA) Producers, Peter Bart, Patrick Wells; Director/Screenplay, Peter Markle; Story, Peter Markle, John Whitman; Photography, Mark Irwin; Visual Consultant, Vincent J. Cresciman; Editors, Stephen E. Rivkin, Jack Hofstra; Music, William Orbit/Torchsong, Chris Boardman; Executive Producers, Jon Peters, Peter Gruber; Associate Producers, Mark Allan, Stephen E. Rivkin; Production Company, Markle-Wells, Inc.; Production Manager, Mark Allan; Assistant Directors, Bill Corcoran, Louise Casselman, Neil Huhta; Production Coordinator, Fran Solomon; Sound, Tom Mather, Emile Razpopov, Dessie Markovsky; Designers, Alicia Keywan, Alta Louise Doyle; Costumes, Eileen Kennedy; Songs by various artists; A presentation of the New United Artists; Metrocolor; Dolby Stereo; Rated R; 110 minutes; January release. CAST: Rob Lowe (Dean Youngblood), Cynthia Gibb (Jessie Chadwick), Patrick Swayze (Derek Sutton), Ed Lauter (Murray Chadwick), Jim Youngs (Kelly Young-

blood), Eric Nesterenko (Blane Youngblood), George Finn (Racki), Fionnula Flanagan (Miss Gill), Ken James (Frazier), Peter Faussett (Huey), Walker Boone (Assistant Coach), Keanu Reeves (Heaver), Martin Donlevy (Referee Hannah), and Harry Spiegel, Rob Sapienszke, Bruce Edwards, Lorraine Foreman, Catherine Bray, Jain Dickson, Barry Swatik, Michael Legros, Murray Evans, Jason Warren, Warren Dukes, Sid Lynas, Jamie McAllister, Jay Hanks, Frank Cini, Greg Salter, Howie McCarrol Jr., Charlie Wasley, Ricky Davis, Joe Bowen

MONSTER IN THE CLOSET (Troma Team) Producers, David Levy, Peter L. Bergquist; Direction/Screenplay, Bob Dahlin; Story, Bob Dahlin, Peter L. Bergquist; Executive Producers, Lloyd Kaufman, Michael Herz; Photography, Ronald W. McLeish; Music, Barrie Guard; Editors, Raja Gosnell, Stephanie Palewski; Designer, Lynda Cohen; Associate Producers, Michel Billot, Terrence Corey, Robert Rock; Casting, Sally Ann Stiner, Cindy Pierson; Production Manager, Mitch Factor; Assistant Directors, Peter L. Bergquist, Bob Simon; Coordinators, Sly Lovegren, Cynthia Colegrove; Sound, Don Parker; Editors, Mark Conte, Jacque Toberen; Music, Barrie Guard, Simon Heyworth; Art Director, Lynda Cohen; Set Decorator, Patricia Hall; Monster Design, William Stout; Stunt Coordinator, Doc Duhame; In color; A Closet Production; Rated PG; 87 minutes; January release. CAST: Donald Grant (Richard Clark), Denise DuBarry (Diane), Henry Gibson (Dr. Pennyworth), Howard Duff (Father Finnegan), Donald Moffat (Gen. Turnbull), Claude Aikins (Sheriff), Paul Walker (Professor), Frank Ashmore (Scoop), John Carradine (Old Joe), Paul Dooley (Roy), Stella Stevens (Margo), Jesse White (Ben), Kevin Peter Hall (Monster/Tony Carlin, voice), Stacy Ferguson (Lucy), Ritchie Montgomery (Deputy), Arthur Berggren/Daryle Ann Lindley (Jimmy's Parents), Benny Baker (McGinty), Gordon Metcalfe (Turnbull's Aide), David Anthony (Paperboy), Stephanie White (Maggie), Corky Pigeon (Danny), Evan Arnold (Beaver), Jonathan Aluzas (Chip), Richie Egan (Charlie)

PRAY FOR DEATH (American Distribution Group) Executive Producers, Moshe Diamant, Sunil Shah, Moshe Barkat; Producer, Don Van Atta; Director, Gordon Hessler; Screenplay, James Booth; Martial Arts Choreography, Sho Kosugi; Photography, Roy Wagner; Art Director, Adrian Gorton; In color; Rated R; 123 minutes; January release. CAST: Sho Kosugi (Akira), James Booth (Limehouse), Robert Ito (Koga), Michael Constantine (Newman), Donna Kei Benz (Reiko), Kane Kosugi (Takeshi), Shane Kosugi (Tomoya), Norman Burton (Lt. Dalmain), Parley Baer (Sam Green)

Rob Lowe, Cindy Gibb
in "Youngblood" © *United Artists*

Sho Kosugi in "Pray for Death"
© *American Distribution Group*

Yvonne De Carlo in "Play Dead"
© Troma Team

Teller, Penn Jillette
in "My Chauffeur"
© Crown International

PLAY DEAD (Troma Team) Producer, Francine C. Rudine; Director, Peter Wittman; Screenplay, Lothrop W. Jordan; Photography, Robert E. Bethard; Music, Bob Farrar; Editor, Eugenie Nicoloff; Art Director, Robert A. Burns; Production Manager, Michael Phillips; Assistant Directors, Robert Elkins, Samai Brown, Susan Robinson; Stunt Coordinator, Randy Fife; Production Coordinator, Mary Church; TVC Color; Rated R; 86 minutes; January release. CAST: Yvonne DeCarlo (Hester), Stephanie Dunham (Audrey), David Cullinane (Jeff), Glenn Kezer (Otis), Ron Jackson (Richard), David Ellzey (Stephen), Jo Livingston (Pathologist), Carolyn Greenwood (Monique), Jeff McVey (Eric), Robert Hibbard (Policeman), Desmond Dhooge (Dog Trainer), John Carroll Perry (Sam), Alex Bond Winslow (Clarisse), Harry Gibbs (Funeral Attendant), and Greta

MY CHAUFFEUR (Crown International) Producer, Marilyn J. Tenser; Co-Producer, Michael Bennett; Director/Screenplay, David Beaird; Photography, Harry Mathias; Editor, Richard E. Westover; Production Manager, Steven J. Wolfe; Designer, C. J. Strawn; Assistant Directors, David M. Robertson, Scott Javine, Kelly Schroeder; Costumes, Camile Schroeder; Sound, Don Summer; Production Coordinator, Marybeth Blackburn; Choreographer, Damita Joe Freeman; Music, Paul Hertzog; Music Supervision, Matthew D. Causey; Songs by various artists; DeLuxe Color; Panavision; Rated R; 97 minutes; January release. CAST: Deborah Foreman (Casey Meadows), Sam J. Jones (Battle Witherspoon), Sean McClory (O'Brien), Howard Hesseman (McBride), E. G. Marshall (Witherspoon), Penn Jillette (Bone), Teller (Abdul), John O'Leary (Giles), Julius Harris (Johnson), Laurie Main (Jenkins), Stanley Brock (Downs), Jack Stryker (Moses), Vance Colvig (Doolittle), Ben Slack (Dupont), Elaine Wilkes (Colleen), Diana Bellamy (Blue Lady), Leland Crooke (Catfight), Robin Antin (Bimbo), Cindy Beal (Beebop), Sue Jackson (Boom Boom), Darian Mathias (Dolly), Mark Holton (Doughboy), Carlton Miller (Amy), Stan Foster (LaRue), Regina Hooks (Charmaine), John Martin (Manager), Leslee Bremer, Jeannine Bisignano, Sheila Lussier, Vickie Benton (Party Girls), Daria Martel (Georgia), David Donham (Dobbs), Daniel Hirsch (Fryer), Jim Holmes (Punk), and Nick DeMauro, Carmen Filpi, Robert Q. Lewis, Robin Nolan, Kevin G. Tracey, Rick Garia, B. J. David, Jacqueline Jacobs, Jim Cushinery, Marty Ross, Val McCallum, Bobby J. Tews

RETURN (A Silver Prod.) Executive Producers, Andrew Silver, Yong-Hee Silver; Producer, Philip Spinelli; Director/Screenplay, Andrew Silver; Based on Donald Harrington's Novel *Some Other Place, The Right Place;* Photography, Janos Zsombolyai; Sets, Charles Tomlinson; Editor, Gabrielle Gilbert; Music, Ragnar Grippe, Michael Shrieve; Color; Rated R; 82 minutes; January release. CAST: Karlene Crockett (Diana Stoving), John Walcutt (Day Whittaker), Lisa Richards (Ann Stoving), Frederic Forrest (Brian Stoving), Anne Lloyd Francis (Eileen Sedgely), Lenore Zann (Susan), Thomas Rolopp (Lucky), Harry Murphy (MDC Officer), Lee Stetson (Daniel Montross), Ariel Aberg-Riger (Diana at 3)

SEVEN MINUTES IN HEAVEN (Warner Bros) Producer, Fred Roos; Director, Linda Feferman; Screenplay, Jane Bernstein, Linda Feferman; Photography, Steven Fierberg; Editor, Marc Laub; Design, Vaughan Edwards; Art Director, Thomas A. Walsh; Set Decoration, Deborah Schutt; Costumes, Dianne Finn Chapman; Sound, Mike Rowland; Associate Producer, Mark Silverman; Assistant Director, Kelly Van Horn; Casting, Aleta Wood-Chappelle; An FR Production from Zoetrope; In Technicolor; PG13; 90 minutes; January release. CAST: Jennifer Connelly (Natalie), Maddie Corman (Polly), Byron Thames (Jeff), Alan Boyce (Casey), Polly Draper (Aileen), Marshall Bell (Gerry), Michael Zaslow (Bob), Denny Dillon (Aunt Gail), Margo Skinner (Lenore), Matthew Lewis (Stew), Tim Waldrip (Richie), Billy Wirth (Zoo), Paul Martel (Tim), Terry Kinney (Bill)

UPHILL ALL THE WAY (New World) Producers, Burt Smidt, David L. Ford; Executive Producers, Renee Valente, Mel Tillis, Roy Clark; Director/Screenplay, Frank Q. Dobbs; Photography, Roland (Ozzie) Smith; Editor, Chuck Weiss; Music, Dennis M. Pratt; Sound, Wayne Bell; Designer, Hal Matheny; Set Decorator, Pat O'Neal; Assistant Director, Tad Devlin; Production Manager, Walt Gilmore; Stunts, Dave Cass; Casting, Rachelle Farberman; Associate Producer, Bob Younts; A Melroy production in association with Guardian Films; DeLuxe Color; Rated PG; 86 minutes; January release. CAST: Roy Clark (Ben), Mel Tillis (Booger Skaggs), Burl Ives (Sheriff), Glen Campbell (Capt. Hazleton), Trish Van Devere (Widow Quinn), Richard Paul (Dillman), Burt Reynolds (Poker player), Elaine Joyce (Jesse), Jacque Lynn Colton (Lucinda), and Frank Gorshin, Sheb Wooley, Burton Gilliam, Gailard Sartain, Rockne Tarkington, Christopher Weeks, Pedro Gonzalez-Gonzalez

Shane and Kane Kosugi
in "Pray for Death"
© American Distribution Group

Deborah Foreman, Sam J. Jones
in "My Chauffeur"
© Crown International

117

Michael Nouri, Anne Twomey
in "The Imagemaker"© *Castle Hill*

Jessica Harper in "The Imagemaker"
© *Castle Hill*

THE IMAGEMAKER (Castle Hill) Producers, Marilyn Weiner, Hal Weiner; Executive Producer, Melvyn J. Estrin; Director, Hal Weiner; Screenplay, Dick Goldberg, Hal Weiner; Music, Fred Karns; Color; Rated R; 93 minutes; January release. CAST: Michael Nouri (Roger Blackwell), Jerry Orbach (Byron Caine), Anne Twomey (Molly Grainger), Jessica Harper (Cynthia), Farley Granger (The Ambassador)

ELIMINATORS (Empire Pictures) Producer, Charles Band; Director, Peter Manoogian; Screenplay, Paul De Meo, Danny Bilson; Photography, Mac Ahlberg; Editor, Andy Horvitch; Music, Bob Summers; Designer, Phillip Foreman; Art Director, Gumersindo Andres Lopez; Line Producer, Alicia Alon; Special Effects, Juan Ramon Molina; Costumes, Jill Ohanneson; Sound, Antonio Bloch Rodriquez; Associate Producer, Debra Dion; Assistant Director, Betsy Magruder; Casting, Anthony Barnac; Fotofilm color; Rated PG; 96 minutes; January release. CAST: Andrew Prine (Harry Fontana), Denise Crosby (Nora Hunter), Patrick Reynolds (Mandroid), Conan Lee (Kuji), Roy Dotrice (Abbott Reeves), Peter Schrum (Ray), Peggy Mannix (Bayou Betty), Fausto Bara (Luis), Tad Horino (Takada), Luis Lorenzo (Maurice)

HOWLING II . . . YOUR SISTER IS A WEREWOLF (Thorn EMI) Producer, Steven Lane; Executive Producer, Grahame Jennings; Director, Philippe Mora; Screenplay, Robert Sarno, Gary Brandner; From the book by Gary Brandner; Photography, G. Stephenson; Music, Steve Parsons; Designer, Karel Vacek; Associate Producer, Robert Pringle; Special Effects Makeup, Jack Bricker; A Hemdale Presentation of a Granite Prods. production; Color; Rated R; 90 minutes; January release. CAST: Christopher Lee (Stefan Crosscoe), Annie McEnroe (Jenny Templeton), Reb Brown (Ben White), Sybil Danning (Stirba), Marsha A. Hunt (Mariana), Judd Omen (Vlad), Ferdinand Mayne (Erle), Babel (Punk Group)

ORNETTE: MADE IN AMERICA (Caravan of Dreams Productions) Producer, Kathelin Hoffman; Director/Editor, Shirley Clarke; Photography, Ed Lachman; Music, Ornette Coleman; Documentary; Not rated; 85 minutes; February release. CAST: Ornette Coleman, Demon Marshall, Eugene Tatum (Young Ornette Coleman) (no other credits submitted)

TERRORVISION (Empire Pictures) Producer, Albert Band; Executive Producer, Charles Band; Director/Screenplay, Ted Nicolaou; Photography, Romano Albani; Editor, Tom Meshelski; Music, Richard Band; Designer, Giovanni Natalucci; Assistant Director, Mauro Sacrapanti; Associate Producer, Debra Dion; Special Effects Makeup, John Buechler, Mechanical and Makeup Imageries Inc; Casting, Anthony Bay Barnao; An Altar Prods. production; Technicolor; Rated R; 83 minutes; February release. CAST: Diane Franklin (Suzy), Gerrit Graham (Stanley), Mary Woronov (Raquel), Chad Allen (Sherman), Jonathan Gries (O.D.), Jennifer Richards (Medusa), Alejandro Rey (Spiro), Bert Remsen (Gramps), Randi Brooks (Cherry), and Ian Patrick Williams, Sonny Carl Davis.

THE GOODBYE PEOPLE (Castle Hill) Producer, David V. Picker; Director/Screenplay, Herb Gardner; Editor, Rick Shaine; Color; Rated PG; 105 minutes; January release. CAST: Judd Hirsch (Arthur Korman), Martin Balsam (Max Silverman), Pamela Reed (Nancie Scot), Ron Silver (Eddie Bergson), Michael Tucker (Michael Silverman), Gene Saks (Marcus Soloway), Sammy Smith (George Mooney) (no other credits available)

TROLL (Marvin Films) Producer, Albert Band; Director, John Buechler; Screenplay, Ed Naha; Photography, Romano Albani; Music, Richard Band; Color; Rated PG-13; 86 minutes; January release. CAST: June Lockhart (Eunice St. Clair), Jenny Beck (Wendy Potter), Anne Lockhart (Young Eunice St. Clair), Shelley Hack (Mrs. Potter), Michael Moriarty (Mr. Potter), Sonny Bono (Peter Dickenson), Noah Hathaway (Harry Potter Jr.) (no other credits submitted)

QUICKSILVER (Columbia) Producers, Michael Rachmil, Daniel Melnick; Director/Screenplay, Tom Donnelly; Photography, Thomas Del Ruth; Designer, Charels Rosen; Editor, Tom Rolf; Associate Producer, Christopher Meledandri; Costumes, Betsy Cox; Casting, Pennie du Pont; Music, Tony Banks; Music Supervision, Becky Mancuso; Vocals, Roger Daltrey; Production Manager, Richard Stenta; Assistant Directors, Duncan Henderson, Dennis MaGuire, Victoria Rhodes; Art Director, James Shanahan; Set Decorator, Marvin March; Sound, John V. Speak; Production Coordinator, Delia Circelli; Choreographer, Grover Dale; Special Effects, Dennis Dion; Stunts, Greg Walker; Songs, Giorgio Moroder, Dean Pitchford, John Parr, Geoff Lyth, and

Denise Crosby, Andrew Prine, Conan Lee,
Patrick Reynolds in "Eliminators"
© *Empire Pictures*

Jami Gertz, Kevin Bacon
in "Quicksilver" © *Columbia*

**Robert Beltran (C), Tony Plana (R)
in "Latino" © *Cinecom International***

**John Mengatti, Leon Isaac Kennedy, Nicholas
Campbell in "Knights of the City"
© *New World***

other artists; Soundtrack on Atlantic Records; Dolby Stereo; From Columbia-Delphi IV Productions; Metrocolor; Panavision; Rated PG; 106 minutes; February release. CAST: Kevin Bacon (Jack Casey), Jami Gertz (Terri), Paul Rodriguez (Hector), Rudy Ramos (Gypsy), Andrew Smith (Gabe), Gerald S. O'Loughlin (Mr. Casey), Larry Fishburne (Voodoo), Louis Anderson (Tiny), Charles McCaughan (Airborne), David Harris (Apache), Whitney Kershaw (Rand), Joshua Shelley (Shorty), Georgann Johnson (Mrs. Casey), and Nelson Vails, Lou Dinos, Michael Kaye, Joel Weiss, Leila Kane, Daniel Leegant, John Walter Davis, Gregory Wagrowski, Frank D'Annibale, Jimmy Romano, Patricia Allison, Abel Fernandez, Patricia West-Del Ruth, Joe Leahy, Michael Fox, Richard Warlock, Jacque Lynn Colton, Joseph Hieu, Michael Paul Chan, Joseph Peck, George Moffatt, Robert Cotney, Valerie McIntosh, Shirley Walker, Launa Morosan, Vanessa Newman, Michael O'Rourke, Irwin Schier, Martin Aparijo, Woody Itson, Franz Krotochvil

LATINO (CinecomInternational) Producer, Benjamin Berg; Direction/Story/Screenplay, Haskell Wexler; Photography, Tom Sigel; Editor, Robert Dalva; Music, Diane Louie; Production Manager, Julio Alejandro Sosa; Assistant Directors, Emilio Rodriguez, Ana Maria Garcia; Art Director, Fernando Castro; Set Decorator, Marianela Salgado; Sound, Pamela Yates; In color; A Lucasfilm presentation; 105 minutes; February release. CAST: Annette Cardona (Marlena), Robert Beltran (Eddie Guerrero), Tony Plana (Ruben), Julio Medina (Edgar), Gavin McFadden (Metcalf), Luis Torrentes (Luis), Juan Carlos Ortiz (Juan Carlos), Marta Tenorio (Rosa-Madre), Roberto Munguia (Guillermo), Mayra Juarro (Ana Maria), Maria Ines Tenerio (Josefina), Roberto Lopez (Tomas), Ricardo Lopez (Attila), Bob Young (Fred), Graciela Amaya (Dona Flora), Walter Marin (Gilberto)

HUEY LONG (Corinth Films) Producers, Ken Burns, Richard Kilberg; Director, Ken Burns; Script, Geoffrey C. Ward; Photography, Ken Burns, Buddy Squires; Editor, Amy Stechler Burns; Sound, Greg Moring; Music, John Colby, Randy Newman; Consultants, William Leuchtenburg, Alan Brinkley, Arthur Schlesinger, Jr., William Snyder, Jerome Liebling; Narrator, David McCullough; A RKB/Florentine Films Production; Documentary; Black & white & color; Not Rated; 88 minutes; February release

KNIGHTS OF THE CITY (New World) Producers, Leon Isaac Kennedy, John C. Strong III; Executive Producers, Michael Franzese, Robert E. Schultz; Director, Dominic Orlando; Screenplay, Leon Isaac Kennedy; Story, Leon Isaac Kennedy, David Wilder; Photography, Rolf Kesterman; Editors, John O'Connor, Nicholas Smith, Paul LaMori; Choreographers, Jeff Kutash, Dallace Winkler; Music, Misha Segal; Production Manager/Assistant Director, Allan Harman; Assistant Director, Ginny Moro; Production Coordinators, Roslyn Meyer, Kim Wolf-Tau; Art Director, Barbara Shelton; Set, Regina McLarney; Costumes, Celia Bryant, Beverly Safier; Sound, Joe Foglia; Stunts, Steve Boyun, Jeff Moldovan; Songs by various artists; Dolby Stereo; Rated R; 87 minutes; February release. CAST: Leon Isaac Kennedy (Troy), Nicholas Campbell (Joey), John Mengatti (Mookie), Stoney Jackson (Eddie), Dino Henderson (Dino), Curtis Lema (Ramrod), Marc Lemberger (Mr. Freeze), Jeff Moldovan (Carlos), Sonny Anthony (Sonny), Jay Armor (Red Cap), Eddie Guy (Eddie), Peter Nicholas (Hairboy), Stan Ward (Buddha), James Reese (Alien), John Franzese (Pharoah), Antone Corona (Eyepatch), Floyd Levine (McGruder), Michael Ansara (Mr. Delamo), Dario Carnevale (Dario), Wendy Barry (Jasmine), Olga Ruiz (Joey's Girl), Katie Lauren (Baby Jane), Smokey Robinson (Himself), Jessie Diaz (Jessie), Gustavo Rodriguez (T. K.), Kurtis Blow (Himself), Jerry Silverman (Jailer), Janine Turner (Brooke), Jeff Kutash (Flash), Cammy Garcia (Beverly), Michelle Garcia (Juliette), K. C. (Himself), Denny Terrio (Himself), and Leslie Wanger, Darren "Human Beat Box" Robinson, Damon Wimbley, Mark Morales, Lou Ann Carrou, Michael Safier, Dallace Winkler, Carol Gun, Cindy Colbert, Angie Sproul, Mr. X, Jeff Marton, Sheli Marton, John Emeney II, Deborah Golden, James Cisco, Heather Lazlo, Joanna Tea, Dedric Fulton, Joe Foglia, Nancy Raffa, Christina Wilfong, Dean Dean, Bob Johnson, Jim Snowden

THE ADVENTURES OF THE AMERICAN RABBIT (Atlantic/ Clubhouse Pictures) Producers, Masaharu Etoh, Masahisa Saeki, John G. Marshall; Co-Producer, Robert Kaplan; Directors, Fred Wolf, Nobutaka Nishizawa; Screenplay, Norm Lenzer; Based on characters by Stewart Moskowitz; Animation, TOEI Doga Co, Ltd.; Executive Producers, Thomas Coleman, Michael Rosenblatt; Music and Lyrics; written and performed by Mark Volman, Howard Kaylan, John Hoier; Color; Rated G; 85 minutes

**Annette Cardona, Robert Beltran
in "Latino" © *Cinecom International***

**Huey Long
© *Corinth Films***

Pierce Brosnan, Anna-Marie Montecelli
in "Nomads" © *Atlantic*

KING OF THE STREETS (Shapiro Entertainment) Producers, Yakov Ventsvi, Edward Hunt; Director, Edward Hunt; Screenplay, Edward Hunt, Ruben Gordon, Steven Shoenberg, Barry Pearson; Executive Producer, Edward Coe; Co-Producers, Shaul Yaron, Noam and Rony Schwartz, Barry Pearson; Eastman Color; Rated R; 100 minutes; February release. CAST: Brett Clark, Pamela Saunders, Reggie De-Morton, Nelson Anderson, Norman Budd, Elodie McKee, Bill Woods, Jr. No further credits supplied.

NOMADS (Atlantic) Executive Producer, Jerry Gershwin; Producers, George Pappas, Cassian Elwes; Associate Producer, Stanley Mark; Direction/Screenplay, John McTiernan; Music, Bill Conti; Production Manager, Susan Baden-Powell; Production Coordinator, Mary McLaglen; Designer, Marcia Hinds; Art Director, Bo Johnson; Set Decorator, Mimi Kolombatovic; Photography, Stephen Ramsey; Costumes, Rhaz Zeisler; Stunt Coordinator, B. J. Davis; Special Effects, Paul Staples; In color; Rated R; 95 minutes; March release. CAST: Pierce Brosnan (Pommier), Lesley-Anne Down (Flax), Anna-Maria Montecelli (Niki), Adam Ant (Number One), Hector Mercado (Ponytail), Josie Cotton (Silver Ring), Mary Woronov (Dirty Blond), Frank Doubleday (Razor), Frances Bay (Bertril), Tim Wallace (Intern), Reed Morgan (Cop), Freddie Duke, Josee Beaudry, Anita Jesse (Nurses), Dana Chelette (Orderly), Alan Autry (Olds), Jeannie Elias (Cassie), Nina Foch (Real Estate Agent), J. J. Saunders (Cort), Kario Salem (Schacter), Helen Vick (Young Nurse), Gayle Vance (Older Nurse), Athan Karras (Apartment Manager), Michael Gregory (Cop), John Vidor (Kid), Elizabeth Russell (Cathy)

WHAT HAPPENED TO KEROUAC? (New Yorker) Producer, Richard Lerner; Direction, Richard Lerner, Lewis MacAdams; Interviewer, Lew MacAdams; Co-producers, Lewis MacAdams, Nathaniel Dorsky, Malcolm Hart; Associate Producer, Eve Levy; Editors, Nathaniel Dorsky, Robert Estrin; Photography, Richard Lerner, Nathaniel Dorsky; Music, Thelonius Monk; 96 minutes; Not rated; March release. CAST: Steve Allen, William Burroughs, Carolyn Cassady, Neal Cassady, Ann Charters, Gregory Corso, Robert Creeley, Diana DiPrima, Lawrence Ferlinghetti, Allen Ginsberg, John Clellon Holmes, Herbert Huncke, Joyce Johnson, Jan Kerouac, Fran Landesman, Michael McClure, Father "Spike" Morissette, Edie Kerouac Parker, Ed Sanders, Gary Snyder, Edward White

CHOPPING MALL aka *Killbots* **(Concorde)** Producer, Julie Corman; Director, Jim Wynorski; Screenplay, Jim Wynorski, Steve Mitchell; Associate Producers, Charles Skouras III, Ginny Nugent; Music, Chuck Cirino; Editor, Leslie Rosenthal; Photography, Tom Richmond; Killbots created by Robert Short; Production Manager, Charles Skouras III; Assistant Directors, Kristine Peterson, Terence Edwards; Art Director, Carol Clements; Production Coordinator, Lisa C. Cook; Wardrobe, Katie Sparks; Special Effects Makeup, Anthony Showe; Special Effects, Roger George; Sound, Walt Martin; Color; Rated R; 76 minutes; March release. CAST: Kelli Maroney (Allison Parks), Tony O'Dell (Ferdy Meisel), John Terlesky (Mike Brennan), Russell Todd (Rick Stanton), Karrie Emerson (Linda Stanton), Barbara Crampton (Suzie Lynn), Nick Segal (Greg Williams), Suzee Slater (Leslee Todd), Mary Woronov (Mrs. Bland), Paul Bartel (Mr. Bland), Dick Miller (Walter Paisley), Gerrit Graham (Technician Nessler), Mel Welles (Cook), Angela Aames (Miss Vanders), Paul Coufos (Dr. Simon), Arthur Roberts (Mr. Todd), Ace Mask, Will Gill, Jr., Lenny Juliano, Lawrence Guy, Morgan Douglas, Toni Naples, Robert Greenberg, Maurie Gallagher

ODD JOBS (Tri-Star) Producer, Keith Fox Rubinstein; Director, Mark Story; Screenplay, Robert Conte, Peter Martin Wortmann; Photography, Arthur Albert, Peter Lyons Collister; Editor, Dennis M. Hill; Music, Robert Folk; Associate Producer, Patricia Whitcher; Designer, Robert R. Benton; Assistant Directors, Brian Frankish, Anthony Brand, Dustin Bernard, Don Wilkerson; Costumes, Betty Pecha; Production Coordinator, Stephanie Lynn Swor; Special Effects, R. Beetz Co.; Stunt Coordinator, Burt McDancer; Songs performed by various artists; In Metrocolor; PG13; 88 minutes; March release. CAST: Paul Reiser (Max), Robert Townsend (Dwight), Scott McGinnis (Woody), Rick Overton (Roy), Paul Provenza (Byron), Leo Burmester (Wylie), Thomas Quinn (Frankie), Savannah Smith Boucher (Loretta/Lynette), Richard Dean Anderson (Spud), Richard Foronjy (Manny), Ken Olfson (Mayor), Jake Steinfeld (Nick), Eleanor Mondale (Mandy), Charlie Dell (Earl), Starletta DuPois (Dwight's Mom), Don Imus (Monty Leader), Wayne Grace (Roy's Father), Julianne Phillips (Sally), Leon Askin (Don), Andra Akers (Mrs. Finelli), Patti Clifton (Mrs. Brady), Martha Jane Urann (Dalene), Tom Dugan (Lester), Jim Holmes (Jeff), and Chuck Pfeifer, Chris Hubbell, Jeff Maxwell, Fred Pierce, Diana Bellamy, Janet Clark, Zero Hubbard, Dermott Downs, John Furlong, Eve Smith, Harvey Levine, Vance Colvig, Susan Krebs, Darlene Chehardy, Arleen Sorkin, Donald J. Westerdale, Jill Goodacre, Andre Veluzet, Michael Ragsdale, Keith Joe Dick, Diane Willson Dick, Debbie Tilton, Cindy Bernstein, Wesley A. Pfenning, Arlin Miller, Bob Banas

APRIL FOOL'S DAY (Paramount) Producer, Frank Mancuso, Jr.; Director, Fred Walton; Screenplay, Danilo Bach; Photography, Charles Minsky; Art Director, Stewart Campbell; Editor, Bruce Green; Music, Charles Bernstein; Production Manager, Randolph F. Cheveldave; Assistant Directors, Lee Knippelberg, David Webb, Geoff Wilkinson, Reid Dunlop; Special Effects, Martin Becker; Sound, David Lewis Yewdall, Peter Shewchuk; Production Coordinator, Victoria Barney; Stunts, John Wardlow, Louis Bollo, Jim Dunn; Orchestration, Charles Bernstein, Julie Giroux-West; Sound Effects, F. Hudson Miller; Special Effects/Make-Up Effects, Reel EFX, Martin Becker, Christopher Swift, Jim Gill, Bettie Kauffman; Songs, Charles Bernstein, Randy Newman; Dolby Stereo; Metrocolor; Panavision; Rated R; 90 minutes; March release. CAST: Jay Baker (Harvey), Pat Barlow (Clara), Lloyd Berry (Ferryman), Deborah Foreman (Muffy/Buffy), Deborah Goodrich (Nikki), Tom Heaton (Constable Potter/Uncle Frank), Mike Nomad (Buck), Ken Olandt (Rob), Griffin O'Neal (Skip), Leah King Pinsent (Nan), Clayton Rohner (Chaz), Amy Steel (Kit), Thomas F. Wilson (Arch)

Rick Overton, Paul Reiser, Scott McGinnis
in "Odd Jobs" © *Tri-Star*

Griffin O'Neal, Thomas F. Wilson (C)
in "April Fool's Day" © *Paramount/Jack Roward*

LUCAS (20th Century Fox) Producer, David Nicksay; Director/screenplay, David Seltzer; Photography, Reynaldo Villalobos; Art Director, James Murakami; Editor, Priscilla Nedd; Associate Producer, Kristi Zea; Casting, Mary Gail Artz; Music, Dave Grusin; Production Manager, Phil Wylly; Assistant Directors, David Sosna, Rob Corn, Maggie Parker; Costumes, Molly Maginnis; Additional Editing, Scott Conrad; Set Decorator, Linda Sutton; Sound, Ray Cymoszinski; Production Coordinator, Else Rohden; DeLuxe Color; Panavision; Dolby DeLuxe Stereo; Rated Pg-13; 100 minutes; March release. CAST: Corey Haim (Lucas), Kerri Green (Maggie), Charlie Sheen (Cappie), Courtney Thorne-Smith (Alise), Winona Ryder (Rina), Thomas E. Hodges (Bruno), Ciro Poppiti (Ben), Guy Boyd (Coach), Jeremy Piven (Spike), Kevin Gerard Wixted (Tonto), Emily Seltzer (Marie), Erika Leigh (Mary Ellen), Anne Ryan (Angie), Jason Robert Alderman (Tony), Tom Mackie (Billy), Garrett M. Brown (Mr. Kaiser), and Ronald Harrigan, Judy Leavitt-Wells, Christina Baglivi, Shirley Maddock, Rosanne E. Krevitt, Gregg Potter, Polly Augusta Noonan, James Krag, R. G. Clayton, Patti Wilkus, Martha Murphy, Lucy Butler, Gary Cole, Jerald Edward Cundiff, Jr.

GHOST WARRIOR aka SWORDKILL (Empire Pictures) Producer, Charles Band; Director, J. Larry Carroll; Executive Producers, Albert Band, Arthur H. Maslansky, Efrem Harkham, Uri Harkham; Associate Producer, Gordon W. Gregory; Screenplay, Tim Curren; Photography, Mac Ahlberg; Editor, Brad Arensman; Music, Richard Band; Designers, Pamela B. Warner, Robert Howland; CFI Color; Rated PG-13; 80 minutes; March release. CAST: Hiroshi Fujioka (Yoshimitsa), John Calvin (Dr. Richards), Janet Julian (Chris), Charles Lampkin (Willie), Frank Schuller (Det. Berger), Bill Morey (Dr. Anderson), Andy Wood (Dr. Denza), Robert Kino (Prof. Tagachi), Joan Foley (Ellie), Peter Liapis (Johnny), Meiko Kobayashi (Chidori)

DEATH OF AN ANGEL (20th Century Fox) Producer, Peter Burrell; Executive Producers, Dimitri Villard, Robby Wald, Charles J. Weber; Director/Screenplay, Petru Popescu; Photography, Fred Murphy; Editor, Christopher Lebonzon; Music, Peter Myers; Designer, Linda Pearl; Art Direction, Dena Roth; Costumes, Jack Bushler; Sound, Susumu Tokonow; Associate Producer, Patrick Markey; Assistant Director, Jeffrey Sudzin; Casting, Paul Bangston, David Cohn; An Angeles Entertainment Group and RDR Prods. presentation of an Everness production in association with The Sundance Institute for Film and Television; DeLuxe Color; Rated PG; 92 minutes; March release. CAST: Bonnie Bedelia (Grace), Nick Mancuso (Father Angel), Pamela Ludwig (Vera), Alex Colon (Robles), and Abel Franco

16 DAYS OF GLORY (Paramount) Produced, Directed and Written by Bud Greenspan; Executive Producer/Second Unit Director, Nancy Beffa; Senior Producer, Milton Okun; Editor, Andrew Squicciqrini; Photography, Robert E. Collins, Gil Hubbs, Michael D. Margulies, Robert Primes; Music Score, Lee Holdridge; Soloist, Placido Domingo; Narrator, David Perry; Rated G; In color; 145 minutes; March release. A documentary on the 1984 Los Angeles Olympics.

BAD GUYS (InterPictures) Producers, John D. Backe, Myron A. Hyman; Director, Joel Silberg; Screenplay, Brady W. Setwater, Joe Gillis; Photography, Hanania Baer; Associate Producer, Shirley J. Eaton; Music, William Goldstein; Music Supervisor, Russ Regan; Soundtrack on Casablanca Records; Color; Dolby Stereo; Rated PG; 86 minutes; March release. CAST: Adam Baldwin, Mike Jolly, Ruth Buzzi, Sgt. Slaughter. (No other credits supplied)

GOBOTS:BATTLE OF THE ROCKLORDS (Clubhouse Pictures/Atlantic) Executive Producers, William Hanna, Joseph Barbera; Producer, Kay Wright; Screenplay, Jeff Segal; Director, Ray Patterson;

John Terlesky, Suzee Slater
in "Chopping Mall" © *Concorde*

Story Consultant, Kelly Ward; Directors, Don Lusk, Alan Zaslove; Assistant Directors, Bob Goe, Don Patterson; Co-Executive Producer, Joe Taritero; Production Executives, Jayne Berbera, Jean MacCurdy; Animation Casting, Andrea Romano; Recording Director, Gordon Hunt; Musical Director, Hoyt Curtin; Music Coordinator, Joanne Miller; Design, Davis Doi; Produced in association with Cuckoos Nest Studio, Wang Film Productions Co., Ltd; Associate Producer, Lynn Hoag; Sound, Alvy Dorman, Phil Flad; Show Editor, Gil Iverson; Animated; Color; Rated G; 75 minutes; March release. VOICE CAST: Margot Kidder (Solitaire), Roddy McDowall (Nuggit), Michael Nouri (Boulder), Telly Savalas (Magmar), Arthur Bughardt (Turbo), Ike Eisenmann (Nick), Bernard Erhard (Cy-Kill), Marilyn Lightstone (Crasher), Morgan Paul (Matt), Lou Richards (Leader-1), Leslie Speights (A. J.), Frank Welker (Scooter), and Michael Bell, Foster Brooks, Arthur Burghardy, Ken Campbell, Philip Lewis Clarke, Peter Cullen, Dick Gautier, Darryl Hickman, B. J. Ward, Kelly Ward, Kirby Ward

GUNG HO (Paramount) Producers, Tony Ganz, Deborah Blum; Director/Executive Producer, Ron Howard; Screenplay, Lowell Ganz, Babaloo Mandel; Story, Edwin Blum, Lowell Ganz, Babaloo Mandel; Photography, Don Peterman; Designer, James Schoppe; Editor, Daniel Hanley, Michael Hill; Music, Thomas Newman; Associate Producer, Jan R. Lloyd; Production Manager, Neila Machlis; Assistant Directors, Jan R. Lloyd, Aldric La'Auli Porter, Janet G. Knutsen; Art Director, Jack G. Taylor, Jr.; Sound, Anthony John Ciccolini III, Richard S. Church; Costumes, Daniel J. Lester; Special Effects, Stan Parks; Musical Performances, Stevie Ray Vaughan; Songs by various artists; Technicolor; Panavision; Dolby Stereo; Rated PG-13; 120 minutes; March release. CAST: Michael Keaton (Hunt Stevenson), George Watanabe (Kazihiro), George Wendt (Buster), Mimi Rogers (Audrey), John Turturro (Willie), Soh Yamamura (Mr. Sakamoto), Sab Shimono (Saito), Rick Overton (Googie), Clint Howard (Paul), Jihmi Kennedy (Junior), Michelle Johnson (Heather), Rodney Kageyama (Ito), Rance Howard (Mayor Zwart), Patti Yasutake (Umeki), Jerry Tondo (Kazuo), Dennis Sakamoto (Matsumura), Stanford Egi (Kenji), Martin Ferrero (Crandall), James Ritz (Tony), Dock P. Ellis, Jr. (Luke), Richard M. McNally (Milt), Jean Speegle, Thomas Ikeda, Noboru Kataoka, Mariye Inouye, Juhachiro Takada, Linda Carola, Jun Lyle Kamesaki, Tamie Saiki, Charlie Samaha, Nann Mogg, Paul C. Nolan, R. Scott Peck, Josef Pilato, William S. Bartman, Tommy LaFitte, James Cash, Kim Chan, Bill Balzell, Tak Kubota, Frank Seals, Maria Barney

Mike Jolly (C), Adam Baldwin (R)
in "Bad Guys" © *InterPictures*

George Wendt, Michael Keaton, Jerry Tondo,
Sab Shimono in "Gung Ho" © *Paramount/Adger W. Cowans*

Leon Isaac Kennedy, Frank Gorshin
in "Hollywood Vice Squad" © *Cinema Group*

Lori Loughlin, Bill Allen
in "Rad" © *Tri-Star*

WHATEVER IT TAKES (Aquarius Films) Producer/Director/ Editor, Bob Demchuk; Screenplay, Chris Weatherhead, Bob Demchuk; Photography, John Drake; Music, Garry Sherman; Color; Not Rated; 93 minutes; March release. CAST: Tom Mason (Jeff Perchick), Martin Balsam (Hap Perchicksky), Chris Weatherhead (Lee Bickford), James Rebhorn (Michael Manion), Maura Shea (Eren Haberfield), Bill Bogert (Timmy Shaughnessy), Rosetta LeNoire (Millie), Joey Ginza (Curley), Fred Morsell (Mr. Bunyon), Edward Binns (Mr. Kingsley)

HOLLYWOOD VICE SQUAD (Cinema Group) Producers, Arnold Orgolini, Sandy Howard; Director, Penelope Spheeris; Associate Producers, Jeff Gary, David Witz; Screenplay, James J. Docherty; Photography, John Hendricks; Production Manager, Scott White; Art Direction, Michael Corenblith; Production Executive, Venetia Stevenson; Editor, John Bowey; Sound, Jan Brodin; Set, Donna Stamps; Costumes, Jill Ohanneson; Assistant Director, Elliot Rosenblatt; Color; Rated R; 100 minutes; March release. CAST: Ronny Cox (Capt. Mike Jensen), Carrie Fisher (Officer Betty Melton), Ben Frank (Daley), Frank Gorshin (Jim Walsh), H. B. Haggerty (Det. Romero), Julius Harris (Harris), Marven Kaplan (Man with the doll), Leon Isaac Kennedy (Det. Jerry Hawkins), Evan Kim (Det. Ray Chang), Joey Travolta (Stevnes), Trish Van Devere (Pauline Stanton), Cec Verrel (Det. Judy O'Malley)

THE NAKED CAGE (Cannon Group) Producer, Chris D. Nebe; Director/Screenplay, Paul Nicholas; Executive Producers, Menahem Golan, Yoram Globus; Production Executive, Jeffrey Silver; Photography, Hal Trussell; Production Manager, Daniel Schneider; Assistant Directors, Bradley Gross, Karen T. Gaviola; Sound, Morteza Rezvani; Art Director, Alex Hajdu; Wardrobe, Shelly Komarov; Special Effects, A&A Special Effects; Songs by various artists; Color; Rated R; 97 minutes; March release. CAST: Shari Shattuck (Michelle), Angel Tompkins (Diane), Lucinda Crosby (Rhonda), Christina Whitaker (Rita), Faith Minton (Sheila), Stacey Shaffer (Amy), Nick Benedict (Smiley), John Terlesky (Willy), Lisa London (Abbey), Aude Charles (Brenda), Angela Gibbs (Vonna), Leslie Huntly (Peaches), Carole Ita White (Trouble), Seth Kaufman (Randy), Larry Gelman (Doc), Susie London (Martha), Valerie McIntosh (Ruby), Flo Gerrish (Mother), James Ingersoll (Father), William Bassett (Jordan), Nora Niesen (Bigfoot), Jennifer Anne Thomas (Mock), Chris Anders (Miller), Al Jones, Sheila Stephenson, Bob Saurman, Rick Avery, Christopher Doyle, Gretchen Davis, Beryl Jones, Michael Kerr

RAD (TriStar) Producer, Robert L. Levy; Director, Hal Needham; Screenplay, Sam Bernard, Geoffrey Edwards; Executive Producer, Jack Schwartzman; Co-Producer, Sam Bernard; Music, James Di Pasquale; Photography, Richard Leiterman; Editor, Carl Kress; Art Director, Shirley Inget; Associate Producer, Mary Eilts; Assistant Directors, Gordon Robinson, Val Stefoff; Costumes, Jerry Allen; Sound, Frank H. Griffiths, Robert Glass; Choreographer, Sidney Kaleff; Songs by various artists; Soundtrack on MCA/Curb Records; Technicolor, Panavision; Dolby Stereo; Rated PG; 93 minutes; March release. CAST: Bill Allen (Cru), Lori Loughlin (Christian), Talia Shire (Mrs. Jones), Ray Walston (Burton Timmer), Alfie Wise (Eliott Dole), Jack Weston (Duke Best), Bart Conner (Bart Taylor), Marta Kober (Becky), Jamie Clarke (Luke), Laura Jacoby (Wesley Jones), H. B. Haggerty (Sgt. Smith), Chad Hayes (Rex Reynolds), Kellie McQuiggin (Foxy), Beverly Hendry (Tiger), Shawna Burnett (Amy), Graeme Davies (Harold), Logan T. Wotton (Miles), Jeff Kress (Rick), Gordon Signer (Mayor Coop Jenkins), Nancy MacDonald (Mrs. Grey), Rick McNair (Bob the Cook), Pat Pearson (Mr. Pratt), Maureen Thomas, Bill Berry, Georgie Collins, Darlene Bradley, Ashley Bristowe, G. A. Dahlseide, Norman Edwards, Jack Goth, Pat Kirst, Laird Mackintosh, Roberta Mauer-Phillips, Danny McDonogh, Tara McHugh, Barry Onody, Rod Padmos, Mary Siegel, Benita Von Sass, Gerry Whelpton, Bev Wotton, Ken Squier

SCREEN TEST (CinTelFilms) Producers/Screenplay, Sam Auster, Laura Auster; Director, Sam Auster; Photography, Jeff Fur; Editor, Carol Eastman; Music, Don Harrow; Executive Producers, Dino Delicata, Benjamin Lecompte III, Frank Madda; Color; Rated R; 88 minutes; March release. CAST: Michael Allan Bloom (Terry), Monique Gabrielle (Roxanne), David Simpatico (Stevie), Paul Leuken (Dan), William Dick (Dr. DeSade), Robert Bundy (Clayton), Cynthia Kahn, Mari Laskarin, Katharine Sullivan, Michelle Bauer

3:15 THE MOMENT OF TRUTH (Dakota Entertainment Corporation) Producers, Dennis Brody, Robert Kenner; Director, Larry Gross; Screenplay, Sam Bernard, Michael Jacobs; Photography, Misha Suslov; Executive Producers, Charles C. Thieriot, Sandy Climan, Jean and Andrew Bullians; Editor, Steven Kemper; Music, Gary Chang; a Wescom Production in association with Ronax; Color; Rated R; 92 minutes; March release. CAST: Adam Baldwin (Jeff Hanna), Deborah Foreman (Sherry Havilland), Rene Auberjonois (Horner), Ed Lauter (Moran). (No other credits supplied)

Nick Benedict, Angel Tompkins
in "The Naked Cage" © *Cannon*

Adam Baldwin, Deborah Foreman
in "3:15 Moment of Truth"
© *Dakota*

CROSSROADS (Columbia) Producer, Mark Carliner; Director, Walter Hill; Screenplay, John Fusco; Photography, John Bailey; Editor, Freeman Davies; Music, Ry Cooder; Color; Rated R; 98 minutes; March release. CAST: Ralph Macchio (Eugene Martone), Joe Seneca (Willie Brown), Jami Gertz (Frances), Joe Morton (Scratch's Assistant), Robert Judd (Scratch), Steve Vai (Jack Butler), Dennis Lipscomb (Lloyd), Tim Russ (Robert Johnson)

THE CHECK IS IN THE MAIL (Ascot Entertainment Group) Executive Producers, Joseph Wolf, Simon Tse; Producers, Robert Kaufman, Robert Krause; Director, Joan Darling; Screenplay, Robert Kaufman; Photography, Jan Kiesser; Music, David Frank; Associate Producer, David Wolf; Color; Rated R; 91 minutes; March release. CAST: Brian Dennehy, Anne Archer, Hallie Todd, Chris Hebert, Michael Bowen, Nita Talbot, Dick Shawn

CRY FROM THE MOUNTAIN (World Wide Pictures) Producer, William F. Brown; Director, James F. Collier; Screenplay, David L. Quick; Photography, Gary D. Baker; Editor/Designer, J. Michael Hooser; Music, J. A. C. Redford; Sound, Michael Strong, Les Kisling; Costumes, M. Butler; Production Coordinator, Twila Knaack; Set Design, James Sewell; Produced by the Billy Graham Film Ministry; Color; Rated PG; 90 minutes; March release. CAST: Wes Parker (Larry Sanders), Rita Walter (Carolyn Sanders), Chris Kidd (Cal Sanders), James Cavan (Jonathan), Coleen Gray (Marian Rissman), Jerry Ballew (Dr. Carney), Allison Argo (Laurie Matthews), Glen Alsworth (Pilot), Myrna Kidd (Dr. Blake)

NINJA TURF aka *L.A. Streetfighters* (Ascot Entertainment Group) Producer, Phillip Rhee; Executive Producer, Jun Chong; Director, Richard Park; Screenplay/Story, Simon Blake Hong; Photography, David D. Kim, Maximo Munzi; Editor, Alex Chang; Music, Charles Pavlosky, Gary Falcone, Chris Stone; Sound, John Dunne, Hilliary Wong; Designer, David Moon Park; Associate Producer, Richard Park; An Action Brothers production; DeLuxe Color; Rated R; 86 minutes; March release. CAST: Jun Chong (Young), Phillip Rhee (Tony), James Lew (Chan), Rosanna King (Lily), Bill "Superfoot" Wallace (Kruger), Dorin Mukama (Dorin), Arlene Montano (Chan's girlfriend)

HIGHLANDER (20th Century Fox) Producers, Peter S. Davis, William N. Panzer; Director, Russell Mulcahy; Screenplay, Gregory Widen, Peter Bellwood, Larry Ferguson; Story, Gregory Widen; Executive Producer, E. C. Monell; Associate Producers, Harold Moskovitz, John Starke, Eva Monley; Editor, Peter Honess; Designer, Allan Cameron; Photography, Gerry Fisher; Casting, Michael McLean, Diane Dimeo, Anne Henderson; Music, Michael Kamen; Songs/Additional Music, Queen; Music Supervisor, Derek Power; Assistant Directors, David Tringham, Michael Stevenson, John Lawlor, Jane Studd; Sound, Tony Dawe; Production Co-ordinators, Liz Kerry, Patsy deLord; Art Directors, Tim Hutchinson, Martin Atkinson, Mark Raggett; Set Decorator, Ian Whittaker; Costumes, Jim Acheson, Gilly Hebden; Special Effects, Martin Gutteridge, Graham Longhurst, Garth Inns, Bert Luxford; Makeup Effects, Bob Keen, Alix Harwood, Robert Verner Gresty, John Schoonraad; Stunts, Peter Diamond; Technicolor; Dolby Stereo; Rated R; 111 minutes; March release. CAST: Christopher Lambert (Connor MacLeod), Roxanne Hart (Brenda Wyatt), Clancy Brown (Kurgen), Sean Connery (Ramirez), Beatie Edney (Heather), Alan North (Lt. Moran), Sheila Gish (Rachel), Jon Polito (Det. Bedsoe), Jugh Quarshie (Sunda), Christopher Malcolm (Kirk), Peter Diamond (Fasil), Billy Hartman (Dugal), James Cosmo (Angus), Celia Imrie (Kate), Alistair Findley (Chief Murdoch), Edward Wiley (Garfield), James McKenna (Father Rainey), John Cassady (Kenny), Ian Reddington (Bassett), Sion Tudor Owen (Hotchkiss), Damien Leake (Tony), Gordon Sterne (Dr. Kenderly), Ron Berglas (Erik), and Louis Guss, Peter Banks, Ted Maynard, Nicola Ramsey, Waldo Roeg, Anthony Mannino, Helena Stevens, Frank Dux, Prince Howell, Anthony Fusco, Ian Tyler, Corrinne Russell, Buckley Norris

Ralph Macchio, Jami Gertz, Joe Seneca
in "Crossroads" © *Columbia*

GIRLS SCHOOL SCREAMERS (Troma Team) Producers, John P. Finegan, Pierce J. Keating, James W. Finegan; Director, John P. Finegan; Executive Producers, Lloyd Kaufman, Michael Herz; Story, John P. Finegan, Katie Keating, Pierce Keating; Screenplay/Designer, John P. Finegan; Music/Sound Effects, John Hodian; Photography, Albert R. Jordan; Editor, Thomas R. Rondinella; Production Manager, Megwin Finegan; Sound, Bruce A. Levin, John Hodian, Michael Aharon; Assistant Directors, Thomas R. Rondinella, William R. Pace; Additional Dialogue, Charles Braun, Robert Fisher; Art Director, Glenn Bookman; Special Effects Makeup, Joanne Grossman, Maryanne Ebner, Jennifer McCole; Color; Rated R; 85 minutes; March release. CAST: Mollie O'Mara (Jackie/Jennifer), Sharon Christopher (Elizabeth), Mari Butler (Kate), Beth O'Malley (Karen), Karen Krevitz (Susan), Marcia Hinton (Adelle), Monica Antonucci (Rosemary), Peter C. Cosimano (Paul), Vera Gallagher (Sister Urban), Charles Braun (Tyler Wells), Tony Manzo (Dr. Robert Fisher), John Turner (Bruce), James Finegan, Sr., Jeff Menapace, Colleen Harrity, Eva Keating McKendrick, John McKeever, Vicki McKeever, Daniel J. Keating, Sr., Miriam Spiller, Ray Spiller, Katie Keating, Kim Robinson

P.O.W. THE ESCAPE (Cannon Group) Producers, Menahem Golan, Yoram Globus; Director, Gideon Amir; Screenplay, Jeremy Lipp, James Bruner, Malcolm Barbour, John Langley; Story, Avi Kleinberger, Gideon Amir; Music, Michael Linn; Editor, Marcus Manton; Designer, Marcia Hinds; Photography, Yechiel Ne'eman; Production Manager, Michael Kansky; Assistant Director, Adi Shoval; Art Director, Bo Johnson; Costumes, Audrey Bansmer; Sound, Jacob Goldstein; Songs, John Fogarty, Fontaine Brown, David Storrs; TVC Color; Rated R; 89 minutes; April release. CAST: David Carradine (Col. Cooper), Charles R. Floyd (Sparks), Mako (Capt. Vinh), Steve James (Jonston), Phil Brock (Adams), Daniel Demorest (Thomas), Tony Pierce (Waite), Steve Freedman (Scott), James Acheson (McCoy), Rudy Daniels (Gen. Morgan), Ken Metcalfe (Gen. Weaver), Kenneth Weaver (Teague), Michael James, Irma Alegre, Spanky Manikan, Estrella Antonio, Tony Beso, Jr., John Falch, Chris Aguillar, Crispin Medina, Rey Ventura, Luisito Hilario, Chris Gould, Brian Robillard, Leif Eriandson, Brian Tasker, James Gaines, Eric Hahn, Mansour Khalili, Tony Realle, Tony Williams, Willy Williams, Avi Karpick, Bill Kipp, Andrew Sommer, Victor Barjo, John Barett, Zenon Gil, Henry Strazalkowski

Sean Connery, Christopher Lambert
in "Highlander" © *Highlander*

Steve James, David Carradine, Brian Tasker,
Phil Brock in "P.O.W. the Escape"
© *Cannon*

123

Hallie Foote, William Converse-Roberts in "On Valentine's Day" © Angelika

LOW BLOW (Crown International) Producer/Screenplay, Leo Fong; Director, Photography, Frank Harris; Associate Producer, Hope Holiday; Production Coordinator/Assistant Director/Art Director, Diane Harris; Production Manager, David Cox; Sound, John Torrijos, Gary Torrijos; Stunts, Gene Lefeldt; Fight Choreographer, George Chung; Editor, Frank Harris; Music, Steve Amundsen, Samuel S. Cardon; Color; Rated R; 90 minutes; April release. CAST: Leo Fong (Joe Wong), Cameron Mitchell (Yarakunda), Troy Donahue (John Templeton), Diane Stevenett (Diane), Akosua Busia (Karma), Patti Bowling (Karen Templeton), Stack Pierce (Corky), Woody Farmer (Fuzzy), Elaine Hightower (Cody), Manny Dela Pena (Sticks), David Cochran (Chico), and Roger Gundert, Gerry Monti, Mike York, Sam Baco, Lyle Compo, Nestor C. Albalos, Gary R. Stroupe, Jack L. Farley, Nestor Gandia, Ann Bridges, Larry Meredity, Grady Butler, Joel Hinger, Steve Tognini, Tony Petrali, John Zgraggen, John Drebinger, Jr., Scott Hall, Anita Cerqui, Lisa Chun, Karen Yee, Helen Yee, Lynda Wong, Gene Lee, William Hunt, Ella Marie Hunt, Ron Ackerman, Harold Storme, Al Allen, Doug Jukich, Randall Witt, Tim Perez, Darrin Westbrook, Elizabeth Wilkinson, Frank Dianette, Billy Blanks, Jay Garber, Cory Troxclair, Ray Lewis, Michael Hughes, Ansel Chin, Raul Magadia, Gerald Sakata, Tom Lingenfelter, Wesley Suttles, Marilyn Tanner, Emil Jaurequi, Jr., Doug Parker, Michael Zezima, Curtis Johnson, Scott Cherney, Loyd Garmany, Wilbert Chin, Lim Sisson, Andre Waters, Jeffery Moznett, Charlie Cook, Bernard Bang, Shirley Nelson, Rick Knoernschild, Doug Weeks, George Chung, Samuel Hawkes, Craig Brandt, Keith Howe, John Louie, Kimball Joyce, Rico Renaldo, Rich Gauardo, Rick Schiller, Peter Ho, Rich Kuehn, Kyle Miller, Leo Beltran, Larry Lopez

LEGEND (Universal) Producer, Arnon Milchan; Director, Ridley Scott; Screenplay, William Hjortsberg; Co-Producer, Tim Hampton; Music, Tangerine Dream; Special Make-up, Rob Bottin; Editor, Terry Rawlings; Designer, Asheton Gorton; Photography, Alex Thomson; Associate Producer, Joseph P. Grace; Costumes, Charles Knode; Special Effects, Nick Allder; Production Supervisor, Hugh Harlow; Choreographer, Arlene Phillips; Assistant Directors, Garth Thomas, Bill Westley; Editor, Pam Power; Sound, Roy Charman; Songs, Bryan Ferry, Jon Anderson, Tangerine Dream; Soundtrack on MCA Records; Dolby Stereo; Technicolor; Rated PG; 89 minutes; April release. CAST: Tom Cruise (Jack), Mia Sara (Lili), Tim Curry (Darkness), David Bennent (Gump), Alice Playten (Blix), Billy Barty (Screwball),

Tom Cruise, Mia Sara in "Legend"
© Universal

Cork Hubbert (Brown Tom), Peter O'Farrell (Pox), Kiran Shah (Blunder), Annabelle Lanyon (Oona), Robert Picardo (Meg Mucklebones), Tina Martin (Nell), Ian Longmuir, Mike Crane (Demon Cooks), Liz Gilbert (Dancing Black Dress), Eddie Powell (Mummified Guard), Vic Armstrong, Terry Cade, Perry Davey, Nick Gillard, Wendy Leach, Danny Potts, Anthony Georghiou, Paul Grant, Kevin Hudson, Jordan Scott, Dean Shackleford

ON VALENTINE'S DAY (Angelika Films) Producers, Lillian V Foote. Calvin Skaggs; Executive Producers, Lewis Allen, Lindsay Law, Ross Milloy, Peter Newman; Director, Ken Harrison; Screenplay, Horton Foote, from his play *"Valentine's Day"*; Photography, George Tirl; Editor, Nancy Baker; Music, Jonathan Sheffer; Art Director, Howard Cummings; Set Decoration, Donnasu Schiller; Costumes, Van Broughton Ramsey; Sound, Skip Frazee; Associate Producers, Carl Clifford, James Crosby; An American Playhouse presentation of a Guadalupe/Hudson production in association with Lumiere Productions; DuArt Color; Rated PG; 105 minutes; April release. CAST: Hallie Foote (Elizabeth Robedaux), William Converse-Roberts (Horace Robedaux), Michael Higgins (Mr. Vaughn), Steven Hill (George Tyler), Rochelle Oliver (Mrs. Vaughn), Richard Jenkins (Bobby Pate), Carol Goodheart (Miss Ruth), Jeanne McCarthy (Bessie), Horton Foote Jr. (Steve Tyler), Matthew Broderick (Brother Vaughn)

ZONE TROOPERS (Empire Pictures) Producer, Paul DeMeo; Executive Producer, Charles Band; Director, Danny Bilson; Screenplay, Danny Bilson, Paul DeMeo; Photography, Mac Ahlberg; Editor, Ted Nicolaou; Music, Richard Band; Sound, Mario Bramonti; Special Effects, John Buechler; Costumes, Jill Ohanneson; Assistant Director, David Boyd; Associate Producer, Debra Dion; Casting, Rita Forzano; Technicolor Rome; Rated PG; 88 minutes; April release. CAST: Tim Thomerson (Sarge), Timothy Van Patten (Joey), Art LaFleur (Mittens), Biff Manard (Dolan), William Paulson (Alien)

BAND OF THE HAND (Tri-Star) Producer, Michael Rauch; Director, Paul Michael Glaser; Screenplay, Leo Garen, Jack Baran; Photography, Reynaldo Villalobos; Designer, Gregory Bolton; Editor, Jack Hofstra; Executive Producer, Michael Mann; Costumes, Robert DeMora; Original Music and performed by Michael Rubini; Associate Producer, Don Kurt; Casting, Pat McCorkle; Assistant Directors, Patrick Kehoe, Robert Yannetti; Art Director, Mark Harrington; Special Effects Coordinator, Ken Pepiot; Production Coordinator, Cynthia E. Streit; Soundtrack on MCA Records; Songs performed by various artists; In Metrocolor; Dolby Stereo; Rated R; 109 minutes; April release. CAST: Stephen Lang (Joe), Michael Carmine (Ruben), Lauren Holly (Nikki), John Cameron Mitchell (J. L.), Daniele Quinn (Carlos), Leon Robinson (Moss), Al Shannon (Dorcey), Danton Stone (Aldo), Paul Calderon (Tito), Larry Fishburne (Cream), James Remar (Nestor), Tony Bolano (Felix), Frank Gilbert (Antoine), Erla Julmiste (Celeste), Deborah King (Yvette), Jimi Ruccolo (Diablo), Bill Smitrovich (Chavez), Luis Valderrama (Chooch), Roy Datz (Rene), James Eros (Hakim), Ken Calman (Pilot), and Carl Cofield, T. R. Durphy, Eddie Edenfield, Matt Butler, Dan Fitzgerald, Christopher Berry, Peter Fournier, Julian Byrd, Joan Murphy, Allyson Garret, Michael Gregory, Sandy Mielke, D. L. Balkely, Jim Zubiena, Nelson Oramas, Antoni Corone, Joe Petrullo

WISE GUYS (MGM/UA) Producer, Aaron Russo; Director, Brian DePalma; Screenplay, George Gallo; Photography, Fred Schuler; Designer, Edward Pisoni; Editor, Jerry Greenberg; Music, Ira Newborn; Costumes, Richard Bruno; Associate Producer, Patrick McCormick; Executive Producer, Irwin Russo; Production Managers, Roger Paradiso, Patrick McCormick; Assistant Directors, Joe Napolitano, Lewis Gould, Ron Bozman; Art Director, Paul Bryan Eads; Set Decorator, Leslie Bloom; Sound, Les Lazarowitz; Orchestrations, Alf Clausen, David Newman; Special Effects, Connie Brink; Second Unit Director, David Hans Dreyfuss; Song, Bruce Springsteen; Technicolor; Rated R; 92 minutes; April release. CAST: Danny DeVito (Harry Valentini), Joe Piscopo (Moe Dickstein), Harvey Keitel (Bobby DiLea), Ray Sharkey (Marco), Dan Hedaya (Anthony Castelo), Capt. Lou Albano (Frank "the Fixer"), Julie Bovasso (Lil Dickstein), Patti LuPone (Wanda Valentini), Antonia Rey (Aunt Sadie), Mimi Cecchini (Grandma Valentini), Matthew Kaye (Harry Jr.), Tony Munafo (Santo Ravallo), Tony Rizzoli (Joey "New Shoes"), Frank Vincent (Louie Fontucci), Rick Petrucelli (Al the Bookie), Anthony Holland (Desk Clerk), Marcelino Rivera (Bellhop), Joseph Cipriano (Valet), Julis Cristinzio (Roulette Operator), Dan Resin (Maitre D'), Father Alessandro Falcini (Priest), Jill Larson (Mrs. Fixer), and Maria Pitillo, Christine Poor, Stephanie Quinn, Cecilia I. Battaglini, Frank D. Formica, Deborah Groen, Bradley Neilson, Maryellen Nugent, Frank Ferrara, Gaetano Lisi, Vince Pacimeo, Henry Stewart, Carol Cass, Mary Engel, Bruce Katzman, Dayna Lee, Louisiana, Myles O'Conner, Don R. Richardson, Johnny George Sarno, Reuben Schafer, Catherine Scorsese, Gary Cookson, Kiya Ann Joyce, Debra MacHale, Bob O'Connell, Joe Schmieg, Richardson Taylor

Michael Caine, Brenda Vaccaro
in "Water" © *Handmade*

Terrence Mann, Don Opper
in "Critters" © *New Line*

WATER (Atlantic) Producer, Ian La Frenais; Director, Dick Clement; Executive Producers, George Harrison, Denis O'Brien; Co-Producer, David Wimbury; Screenplay, Dick Clement, Ian La Frenais, Bill Persky; Story, Billy Persky; Photography, Douglas Slocombe; Designer, Norman Garwood; Costumes, Jim Acheson; Editor, John Victor Smith; Songs, Eddy Grant, Eric Clapton, George Harrison, Mike Moran: Music, Mike Moran; Production Managers, Matthew Binns, Peter Kohn; Production Co-ordinators, Laura Grumitt, Valerie Craig, Kathy Sykes; Assistant Directors, Garth Thomas, Paul Tivers, Paul Frift; Color; Rated PG-13; 91 minutes; April release. CAST: Michael Caine (Baxter), Valerie Perrine (Pamela), Brenda Vaccaro (Dolores), Billy Connolly (Delgado), Leonard Rossiter (Sir Malcolm), Dennis Dugan (Rob), Fulton MacKay (Eric), Chris Tummings (Garfield), Trevor Laird (Pepito), Kevin Olmard (Nado), Oscar James (Miguel), Stefan Kalipha (Angola), Alan Igbon (Jesus), Alan Shearman (Charlesworth), Paul Heiney (Kessler), Jimmie Walker (Jay Jay)

TORMENT (New World) Producer/Director/Screenplay, Samson Aslanian, John Hopkins; Co-Producer, Stacey Giachino; Associate Producers, John Penney, Deane Weaver; Photography, Stephen Carpenter; Music, Christopher Young; Production Consultant, Jeffrey Obrow; Production Associate, Earl Ghaffari; Production Managers, Bret Shelton, David Cunningham; Assistant Directors, Jay Vincent, Earl Ghaffari, Carrie Francis King, Wesley Lou David; Art Director, Chris Hopkins; Production Coordinator, Gigi De Young; Sound, Walter Gorey, Larry Hoki, Paul Fischer, Calvin Toya; Special Make-Up Effects, Matthew Mungle; Song, Pamela Rose, the Wild Kingdom; Color; Rated R; 90 minutes; April release. CAST: Taylor Gilbert (Jennifer), William Witt (Father), Eve Brenner (Mrs. Courtland), Warren Lincoln (Michael), Najean Cherry (Helen), Stan Weston (Bogartis), Doug Leach (Officer Tilman), Lisa Ramirez (Dianne), Dan Kosloff (Barry), Paul McCarthy (Officer Gilchrist), Kent Minault (Fort Point Officer), Sherman Brown (Coroner), Al Droyan, Pepe McIlvaine, Gar Grover (Cops), Michael Orloff (Cab Driver), Michael Holloway (Clerk), Ramon Vargas (Customer), Mark Elliot Grauer (Disc Jockey)

ROUTINE PLEASURES (Film Forum) Producer, ZDF, Institut National de la Communication Audiovisuelle, Channel Four Television & Jean-Pierre Gorin Productions; Director/Editor, Jean-Pierre Gorin; Screenplay, Jean-Pierre Gorin, Patrick Amos; Photography, Babette Mangolte; Documentary; Color; Not Rated; 81 minutes; April release

CRITTERS (New Line Cinema) Producer, Rupert Harvey; Director, Stephen Herek; Executive Producer, Robert Shaye; Screenplay, Stephen Herek, Domonic Muir; Additional Scenes, Don Opper; Associate Producer, Sara Risher; Photography, Tim Suhrstedt, Chris Tufty; Music, David Newman; Critters Effects, Chiodo Brothers Prods.; Editor, Larry Bock; Designer, Gregg Fonseca; Production Manager, Daryl Kass; Assistant Director, Leon Dudevoir; Art Director, Philip Foreman; Second Director, Mark Helfrich; A Sho Films Production; Presented in association with Smart Egg Pictures; Color; Rated PG-13; 86 minutes; April release. CAST: Dee Wallace Stone (Helen Brown), M. Emmet Walsh (Harv), Billy Green Bush (Jay Brown), Scott Grimes (Brad Brown), Nadine Van Der Velde (April Brown), Don Opper (Charlie McFadden), Billy Zane (Steve Elliot), Ethan Phillips (Jeff Barnes), Jeremy Lawrence (Preacher), Lin Shaye (Sally), Michael Lee Gogin (Warden Zanti), Art Frankel (Ed), Douglas Koth (Bowler #1 and #2), Montrose Hagins (Organist/Woman #2), Roger Hampton (Jake), Chuck Lindsly (Pool Player)

OFF BEAT (Buena Vista) Producers, Joe Roth, Harry Ufland: Director, Michael Dinner; Screenplay, Mark Medoff; Based on a story by Dezso Magyar; Editors, Dede Allen, Angelo Corrao; Photography, Carlo DiPalma; Designer, Woods MacKintosh; Costumes, Joseph G. Aulisi; Choreographer, Jacques d'Amboise; Music, James Horner; Production Manager, A. Kitman Ho; Assistant Directors, Peter Giuliano, Nathalie Vadim, Ellen Schwartz; Sound, Tod A. Maitland, Michael Bedard; Orchestrations, Greig McRitchie; Ballet Lighting, Richard Nelson; Presented by Touchstone Films; Technicolor; Panavision; Dolby Stereo; Rated PG; 93 minutes; April release. CAST: Judge Reinhold (Joe Gower), Meg Tilly (Rachel Wareham), Cleavant Derricks (Abe Washington), Joe Mantegna (Pete Peterson), Jacques d'Amboise (August), Amy Wright (Mary Ellen Gruenwald) John Turturro (Neil Pepper), James Tolkan (Harry), Julie Bovasso, (Mrs. Wareham), Anthony Zerbe (Mr. Wareham), Fred Gwynne (Commissioner), Harvey Keitel (Leon), Victor Argo (Leon), Austin Pendleton (Gun Shop Salesman), Penn Jillette (Norman), Jack Fletcher (Alvin), Mel Winkler (Earl), Irving Metzman (DeLuca), Mike Starr (James Bonnell), Shawn Elliot (Hector), Stanley Simmonds (Pud), Nancy Giles (Celestine), Paul Butler (Jordan), John Kapelos (Lou Wareham), Bill Sadler (Dickson), Christopher Noth (Ely Wareham, Jr.), Mark Medoff (Sgt. Tiegher), Yvonne Talton Kersey (Lucinda), and Fyvush Finkel, Ann McDonough, Mary Duncan, Laura Crimmins, Darmine Foresta, Madeleine Berger, Helen Hanft, Peter Wise

"Band of the Hand"
© *Tri-Star*

Judge Reinhold, Fred Gwynne
in "Off Beat" © *Touchstone*

Phil Hartman, Mario Van Peebles, Charles Grodin,
Steve Levitt, Mimi Lieber in "Last Resort"
© Concorde

LAST RESORT (Concorde Pictures) formerly *Club Sandwich;* Producer, Julie Corman; Director, Zane Buzby; Screenplay, Steve Zacharias, Jeff Buhai; Executive Producer, Nessa Cooper; Music, Steve Nelson, Thom Sharp; Photography, Stephen Katz, Alex Nepomniaschy; Editor, Gregory Scherick; Production Executive, Jack M. Bohrer; Production Managers, C. William Cummings III, Keith A. Baumgartner; Assistant Directors, John Jakes, Katherine Palmer-Collins, Judith Collins; Designer, Curtis A. Schnell; Art Director, Colin D. Irwin; Costumes/Jewelry, Julie Gombert; Sound, Walter Martin; Special Effects, Ronald O. Coe; Choreographer, JoAnn Harris; Music Consultant, Conan Berkely; Songs by various artists; Color; Rated R; 84 minutes; April release. CAST: Charles Grodin (George Lollar), Robin Pearson Rose (Sheila Lollar), John Ashton (Phil Cocoran), Ellen Blake (Dorothy Cocoran), Megan Mullally (Jessica Lollar), Christopher Ames (Brad Lollar), Scott Nemes (Bobby Lollar), Jon Lovitz (Bartender), Gerrit Graham (Curt), Mario Van Peebles (Pino), Brenda Bakke (Veroneeka), William Bumiller (Etienne), Phil Hartman (Jean-Michel), Mimi Lieber (Mimi), Steve Levitt (Pierre), Zane Buzby (Martine), Victor Rivers (Klaus), Brett Clark (Manuello), Ian Abercrombie (Maitre d'), Jacob Vargas (Carlos), Irina Maleeva (Maria), Eduardo Richard (Juan), Morgan Douglas (Pilot), Joycee Katz (Connie), David Mirkin (Walter Ambrose), Buck Young (Mr. Emerson), Twinkle Bayoud (Twinkle Bayoud), Gregory Michaels, Michael Markowitz, Sandy Ignon, Wally Wharton, Patti R. Lee, Chip Johannessen, John "Bud" Cardos

THE LADIES CLUB (New Line Cinema) Producers, Nick J. Mileti, Paul Mason; Director, A. K. Allen; Screenplay, Paul Mason, Fran Lewis Ebeling; Based on the novel *Sisterhood* by Betty Black and Casey Bishop; Associate Producers, John Broderick, Richard Kahn, Rosemary Dennis; Music, Lalo Schifrin; Photography, Adam Greenburg; Editors, Mario Segal, Randall Torno; Designer, Stephen Myles Berger; Production Executive, Robert Greenburg; Production Consultant, Amy Rabins; Production Manager/Assistant Director, H. Gordon Boos; A Media Home Entertainment Inc./Heron International Co. Production; Color; Rated R; 90 minutes; April release. CAST: Karen Austin (Joan Taylor), Diana Scarwid (Lucy Bricker), Christine Belford (Dr. Constance Lewis), Bruce Davison (Richard Harrison), Shera Danese (Eva), Beverly Todd (Georgiane), Marilyn Kagan (Rosalie), Kit McDonough (Carol), Arliss Howard (Ed Bricker), Randee Heller (Harriet), Paul Carafotes (Eddie), Nicholas Worth (Jack Dwyer), Scott Lincoln (Pete Campanella)

THE WAY IT IS (Spring Films, Inc.) Producers, Daniel Sales, E Mitchell; Director/Screenplay, Eric Mitchell; Photography, Bol Bukowski; Editors, Bob Gould, Sue Graef; Music, Vincent Ga Black & White; Not rated; 80 minutes; April release. CAST: Kai F (Orpheus), Boris Major (Eurydice), Vincent Gallo (Vic), Jess Stutchbury (Vera), Mark Boone, Jr. (Hank), Steve Buscemi (Will Rockets Redglare (Frank), Daniel Rosen (Dave), Edwige Belme (Rebecca), Brett Bartlett (Ann)

PRIVATE PROPERTY formerly *Young Lady Chatterley II* (Pa Lane Productions) Producers, Alan Roberts, Stanton Korey; Direct Alan Roberts; Screenplay, Anthony Williams; Photography, E Brownell, Bryan England; Editor, Gregory Saunders; Music, Mis Segal; Designer, Warren Skip Wildes; Costumes, Eduart Castro; Col Rated R; 90 minutes; April release. CAST: Harlee McBride (Cynt Chatterley), Brett Clark (Thomas), Adam West (Arthur Bohart J Sybil Danning (Judith), Alex Sheaf (French Count)

RYDER, P.I. (YGB Distribution) Producer, Karl Hosch; Execut Producers, Taimi Kivikko, Tony DeMartino, Angelo DeMartino; rectors, Karl Hosch, Chuck Walker; Screenplay, Karl Hosch, Chu Walker, Dave Hawthorne, Bob Nelson; Story, Karl Hosch, Chu Walker; Photography, Phil Arfman; Editor, Keith Brooke; Mus Kevin Kelly; Sound, David Greenbaum; Art Director, Kenneth Hos Production Manager, George Steinholz; Associate Producer, Chu Walker; A Long Island Entertainment Group production; Color; Ra PG-13; 92 minutes; April release. CAST: Dave Hawthorne (Sky Ry er), Bob Nelson (Eppie), Frances Raines (Valerie), John Mulroor (Gang leader), Bob Woods (Prof. Throckmorton), Howard Stern (P Wah), Kim Lurie (Maria), Chuck Rader (Det. Hoolihan)

BLOODY BIRTHDAY (Judica Prods.) Producer, Gerald T. Olso Executive Producer, Chris Tufty; Director, Ed Hunt; Screenplay, Hunt, Barry Pearson; Photography, Stephen Posey; Editor, Ann Mills; Music, Arlon Ober; Art Directors, Lynda Burbank, J. Rae F Set, Alex Hajdu; Casting, Judith Holstra; Special Effects, Ro George; Color; Rated R; 85 minutes; April release. CAST: Sus Strasberg (Mrs. Davis), Jose Ferrer (Doctor), Lori Lethin (Joyc Melinda Cordell (Mrs. Brody), Julie Brown (Beverly), Joe Pen (Harding), Billy Jacoby (Curtis), Andy Freeman (Steven), Elizab Hoy (Debby), and Bert Kramer, K. C. Martel, Ben Marley, Er Hope, Cyril O'Reilly, Shane Butterworth, Michael Dudikoff, Dan Currie, Norman Rice, George Paul, Bill Boyett, Ellen Geer, Wa Costello, Ruth Silveira

AMERICA 3000 (Cannon) Producers, Menahem Golan, Yora Globus; Director/Screenplay, David Engelbach; Associate Produc Itzhak Kol; Art Directors, Kuli Sander, Stephen Dane; Costume Debbie Leon; Editor, Alain Jakubowicz; Photography, David G finkel; Stunts, Mario DeBarros; Fights, Ernie Reyes, Karen Shephe Production Associate, Dan Vance; Production Manager, Chaim Sha Sound, Danny Natovich; Special Effects, Carlo DeMarchis, Yora Pollack; Special Sound Effects, Dale Strumpell; Aargh the Awful Laine Liska; Assistant Art Director, Emmanuel Amrami; Set Design Pat Tagliaferro; Production Coordinator, Dvora Pazi; Color; Rat PG-13; 92 minutes; April release. CAST: Chuck Wagner (Korvi Lauren Landon (Vena), William Wallace (Gruss), Sue Giosa (Morh Victoria Barrett (Lakella), Galyn Gorg (Lynka), Shai K. Ophir (Lel Camilla Sparv (Reya), Karen Lee Sheperd (Keva), Ari Sorko-Ra (Relk), Ezra Dagan (Amie), Joanna Reis (Freyha), Steve Malov (Aargh the Awful), Anat Zachor (Bowa), Pierre Henry (Troke), Zip Peled (Gramma), Steve Stroppiana (Young Korvis), Eli Pilo (You Gruss), Marvin Friedman (Gen. Greer), Silvian Imberg (Seeder), E Jacobs (Redcross), Dada Rubin (Yuke), Barak Negby (Tuke), Hel Eleazari (Paradise Elder), Dodik Samdar (Dob), Mafi Salah (Ou Zazy Shavit (Mela)

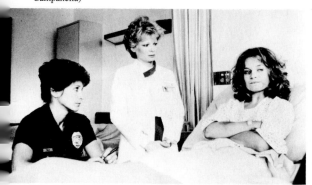

Randee Heller, Christine Belford, Karen Austin
in "The Ladies Club" © *New Line Cinema*

Laurene Landon, Chuck Wagner
in "America 3000" © *Cannon*

Anna Chappell in "Mountaintop Motel Massacre"
© New World Pictures

Debbie Allen, Richard Pryor
in "Jo Jo Dancer . . ." © Columbia

EYES OF FIRE (Aquarius Films) Producer, Philip J. Spinelli; Director/Screenplay, Avery Crounse; Photography, Wade Hanks; Editor, Michael Barnard; Color; Rated R; 86 minutes; April release. CAST: Dennis Lipscomb (Will Smythe), Guy Boyd (Marion Dalton), Rebecca Stanley (Eloise Dalton), Sally Klein (Fanny Dalton), Karlene Crockett (Leah), Fran Ryan (Sister), Rob Paulsen (Jewell Buchanan), Kerry Sherman (Margaret Buchanan), Caitlin Baldwin (Cathleen)

HEATHCLIFF THE MOVIE (Atlantic) Producer, Jean Chalopin; Director, Bruno Bianchi; Animated; Color; Rated G; 76 minutes; April release. VOICE CAST: Mel Blanc (Heathcliff) (no other credits available)

MOUNTAINTOP MOTEL MASSACRE (New World) Producer/Director, Jim McCullough, Sr.; Co-Producer/Screenplay, Jim McCullough, Jr.; Photography, Joe Wilcots; Editor, Mindy Daucus; Special Makeup Effects, Drew Edward Hunter; Music/Sound, Ron DiIulio; Sound, Bob Smith, Gary Hood, Gary French; Costumes, Melinda McKeller; Color; Rated R; 95½ minutes; May release. CAST: Bill Thurman (Rev. Bill McWilley), Anna Chappell (Evelyn), Will Mithcel (Al), Virginia Loridans (Tanya), Major Brock (Crenshaw), James Bradford (Sheriff), Amy Hill (Prissy), Marian Jones (Mary), Greg Brazzel (Vernon), Jill King (Lori), Rhonda Atwood, Foster Litton, Linda Blankenship, Angela Christine

JAKE SPEED (New World) Producers, Andrew Lane, Wayne Crawford, William Fay; Director, Andrew Lane; Screenplay, Wayne Crawford, Andrew Lane; Executive Producer, John Roach; Photography, Brian Loftus; Editor, Fred Stafford, Michael Ripps; Music, Mark Snow; Designer, Norm Baron; Associate Producers, Rob Milne, Roy London; Music Supervision, Don Perry; Production Executive, Larry Larson; Production Manager, Debi Nethersole; Assistant directors, Martin Walters, Wynton Tavill, Steve Chigorimbo, Nandi Bowe; Sound, Ian Voigt; Set, Mike Phillips; Costumes, Dianna Cilliers; Stunts, Grant Page, Zenda Graves, Scott Ateah, Spike Cherrie; Special Effects, John Hartigan; Presented in Association with Force Ten Productions and Balcor Film Investors; Songs by various artists; Color; Rated PG; 104 minutes; May release. CAST: Wayne Crawford (Jake Speed), Dennis Christopher (Desmond Floyd), Karen Kopins (Margaret Winston), John Hurt (Sid), Leon Ames (Pop), Roy London (Maurice), Donna Pescow (Wendy), Barry Primus (Lawrence), Monte Markham (Mr. Winston), Millie Perkins (Mrs. Winston), Rebecca

Ashley (Maureen), Alan Shearman (Rodrigo), Karl Johnson (Charles), Sal Viscuso (Newsstand Attendant), Ken Lerner (Ken), Peter Fox (Priest), Ian Yule (Bill Smith), Ken Gampu (Joe Smith), Joe Ribeiro (Nigel), and Jean Marc Morel, Bernard Crombey, Thys Du Plooy, Jason Ronard, Robert Winley, Lisa Lucas, Wendy Stockle, Jean Pierre Lorit, Vincent Nemeth, Etienne Le Foulon, Franz Dubrovsky, Will Bernard, Sammy Davis, Nancy Riach, Ivan Joseph, June Maforimbo, Mark Orthwaite

JO JO DANCER, YOUR LIFE IS CALLING (Columbia) Producer/Director, Richard Pryor; Screenplay, Rocco Urbisci, Paul Mooney, Richard Pryor; Photography, John Alonzo; Designer, John DeCuir; Editor, Donn Cambern; Costumes, Marilyn Vance; Casting, Reuben Cannon; Music, Herbie Hancock; Music Supervision, Jerry Wexler; Production Manager/Associate Producer, John Wilson; Assistant Directors, Jerry Ziesmer, Bryan Denegal; Set Decorator, Cloudia; Sound, Willie D. Burton; Special Effects, Larry Fuentes; Set Designers, Dianne I. Wager, Mark Fabus, Daniel Gluck, Joe Lucky, Sig Tingloff; Stunts, Ron Oliney; Choreographer, Jennifer Stace; Songs, Chaka Khan and other artists; From Columbia-Delphi V Productions; Dolby Stereo; DeLuxe Color; Panavision; Rated R; 97 minutes; May release. CAST: Richard Pryor (Jo Jo Dancer/Alter Ego), Debbie Allen (Michelle), Art Evans (Arturo), Fay Hauser (Grace), Barbara Williams (Dawn), Carmen McRae (Grandmother), Paula Kelly (Satin Doll), Diahnne Abbott (Mother), Scoey Mitchell (Father), Billy Eckstine (Johnny Barnett), Tanya Boyd (Alicia), Wings Hauser (Cliff), E'lon Cox (Little Jo Jo), Michael Ironside (Det. Lawrence), J. J. Barry (Sal), Michael Genovese (Gino), Marlene Warfield (Sonja), Virginia Capers (Emma Ray), Dennis Farina (Freddy), Frederick Coffin (Dr. Weissman), Dr. Richard Grossman (Dr. Carlyle), Ken Foree (Big Jake), Gloria Charles, Mary Bond Davis, Cheri Wells, Valerie McIntosh, Bebe Drake-Massey, Charlie Dell, Teri Hafford, Edy Roberts, Michael Prince, Rocco Urbisci, Rod Gist, Elizabeth Robinson, Beau Starr, Ludie C. Washington, Kiblena Peace, Larry Murphy, Linda Hoy, Dennis Hayden, Sam Hennings, Rashon Kahn, Charles Knapp, Tracy Morgan, Gary Allen, Jack Andreozzi, Martin Azarow, Dean Wein, Sig Frohlich, JoAnna Lipari, Jo Ann Mann, Richard Daugherty, Alicia Shonte Harvey, Robin Torell, Laura Rae, Erika Marr, Angella Mitchell, Roxanne Rolle, Geraldine Mason, Michael Williams, Deon Pearson, Dorothy McLennan, Erastus Spencer, Edwin Hausam, Howard L. W. Fortune, Dewayne Taylor, Jimmy Binkley Group

Dennis Christopher, Wayne Crawford in "Jake Speed"
© New World

Richard Pryor, Paula Kelly
in "Jo Jo Dancer . . ." © Columbia

127

Babette Props, Brian MacGregor, Reed Rudy
in "Free Ride" © *Galaxy International*

SEX APPEAL (Platinum Pictures) Producer/Director, Chuck Vincent; Screenplay, Chuck Vincent, Craig Horrall; Based on film by Jimmy James, Chuck Vincent; Photography, Larry Revene; Editor, Mark Ubell; Music, Ian Shaw, Kai Joffe; Costumes, Robert Pusilo Studio; Set, Nell Stifel, Pat Hyland; Sound, Peter Penguin; Production Manager/Art Director, Philip Goetz; Assistant Director, Bill Slobodian; Presented by Vestron Entertainment; Color; Rated R; 84 minutes; May release. CAST: Louie Bonanno (Tony), Tally Brittany (Corinne), Marcia Karr (Christina), Jerome Brenner (Joseph), Marie Sawyer (Louise), Philip Campanaro (Ralph), Jeff Eagle (Donald Cromronic), Gloria Leonard (Maggie Mason), Molly Morgan (Bunny), Veronica Hart (Monica), Candida Royalle (Hooker), Taija Rae (Rhonda), Stasia Micula (Sheila), Kim Kafkaloff (Stephanie), Jill Cumer (Miss Crenshaw), Norris O'Neil (Fran), Stephen Raymone (Short Jock), and Edwina Thorne, Cindy Joy, Terry Powers, Ron Chalon, Robin Leonard, Janice Doskey, Johnny Nineteen, Larry Catanzano, Anne Tylar, Suzanne Vale, Dimitri Klidonas, Jane Kreisel, Adrian Lee, Phil Goetz, Carl Fury, Walter Cedric Harris, Daniel Lake, Adam Fried, Josh Andrews, Ron Jeremy, Adam DeHaven, Sharon Mitchell

WHAT COMES AROUND (W.O. Associates) Executive Producer/Director, Jerry Reed; Producer, Ted Evanson; Screenplay, Peter Herrecks; Story, Gary Smith, Dave Franklin; Photography, James Pergola; Editor, William Carruth; Designer, Don K. Ivey; Music, Al Delory; Associate Producer, Gary Neill; Color; 86 minutes; May release. CAST: Jerry Reed (Joe Hawkins), Barry Corbin (Leon), Bo Hopkins (Tom Hawkins), Arte Johnson (Malone), Nancy (Ester Houston), Ernest Dixon (Big Jay), Hugh Jarrett (Ralph), Buck Ford (Chester)

AT CLOSE RANGE (Orion) Producers, Elliott Lewitt, Don Guest; Director, James Foley; Screenplay, Nicholas Kazan; Photography, Juan Ruiz-Anchia; Editor, Howard Smith; Music, Patrick Leonard; Sound, David Brownlow; Designer, Peter Jamison; A Hemdale Production; CFI Color; Panavision; 111 minutes; May release. CAST: Sean Penn (Brad Whitewood Jr.), Christopher Walken (Brad Whitewood Sr.), Mary Stuart Masterson (Terry), Christopher Penn (Tommy), Millie Perkins (Julie), Eileen Ryan (Grandmother), Alan Autry (Ernie), Candy Clark (Mary Sue), R. D. Call (Dickie), Tracey Walter (Patch), J. C. Quinn (Boyd), David Strathairn (Tony Pine), Jake Dengel (Lester), Crispin Glover (Lucas), Kiefer Sutherland (Tim), Noelle Parker (Jill)

BREEDERS (Empire Pictures) Producer, Cynthia DePaula; Directo[r] Screenplay, Tim Kincaid; Photography, Arthur D. Marks; Edito[r] Barry Zetlin; Music, Tom Milano, Don Great; Sound, Russell Fage[r] Art Director, Marina Zurkow; Set Decorator, Ruth Lounsbury; Assis[s]tant Director, Budd Rich; Production Manager, Rebecca Rothbaum Special Effects, Matt Vogel; Production Coordinator, Juliette Claire An Entertainment Concepts (Tycin Entertainment) production; Prec[i]sion Color; Not rated; 77 minutes; May release. CAST: Teresa Farle[y] (Dr. Gamble Pace), Lance Lewman (Det. Dale Andriotti), France[s] Raines (Karinsa Marshall), Natalie O'Connell (Donna), Amy Brentan[o] (Gail), Leeanne Baker (Kathleen), Ed French (Dr. Ira Markum), Ma[tt] Mitler (Ted), Adriane Lee (Alec), Owen Flynn (Monster)

FRENCH QUARTER UNDERCOVER (Shapiro Entertainmen[t]) Producer, Thomas Hebert; Director, Joseph Catalanotto; Screenplay Bill Holliday; A Worldwide Production, Inc.; Color; Rated R; 9[?] minutes; May release. CAST: Michael Parks, Bill Holliday, Suzann[e] Regard, Miz Mary (no other credits submitted)

FREE RIDE (Galaxy) Producers, Tom Boutross, Bassem Abdallah Director, Tom Trbovich; Screenplay, Ronald Z. Wang, Lee Fulkerson Robert Bell; Story, Ronald Z. Wang; Photography, Paul Lohmann Designer, Daniel Webster; Editor, Ron Honthaner; Executive Pro[ducer], Moustapha Akkad; Associate Producer, M. Sanousi; Productio[n] Manager, John J. Smith; Assistant Directors, Robert Smawley, Law rence Lipton; Sound, Steve Nelson, Clark King; Costumes, Barbar[a] Scott; Special Effects, A&A Special Effects, Richard Albain, Ro[n] Nary, Don Powers, John Alexander; Color; Rated R; 82 minutes; Ma[y] release. CAST: Gary Hershberger (Dan Garten), Reed Rudy (Greg[?]) Dawn Schneider (Jill Monroe), Peter De Luise (Carl), Brian Ma[c]Gregor (Elmer), Warren Berlinger (Dean Stockwell), Mamie Va[n] Doren (Debbie Stockwell), Babette Props (Kathy), Chick Venner (Edgar Ness), Anthony Charnota (Vinnie Garbagio), Mario Marcelin[o] (Vito Garbagio), Joseph Tornatore (Murray Garbagio), Ken Olfso[n] (Mr. Lennox), Liam Sullivan (Mr. Monroe), Frank Campanella (O[ld] Man Garbagio), Diana Bellamy (Woman Guard), Teressa Haffor[?] (Monique), Karen L. Scott, Robert De Frank, Jeff Winkless, Vick[i] Seton, Mary Garripoli, Kevin Welch, Sasha Jenson, John Washingto[n] Christina MacGregor, Robert Apisa, Michael Carr, Anthony S[?] Ragonese, Robert E. Bastanchury, Crystal Smart, Norman Panto[?] Elizabeth Cochrell, Rebecca Lynne, Millie Moss, Roberta Smar[t] Caroline Davis, Scott Walker, Tommy Girvin, David Blade, Mar[?] Poynter, Tony Pacheco

FIRE WITH FIRE (Paramount) Producer, Gary Nardino; Directo[r] Duncan Gibbins; Screenplay, Bill Phillips, Warren Skaaren, Paul [&] Sharon Boorstin; Executive Producer, Tova Laiter; Photography, Hir[o] Narita; Designer, Norman Newberry; Editor, Peter Berger; Music Howard Shore; Casting, Jackie Burch; Production Manager, Willia[m] Watkins; Assistant Directors, Jules Lichtman, Neil Huhta, Sandr[a] Mayo, Paul D. Etherington; Art Director, Michael Bolton; Costumes Enid Harris, Andrew Brown; Sound Effects, Bruce Lacey; Orchestra tions, Lewis Del Gatto; Sound, Larry Sutton; Stunts, Fred Waugh Tony Morelli; Choreographer, Sarah Elgart; Special Effects, Joh[n] Thomas, Stewart Bradley, Bill Orr; Songs by various artists; Metro color; Rated PG-13; 104 minutes; May release. CAST: Crai[g] Sheffer (Joe), Virginia Madsen (Lisa), Jon Polito (Boss), Jeffrey Ja[y] Cohen (Mapmaker), Kate Reid (Sister Victoria), Jean Smart (Siste[r] Marie), Tim Russ (Jerry), David Harris (Ben), D. B. Sweeney (Baxter[?]) Dorrie Joiner (Sandy), Evan Mirand (Manuel), Ann Savage (Siste[r] Harriet), William Schilling (Watley), Penelope Sudrow (Stephanie) Star-Shemah Bobatoon (Margo), Kari Wuhrer (Gloria), Smitty Smit[h] (Keyes), Franklin Johnson (Old Man), Enid Saunders (Old Woman[?]) Birdie M. Hale (Arlene), and Dwight McFee, David Longworth, Gar[?] Chalk, Howard Storey, Steven J. Wright, Ian Tracey, Andy Gray, Ke[?] Douglas, Lesley Ewen, Janne Mortil, Robyn Stevan, Jacob Rupp[?] Debby Lynn Ross, Alex Green, Tony Morelli, Anne Lore Kemsies[?]

Christopher Walken, Sean Penn
in "At Close Range" © *Orion*

Virginia Madsen, Craig Sheffer
in "Fire with Fire" © *Paramount/Shane Harvey*

AGENT ON ICE (Shapiro Entertainment) Executive Producer, Robert J. Dupere; Producer, Louis Pastore; Director, Clark Worswick; Screenplay, Clark Worswick, Louis Pastore; Photography, Erich Kollmar; Editor, Bill Freda; Music, Ian Carpenter; Sound, Don Paradise; Production Manager, Jeff Switzer; Casting, Donna De Seta; A Louis and Clark Expedition production; Du Art Color; Rated R; 97 minutes; May release. CAST: Tom Ormeny (John Pope), Clifford David (Kirkpatrick), Louis Pastore (Frank Matera), Matt Craven (Joey), Debra Mooney (Secretary), Donna Forbes (Jane), Jennifer Leak (Helen Pope)

IN THE SHADOW OF KILIMANJARO (Scotti Bros.) Executive Producer, Sharad Patel; Producers, Gautam Das, Jeffrey M. Sneller; Director, Raju Patel; Screenplay, Jeffrey M. Sneller, T. Michael Harry; Photography, Jesus Elizondo; Editors, Paul Rubell, Pradip Roy Shah; Music, Arlon Ober; Sound, Russell Williams; Art Director, Ron Foreman; Production Manager, Joyce Warren; Assistant Director, Mila Rocho; Animal Trainer, Clint Rowe; Baboon Voices, Percy Edwards; Casting, Laurie Ronson; An Intermedia production; Technicolor; Rated R; 97 minutes; May release. CAST: John Rhys-Davies (Chris Tucker), Timothy Bottoms (Jack Ringtree), Irene Miracle (Lee Ringtree), Michele Carey (Ginny), Leonard Trolley (Maitland), Patty Foley Lucille Gagnon), Calvin Jung (Mitushi), Don Blakely (Julius), Patrick Gorman (Eugene), Jim Boeke (Gagnon)

SIGNAL SEVEN (One Pass Pictures) Producers, Don Taylor, Ben Myron; Director/Screenplay, Rob Nilsson; Photography, Geoff Schaaf, Tomas Tucker; Editor, Richard Harkness; Music, Andy Narell; Color; Not rated; 92 minutes; May release. CAST: Bill Ackridge (Speed), Dan Leegant (Marty), John Tidwell (Johnny), Herb Mills (Steve), Don Bajema (Roger), Phil Polakoff (Phil), Don Defina (Setts), Frank Triest (Tommy), Jack Tucker (Hank), David Schickele (Bert), Paul Prince (Paul)

HARD CHOICES (Lorimar) Producer, Robert Mickelson; Director/Screenplay, Rick King; Story, Robert Mickelson, Rick King; Photography, Tom Hurwitz; Editor, Dan Loewenthal; Music, Jay Chattaway; Color; Not rated; 90 minutes; May release. CAST: Margaret Klenck (Laura), Gary McCleery (Bobby), John Seitz (Sherif Mavis Johnson), John Sayles (Don), Jon Snyder (Ben), Martin Donovan (Josh), Larry Golden (Carl), Judson Camp (Jimmy), Wiley Reynolds 3d (Horton), Liane Curtis (Maureen), J. T. Walsh (Dep. Anderson), Spalding Gray (Terry Norfolk), John Connolly (Preach), Ruth Miller (Mrs. Lipscomb), Tom McCleister (Blinky)

EVILS OF THE NIGHT (Shapiro Entertainment) Executive Producer, Mohammed Rustam; Producer/Director, Mardi Rustam; Photography, Don Stern; Music, Robert O. Ragland; Editor, Henri Chapro; A Mars Production; Color; Rated R; 85 minutes; May release. CAST: Neville Brand (Kurt), Aldo Ray (Fred), John Carradine (The Leader), Tina Louise (Cora), and Julie Newmar, Karrie Emerson, David Hawk, Tony O'Dell (no other credits submitted)

METROPOLITAN AVENUE (NEW DAY) Producer/Director/Narrator, Christine Noschese; Photography, John Bonanno; Editor, Stan Salfas; Music, Glen Daum; A production of Metropolitan Avenue Film Project, N.Y.; John Grierson Award/American Film Festival; Documentary; Color/B&W; Not rated; 60 minutes; May release

DETECTIVE SCHOOL DROP OUTS aka *Dumb Dicks* (Cannon) Producers, Menahem Golan, Yoram Globus; Director, Philip Ottoni; Associate Producer, John Thompson; Screenplay, Lorin Dreyfuss, David Landsberg; Production Supervisor, Mario Cotone; Photography, Giancarlo Ferrando; Editor/Sound Editor, Cesare D'Amico; Music, Geo; Designer, Antonello Geleng; Costumes, G. P. 11, Adriana Spadaro, Michela Gisotti, Raffaella Leone; Assistant Director, Allan Elledge; Production Manager, Attilio Viti; Production Coordinator,

Pat McGuiness in "Metropolitan Avenue"
© New Day/Janie Eisenberg

Pietro Sassaroli; Assistant Designer, Denise Lupi; Special Effects, Giovanni Corridori; Sound, Carlo Palmieri; Stunts, Franco Salomon, Benito Pacifico; Telecolor; Rated PG; 90 minutes; May release. CAST: Lorin Dreyfuss (Paul), David Landsberg (Donald), George Eastman (Bruno), Christian DeSica (Carlo), Valeria Golino (Caterina), Annette Meriweather (Carlotta), Mario Brega (Don Lombardi), Alberto Farnese (Don Falcone), Rick Battaglia (Don Zanetti), Giancarlo Prete (Mario Zanetti), Carolin De Fonseca (Tourist), Julian Jenkins (Tourist's Husband), Sofia Lombardo (Sonia Falcone), Barbara Hererra (Mother), Micky Knox (Bernie Rappaport), Geoffrey Coplestone (Mr. Himelfarb), Ute Cremer (Airline Hostess), Louis Ciannelli (Embassy Official), John Karlsen (Museum Guide), Nicola Romani, Amy Werba (Nun's), Ennio Antonelli (Little Ricky), Andrea Coppola (Airport Official), Loris Bazzocchi (Henchman), Joe Wheeler (Texan), Valentina Forte (Mystery Girl), Norman Mozzato (Monk), Pamela Prati (Secretary), Victor Falanga (Don Zanetti's Right Arm), Adriana Giuffre (Don Lombardi's Wife)

DANGEROUSLY CLOSE (Cannon Group) Producer, Harold Sobel; Director, Albert Pyun; Screenplay, Scott Fields, John Stockwell, Marty Ross; Story, Marty Ross; Executive Producers, Menahem Golan, Yoram Globus; Associate Producers, Susan Hoffman, Karen Koch; Production Executive, Jeffrey Silver; Production Manager, Christopher Pearce; Photography, Walt Lloyd; Assistant Directors, Bradley Gross, Robert Roda; Sound, Ed Novick; Production Coordinator, Claire Baker; Designer, Marcia Hinds; Art Director, Bo Johnson; Costumes, Dana Sanchez; Music, Michael McCarty; Songs by various artists; Soundtrack on Enigma Records; TVC Color; Dolby Stereo; Rated R; 95 minutes; May release. CAST: John Stockwell (Randy), J. Eddie Peck (Donny), Carey Lowell (Julie), Bradford Bancroft (Krooger), Don Michael Paul (Ripper), Thom Mathews (Brian), Jerry Dinome (Lang), Madison Mason (Corrigan), Anthony DeLongis (Smith Raddock), Carmen Argenziano (Matty), Miguel Nunez (Leon Biggs), Dedee Pfeiffer (Nikki), Karen Witter (Betsy), Greg Finley (Morelli), Debra Berger (Ms. Hoffman), Angel Tompkins (Mrs. Waters), Rosalind Ingledew (Mrs. McDeavitt), David Boyle (Mr. McDeavitt), G. Adam Gifford (Morgan Page), Mark Durbin (Zander), Eric Bartsch (Pete Bentley), Joe Nipote (Steve), Tony Kienitz (Paul), Dru-Anne Perry (Barbie), Paul Rosenblum (Toby), Kelly Chapman (Bobbi Page), Rebecca Cruz (Vanessa), Noelle Nelson, Tom Fridely, Dan Bradley, Brian MaGuire; William Zimmerman, Deborah Hanan, Larry Key Hancock, Russell Scott Ziecker, Brad Willis

**Lorin Dreyfuss, David Landsberg
in "Detective School Drop Outs"**
© Cannon

**J. Eddie Peck, Carey Lowell
in "Dangerously Close"** *© Cannon*

129

Audrey Landers, Edward Albert
in "Getting Even" © *American*

Gail Youngs, Armand Assante
in "Belizaire the Cajun" © *Cote Blanche*

GETTING EVEN (American Distribution Group) Producer/Story, J. Michael Liddle; Director, Dwight H. Little; Screenplay, M. Phil Senini, Eddy Desmond; Executive Producer, Alan Belkin; Line Producer, Jean Higgins; Photography, Peter Lyons Collister; Editor, Charles Bornstein; Design, Richard James; Music, Christopher Young; Production Manager, Joe O'Har; Assistant Directors, David Robertson, Joe O'Har, Terri Martin; Sound, David Lewis Yewdall, John Pritchett; Costumes, Sawnie Baldridge; Special Effects, Jack Bennett, Jack Bennett, Jr., Ken Miller; Special Effects Makeup, Larry Aeschlimann; C. F. I. An AGH Entertainment Production; Color; Rated R; 89 minutes; May release. CAST: Edward Albert ('Tag' Taggar), Audrey Landers (Paige Starson), Joe Don Baker (King R. Kenderson), Rod Pilloud (Doc), Billy Streater (Ryder), Blue Deckert (Kurt), Dan Shackelford (Raoul), Caroline Williams (Molly), Woody Watson (Max), Joe Asberry (Potts), Tommy Splittgerber (Calvin Deats), Paul Napier (Reynolds), Christopher Wycliff (Phil), Sean McGraw (Gary), Michael Loggins (Tom), Ralph U. Brown (Potter), Jerry Biggs (Vernon), Martin Rayner (Niles), Chuck Tamburro (Pilot), Jane Simoneau (Mrs. Conroy), Jeri Leer, Sherry Marshall, Mary Ann Smith, Rudy Young, David Coffee, Harlan Jordan, George Davis, Joe Don Griffin, Tom Gark, Michael McHugh, Alex Slephukof, Sam Seidel, Angelo Lamoneau

BLUE CITY (Paramount) Producers, William Hayward, Walter Hill; Director, Michelle Manning; Screenplay, Lukas Heller, Walter Hill; Based on novel by Ross MacDonald; Executive Producers, Robert Kenner, Anthony Jones; Photography, Steven Poster; Art Director, Richard Lawrence; Editor, Ross Albert; Music, Ry Cooder; Casting, Jackie Burch; Associate Producer, Katherine Morris; Production Manager, Robert Latham Brown; Assistant Directors, Doug Claybourne, Mark A. Radcliffe, Victoria Rhodes; Additional Editors, Ned Humphreys, James W. Miller; Costumes, Dan Moore; Stunts, Bennie Dobbins, Jerry Wills; Sound Effects, George Watters II, Cecelia Hall; Sound, C. Darin Knight; Special Effects, Joseph P. Mercurio, John R. Elliott; Set Designers, Cathryn M. Bangs, Dan Maltese; Choreography, Vicky Tarazi; Songs by various artists; Panavision; Technicolor; Rated R; 83 minutes; May release. CAST: Judd Nelson (Billy Turner), Ally Sheedy (Anne Rayford), David Caruso (Joey Rayford), Paul Winfield (Luther Reynolds), Scott Wilson (Perry Kerch), Anita Morris (Malvina Kerch), Luis Contreras (Lt. Ortiz), Julie Carmen (Debbie Torres), Allan Graf (Graf), Hank Woessner (Hank), Tommy Lister, Jr. (Tiny), Rex Ryon (Rex), Felix Nelson (Caretaker), Willard E. Pugh (LeRoy), Sam Whipple (Jailer), David Crowley (Bartender), Paddi Edwards

(Kate), and John H. Evans, Rick Hurst, Lincoln Simonds, Ken Lloyd, Vaughn Tyree Jelks, Roxanne Tunis, Roberto Contreras, Carla Olson, Tom Junior Morgan, Phil Seymour, Joe Read, George Callins

BELIZAIRE THE CAJUN (Skouras Pictures) Producers, Allan L. Durand, Glen Pitre; Director/Screenplay, Glen Pitre; Creative Consultant, Robert Duvall; Editor, Paul Trejo; Photography, Richard Bowen; Executive Producer, James B. Levert, Jr.; Line Producer, Sandra Schulberg; Designer, Randall LaBry; Costumes, Sara Fox; Music, Michael Doucet; Music Producer, Howard Shore; a Cote Blanche Feature Films, Ltd. Production; Color; Rated PG; 103 minutes; May release. CAST: Armand Assante (Belizaire Breaux), Gail Youngs (Alida Thibodaux), Michael Schoeffling (Hypolite Leger), Stephen McHattie (James Willoughby), Will Patton (Matthew Perry), Nancy Barrett (Rebecca), Loulan Pitre (Sheriff), Andre DeLaunay (Dolsin), Jim Levert (Amadee Meaux), Ernie Vincent (Old Perry), Paul Landry (Sosthene), Allan Durand (Priest), Robert Duvall (Preacher), Bob Edmundson (Head Vigilante), Robin Wood, Charlie Goulas, Robert Earl Willis (Vigilantes), Harold Broussard (Parrain), Merlyn Fore (Parrain's Wife), Marcus Delahoussaye (Theodule), Ken Maux, Craig Soileau (Card Players)

NO RETREAT, NO SURRENDER (New World) Producer, Ng See Yuen; Director, Corey Yuen; Story, Ng See Yuen, Corey Yuen; Screenplay, Keith W. Strandberg; Production Executives, Thaddeus Hejker, Jean Ferguson; Photography, John Huneck, David Golia; Production Manager, Thaddeus Hejker; Production Coordinator, Mary Temkin; Assistant Directors, Tony Lee, Lang Yun, Keith W. Strandberg; Martial Arts Choreographer, Harrison Mang; Editors, Alan Poon, Mark Pierce, James Melkonian, Dane Davis; Special Effects, John Ting; Song, Paul Gilreath; Vocals, Joe Torono; Presented by Seasonal Films/Balcor Film Investors/New World; Color; Rated PG; 90 minutes. CAST: Kurt McKinney (Jason Stillwell), Jean-Claude Van Damme (Ivan), J. W. Fails (R. J. Madison), Kathie Sileno (Kelly Reilly), Kim Tai Chong (Sensei Lee), Kent Lipham (Scott), Ron Pohnel (Ian Reilly), Dale Jacoby (Dean), Pete Cunningham (Frank), Tim Baker (Tom Stillwell), Gloria Marziano (Mrs. Stillwell), and Joe Vance, Farid Panahi, Tom Harris, John Andes, Mark Zacharatos, Ty Martinez, Bob Johnene, Dennis Park, Alex Stelter, Harold Engel, Jerry Cole, Ken Firestone, Wayne Yee, Charlie Sparks, Lynetta Welch, Carin Badger, Tina Erickson, Corey Jacoby, Neil Rozbaruch, George Mason, Robert Villeaux, Dave Robinson, Keith Strange, Ruckins McKinley, Roz McKinley, Terry Bixler, Paul Dahomme

Judd Nelson, Ally Sheedy
in "Blue City" © *Paramount/Robbie Robinson*

Jean-Claude Van Damme, Kurt McKinney
in "No Retreat No Surrender" © *New World*

KILLER PARTY (UA/MGM) Producer, Michael Lepiner; Executive Producer, Kenneth Kaufman; Director, William Fruet; Screenplay, Barney Cohen; Photography, John Lindley; Editor, Eric Albertson; Music, John Beal; Designer, Reuben Freed; Assistant Art Director, Alicia Keywan; Set Decorator, Enrico Campana; Costumes, Gina Keillerman; Sound, Bryan Day, Michael Lecroix; Coordinating Producer, Majorie Kalins; Associate Producer, Grace Gilroy; Assistant Director, Gordon Robinson; A Marquis Prods. presentation; Casting, Peg Halligan, Armstrong/Clysdale; Technicolor; Rated R; 91 minutes; May release. CAST: Martin Hewitt (Blake), Ralph Seymour (Martin), Elaine Wilkes (Phoebe), Paul Bartel (Prof. Zito), Sherry Willis-Burch (Vivia), Alicia Fleer (Veronica), Woody Brown (Harrison), Joanna Johnson (Jennifer), Terri Hawkes (Melanie)

THE EYES OF THE BIRDS (Icarus Films) Producer, Daniel Vaissaire; Director, Gabriel Auer; Screenplay, Gabriel Auer, Carlos Andreu; France/England; French with subtitles; Color; Not Rated; 80 minutes; June release. CAST: Roland Amstutz (Dr. Norberto Palacios), Philippe Clevenot (Enrique Materneo), Raquel Iruzubieta (Gloria Materneo), Philippe de Janerand (Victor Benavente), Jean-Claude Legay (Dr. Rudolph Hoegen), Christian Colin (Hector Del Rio), Mario Gonzalez (Julio Rojas), Bernard Waver (Claude Dubath)

FLIGHT OF THE SPRUCE GOOSE (Michael Hausman/Filmhaus) Producer, Michael Hausman; Director, Lech Majewski; Screenplay, Lech Majewski, Chris Burdza; Photography, Jerzy Zielinski; Editor, Corky O'Hara; Music, Henri Seroka; In color; Not rated; 97 minutes; June release. CAST: Dan O'Shea (Adam), Jennifer Runyon (Terry), Karen Black (Mother), Dennis Christopher (Friend), George A. Romero

FLOODSTAGE (Spring Films) Produced, Directed, Written, Edited by David Dawkins; Photography, Wade Hanks; Sound, Joe Brennan; Art Director, Gregory Frank; Costumes, Lois Simbach; Production Supervisor, Avery Crounse; In color; Not rated; 80 minutes; June release. CAST: David Dawkins (Lenny), Patience Pierce (Pinky), Lenard Petit (Merrit), Gregory Frank (Cookie), Deborah Barham (Faye), Diane Brown (Mona), David Jaffe (Red), Marty Rossip (Marty), Joanne Zonis (Maggie), Roger Rabb (Narrator)

CRIMEWAVE (Embassy) Producer, Robert Tapert; Director, Sam Raimi; Screenplay, Sam Raimi, Joel Coen, Ethan Coen; Editor, Kathie Weaver; Music, Arlon Obler; In color; Rated PG; 83 minutes; June release. CAST: Louise Lasser (Mrs. Trend), Edward R. Pressman (Ernest Trend), Paul L. Smith (Crush), Brion James (Coddish), Sheree J. Wilson (Nancy), Bruce Campbell (The Heel), Reed Birney (Vic), Hamid Dana (Donald Odegard)

MY LITTLE PONY (DeLaurentiis) Producers, Joe Bacal, Tom Griffin, Michael Joens; Director, Michael Joens; Screenplay, George Arthur Bloom; Music, Tommy Goodman, Rob Walsh; Lyrics, Barry Harman; In color and animated; Rated G; 87 minutes; June release. VOICES of Danny DeVito (Grundle King), Madeline Kahn (Draggle), Cloris Leachman (Hydia), Rhea Perlman (Reeka), Tony Randall (Moochick), Tammy Amerson (Megan), Jon Bauman (Smooze), Alice Playten (Baby Lickety Split/Bushwoolie 1)

SAY YES (CineTel) Producers, Rosemary Le Roy Layng, Larry Yust; Direction/Screenplay, Larry Yust; Photography, Isidore Mankofsky; Editor, Margaret Morrison; In color; Rated PG13; 90 minutes; June release. CAST: Jonathan Winters (W. D. Westmoreland), Art Hindle (Luke), Lissa Layng (Annie), Logan Ramsey (George)

SPIKER (Seymour Borde and Associates) Executive Producers, Clarkson Higgins, Mary Lee Coleman; Producer/Director, Roger Tilton; Screenplay, Marlene Matthews; Story, Roger Tilton, Marlene Matthews; Photography, Robert A. Sherry; Editor, Richard S. Brummer; Music, Jeff Barry; Casting, Hank McCann; Associate Producers, Dusty Dvorak, Wendi Dvorak; Color; Rated R; 104 minutes; June release. CAST: Patrick Houser, Kristi Ferrell, Jo McDonnel, Natasha Shneider, Stephan Burns, Christopher Allport, Michael Parks, Ken Michelman, Eric Matthew, Philip Mogul, Jan Ivan Dorin, Tim R. Ryan, Mark Hesse, Sandy-Alexander Champion, U.S. Men's National Volleyball Team, Doug Beal

THE PERILS OF P. K. (Joseph Green Pictures) Executive Producer/Screenplay/Editor/Music & Lyrics, Naura Hayden; Producer, Sheila MacRae; Coproducer, Marge Cowan; Director, Joseph Green; Photography, Paul Glickman; Arrangements/Conductor, Dunn Pearson; Sound, Laszlo Haverland; Associate Producers, Joseph Green, Sam E. Beller; Color; Rated R; 90 minutes; June release. CAST: Naura Hayden, Kaye Ballard, Sheila MacRae, Heather MacRae, Larry Storch, Norma Storch, Dick Shawn, Sammy Davis Jr., Altovise Davis, Louise Lasser, Prof. Irwin Corey, Virginia Graham, Jackie Mason, Joey Heatherton, Anne Meara, Al Nuti, Mike Murphy

Philippe Clevenot, Raquel Iruzubieta
in "Eyes of the Birds"

THE COSMIC EYE (Upfront) Producer/Director/Designer, Faith Hubley; Associate Producer, Emily Hubley; Animation, William Littlejohn, Emily Hubley, Fred Burns; Music, Benny Carter, Elizabeth Swados, Dizzy Gillespie, Conrad Cummings, William Russo; Additional Animation, Georgia Hubley, Robert Cannon, Ed Smith, Tissa David, Phil Duncan, Kate Wodell; Production Supervisors, Janet Benn, Ida Greenberg; Photography, Nick Vasu; Production Supervisor, Ray Hubley; A Hubley Studio Production; Animated; Color; Not rated; 72 minutes; June release. VOICES of Maureen Stapleton (Mother Earth), Dizzy Gillespie (Father Time), and musicians Dizzy Gillespie, Linda Atkinson

INVADERS FROM MARS (Cannon Group) Producers, Menahem Golan, Yoram Globus; Director, Tobe Hooper; Screenplay, Dan O'Bannon, Don Jakoby; Based on a Screenplay by Richard Blake; Music, Christopher Young; Costumes, Carin Hooper; Invader Creatures by Stan Winston; Special Visual Effects, John Dykstra; Production Manager, Cyrus Yavneh; Assistant Directors, David Womark, David Lipman; Editor, Alain Jakubowicz; Photography, Daniel Pearl; Designer, Leslie Dilley; Associate Producers, Edward L. Alperson, Jr., Wade H. Williams, III; Production Executive, Mati Raz; Art Director, Craig Stearns; Sets, Randy Moore, Cricket Rowland, Portia Iversen; Sound, Russell Williams II; Special Martian Vocal Effects, Ron Bartlett, Jim Cushinery, Craig Bodkin, Tony Campisi; Additional Music, David Storrs; Special Effects, Robert Shepherd, Phil Corey; TVC Color; 94 minutes; Rated PG; June release. CAST: Karen Black (Linda), Hunter Carson (David), Timothy Bottoms (George), Laraine Newman (Ellen), James Karen (Gen. Wilson), Bud Cort (NASA Scientist), Louise Fletcher (Mrs. McKeltch), Eric Pierpoint (Sgt. Rinaldi), Christopher Allport (Capt. Curtis), Donald Hotton, William Bassett (Scientists), Kenneth Kimmins (Officer Kenney), Charlie Dell (Mr. Cross), Jimmy Hunt (Chief), Virginia Keehne (Heather), Chris Hebert (Kevin), Mason Nupuf (Doug), William Frankfather (Ed), Joseph Brutsman, Eric Norris (M.P.'s), Debra Berger (Corp. Walker), Eddy Donno (Hollis), Mark Giardino (Johnson), Daryl Bartley, Roy Mansano, Shonda Whipple, Amy Fitzpatrick, Shawn Campbell, Brett Johnson (Classmates), and Dale Dye, Douglas Simpson, Lonny Low, Scott Leva, Scott Wulff, Frederick Menslage, Michael McGrady, Lawrence Poindexter, J. Ahceson, Matt Bennett, Aaron Scott Bernard, Steve Lambert, Debbie Carrington, Margarite Fernandez, Joe Anthony Cox, Salvatore Fondacaro

Karen Black, Hunter Carson
in "Invaders from Mars" © *Cannon*

131

Michael White, Robert Doqui
in "Good to Go" © *Island*

NEVER TOO YOUNG TO DIE (Paul Entertainment) Executive Producers, Hank Paul, Dorothy Koster-Paul; Producer, Steven Paul; Director, Gil Bettman; Screenplay, Lorenzo Semple, Jr., Steven Paul, Anton Fritz, Gil Bettman; Story, Stuart Paul, Steven Paul; Photography, David Worth; Editors, Bill Anderson, Paul Seydor, Ned Humphreys; Music, Chip Taylor, Ralph Lane, Michael Kingsley, Irene Koster; Designer, Dale Allen Pelton; Art Directors, Dean Tschetter, Michelle Starbuck; Set Decorators, Deborah K. Evans, Carol Westcott; Sound, Don Parker, Edwin J. Somers; Costumes, Fred Long; Assistant Directors, Thom Anable, Fred Wardell; Assistant Producer, Vikki Hansen; Casting, Dorothy Koster-Paul; Metrocolor; Rated R; 92 minutes; June release. CAST: John Stamos (Lance Stargrove), Vanity (Danja Deering), Gene Simmons (Velvet Von Ragner/Carruthers), George Lazenby (Drew Stargrove), Peter Kwong (Cliff), Ed Brock (Pyramid), John Anderson (Arliss), Robert Englund (Riley)

STOOGEMANIA (Atlantic) Producers, Chuck Workman, James Ruxin; Director, Chuck Workman; Screenplay, Jim Geoghan, Chuck Workman; Photography, Christopher Tufty; Editor, James Ruxin; Music, Hummie Mann, Gary Tigerman; Sound, Jan Brodin; Assistant Director/Production Manager, Ronald Colby; Art Director, Charles D. Tomlinson; Set Decorator, Tom Talbert; Additional Photography, Steve Posey; Casting, Paul Ventura; A Thomas Coleman and Michael Rosenblatt presentation; Color, B&W; Rated PG; 83 minutes; June release. CAST: Josh Mostel (Howard F. Howard), Melanie Chartoff (Beverly), Mark Holton (Son of Curly), Sid Caesar (Dr. Fixyer Minder), and Patrick DeSantis, Armin Shimerman, Thom Sharp, Josh Miller, Victoria Jackson, Ron House, Diz White, The Three Stooges (in compilation footage)

SNO-LINE (Vandom Intl. Pictures) Producer, Robert Burge; Director, Douglas F. O'Neons; Screenplay, Robert Hilliard; Photography, Gary Thieltges; Editor, Beth Conwell; Music, Richard Bellis; Sound, Tim Himes; Designer, Chuck Stewart; Assistant Director/Associate Producer, Lou Wills; Casting, Bob Burge Prods.; United Color; Rated R; 89 minutes; June release. CAST: Vince Edwards (Steve King), Paul Smith (Duval), June Wilkinson (Audrey), Phil Foster (Ralph Salerno), Louis Guss (Gus), Carey Clark (Michael), Charity Ann Zachary (Tina), and Gary Lee Love, Edward Talbot Matthews 3rd, Scott Strozer, Maggie Egan, Dominic Barto, Roy Morgan, Kelly Nichols, Gary Angelle, Michele Ewing, Fredrika Duke, Cassandra Edwards, Kay Elrod, Billy J. Holman

ROLLER BLADE (New World) Producer/Director/Story Photography, Donald G. Jackson; Screenplay, Donald G. Jackson Randall Frakes; Editor/Associate Producer, Ron Amick; Music, Rober Garrett; Production Manager, Elaine Edford; Assistant Director/Stunts Clifford Davidson; Set Design, Donald G. Jackson, Ron Amick Special Visual Effects, Tony Tremblay, Ron Amick; Color; Not rated 97 minutes; July release. CAST: Suzanne Solari (Sister Sharon Cross) Jeff Hutchinson (Marshall Goodman), Shaun Michelle (Hunter/Sister Fortune), Katina Garner (Mother Speed), Sam Mann (Waco), Robby Taylor (Deputy/Dr. Saticoy), Chris Douglas, Olen Ray, Michelle Bauer, Barbara Peckinpaugh, Lisa Marie

RAINY DAY FRIENDS (Signature Prods.) Producers, Tomi Barrett, Walter Boxer; Director/Screenplay, Gary Kent; Photography, Designer, Ronald Victor Garcia; Art Director, Russell Pyle; Editor Peter Appleton; Music, Jimmie Haskell; Casting, Pat Orseth; Eastmancolor; Not rated; 101 minutes; July release. CAST: Esai Morales (Neekos Valdez), Chuck Bail (Jack Marti), Janice Rule (Elaine Hammond), Carrie Snodgress (Margot Fisher), Tomi Barrett (Shirley Felton), John Phillip Law (Stephen Kendricks), Lelia Goldoni (Barbara Marti), Kimberley Hill (Angel)

SPECIAL EFFECTS (New Line Cinema) Producer, Paul Kurta Director/Screenplay, Larry Cohen; Photography, Paul Glickman; Editor, Armond Lebowitz; Music, Michael Minard; Color; Rated R; 95 minutes; July release. CAST: Zoe Tamarlis (Andrea/Elaine), Eric Bogosian (Chris Neville), Brad Rijn (Keefe), Kevin O'Connor (Lt. Delroy), Bill Olland (Vickers), Richard Greene (Emil Gruskin)

PERFECT STRANGERS (ITC Entertainment) Producer, Paul Kurta; Director/Screenplay, Larry Cohen; Photography, Paul Glickman; Editor, Armond Lebowitz; Music, Dwight Dixon; Color; Not rated; 100 minutes; July release. CAST: Anne Carlisle (Sally), Brad Rijn (Johnny), John Woehrle (Fred), Matthew Stockley (Matthew), Stephen Lack (Lt. Burns), Anne Magnuson (Maida), Zachary Hains (Maletti), Otto Von Wernherr (Pvt. Det.), Kitty Summerall (Joanna)

GOOD TO GO (Island Pictures) Producers, Doug Dilge, Sean Ferrer Direction/Screenplay, Blaine Novak; Photography, Peter Sinclair; Executive Producers, Chris Blackwell, Jeremy Thomas; Editors, Gib Jaffe, Kimberly Logan, D. C. Stringer; Art Director, Ron Downing Associate Producer, Maxx Kidd; Music Producer, Rob Fraboni; Production Manager, Carol Flaisher; Costumes, Mary Vinson, Cate Adair Stunt Coordinator, John Branagan; Music performed by various artists Special Effects, Yves DeBono; Production Coordinator, Terry Becker Rated R; 87 minutes; July release. CAST: Art Garfunkel (S.D.), Rober Doqui (Max), Harris Yulin (Harrigan), Reginald Daughtry (Little Beats), Richard Brooks (Chemist), Paula Davis (Evette), Richard Bauer (Editor), Michael White (Gil), Hattie Winston (Mother), Fred Brathwaite (Mr. Ain't), Roderick Garr (Trim), Winston Jackson (Lite) Eric Delums (Bam-Bam), Terry Barnes (High), Chuck Byrd (Zero) Leslie Ross (Evette's Friend), Arthur Dailey (Mercer), Albert Butler (Big Al), Roosevelt Littlejohn (Rosie), Linda Gravatt (Nurse Shades) Sid Bernstein (Sidney), Gino Sullivan (Brad), Annie Allman (Brad's Girlfriend), Mark Rowen (Cop), Guy Louthan (Rabbit), Kim Brown (Melons), Isabel Monk (Lady with groceries), Stevie Blake (Drug Dealer), Lauren White (Reporter), Trouble Funk, Redds & the Boys, Chuck Brown & Soul Searchers

CLUB PARADISE (Warner Bros.) Producer, Michael Shamberg Director, Harold Ramis; Screenplay, Harold Ramis; Brian Doyle-Murray; Story, Ed Roboto, Tom Leopold, Chris Miller, David Standish; Executive Producer, Alan Greisman; Photography, Peter Hannan; Designer, John Graysmark; Editor, Marion Rothman; Associate Producer, Trevor Albert; Music, David Mansfield, Van Dyke Parks; Production Manager, John Comfort; Assistant Directors, Pat Clayton, Chris Brock, Callum McDougall; Art Director, Tony Reading; Set Decorator, Peter Young; Sound, Roy Charman; Special Effects, John Morris, Daniel Dark; Wardrobe, Catherine Halloran, Geoffrey Lawrence, Sally Downing, Susan Nininger; Songs by various artists; Technicolor; Dolby Stereo; Rated PG-13; 104 minutes; July release. CAST: Robin Williams (Jack Moniker), Peter O'Toole (Gov. Anthony Croyden Hayes), Rick Moranis (Barry Nye), Jimmy Cliff (Ernest Reed), Twiggy (Phillipa Lloyd), Adolph Caesar (Prime Minister Solomon Gundy), Eugene Levy (Barry Steinberg), Joanna Cassidy (Terry Hamlin), Andrea Martin (Linda White), Brian Doyle-Murray (Voit Zerbe), Joe Flaherty (Pilot), Steven Kampmann (Randy White), Robin Duke (Mary Lou), Mary Gross (Jackie), Simon Jones (Toby Prooth), Antoinette Bower (Pamela), Peter Bromilow (Nigel), Verna Hampton (Pansy Brown), Louise Bennett (Portia), Bunny Melville (Tree), and Wilburn "Squidley" Cole, Ansel "Double Barrel" Collins, Bertram "Ranchie" McLean, Christopher Meredity, Earl "Chinna" Smith, Sydney Wolfe, Carey Lowell, Alecia Munn, Bill Curry

Jimmy Cliff, Robin Williams, Peter O'Toole
in "Club Paradise" © *Warner Bros.*

SAVING GRACE (Embassy) Producer, Herbert Solow; Director, Robert M. Young; Screenplay, David S. Ward, Richard Kramer; From the novel *"Saving Grace"* by Celia Gittelson; Photography, Reynaldo Villalobos; Designer, Giovanni Natalucci; Editorial Supervisor, Peter Zinner; Production Manager, Mario Pisani; Sound, Peter Sutton; Costumes, Vittoria Guaita; Associate Producer, Newton Arnold; Assistant Director, Gianni Cozzo, Mauro Sacripanti, Luca Lachin; Editor, Claudio Cutry; Casting, Francesco Cinieri; Set Decorator, Joe Chevalier; Assistant Art Director, Mariangela Capuano; Special Effects, Eros Bacciucchi, Giovanni Diodato; Technovision; Rated PG; 112 minutes; July release. CAST: Tom Conti (Pope Leo XIV), Giancarlo Giannini (Abalardi), Erland Josephson (Monsignor Francesco Ghezzi), Fernando Rey (Cardinal Stefano Biondi), Patricia Mauceri (Lucia Fedelia), Edward James Olmos (Ciolino), Donald Hewlett (Monsignor Colin McGee), Angelo Evans (Giuliano), Marta Zoffoli (Isabella), Guido Alberti (Augusto Morante), Massimo Sarchielli (Fortunato), Massimo Serato (Monsignor Betti), and Agnes Nobercourt, Jorge Krimer, Robert Sommer, Tom Felleghy, Margherita Horowitz, Domenico Modena, Angelo Panarella, Fernando Cartocci, Julian Jenkyns, Peter Boom, Claudio Masin, Carlo Monni, Eric Galati, Tessa Passante, Benito Pucciariello, Natale Nazzareno, Judy Natalucci, Ettore Martini, Paolo Merosi, Fabio Caretti, Joe Chevalier

NIGHT OF THE CREEPS aka HOMECOMING NIGHT (Tri-Star) Producer, Charles Gordon; Executive Producer, William Finnegan; Director/Screenplay, Fred Dekker; Photography, Robert C. New; Editor, Michael N. Knue; Music, Barry DeVorzon; Designer, George Costello; Art Director/Set Decorator, Maria Caso; Costumes, Eileen Kennedy; Makeup Effects/Creeps Design, David B. Miller; Associate Producer/Production Manager, Donna Smith; Production Supervisor, Vahan Moosekian; Assistant Director, Mark Allan; Special Visual Effects, David Stripes Prods.; Creeps Supervisor/Dimensional Animation Effects, Ted Rae; Casting, Ilene Starger; CFI Color; Rated R; 85 minutes; August release. CAST: Jason Lively (Chris), Steve Marshall (J.C.), Jill Whitlow (Cynthia), Tom Atkins (Ray), Wally Taylor (Det. Landis), Bruce Solomon (Sgt. Raimi), Vic Polizos (Coroner), Allan J. Kayser (Brad), and Ken Heron, Alice Cadogan, June Harris, David Paymer, David Oliver, Evelyne Smith, Ivan E. Roth

A FINE MESS (Columbia) Producer, Tony Adams; Director/Screenplay, Blake Edwards; Photography, Harry Stradling; Designer, Rodger Maus; Editors, John F. Burnett, Robert Pergament; Executive Producer, Jonathan D. Krane; Associate Producer, Trish Caroselli; Costumes, Patricia Norris; Music, Henry Mancini; Casting, Nancy Klopper; Production Manager, Alan Levine; Assistant Directors, Mickey McCardle, David Kelley, Margaret Nelson; Set Decorator, Stuart A. Reiss; Music Supervision, Al Bunetta, Tom Bocci, Dan Einstein; Sound, Jerry Jost; Roller-skate Choreographer, Phil Gerard; Special Effects, Roy L. Downey; Production Coordinator, Jane Prosnit; Songs, Henry Mancini, Dennis Lambert, and various artists; Soundtrack on Motown Records; From Columbia-Delphi V Productions; DeLuxe Color; Panavision; Rated PG; 100 minutes; August release. CAST: Ted Danson (Spence Holden), Howie Mandel (Dennis Powell), Richard Mulligan (Wayne "Turnip" Farragalla), Stuart Margolin (Maurice "Binky" Dzundza), Maria Conchita Alonso (Claudia Pazzo), Jennifer Edwards (Ellen Frankenthaler), Paul Sorvino (Tony Pazzo), Rick Ducommun (Wardell), Keye Luke (Ishimine), Ed Herlihy (TV Reporter), Walter Charles (Auctioneer), and Tawny Moyer, Emma Walton, Carrie Leigh, Sharan Lea, Rick Overton, John Short, Theodore Wilson, Valerie Wildman, Larry Storch, C. James Lewis, Robert Hoy, John Davey, Frederick Coffin, Darryl Henriques, Sharon Hughes, Garth Wilton, Castulo Guerra, Sharon Barr, Jack O'Leary, Doug Cox, Elaine Wilkes, Jeffrey Lampert, Jim Byers, Shep Tanney, Vic Polizos, James Cromwell, Dennis Franz, Brooke Alderson, Joe Dunne

KGB: THE SECRET WAR aka LETHAL (Cinema Group) Producers, Sandy Howard, Keith Rubinstein; Director, Dwight Little; Executive Producer/Photography, Peter Collister; Story, Dwight Little, Sandra K. Bailey; Screenplay, Sandra K. Bailey; Associate Producers, Joel Soisson, Michael Murphy; Production Manager, Bill Fay; Assistant Directors, Martin Walters, Scott White, Kate Linforth; Production Coordinator, Angela Heald; Art Director, Phillip Duffin; Stunt Coordinator, Dan Bradley; Special Effects, Miek Menzel; In color; Rated PG13; 89 minutes; August release. CAST: Michael Billington (Peter Hubbard), Denise DuBarry (Adele Martin), Michael Ansara (Lyman Taylor), Walter Gotell (Nicholai), Sally Kellerman (Fran Simpson), Christopher Cary (Alex Stefanac), Phillip Levien (Ryder), Julian Barnes (Ilya Koslov), Paul Linke (Frank), Richard Pachorek (Marine), Gerrod Miskovsky (Thedor), Kim Joseph (Shirley), Clement St. George (Yuri), Dorit Stevens (Gretchen), Ralph Redpath (Kerensky),

Michael O'Keefe, Paul Rodriguez
in "The Whoopee Boys" © *Paramount/Robert de Stolfe*

Paul Kaufman (Kramer), George C. Grant (Bruslov), and Andrew Schneider, Jimmy Yung, Joe Nesnow, Floyd Foster, Peter Whittle, David Perceval, Lev Mailer, Sandra Gimpel, Ronald Ross, Nathan Adler, Brandon Brady, Bea Hagen, Arnolda Lawry, Tony Maccario, Claudia Templeton, Dale E. House

THE WHOOPEE BOYS (Paramount) Producers, Adam Fields, Peter MacGregor-Scott; Director, John Byrum; Screenplay/Executive Producers, Steve Zacharias, Jeff Buhai, David Obst; Photography, Ralf Bode; Designer, Charles Rosen; Editor, Eric Jenkins; Costumes, Patricia Norris; Music, Jack Nitzsche; Casting, Sally Dennison, Julie Selzer, Risa Bramon, Billy Hopkins; Production Manager, P. M. Scott; Assistant Directors, Richard Espinoza, Ian Brister; Set Decorator, Don Ivey; Sound, Bill Kaplan; Production Coordinator, Jacqueline George; Special Effects, J. B. Jones, Bruce Merlin; Choreographer, Dorain Grusman; Additional Music, Udi; Songs by various artists; Technicolor; Panavision; Rated R; 98 minutes; August release. CAST: Michael O'Keefe (Jake), Paul Rodriguez (Barney), Denholm Elliott (Col. Phelps), Carole Shelley (Henrietta Phelps), Andy Bumatai (Roy Raja), Eddie Deezen (Eddie), Marsha Warfield (Officer White), Elizabeth Arlen (Shelley), Karen A. Smythe (Clorinda Antonucci), Joe Spinell (Guido Antonucci), Robert Gwaltney (Humping the Butler), Lucinda Jenney (Olivia), Dan O'Herlihy (Judge Sternhill), Stephen Davies (Strobe), Taylor Negron (Whitey), Greg Germann (Tipper), Bill Cwikowski (Snookie), Kevin O'Keefe (Duncan), and Paul J. Q. Lee, Ann Pearl Gary, David Keith, Raymond Anthony Thomas, Bruce MacVittie, Mary Joy, Terry Fiorentino, Noelle Parker, Jack Nitzsche, Ben Coney, Tony Dreyspool, Kera Trowbridge, Sondra Barrett, Harold Bergman, Fernie Berlin, Gonzalo Ruiz, Donitroy Ragoonanan, Stephen Tiger, Lee Tiger, Mary Madrid, Bobby Tiger, Bill Cross, Al Romero, Walter Zukovski, Bill M. Hindman, Dee Dee Deering, Lorna Gillam, Jody Wilson, Mimi Honce, Ida Clemons, Sherry Faber, Carla Dingler, Katharine Long, Gordon Clark, Barry Marder, Lou Sussman, Stephen Roberts, Deborah P. Davies, Howard Allen, Patience Cleveland, Russel Davies, Linda Buchanan, Ava Fabian

LIGHTNING—THE WHITE STALLION (Cannon) Producer, Harry Alan Towers; Director, William A. Levey; Screenplay, Peter Welbeck (Towers); Photography, Steven Shaw; Editor, Ken Bornstein; No other credits given; Rated PG; 95 minutes; August release. CAST: Mickey Rooney (Barney Ingram), Isabel Lorca (Steff), Susan George (Madame Rene), Billy Wesley (Lucas)

Howie Mandel, Ted Danson, Paul Sorvino
in "A Fine Mess" © *Columbia* **133**

Steve Durham, David Coburn, Mike Norris
in "Born American" © *Cinema Group*

BORN AMERICAN (Cinema Group) Producer, Markus Selin; Director, Renny Harlin; Executive Producer, Venetia Stevenson; Screenplay, Renny Harlin, Markus Selin; Photography, Henrik Paerchs; Music, Richard Mitchell; Editor, Paul Martin Smith; Assistant Directors, Paul Martin Hardesty, Harry Paivalainen; Production Coordinators, Debra Mendel, Ulla Virtanen; Casting, Bob Morones; Designer, Torsti Nyholm; Costumes, Anja Pekkala; Stunt Coordinator, Eddie Braun; U.S./Finland; In color; Rated R; 96 minutes; August release. CAST: Mike Norris (Savoy), Steve Durham (Mitch), David Coburn (K.C.), Thalmus Rasulala (Admiral), Albert Salmi (Drane), Piita Vuosalmi (Nadja), Vesa Vierikko (Kapsky), Ismo Kallio (Zarkov), Laura Heimo (Irina), Antti Horko (Cossack), Pauli Virtanen (Sergei), Jouni Takamaki (Interrogator), Inkeri Luoma-Aho (Female Guard), Markku Blomqvist (Irina's Father), Marjo Vuollo (Tamara), Casper Anttila (Chess Player), Aapo Autola (Car Salesman), Sari Havas (Girl at party)

FRIDAY THE 13TH, PART VI: JASON LIVES (Paramount) Producer, Don Behrns; Director/Screenplay, Tom McLoughlin; Photography, Jon Kranhouse; Designer, Joseph T. Garrity; Editor, Bruce Green; Special Effects, Martin Becker; Music, Harry Manfredini; Casting, Fern Champion, Pamela Basker, Debra Rubenstein; Production Manager, Iya Labunka; Production Coordinator, Vikki Williams; Assistant Directors, Martin Walters, Cathy Gesualdo, Anthony Smoller; Art Director, Pat Tagliaferro; Set Decorator, Jerie Kelter; Costumes, Maria Mancuso; Sound, James Thornton; Stunts, Michael Nomad; Special Effects Makeup, Chris Swift, Brian Wade; Special Effects Mechanical, David Wells, Ken Sher; Special Lighting Effects, William Wysock; Songs, Alice Cooper; Ultra-Stereo; Metrocolor; Rated R; August release. CAST: Thom Mathews (Tommy), Jennifer Cooke (Megan), David Kagen (Sheriff Garris), Kerry Noonan (Paula), Renee Jones (Sissy), Tom Fridley (Cort), C. J. Graham (Jason), Darcy Demoss (Nikki), Vincent Guastaferro (Dep. Rick Cologne), Tony Goldwyn (Darren), Nancy McLoughlin (Lizbeth), Ron Palillo (Allen Hawes), Alan Blumenfeld (Larry), Matthew Faison (Stan), Ann Ryerson (Katie), Whitney Rydbeck (Roy), Courtney Vickery (Nancy), Bob Larkin (Martin), Michael Swan (Officer Pappas), Michael Nomad (Thornton), Wallack Merck (Burt), Roger Rose (Steven), Cynthia Kania (Annette), Tommy Nowell (Tyen), Justin Nowell (Billy), Sheri Levinsky (Bus Monitor), and Temi Epstein, Taras O'Har

ARMED AND DANGEROUS (Columbia) Producers, Brian Grazer James Keach; Director, Mark L. Lester; Screenplay, Harold Ramis Peter Torokvei; Story, Brian Grazer, Harold Ramis, James Keach Photography, Fred Schuler; Designer, David L. Snyder; Associat Producers, Christopher Mankiewicz, Jerry Baerwitz; Editors, Michae Hill, Daniel Hanley, Gregory Prange; Casting, Jane Jenkins, Jane Hirshenson; Music, Bill Meyers; Music Supervisor/Producer, Mauric White; Costumes, Deborah L. Scott; Production Manager, Jerry Baer witz; Assistant Directors, Robert P. Cohen, Steve Cohen, Carol D Bonnefil; Sound, Richard Raguse; Set Decorator, Tom Pedigo; Specia Effects, Mike Wood, Mike Edmonson; Set Designer, Nancy Patton Production Coordinator, Jane Prosnit; Stunts, Alan Gibbs; From Co lumbia-Delphi V Productions; Songs, Maurice White, Bill Meyers, an other artists; Additional Music, James DiPasquale; Soundtrack on Manhattan Records, a Division of Capitol Records, Inc.; Dolby Stereo DeLuxe Color; Rated PG-13; 88 minutes; August release. CAST: Joh Candy (Frank Dooley), Eugene Levy (Norman Kane), Robert Loggi (Michael Carlino), Kenneth McMillan (Clarence O'Connell), Me, Ryan (Maggie Cavanaugh), Brion James (Anthony Lazarus), Jonathan Banks (Clyde Klepper), Don Stroud (Sergeant Rizzo), Larry Hanki (Kokolovitch), Steve Railsback (The Cowboy), Robert Burgos (Me Nedler), Tony Burton (Cappy), Robert Gray (Butcher), Larry Flash Jenkins (Raisin), Stacy Keach, Sr. (Judge), Bruce Kirby (Police Cap tain), Savely Kramarov (Olaf), Judy Landers (Noreen), Tom "Tiny Lester, Jr. (Bruno), James Tolkan (Brackman), K. C. Winkler (Vicki) Glenn Withrow (Larry Lupik), David Wohl (Prosecutor), and Melani Gaffin, Ira Miller, Royce O. Applegate, John Solari, David Hess Sharon Wyatt, Joe Seely, Christine Dupree, Richard Blum, Randolph L. Pitkin, Nicholas Worth, Seth Kaufman, Mark Carlton, Sylvia Kau ders, Wilson Camp, Murray Lebowitz, Edith Fields, Lisa Figus, J. Jay Saunders, Lyn Vandegrift, Richard Walsh, Teagan Clive, Tina Plackinger, Susie Jaso, Tito Puente, Nils Nichols, Martin Charles Warner, Rick Avery, Christopher Mankiewicz

FULL MOON HIGH (Orion) Producer/Director/Screenplay, Larry Cohen; Photography, Daniel Pearl; Music, Gary W. Friedman; Ar Director, Robert Burns; Makeup, Steve Neill; A Filmways/Larco Pro duction; Color; Rated PG; 93 minutes; August release. CAST: Adam Arkin, Roz Kelly, Elizabeth Hartman, Ed McMahon, Kenneth Mars, Joanne Nail, Pat Morita, Alan Arkin, Louis Nye, John Blythe Barry more

HARD TRAVELING (New World) Producer/Assistant Director, Helen Garvy; Director/Screenplay, Dan Bessie; Based on the novel "Bread And A Stone" by Alvah Bessie; Photography, David Myers Music, Ernie Sheldon; Editor, Susan Heick; Production Manager, Ellen Winchell; Costumes, Karen Mitchell; Art Director, Kevin Constant Assistant Art Director, Luana Speelman; Sound, Anne Evans; Harmonica Player, David Berger, A Shire Films Production; Color; Rated PG 99 minutes; August release. CAST: J. E. Freeman (Ed Sloan), Eller Geer (Norah Gilbert Sloan), Barry Corbin (Atty. Frank Burton), James Gammon (Sgt. Slattery), Jim Haynie (Lt. Fisher), W. Scott DeVenney (Bill Gilbert), Joe Miksak (Judge), William Paterson (Sheriff Hoskins), Al Blair (Jim Baldwin), Anthony Danna (Joey Gilbert), T. J. Thompson (Tim Gilbert), John Allen Vick (Capt. Patrick), Jack Tate (Mike), Charles Martinet (District Atty. Cobb), Kathryn Trask (Winnie Hoskins), Marcia Taylor (Ella Horton), William Ackridge (Earl Horton), Elizabeth Holmes (Alice Gilbert), Sheldon Feldner (Salesman), Walter Johnson (Minister), Michael Griggs, Simon Kelly (Civilian's)

CHOKE CANYON aka *On Dangerous Ground* **(United Film)** Producer, Ovidio G. Assonitis; Director, Chuck Bail; Screenplay, Sheila Goldberg, Ovidio G. Assonitis, Alfonso Brescia; Music, Sylvester Levay; Associate Producer, Peter Shepherd; Production Manager, Maxwell Meltzer; Assistant Directors, Stuart Fleming, Mitchell Factor; Designer, Frank Vanorio; Editor, Robert Silvi; Photography, Dante Spinotti; Production Executive, Maria Cotone, Aldo Passalacqua; Col-

David Hagen, Thom Mathews, Vincent Guastafferro
in "Friday the 13th Part VI" © *Paramount/James Armfield*

Barry Corbin, J. E. Freeman, Ellen Geer
in "Hard Traveling" © *New World*

r; Rated PG; 94 minutes; August release. CAST: Stephen Collins, Janet Julian, Lance Henriksen, Bo Svenson, Victoria Racimo, Nicholas Pryor, Robert Hoy, Michael Gates, Mark Baer, Michael Flynn, Marc De Nunzio, Frank Kanig, Jill Freeman, Emmet Larimer, Gloria Fioramonti, Walter Robles, Ted Petersen, Kurt Woodruff, Sherry Sailer, Alan Gregory Greenwood, John Fountain, Mitchell Scott Thompson, Robert Conder, Denver Mattson.

HOWARD THE DUCK (Universal) Producer, Gloria Katz; Director, Willard Huyck; Screenplay, Willard Huyck, Gloria Katz; Based on the Marvel Comics Character *"Howard the Duck"* Created by Steve Gerber; Executive Producer, George Lucas; Co-Producer, Robert Latham Brown; Photography, Richard H. Kline; Designer, Peter Jamison; Editors, Michael Chandler, Sidney Wolinsky; Music, John Barry; Songs Produced by Thomas Dolby; Costumes, Joe Tompkins; Associate Producer, Ian Bryce; Production Managers, Robert Latham Brown, Richard Hashimoto; Assistant Directors, Dan Kolsrud, Pat Cosgrove, Dean Jones; Visual Effects, Industrial Light & Magic/Michael J. McAlister, Phillip Norwood; Duck Design, Nikki Rodis-Jamero; Duck Coach, Miles Chapin; Sound, Randy Thom, Gloria Borders, Agamemnon Andrianos; Art Directors, Blake Russell, Mark Billerman; Set Designers, Jim Pohl, Pamela Marcotte; Special Effects, Bob MacDonald, Jr., Bob MacDonald, Sr., Richard Ratliff, John McLeod, Jeff Jarvis, Marty Brenneis, Greg Childers, Reuben Goldberg, Jeff Marz, Dan Nelson, Raymond Robinson; Rock Staging, Thomas Dolby; Choreographer, Sarah Elgart; Songs by various artists; Original Soundtrack on MCA; A Lucas film Ltd. Production; Panavision; Color by DeLuxe; Dolby Stereo; Rated PG; 111 minutes; August release. CAST: Lea Thompson (Beverly Switzler), Jeffrey Jones (Dr. Jenning), Tim Robbins (Phil Blumburtt), Ed Gale/Chip Zien/Tim Rose/Steve Sleap/Peter Baird/Mary Wells/Lisa Sturz/Jordan Prentice (Howard T. Duck), Paul Guilfoyle (Lt. Welker), Liz Sagal (Ronette), Dominique Davalos (Cal), Holly Robinson (K. C.), Tommy Swerdlow (Ginger Moss), Richard Edson (Ritchie), Miles Chapin (Carter), Richard McGonagle (Cop), Virginia Capers (Coramae), Richard Kiley (Voice of the Cosmos), and Debbie Carrington and Jorli McLain, Michael Sandoval, Sheldner Feldner, Lee Anthony, Paul Comi, Maureen Coyne, James Lashly, Tom Parker, Ed Holmes, David Paymer, William Hall, Denny Delk, Martin Ganapoler, Tom Rayhall, Gary Littlejohn, Thomas Dolby, Kristopher Logan, Reed Kirk Rahlmann, John Fleck, William McCoy, Steve Kravitz, Anne Tofflemire, Marcia Banks, Nancy Fish, Monty Hoffman, Ted Kurtz, Wood Moy, Wanda McCaddon, James Brady, Carol McElheney, Jeanne Lauren, Margarita Fernandez, Felix Silla.

MANHUNTER (De Laurentiis Entertainment Group) Executive Producer, Bernard Williams; Producer, Richard Roth; Director/Screenplay, Michael Mann; Based on the book *Red Dragon* by Thomas Harris; Editor, Dov Hoenig; Designer, Mel Bourne; Photography, Dante Spinotti; Music, The Reds, Michel Rubini; Costumes, Colleen Atwood; Production Managers, Bernard Williams, Jon Landau, Peter McIntosh; Assistant Directors, Herb Gaines, Nathalie Vadim, Michael Waxman; Associate Producer, Gusmano Cesaretti; Production Supervisor, Don Kurt; Art Director, Jack Blackman; Sound, John Mitchell; Special Make-up, John Caglione, Jr., Doug Drexler; Special Effects, Joseph Digaetano, III, R. J. Hohman, Larry Daniel Reid; Songs by various artists; Soundtrack on MCA Records; Dolby Stereo; Technicolor; Rated R; 118 minutes; August release. CAST: William Petersen (Will Graham), Kim Greist (Molly Graham), Joan Allen (Reba), Brian Cox (Dr. Lektor), Dennis Farina (Jack), Stephen Lang (Freddie), Tom Noonan (Francis), David Seaman (Kevin Graham), Benjamin Hendrickson (Dr. Chilton), Michael Talbott (Geehan), Dan E. Butler (Jimmy), Michele Shay (Beverly), Robin Moseley (Sarah), Paul Perri (Dr. Bloom), Patricia Charbonneau (Mrs. Sherman), Bill Cwikowski (Ralph), Alex Neil (Eileen), Norman Snow (Springfield), Jim Zubiena (Spurgen), Frankie Faison (Lt. Fisk), and Garcelle Beauvais, Joanne Camp, David A. Brooks, Lisa Ryall, Chris Elliot, Gary

Lea Thompson in "Howard the Duck"
© *Universal*

Chavaras, Chris Cianciolo, Ken Colquitt, Ron Fitzgerald, Dennis Quick, David Meeks, Sherman Michaels, Robin Trapp, Lisa Winters, Daniel T. Snow, Cynthia Chvatal, King White, Mickey Lloyd, Dawn Carmen, David Fitzsimmons, Robert A. Burton, Steve Hogan, Micky Pugh, Kin Shriner, John Posey, Kristin Holby, Greg Kelly, Brian Kelly, Ryan Langhorne, Hannah Cacciano, Lindsey Fonora, Jason Friar, Bryant Arrants, Christopher Arrants, Capt. Melvin Clark, Officer Renee Ayala, Officer Dana Dewey, Officers Stephen Hawkins, Leonard Johnson, Keith Pyles, Michael Russell, Michael Vitug, Pat Williams, and Charles Yarbaugh, Bill Smitrovich, Peter Maloney, Michael D. Roberts

ONE CRAZY SUMMER (Warner Bros.) Producer, Michael Jaffe; Director/Screenplay, Savage Steve Holland; Executive Producers, Gil Friesen, Andrew Meyer; Photography, Isidore Mankofsky; Designer, Herman Zimmerman; Editor, Alan Balsam; Music, Cory Lerios, James Di Pasquale; Associate Producer, William Strom; Production Manager, Robert Brown; Assistant Directors, Albert Shapiro, Jann Dutmer, Matt Beesley; Set Decorator, Gary Moreno; Sound, Bill Phillips, Hal Sanders, Jim Isaacs, John Phillips, David Ronne; Costumes, Brad R. Loman; Special Effects, Joe Mercurio; Animated Characters, Bill Kopp, Savage Steve Holland; Animation Producer, Claudia Sloan; Orchestrations, Chris Boardman; Songs by various artists; Panavision; Color; Rated PG; 95 minutes; August release. CAST: John Cusack (Hoops McCann), Linda Warren (Mrs. McCann), Joel Murray (George Calamari), Grenville Cuyler (Graduation Orator), Kristen Goelz (Squid Calamari), Sky (Boscoe), Laura Waterbury (Crossing Guard), Jennifer Yahoodik (Andrea), Rachel C. Telegen (Brunhelda), Demi Moore (Cassandra), John Matuszak (Stain), Paul Lane, Don Ruffin, Gary Littlejohn, Pat McGroarty (Bikers), Bobcat Goldthwait (Egg Stork), Tom Villard (Clay Stork), Isidore Mankofsky (Camerman), Matt Mulhern (Teddy Beckersted), Kimberly Foster (Cookie Cambell), Jeremy Piven (Ty), Billie Bird (Grandma), Bruce Wagner (Uncle Frank), Joe Flaherty (Gen. Raymond), Curtis Armstrong (Ack Ack Raymond), Al Mohrmann (Yuppie Preacher), Mark Metcalf (Aguilla Beckersted), Anthony Viveiros, Sharon Hope, Donna Clements, Alberta Glover, Pamela Shadduck, William Hickey, Jerry Winsett, Bill Hoversten, Donald Watson, Lisa Melilli, Deborah Bial, Taylor Negron, Rich Hall, Bob Gage, Bob Duncan, Herb Mingace, Earl Blank, Donald Li, Barry Doe, Scott Richards, Elizabeth Field, Len Lawrence, Barry Karas, John Blood, Joan Drott, Jim Cooke, Robert Boardman, John Fiore, Rich Little

William Petersen in "Manhunter"
© *DeLaurentiis*

John Cusack, Joel Murray, Tom Villard in "One Crazy Summer" © *Warner Bros.*

135

Sybil Danning, (C), Pat Ast (R)
in "Reform School Girls" © *New World*

"The Transformers"
© *Hasbro/Sunbow*

INFERNO (20th Century Fox) Producer, Claudio Argento; Director/Screenplay, Dario Argento; Photography, Romano Albani; Editor, Franco Francelli; Music Keith Emerson; Color; Rated R; 83 minutes; August release. CAST: Leigh McClosky (Mark), Irene Miracle (Rose), Ellonora Giorgi (Sara), Daria Nicolodi (Elise), Sacha Pitoeff (Kazanian), Alida Valli (Carol), Veronica Lazar (Nurse), Gabriele Lavia (Carlo)

REFORM SCHOOL GIRLS (New World) Producer, Jack Cummins; Director/Screenplay, Tom DeSimone; Executive Producers, Gregory Hinton, Leo Angelos; Photography, Howard Wexler; Editor, Michael Spence; Associate Producers, Charles Skouras III, Kathy Lee Kennedy; Additional Dialogue, Daniel Arthur Wray, Jack Cummins; Music Supervisor, Martin Schwartz; Assistant Directors, Kristine Peterson, Terry Edwards, John Keefer; Production Manager, Charles Skouras III; Art Director, Becky Block; Production Coordinator, J. Marina Muhlfriedel; Costumes, Katie Sparks; Sound, Steve Nelson; Stunts, Sandy Gimpel; Special Effects, Rodger George, Lise Romanoff; Songs by various artists; Presented by International Cinevision Productions, Inc. in association with Balcor Film Investors; Color; Rated R; 98 minutes; August release. CAST: Linda Carol (Jenny), Wendy O. Williams (Charlie), Pat Ast (Edna), Sybil Danning (Sutter), Charlotte McGinnis (Dr. Norton), Sherri Stoner (Lisa), Denise Gordy (Claudia), Laurie Schwartz (Nicky), Tiffany Helm (Fish), Darcy DeMoss (Knox), Andrea Darnell (Paula), Robin Watkins (Kelly), Winifred Freedman (Terri), Jim Staskel (Truck Driver), Fred D. Scott (Judge Carter), Lorrie Marlow (Shelly), Daniel Arthur Wray (Dr. Fisher), Alicia Shonte (Stella), Jon Epstein (Billy), and Terri Lynne, Sylvia Dohi, Victoria Fischer, Lila Waters, Linda L. Rand, Don Pugsley, Su San Cheung, Micki Varro, Leslie Rivers, Dharvi Darrelle, Archie Lang, Justine Lenore, Vance Valencia, Lavelle Roby, Mary Brando, Jennifer Sophia, Kristi Hayden, Katherine Hittleman, Lisa Sanderson

THE TEXAS CHAINSAW MASSACRE PART 2 (Cannon Group) Producers, Menahem Golan, Yoram Globus; Director/Co-producer, Tobe Hooper; Screenplay/Associate Producer, L. M. Kit Carson; Executive Producers, Henry Holmes, James Jorgensen; Editor, Alain Jakybowicz; Photography, Richard Kooris; Designer, Cary White; Music, Tobe Hooper, Jerry Lambert; Special Makeup Effects, Tom Savini; Costumes, Carin Hooper; Production Manager, Henry Kline; Assistant Directors, Richard Espinoza, Mark Lyon; Set Decorator, Michael Peal; Special Effects, Eddie Surkin, Gerald McClanahan; Sound, Wayne Bell; Costumes, Julia Gombert, Karen Miller; Songs by

various artists; Soundtrack on I.R.S. Records; TVC Color; Not Rated; 95 minutes; August release. CAST: Dennis Hopper (Lt. "Lefty" Enright), Caroline Williams (Vanita "Stretch" Brock), Bill Johnson (Leatherface), Jim Siedow (Cook/Drayton Sawyer), Bill Moseley (Chop-Top), Lou Perry (L. G. McPeters), and Barry Kinyon, Chris Douridas, Harlan Jordan, Kirk Sisko, James N. Harrell, Judy Kelly, Wirt Cain, Dan Jenkins, Kinky Friedman, Brad Leland, Cody Haynes, Steven McDaniel, Matthew Kennedy Johnson, John Martin Ivey, Joe Bob Briggs, Ken Evert, Twinkle Bayoud, Victoria Powells

THE TRANSFORMERS The Movie (DeLaurentiis Entertainment Group) Producers, Joe Bacal, Tom Griffin; Director/Co-Producer, Nelson Shin; Supervising Producer, Jay Bacal; Executive Producers, Margaret Loesch, Lee Gunther; Screenplay, Ron Friedman; Story Consultant, Flint Dillie; Music, Vince DiCola; Animated; Color; Rated PG; 86 minutes; August release. CAST: Eric Idle (Wreck Gar), Judd Nelson (Hot Rod/Rodimus Prime), Leonard Nimoy (Galvatron), Robert Stack (Ultra Magnus), Lionel Stander (Kup), Orson Welles (Unicorn), Scatman Crothers (Jazz), Clive Revill (Kickback), and Norm Alden, Jack Angel, Michael Bell, Gregg Berger, Susan Blu, Arthur Burghardt, Corey Burton, Roger C. Carmel, Rege Cordic, Peter Cullen, Bud Davis, Walker Edmiston, Paul Eiding, Ed Gilbert, Dan Gilvezan, Buster Jones, Stan Jones, Casey Kasem, Chris Latta, David Messick, John Moschitta, Hal Rayle, Neil Ross, Frank Welker

WE WERE SO BELOVED (First Run Features) Producer/Director/Screenplay/Editor, Manfred Kirchheimer; Photography, James Callanan, Steven Giuliano; Recorded by James Steele; Documentary; Color; Not Rated; 145 minutes; August release

SHANGHAI SURPRISE (MGM) Producer, John Kohn; Director, Jim Goddard; Screenplay, John Kohn, Robert Bentley; From the novel *"Faraday's Flowers"* by Tony Kenrick; Executive Producers, George Harrison, Denis O'Brien; Co-Producer, Robin Douet; Photography, Ernie Vincze; Produced in association with the Vista Organization, Ltd.; Associate Producer, Sara Romilly; Music, George Harrison, Michael Kamen; Songs, George Harrison; Editor, Ralph Sheldon; Costumes, Judy Moorcroft; Designer, Peter Mullins; Production Managers, Peter Kohn, David Brown; Assistant Directors, Gino Marotta, Gerry Toomey, Rupert Tyle-Hodges; Sound, Andrew Boulton; Casting, Ann Fielden, Judy Dennis, Pat Pao; Art Directors, John Siddall, David Minty; Special Effects, David Watkins; Production Coordinators, Diane Chittell, Kathy Sykes; Stunts, Alf Joint; Presented by

Caroline Williams, Bill Moseley in "Texas Chainsaw Massacre 2"
© *Cannon*

"We Were so Beloved"
© *First Run*

Sean Penn, Madonna in "Shanghai Surprise"
© MGM Entertainment

Sally Kellerman, Patrick Dempsey
in "Meatballs III" © Movie Store

Handmade Films; Soundtrack on Dark Horse Records; Dolby Stereo; Panavision; Color; Rated PG-13; 97 minutes; September release. CAST: Sean Penn (Glendon Wasey), Madonna (Gloria Tatlock), Paul Freeman (Walter Faraday), Richard Griffiths (Willis Tuttle), Philip Sayer (Justin Kronk), Clyde Kusatsu (Joe Go), Kay Tong Lim (Mei Gan), Sonserai Lee (China Doll), Victor Wong (Ho Chong), Professor Toru Tanaka (Yamagani San), Michael Aldridge (Mr. Burns), Sarah Lam (Maid), George She (Wu Ch'En She), Won Gam Bor (Rickshaw King), To Chee Kan (Boatman), and David Li, Keith Bonnard, Claire Lutter, Pamela Yang, Michael Chow, Samuel Tsao, Philip Tan, George Harrison

FAT GUY GOES NUTZOID (Troma Team) Producer, Emily Dillon; Director, John Golden; Executive Producers, Robert Shinerock, Robert A. Mitchell; Photography, John Drake; Designer, Martin De Maat; Editors, Jeffrey Wolf, Krissy Boden, Kathie Weaver; Music, Leo Kottke; Screenplay, John Golden, Roger Golden; Production Manager/Associate Producer, Brooke Kennedy; Casting, Susan Shopmaker; Costumes, Lyndsay W. Davis; Assistant Directors, Aaron Barsky, Rick Dallago; Sound, Felipe Borrero; Stunts, Jery Hewitt; Color; Rated PG-13; September release. CAST: Tibor Feldman (Roger), Douglas Stone (Doogle), Max Alexander (Harold), John McEvily (Oscar), John MacKay (Ronald), Lynne Marie Brown (Hooker), Mark Alfred (Milton), Joan Allen (Lala), and Josh Blake, Anthony Ettari, Thomas Ettari, Annette Mauer, Joniruth White, Libby Miller, Mazie Murphy Klein, Emanuel Ferrante, Jay Natelli, Joyce Sozen, Max Jacobs, Chris Liano, Peter Linari, Jerold Goldstein, Chris Burke, David Stern, Gerard Gilch, Hektor Munoz, Clement Roberson, Loren Bass, George Ross, Danny Shea, Eve Van Sickle, Willard Morgan, Karla White, Mic Muldoon, James Sullivan, Phillip Dachille, Michael Carrafa, Jack Du-Vall, T. G. Welles, Peter A. Levine, Sam Goldrich, Beverly Vail, Anthony DiPietro, Craig Barnett, Crawford Young, Stephen Salter, David Sheridan, Howard Spiegel, Marc Duncan, Mark Deikman

MEATBALLS III (The Movie Store) Executive Producers, Andre Link, Lawrence Nesis; Producers, Don Carmody, John Dunning; Director, George Mendeluk; Screenplay, Michael Paseornek, Bradley Kesden; Story, Chuck Workman; Photography, Peter Benison; Designer, Charles Dunlop; Production Executive, Jim Hanley; Music, Paul Zaza; Editor, Debra Karen; Casting, Barbara Claman, Lucinda Sill, Michael Wener, Ginette D'Amico, Chantal Condor; Production Manager, William Zborowsky; Assistant Directors, Don Granbery,

Erika Zborowsky, Norman Belair, Tommy Groszman; Production Coordinator, Irene Litinsky; Sound, Marcel Pothier, David Lee; Stunts, Jerry Wills; Set Decorator, Mark Freeborn; Costumes, Mary McLeod; Special Effects, Martin Mallivoire; A Dalco Production; Sonolab Color; Rated R; 95 minutes; September release. CAST: Sally Kellerman (Roxy Du Jour), Patrick Dempsey (Rudy), Al Waxman (Saint Peter), Isabelle Mejias (Wendy), Shannon Tweed (Love Goddess), Jan Taylor (Rita), Rummy Bishop (Murray), Mark Blutman (Andy), Justine Campbell (Val), Peter Snider (Tom), Caroline Arnold (Lisa), Pamela Collyer (Karen), Colleen Karney (Cheryl), and Wayne Fleming, George Buza, Maury Chaykin, Keith Brown, Little Beaver, Michael Whitehead, Bob Benedetti, David Bailey, Paul Charters, Zack Nesis, Pierre Larocque, Peter Mahoney, Rona Waddington, Buster the Bull, Ronnie Hawkins

ONCE MORE SATURDAY NIGHT (Columbia) Producers, Tova Laiter, Robert Kosberg, Jonathan Bernstein; Director, Dennis Klein; Screenplay, Al Franken, Tom Davis; Executive Producer, Dan Aykroyd; Photography, James Glennon; Art Director, Maher Ahmad; Editor, Gregory Prange; Music/Orchestrations, David McHugh; Casting, Jane Alderman, Shelley Andreas; Production Manager, Jonathan Bernstein; Assistant Directors, William Hassell, Jeanne Caliendo, Howard Ellis; Production Supervisor, Julie Chandler; Sound, Scott Smith; Set Decorator, Karen O'Hara; Costumes, Mickey Antonetti; Jay Hurley; Puppeteer, Norman Tempia; Songs by various artists; Soundtrack on Motown Records; Dolby Stereo; From Columbia-Delphi IV Productions; DeLuxe Color; Panavision; Rated R; 95 minutes; September release. CAST: Tom Davis (Larry), Al Franken (Paul), Moira Harris (Peggy), Frank Howard (Eddie), Bess Meyer (Tobi), Dave Reynolds (Russ Caldwell), Chelcie Ross (Dad Lundahl), Eric Saiet (Doug), Jessica Schwartz (Traci), Dianne B. Shaw (Lynn), Nina Siemaszko (Karen), Jonathan Singer (Kevin), Meshach Taylor (Bill), Nan Woods (Diane), Wynton & Wynetta Harris (Jason), Jon Tiven (John), Sally Tiven (Sally), Del Close (Mr. Schneider/Large Tattooed Man), Patrick Billingsly (Mr. McGrath), Shirley Spiegler-Jacobs (Mrs. McGrath), and Nathan Davis, Ann Coyle, Jack Callahan, Rondi Reed, Kevin J. O'Connor, Joey Garfield, Tom Tucker, Steve Pink, Charles Fink, Amy Benedict, Bridget M. McCarthy, Aviva Brill, John Cameron Mitchell, Julie Busch, Tim Markiewicz, Jonathan Bernstein, Tyler Ann Carroll, Chad Smith, Shawn Simons, Nancy Baird, Chris Holloway, Mike Hagerty, Eric Bernt, Ted Levine, Tom Joyce, Joe Krowka, Dean Hill, James Willis, Evelyn Kashefska, Rick Lefevour

"Fat Guy Goes Nutzoid"
©Troma Team

Sally Tiven, Al Franken, Nan Woods, Bess Meyer,
Tom Davis in "Once More Saturday Night"
© Columbia

137

Jameson Parker, Jeannie Wilson
in "American Justice" © *Movie Store*

Steve James, Michael Dudikoff
in "Avenging Force" © *Cannon*

AMERICAN JUSTICE (The Movie Store) Producers, Jack Lucarelli, Jameson Parker; Director, Gary Grillo; Executive Producer, Martin F. Goldman; Screenplay, Dennis A. Pratt; Associate Producer/Editor, Steve Mirkovich; Music, Paul Chihara; Art Director, Bruce Crone; Stunts, Billy Burton; Photography, Steve Yaconelli; Assistant Directors, Robert Webb, John Eyler; Costumes, Kent James; Special Effects, Richard Helmer, Grant McCune; Production Coordinator, Anita Terrian; Casting, Mary Nelson; Technical Advisor, Sgt. John Bonhorst; Sound, Michael Hilkene, Gregg Barbanell, Blake Leigh, Jeff Rosen; Color; Rated R; 95 minutes; September release. CAST: Jack Lucarelli (Joe Case), Jameson Parker (Dave Buchanon), Gerald McRaney (Jake Wheeler), Jeannie Wilson (Jess Buchanon), Wilford Brimley (Sheriff Mitchell), Dennis A. Pratt (Connie Baldwin), Danelle Hand (Angelina), Rick Hurst (Harley), Sherry Adamo (Little Wheeler), Sharon Hughes (Valerie), Warner Glenn (Warner), David Steen (Hobie Landrith), Rosanna DeSoto (Manuela), Roman Cisneros (Raul)

DOIN' TIME (Warner Bros.) Producers, Bruce Mallen, George Mendeluk; Director, George Mendeluk; Screenplay, Franelle Silver, Ron Zwang, Dee Caruso; Story, Franelle Silver, Ron Zwang, George Mendeluk, Dee Caruso, Peter Wilson; Executive Producers, Ken Sheppard, Carol Mallen; Photography, Ronald V. Garcia; Designer, Jack McAdam; Editor, Stanford C. Allen; Music, Charles Fox; Casting, Al Onorato, Jerry Franks; Executive Production/Post Production Supervisor, Leonard C. Kroll; Production Manager, Michael Bennett; Assistant Directors, David M. Robertson, Marlon Staggs, Nancy Forelich; Set Decorator, Linda Allen; Sound, Donald B. Summer; Costumes, Arlene Zamiara; Special Makeup, Kenny Myers; Production Coordinator, Susan W. Dukow; Stunts, Erik Cord; Special Effects, Bob McCarthy; Song, Max Carl, Andrew Kastner, Jack Mack and The Heart Attack; Presented by Filmcorp Productions, Inc.; A Ladd Company Release; DeLuxe Color; Rated R; 77 minutes; September release. CAST: Muhammad Ali (Himself), Jeff Altman (Duke), Henry Bal (Guard Kowalaski), Gene Bell (Vaudevillian), Big Yank (Bubba), Simmy Bow (Snake Eyes), Drew Bundini Brown (Himself), David Lee Bynum (Prisoner), Colleen Camp (Catlett), Max Carl (Vocalist), Melanie Chartoff (Linda), Robert Clotworthy (Attorney), Dee Cooper (Truck Driver), Ji Tu Cumbuka (Bernie), Robert Czakel (Trainer), Eugene Davis, Jr. (Prisoner), Nora Denney (Martha), Melinda Fee (Denise), Gayle Fox (Bambi), Irma Garcia (Maid), Stuart Gillard (Sen.

Hodgkins), Graham Jarvis (Prescott), Dulcie Jordan (Inspector), Judy Landers (Bride), Lex Landi (Krat Producer), Lee Robert Laningham (Prisoner), Julius LeFlore (Murray), Frank Lugo (Garcia), Mike Mazurki (Bruno), Pat McCormick (Fallis), Travis McKenna (Slob), Charlie Messenger (Referee), Richard Mulligan (Mongo), Kitten Natividad (Tassie), Joseph Nipote (Angelo Chrispini), Ron Palillo (Pappion), John Reilly (Gov.), Don Richey (Gibbons), Dennis Robertson (Father O'Brien), Rhonda Shear (Adrianne), Dona L. Spier (Card Holder), Paul Stader (Oldman), Duke Stroud (George), Jaynie Sustar (Monique), Eddie Velez (Wetback), John Vernon (Big Mac), Jimmie Walker (Shaker), James Welch (Billy), Peter M. Wilcox (Melvin), Nicholas Worth (Animal), Dey Young (Vicki), Joel Zurlo (Manager), Ron Zwang (Arthur)

AVENGING FORCE (Cannon) Producers, Menahem Golan, Yoram Globus; Director, Sam Firstenberg; Screenplay, James Booth; Editor, Michael J. Duthie; Photography, Gideon Porath; Designer, Marcia Hinds; Music, George S. Clinton; Art Director, Bo Johnson; Set Decorator, Michele Starbuck; Sound, Jacob Holdstein; Costumes, Audrey Bansmer, Dana Sanchez, Lynn Goddard; Special Effects, William O. Purcell; Orchestrations, Joey Rand; TVC Color; Rated R; 103 minutes; September release. CAST: Michael Dudikoff (Matt Hunter), Steve James (Larry Richards), James Booth (Adm. Brown), John P. Ryan (Glastenbury), Bill Wallace (Delaney), Karl Johnson (Wallace), Mark Alaimo (Lavall), Allison Gereighty (Sara Hunter), Loren Farner (Parker), Richard Boyle (Grandpa Jimmy), Sylvia Joseph (Daisy Richards), Robert Taylor (Larry Richards, Jr.), Bruce Johnson (Jeff Richards), Robert Cronin (T. C. Cooper), John Wilmot (Gen. Wyatt), James Borders (Charles Kray), Nelson Camp (Fifi), Lyla Hay Owen, Becki Davis (Doctors), and Claudia Vasilovik, Ramon Olavarietta, John Barber, Paul Staples, B. J. Davis, Kane Hodder, Steve Hulin, Alan Marcus, Charlie Skeen, Gary Alexander

PRIVATE PRACTICES (Kino International) Producer/Director, Kirby Dick; Photography, Christine Burrill, Catherine Coulson; Sound, Alan Barker, David Brownlow; Associate Producer, Barbara Zheutlin; Video Technicians, John Jebb, Alan Barker; Production Associate, Deborah Roetman; Technical Consultant, Christopher Gray; Interviewers, Catherine Coulson, Kirby Dick; Editors, Lois Freeman, Kirby Dick; Assistant Editor, Linda Tadic; Post Production Consultant, Patrick Gregston; Narration, Noreen Hennesey; Documentary; *Best Documentary* USA Film Festival, 1985; Color; Not Rated; 78 minutes; September release.

SHERMAN'S MARCH (First Run Features) "An Improbable Quest for Love"; Produced, Filmed, Sound recorded and Edited by Ross McElwee; Narration written and spoken by Ross McElwee; Introductory historical narration, Richard Leacock; Assistant Editors, Kate Davis, Alyson Denny, Meredith Woods; Not rated; In color; 155 minutes; September release. A documentary.

PARTISANS OF VILNA (European Classics) Producer, Aviva Kempner; Director, Editor, Josh Waletzky; Photography, Danny Shneuer; Sound, Danny Natovich; Narrator, Roberta Wallach; Production Managers, Asher Cohen, Abraham Ravett; Music Consultant/Research, Aviva Kempner, Josh Waltezky; In Duart Color; Not rated; 120 minutes; September release. A holocaust documentary.

STATIC (Film Forum) Producer, Amy Ness; Director, Mark Romanek; Screenplay, Keith Gordon, Mark Romanek; Executive Producer, Julio Caro; Not rated; 93 minutes; September release. CAST: Keith Gordon (Ernie), Amanda Plummer (Julia), Bob Gunton (Frank). No other credits submitted.

Amanda Plummer in "Static"
© *Mark Romanek*

VENDETTA (Concorde) Producers, Jeff Begun, Ken Solomon, Ken Dalton; Director, Bruce Logan; Associate Producers, Richard Harrison, Greg Hinton; Editor, Glenn Morgan; Production Manager, Ken Solomon; Assistant Directors, Elliot Rosenblatt, Katherine Palmer-Collins; Art Director, Chris Clarens; Costumes, Meg Mayer; Sound, Dennis Carr; Stunts, Emil Farkas; Effects, John Hartigan; Production Coordinator, Pamela Jaeckle; Color; Rated R; 88 minutes; September release. CAST: Greg Bradford (Joe-Bob), Holly Butler (Movie Star), Karen Chase (Laurie), Lisa Clarson (Bobo), Roberta Collins (Miss Dice), Pilar Delano (Inmate), Joshua Brooks, J. W. Fails (Parking Attendants), Eugene Robert Glazer (David Greene), Will Hare (Judge Waters), Cynthia Harrison (Debra), Hoke Howell (Deputy Curly), Lisa Hullana (China), Marta Kober (Sylvia), Jack Kosslyn (Warden Haines), Dixie Lee (Rosie), Linda Lightfoot (Wanda), Charles Joseph Martin (Willis), Sandy Martin (Kay), Durga McBroom (Willow), Adzine Melliti (Gino), Michelle Newkirk (Bonnie), Dave Nicolson (D.A.), Carol Porter (Candy), Joanelle Nadine Romero (Elena), Kin Shriner (Steve Nelson), Gamy L. Taylor (Judge Stivers), Marianne Taylor (Star), Marshall Teague (Paul)

BEDROOM EYES (Aquarius Releasing) Producers, Robert Lantos, Stephen J. Roth; Director, William Fruet; Screenplay, Michael Alan Eddy; Photography, Miklos Lente; Editor, Tony Lower; Color; Rated R: 90 minutes; September release. CAST: Kenneth Gilman (Harry), Dayle Haddon (Alixe), Barbara Law (Jobeth)

RADIOACTIVE DREAMS (De Laurentiis Entertainment Group) Producers, Thomas Karnowski, Moctesuma Esparza; Director/Screenplay, Albert F. Pyun; Photography, Charles Minsky; Music, Pete Robinson; Color; Rated R; 94 minutes; September release. CAST: John Stockwell, Michael Dudikoff, George Kennedy, Don Murray, Michele Little, Norbert Weiser, Lisa Blount

VASECTOMY: A DELICATE MATTER (Vandom International Pictures) Producers, Robert Burge, Lou Wills; Director, Robert Burge; Screenplay, Robert Hilliard, Robert Burge; Photography, Gary Thieltges; Editor, Beth Conwell; Music, Fred Karlin; Color; Rated PG-13; 90 minutes; September release. CAST: Paul Sorvino, Cassandra Edwards, Abe Vigoda, Ina Balin, June Wilkinson, William Marshall, Lorne Greene

A ZED AND TWO NOUGHTS (BFI Productions) Producers, Peter Sainsbury, Kees Kasander; Director/Screenplay, Peter Greenaway; Photography, Sacha Vierny, Editor, John Wilson; Music, Michael Nyman; Not rated; 115 minutes; September release. CAST: Andrea Ferreol (Alba Bewick), Brian Deacon (Oswald Deuce), Eric Deacon (Oliver Deuce), Frances Barber (Venus de Milo), Joss Ackland (Van Hoyten), Jim Davidson (Joshua Plate) Agnes Brulet (Beta Bewick), Guusje Van Tilborgh (Caterina Bolnes), Gerard Thoolen (Van Meegeren), Ken Campbell (Stephen Pipe)

THE PATRIOT (Crown International) Producer, Michael Bennett; Director/Photography, Frank Harris; Associate Producer, Diane Harris; Screenplay, Andy Ruben, Katt Shea Ruben; Casting, Paul Bengston, David Cohn; Editor, Richard E. Westover; Music, Jay Ferguson; Production Manager/Assistant Director, Scott Javine; Art Director, Brad Einhorn; Set Decorator, Tori Nourafchan; Special Effects, Fred Cramer; Costumes, Robin Lewis; Assistant Director, William Shea; Production Co-ordinator, Alan Z. McCurdy; Sound, Glenn Berkovitz; Stunts, John Barrett; Executive Producer, Mark Tenser; Music Supervisor, Budd Carr; Songs by various artists; Foto Kem Color; Rated R; 90 minutes; September release. CAST: Gregg Henry (Ryder), Simone Griffeth (Sean), Michael J. Pollard (Howard), Jeff Conaway (Mitchell), Stack Pierce (Atkins), Leslie Nielsen (Adm. Frazer), Glenn Withrow (Pink), Larry Mintz (Bite), Diane Stevenett (Maggie), Anthony Calderella (Eight Ball), Mike Gomez (Kenwood), Larry Moss (Devon), Smith Osborne (Rosa), and Sally Brown, Mike Muscat, Lorin Vail, Gene Lehfeldt, Gary Kalpakoff, B. L. Foley, Andy Lentz, Rick McCallum, Peter Griffin, Ron Adams, Ross Borden, Jacqueline Jacobs

THRASHIN' (Fries Entertainment) Executive Producers, Charles Fries, Mike Rosenfeld; Producer, Alan Sacks; Director, David Winters; Screenplay, Paul Brown, Alan Sacks; Photography, Chuck Colwell; Editor, Nicholas Smith; Designer, Katheryn Hardwick; Music, Barry Goldberg; Casting, Gino Havens; Color; Rated PG-13; 90 minutes; September release. CAST: Josh Brolin (Cory Webster), Robert Rusler (Tommy Hook), Pamela Gidlay (Chrissy), Brooke McCarter (Tyler), Brett Marx (Bozo), Josh Richman (Radley), David Wagner (Little Stevie), Sherilyn Fenn (Velvet)

DANCES SACRED AND PROFANE Producer, Thunder Basin Films; Producer/Director/Editor, Mark Jury, Dan Jury; Based on books of photographer-anthropologist Charles Gatewood; Photography, Dany Jury; Sound, Mark Jury; Music, Larry Gelb; A presentation of Valley Filmworks; Documentary; Color; Not rated; 80 minutes; October release. Narrator: Charles Gatewood

Kathrine Forster, Robert Forster
in "Harry's Machine" © *Cannon*

HARRY'S MACHINE aka *Hollywood Harry* (Cannon Group) Producers, Robert Forster, The Starquilt Company; Director, Robert Forster; Screenplay, Curt Allen; Music, Michael Lang; Photography, Gideon Porath; Editor, Rich Meyer; Color; Not rated; 96 minutes; October release. CAST: Robert Forster (Harry), Joe Spinell (Max), Shannon Wilcox (Candy), Kathrine Forster (Danielle) (no other credits submitted)

THE TOMB (Trans World Entertainment) Producers, Fred Olen Ray, Ronnie Hadar; Executive Producers, Richard Kaye, Paul Hertzberg; Director, Fred Olen Ray; Screenplay, Kenneth J. Hall; Additional Dialog & Material, T. L. Lankford; Photography, Paul Elliott; Editor/Coproducer, Miriam L. Preissel; Music, Drew Neumann; Sound, Stephan Von Hase; Art Director, Maxine Shepard; Production Manager, Robert Tinnell; Assistant Director, Tony Brewster; Special Effects Animation, Bret Mixon; Special Makeup Effects, Makeup & Effects Lab; Costumes, Elizabeth A. Reid; Stunts, John Stewart; Color; Not rated; 84 minutes; October release. CAST: Cameron Mitchell (Prof. Phillips), John Carradine (Mr. Androheb), Sybil Danning (Jade), Susan Stokey (Helen), Richard Alan Hench (David Manners), Michelle Bauer (Nefratis), David Pearson (John Banning), George Hoth (Dr. Stewart), and Stu Weltman, Frank McDonald, Victor Von Wright, Jack Frankel, Peter Conway, Brad Arrington, Emanuel Shipow, Craig Hamann, Kitten Natividad, Dawn Wildsmith

AMERICA (ASA Communications) Producer, Paul A. Leeman; Executive Producer, Paul E. Cohen; Director/Screenplay, Robert Downey; Additional Dialog, Sidney Davis; Photography, Richard Price; Editor, C. Vaughn Hazell; Music, Leon Pendarvis; Sound, Lawrence Hoff, Ron Harris, Frank Stettner; Creative Consultant, Ralph Rosenblum; Art Director, C. J. Strawn; Assistant Director, Forrest Murray; Production Manager/Associate Producer, Ron Nealy; Additional Photography, Michael Sullivan, Terry Kosher, Michael Davis; Production Supervisor, Elliott Schwartz; A Moonbeam Associates production; Movielab/Guffanti Color; Rated R; 83 minutes; October release. CAST: Zack Norman (Terrance Hackley), Tammy Grimes (Joy Hackley), Michael J. Pollard (Bob Jolly), Richard Belzer (Gypsy Baum), Monroe Arnold (Floyd), Liz Torres (Dolores), Pablo Ferro (Hector), David Kerman (Mr. Management), Howard Thomashefsky (Earl), Michael Bahr (Martin), Laura Ashton (Tina), and Robert Downey Jr., Corinne Alphen, Minnie Gentry, Chuck Griffin, Ron Nealy, Forrest Murray, Melvin Van Peebles, Michael Rubenstein, Rudy Wurlitzer

Leslie Nielsen, Gregg Henry, Simone Griffeth
in "The Patriot" © *Crown International* **139**

**Mako, David Carradine
in "Armed Response"** © *CineTel*

**Lloyd Bridges, Chris Lemmon
in "Weekend Warriors"** © *Movie Store*

ARMED RESPONSE (Cinetel Films) Producer, Paul Hertzberg; Executive Producer, Lisa Hansen; Director/Co-producer, Fred Olen Ray; Screenplay, T. L. Lankford; In color; Rated R; 85 minutes; October release. CAST: Lee Van Cleef (Burt Roth), David Carradine (Jim), Brent Huff (Tommy Roth), Laurene Landon (Deborah Silverstein), Mako (Akira Tanaka), Lois Hamilton (Sara Roth), Michael Berryman (Akira's Assistant)

COMBAT SHOCK (Troma Team) Produced/Directed/Written by Buddy Giovanazzo; Photography, Stella Varveris; Associate Producers, Jerry Giovinazzo, Lori Labar, John Giovanazzo; Sound, Howie Murphy, Music, Ricky Giovinazzo; Special Effects, Ed Varuolo, Jeff Matthes; Executive Producers, Lloyd Kaufman, Michael Herz; In color; Rated R; 96 minutes; October release. CAST: Ricky Giovinazzo (Frankie Dunlan), Veronica Stork (Cathy Dunlan), Mitch Maglio (Paco), Aspah Livni (Labo), Nick Nasta (Morbe), Mike Tierno (Mike), Mary Cristadoro (Mary), and Ginny Cattano, Doo Kim, Leo Lunney, Bob Mireau, Nancy Zawada, Ed Pepitone, Brendan Tesoriero, Ray Pinero, Jim Cooney, Yon Lai, Shinri Saito, Martin Blank, Clare Harnedy, Carmine Giovinazzo, Melissa Tait, Stacy Tait, Arthur Saunders, Lori Labar, Janet Ramage, Collette Geraci, Dean Mercil, Vinnie Petrizzo.

VACATION NICARAGUA (Rock Solid) Producer/Director, Anita Clearfield; Executive Producer, David A. Griffin; Editor/Photography, Geoffrey Leighton; Sound, John Luck; Lighting, Cathy Zheutlin; In color; Not rated; 77 minutes; October release. A documentary.

FROM BEYOND (Empire Pictures) Producer, Brian Yuzna; Executive Producer, Charles Band; Line Producer, Roberto Bessi; Director, Stuart Gordon; Screenplay, Dennis Paoli; Adapted from story by H. P. Lovecraft; Adaptation, Brian Yuzna, Dennis Paoli, Stuart Gordon; Photography, Mac Ahlberg; Editor, Lee Percy; Music, Richard Band; Designer, Giovanni Natalucci; Set Decorator, Robert Burns; Special Effects, John Buechler, Anthony Doublin, John Naulin, Mark Shostrom; Costumes, Angee Beckett; Sound, Mario Bramonti; Associate Producer, Bruce Curtis; Assistant Director, Mauro Sacripanti; Technicolor; Ultra-Stereo; Rated R; 85 minutes; October release. CAST: Jeffrey Combs (Crawford Tillinghast), Barbara Crampton (Dr. Katherine McMichaels), Ted Sorel (Dr. Edward Pretorious), Ken Foree (Bubba Brownlee), Carolyn Purdy-Gordon (Dr. Roberta Bloch), Bunny Summers (Hester Gilman), Bruce McGuire (Jordan Fields)

WEEKEND WARRIORS (The Movie Store) Executive Producers, Bert Convy, Stanley Fimberg; Producer, Hannah Hempstead; Director, Bert Convy; Story, Bruce Belland; Screenplay, Bruce Belland, Roy M. Rogosin; Photography, Charles Minsky; Designer, Chester Kaczenski; Production Executive, Cami Taylor; Editor, Raja Gosnell; Casting, Junie Lowry; Music, Perry Botkin; Color; Rated R; 85 minutes; October release. CAST: Chris Lemmon (Vince Tucker), Vic Tayback (Sgt. Burge), Lloyd Bridges (Col. Archer), Graham Jarvis (Congressman Balljoy), Daniel Greene (Phil McCracken), Marty Cohen (Decola), Brian Bradley (Cory Seacomb), Matt McCoy (Ames), Alan Campbell (Duckworth), Tom Villard (Mort Seblinsky), Jeff Meyer (Tom Dawson), Mark Taylor (Capt. Cabot), Gail Barle (Nurse Nancy), La Gena Hart (Debbie), Brenda Strong (Danielle), Frank Mugavero (Timmy Barker), Art Kimbro (Izzy), Juney Smith (Ain't), Jennifer Convy (Vanessa), Gretchen Gray (Secretary), Lou Tiano (Beckman), Camille Saviola (Betty Beep)

TRICK OR TREAT (De Laurentiis Entertainment Group) Producers, Michael S. Murphey, Joel Soisson; Director, Charles Martin Smith; Screenplay, Michael S. Murphey, Joel Soisson, Rhet Topham; Story, Rhet Topham; Associate Producer, Scott White; Photography, Robert Elswit; Editor, Jane Schwartz Jaffe; Designer, Curt Schnell; Music, Christopher Young, Fastway; Music Producer, Stephen E. Smith; Stunts, Dan Bradley; Special Make-Up, Kevin Yahger; Optical Effects, Richard Malzahn, David S. Williams, Jr.; Costumes, Jill Ohanneson; Production Manager, Scott White; Assistant Directors, Matia Karrell, Benita Ann Allen, Ken Hudson; Production Coordinator, Barbara D'Alessandro; Art Director, Colin D. Irwin; Sound, Ed White; Assistant Costume Designer, Robin Lewis Burton; Mechanical Effects, Steve Wolke; Songs by various artists; Soundtrack on CBS/Columbia Records; Ultrastereo; Technicolor; Rated R; 97 minutes; October release. CAST: Marc Price (Eddie Weinbauer), Tony Fields (Sammi Curr), Lisa Orgolini (Leslie Graham), Doug Savant (Tim Hainey), Elaine Joyce (Angie Weinbauer), Glen Morgan (Roger Mockus), Gene Simmons (Nuke), Ozzy Osbourne (Rev. Aaron Gilstrom), Elise Richards (Genie Wooster), Richard Pachorek (Ron Avery), Clare Nono (Maggie Wong-Hernandez), Alice Nunn (Mrs. Clavell), Larry Sprinkle (Marv McCain)L Charles Martin Smith (Mr. Wimbley), and Claudia Templeton, Denny Pierce, Ray Shaffer, Brad Thomas, Terry Loughlin, Graham Smith, Kevin Yahger, Amy Bertolette, Leroy Sweet, Barry Bell, Steve Boles, James D. Nelson, Richard Doyle

"Combat Shock"
© *Troma Team*

**Ozzy Osbourne, Tony Fields, Gene Simmons
in "Trick or Treat"** © *DeLaurentiis*

**Katharine Ross, Bryan Fowler, Willie Nelson
in "Red Headed Stranger"** © *Alive Films*

**Michael Sharrett, Krysty Swanson, Matthew Laborteaux
in "Deadly Friend"** © *Warner Bros.*

RED HEADED STRANGER (Alive Films) Producers, Willie Nelson, Bill Wittliff; Director/Screenplay, Bill Wittliff; Music, Willie Nelson; Associate Producers, David Anderson, Ethel Vosgitel, Barry Fey; Photography, Neil Roach; Editor, Eric Austin Williams, Stephen H. Purvis; Designer, Cary White; Casting, Connie Todd Ray; Costumes, Lana Nelson; Production Manager, Dick Gallegly; Assistant Directors, Tommy Thompson, William Cosentino; Sound, Art Rochester; Sound Effects, Doug Hemphill; Special Effects, Jack Bennett, Jack Bennett, Jr., Ken Miller; Stunts, Joe Kidd, J. P. Swann; Color; Rated R; 105 minutes; October release. CAST: Willie Nelson (Julian), Morgan Fairchild (Raysha), Katharine Ross (Laurie), R. G. Armstrong (Scoby), Royal Dano (Larn Claver), Sonny Carl Davis (Odie Claver), Marinell Madden (Cindy), Ted J. Crum (Cauley Felps), Bryan Fowler (Nathan), Paul English (Avery Claver), Bee Spears (Eugene Claver), Dennis Hill (Carl Claver), Mark Jenkins (Victor Claver), Berkley Garrett (Rev. Longley), Elberta Hunter (Mrs. Longley), and Mark Voges, John Dodson, John Browing, Julius Tennon, JoAnne Russell, Bob Boothe, Bill Richardson, Robert Kuhn, Ralph Ware, Joe K. Longley, Steve Uzzell, Jubal Clark, James Wong, Martha Fowler, Allison Wittliff, Amy McMichael, Ada Harden, Ken Thomas, Billy Cooper, Bill Russell, Bo Franks, Russ Russell, Ralph Franzetti, Ralph Willard, Priscilla Dougherty, Pam Hale, Sandra Hale, Lana Nelson, Janna Phillips, Jo Carroll Pierce, Lauren Stone, Linette Themer

RECRUITS (Concorde) Producer, Maurice Smith; Director, Rafal Zielinski; Screenplay, Charles Wiener, B. K. Roderick; Music, Steve Parsons; Art Director, Craig Richards; Costumes, Eva Gord; Production Supervisor, Ken Gord; Assistant Directors, Rob Malenfant, George Collins, Chris Geggie; Production Co-ordinator, Mike Dolgy; Sound, Urmas John Rosin; Editors, Stephen Fanfara, Christie Wilson; Stunts, Marco Bianco; Color; Rated R; 82 minutes; October release. CAST: Steve Osmond (Steve), Doug Annear (Mike), Alan Deveau (Howie), John Terrell (Winston), Lolita Davidoff (Susan), Tracey Tanner (Brazil), Annie McAuley (Tanya), Tony Travis (Stonewall), Mike McDonald (Magruder), Colleen Karney (Sgt. S.), Jason Logan (Mayor Bagley), Caroline Tweedle (Mrs. Bagley), Mark Blutman (Clint), John Mikl Thor (Thunderhead), Tom Melisus, Frank Savage (Biker's), Adrien Dorval (Beast), Herb Field (Rummy), Terry Howsen (Billy Bob), Kim Cayer (Lady Biker), Al Therian (Yacht Owner), Bob Segarini (Creep), Bruce Bell (Husband), Kimberly McCoy (Wife), John Wing (Accountant), Frank Thompson (Gov. Foster), Dominique St. Croix (Mrs. Foster), Karen Wood (Cheerleader)

DEADLY FRIEND (Warner Bros.) Producer, Robert M. Sherman; Director, Wes Craven; Screenplay, Bruce Joel Rubin; Based on the novel *"Friend"* by Diana Henstell; Photography, Philip Lathrop; Designer, Daniel Lomino; Editor, Michael Eliot; Music, Charles Bernstein; Executive Producer, Patrick Kelley; Co-producer, Robert L. Crawford; Production Manager, Phil Rawlins; Assistant Directors, Nicholas Batchelor, Peter Graupner; Set Decorator, Edward J. McDonald; Set Designer, Roy Barnes; "BB" Robot, Robotics 21, Ray Raymond; "BB" Shell Design, Keith Huber; Mime Coach, Richmond Shepard; Sound, Richard Church; Costumers, Barton "Kent" James, Carol Brown-James; Special Effects, Peter Albiez; Special Makeup Effects, Lance Anderson; A Pan Arts/Layton Production; Color; Panavision; Rated R; 99 minutes; October release. CAST: Matthew Laborteaux (Paul), Kristy Swanson (Samantha), Michael Sharrett (Tom), Anne Twomey (Jeannie), Anne Ramsey (Elvira), Richard Marcus (Harry), Russ Martin (Dr. Johanson), Lee Paul (Sgt. Volchek), Andrew Roperto (Carl), Charles Fleischer (Voice of "BB"), Robin Nuyen (Thief), and Frank Cavestani, Merritt Olsen, William H. Faeth, Joel Hile, Tom Spratley, Jim Ishida

A COMPOSER'S NOTES: PHILIP GLASS AND THE MAKING OF AN OPERA (Film Forum) Producer/Director, Michael Blackwood; Photography, Mead Hunt; Editor, Peter Geismar; Associate Producers, Mead Hunt, Peter Geismar; Color; Not Rated; 87 minutes; October release. CAST: Philip Glass (Narrator), and with the participation of the artists of the Wurttemberg State Theatre in Stuttgart and the Houston Grand Opera

COOL RUNNINGS: THE REGGAE MOVIE *(R5/S8)* Producer/Director/Writer/Editor, Robert Mugge; Executive Producer, Tony Johnson; Associate Producers, Ronnie Burke, Don Green, John Wakeling; Photography/Steadicam, Lawrence McConkey; Steadicam Assistant, Anastas Michos; Camera, Lawrence McConkey, Eric Roland, Chris Li, David Sperling; Sound, William Barth; Music Mixing, Dominick Maita; Sound Mixing, Tom Fleischman; Lighting, John Swaby; Stage/Lighting Design, Neville Garrick; Assistants to Director, Pauline Johnson-Henry, Adrian Irvine, Dana Yuricich; Produced by Mug-Shot Productions for Sunsplash Filmworks Ltd.; Songs by various artists; Color; 24-track audio recording; Dolby "Surround" Stereo; Not Rated; 105 minutes. CAST: Third World, Rita Marley, Musical Youth, Gil Scott-Heron, Mutabaruka, Gregory Isaacs, Chalice, Sugar Minott, Bankie Banx, Judy Mowatt, Melody Makers, The Skatalites, Alton Ellis, Tony Johnson, Larry MacDonald, Barry Gordon, Tommy Cowan, Bagga Brown

**Willie Nelson, Morgan Fairchild
in "Red Headed Stranger"** © *Alive Films*

Third World in "Cool Runnings"
© *R5/S8*

Paula de Koenigsberg, Lucy Winer
in "Rate It X" © *Tom Waldron*

Louie Anderson, S. L. Baird, Sondra Locke,
Gerrit Graham, Robert Townsend in "Ratboy"
© *Warner Bros.*

RATE IT X (Nicole Jouve Interama) Producers/Directors, Lucy Winer, Paula de Koenigsberg; Executive Producers, Lynn Campbell, Claudette Charbonneau; Music/Lyrics, Elizabeth Swados; Photography, Paula de Koenigsberg; Editor/Interviewer, Lucy Winer; Associate Editor, Allyson Smith; Associate Producer, Karen Eaton; Based on a concept by Claudette Charbonneau; Documentary; Not Rated; 95 minutes; October release

RATBOY (Warner Bros.) Producer/Production Manager, Fritz Manes; Director, Sondra Locke; Screenplay, Rob Thompson; Music, Lennie Niehaus; Editor, Joel Cox; Designer, Edward Carfagno; Photography, Bruce Surtees; Associate Producers, David Valdez, Rob Thompson; Assistant Directors, David Valdes, L. Dean Jones, Jr.; Ratboy Design, Rick Baker; Sound, C. Darin Knight; Special Effects, Wayne Edgar; Set Designer, Bob Sessa; Costumes, Glenn Wright, Deborah Ann Hopper, Darryl Athons; Songs by various artists; A Malpaso Production; Technicolor; Panavision; Rated PG-13; 104 minutes; October release. CAST: Sondra Locke (Nikki Morrison), Robert Townsend (Manny), Christopher Hewett (Acting Coach), Larry Hankin (Jewell), Sydney Lassick (Dial-A-Prayer), Gerrit Graham (Billy Morrison), Louie Anderson (Omer Morrison), S. L. Baird (Ratboy), Billie Bird (Psychic), John Witherspoon (Heavy), Charles Bartlett, Lee de Broux, Jeffrey Josephson, Peter Looney (Catullus Cops), Tiger Haynes (Derelict Ralph), Gary Riley (Bill), Gordon Anderson (Ratboy's Voice), Nina Blackwood (MTV Vee-Jay), Damita Jo Freeman (Louise), Lisa Cloud (Zu-Zu), and Courtney Gains, Winifred Freedman, Lisa Figueroa, Diane Delano, Brett Halsey, Steve Bassett, Lloyd Nelson, Don Sparks, Durk Pearson, Sandy Shaw, Michael Canavan, Theresa DePaolo, Virginia Peters, Grant Loud, Ed Williams, Albert Michel, Jr., M. C. Gainey, Sam Ingraffia, Dahlia Pujol, Clifford Shegog

PLAYING FOR KEEPS (Universal) Producers, Alan Brewer, Bob Weinstein, Harvey Weinstein; Directors, Bob Weinstein, Harvey Weinstein; Screenplay, Bob Weinstein, Harvey Weinstein, Jeremy Leven; Executive Producers, Julia Palau, Michael Ryan, Patrick Wachsberger; Photography, Eric Van Haren Noman; Editors, Gary Karr, Sharyn Ross; Musical Director, Alan Brewer; Original Score, George Acogny, Daniel Bechet; Designer, Waldemar Kalinowski; Associate Producer/Production Manager, Ira Halberstadt; Costumes, Aude Bronson-Howard; Choreographers, Lynnette Barkley, Ronn Forella, Alison Pearl; Assistant Directors, James Chory, Ellen H. Schwartz; Art Director, Steve Miller; Sound, Neil Kaufman; Consultant, Jeffrey Silver; Fireworks, Grucci; Costume Painting, Gail Bartly; Songs by various artists; Original Soundtrack on Atlantic Records or EMI Records; Panavision; Color; Dolby Stereo; Rated PG-13; 103 minutes; October release. CAST: Daniel Jordana (Danny), Matthew Penn (Spikes), Leon W. Grant (Silk), Mary B. Ward (Chloe), Marisa Tomei (Tracy), Jimmy Baio (Steinberg), Harold Gould (Rockefeller), Kim Hauser (Marie), Robert Milli (Cromwell), John Randolf Jones (Sheriff), and Bruce Kluger, Anthony Marciona, Glen Robert Robillard, J. D. Rosenbaum, Frank Scasso, Lisa Schultz, Doug Warhit, Peter Antico, John Anzaloni, Anthony Arcure, Harrison Balthaser, Jack Banning, Ronnie Baron, Raymond Barry, John Bennes, Robert Berger, Joel Blake, Hildy Brooks, Bonnie Jean Brown, Joseph R. Burns, Teresa Burns, William Burton, Peter Carew, Timothy Carhart, Madelaine Carol, Edna Chew, Sheila Coonan, John Corcoran, William Cosgriff, Agnes Cummings, Pat De Vita, Gena D'Orazio, Anita Ehrler, Frank Faldermeyer, Paul Finan, Edie Fleming, Clement Fowler, Martha Frei, Germaine Goodson, Kevin Hagan, Frank Rollins Harrison, Jery Hewitt, Hal Holden, Steven Hurwitz, Ruth Judd, Philip Kraus, Jerry Leonti, Bonnie Lewis, David Lile, David Lipman, Monique Mannen, Michael May, Tom McDermott, Jerry McGee, Liz McLellan, Court Miller, Donna Moore, Charles Morelli, Katherine Elizabeth Neuman, William Newman, Joseph J. O'Brien, Max Olivas, Brad Orrison, Lenore Pemberton, Charles Picerni Jr., Jeff Pope, Albert Rutherford, Carol Schuberg, William Soose, Donald Sharton, Jeanne Spillane, Susan Skeed, Larry Swansen, Willy Wsitkes, Raymond Thorne, Sel Vitella, Vickie Weinstein, Kelly Wolf, Louise Woolf

HARDBODIES 2 (CineTel Films) Producers, Jeff Begun, Ken Solomon, Dimitri Logothetis, Joseph Medawar; Director, Mark Griffiths; Screenplay, Mark Griffiths, Curtis Wilmot; Photography, Tom Richmond; Editor, Andy Blumenthal; Music, Jay Levy, Eddie Arkin; Art Director, Theodosis Davlos; Production Manager, Dimitri Dimitriadis; Hair, Loraine Watson; Makeup, Stella Votsou; Wardrobe, Dimitra Stayropoulou; Associate Producer, Costa Catsaris; Assistant Editor, Claudia Hoover; Assistant Art Director, Beau Peterson; Casting, F. Daniel Somrack; A Lee Fry/Chroma III/First American Film Production; Color; Rated R; 88 minutes; October release. CAST: Brad Zutaut (Scott), Sam Temeles (Rags), Curtis Scott Wilmot (Sean), Brenda Bakke (Morgan), Fabiana Udenio (Cleo), Louise Baker (Cookie), James Karen (Logan), Alba Francesca (Zacherly), Sorrells Pickard (Carlton Ashby), Roberta Collins (Lana Logan), Julie Rhodes (Ms. Rollins), Alexi Mylones (Brucie), George Tzifos (Father), Ula Gavala (Kidnapper's Wife), George Kotandis (Kidnapper)

Marisa Tomei, Matthew Penn
in "Playing for Keeps" © *Universal*

Robert Townsend, John Witherspoon, S. L. Baird
in "Ratboy" © *Warner Bros.*

DEADTIME STORIES (Bedford Entertainment) Producer, Bill Paul; Director, Jeffrey Delman; Executive Producers, William J. Links, Steven D. Mackler; Associate Producers, Edwin Picker, Bernard E. Goldberg; Photography, Daniel B. Canton; Music, Larry Juris; Screenplay, Jeffrey Delman, Charles F. Shelton, J. Edward Kiernan; Editor, Jim Rivera; Special Effects Make-up, Edward French, Bryant Tausek; Color; Rated R; 81 minutes; October release. CAST: Scott Valentine, Melissa Leo, Cathryn De Prume, Anne Redfern, Nicole Picard, Matt Mitler, Kathy Fleig, Phyllis Craig (No other credits submitted)

THE WRAITH (New Century Productions Ltd.) Producer, John Kemeny; Director/Screenplay, Mike Marvin; Photography, Reed Smoot; Editors, Scott Conrad, Gary Rocklin; Music, Michael Hoenig, J. Peter Robinson; Color; Rated PG-13; 90 minutes; November release. CAST: Charlie Sheen (The Wraith/Jake), Nick Cassavetes (Packard), Sherilyn Fenn (Keri), Randy Quaid (Loomis), Matthew Barry (Billy), David Sherrill (Skank), Jamie Bozian (Gutterboy), Clint Howard (Rughead)

INSIDE OUT (Beckerman) Producer, Sidney Beckerman; Director, Robert Taicher; Screenplay, Robert Taicher, Kevin Bartelme; Photography, Jack Wallner; Editor, David Finfer; Music, Peer Raben; Sound, Steve Nelson; Art Director, Jack Wright 3rd; Costumes, Arlene Ansel; In color; Not rated; 87 minutes; November release. CAST: Elliott Gould (Jimmy Morgan), Howard Hesseman, Jennifer Tilly, Beah Richards, Nicole Norman, John Bleifer, Dana Elcar

IMPURE THOUGHTS (ASA Communications) Executive Producers, Kirk K. Smith, Stan M. Wakefield; Producers, William VanDer-Kloot, Michael A. Simpson, Michael J. Simpson; Director, Michael A. Simpson; Editor/Photography, William VanDerKloot; Music, James Oliverio; Design, Guy Tuttle; Sound, David Terry; Sister of Purgatory narrated by Dame Judith Anderson; Not rated; In Eastmancolor; 83 minutes; November release. CAST: John Putch (Danny Stubbs), Terry Beaver (William Miller), Brad Dourif (Kevin Harrington), Lane Davies (Steve Barrett), Benji Wilhoite (Young Bill), J. J. Sacha (Young Danny), Sam McPhaul (Young Kevin), Jason Jones (Young Steve), Mary McDonough (Sister Juliet), Joe Conley (Father Minnelli), Mary Nell Santacroce (Sister Gertrude), Charlie Hill (Bill Miller, Sr.), Carmen Thomas (Marie Borkowsky), Sandra Dorsey, Randi Layne, Muriel Moore, Carol Haynes, Dennis Harrington, Bob Bost, Shirlene Foss

KAMIKAZE HEARTS (Legler/Bashore) Producer, Heinz Legler; Director, Juliet Bashore; Conceived and Written by Juliet Bashore, Tigr Mennett; Photography, David Golia; Editor, John Knoop; Art-Set Directors, Hans Fuss, Miriam Tinguely; Music, Paul M. Young, Walt Fowler; Sound, Leslie Schatz; Coproducers, Sharon Hennessey, Bob Rivkin; In color; Not rated; 87 minutes; November release. A documentary on porno performers.

EYE OF THE TIGER (Scotti Bros.) Producer, Tony Scotti; Executive Producers, Herb Nanas, Ben Scotti; Director, Richard Sarafian; Screenplay, Michael Montgomery; Photography, Peter Collister; Sound, Dennis Carr; Editor, Greg Prange; Assistant Directors, Scott Maitland, Leo Zisman; Production Coordinator, Pilar Stallwort; Art Director, Wayne Springfield; Set Director, Kurt Gauger; In United Color; Rated R; 90 minutes; November release. CAST: Gary Busey (Buck Matthews), Yaphet Kotto (J. B. Deveraux), Seymour Cassel (Sheriff), Bert Remsen (Father Healy), William Smith (Blade), Kimberlin Ann Brown (Dawn), Denise Galik (Christie), Judith Barsi (Jennifer), Eric Bolles (Doctor), Joe Brooks (Jake)

EYES ON THE PRIZE: AMERICA'S CIVIL RIGHTS YEARS, 1954–1965 (Film Forum) a documentary compilation of six one-hour films; Executive Producer, Henry Hampton; Series Senior Producer, Judith Vecchione; Series Producer, Jan Else; Documentary; For Black-side, Inc.; 6 hours, presented in two 3-hour screenings; Not rated; November release

50 YEARS OF ACTION! (DMS Production Services) Producer/Director/Screenplay, Douglass M. Stewart, Jr.; Photography, John A. Alonzo, Caleb Deschanel, Chuck Clifton; Additional Photography, James Mathers; Editors, John Soh, Douglas M. Stewart, Jr.; Music, Bill Conti; Art Director, Jim Clayter; Associate Producer, Soh; Assistant Directors, Walter Gilmore, Steven Tramz, Joe Napolitano, Dwight Williams; Sound, Fred Ginsburg, John Lifavi, Mike Lonsdale; A Directors Guild of America Golden Jubilee Committee presentation; Documentary; CFI Color; Not rated; 60 minutes; November release CAST: Richard Crenna (Narrator), Morris R. Abrams, Stanley Ackerman, Woody Allen, John A. Alonzo, Warren Beatty, Steve Besner, Richard Brooks, Hiram Brown, Gilbert Cates, Michael Cimino, Martha Coolidge, Norman Corwin, William Crain, Chico Day, Tom Donovan, Edward Dmytryk, Milos Forman, Arthur Forrest, Michael H. Franklin, George L. George, Alan Gordon, John Huston,

"Hollywood Zap"
© *Troma Team*

Elia Kazan, Kim Kurumada, Sheldon Leonard, Dan Lew, Lynne Littman, Sidney Lumet, Rouben Mamoulian, Joseph L. Mankiewicz, Fletcher Markle, Patricia McBrearty, Adam Merims, Richard Mutschler, Gordon Parks, Ernest Ricca, Martin Ritt, John Rich, John Schlesinger, Gene Searchinger, Susan Seidelman, George Sidney, Joan Micklin Silver, Elliot Silverstein, James E. Wall, Robert Wise, Joseph C. Youngerman

HOLLYWOOD ZAP (Troma) Producers, Bobbi Frank, Ben Frank; Director/Screenplay, David Cohen; Special Consultant to Director/Executive Producer, Dror Soref; Photography, Tom Frisby Fraser; Production Supervisor/Editor, Rick Westover; Casting, Janet Cunningham; Music, Art Podell, James Ackley, Paul Hertzog; Production Manager, Rick Murken; Assistant Directors, Steve Budde, KC Nichols, Modi Frank; Art Director, Vicki Auth; Assistant Art Director, Lucinda Foy; Costumes, Judith B. Curtis; Sound, Don Sanders; Assistant Editor, Bob Bowman; Fotokem Color; Rated R; 93 minutes; November release. CAST: Ben Frank (Nash), Ivan E. Roth (Tucker), De Waldron (Tee Tee), Annie Gaybis (Debbie), and Millie Moss, Shirley Prestia, Addington Wise, Sandy Rose, Claude Earl Jones, Don Carmona, Nancye Ferguson, Chuck "Porky" Mitchell, Carmen Filpi, Stan Ross, Helen Verbit, Jason Edwards, Louise Hartley, Walter Stocker, Neil Flanagan, Tony Cox, Wayne Montanio, Eric Marvin

WIRED TO KILL (American Distribution Group) Producer, Jim Buchfuehrer; Director/Screenplay, Franky Schaeffer; Co-Producer, Peter Chesney; Executive Producer, Paul McGuire; Music, Russell Ferrante, The Yellow Jackets; Photography, Tom Fraser; Editor, Daniel Agulian, Franky Schaeffer; Assistant Director, Guy Louthan; Production Manager, Susan McShayne; Make-up/Make-up Effects, Michele Burke; Special Sound Effects, Alan Howarth; Special Mechanical Effects, Bruce Hayes; Art Director, Diana Williams; Set Decorator, Ainslee Colt DeWolf; Costumes, Dorothy Bulac, Steve Sleap; Special Effects, Scott Hass, Bernardo Munoz, Emmet Kane; Color; Dolby Stereo; Rated R; 96 minutes; November release. CAST: Emily Longstreth (Rebecca), Devin Hoelscher (Steve), Merritt Butrick (Reegus), Frank Collison (Sly), Garth Gardner (Loady), Tom Lister, Jr./Tiny (Sleet), Kim Milford (Rooster), Michael Wollet (Zero), Kristina David (Mother), Don Blakely (Sergeant), Dorothy Patterson (Grandmother), June C. Ellis (Snatch), and John Michael Stewart, Paul Short, Bob Bragg, Bob Ivey, Elliot Berk, Nolberto Huerta, Gary Bergher, Phillip Clark, Richard McGregor, Jeff Silverman, Ron Ross, Angela Adams, J. P. Bumstead, Gayle Vance, Charles Allen Anderson

Emily Longstreth, Devin Hoelscher in "Wired to Kill" © *American*

Ellen McElduff in "Dead End Kids"
© *Carol Rosegg*

Adam Coleman Howard, James Remar
in "Quiet Cool" © *New Line*

NEON MANIACS (Bedford Entertainment) Producers, Steven Mackler, Chris Arnold; Executive Producers, H. Frank Dominquez, Bernard E. Goldberg; Director Joseph Mangine; Screenplay, Mark Patrick Carducci; Photography, Joseph Mangine, Oliver Wood; Editor, Timothy Snell; Music, Kendall Schmidt; Sound, Peter Bentley, Ed White; Art Director, Katherine Vallin; Special Makeup Effects, Allan A. Apone, Douglas J. White; Special Effects, Image Engr.; Assistant Director, Linda Graeme; Costumes, Joseph Porro; Casting, Paul Bengston, David Cohn; Associate Producer/Production Manager, Herb Linsey; Associate Producers, Bran Arandjelovich, Edwin Picker, Brian Leonard; A Cimmaron production; Cinema color; Rated R; 91 minutes; November release. CAST: Allan Hayes (Steven), Leilani Sarelle (Nathalie), Donna Locke (Paula), Victor Elliot Brandt (Devin)

DEAD END KIDS (Film Forum) Producers, Monty Diamond, Marian Godfrey; Director/Screenplay, JoAnne Akalaitis; Based on play by Mabou Mines; Music, David Byrne, Philip Glass; Photography, Judy Irola; Not rated; 90 minutes; November release. CAST: Ellen McElduff (TV Hostess/Army Stenographer/School Teacher), Ruth Maleczech (Madame Curie), George Bartenieff (Faust/General Groves), David Brisbin (Comic/Gen. Farrell), B-St. John Schofield (Lecturer/Devil), Frederick Neumann (Alchemist/Academician), Terry O'Reilly (Magician Devil), Greg Mehrten (TV Technician/Devil)

STREETS OF GOLD (20th Century-Fox) Producers, Joe Roth, Harry Ufland; Director, Joe Roth; Co-Producers, Patrick McCormick, Dezo Magyar; Screenplay, Heywood Gould, Richard Price, Tom Cole; Story, Dezsö Magyar; Photography, Arthur Albert; Designer, Marcos Flaksman; Music, Jack Nitzsche, Brian Banks, Anthony Marinelli; Costumes, Jeffrey Kurland; Editor, Richard Chew; Production Manager, Patrick McCormick; Assistant Director, James Chory, Ellen Schwartz; Associate Producer, Paul Schiff; Fight Choreographer, Jimmy Nickerson; Associate Editor, Gary Karr; Production Coordinator, Kate Guinzburg; Art Director, Bill Pollock; Sound, Frank Stettner; Color; Rated R; 95 minutes; November release. CAST: Klaus Maria Brandauer (Alek Neuman), Adrian Pasdar (Timmy Boyle), Wesley Snipes (Roland Jenkins), Angela Molina (Elena Gitman), Elya Baskin (Klebanov), Rainbow Harvest (Brenda), Adam Nathan (Grisha), John Mahoney (Lineman), Jaroslav Stremien (Malinovsky), Dan O'Shea (Vinnie), Mike Beach (Sonny), John McCurry (Bobby Rainey), Jimmy Nickerson (Suvorov), Jeff Ward (Preston), Pete Antico (Balsamo), Dan Nutu (Semyon), Liya Glaz (Polina), Elizbieta Czyzewska (Mrs. Peshkov), Yacov Levitan (Mr. Peshkov), Alexander Yampolsky (Dimitri), David S. Chandler (Intern), Rene Rivera (Attendant), Frances Foster

(Nurse), and Bill Cobbs, Gregory Holtz, Sr., Grafton Trew, Ramon Rodriguez, Paul Davidovsky, Paul Herman, Frank Patton, John Garcia, Hechter Ubarry, Thomas Mendola, Jud Henry Baker, Luther Rucker, Eddie Mustafa Muhammad, Kevin Mahon, Vern De Paul, Jack Wilkes, James Babchak, Al Bernstein, Gene LeBell, Marty Denkin, Mike Radner

QUIET COOL (New Line Cinema) Producers, Robert Shaye, Gerald T. Olson; Director, Clay Borris; Screenplay, Clay Borris, Susan Vercellino; Associate Producer, Sara Risher; Executive Producers, Pierre David, Arthur Sarkissian, Larry Thompson; Music, Jay Ferguson; Photography, Jacques Haitkin; Editor, Bob Brady; Color; Rated R; 86 minutes; November release. CAST: James Remar, Adam Coleman Howard, Daphne Ashbrook, Jared Martin, Nick Cassavetes, Fran Ryan

PORKY PIG IN HOLLYWOOD (Films Incorporated) Originally Produced by Leon Schlesinger Productions for Warner Bros.; Compiled by George Feltenstein; Special Consultant, Greg Ford; Directors, Fred "Tex" Avery, I. "Friz" Freleng, Robert "Bob" Clampett, Frank Tashlin (aka Frank Tash), Charles M. "Chuck" Jones; Music, Carl Stallings; Writers include, Rich Hogan, Tubby Millar, Ben "Bugs" Hardaway, Frank Tashlin, Dave Monahan, Ernest Gee; Animators include, Rod Scribner, Charles M. "Chuck" Jones, Vive Risto, Bob McKimson, Robert "Bobo" Cannon, Norman McCabe, Virgil Ross, John Carey, I. Ellis; Animated; Black & White; Not Rated; 116 minutes; November release. VOICES: Mel Blanc and others.

THE BOSS' WIFE (Tri-Star) Producer, Thomas H. Brodek; Direction/Screenplay, Ziggy Steinberg; Photography, Gary P. Thieltges; Designer, Brenton Swift; Editor, John A. Martinelli; Music, Bill Conti; Casting, Karen Rea; Assistant Directors, Thomas A. Irvine, Steven Pomeroy, Eric Heffron, Scott Patterson; Art Directors, Albert J. Locatelli, Kathy Cahill; Decorator, K. C. Fox; Costumes, Jean-Pierre Dorleac; Production Coordinator, Laurel Walter; Metrocolor; Dolby Stereo; Rated R; 83 minutes; November release. CAST: Daniel Stern (Joel), Arielle Dombasle (Louise), Fisher Stevens (Carlos), Melanie Mayron (Janet), Lou Jacobi (Harry), Martin Mull (Tony), Christopher Plummer (Roalvang), Diane Stilwell (Suzy), Robert Costanzo (Eddie), Thalmus Rasulala (Barney), Jack Andreozzi (Doorman), Freddye Chapman (Marge), John Harwood (Roalvang Aide), Stanley Ralph Ross (Ticket Taker), Jim Hudson (Cop), Bill Grant (Red Cap), Clare Fields (Waitress), Chris Conte (Waiter), Obaka Adedunyo (Valet), Dave Adams (Conductor), Kedrick Wolfe (Maitre d'), John A. Martinelli (Barber), John Branagan, Joseph C. Gilbride

Wesley Snipes, Klaus Maria Brandauer, Adrian Pasdar
in "Streets of Gold" © *Roundhouse/Ken Howard*

Arielle Dombasle, Daniel Stern
in "The Boss' Wife" © *Tri-Star*

**Anat Atzmon, Benedict Taylor, Tom Hanks,
Cristina Marsillach in "Every Time We Say Goodbye"**
© *Tri-Star*

**John Putch, Mariska Hargitay
in "Welcome to 18"** © *American*

EVERY TIME WE SAY GOODBYE (Tri-Star) Producers, Jacob Kotzky, Sharon Harel; Director/Story, Moshe Mizrahi; Screenplay, Moshe Mizrahi, Rachel Fabien, Leah Appet; Music, Philippe Sarde; Editor, Mark Burns; Sound, Daniel Brisseau; Art Director, Micky Zahar; Photography, Giuseppe Lanci; Casting, Joy Todd, Sharon Howard Field, Levia Hon; Production Manager, Avner Peled; Line Producer, Eitan Evan; Production Coordinator, Ruthy Dassa-Lustig; Assistant Directors, Adi Shoval, Avi Mograbi; Costumes, Rona Doron; Stunts, Alberto Vaknin, Hadar Anafi, Avraham Itzhaki; Conductors, Bill Byers, David Kribushe; Color; Rated PG-13; 97 minutes; November release. CAST: Tom Hanks (David), Cristina Marsillach (Sarah), Benedict Taylor (Peter), Anat Atzmon (Victoria), Gila Almagor (Lea), Monny Moshanov (Nessin), Avner Hizkiyahu (Raphael), Caroline Goodall (Sally), Esther Parnass (Rosa), Daphne Armony (Clara), Orit Weisman (Mathilda), Ronit Lors (Ester), Moshe Ivgi (Daniel), David Menachem (Elie), Nissim Azikry (Shaltiel), Avi Keidar (Sammy), Alan Abovtboul (Joseph), Jacky Banian (Albert), Rivka Gour (Dinah), Jack Cohen (Solomon), Danni Muja (Sabriel), Orna Porat (Mrs. Finkelstein), and Gordy Mass, Ofera Ariav, Ilan Machora, "Hora Jerusalem", Anat Ben-Yehoshua

SOLARBABIES (MGM/UA) Producers, Irene Walzer, Jack Frost Sanders; Director, Alan Johnson; Screenplay, Walon Green, Douglas Anthony Metrov; Photography, Peter MacDonald; Designer, Anthony Pratt; Editor, Conrad Buff; Visual Effects, Richard Edlund; Costumes, Bob Ringwood; Music, Maurice Jarre; Production Supervisor, Dennis J. Parrish; Assistant Directors, Juan Carlos L. Rodero, Ian Woolf, Victor Albarran, Salvador Pons; Art Directors, Don Dossett, Les Tompkins, Paco Prosper, Fernando Gonzalez, Jose Maria Alarcon, Raul Paton; Set Decorator, Graham Sumner; Sound, Jim Willis; Special Effects, Nick Allder, Dick Parker, Alan Bryce, Antonio Parra, Antonio Balandin, Daniel Hutten; Sound Effects, Mark Magini; Make-up Effects, Steve Johnson, Eric Fiedler; Song, Smokey Robinson, Ivory Stone; Metrocolor; Dolby Stereo; Rated PG-13; 94 minutes; November release. CAST: Richard Jordan (Grock), Jami Gertz (Terra), Jason Patric (Jason), Lukas Haas (Daniel), James Le Gros (Metron), Claude Brooks (Rabbit), Peter DeLuise (Tug), Pete Kowanko (Gavial), Adrian Pasdar (Darstar), Sarah Douglas (Shandray), Charles Durning (Warden), Frank Converse (Greentree), Terrence Mann (Ivor), Alexei Sayle (Malice), Bruce Payne (Dogger), Willoughby Gray (Canis), Kelly Bishop (Tutor Nover), Sam Hamann (Technician), Vin Burnham (Vendor), Carlin Andersen (Hooker), and Jose Ignacio Alvarez, Robert Seaquist, Salvador Martos, Anna Montalvo

WELCOME TO 18 (American Distribution Group) Executive Producer, Bruce W. Brown; Producer, David C. Thomas; Director, Terry Carr; Screenplay, Judith Sherman Wolin, Terry Carr; Photography, Stephen L. Posey; Associate Producers, Cheryl Downey, Kathleen Lawrence; Editor, Lois Freeman-Fox; Designer, Steven Legler; Music, Tony Berg; Production Manager, David C. Thomas; Assistant Directors, Cheryl Downey, Patrick Regan; Sound, Ron Judkins; Set Designer, Don Ferguson; Set Decorators, Etta Leff, Don Elmblad; Assistant Art Director, Marty Cusack; Costumes, Karen Patch, Rosalie Wallace; Special Effects, A & A Special Effects; Production Coordinator, Joan Wolpert; Songs by various artists; Color; Rated PG-13; 91 minutes; November release. CAST: Courtney Thorne-Smith (Lindsey), Mariska Hargitay (Joey), Jo Ann Willette (Robin), Cristen Kauffman (Talia), E. Erich Anderson (Roscoe), Jeff MacGregor (Cliff), John Putch (Cory), Eli Cummins (Trump), Graham Ludlow (Pipes), Michael MacRae (Gallpin), Micole Mercurio (Miss Bulah), Brandis Kemp (Miss Reba), Mickey Jones (Harper), Deanna Booher (Tough Broad), Cletus Young (Hud), Clay Stone (Cassidy), Michael Greene (Luke), Max Trumpower, Bob Gould (Cowboys), and Billy Silva, Georja Danzer, Stephen Flanigan, Patrick Regan, Gene Le Bell, Tom DeWier, Noon Orsatti, Patrick Romano

MODERN GIRLS (Atlantic) Producer, Gary Goetzman; Director, Jerry Kramer; Screenplay, Laurie Craig; Photography, Karen Grossman; Editor, Mitchell Sinoway; Music, Jay Levy, Ed Arkin; Designer, Laurence Bennett; Art Director, Joel Lang; Production Manager, Marie Cantin; Associate Producers, June Petersen, Anita Rosenberg; Casting, Paul Ventura; Assistant Directors, Mary Ellen Woods, John Scherer, R. P. Sekon; Stunts, Kenny Endoso, Mike Runyard, Jimmy Nickerson; Production Coordinator, Patricia Bischetti; Sound, Steve Nelson; Costumes, Theda Deramus; Animals, David J. McMillan; Special Effects, Steve Gallich; Soundtrack on Warner Bros. Records; Rated PG-13; December release. CAST: Daphne Zuniga (Margo), Virginia Madsen (Kelly), Cynthia Gibb (Cece), Clayton Rohner (Clifford/Bruno X), Chris Nash (Ray), Steve Shellen (Brad), Rick Overton (Marsalis), Quin Kessler (Retro Vamp), Pamela Springsteen (Tanya), and Charles Zucker, Carl Weintraub, Michael Clarke, Mike Muscat, Sharron Shayne, Troy Evans, Vojo Goric, Gary Goetzman, Michael Frost, Richard Fullerton, Steve Nemeth, John Dye, Cameron Thor, Ron Campbell, Janet Bowen, Mark Holton, Josh Richman, Martin Ferrero

**Peter DeLuise, Jami Gertz, Lukas Haas, Jason
Patric, Claude Brooks, James LeGros in "Solarbabies"**
© *MGM Entertainment*

**Cynthia Gibb, Daphne Zuniga, Clayton Rohner
in "Modern Girls"** © *Atlantic*

NATIVE SON (Cinecom) Producer, Diane Silver; Executive Producer, Lindsay Law; Director, Jerrold Freedman; Screenplay, Richard Wesley; Based on novel by Richard Wright; Photography, Thomas Burstyn; Editor, Aaron Stell; Music, James Mtume; Song "Jones Comes Down" by Mtume and Silver; Performed by Stephanie Mills; Design, Stephen Marsh; Casting, Hank McCann; In color; Rated PG; 112 minutes; December release. CAST: Carroll Baker (Mrs. Dalton), Akousua Busia (Bessie), Matt Dillon (Jan), Art Evans (Doc), John Karlen (Max), Victor Love (Bigger Thomas), Elizabeth McGovern (Mary Dalton), John McMartin (Mr. Dalton), Geraldine Page (Peggy), Willard E. Pugh (Gus), David Rasche (Buckley), Lane Smith (Britton), Oprah Winfrey (Mrs. Thomas)

CLUB LIFE (Troma, Inc.) Producer/Director/Screenplay, Norman Thaddeus Vane; Story, Bleu McKenzie, Norman Thaddeus Vane; Music, Jack Conrad; Choreography, Dennon Rawles; Executive Producers, Charles Aperia, Guy Collins; Editor, David Kern; Line Producer, Patrick Wright; Photography, Joel King; Music Producers, Frank Musker, Evros Stakis; Casting, Stanzi Stokes; Associate Producers, Sandy Horowitz, Herb Linsey, Mark Madero; Music Supervisor, Philip Moores; Music Coordination, David Minns; Production Executive, Jean Ovrum; Production Managers, Herb Linsey, Larry Gitlin; Assistant Directors, Patrick Wright, Kelly Schroeder, Kurt Benjamin, Tony DiSalvo, Michael Rooney; Costumes, Elisabeth Scott; Production Coordinator, Mark Madero; Set Directors, Sherry Dreizen, Michelle Hormel; Art Directors, Cynthia Sowder, Phillip Duffin; Set Designer, Katherine Vallin; Sound, Jim Murphy; Special Effects, SPFX, Inc., Court Wizard; Songs by various artists; CFI Color; Rated R; 77 minutes; December release. CAST: Tom Parsekian (Cal), Michael Parks (Tank), Jamie Barrett (Sissy), Tony Curtis (Hector), Dee Wallace (Tilly), Ron Kuhlman (Doctor), Pat Ast (Butch), Bruce Reed (Punk), Sal Landi (Sonny), Robert Miano (Ferd), Ron Gilbert (Mace), and Bleu McKenzie, Michael Aaron, Herb Abrams, Dominick Allen, Gene Scott Casey, Ross Fenton, Kate Finlayson, Whip Hubley, Jay Arlen Jones, Elizabeth Lamers, Barbara Powers, Yavonne Smith, Valerie Shaldene, John Vidor, Charles Prior

CLASS OF NUKE 'EM HIGH (Troma Inc.) Producers, Lloyd Kaufman, Michael Herz; Directors, Richard W. Haines, Samuel Weil; Executive Producer, James Treadwell; Screenplay/Story/Editor, Richard W. Haines; Screenplay, Mark Rudnitsky, Lloyd Kaufman, Stuart Strutin; Photography, Michael Mayers, Jim Grib; Associate Producer, Stuart Strutin; Special Effects/Special Effects Makeup, Scott Coulter, Brian Quinn; Art Directors, Art Skopinsky, Arthur Lorenz; Anamatronic Creatures, Tom Lauten; Production Supervisors, Eileen Nad Castaldi, Elizabeth Whitman; Production Managers, Sandra Byrd Curry, Art Skopinsky; Casting/Assistant Director, Ann McCabe; Sound, Mark Pancza, Tom Chichester; Casting/Additional Material, Graham Flashner; Lighting, Jim Grib, Marc Kroll; Stunts, Jeff Gibson; Costumes, Ivy Rosovsky, John Reefer; Songs, Clive Burr, David Barreto, David Behennah; Color; Rated R; 92 minutes; December release. CAST: Janelle Brady (Chrissy). Gilbert Brenton (Warren), Robert Prichard (Spike), R. L. Ryan (Paley), James Nugent Vernon (Eddie), Brad Dunker (Gonzo), Gary Schneider (Pete), Theo Cohan (Muffey), Gary Rosenblatt (Greg), Mary Taylor (Judy), Rick Howard (Spud), Heather McMahan (Taru), Chris McNamee (Joe), Anthony Ventola (George), Arthur Lorenz (Dewy), Donald O'Toole (Westley), Seth Oliver Hawkins (Lumpy), LaRae Dean (Cathy), Reuben Guss (Hyde), Diana DeVries (Miss Stein), Lauraine Austin (Ms. Austin), Dianna-Jean Flaherty (Denise) and Sloane Herz, Lily Hayes Kaufman, Don Costello, Frank Cole, Sam Scardino, Barbara Ann Missbach, Andy Newton, Skip Hamra, Donnie Reynolds, Joe Severino, Jeffrey Grossi, Maezie Murphy, Rick Collins, Bob Schenck, Belle Maria Wheat, Libby Miller, Ron Giles, Donna Nardo, Ann McCabe, Kitty Alson, Thomas Feeney, Richard W. Haines, Leonard Tepper, Nicky Baker, Seth Kadish, Louise Edwards, Ava Kelly, Elizabeth (Locky) Lambert, Gerald Willaidom, Gersa Arias, Glaurys Arias, Brian Quinn, Erika Zatt, Michael Popowitz, Jon Kurtis, Virginia Kurtis

WHERE ARE THE CHILDREN (Columbia) Producer, Zev Braun; Director, Bruce Malmuth; Screenplay, Jack Sholder; Based on the novel by Mary Higgins Clark; Associate Producer, Bryant Christ; Photography, Larry Pizer; Editor, Roy Watts; Costumes, Mary Ellen Winston; Designer, Robb Wilson King; Casting, Bonnie Timmermann; Music, Sylvester Levay; Production Manager, Lester Berman; Assistant Director, Donald J. Newman, James Freitag; Set Decorator, Jane Cavedon; Sound, Carey Lindley, Jeff Clark; Special Effects, Image Engineering, Inc., Peter Chesney, Mike Menzel, Dan Malmuth; Song, Fred F. Forrest, Sr., Frederic Forrest, Jr.; Metrocolor; Panavision; Rated R; 92 minutes; December release. CAST: Jill Clayburgh (Nancy Eldridge), Max Gail (Clay Eldridge), Harley Cross (Michael Eldridge), Elisabeth Harnois (Missy Eldridge), Elizabeth Wilson (Dorothy Prentiss), Barnard Hughes (Jonathan Knowles), Frederic Forrest (Courtney Parrish), James Purcell (Robin Legler), Clifton James (Chief Coffin), Eriq LaSalle (Bernie Miles), Joseph Hindy (Det. Morello), Devin Ratray (Neil Kenney), Zev Braun (J. D. Quill), Christopher Murney (Lenny Barron), and Ted O'Brien, Dan Lounsbery, Evan Malmuth, Bruce Malmuth, Ruth Edinberg, Louis Zorich, Axel Van Dereck, Peter Kovner, D. Neal Brown, Mike Stines, Lori Michaels, Carol Higgins Clark, Doug Riley, Dan Malmuth, Paul O'Brien, Robert Pena, Coleen Cavanaugh

SCORPION aka *The Summons* (Crown International) Producer/Director/Screenplay, William Riead; Executive Producer, John R. Burrows, Jr.; Photography, Bill Philbin; Sound, Stan Gordon; Editor, Gigi Coello; Associate Producer, Peter Martineau; Production Manager, Roger Cannon; Assistant Directors, Wendy West, Ron Simonson; Music, Sean Murray; Music Supervisor, Richard McCurdy; Casting, Lisa Pontrelli; Costumes, Elaine Turner; Special Effects, Wayne Beauchamp; Stunts, Dar Robinson; Art Director, Heather Cameron; Color; Rated R; 98 minutes; December release. CAST: Tonny Tulleners (Steve), Don Murray (Gilford), Robert Logan (Gordon), Allen Williams (Keller), Kathryn Daley (Jackie), Ross Elliott (Sam), John Anderson (Neal), Bart Braverman (Mehdi), Thom McFadden (Lt. Woodman), Billy Hayes (Wolfgang), Adam Pearson (Jack), Ari Barak (Hanis), and Adam Ageli, John LaZar, Pamela Bryant, Lisa Pontrelli, Joseph Whipp, Stephen Riead, Thomas Riead, Jack Lightsy, Kelela Wright, Douglas Joho, Gloria Thomas, Michael J. Epps, William Moy, William Griffith, Tom Cassell, Douglas Happ, Bill Sherwood, Bob Golden, Leroy Tardy, Bart McManus, Jane Gierlich, Lawrence Cohen, Wendy West, Shawn Player, Cam Colee, Robert Colbert, Robert Darnell, Allan Thomas, Tony Martineau, Tom Serrano, Duke Jubran, Anna Ortega, Raymond Petterson, Stephen Woods, Joy Rinaldi, Byron Nelson, Jeffrey Rizzo, Pedro Velis, Anthony Vatsula, Marthy Imsland, Herb Mitchell, Patricia Murray, William Utay, Vivian Patrick, Dimitra Mina, Colleen Nelson, Harvey Whitaker, Robert Hinshaw, Erik White, Brad Wilson, Steve Mattson, Robert Storick, Richard Bravo, Louis Alexander, J. Victor Lopez, Sonia Vera, Luis Marugon, Felix Martin, Carmen More, Clemens Meuleman, Wayne Ward, Taia Chard, Peter Kamealoha Clark, Patrick Bishop, Nabwa Abou-Seif, Alfredo Sedo, Dea McCallister, Marianne Fornstedt

PROMISING NEW ACTORS OF 1986

JOAN ALLEN

KEVIN COSTNER

PAUL HOGAN

SUZY AMIS

147

C. THOMAS HOWELL

MARY ELIZABETH MASTRANTONIO

MARLEE MATLIN

RIVER PHOENIX

148

DEMI MOORE

AIDAN QUINN

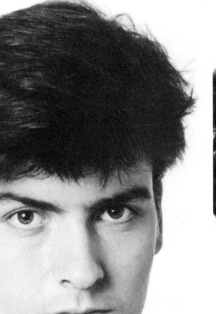

CHARLIE SHEEN

ELIZABETH PERKINS

149

Charlie Sheen, Keith David
Above: The Platoon

PLATOON

(ORION) Producer, Arnold Kopelson; Director/Screenplay, Oliver Stone; Executive Producers, John Daly, Derek Gibson; Co-Producer, A. Kitman Ho; Production Executive, Pierre David; Photography, Robert Richardson; Designer, Bruno Rubeo; Editor, Claire Simpson; Assistant Directors, H. Gordon Boos, Gerry Toomey, Pepito Diaz; Sound, Simon Kaye; Military Technical Advisor, Captain Dale Dye, USMC(Ret); Special Effects, Yves De Bono, Andrew Wilson; Special Make-up Effects, Gordon J. Smith; Production Executive, Graham Henderson; Music, Georges Delerue, Budd Carr; Casting, Pat Golden, Bob Morones, Warren McLean; Production Supervisor, Ooty Moorehead; Production Manager, Joe Constantino; Production Coordinator, Angelica De Leon; Associate Editor, Tom Finan; Sound Editors, Gordon Daniel, David Campling, Greg Dillon, James J. Klinger, Tony Palk; Music Coordinator, JoAnne Weiss; Art Directors, Rodel Cruz, Doris Sherman Williams; Stunts, Gil Arceo; Songs, Samuel Barber, Grace Slick, Merle Haggard, William Robinson, Marvin Tarplin, Warren Moore; CFI Color; Rated R; 120 minutes; November release

CAST

Sergeant Barnes	Tom Berenger
Sergeant Elias	Willem Dafoe
Chris	Charlie Sheen
Big Harold	Forest Whitaker
Rhah	Francesco Quinn
Sergeant O'Neill	John C. McGinley
Sal	Richard Edson
Bunny	Kevin Dillon
Junior	Reggie Johnson
King	Keith David
Lerner	Johnny Depp
Tex	David Neidorf
Lieutenant Wolfe	Mark Moses
Crawford	Chris Pedersen
Manny	Corkey Ford
Francis	Corey Glover
Gardner	Bob Orwig
Warren	Tony Todd
Morehouse	Kevin Eshelman
Ace	James Terry McIlvain
Sanderson	J. Adam Glover
Tony	Ivan Kane
Doc	Paul Sanchez
Captain Harris	Dale Dye
Parker	Peter Hicks
Flash	Basile Achara
Fu Sheng	Steve Barredo
Rodriguez	Chris Castillejo
Tubbs	Andrew B. Clark
Village Chief	Bernardo Manalili
His Wife	Than Rogers
Their Daughter	Li Thi Van
Old Woman	Clarisa Ortacio
One-legged Man	Romy Sevilla
Rape Victim	Li Mai Thao
Medic	Ron Barracks
Soldiers	Mathew Westfall, Nick Nickelson, Warren McLean

Academy Awards for Best Picture, Best Direction, Best Editing, and Best Sound

Top Left: Oliver Stone
Below: Charlie Sheen, Tom Berenger, Willem Dafoe,
(kneeling) Francesco Quinn, Kevin Dillon
© Orion/Ricky Francisco

BEST PICTURE OF 1986

Charlie Sheen, Corey Glover, Chris Pedersen, Willem Dafoe, Forrest Whittaker,
Keith David Top: Willem Dafoe, Charlie Sheen, Tom Berenger

THE COLOR OF MONEY

(BUENA VISTA) Producers, Irving Axelrad, Barbara DeFina; Director, Martin Scorsese; Screenplay, Richard Price; Based on novel by Walter Tevis; Photography, Michael Ballhaus; Design, Boris Leven; Editor, Thelma Schoonmaker; Costumes, Richard Bruno; Score, Robbie Robertson; Associate Producer/Production Manager, Dodie Foster; Assistant Directors, Joseph Reidy, Richard Feld; Special Effects, Curt Smith; Production Coordinator, Elise Rohden; Technical Adviser, Michael Sigel; Presented by Touchstone Pictures in association with Silver Screen Partners II; Sound Track on MCA Records/Cassettes; In DeLuxe Color/Dolby Stereo; Rated R; 119 minutes; October release.

CAST

Eddie	Paul Newman
Vincent	Tom Cruise
Carmen	Mary Elizabeth Mastrantonio
Janelle	Helen Shaver
Julian	John Turturro
Orvis	Bill Cobbs
Earl	Robert Agins
Kennedy	Alvin Anastasia
Diane	Elizabeth Bracco
Lou	Vito D'Ambrosio
Chuck	Joe Guastaferro
Grady Seasons	Keith McCready
Dud	Grady Mathews
Band Singer	Carol Messing
Duke	Steve Mizerak
Tom	Jerry Piller
Amos	Forest Whitaker
Moselle	Bruce A. Young

and Randall Arney, Ron Dean, Lisa Dodson, Donald Feeney, Paul Geier, Carey Goldenberg, Paul Herman, Mark Jarvis, Jimmy Mataya, Lloyd Moss, Michael Nash, Mario Nieves, Miguel A. Nino, Andy Nolfo, Ernest Perry Jr., Iggy Pop, Richard Price, Juan Ramirez, Alex Ross, Charles Scorsese, Christina Sigel, Harold Simonsen, Fred Squillo, Lawrence Linn, Rick Mohr, Rodrick Selby

PAUL NEWMAN
in "The Color of Money"
© *Touchstone Films*

MARLEE MATLIN
in "Children of a Lesser God"
© *Paramount/Takashi Seida*

1986 ACADEMY AWARD FOR BEST ACTRESS   153

MICHAEL CAINE
in "Hannah and Her Sisters"
© *Orion/Brian Hamill*

1986 ACADEMY AWARD FOR BEST SUPPORTING ACTOR

DIANNE WIEST
in "Hannah and Her Sisters"
© *Orion/Brian Hamill*

1986 ACADEMY AWARD FOR BEST SUPPORTING ACTRESS   155

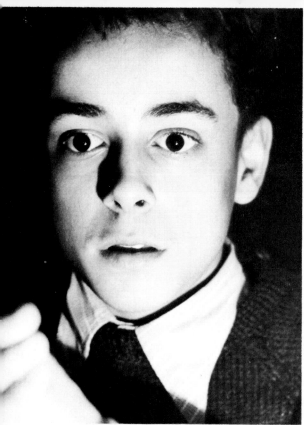

THE ASSAULT

(CANNON) Producer/Director, Fons Rademakers; Executive Producer, Jos Van Der Linden; Screenplay, Gerard Soeteman; Based on novel by Harry Mulisch; Photography, Theo Van De Sande; Editor, Kees Linthorst; Music, Jurriaan Andriessen; Art Director, Dorus Van Der Linden; Assistant Directors, Lili Rademakers, Arthur Hornstra; Costumes, Annemarie Van Beverwijk; Casting, Hans Kemna; Assistant Art Directors, Annechien Braak, Joke Koterus; English Adaptation, Maggie Dickie; Production Manager, Panos Nicolaou; Special Effects, Harry Wiessenhaan; Sound, Kees Linthorst, Rupert Scrivener,; Conductor, Rogier Van Oterloo; Song, Adamo; Dolby Stereo; Dutch with subtitles; Color; Rated PG; 146 minutes

CAST

Anton Steenwijk	Derek De Lint
Anton Jr.	Marc Van Uchelen
Truus Coster/Saskia de Graaff	Monique Van De Ven
Cor Takes	John Kraaykamp
Fake Ploeg	Huub Van Der Lubbe
Mrs. Beumer	Elly Weller
Karin Korteweg	Ina Van Der Molen
Father Steenwijk	Frans Vorstman
Mother Steenwijk	Edda Barends
Peter Steenwijk	Casper De Boer
Mr. Korteweg	Wim De Haas
Karin Jr.	Hiske Van Der Linden
Mr. Beumer	Piet De Wijn
Sandra	Akkemay
Gerrit-Jan	Kees Coolen
Mr. De Graaff	Eric Van Heijst
Elisabeth	Mies De Heer
SD Officer	Olliver Domnick
Hauptsturmfuhrer	Amadeus August
Sergeant	Matthias Hell
Officer	Horst Reichel
General	Ludwig Haas
Cor Takes Jr.	Michel Van Rooij
Mr. Van Lennep	Guus Hermus
Mrs. De Graaff	Manon Alving
Jaap	Tabe Bas
Henk	Cas Baas
Vicar	Okke Jager
Simon	Eric Van Der Donk

and Ab Abspoel (Man in cafe), Pierre Bokma, Fillip Bolluyt, Willem Van De Sande Bakhuijzen, Jan Pieter Koch, Gijs De Lange, Kees Hulst (Students), Kenneth Oakley (Guide), Erik Van Der Hoff (Bastiaan), Krijn Ter Braak (Uncle Peter), Nico Jansen (Police Sgt.), Willem Van Rinsum (Guard), Lex Wiertz (Herring Dealer), Karl Golusda, Harold Bendig (Officers), Paula Petri (Woman in window), Mike Bendig (Fake Ploeg, Jr.), Norman Longdon (General), Lisa Takacs (Sandra, Jr.), Rogier Van Gestel (Peter at 12), Marco Ramos (Peter at 8), Dott Martini (Doctor)

Academy Award for Best Foreign-language Film

Top Left: Mark Van Uchelen © *Cannon*

Derek De Lint

Mark Van Uchelen (center)

Monique Van De Ven (center)
Top: John Kraaycamp (Right)

ARTIE SHAW: TIME IS ALL YOU'VE GOT

(BRIDGE FILMS) Producer/Director, Brigitte Berman; Associate Producer, Don Haig; Writer/Narrator, Brigitte Berman; Photography, Mark Irwin, Jim Aquila; Sound, Jon Brodin, Gerry Jest; Editing, Brigitte Berman, Barry Backus; Music, Artie Shaw and his various orchestras; Canadian; In black and white and color; Not rated; 114 minutes; Carried in Volume 37, page 205. CAST: Artie Shaw, Evelyn Keyes, Polly Haynes, John Wexley, Lee Castle, John Best, Helen Forrest, Buddy Rich, Mel Torme, Mack Pierce, Frederick Morton
Tied with "Down and Out in America" for 1986 Academy Award for Best Feature-length Documentary

Right: Artie Shaw (C), and also
at top
© *Brigitte Berman*

DOWN AND OUT IN AMERICA

(JOSEPH FEURY PRODUCTIONS) Producers, Joseph Feury, Milton Justice; Directed and Narrated by Lee Grant; Photography, Tom Hurwitz; Associate Producer, Carol Cuddy; Editor, Milton Ginsberg; Production Manager/Assistant Director, Joseph Feury; Associate Editor, Dean Wetherell; Sound, Maryte Kavaliauskus; Sound Effects, Richard Goldberg; Music, Tom Manoff, Jonathan Mann; In color; Not rated; 56 minutes; October release. A documentary about the millions of American citizens who have unexpectedly joined the ranks of the nation's poor.
Tied with "Artie Shaw: Time Is All You've Got" for 1986 Academy Award for Best Feature-length Documentary

© *HBO/Mariette Pathy Allen*

Lee Grant (second from right)

1986 ACADEMY AWARD FOR BEST FEATURE-LENGTH DOCUMENTARY **159**

| Ernest Borgnine | Faye Dunaway | Joel Grey | Louise Fletcher | Rex Harrison | Helen Hayes |

PREVIOUS ACADEMY AWARD WINNERS

(1) Best Picture, (2) Actor, (3) Actress, (4) Supporting Actor, (5) Supporting Actress, (6) Director, (7) Special Award, (8) Best Foreign Language Film, (9) Best Feature Documentary

1927–28: (1) "Wings," (2) Emil Jannings in "The Way of All Flesh," (3) Janet Gaynor in "Seventh Heaven," (6) Frank Borzage for "Seventh Heaven," (7) Charles Chaplin.

1928–29: (1) "Broadway Melody," (2) Warner Baxter in "Old Arizona," (3) Mary Pickford in "Coquette," (6) Frank Lloyd for "The Divine Lady."

1929–30: (1) "All Quiet on the Western Front," (2) George Arliss in "Disraeli," (3) Norma Shearer in "The Divorcee," (6) Lewis Milestone for "All Quiet on the Western Front."

1930–31: (1) "Cimarron," (2) Lionel Barrymore in "A Free Soul," (3) Marie Dressler in "Min and Bill," (6) Norman Taurog for "Skippy."

1931–32: (1) "Grand Hotel," (2) Fredric March in "Dr. Jekyll and Mr. Hyde" tied with Wallace Beery in "The Champ," (3) Helen Hayes in "The Sin of Madelon Claudet," (6) Frank Borzage for "Bad Girl."

1932–33: (1) "Cavalcade," (2) Charles Laughton in "The Private Life of Henry VIII," (3) Katharine Hepburn in "Morning Glory," (6) Frank Lloyd for "Cavalcade."

1934: (1) "It Happened One Night," (2) Clark Gable in "It Happened One Night," (3) Claudette Colbert in "It Happened One Night," (6) Frank Capra for "It Happened One Night," (7) Shirley Temple.

1935: (1) "Mutiny on the Bounty," (2) Victor McLaglen in "The Informer," (3) Bette Davis in "Dangerous," (6) John Ford for "The Informer," (7) D. W. Griffith.

1936: (1) "The Great Ziegfeld," (2) Paul Muni in "The Story of Louis Pasteur," (3) Luise Rainer in "The Great Ziegfeld," (4) Walter Brennan in "Come and Get It," (5) Gale Sondergaard in "Anthony Adverse," (6) Frank Capra for "Mr. Deeds Goes to Town."

1937: (1) "The Life of Emile Zola," (2) Spencer Tracy in "Captains Courageous," (3) Luise Rainer in "The Good Earth," (4) Joseph Schildkraut in "The Life of Emile Zola," (5) Alice Brady in "In Old Chicago," (6) Leo McCarey for "The Awful Truth," (7) Mack Sennett, Edgar Bergen.

1938: (1) "You Can't Take It with You," (2) Spencer Tracy in "Boys' Town," (3) Bette Davis in "Jezebel," (4) Walter Brennan in "Kentucky," (5) Fay Bainter in "Jezebel," (6) Frank Capra for "You Can't Take It with You," (7) Deanna Durbin, Mickey Rooney, Harry M. Warner, Walt Disney.

1939: (1) "Gone with the Wind," (2) Robert Donat in "Goodbye, Mr. Chips," (3) Vivien Leigh in "Gone with the Wind," (4) Thomas Mitchell in "Stagecoach," (5) Hattie McDaniel in "Gone with the Wind," (6) Victor Fleming for "Gone with the Wind," (7) Douglas Fairbanks, Judy Garland.

1940: (1) "Rebecca," (2) James Stewart in "The Philadelphia Story," (3) Ginger Rogers in "Kitty Foyle," (4) Walter Brennan in "The Westerner," (5) Jane Darwell in "The Grapes of Wrath," (6) John Ford for "The Grapes of Wrath," (7) Bob Hope.

1941: (1) "How Green Was My Valley," (2) Gary Cooper in "Sergeant York," (3) Joan Fontaine in "Suspicion," (4) Donald Crisp in "How Green Was My Valley," (5) Mary Astor in "The Great Lie," (6) John Ford for "How Green Was My Valley," (7) Leopold Stokowski, Walt Disney.

1942: (1) "Mrs. Miniver," (2) James Cagney in "Yankee Doodle Dandy," (3) Greer Garson in "Mrs. Miniver," (4) Van Heflin in "Johnny Eager," (5) Teresa Wright in "Mrs. Miniver," (6) William Wyler for "Mrs. Miniver," (7) Charles Boyer, Noel Coward.

1943: (1) "Casablanca," (2) Paul Lukas in "Watch on the Rhine," (3) Jennifer Jones in "The Song of Bernadette," (4) Charles Coburn in "The More the Merrier," (5) Katina Paxinou in "For Whom the Bell Tolls," (6) Michael Curtiz for "Casablanca."

1944: (1) "Going My Way," (2) Bing Crosby in "Going My Way," (3) Ingrid Bergman in "Gaslight," (4) Barry Fitzgerald in "Going My Way," (5) Ethel Barrymore in "None but the Lonely Heart," (6) Leo McCarey for "Going My Way," (7) Margaret O'Brien, Bob Hope.

1945: (1) "The Lost Weekend," (2) Ray Milland in "The Lost Weekend," (3) Joan Crawford in "Mildred Pierce," (4) James Dunn in "A Tree Grows in Brooklyn," (5) Anne Revere in "National Velvet," (6) Billy Wilder for "The Lost Weekend," (7) Walter Wanger, Peggy Ann Garner.

1946: (1) "The Best Years of Our Lives," (2) Fredric March in "The Best Years of Our Lives," (3) Olivia de Havilland in "To Each His Own," (4) Harold Russell in "The Best Years of Our Lives," (5) Anne Baxter in "The Razor's Edge," (6) William Wyler for "The Best Years of Our Lives," (7) Laurence Olivier, Harold Russell, Ernst Lubitsch, Claude Jarman, Jr.

1947: (1) "Gentleman's Agreement," (2) Ronald Colman in "A Double Life," (3) Loretta Young in "The Farmer's Daughter," (4) Edmund Gwenn in "Miracle On 34th Street," (5) Celeste Holm in "Gentleman's Agreement," (6) Elia Kazan for "Gentleman's Agreement," (7) James Baskette, (8) "Shoe Shine," (Italy).

1948: (1) "Hamlet," (2) Laurence Olivier in "Hamlet," (3) Jane Wyman in "Johnny Belinda," (4) Walter Huston in "The Treasure of the Sierra Madre," (5) Claire Trevor in "Key Largo," (6) John Huston for "The Treasure of the Sierra Madre," (7) Ivan Jandl, Sid Grauman, Adolph Zukor, Walter Wanger, (8) "Monsieur Vincent," (France).

1949: (1) "All the King's Men," (2) Broderick Crawford in "All the King's Men," (3) Olivia de Havilland in "The Heiress," (4) Dean Jagger in "Twelve O'Clock High," (5) Mercedes McCambridge in "All the King's Men," (6) Joseph L. Mankiewicz for "A Letter to Three Wives," (7) Bobby Driscoll, Fred Astaire, Cecil B. DeMille, Jean Hersholt, (8) "The Bicycle Thief," (Italy).

1950: (1) "All about Eve," (2) Jose Ferrer in "Cyrano de Bergerac," (3) Judy Holliday in "Born Yesterday," (4) George Sanders in "All about Eve," (5) Josephine Hull in "Harvey," (6) Joseph L. Mankiewicz for "All about Eve," (7) George Murphy, Louis B. Mayer. (8) "The Walls of Malapaga," (France/Italy).

1951: (1) "An American in Paris," (2) Humphrey Bogart in "The African Queen," (3) Vivien Leigh in "A Streetcar Named Desire," (4) Karl Malden in "A Streetcar Named Desire," (5) Kim Hunter in "A Streetcar Named Desire," (6) George Stevens for "A Place in the Sun," (7) Gene Kelly, (8) "Rashomon," (Japan).

1952: (1) "The Greatest Show on Earth," (2) Gary Cooper in "High Noon," (3) Shirley Booth in "Come Back, Little Sheba," (4) Anthony Quinn in "Viva Zapata," (5) Gloria Grahame in "The Bad and the Beautiful," (6) John Ford for "The Quiet Man," (7) Joseph M. Schenck, Merian C. Cooper, Harold Lloyd, Bob Hope, George Alfred Mitchell, (8) "Forbidden Games," (France).

1953: (1) "From Here to Eternity," (2) William Holden in "Stalag 17," (3) Audrey Hepburn in "Roman Holiday," (4) Frank Sinatra in "From Here to Eternity," (5) Donna Reed in "From Here to Eternity," (6) Fred Zinnemann for "From Here to Eternity," (7) Pete Smith, Joseph Breen, (8) no award.

1954: (1) "On the Waterfront," (2) Marlon Brando in "On the Waterfront," (3) Grace Kelly in "The Country Girl," (4) Edmond O'Brien in "The Barefoot Contessa," (5) Eva Marie Saint in "On the Waterfront," (6) Elia Kazan for "On the Waterfront," (8) "Gate of Hell," (Japan).

1955: (1) "Marty," (2) Ernest Borgnine in "Marty," (3) Anna Magnani in "The Rose Tattoo," (4) Jack Lemmon in "Mister Roberts," (5) Jo Van Fleet in "East of Eden," (6) Delbert Mann for "Marty," (8) "Samurai," (Japan).

1956: (1) "Around the World in 80 Days," (2) Yul Brynner in "The King and I," (3) Ingrid Bergman in "Anastasia," (4) Anthony Quinn in "Lust for Life," (5) Dorothy Malone in "Written on the Wind," (6) George Stevens for "Giant," (7) Eddie Cantor, (8) "La Strada," (Italy).

John Houseman   **Barbra Streisand**   **George C. Scott**

1957: (1) "The Bridge on the River Kwai," (2) Alec Guinness in "The Bridge on the River Kwai," (3) Joanne Woodward in "The Three Faces of Eve," (4) Red Buttons in "Sayonara," (5) Miyoshi Umeki in "Sayonara," (6) David Lean for "The Bridge on the River Kwai," (7) Charles Brackett, B. B. Kahane, Gilbert M. (Bronco Billy) Anderson, (8) "The Nights of Cabiria," (Italy).
1958: (1) "Gigi," (2) David Niven in "Separate Tables," (3) Susan Hayward in "I Want to Live," (4) Burl Ives in "The Big Country," (5) Wendy Hiller in "Separate Tables," (6) Vincente Minnelli for "Gigi," (7) Maurice Chevalier, (8) "My Uncle," (France).
1959: (1) "Ben-Hur," (2) Charlton Heston in "Ben-Hur," (3) Simone Signoret in "Room at the Top," (4) Hugh Griffith in "Ben-Hur," (5) Shelley Winters in "The Diary of Anne Frank," (6) William Wyler for "Ben-Hur," (7) Lee de Forest, Buster Keaton, (8) "Black Orpheus," (Brazil).
1960: (1) "The Apartment," (2) Burt Lancaster in "Elmer Gantry," (3) Elizabeth Taylor in "Butterfield 8," (4) Peter Ustinov in "Spartacus," (5) Shirley Jones in "Elmer Gantry," (6) Billy Wilder for "The Apartment," (7) Gary Cooper, Stan Laurel, Hayley Mills, (8) "The Virgin Spring," (Sweden).
1961: (1) "West Side Story," (2) Maximilian Schell in "Judgment at Nuremberg," (3) Sophia Loren in "Two Women," (4) George Chakiris in "West Side Story," (5) Rita Moreno in "West Side Story," (6) Robert Wise for "West Side Story," (7) Jerome Robbins, Fred L. Metzler, (8) "Through a Glass Darkly," (Sweden).
1962: (1) "Lawrence of Arabia," (2) Gregory Peck in "To Kill a Mockingbird," (3) Anne Bancroft in "The Miracle Worker," (4) Ed Begley in "Sweet Bird of Youth," (5) Patty Duke in "The Miracle Worker," (6) David Lean for "Lawrence of Arabia," (8) "Sundays and Cybele," (France).
1963: (1) "Tom Jones," (2) Sidney Poitier in "Lilies of the Field," (3) Patricia Neal in "Hud," (4) Melvyn Douglas in "Hud," (5) Margaret Rutherford in "The V.I.P.'s," (6) Tony Richardson for "Tom Jones," (8) "8½," (Italy).
1964: (1) "My Fair Lady," (2) Rex Harrison in "My Fair Lady," (3) Julie Andrews in "Mary Poppins," (4) Peter Ustinov in "Topkapi," (5) Lila Kedrova in "Zorba the Greek," (6) George Cukor for "My Fair Lady," (7) William Tuttle, (8) "Yesterday, Today and Tomorrow," (Italy).
1965: (1) "The Sound of Music," (2) Lee Marvin in "Cat Ballou," (3) Julie Christie in "Darling," (4) Martin Balsam in "A Thousand Clowns," (5) Shelley Winters in "A Patch of Blue," (6) Robert Wise for "The Sound of Music," (7) Bob Hope, (8) "The Shop on Main Street," (Czech).
1966: (1) "A Man for All Seasons," (2) Paul Scofield in "A Man for All Seasons," (3) Elizabeth Taylor in "Who's Afraid of Virginia Woolf?," (4) Walter Matthau in "The Fortune Cookie," (5) Sandy Dennis in "Who's Afraid of Virginia Woolf?," (6) Fred Zinnemann for "A Man for All Seasons," (8) "A Man and A Woman," (France).
1967: (1) "In the Heat of the Night," (2) Rod Steiger in "In the Heat of the Night," (3) Katharine Hepburn in "Guess Who's Coming to Dinner," (4) George Kennedy in "Cool Hand Luke," (5) Estelle Parsons in "Bonnie and Clyde," (6) Mike Nichols for "The Graduate," (8) "Closely Watched Trains," (Czech).
1968: (1) "Oliver!," (2) Cliff Robertson in "Charly," (3) Katharine Hepburn in "The Lion in Winter" tied with Barbra Streisand in "Funny Girl," (4) Jack Albertson in "The Subject Was Roses," (5) Ruth Gordon in "Rosemary's Baby," (6) Carol Reed for "Oliver!," (7) Onna White for "Oliver!" choreography, John Chambers for "Planet of the Apes" make-up, (8) "War and Peace," (USSR).
1969: (1) "Midnight Cowboy," (2) John Wayne in "True Grit," (3) Maggie Smith in "The Prime of Miss Jean Brodie," (4) Gig Young in "They Shoot Horses, Don't They?," (5) Goldie Hawn in "Cactus Flower," (6) John Schlesinger for "Midnight Cowboy," (7) Cary Grant, (8) "Z," (Algeria).
1970: (1) "Patton," (2) George C. Scott in "Patton," (3) Glenda Jackson in "Women in Love," (4) John Mills in "Ryan's Daughter," (5) Helen Hayes in "Airport," (6) Franklin J. Schaffner for "Patton," (7) Lillian Gish, Orson Welles, (8) "Investigation of a Citizen above Suspicion," (Italy).
1971: (1) "The French Connection," (2) Gene Hackman in "The French Connection," (3) Jane Fonda in "Klute," (4) Ben Johnson in "The Last Picture Show," (5) Cloris Leachman in "The Last Picture Show," (6) William Friedkin for "The French Connection," (7) Charles Chaplin, (8) "The Garden of the Finzi-Continis," (Italy).
1972: (1) "The Godfather," (2) Marlon Brando in "The Godfather," (3) Liza Minnelli in "Cabaret," (4) Joel Grey in "Cabaret," (5) Eileen Heckart in "Butterflies Are Free," (6) Bob Fosse for "Cabaret," (7) Edward G. Robinson, (8) "The Discreet Charm of the Bourgeoisie," (France).
1973: (1) "The Sting," (2) Jack Lemmon in "Save the Tiger," (3) Glenda Jackson in "A Touch of Class," (4) John Houseman in "The Paper Chase," (5) Tatum O'Neal in "Paper Moon," (6) George Roy Hill for "The Sting," (8) "Day for Night," (France).

1974: (1) "The Godfather Part II," (2) Art Carney in "Harry and Tonto," (3) Ellen Burstyn in "Alice Doesn't Live Here Anymore," (4) Robert DeNiro in "The Godfather Part II," (5) Ingrid Bergman in "Murder on the Orient Express," (6) Francis Ford Coppola for "The Godfather Part II," (7) Howard Hawks, Jean Renoir, (8) "Amarcord," (Italy).
1975: (1) "One Flew over the Cuckoo's Nest," (2) Jack Nicholson in "One Flew over the Cuckoo's Nest," (3) Louise Fletcher in "One Flew over the Cuckoo's Nest," (4) George Burns in "The Sunshine Boys," (5) Lee Grant in "Shampoo," (6) Milos Forman for "One Flew over the Cuckoo's Nest," (7) Mary Pickford, (8) "Dersu Uzala," (U.S.S.R.), (9) "The Man Who Skied Down Everest."
1976: (1) "Rocky," (2) Peter Finch in "Network," (3) Faye Dunaway in "Network," (4) Jason Robards in "All the President's Men," (5) Beatrice Straight in "Network," (6) John G. Avildsen for "Rocky," (8) "Black and White in Color" (Ivory Coast), (9) "Harlan County U.S.A."
1977: (1) "Annie Hall," (2) Richard Dreyfuss in "The Goodbye Girl," (3) Diane Keaton in "Annie Hall," (4) Jason Robards in "Julia," (5) Vanessa Redgrave in "Julia," (6) Woody Allen for "Annie Hall," (7) Margaret Booth (film editor), (8) "Madame Rosa" (France), (9) "Who Are the DeBolts?"
1978: (1) "The Deer Hunter," (2) Jon Voight in "Coming Home," (3) Jane Fonda in "Coming Home," (4) Christopher Walken in "The Deer Hunter," (5) Maggie Smith in "California Suite," (6) Michael Cimino for "The Deer Hunter," (7) Laurence Olivier, King Vidor, (8) "Get Out Your Handkerchiefs" (France), (9) "Sacred Straight."
1979: (1) "Kramer vs. Kramer," (2) Dustin Hoffman in "Kramer vs. Kramer," (3) Sally Field in "Norma Rae," (4) Melvyn Douglas in "Being There," (5) Meryl Streep in "Kramer vs. Kramer," (6) Robert Benton for "Kramer vs. Kramer," (7) Robert S. Benjamin, Hal Elias, Alec Guinness, (8) "The Tin Drum" (Germany), (9) "Best Boy."
1980: (1) "Ordinary People," (2) Robert DeNiro in "Raging Bull," (3) Sissy Spacek in "Coal Miner's Daughter," (4) Timothy Hutton in "Ordinary People," (5) Mary Steenburgen in "Melvin and Howard," (6) Robert Redford for "Ordinary People," (7) Henry Fonda, (8) "Moscow Does Not Believe in Tears" (Russia), (9) "From Mao to Mozart: Isaac Stern in China."
1981: (1) "Chariots of Fire," (2) Henry Fonda in "On Golden Pond," (3) Katharine Hepburn in "On Golden Pond," (4) John Gielgud in "Arthur," (5) Maureen Stapleton in "Reds," (6) Warren Beatty for "Reds," (7) Fuji Photo Film Co., Barbara Stanwyck, (8) "Mephisto" (Germany/Hungary), (9) "Genocide."
1982: (1) "Gandhi," (2) Ben Kingsley in "Gandhi," (3) Meryl Streep in "Sophie's Choice," (4) Louis Gossett, Jr. in "An Officer and a Gentleman," (5) Jessica Lange in "Tootsie," (6) Richard Attenborough for "Gandhi," (7) Mickey Rooney, (8) "Volver a Empezar" (To Begin Again) (Spain), (9) "Just Another Missing Kid."
1983: (1) "Terms of Endearment," (2) Robert Duvall in "Tender Mercies," (3) Shirley MacLaine in "Terms of Endearment," (4) Jack Nicholson in "Terms of Endearment," (5) Linda Hunt in "The Year of Living Dangerously," (6) James L. Brooks for "Terms of Endearment," (7) Hal Roach, (8) "Fanny and Alexander" (Sweden), (9) "He Makes Me Feel Like Dancin'."
1984: (1) "Amadeus," (2) F. Murray Abraham in "Amadeus," (3) Sally Field in "Places in the Heart," (4) Haing S. Ngor in "The Killing Fields," (5) Peggy Ashcroft in "A Passage to India," (6) Milos Forman for "Amadeus," (7) James Stewart, (8) "Dangerous Moves" (Switzerland), (9) "The Times of Harvey Milk."
1985: (1) "Out of Africa," (2) William Hurt in "Kiss of the Spider Woman," (3) Geraldine Page in "The Trip to Bountiful," (4) Don Ameche in "Cocoon," (5) Anjelica Huston in "Prizzi's Honor," (6) Sydney Pollack for "Out of Africa," (7) Paul Newman, Alex North, (8) "The Official Story" (Argentina), (9) "Broken Rainbow."

FOREIGN FILMS RELEASED IN U.S. DURING 1986

LADY JANE

(PARAMOUNT) Producer, Peter Snell; Director, Trevor Nunn; Screenplay, David Edgar; Story, Chris Bryant; Photography, Douglas Slocombe; Editor, Anne V: Coates; Music, Stephen Oliver; Designer, Harry Rabinowitz; Designer, Allan Cameron; Costumes, Sue Blane, David Perry; Associate Producer, Ted Lloyd; Production Manager, Malcolm Christopher; Production Coordinator, Monica Rogers; Assistant Directors, Barry Langley, Mike Higgins, Jerry Daly, Peter Freeman; Casting, Rebecca Howard, Joyce Nettles; Art Directors, Fred Carter, Martyn Hebert, Mark Raggett; Set Decorator, Harry Cordwell; Choreographers, Geraldine Stephenson, Sheila Falconer; Stunt Coordinator, Alf Joint; Music performed by Royal Philharmonic Orchestra; In Technicolor; Dolby Stereo; Rated PG13; 144 minutes; January release

CAST

Lady Jane Grey	Helena Bonham Carter
Guilford Dudley	Cary Elwes
John Dudley, Duke of Northumberland	John Wood
Dr. Feckenham	Michael Hordern
Mrs. Ellen	Jill Bennett
Princess Mary	Jane Lapotaire
Frances Grey, Duchess of Suffolk	Sara Kestelman
Henry Grey, Duke of Suffolk	Patrick Stewart
King Edward VI	Warren Saire
Sir John Bridges	Joss Ackland
Sir John Gates	Ian Hogg
Renard, Spanish Ambassador	Lee Montague
Marquess of Winchester	Richard Vernon
Archbishop Cranmer	David Waller
Earl of Arundel	Richard Johnson
Thomas	Pip Torrens
Dr. Owen	Matthew Guinness
Robert Dudley	Guy Henry
John Dudley	Andrew Bicknell
Peasant Leader	Clyde Pollitt
Executioner	Morgan Sheppard
Lady Anne Wharton	Zelah Clarke
Katherine Grey	Laura Clipsham
Housekeeper	Janet Henfrey
Under Treasurer	Brian Poyser
Herald	Phillip Voss
Steward	Robert Putt
Tavern Keeper	Stewart Harwood
Brothel Keeper	Carole Hayman
Lady Warwick	Adele Anderson
Lady Robert Dudley	Anna Gilbert

and Richard Moore, Michael Goldie, Denyse Alexander, Gabor Vernon, Robin Martin Oliver, Nicky Croydon, John Abbott, Jeannette Fox, Alison Woodgate, Philippa Luce, Eliza Kern, Krzysia Bialeska, Cryss Jean Healey

Top Right: Richard Vernon, Frances Grey, John Wood, Helena Bonham Carter, David Waller Below: Carter, Elwes, Michael Hordern © *Paramount/Graham Attwood*

Cary Elwes, Helena Bonham Carter

Helena Bonham Carter

ANGRY HARVEST

(EUROPEAN CLASSICS) Producer, Arthur Brauner; Director, Agnieszka Holland; Screenplay, Miss Holland, Paul Hengge; Based on the novel by Hermann Field, Stanislaw Mierzenski; Photography, Josef Ort-Snep; Editor, Barbara Kunze; Music, Jorg Strassburger; In German with English subtitles; Not rated; Color; 107 minutes; January release.

CAST

Leon	Armin Mueller-Stahl
Rosa	Elisabeth Trissenaar
Anna	Kathe Jaenicke
Kaspar	Hans Beerhenke
Magda	Isa Haller
Eugenia	Margit Carstensen
Cybolowski	Wojtech Pszoniak
Geislicher	Gerd Baltus
Pauline	Anita Hofer
Maslanko	Kurt Raab
Walden	Gunter Berger
Dan	Wolf Donner

Top Right: Armin Mueller-Stahl, Elisabeth Trissenaar © *European Classics*

FOREVER YOUNG

(CINECOM) Executive Producer, David Puttnam; Producer, Chris Griffin; Director, David Drury; Script Editor, Jack Rosenthal; Screenplay, Ray Connelly; Associate Producer, David Bill; Production Manager, Dominic Fulford; Location Manager, Scott Wodehouse; Photography, Norman Langley; Sound, David Crozier; Art Director, Jeffrey Woodbridge; Costumes, Tudor George; Editor, Max Lemon; British; Color; Not Rated; 84 minutes; January release

CAST

James (Jimmy)	James Aubrey
Father Michael	Nicholas Gecks
Father Vincent	Alec McCowen
Mary	Karen Archer
John	Joseph Wright
Paul	Liam Holt

Right Center: Nicholas Gecks, Karen Archer © *Cinecom*

Robert Urquhart, Suzanne Burden, Michael Maloney

SHARMA AND BEYOND

(CINECOM) Executive Producer, David Puttnam; Producer, Chris Griffin; Director/Screenplay, Brian Gilbert; Production Manager, David Barron; Location Manager, Scott Wodehouse; Photography, Ernest Vincze; Sound, David Crozier; Art Director, Maurice Cain; Editor, Max Lemon; British; Color; Not Rated; 82 minutes; January release

CAST

Natasha Gorley-Peters	Suzanne Burden
Evan Gorley-Peters	Robert Urquhart
Stephen Archer	Michael Maloney
Myrna	Antonia Pemberton
Anton Heron	Benjamin Whitrow
Vivian	Tom Wilkinson

© *Cinecom*

THOSE GLORY, GLORY DAYS

(CINECOM) Executive Producer, David Puttnam; Producer, Chris Griffin; Director, Philip Saville; Series Script Editor, Jack Rosenthal; Screenplay, Julie Welch; Associate Producer, David Bill; Production Manager, Dominic Fulford; Location Manager, Scott Wodehouse Photography, Phil Meheux; Art Director, Maurice Cain; Sound, David Crozier; Costumes, Tudor George; Editor, Max Lemon; British; Color; Not Rated; 91 minutes; January release

CAST

Mrs. Herrick	Julia McKenzie
Coalhole	Elizabeth Spriggs
Julia, journalist	Julia Goodman
Young Danny	Rachael Meidman
Danny	Zoe Nathenson
Jailbird	Liz Campion
Toni	Sara Sugarman
Tub	Cathy Murphy
Petrina	Amelia Dipple
Petrina's Mum	Eva Lohman
Mr. Herrick	Peter Tilbury
Petrina's Dad	Stephan Chase
Himself	Danny Blanchflower

Sara Sugarman, Zoe Nathenson (below)
© *Cinecom*

SUMMER

(ORION CLASSICS) Producer, Margaret Menegoz for Les Films du Losange with the cooperation of the French Ministry of Culture and P.T.T.; Director/Screenplay, Eric Rohmer; Photography, Sophie Maintigneux; Sound, Claudine Nougaret; Editor, Maria-Luisa Garcia; Music, Jean-Louis Valero; Mixing, Dominique Hennequin; Administration, Francoise Etchegarary; With the aid of Pierre Chatard, Gerard Lomond; Color; Rated R; 98 minutes; August release

CAST

Delphine	Marie Riviere
Manuella	Lisa Heredia
Beatrice	Beatrice Romand
Francoise	Rosette
Edouard	Eric Hamm
Young girl in Cherbourg	Vanessa Leleu
Irene	Irene Skobline
Lena	Carita
Joel	Joel Comarlot
Pierrot	Marc Vivas
Jacques	Vincent Gauthier

Vincent Gauthier, Marie Riviere

Top Left: Marie Riviere, Rosette
Below: Marie Riviere, Beatrice Romand
© *Orion Classics*

TURTLE DIARY

(SAMUEL GOLDWYN) Producer, Richard Johnson; Director, John Irvin; Screenplay, Harold Pinter; Based on the novel *Turtle Diary* by Russell Hoban; Editor, Peter Tanner; Executive Producer, Peter Snell; A CBS Theatrical Films Presentation of a United British Artists/ Britannic Production; British; Color; Rated PG; 97 minutes; February release

CAST

Neaera Duncan	Glenda Jackson
William Snow	Ben Kingsley
Mr. Johnson	Richard Johnson
George Fairbairn	Michael Gambon
Mrs. Inchcliff	Rosemary Leach
Miss Neap	Eleanor Bron
Harriet	Harriet Walter
Sandor	Jeroen Krabbe
Publisher	Nigel Hawthorne
Mr. Meager	Michael Aldridge

Right: Ben Kingsley, Glenda Jackson
© Samuel Goldwyn

Ben Kingsley, Harold Pinter Above: Michael
Gambon, Glenda Jackson, Ben Kingsley

Richard Johnson, Glenda Jackson
Above: Harriet Walter, Ben Kingsley

165

MY AMERICAN COUSIN

(SPECTRAFILM) Producer, Peter O'Brian; Co-Producer/Director/ Screenplay, Sandy Wilson; Photography, Richard Leiterman; Designer/Associate Producer, Phillip Schmidt; Editor, Haida Paul; Production Manager, Tom Braidwood; Assistant Directors, Edward Folger, Matthew O'Connor; Costumes, Philip Clarkson, Sheila Bingham; Sound, Bruce Nyznik, Garrell Clark, Paul Sharpe; Production Coordinator, Gabriella Martinelli; Produced in Association with Borderline Productions Inc.; Produced by Okangan Motion Picture Company Ltd.; Songs by various artists; Canadian; Color; Rated R; 112 minutes; February release

CAST

Sandy Wilcox	Margaret Langrick
Butch Walker	John Wildman
Major Wilcox	Richard Donat
Kitty Wilcox	Jane Mortifee
Lenny McPhee	T. J. Scott
Shirley Darling	Camille Henderson
Thelma	Darsi Bailey
Lizzie	Alison Hale
Sue	Samantha Jocelyn
Dolly Walker	Babs Chula
Al Walker	Terry Moore
Johnny Wilcox	Brent Severson
Danny Wilcox	Brian Hagel
Eddie Wilcox	Carter Dunham
Ruth Wilcox	Julie Nevlud
Pixie Wilcox	Alexis Peat
Granny Wilcox	Micki Maunsell
Aunt Nell	Kitty Wilson
Jim June	Jake Van Weston
Mucker	Ritchie Hobden
Rosie Hardman	Linda Geggie
Dance M. C.	Nikos Theodosakis

and Lisa Nevin, Tom Braidwod, Nicola Cavendish, Dave Sher, Linda Wiebe, Lisa Wiebe, Sergei Ryga, Lorne Davidson, Kellie Benz, Jacqueline Conrad, Gabriella Martinelli, Rob Wylie, James Forsyth

Left: John Wildman (C), Margaret Langrick (R)
© *International Spectrafilm*

John Wildman (also Top Left), Margaret Langrick

LA CAGE AUX FOLLES 3
The Wedding

(TRI-STAR) Producer, Marcello Danon; Director, Mario D'Alessio; Story, Philippe Nicaud, Christine Carere, Marcello Danon; Inspired by characters in Jean Poiret's play "La Cage aux Folles"; Screenplay, Michael Audiard, Jacques Audiard, Marcello Danon, Georges Lautner, Gerard Lamballe; Dialogue, Michel Audiard, with Antonella Interlenghi, Saverio Vallone, Benny Luke, Gianluca Favilla, Umberto Raho, and the participation of Stephane Audran and Michel Galabru; Design, Mario Garbuglia; Costumes, Ambra Danon; Wardrobe for M. Serrault and M. Tognazzi, Piero Tosi; Editors, Michelle David, Elisabeth Guido, Lidia Pascolini; Photography, Luciano Tovoli; Music, Ennio Morricone; Assistant Directors, Henri Jacques Cukier, Albino Cocco; In color; PG13; 90 minutes; February release

CAST

Renato	Ugo Tognazzi
Albin	Michel Serrault
Charrier	Michel Galabru
Cindy	Antonella Interlenghi
Jacob	Benny Luke
Mortimer	Saverio Vallone
Matrimonia	Stephane Audran
Kennedy	Umberto Raho
Dulac	Gianluca Favilla
Laurent	Pierfrancesco Aiello
Dottore	Roberto Posse
Flora	Flora Mastroianni

Michel Serrault

Top: Ugo Tognazzi, Michel Serrault
Below: Antonella Interlenghi, Saverio Vallone
Right: Tognazzi, Serrault (also at Top)
© Tri-Star

167

ARTHUR'S HALLOWED GROUND

(CINECOM) Executive Producer, David Puttnam; Producer, Chris Griffin; Director, Freddie Young; Script Editor, Jack Rosenthal; Screenplay, Peter Gibbs; Associate Producer, David Bill; Production Manager, Dominic Fulford; Location Manager, Scott Wodehouse; Photography, Chick Anstiss; Sound, David Crozier; Costumes, Tudor George; Editor, Chris Ridsdale; British; Color; Not rated; 84 minutes; February release

CAST

Arthur	Jimmy Jewel
Betty	Jean Boht
Lionel	David Swift
Len	Michael Elphick
Eric	Derek Benfield
Henry	Vas Blackwood
Norman	John Flanagan
George	Bernard Gallagher
Sales Representative	Sam Kelly
Billy	Al Ashton
Kev	Mark Drewry

Vas Blackwood, Jimmy Jewel
© *Cinecom*

Reece Dinsdale, Sean Bean
© *Cinecom*

WINTER FLIGHT

(CINECOM) Executive Producer, David Puttnam; Co-Producers, Robin Douet, Susan Richards; Director, Roy Battersby; Screenplay, Alan Janes; Music, Richard Harvey; Location Manager, David Brown; Photography, Chris Menges; Art Director, Adrienne Atkinson; Costumes, Sue Yelland; Editor, Lesley Walker; British; Color; 89 minutes; February release

CAST

Mal Stanton	Reece Dinsdale
Angie Bowyer	Nicola Cowper
Dave	Gary Olsen
Hooker	Sean Bean

BLISS

(NEW WORLD) Producer, Anthony Buckley; Director, Ray Lawrence; Screenplay, Ray Lawrence, Peter Carey; Based on the novel by Petery Carey; Photography, Paul Murphy; Editor, Wayne LeClos; Sound, Gary Wilkens, Dean Gawen, Peter Fenton; Music, Peter Best; Designer, Owen Paterson; Costumes, Helen Hooper; Presented by Window III Productions and New South Wales Film Corporation; Australian; Color; Rated R; 112 minutes; February release

CAST

Harry Joy	Barry Otto
Bettina Joy	Lynette Curran
Honey Barbara	Helen Jones
David Joy	Miles Buchanan
Lucy Joy	Gia Carides
Alex Duval	Tim Robertson
Joel	Jeff Truman
Rev. Des	Paul Chubb
Adrian Clunes	Bryan Marshall
Damian	Robert Menzies
Ken McClaren	Nique Needles
Alice Dalton	Kerry Walker
Aldo	Jon Ewing
Harry's Father	George Whaley

Miles Buchanan, Lynette Curran, Gia Carides
Above: Barry Otto © *New World*

168

THE GO MASTERS

(CIRCLE FILMS) Producers, Mashairo Sato, Wang Zhi-Min; Presented by Ben Barenholtz; Directors, Junya Sato, Duan Jishun; Screenplay, Li Hongzhou, Ge Kangtong, Fumio Konami; Final Script, Yasuko Ohno, Tetsuro Abe; Photography, Shoehei Ando, Luo De-An; Lighting, Hideo Kumagai, Xu He-Quing; Art Direction, Takeo Kimura, Xiao Bin; Music, Hikaru Hayashi, Jiang Dingxian; Sound, Fumio Hashimoto, Lu Xian-Chan; Produced by Toko Tokuma Co., Ltd. & Beijing Film Studio; China/Japan; Japanese with subtitles; Color; Not rated; 123 minutes; February release

CAST

Kuang Yi-shan	Sun Dao-Lin
Kuang Yuan-zhi	Huang Zong-Ying
Guan Xiao-Chuan	Du Peng
Doctor Zhang	Yu Shao-Kang
Kuang A-ming	Liu Xin, Shen Guan-Chu
Kuang A-hui	Mao Wei-Hui, Shen Dan-Ping
Xiao A-hui	Zhang Lei
Rinsaku Matsunami	Rentaro Mikuni
Shinobu onda	Yoshiko Mita
Kuang Ba	Misako Konno
Ms. Tachibano	Keiko Matsuzaka
Mrs. Yang	Mayumi Ogawa
Kuang Hua-cin	Tsukasa Ito
Yuji Onda	Wataru Yamamoto
Morikawa	Junichi Ishida
Yone Morikawa	Nobuko Otowa

Sun Dao-Lin (R)
© *Circle Films*

LOVE ON THE GROUND

(SPECTRAFILM) *L'Amour Par Terre;* Production Company, La Cecilia; Director, Jacques Rivette; Story/Screenplay, Pascal Bonitzer, Marilu Parolini, Jacques Rivette, Suzanne Schiffman; Dialogue, Pascal Bonitzer, Marilu Parolini; Photography, William Lubtchansky; Sound, Pierre Gamet; Art Director, Roberto Plate; Costumes, Manu Decor; Editor, Nicole Lubtchansky; 1st Assistant, Suzanne Schiffman; Executive Producer, Martine Marignac; France, 1984; French with subtitles; Color; Rated PG; 186 minutes; March release

CAST

Charlotte	Geraldine Chaplin
Emily	Jane Birkin
Paul	Andre Dussollier
Clement	Jean-Pierre Kalfon
Facundo	Facundo Bo
Virgil	Laszlo Szabo
Eleonore	Sandra Montaigu
Beatrice	Isabelle Linnartz
Justine	Eva Roelens

**Above: Jane Birkin, Geraldine Chaplin,
Jean-Pierre Kalfon (also Right)**
© *International Spectrafilm*

Jane Birkin (L), Geraldine Chaplin (R)

MY BEAUTIFUL LAUNDRETTE

(ORION CLASSICS) Producers, Sarah Radclyffe, Tim Bevan; Director, Stephen Frears; Screenplay, Hanif Kureishi; Photography, Oliver Stapleton; Editor, Mick Audsley; Music, Ludus Tonalis; Design, Hugo Luczyc Whyhowski; Sound, Albert Bailey; Costumes, Lindy Hemming; Make-up, Elaine Carew; Assistant Director, Simon Hinkly; Production Manager, Jane Frazer; Assistant Art Director, Alison Dominitz; A Working Title Ltd./SAF Productions production for Film Four International; British; Color; Rated R; 93 minutes; March release

CAST

Johnny	Daniel Day Lewis
Nasser	Saeed Jaffrey
Papa	Roshan Seth
Omar	Gordon Warnecke
Rachel	Shirley Anne Field
Tania	Rita Wolf
Genghis	Richard Graham
Jamaican One	Winston Graham
Jamaican Two	Dudley Thomas
Salim	Derrick Branche
Squatter	Garry Cooper
Bilquis, Nasser's wife	Charu Bala Choksi
Cherry, Salim's wife	Souad Faress
Nasser's elder daughter	Persis Marvala
Nasser's younger daughter	Nisha Kapur
Englishman	Neil Cunningham
Dick O'Donnell	Walter Donohue
Zaki	Gurdial Sira
Moose	Stephen Marcus
Gang Member's	Dawn Archibald, Jonathan Moore
Telephone Man	Gerard Horan
Poet	Ram John Holder
Tariq	Bhasker
Student	Ayub Khan Din
Girl in Disco	Dulice Leicier
Dealer	Badi Uzzaman
Kid's	Chris Pitt, Kerryann White
Madame Butterfly Man	Colin Campbell
Zaki's Wife	Sheila Chitnis

Daniel Day Lewis

Top: Gordon Warnecke, Shirley Anne Field, Saeed Jaffrey © *Orion Classics*

Gordon Warnecke, Daniel Day Lewis Top: Roshan Seth, Daniel Day Lewis

A ROOM WITH A VIEW

(CINECOM) Producer, Ismail Merchant; Director, James Ivory; Screenplay, Ruth Prawer Jhabvala; Based on the novel by E. M. Forster; Photography, Tony Pierce-Roberts; Music, Richard Robbins; Editor, Humphrey Dixon; Costumes, Jenny Beavan, John Bright; Designers, Gianni Quaranta, Brian Ackland-Snow; Assistant Director, Kevan Barker; Production Managers, Ann Wingate, Lanfranco Diotallevi; Associate Producers, Paul Bradley, Peter Marangoni; Casting, Celestia Fox; Sound, Ray Beckett, Richard King; A Goldcrest presentation in association with National Film Finance Corporation and Curzon Film Distributors; Soundtrack on Filmtrax DRG Records; Dolby Stereo; Color; Not Rated; 115 minutes; March release

CAST

Charlotte Bartlett	Maggie Smith
Lucy Honeychurch	Helena Bonham Carter
Mr. Emerson	Denholm Elliott
George Emerson	Julian Sands
Cecil Vyse	Daniel Day Lewis
Reverend Beebe	Simon Callow
Miss Lavish	Judi Dench
Mrs. Honeychurch	Rosemary Leach
Freddy Honeychurch	Rupert Graves
Mr. Eager	Patrick Godfrey
Catherine Alan	Fabia Drake
Teresa Alan	Joan Henley
Mrs. Vyse	Maria Britneva
The Cockney Signora	Amanda Walker
Sir Harry Otway	Peter Cellier
Minnie Beebe	Mia Fothergill
Mrs. Butterworth	Patricia Lawrence
Santa Croce Guide	Mirio Guidelli
The New Charlotte and Lucy	Matyelock Gibbs, Kitty Aldridge
Mr. Floyd	Freddy Korner
Miss Pole	Elizabeth Marangoni
"Phaeton"	Lucca Rossi
"Persephone"	Isabella Celani
Murdered Youth	Luigi Di Fiori

© *Cinecom*

Denholm Elliott, Joan Henley, Julian Sands, Fabia Drake
Top Left: Rupert Graves, Helena Bonham Carter, Daniel Day Lewis

1986 Academy Awards For Best Screenplay Adaptation,
Art Direction, Costume Design

Helena Bonham Carter, Maggie Smith Top Left: Julian Sands, Helena Bonham Carter (also below) Right: Helena Bonham Carter, Daniel Day Lewis Top: Carter, Judi Dench

GINGER & FRED

(MGM/UA) Producer, Alberto Grimaldi; Director, Federico Fellini; Story, Federico Fellini, Tonino Guerra; Screenplay, Federico Fellini, Tonino Guerra, Tullio Pinelli; Photography, Tonio Delli Colli, Ennio Guarnieri; Costumes, Danilo Donati; Designer, Dante Ferretti; Music, Nicola Piovani; Editors, Nino Baragli, Ugo De Rossi, Ruggero Mastroianni; Assistant Director, Gianni Arduini; Assistants to Director, Filippo Ascione, Daniela Barbiani, Eugenio Cappuccio, Anke Zindler; Production Supervisor, Luigi Millozza; Production Managers-Walter Massi, Gianfranco Coduti, Roberto Mannoni, Raymond Leplont; Set Decorator, Gian Franco Fumagalli; Art Director, Nazzareno Piani; Costume Assistant, Rosanna Andreoni; Make-up, Rino Carboni; Sound, Fausto Ancillai, Fabio Ancillai, Tommaso Quattrini; Special Effects, Adriano Pischiutta; Choreographer, Tony Ventura; Assistant Choreographer, Isabella Paolucci; A Co-Production of PEA Produzioni Europee Associate S.r.l., Rome/Revcom Films S.A. in association with Les Films Arianne and with FR3 Films Production, Paris/Stella Film in association with Anthea/with the collaboration of Rai Uno; Color; Rated PG-13; 130 minutes; March release

CAST

Amelia (Ginger)	Giulietta Masina
Pippo (Fred)	Marcello Mastroianni
Host of the television program	Franco Fabrizi
Admiral Aulenti	Frederick Ledebur
Transvestite	Augusto Poderosi
Assistant Director	Martin Maria Blau
Brother Gerolamo	Jacques Henry Lartigue
Toto	Toto Mignone
Writer	Ezio Marano
Bandaged Man	Antoine Saint Jean
Kidnapped Industrialist	Frederich Thun
Television Inspector	Antonio Iuorio
Pretty Journalist	Barbara Scoppa
Journalist	Elisabeth Flumeri
Gable Double	Salvatore Billa
Clairvoyant	Ginestra Spinola
CST Secretary	Stefania Marini
Mobster	Francesco Casale

and Gianfranco Alpestre, Filippo Ascione, Elena Cantarone, Cosima Chiusoli, Claudio Ciocca, Sergio Ciulli, Roberto DeSandro, Bittorio DeBisogno, Fabrizio Fontana, Laurentina Guidotti, Giorgio Iovine, Danika LaLoggia, Isabelle Therese LaPorte, Luigi Leoni, Luciano Lombardo, Mariele Loreley, Elena Magoia, Franco Marino, Mauro Misul, Jurgen Morhofer, Pippo Negri, Antonietta Patriarca, Nando Pucci Negri, Luigi Rossi, Franco Trevisi, Patty Vailati, Narcisio Vicario, Hermann Weiskopf

Giulietta Masina, Marcello Mastroianni
(also above)

3 MEN AND A CRADLE

(GOLDWYN) Producer, Jean-Francois Lepetit; Director/Screenplay, Coline Serreau; Photography, Jean-Yves Escoffier; Camera, Jean-Jacques Bouhon; Sound, Daniel Ollivier; Designer, Yvan Maussion; Editor, Catherine Renault; Production Managers, Henri Vart, Jacques Attia; Assistant Directors, Graziella Molinaro, Dominique Chaulot Talmon, Pierre De Riviere; Art Direction, Michele Hautin, Vincent Litchle, Pascal Morin, Francis Pesquer, Jacques Violette, Laurent Teysseire; Costumes, Edith Vesperini, Poussine Mercanton; A Flach Film—Soprofilms—TF 1 Productions Coproduction; Winner of three Cesars (French Oscars); French; Color; PG-13; 100 minutes; April release.

CAST

Pierre	Roland Giraud
Michel	Michel Boujenah
Jacques	Andre Dussollier
Sylvia	Philippine Leroy Beaulieu
Madame Rapons	Dominique Lavant
Antoinette	Marthe Villalonga
The Pharmacist	Annik Alane
Madame Rodriquez	Josine Comellias
Marie 1	Gwendoline Mourlet
Marie 2	Jennifer Moret
Paul	Francois Domange
Hoodlum 1	Christian Zanetti
Hoodlum 2	Gilles Cohen
Traffic Cop	Bernard Sancy
Man following Michel	Xavier Maly

Roland Giraud, Michel Boujenah, Andre Dussollier,
Jennifer Moret (baby)

174

MR. LOVE

(WARNER BROS.) Producers, Susan Richards, Robin Douet; Director, Roy Battersby; Executive Producer, David Puttnam; Screenplay, Kenneth Eastaugh; Music, Willy Russell; Designer, Adrienne Atkinson; Editor, Alan J. Cumner-Price; Sound, Tony Jackson; Assistant Directors, Roy Stevens, Andrew Wood, Kevin Westley; Costumes, Ann Hollowood; Additional Photography, John Davey; Production Cordinator, Mary Richards; Special Effects, Tony Neale, Steve May, Tim Jones; Vocals, Rebecca Storm; Lyrics, Ruth and Willy Russell; Musical Director, David Goldberg; Choreography, Gillian Lynne; Songs by various artists; a Warner Bros. and Goldcrest presentation of an Enigma Production; British; Color; Rated PG-13; 92 minutes; April release

CAST

Donald Lovelace	Barry Jackson
Theo	Maurice Denham
Pink Lady	Margaret Tyzack
Barbara	Linda Marlowe
Ester	Christina Collier
Lucy Nuttall	Helen Cotterill
Melanie	Julia Deakin
Leo	Donal McCann
Doris Lovelace	Marcia Warren
Ferris	Tony Melody
Maggie Capstick	Kay Stonham
Mrs. Lunt	Patsy Byrne
Boy in projection room	Jeremy Swift
Little Alice	Janine Roberts
Parson	John Joyce
Undertaker	Dave Atkins
Old Gardener	George Malpas
Apprentice Gardeners	Chris Jury, James Benson
Leo's Girlfriend	Jacki Piper
Landau Proprietor	Robert Bridges
Landau Man	Alan Starkey
Nubile Housewife	Lill Roughley
Art Teacher	Tina Simmons

Maurice Denham, Linda Marlowe
Top: Janine Roberts, Barry Jackson
© *Warner Bros.*

MARIA CHAPDELAINE

(THE MOVIE STORE) Producers, Murray Shostak, Robert Baylis; Executive Producer, Harold Greenberg; Director, Gilles Carle; Screenplay, Guy Fournier, Gilles Carle; Based on novel by Louis Hemon; Art Director, Jocelyn Joly; Assistant Art Director, Raymond Dupuis; Photography, Pierre Mignot; Costumes, Michele Hamel; Editor, Evde Chiriaeff, Michel Arcand; Music, Lewis Furey; Production Manager, Lorraine Richard; Assistant Directors, Jacques W. Benoit, Monique Maranda, Jacques Laberge; Sound, Patrick Rousseau; Special Effects, Bill Orr, John Thomas; Production Coordinator, Mary Helene Roy; Musical Arranger, Richard Gregoire; Canadian; Four Canadian Academy (Genie) Awards/Film Advisory Board Award of Excellence/California Motion Picture Council Golden Halo Award; Color; Rated PG; 114 minutes; April release

CAST

Maria Chapdelaine	Carole Laure
Francois Paradis	Nick Mancuso
Father Cordelier	Claude Rich
Laura Chapdelaine	Amulette Garneau
Samuel Chapdelaine	Yoland Guerard
Eutrope Gagnon	Pierre Curzi
Lorenzo Suprenant	Donald Lautrec
Da'Be Chapdelaine	Gilbert Sicotte
Esdras Chapdelaine	Guy Thauvette
Tit-Be Chapdelaine	Stephane Query
Alma-Rose Chapdelaine	Josee-Anne Fortin
Telesphore Chapdelaine	Louis-Philippe Milot
Edwidge Legare	Gilbert Comtios
Marie-Ange	Marie Tifo
Boat Captain	Guy L'Ecuyer
Bedeau	Roland Bedard
Doctor	Michel Rivard
Pierre Caumartin	Michel Langevin
Edmond Caumartin	Cedric Noel

Nick Mancuso, Carole Laure
(also above)

© *The Movie Store*

ABSOLUTE BEGINNERS

(ORION) Producers, Stephen Woolley, Chris Brown; Director, Julien Temple; Screenplay, Christopher Wicking, Richard Burridge, Don MacPherson; Based on the novel by Colin MacInnes; Additional Dialogue, Terry Johnson; Executive Producers, Nik Powell, Al Clark, Robert Devereux; Associate Producer, David Wimbury; Developed for the screen by Michael Hamlyn; Choreographer, David Toguri; Photography, Oliver Stapleton; Music, Gil Evans, Clive Langer, Alan Winstanley; Editors, Michael Bradsell, Gerry Hambling, Richard Bedford, Russell Lloyd; Costumes, Sue Blane, David Perry; Designer, John Beard; Production Manager, Peter Kohn; Assistant Directors, Ray Corbett, Kieron Phipps, Tony Aherne; Sound, David John; Art Directors, Stuart Rose, Ken Wheatley; Production Co-Ordinators, Kathy Sykes, Valerie Craig; Assistant Choreographer, Jonathan Thornton; Executive Music Supervisor, Ray Williams; Songs by various artists; Presented by Virgin and Goldcrest; A Palace Production; British; System 35; Color; Dolby Stereo; Rated PG-13; 111 minutes; April release

CAST

Colin	Eddie O'Connell
Suzette	Patsy Kensit
Vendice Partners	David Bowie
Henley of Mayfair	James Fox
Arthur	Ray Davies
Mum	Mandy Rice-Davies
Big Jill	Eve Ferret
Mr. Cool	Tony Hippolyte
Wizard	Graham Fletcher-Cook
Fabulous Hoplite	Joe McKenna
The Fanatic	Steven Berkoff
Athene Duncannon	Sade
Ed the Ted	Tenpole Tudor
Flikker	Bruce Payne
Call Me Cobber	Alan Freeman
Dido Lament	Anita Morris
Dean Swift	Paul Rhys
The Misery Kid	Julian Firth
Baby Boom	Chris Pitt
Harry Charms	Lionel Blair
Johnny Wonder	Gary Beadle
Mario	Robbie Coltrane
Cappuccino Man	Jess Conrad
D.J. Entertainer	Smiley Culture
Amberly Drove	Ronald Fraser
Party Singer	Slim Gaillard
Mrs. Larkin	Irene Handl
Vern	Peter Hugo-Daly
Dorita	Amanda Jane Powell
Saltzman	Johnny Shannon
Cynthia Eve	Sylvia Syms
Santa Lucia Club Owner	Ekow Abban
Slim Brother	Robert Austin
Ton-Up Vicar	Gerry Alexander
Slim Brother	Jim Dunk

and Johnny Edge, Carmen Ejogo, Paul Fairminer, Hugo First, Pat Hartley, Astley Harvey, Colin Jeavons, Alfred Maron, G. B. (Zoot) Money, Sandie Shaw, Bruno Toniolo

Eddie O'Connell, Patsy Kensit
© *Orion*

Hideko Takamine

HORSE

(R5/S8) Producer, Nobuyoshi Morita; Director, Kajiro Yamamoto; Screenplay, Kajiro Yamamoto, Akira Kurosawa; Photography, Hiromitsu Karasawa (Spring), Akira Mimura (Summer/Sets), Hiroshi Suzuki (Autumn), Takeo Ito (Winter); Art Director, Takashi Matsuyama; Music, Jisho Kitamura; Editor, Akira Kurosawa; Production Coordinator, Akira Kurosawa; Equestrian Supervisors, Jun Maki, Shoichiro Ozaki; A Toho Production; Color; Japanese, 1941; Japanese with subtitles; Not Rated; 129 minutes; May release

CAST

Ine	Hideko Takamine
Mr. Onoda	Kamatari Fujiwara
Mrs. Onoda	Chieko Takehisa
Grandma	Kaoru Futaba
Toyokazu	Takeshi Hirata
Kinjiro	Toshio Hosoi
Tsuru	Setsuko Ichikawa
Teacher	Sadao Maruyama
Zenzo	Yoshio Kosugi

LETTER TO BREZHNEV

(CIRCLE RELEASING CORP) Producer, Janet Goddard; Director, Chris Bernard; Screenplay, Frank Clarke; Co-producer, Caroline Spack; Assistant Directors, Pete Cavaciuti, Piers Player, Matt McConaghy; Lighting, Bruce McGowan; Editor, Lesley Walker; Assistant Editor, Oliver Huddleston; Designers, Lez Brotherston, Nick Englefield, Jonathan Swain; Sound, Ray Beckett; Costumes, Mark Reynolds; Production Co-ordinator, Chriss Kerr; Associate Producer, Paul Lister; Music, Alan Gill; Soundtrack on MCA Records; British; Color; 94 minutes; May release

CAST

Sergei	Alfred Molina
Peter	Peter Firth
Teresa	Mergi Clarke
Tracy	Tracy Lea
Elaine	Alexandra Pigg
Girl in yellow pedal pushers	Susan Dempsey
Mick	Ted Wood
Taxi Driver	Carl Chase
Charlie	Robbie Dee
Charlie's Girlfriend	Sharon Power
Dimitri	Syd Newman
Rayner	Eddie Ross
Girls on bus	Wendy Votel, Jeanette Votel
Mother	Mandy Walsh
Josie	Angela Clarke
Father	Joey Kaye
Vinny	Frank Clarke
Boy at party	Paul Beringer
Reporter	Ken Campbell
Foreign Officer Official	Neil Cunningham
"Sweaty Arse"	John Carr

Top Right: Alexandra Pigg, Peter Firth
Below: Margi Clarke, Alfred Molina
© *Circle Films*

FEMMES DE PERSONNE

(EUROPEAN CLASSICS) Executive Producer, Alain Terzian; Director/Screenplay, Christopher Frank; Photography, Jean Tournier; Sound, Michel Desrois; Production Director, Philippe Lievre; Editor, Nathalie LaFaurie; Music, Georges DeLerue; Production Company, T. Films, F.R.3; French; Color; Not Rated; 106 minutes; May release

CAST

Cecile	Marthe Keller
Gilquin	Jean-Louis Trintignant
Isabelle	Caroline Cellier
Adeline	Fanny Cottencon
Antoine	Philippe Leotard
Marc	Patrick Chesnais
Julie	Elisabeth Etienne
Patric	Pierre Arditi
Philippe Dubly	Marcel Bozonnett
Monica Gilquin	Yvette DeLaune
Arnaud	Karol Zuber

© *European Classics*

Marthe Keller, Caroline Cellier, Fanny Cottencon

VAGABOND

(INTERNATIONAL FILM EXCHANGE) *Sans Toit Ni Loi;* Producer, Cine-Tamaris, Films A2; Director/Screenplay, Agnes Varda; Photography, Patrick Blossier; Sound, Jean-Paul Mugel; Music, Joanna Bruzdowicz; Editors, Agnes Varda, Patricia Mazuy; Produced with the participation of The French Ministry of Culture; Released in association with Grange Communications; France; French with subtitles; Color; Not Rated; 105 minutes; May release

CAST

Mona	Sandrine Bonnaire
Madame Landier	Macha Meril
Jean-Pierre	Stephane Freiss
Eliane	Laurence Cortadellas
Tante Lydie	Marthe Jarnias
Yolande	Yolande Moreau
Paulo	Joel Fosse
David	Patrick Lepcynski
Assoun	Yahaoui Assouna
Drifter/Pimp	Christian Chessa

**Top Left: Sandrine Bonnaire, and Below
with Macha Meril**
© *Grange Communications/International Film Exchange*

DARK OF THE NIGHT
(aka Mr. Wrong)

(CASTLE HILL) Producers, Robin Laing, Gaylene Preston; Director, Gaylene Preston; Production Co., Preston Laing with N.Z. Film Commission; Screenplay, Gaylene Preston, Geoff Murphy, Graham Tetley; Based on story by Elizabeth Jane Howard; Photography, Thom Burstyn; Camera, Alun Bollinger; Art Director, Mike Becroft; Editor, Simon Reece; Sound, Ken Saville; Music, Jonathan Crayford; New Zealand; Color; Not Rated; 88 minutes; May release

CAST

Meg	Heather Bolton
Mr. Wrong	David Letch
Samantha	Margaret Umbers
Val	Suzanne Lee
Bruce	Gary Stalker
Wayne	Danny Mulheron
Mary Carmichael	Perry Piercy
Clive	Philip Gordon
Mr. Whitehorn	Michael Haigh
Mrs. Alexander	Kate Harcourt

© *Quartet Films*

Heather Bolton

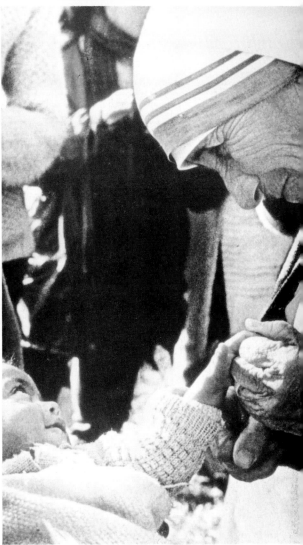

MOTHER TERESA

(TOHO INTERNATIONAL) Producers/Directors, Ann Petrie, Jeanette Petrie; Editor, Tom Haneke; Photography, Ed Lachman, Sandi Sissel; Music, Suzanne Ciani; Associate Producer, Lindsay Fontana; Assistant Editor/Sound Editor, Donald Klocek; Sound, Barbara Becker, Lee Dichter; Consultants, William Petrie, Philip Kravitz, Scott Morris, Jerald F. Wagner; Production Coordinators, Vincent Millard, Jane Abbott; Production Staff, Robert Hiott, Suzanne Johnson, Brenda Nicholls, Warren Black; Songs, John B. Foley, Karen Lafferty; Documentary; Color by Du Art; Not Rated; 81 minutes; May release. CAST: Mother Teresa and the Sisters, Brothers, Fathers and co-workers of the Missionaries of Charity throughout the world.

Top Left and Right: Mother Teresa
© *Petrie Productions/Mary Ellen Mark*

Jeanette Petrie, Anne Petrie

MONA LISA

(ISLAND PICTURES) Producers, Stephen Woolley, Patrick Cassavetti; Director, Neil Jordan; Executive Producers, George Harrison, Denis O'Brien; Co-Producers, Ray Cooper, Chris Brown; Screenplay, Neil Jordan, David Leland; Photography; Roger Pratt; Designer, Jamie Leonard; Art Director, Gemma Jackson; Editor, Lesley Walker; Music, Michael Kamen; Song, Genesis; Production Manager, Linda Bruce; Production Co-Ordinator, Laura Julian; Assistant Directors, Ray Crobett, Chris Brock, Tony Aherne; Assistant Editors, Jeremy Hume, Kevin Lane; Sound, David John; Costumes, Louise Frogley; Special Effects Make-up, Nick Dudman; Stunts, Terry Forrestal; Presented with Handmade Films; A Palace Production; Soundtrack on Filmtrax; Rated R; 104 minutes; June release

CAST

George	Bob Hoskins
Simone	Cathy Tyson
Mortwell	Michael Caine
Anderson	Clarke Peters
Cathy	Kate Hardie
Thomas	Robbie Coltrane
Jeannie	Zoe Nathenson
May	Sammi Davies
Terry	Rod Bedall
Dudley	Joe Brown
Dawn	Pauline Melville
Devlin	David Halliwell
Carpenter	G.B. "Zoot" Money
Raschid	Hossein Karimbeik
Roberts	John Darling
Rosie	Donna Cannon
Flower Shop Girl	Mandy Winch
Girl in Paradise Club	Maggie O'Neill
Girl Prostitute in Joint	Dawn Archibald
Hotel Clerk	Geoff Larder
Hotel Punter	Robert Dorning
Peep Show Girl	Helen Martin
Pron Shop Man	Richard Strange
Shop Assistant	Jeremy Hardy
Stanley	Bryan Coleman
Arab Servant	Raad Raawi
Attendant (Baths)	Alan Talbot
Black Youth	Stephen Persaud
Busker's	Bill Moore, Kenny Baker
Waiter 1st Hotel	Gary Cady
White Pimp	Perry Fenwick

Cathy Tyson Top Right: Bob Hoskins
Center: Hoskins, Michael Caine, Tyson

Michael Caine, Bob Hoskins

THE WALL

(KINO INTERNATIONAL) Producer, Marin Karmitz; Director/ Story/Dialogue Yilmaz Guney; Screenplay, Marie-Helene Quinton; Photography, Izzet Akay; Editor, Sabine Mamou; Music, Ozan Garip Sahin, Setrak Bakirel; Documentary; French/Turkish; Turkish with subtitles; Color; Not Rated; 117 minutes; June release

CAST

Tonton Ali	Tuncel Kuritz
The Political One	Ayse Emel Mesci
The Arab	Malik Berrichi
The Skinny Woman	Nicolas Hossein
The Bride	Isabelle Tissandier
Cafer	Ahmet Ziyrek
The Groom	Ali Berktay
The Prison Director	Selahattin Kuzuogly
Director General of Prisons	Jean-Pierre Colin
Chief Guard	Jacques Dimanche
Pepe Ali	Ali Dede Altuntas

"The Wall"

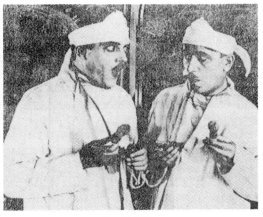

Max Linder

THE MAN IN THE SILK HAT

(KINO INTERNATIONAL) Produced, Directed and Written by Maud Linder; Original Music, Jean-Marie Senia; Narrated by Maud Linder; Orchestral Direction, Carlo Savina; Editors, Suzanne Baron, Pierre Gillette; Production Company, Films Max Linder; A Media Home Entertainment release; France 1984; In black and white; Not rated; 96 minutes; June release.

CAST

Silent Movie Comic Max Linder

THE ASSAM GARDEN

(FILM FORUM) Producer, Nigel Stafford-Clark; Director, Mary McMurray; Screenplay, Elisabeth Bond; Photography, Bryan Loftus; A Moving Picture Company Film; England, 1985; Not Rated; 92 minutes; July release

CAST

Helen	Deborah Kerr
Ruxmani	Madhur Jaffrey
Mr. Philpott	Alec McCowen
Mr. Lal	Zia Mohyeddin
(no other credits or cast submitted)	

Madhur Jaffrey, Deborah Kerr

MEN

(NEW YORKER FILMS) Executive Producer, Harald Kugler; Director/Screenplay, Doris Dorrie; Photography, Helge Weindler; Sound, Michael Etz; Editor, Raimund Barthelmes; Music, Claus Bantzer; Art Director, Jorg Neumann; Costumes, Jorg Trees; Assistant Director, Michael Juncker; Photography Assistant, Ute Wieland; Production Managers, Gerd Huber, Volker Wach; Produced by Olga Film (Munich) in cooperation with ZDF (Second German Television); German with subtitles; Color; Not Rated; 99 minutes; July release

CAST

Julius Armbrust	Heiner Lauterbach
Stefan Lachner	Uwe Ochsenknecht
Paula Armbrust	Ulrike Kriener
Angelika	Janna Marangosoff
Lothar	Dietmar Bar
Marita Strass	Marie-Charlott Schuler
Frau Lennart	Edith Volkmann
Florian	Louis Kelz
Caro	Cornelia Schneider
Juliane Zorn	Sabine Wegener
Woman in bar	Monika Schwarz
Boy in the house	Gabriel Pakleppa
Boy in the bathtub	Bjorn Banhardt
Sales Clerk	Werner Albert Puthe
Sausage Man	Ulrich Gunther
Woman in car	Astrid Pilling
Jeweler	Gerd Huber
Chambermaid	Nasrin Khochsima
Boy at the lake	Roland Schreiber
Neumann	Jorg Neumann

Uwe Ochsenknecht, Ulrike Kriener, Heiner
Lauterbach Top: Lauterback, Ochsenknecht

MALCOLM

(VESTRON) Producers, Nadia Tass, David Parker; Director, Nadia Tass; Screenplay, David Parker; Associate Producer, Timothy White; Executive Producer, Bryce Menzies; Music, Simon Jeffes, The Penguin Cafe Orchestra; Editor, Ken Sallows; Photography, David Parker; Australian; Color; Rated PG-13; 90 minutes; July release

CAST

Malcolm	Colin Friels
Frank	John Hargreaves
Judith	Lindy Davies
Willy	Chris Haywood
Tramways Supervisor	Charles Tingwell
Mrs. T.	Beverly Phillips
Jenny	Judith Stratford
Barmaid	Heather Mitchell
Jenny's Mother	Katerina Tassopoulos

John Hargreaves, Colin Friels (also above),
Lindy Davies

SINCERELY CHARLOTTE

(NEW LINE CINEMA) Executive Producer, Adophe Viezzi; Director, Caroline Huppert; Production Director, Louis Wipf; Screenplay, Caroline Huppert, Luc Beraud, Joelle Goron; Music, Philippe Sarde; Photography, Bruno de Keyzer; Editor, Anne Boissel; A Co-Production of Les Films de la Tour and FR3; French with subtitles; Color; Not Rated; 92 minutes; July release

CAST

Charlotte	Isabelle Huppert
Mathieu	Niels Arestrup
Christine	Christine Pascal
Freddy	Nicolas Wostrikoff
Roger	Jean-Michel Ribes
Mathieu's Friend	Philippe Delevingne
Christine's Mother	Laurence Mercier
Workman	Frederic Bourboulon
Marie-Cecile	Berangere Gros
Marie	Chantal Bronner
Emilie	Justine Heynemann
Vincent	Baptiste Heynemann
Inspector	Michel Fortin
Nurse	Tina Lara
Doctor	Luc Beraud
Jacquelina	Josiane Comellas
Emilio	Eduardo Manet
Nando	Ronald Chammah
Irene (Baby Sitter)	Caroline Faro
Girl on train	Claude Menard
American Woman	Laurence Masliah
Man in restaurant	Francois Borysse
Charlotte's Husband	Herman Brau

**Left: Isabelle Huppert, and Top
with Niels Arestrup**
© *New Line Cinema*

SHE'LL BE WEARING PINK PAJAMAS

(FILM FORUM) Producers, Tara Prem, Adrian Hughes; Director, John Goldschmidt; Screenplay, Eva Hardy; Photography, Clive Tickner; Music, John du Prez; Designer, Colin Pocock; Sound, Paul Filby; Editor, Richard Key; A Film Four Intl.-Pink Pajamas Production; British: Eastmancolor; Not Rated; 90 minutes; July release

CAST

Fran	Julie Walters
Tom	Anthony Higgins
Catherine	Jane Evers
Lucy	Janet Henfrey
Doreen	Paula Jacobs
Ann	Penelope Nice
Joan	Maureen O'Brien
Anita	Alyson Spiro
Judith	Jane Wood
Diane	Pauline Yates

Julie Walters

LOVE SONGS

(SPECTRAFILM) Producers, Elie Chouraqui, Robert Baylis; Director/Screenplay, Elie Chouraqui; Executive Producers, Marie-Christine Chouraqui, Murray Shostak; Music, Michel Legrand; Editor, Noelle Boisson; Art Director, Gerard Daoudal; Photography, Robert Alazraki; Sound, Patrick Rousseau; Assistant Directors, Jacques Cukier, Jacques Benoit, Serge Frydman, Thierry Meunier; Script, Suzanne Burrenberger; Casting, Margot Cappelier; Production Director, Henri Jacquillard; Production Manager, Catherine Pierrat; Costumes, Caroline DeVivaise; Songs, Michel Legrand, Gene McDaniels, S. Staplayet, A. Russell; Vocals, Guy Thomas, Terry Lauber; A 7 Films Canada-Canadian International Studios Inc.-F.R.3 Presentation; A Canada/France Co-Production; Soundtrack on Varese Sarabande Records; Color; Not rated; 107 minutes; July release

CAST

Marqaux	Catherine Deneuve
Michel	Richard Anconina
Jeremy	Christopher Lambert
Yves	Jacques Perrin
Peter	Nick Mancuso
Corinne	Dayle Haddon
Charlotte	Charlotte Gainsbourg
Elliot	Frank Ayas
Florence	Dominique Lavanant
Julie	Nelly Borgeaud
Alain	Lazslo Szabo
Jean-Paul	Inigo Lezzi
Claire	Julie Ravix
Gruber	Lionel Rocheman
Switchboard Operator	Yuni Fujimori

Right: Catherine Deneuve
Below: Richard Anconina, Christopher Lambert
© *International Spectrafilm*

Catherine Deneuve, Jacques Perrin

Catherine Deneuve, Christopher Lambert

Jean-Louis Trintignant, Marie Sophie Pochat
© *Warner Bros.*

A MAN AND A WOMAN: 20 YEARS LATER

(WARNER BROS.) Producer/Director/Screenplay, Claude Lelouch; Adaption/Additional Dialogue, Claude Lelouch, Pierre Uytterhoeven, Monique Lange, Jerome Tonnerre; Music, Francis Lai; Lyrics, Pierre Barouth; Vocals, Richard Berry, Liliane Davis, Pierre Barouh; Arranger/Conductor, Christian Gaubert; Photography, Jean-Yves LeMener, Assisted by Eric Dumage, Berto, Philippe Ros, Alain Ducousset; Sound, Harald Maury, Assisted by Dominique Duchatelle; Video Photography, Patrick Fabry; Art Director, Jacques Bufnoir; Assistant Art Directors, Marc Balzarelli, Tony Egry; Assistant Directors, Didier Grousset, Marie Fernandez, Yann Michel, Jean Sentis, Alain Maline; Editor, Hugues Darmois; Assistant Editors, Sandrine Pery, Annie Darmois; Casting, Arlette Gordon; Costumes, Mic Cheminal, Emanuel Ungaro; Stunts, Remy Julienne, Jean-Claude Lagniez; Special Effects, Georges Demetrau; Production Manager, Tania Zazulinsky; A Films 13 Production; French; Dolby Stereo; Color; Rated PG; 120 minutes; August release

CAST

Anne	Anouk Aimee
Jean-Louis	Jean-Louis Trintignant
Richard Berry	Richard Berry
Francoise	Evelyne Bouix
Marie-Sophie	Marie-Sophie Pochat
Patrick Poivre D'Arvor	Patrick Poivre D'Arvor

and Philippe Leroy-Beaulieu, Charles Gerard, Thierry Sabine, Antoine Sire, Andre Engel, Robert Hossein, Jacques Weber, Tanya Lopert, Nicole Garcia, Yane Barry, Alain Berry, Jean-Philippe Chatrier, Maurice Illouz, Jean-Claude Lagniez, Caroline Lang, Laurence Merchet, Isabelle Sadoyan, Pierre Aknine, Jean-Claude Aube, Marine Falk, Marie Giamarchi, Sylvie Jacob, Salome Lelouch, Sarah Lelouch, Alexandra Lorska, Tom Novembre, Benoit Regent, Olivier Schmitt, Patrice Valota

Jean-Louis Trintignant, Anouk Aimee

Michael Angelis, Bernard Hill, Joanne Whalley
Top: Marjorie Sudell, Ken Jones, James Ellis
© Circle Films

NO SURRENDER

(CIRCLE RELEASING CORP.) Producer, Mamoun Hassan; Executive Producer, Michael Peacock; Director, Peter Smith; Associate Producer, Clive Reed; Designer, Andrew Mollo; Photography, Michael Coulter; Editors, Rodney Holland, Kevin Brownlow; Music, Daryl Runswick; Screenplay, Alan Bleasdale; A Dunbarton Film production in association with National Film Finance Corporation, Film Four International, and William Johnston/Ronald Lillie, Lauron International; British; In color; Rated R; 100 minutes; August release

CAST

Mike	Michael Angelis
Martha Gorman	Avis Bunnage
Paddy Burke	James Ellis
Mr. Ross	Tom Georgeson
Bernard	Bernard Hill
Billy McRacken	Ray McAnally
Norman	Mark Mulholland
Cheryl	Joanne Whalley
George Groman	J. G. Devlin
Frank	Vince Earl
Ronny	Ken Jones
Tony Bonaparte	Michael Ripper
Barbara	Marjorie Sudell
Superwoman	Joan Turner

and Richard Alexander, Pamela Austin, Ina Clough, Paul Codman, Paul Conner, Elvis Costello, James Culshaw, Gabrielle Daye, David Doyle, Lovette Edwards, Gerry Fogarty, Harry Goodier, Eric Granville, Robert Hamilton, Ian Hart, Gerard Hely, Joey Kaye, Vera Kelly, Phil Kernot, Al Kossy, Penny Leatherbarrow, Stephen Lloyd, Johnny Mallon, Joe McGann, Ron Metcalf, Bill Moores, Robert Nield, Doc O'Brien, Steve O'Connor, Peter Price, Christopher Quinn, Helen Rhodes, Linus Roache, Tony Rohr, Tommy Ryan, Andrew Schofield, Tony Scoggo, Mabel Seward, Georgina Smith, Arthur Spreckley, Mike Starke, Frank Vincent, Eileen Walsh, Harry Webster, Gerry White, Dean Williams, Peter Wilson

TWIST AND SHOUT

(MIRAMAX FILMS) Director, Bille August; Screenplay, Bille August, Bjarne Reuter; Assistant Director, Tove Berg; Production Manager, Ib Tardini; Assistant Producer, Janne Find; Photography, Jan Weincke; Sound, Niels Bokkenheuser; Lighting, Soren Sorensen; Designer, Soren Krag Sorensen; Editor, Janus Billeskov Jansen; Music, Bo Holten; Produced by Per Holst Filmproduktion and Palle Fogtdal in collaboration with the Danish Film Institute, the Children's Film Council and the Co-productions Fund of Denmarks Radio; Danish (documented as the most popular film in Denmark's history); Color; Not rated; 103 minutes; August release

CAST

Bjorn	Adam Tonsberg
Erik	Lars Simonsen
Anna	Camilla Soeberg
Kirsten	Ulrikke Juul Bondo
Henning	Thomas Nielsen
Bjorn's Mother	Lone Lindorff
Bjorn's Father	Arne Hansen
Erik's Mother	Aase Hansen
Erik's Father	Bent Mejding
Kirsten's Mother	Malene Schwartz
Kirsten's Father	Troels Munk
Inge, Kirsten's sister	Helle Spanggaard
Kurt, Inge's husband	Kurt Ravn
Anna's Mother	Grethe Mogensen
Bjorn's Grandmother	Elga Olga
Bjorn's Grandfather	Willy Jacobsen
Bjorn's Aunt	Ingelise Ullner
Bjorn's Uncle	Bent Biran
Bjorn's Aunt	Jytte Strandberg
Quack	Nina Christoffersen
Band	Rubber Band

© Miramax Films

Camilla Soeberg, Adam Tonsberg
Above: Lars Simonsen, Adam Tonsberg

NEXT SUMMER

(EUROPEAN CLASSICS) Producer, Alain Sarde; Director/
Screenplay, Nadine Trintignant; Photography, William Lubtchansky;
Designer, Michele Abbe-Vannier; Editor, Marie-Josephe Yoyotte;
Music, Philippe Sarde; Production Company, Sara Films; French with
subtitles; Color; Not Rated; 100 minutes; August release

CAST

Dino .... Fanny Ardant
Paul .... Jean-Louis Trintignant
Jeanne .... Claudia Cardinale
Edouard .... Philippe Noiret
Sidonie .... Marie Trintignant
Jude .... Jerome Ange

Above: Marie Trintignant, Claudia Cardinale
Top: Fanny Ardant, Jean-Louis Trintignant
© *European Classics*

Claudia Cardinale, Pierre-Loup Rajot

CACTUS

(SPECTRAFILM) Producers, Jane Ballantyne, Paul Cox; Director, Paul Cox; Screenplay, Paul Cox, Norman Kaye, Bob Ellis; Associate Producer, Tony Llewellyn-Jones; Photography, Yuri Sokol; Designer, Asher Bilu; Editor, Tim Lewis; Sound, Ken Hammond; Production Manager, Milanka Comfort; Huppert's Wardrobe, Missoni; Australian; Color; Not Rated; 95 minutes; September release

CAST

Colo	Isabelle Huppert
Robert	Robert Menzies
Tom	Norman Kaye
Bea	Monica Maughan
Banduk	Banduk Marika
Martha	Sheila Florance
George	Peter Aanensen
Club Speaker	Julia Blake
Eye Specialist	Lionel Kowal
Jean-Francois	Jean-Pierre Mignon
Elsa	Elsa Davis
Kevin	Ray Marshall
Maurie	Maurie Fields
Doctor	Sean Scully
Pedestrian	Dawn Klingberg
Young Robert	Curtis Easton
Sister	Kyra Cox
Mother	Tarni James
Father	Tony Llewellyn-Jones

Right: Robert Menzies, Isabelle Huppert
© *International Spectrafilm*

FOREIGN BODY

(ORION) Producer, Colin M. Brewer; Director, Ronald Neame; Screenplay, Celine La Freniere; Based on the novel by Roderick Mann; Executive Producer, Christopher Neame; Photography, Ronnie Taylor; Designer, Roy Stannard; Editor, Andrew Nelson; Music/Song, Ken Howard; Vocals, Lynda Hayes; Production Manager, Donald Toms; Assistant Directors, Patrick Clayton, Callum McDougall; Costumes, Maggie Quigley; Sound, Claude Hitchcock; Art Director, Diane Dancklefsen; Orchestrations, John Altman; Production Co-ordinators, Monica Rogers, Liz Bunton; British; Color; Panavision; Rated PG-13; 100 minutes; September release

CAST

Ram Das	Victor Banerjee
I.Q.	Warren Mitchell
Lady Ammanford	Geraldine McEwan
Prime Minister	Denis Quilley
Susan	Amanda Donohoe
Norah	Eve Ferret
Miss Furze	Anna Massey
Mr. Plumb	Stratford Johns
Dr. Stirrup	Trevor Howard
Jo Masters	Jane Laurie
Mr. Nahan	Rashid Karapiet
Lovely Indian Girl	Sinitta Renet
Macho Escort	Marc Zuber
Landlady	Janet Henfrey
Mrs. Plumb	Ann Firbank
Agent at Harley Street	Timothy Bateson
Hilary Pike	Jack Galloway
Antique Shop Lady	Angela Morant
Colonel Partridge	Richard Wilson
Simons	Patrick Godfrey
Basil	Miles Richardson
Jean	Edita Brychta

Harriet Thorpe, Roy Evans, Peggy Aitchison, John Rogan, Eric Mason, Terry Diab, Neville Phillips, Clive Mantle, Barry Upton, Stephen Rashbrook, Jenny Michelmore, Barrie Rutter, Peter Ellis, Meriel Brook, Peter Forbes-Robertson, Roger Hammond, Paul Rattee, Albert Moses

Jane Laurie, Victor Banerjee

© *Orion*

ROUND MIDNIGHT

(WARNER BROS.) Producer, Irwin Winkler; Director, Bertrand Tavernier; Screenplay, David Rayfiel, Bertrand Tavenier; Inspired by incidents in the lives of Francis Paudras and Bud Powell; Photography, Bruno De Keyzer; Designer, Alexandre Trauner; Operator, Philippe Brun; Assistant Directors, Frederic Bourboulon, Philippe Berenger, Veronique Bourboulon; Art Director, Pierre Duquesne; Sound, Michel Desrois, William Flageollett; Editor, Armand Psenny; Costumes, Jacqueline Moreau; Music, Herbie Hancock; Production Manager, Pierre Saint-Blancat; Set, Philippe Turlure; French Translation, Colo Tavernier; Songs by various artists; Original soundtrack album by CBS; Eastmancolor; Panavision; Rated R; 133 minutes; September release.

CAST

Dale Turner	Dexter Gordon
Francis Borier	Francois Cluzet
Berangere	Gabrielle Haker
Buttercup	Sandra Reaves-Phillips
Darcey Leigh	Lonette McKee
Sylvie	Christine Pascal
Eddie Wayne	Herbie Hancock
Ace	Bobby Hutcherson
Francis's Father	Pierre Trabaud
Francis's Mother	Frederique Meininger
Mme Queen	Liliane Rovere
Hershell	Hart Leroy Bibbs
Beau	Ged Marlon
Psychiatrist	Benoit Regent
Chan	Victoria Gabrielle Platt
Booker	Arthur French
Ben	John Berry
Goodley	Martin Scorsese
Redon	Philippe Noiret
Terzian	Alain Sarde
A Drunk	Eddy Mitchell

and Billy Higgins, Bobby Hutcherson, Eric Le Lann, John McLaughn, Pierre Michelot, Wayne Shorter, Ron Carter, Billy Higgins, Palle Mikkelborg, Mads Vinding, Cheikh Fall, Michel Perez, Tony Wiliams, Freddie Hubbard, Cedar Walton, Charles Belonzi, Arnaud Chevrier, Marpessa Djian, Guy Louret, Patrick Massieu, Philippe Moreau, Jacques Poitrenaud, Luc Sarot, Jimmy Slyde, Pascal Tedes, Pascale Vignal, Noel Simsolo.

Right: Dexter Gordon, Lonette McKee
Top: Dexter Gordon, Sandra Reaves-Phillips,
Francois Cluzet © *Warner Bros.*

Dexter Gordon

Gabrielle Haker, Dexter Gordon

1986 Academy Award For Best Original Score

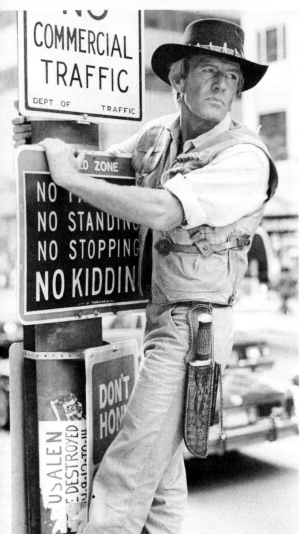

"CROCODILE" DUNDEE

(PARAMOUNT) Producer, John Cornell; Director, Peter Faiman; Screenplay, Paul Hogan, Ken Shadie, John Cornell; Original Story, Paul Hogan; Line Producer, Jane Scott; Editor, David Stiven; Music, Peter Best; Photography, Russell Boyd; Assistant Director, Mark Turnbull; Designer, Graham (Grace) Walker; Costumes, Norma Moriceau; Casting, Paula Herold; Associate Producer, Wayne Young; Production Manager/Post Production Supervisor, Peter Sjoquist; Production Coordinator, Julie Forster, Denise Pinckley; Assistant Directors, Craig Bolles, Peter Voeten, John Kilik, Richard Schlesinger; Sound, Gary Wilkins, Roger Savage, Bill Daly; Stunts, Max Aspin, Jery Hewitt; Production Manager, Kelly Van Horn; Songs, A. Farriss, M. Hutchence, Greedy Smith, Stephen Prestwich; Australia, 1986; Dolby Stereo; Color; Panavision; Rated PG-13; 105 minutes; September release

CAST

Mick "Crocodile" Dundee	Paul Hogan
Sue Charlton	Linda Kozlowski
Walter Reilly	John Meillon
Neville Bell	David Gulpilil
Con	Ritchie Singer
Ida	Maggie Blinco
Donk	Steve Rackman
Nugget	Gerry Skilton
Duffy	Terry Gill
Trevor	Peter Turnbull
Rosita	Christine Totos
Angelo	Graham (Grace) Walker
Burt	David Bracks
Peter	Brett Hogan
Richard Mason	Mark Blum
Sam Charlton	Michael Lombard
Doorman	Irving Metzman
Gus	Reginald VelJohnson
Danny	Rik Colitti
Pimp	John Snyder
Buzzy	J. J. Cole
Wendell Wainwright	Gwyllum Evans
Wino	Jan Saint
Subway Creep	Peter Bucossi
Tall Man	Sullivan Walker
Pug Nose	Bobby Alto
Gwendoline	Anne Carlisle
Fran	Anne Francine
Party Girl	Paige Matthews
New Yorker	Paul Greco
Simone	Caitlin Clarke
Karla	Nancy Mette
Coke Snorter	Barry Kivel
Teenage Mugger	Tony Holmes
Simpson	Dan Lounsbery
Receptionist	Dolores Messina

© *Rimfire Films*

Paul Hogan, and above

Linda Kozlowski, Paul Hogan

Paul Hogan, Linda Kozlowski, Anne Francine
Top: Kozlowski, Hogan

Linda Kozlowski, Paul Hogan
Top: Paul Hogan

191

RESTLESS NATIVES

(ORION CLASSICS) Producer, Rick Stevenson; Director, Michael Hoffman; Screenplay, Ninian Dunnett; Executive Producer, Mark Bentley; Co-Producer/Production Manager, Andy Paterson; Associate Producer, Paddy Higson; Script Editor, Rupert Walters; Photography, Oliver Stapleton; Editor, Sean Barton; Music, Stuart Adamson, Big Country; Designer, Adrienne Atkinson; Assistant Director, Ken Tuohy; Costumes, Mary Jane Reyner; Art Director, Andy Harris; Sound, Louis Kramer, Alastair Chilston, Christopher Ross Leong, Eric Peters, Richard Newnham; Make-Up, Elizabeth Armstrong, Miranda Davidson; Production Co-Ordinator, Christine MacLean; Stunts, Nick Gillard, Marc Boyle, Lex Milloy; An Oxford Film Company production in association with Thorn EMI Screen Entertainment Ltd.; British; Color; Rated PG; 90 minutes; September release

CAST

Will	Vincent Friell
Ronnie	Joe Mullaney
Margot	Teri Lally
Fritz Bender	Ned Beatty
Superintendent Baird	Robert Urquhart
Mr. Bryce	Bernard Hill
Mrs. Bryce	Ann Scott-Jones
Isla	Rachel Boyd
Nigel	Iain McColl
Pyle	Mel Smith
Man in car	Bryan Forbes
Woman in car	Nanette Newman
Detective "A"	Lawrie McNicol
Detective "B"	Neville Watchurst
Illingworth	Dave Anderson
Japanese Presenter	Eiji Kusuhara
Second Japanese Man	Sabu Kimura
TV Reporter (British)	Michael Stroud
TV Reporter (American)	Ed Bishop
Agent's	Derek Starr, Peter Pringle
Mary Harrison	Laura Smith
Angus Paterson	Robin Brown
Mrs. Paterson	Irene Sunters
Guide (First Hold-up)	Frances Lonergan
American Woman	Karen McCrary
Elderly American Woman	Jean Faulds
Courier (Bus Station)	Sally Kinghorn
Isla's Boyfriend	Andrew Brown
Teacher	Sharon MacKenzie
Bouncer	Big "D"
Policeman in shop	Jim Boyce
Lady at bus station	Margaret Robertson
Girl on bus	Victoria Rutherford

Left: Teri Lally, Vincent Friell
Above: Robert Urquhart, Ned Beatty
Top: Joe Mullaney, Vincent Friell
© Orion Classics

90 DAYS

(CINECOM) Producers/Screenplay, David Wilson, Giles Walker; Director, Giles Walker; Photography, Andrew Kitzanuk; Editor, David Wilson; Music, Richard Gresko; Canadian; Color; Not Rated; 99 minutes; September release

CAST

Blue	Stefan Wodoslawsky
Hyang-Sook	Christine Pak
Alex	Sam Grana
Laura	Fernanda Tavares
Mother	Daisy De Bellefeuille

(No other credits submitted)

© Cinecom

Stefan Wodoslawsky, Christine Pak

NINETEEN NINETEEN

(SPECTRAFILM) Producer, Nita Amy; Director, Hugh Brody; Screenplay, Hugh Brody, Michael Ignatieff; Based on an idea by Michael Ignatieff; Photography, Ivan Strasburg; Sound, Mike McDuffie; Art Director, Caroline Amies; Assistant Art Director, Jock Scott; Costumes, Jane Robinson; Music, Brian Gascoigne; Editor, David Gladwell; FX, Beryl Mortimer, Jerry Foster; Assistant Directors, Peter Chadwick, Joanna Smith, Karl Ludwig; Associate Producer, Gerhard Czepe; Production Manager, Donna Grey; Executive Producer, Peter Sainsbury; A British Film Institute Production in association with Channel Four Television; British; Color; Not Rated; 99 minutes; September release

CAST

Alexander	Paul Scofield
Sophie	Maria Schell
The Voice of Dr. Sigmund Freud	Frank Finlay
Anna	Diana Quick
Young Sophie	Clare Higgins
Young Alexander	Colin Firth
Nina	Sondra Berkin
Alexander's Sister	Jacqueline Dankworth
Sophie's Father	Alan Tilvern
Child Alexander	Christopher Lahr
Child's Nurse	Bridget Amies

and Christine Hargreaves, Ronald Nunnery, Willy Bowman, Annet Peters, Keith Kraushaar, Norman Chancer

Left: Paul Scofield, Maria Schell (also below)
Top: Maria Schell, Paul Scofield
© *International Spectrafilm*

MARLENE

(ZEV BRAUN PICTURES, INC.) Director, Maximilian Schell; Script, Mier Dohnal, Maximilian Schell; Photography, Ivan Slapeta; Editors, Heidi Genee, Dagmar Hirtz; Costumes, Heinz Eickmeier; Sound, Norbert Lill; Production Manager, Peter Genee; Production Company, Oko-Film; Presented by Zev Braun, Karel Dirka; A documentary with fictional elements; Color; Not rated; 96 minutes; September release. CAST: Marlene Dietrich, Maximilian Schell, and others.

Top Right: Marlene Dietrich in
the 1930's

Dietrich in
"Morocco"

Dietrich in concert
1950's **193**

MENAGE

(CINECOM) Producer, Rene Cleitman; Director/Screenplay, Bertrand Blier; Executive Producer, Philippe Dussart; Photography, Jean Penzer; Camera, Yves Agostini; Sound, Bertrand Bats, Dominique Hennequin; Set Design, Theobald Meurisse; Editor, Claudine Merlin; Music, Serge Gainsbourg; Assistant Directors, Bertrand Arthuys, Luc Goldenberg; Assistant Editor, Sylvie Quester; Production Manager, Michel Choquet; Assistant Production Manager, Michel Bernede; Makeup, Michel Deruelle, Joel Lavau; Hair, Philippe Van Tran; Wardrobe, Michele Cerf; Casting, Margot Capelier; A co-production of Hachette Premiere, DD Productions, Cine Valse and Philippe Dussart Sarl; French; Color; Not Rated; 84 minutes; October release

CAST

Bob	Gerard Depardieu
Antoine	Michel Blanc
Monique	Miou-Miou
Art Collector	Bruno Cremer
Depressed Man	Jean-Pierre Marielle
Pedro	Michel Creton
Depressed Woman	Caroline Sihol
Man in night club	Jean-Yves Berteloot

Right: Michel Blanc, Gerard Depardieu
Top: Gerard Depardieu, Miou-Miou, Michel Blanc
© *Cinecom*

Gerard Depardieu, Miou-Miou

Miou-Miou, Gerard Depardieu

SID & NANCY

(SAMUEL GOLDWYN) Producer, Eric Fellner; Director, Alex Cox; Screenplay, Alex Cox, Abbe Wool; Co-producer, Peter McCarthy; Music, The Pogues, Joe Strummer, Pray for Rain; Photography, Roger Deakins; Editor, David Martin; Designer, Andrew McAlpine; Art Direction, J. Rae Fox, Lynda Burbank; Sound, Peter Glossop; Make-up, Peter Frampton; Hair, Aaron Glynn; Costumes, Cathy Cook, Theda De Ramus; Presented by Embassy Home Entertainment; A Zenith Production in association with Initial Pictures; British; Original Soundtrack on MCA; Dolby Stereo; Color; Rated R; 111 minutes; October release

CAST

Sid Vicious	Gary Oldman
Nancy Spungen	Chloe Webb
Johnny Rotten	Drew Schofield
Malcolm McLaren	David Hayman
Phoebe	Debby Bishop
Steve	Tony London
Paul	Perry Benson
Linda	Ann Lambton
Brenda	Kathy Burke
Clive	Mark Monero
Olive	Michele Winstanley
Wally	Graham Fletcher Cook
Ma Vicious	Jude Alderson
Abby	Sara Sugarman
Rock Head	Stuart Fox
Hugh Kares	Peter McCarthy
Receptionist	Tenpole Tudor
Duke Bowman	Pete Lee Wilson
Gretchen	Courtney Love
Trell	Jeanny McCarthy
Vito	John Snyder
Wax Max	Ron Moseley, Jr.
Old Stain	Fox Harris
Bowery Snax	Xander Berkeley
Detective	Biff Yeager
Hotelier	Sandy Baron
Granpa Spungen	Milton Selzer
Granma Spungen	Gloria Leroy
Caseworker	Sy Richardson

© *Samuel Goldwyn*

Chloe Webb
Top Right: Gary Oldman

Chloe Webb, Gary Oldman

195

THERESE

(CIRCLE RELEASING CORP.) Producer, Maurice Bernart; Director, Alain Cavalier; Photography, Philippe Rousselot; Editor, Isabelle Dedieu; Sound, Alain Lachassagne, Dominique Dalmasso; Designer, Bernard Evein; Costumes, Yvette Bonnay; Screenplay, Alain Cavalier, Camille'De Casabianca; Production Manager, Florence Malraux; Music, Jacques Offenbach, Gabriel Faure; French; Color; Not rated; 90 minutes; October release.

CAST

Therese	Catherine Mouchet
Celine	Aurore Prieto
Pauline	Sylvie Habault
Marie	Ghislane Mona
Lucie	Helene Alexandridis
The Prieure	Clemence Massart
Aimee	Nathalie Bernart
Singer	Beatrice DeVigan
The Elder	Noele Chantre
Recluse	Anna Bernelat
Nurse	Sylvaine Massart
Doorkeeper	M. C. Brown-Sarda
Painter	M. L. Eberschweiler
Sisters	Josette Lefevre, Gilberte Laurain
The Petals	Renee Cretien
Framer	Evy Carcassonne
Embroiderer	Simone Duboco
Violinist	Jacqueline Legrain
Novices	Veronique Muller, Jacqueline Bouvyer
Father	Jean Pelegri
Pranzini	Michel Rivelin
Choir Boy	Quentin
Priest	Pierre Baillot
Bishop	Jean Pieuchot
Cardinals	Georges Aranyossy, Edmond Levy
Pope	Armand Meppiel
Old Man with bouquet	Lucien Folet
Carmel Doctor	Pierre Maintigneux
Aimee's Fiance	Guy Faucon
Young Doctor	Joel LeFrancois

Catherine Mouchet (kneeling) and above center

DUST

(KINO INTERNATIONAL) Executive Producer, Michele Troncon; Direction/Screenplay, Marion Hansel; Adapted from novel "In the Heart of the Country" by J. M. Coetzee; Photography, Walter Vanden Ende; Editor, Susanna Rossberg; Sound, Henri Morelle; Design, Pierre Thevenet, Luciano Arroyo; Costumes, Yan Tax; Music, Martin St. Pierre; A Jerry Winters presentation; Belgium/France 1985; Co-production of Man's Films (Brussels), Daska Film International (Gent), Flash Films (Paris), FR3 Production (France), La Communaute Francaise de Belgique and De Ministerie van de Vlaamse Gemeenschap; Not rated; 87 minutes; Winner of Silver Lion at Venice Film Festival; October release

CAST

Magda	Jane Birkin
Father	Trevor Howard
Hendrik	John Matshikiza
Klein Anna	Nadine Uwampa
Oud Anna	Lourdes Christina Sayo
Jacob	Rene Diaz

Top Right: Trevor Howard, Jane Birkin
© Kino International

TANGOS: THE EXILE OF GARDEL

(NEW YORKER) Executive Producer, Sabina Sigler; Associate Producer, Vicente Diaz Amo; Producers, Fernando E. Solanas, Enva El Kadri; Direction/Screenplay, Fernando E. Solanas; Assistant Director, Teo Koffman; Costumes, Judy Shrewsbury, Luis Diego Pedreira; Editors, Cesar D'Angiolillo, Jacques Gaillard; Sound, Adrian Nataf; Design, Luis Diego Pedreira, Jimmy Vansteenskiste; Photography, Felix Monti; Music, Astor Piazzolla; Songs, Jose Luis Castineira de Dios, Fernando E. Solanas; Choreography, Susana Tambutti, Margarita Balli, Robert Thomas, Adolfo Andrade; A French/Argentine co-production; In French and Spanish with subtitles; In color; Not rated; 125 minutes; October release

CAST

Mariana	Marie Laforet
Pierre	Philippe Leotard
Juan Dos	Miguel Angel Sola
Florence	Marina Vlady
Jean-Marie	Georges Wilson
Gerardo	Lautaro Murua
Ana	Ana Maria Picchio
Maria	Gabriela Toscano
San Martin	Michel Etcheverry
Discepolo	Claude Melki
Carlos Gardel	Gregorio Manzur
Alicia	Leonor Galindo
Dr. Figueroa	Eduardo Pavlosky
Miseria	Jorge Six
El Negro	Guillermo Nunez
Alcira	Mirta Camedeiros
Susana	Delia Bermejo
Concepcion	Norma Guevara
Nathalie	Catherine Laborde
Celine	Huguette Faget
Arlette	Beatrice Jacobs
Angel	Fernando E. Solanas

and Oscar Castro, Hector Malamud, Lorena Gelso, Emilio Cedron, Anita Beltran, Gaspar Noe, Victoria Solanas, and Ballet Nucleo-Danza

Right Center: Marie Laforet
Below: Miguel Angel
© New Yorker

Roser Montillo, Gabriela Toscano

THE MISSION

(WARNER BROS) Producers, Fernando Ghia, David Puttnam; Director, Roland Joffe; Photography, Chris Menges; Designer, Stuart Craig; Costumes, Enrico Sabbatini; Editor, Jim Clark; Music, Ennio Morricone; Story/Screenplay, Robert Bolt; Production Supervisor, Barrie Melrose; Production Co-ordinator, Judi Bunn; Assistant Directors, Bill Westley, Gerry Toomey, Uberto Pasolini; Sound, Clive Winter, Chris Ackland; Special Effects, Peter Hutchinson, Martin Gant, Peter Fern, Peter Skehan, Andrew Smith; Original Soundtrack on Virgin Records; A Goldcrest Production in Association with Kingsmere Productions Ltd; Color; 128 minutes; Rated PG; October release.

CAST

Mendoza	Robert De Niro
Gabriel	Jeremy Irons
Altamirano	Ray McAnally
Felipe	Aidan Quinn
Carlotta	Cherie Lunghi
Hontar	Ronald Pickup
Cabeza	Chuck Low
Fielding	Liam Neeson
Indian Boy	Bercelio Moya
Witch Doctor	Sigifredo Ismare
Indian Chief	Asuncion Ontiveros
Chief's Lieutenant	Alejandrino Moya
Sebastian	Daniel Berrigan
Young Jesuit	Rolf Gray
Jesuit	Alvaro Guerrero
Father Provincial	Tony Lawn
Nobleman	Joe Daly
Portuguese Commander	Carlos Duplat
Spanish Commander	Rafael Camerano
Ibaye	Monirak Sisowath
Indian	Silvestre Chiripua
Boy Singer	Luis Carlos Gonzalez
Carlotta's Maid	Maria Teresa Ripoll

© *Warner Bros.*

Cherie Lunghi, Aidan Quinn, Robert De Niro
Top Left: Robert De Niro, Bercelio Moya

1986 Academy Award For Best Cinematography

Jeremy Irons (Center) Top Left: Aidan Quinn, Cherie Lunghi Below: Ray McAnally,
Ronald Pickup Right: Jeremy Irons, Robert De Niro, Bercelio Moya Top: De Niro, Irons

THE DECLINE OF THE AMERICAN EMPIRE

(CINEPLEX ODEON FILMS) Producers, Rene Malo, Roger Frappier; Direction/Screenplay, Denys Arcand; Line Producer, Pierre Tendron; Photography, Guy Dufaux, Jacques Leduc; Music, Handel, Francois Dompierre; Art Director, Gaudeline Sauriol; Costumes, Denis Sperdouklis; Editor, Monique Fortier; Production Manager, Lyse LaFontaine; Assistant Directors, Jacques Benoit, Monique Maranda; Production Coordinator, Jean Gerin; Produced by Malo Film Group and the National Film Board of Canada; In color; Canadian; Rated R; 101 minutes; September release

CAST

Dominique	Dominique Michel
Louise	Dorothee Berryman
Diane	Louise Portal
Pierre	Pierre Curzi
Remy	Remy Girard
Claude	Yves Jacques
Alain	Daniel Briere
Mario	Gabriel Arcand

Dorothee Berryman, Remy Girard, Dominique Michel, Genevieve Rioux, Pierre Curzi, Louise Portal, Yves Jacques Top Left: Remy Girard, Daniel Briere, Pierre Curzi, Yves Jacques Below: Yves Jacques, Dorothee Berryman Right: Louise Portal, Dominique Michel, Dorothee Berryman, Genevieve Rioux © Cineplex Odeon

THE SACRIFICE

(ORION CLASSICS) Director/Screenplay, Andrei Tarkovskij; Photography, Sven Nykvist; Camera Assistants, Lasse Karlsson, Dan Myhrman; Assistant Directors, Kerstin Eriksdotter, Michal Leszczylowski; Editors, Andrei Tarkovskij, Michal Leszczylowski; Editing Consultant, Henri Colpi; Executive Producer, Anna-Lena Wibom; Production Manager, Katinka Farago; Interpreter, Layla Alexander; Sound, Owe Svensson, Bosse Persson; Art Director, Anna Asp; Technical Manager, Kaj Larsen; Costumes, Inger Pehrsson; Make-up/Wigs, Kjell Gustavsson, Florence Fouquier; Special Effects, Svenska Stuntgruppen/Lars Hoglund, Lars Palmqvist; Music, J. S. Bach/Swedish and Japanese folk music; A Swedish-French Co-Production/The Swedish Film Institute-Argos Films S.A. in association with Film Four International and Josephseon & Nykvist HB, Sveriges Television/SVT 2, Sandrew Film & Teater AB and with the participation of The French Ministry of Culture; Eastmancolor; Rated PG; 145 minutes; November release

CAST

Alexander	Erland Josephson
Adelaide	Susan Fleetwood
Julia	Valerie Mairesse
Otto	Allan Edwall
Maria	Gudrun Gisladottir
Victor	Sven Wollter
Marta	Filippa Franzen
Little Man	Tommy Kjellqvist

Left: Sven Wollter, Susan Fleetwood
Top: Allan Edwall, Filippa Franzen, Susan Fleetwood © *Orion Classics*

ROUGE BAISER
(Red Kiss)

(CIRCLE RELEASING CORP.) Producer/Director, Vera Belmont; Screenplay, Vera Belmont with Guy Konopnicki, David Milhaud; Line Producer, Nicole Flipo; Photography, Ramon Suarez; Editor, Martine Giordano; Music, Jean-Marie Senia; A Stephan Films Production in association with Films A2, Farena Films, and C&H Films Berlin; France; French with subtitles; Color; Not rated; 110 minutes; November release

CAST

Nadia	Charlotte Valandrey
Stephane	Lambert Wilson
Bronka	Marthe Keller
Herschel	Gunter Lamprecht
Moishe	Laurent Terzieff
Roland	Laurent Arnal
Henriette	Audrey Lazzini
Rosa	Elsa Lunghini
Andre	Yves Nadot
Gaby	Pascal Guiomor
Joel	Riton Liebman
Jeanine	Isabelle Nanty
Pierette	Corinne Juresco
Vivianne	Anne Dumas
Rosette	Deborah Cohen
Marion	Jodi Pavlis
Police Inspector	Georges Staquet
Mr. Victor	Lionel Rocheman

(No photos available)

Allan Edwall, Erland Josephson

201

THE FUTURE OF EMILY

(FILM FORUM) Director/Screenplay, Helma Sanders-Brahms; Photography, Sacha Vierny; West Germany/France; French with subtitles; Color; Not Rated; 107 minutes; December release

CAST

Isabelle	Brigitte Fossey
Paula	Hildegarde Knef
Charles	Ivan Desny
Frederick	Hermann Treusch
Emily	Camille Raymond

(No other credits or cast submitted)

Brigitte Fossey, Hildegarde Knef
© *Film Forum*

REBEL

(VESTRON PICTURES) Producer, Phillip Emanuel; Executive Producer, The Village Roadshow Corporation; Director, Michael Jenkins; Screenplay, Michael Jenkins, Bob Herbert; Adapted from the Play *No Names . . . No Pack Drill* by Bob Herbert; Photography, Peter James; Editor, Michael Honey; Designer, Brian Thomson; Production Manager, Susan Wild; Costumes, Roger Kirk; Music, Chris Neal; Musical Director, Ray Cook; Orchestrations, Billy Byers; Song Coordinator, Bruce Rowland; Songs, Peter Best; Choreographer, Ross Coleman; Sound, Mark Lewis, Penn Robinson, Julian Ellingworth, Chris Schweers; Casting, Michael Lynch, Pat McCorkle; Art Director, Igor Nay; Assistant Directors, David Evans, Hamish McSporran, Henry Osborne; Production Coordinator, Suzanne Donnolley; Assistant Editor, Amanda Sheldon; Set Decorator, Lissa Coote; Assistant Art Directors, Michael Scott-Mitchell, Robert Kemp; Stunts, Max Aspin; Additional Dialogue, Carole Sklan, John Lind; Soundtrack on EMI; Australian; Color; Rated R; 89 minutes; December release

CAST

Rebel	Matt Dillon
Kathy	Debbie Byrne
Tiger	Bryan Brown
Browning	Bill Hunter
Bubbles	Ray Barrett
Joycie	Julie Nihill
Bernie	John O'May
Hazel	Kim Deacon
Mrs. Palmer	Isabelle Anderson
Barbara	Sheree Da Costa
Mary	Joy Smithers
Lambert	Chris Hession
Wood	Spike Cherry
Webb	Stuart McCreery
Harry De Wheels	Ric Carter
Madam	Annie Semler
Mary's GI	Todd Bryce
Bea Miles	Beth Child
Landlord	Fred Welch

and Tom Appleton, James Marsh, Rainee Skinner, Lance Curtis, Colleen Fitzpatrick, Ray Marshall, James Kuri

Matt Dillon, Debbie Byrne

Top Left: Bryan Brown, Debbie Byrne, Matt Dillon Below: Debbie Byrne, Matt Dillon
© *Vestron Pictures*

PLACE OF WEEPING

(NEW WORLD) Producer, Anant Singh; Director/Screenplay, Darrell Roodt; Associate Producer/Production Manager, Les Volpe; Story, Darrell Roodt, Les Volpe; Photography, Paul Witte; Assistant Director, Neil Sonnekus; Art Director, Dave Barkham; Set Decorator, Hazel Crampton; Sound, Craig Walmsley, Chris Pieterse; Editor, David Heitner; Assistant Editor, Mary-Ann Lindenstadt; South African; Color; Rated PG; 88 minutes; December release

CAST

Philip Seago	James Whyle
Gracie	Gcina Mhlophe
Tokkie Van Rensburg	Charles Comyn
Father Eagen	Norman Coombes
Maria Van Rensburg	Michelle Du Toit
Themba	Ramolao Makhene
Lucky	Patrick Shai
Joseph	Siphiwe Khumalo
Prosecutor: Dick Van Heerden	Kernels Coertzen
Ana	Doreen Mazibuko
Joseph's Widow	Thoko Ntshinga
Tokkie's Son Pieter	Jeremy Taylor
Tokkie's Daughter Elize	Nicole Jourdan

Right: James Whyle, Gcina Mhlophe
Top: Thoko Ntshinga, Gcina Mhlophe
© *New World*

EL AMOR BRUJO
(Love, the Magician)

(ORION CLASSICS) Producer, Emiliano Piedra; Director, Carlos Saura; Screenplay/Choreography, Carlos Saura, Antonio Gades; Photography, Teo Escamilla; Music, Manuel De Falla; Conductor, Jesus Lopez Cobos; Orchestra, Spanish National Orchestra; Singer, Rocio Jurado; Sets/Costumes, Gerardo Vera; Editor, Pedro Del Rey; Assistant Director, Carlos Saura Medrano; Sound, Daniel Goldstein; Production Manager, Emiliano Otegui; Spanish with subtitles; Color; Rated PG; 100 minutes; December release

CAST

Carmelo	Antonio Gades
Candela	Cristina Hoyos
Lucia	Laura Del Sol
Jose	Juan Antonio Jimenez
Aunt Rosario	Emma Penella
Pastora	La Polaca
El Lobo	Gomez De Jerez
Jose's Father	Enrique Ortega
Candela's Father	Diego Pantoja
Rocio	Giovana
Chulo	Candy Roman
Singers	Gomez DeJerez, Manolo Sevilla
Guitarists	Antonio Solera, Manuel Rodriguez, Juan Manuel Roldan
Ballet	Antonio Gades Company

with the participation of "*Grupo La Mosca*," "*Grupo Azucar Moreno*," folk performers, and one hundred dancers and singers

© *Orion Classics*

Cristina Hoyos Above: Antonio
Gades, Cristina Hoyos

Scott Glenn (c) in "Wild Geese"
© *Universal*

Tatsuya Nakadai in "A.K. The Making of
Kurosawa's Ran" © *Orion Classics*

AMIGOS (Manicato Films) Producer, Camilo Vila; Director/
Screenplay, Ivan Acosta; Photography, Henry Vargas; Editor, Gloria
Pineyro; Music, Sergio Garcia-Marruz; Spanish with subtitles; Not
rated; 108 minutes; January release. CAST: Ruben Rabasa (Ramon),
Reynaldo Medina (Pablo), Lucy Pereda (Magaly), Juan Granda (Olme-
do), Armando Naser (Gavilan), Blanca de Abril (Cecilia), Lillian Hurst
(Mirta), Dania Victor (Senora Gavilan), Uva Clavijo (Senora Olmeda),
Luisa Gil (Consuelo)

EDITH'S DIARY (Greentree) Director/Screenplay, Hans W. Geissendoerfer; Based on the novel by Patricia Highsmith; Photography,
Michael Ballhaus; Sets, Toni Leudi; Music, Juergen Kniefer; Editor,
Helga Borsche; Costumes, Katharina von Martius; Production Mana-
ger, Rolf M. Degener; TV Producer, Willi Segler; A coproduction of
Hans W. Geissendoerfer Filmproduktion, Roxy Film Luggi Waldeit-
ner, Project Filmproduktion im Filverlag der Autoren, and Zweites
Deutsches Fernsehen (ZDF); West Germany; Color; Rated R; 108
minutes; January release. CAST: Angela Winkler (Edith Baumeister),
Vadim Glowna (Paul Baumeister), Leopold von Verschuer (Chris
Baumeister), Hans Madin (Uncle George), Sona MacDonald (Kathar-
ine Ems), Irm Hermann (Sabine Angerwolf), Wolfgang Condrus
(Bernd Angerwolf), Freidrich G. Beckhaus (Dr. Bleibig), Werner
Eichhorn (Dr. Star)

WILD GEESE II (Universal) Producer, Euan Lloyd; Executive Producer, Chris Chrisafis; Director, Peter Hunt; Screenplay, Reginald
Rose; Based on the book *The Square Circle* by Daniel Carney; Photography, Michael Reed; Editor, Keith Palmer; Music, Roy Budd; De-
signer, Syd Cain; Art Director, Peter Williams; Costumes, Diane
Holmes; Sound, Chris Munro; A Thorn EMI presentation of a Frontier
Film production; British; Technicolor; Not rated; 125 minutes; January
release. CAST: Scott Glenn (John Haddad), Barbara Carrera (Kathy
Lukas), Edward Fox (Alex Faulkner), Laurence Olivier (Rudolf Hess),
Robert Webber (Robert McCann), Robert Freitag (Heinrich Stroebl-
ing), Kenneth Haigh (Col. Reed-Henry), Stratford Johns (Mustapha El
Ali), Derek Thompson (Hourigan), Paul Antrim (Murphy), John Terry
(Michael Lukas), Ingrid Pitt (Hooker)

A.K.: THE MAKING OF KUROSAWA'S RAN (Orion Classics)
Producers, Serge Silverman, Greenwich Films (Paris) & Herald Ace
Inc. (Tokyo); Director/Screenplay, Chris Marker; Photography, Frans-
Yves Maresco; Music, Toru Takemitsu; Narrator, Robert Kramer;
France/Japan, 1985; English and Japanese with subtitles; Color; Not
rated; 77 minutes; January release (For RAN credits see SCREEN
WORLD Vol. 37)

RAONI (Nicole Jouve Interama) Producer/Director/Writer, Jean-
Pierre Dutilleux; Photography, Carlos Saldanha; Introduced & Nar-
rated by Marlon Brando; Color; France/Brazil, 1979; In Portugese,
Kayapo, & English with subtitles; Documentary; Not Rated; 85
minutes; January release. CAST: Raoni & the Mekronoti tribe, Marlon
Brando, Claudio & Orlando Villas-Boas (anthropologists), Ismarth de
Araujo Oliveira (President of the FUNAI)

FOLLOWING THE FUHRER (EML-FILM, Munich with ZDF) A
film by Erwin Leiser; Dramatic Sequence Director, Eberhard Itzenplitz;
Dramatic Sequence Screenplay, Oliver Storz; Photography, Gerard
Vandenberg, Jochen Radermacher; West Germany; German with sub-
titles; Documentary with Dramatic Sequences; Not Rated; 90 minutes;
January release. CAST: Lisi Mangold (Marga), Felix von Manteuffel
(Arthur), Gottfried John (Brocke), Frank Strecker (Deschler), Walter
Schultheiss (Durr), Horst Bollmann (Kramm), Ilsemarie Schnering
(Mrs. Kramm), Karin Baal (Elisabeth Kurz), Armin Mueller-Stahl
(Kurz), Therese Lohner (Ellen Kurz)

THE MYSTERY OF PICASSO (Samuel Goldwyn) Producer/
Director/Screenplay/Editor, Henri-Georges Clouzot; Music, Georges
Auric; Photography, Claude Renoir; Sound, Joseph Bretagne, Henri
Colpi; Color Spotting, Claude Leon; Color; France, 1955; Declared a
national treasure by the French government in 1984; Rated PG; 85
minutes; January release. CAST: Pablo Picasso

RIVE DROITE, RIVE GAUCHE (20th Century Fox) Producer,
Alain Terzain; Director/Screenplay, Philippe Labro; Music, Michel
Berger; French; Color; Not rated; 94 minutes; January release. CAST:
Gerard Depardieu (Paul Senanques), Nathalie Baye (Sacha Venakis),
Carole Bouquet (Babee Senanques), Bernard Fresson (Guarrigue)

"Raoni"
© *Nicole Jouve Interama*

Pablo Picasso in "The Mystery of
Picasso" © *Samuel Goldwyn*

Armin Mueller-Stahl, Karin Baal
in "Following the Fuhrer" © *EMI*

"Unfinished Business"
© *PBS*

ENDGAME (American National Enterprises) Producer, Filmirage; Director, Steven Benson; Screenplay, Alex Carver; Story, Alex Carver, Steven Benson; Photography, Federico Slonisco; Editor, Tony Larson; Music, Carlo Maria Cordio; Production Manager, Charles Kellin; Production Supervisor, Helen Handris; Designer, Robert Connors; Costumes, Linda Jenkins; A Cinema 80 presentation; Italian; Technicolor; Not rated; 99 minutes; January release. CAST: Al Cliver (Ron Shannon), Laura Gemser (Lilith), George Eastman (Kurt Karnak), Jack Davis (Prof. Levin), Al Yamanouchi (Ninja), Gabriel Tinti (Bull), Mario Pedone (Kovak), Gordon Mitchell (Col. Morgan), Christopher Walsh (Tommy)

KAOS directed by Paolo and Vittorio Taviani; Loosely based on stories by Luigi Pirandello. Not rated; 188 minutes; February release. No other credits available.

STRAIGHT THROUGH THE HEART Producer, Denyse Noever; Director, Doris Dorrie; Screenplay, Jelena Kristl; Photography, Michael D Goebel; Editor, Thomas Wigand; Music, Paul Shigihara; German with subtitles; Germany; Not rated; 91 minutes; February release. CAST: Beate Jensen (Anna), Sepp Bierbichler (Armin), Gabrielle Litty (Marlies), Nuran Filiz (Marisol), Jens Mueller-Rastede (Messenger), Joachim Hoepner (Supermarket Manager)

UNFINISHED BUSINESS (Mouchette Films) Producer/Director/Photography, Steven Okazaki; Associate Producer, Jane Kaihatsu; Consultant, Roger Daniels; Screenplay, Steven Okazaki, Jane Kaihatsu, Kei Yokomizo, Laura Ide; Assistant Director/Narrated by Amy Hill; Sound/Lighting, Joseph Kwong; Editor, Steven Okazaki; Assistant Editor, Kim Costalupes; Scenes from *"Point of Order"* by R. A. Shiomi; Costumes/Set Design, Lydia Tanji; Australian; Documentary; Not rated; 60 minutes; February release. CAST: *("Point of Order")* Ken Narasaki (Gordon), Suzie Okazaki (Mother), James Hirabayashi (Father). INTERVIEWEES: Minoru Yasui, Fred Korematsu, Gordon Hirabayashi, Peter Irons, Roger Daniels, Peggy Nagae, Milton S. Eisenhower, Ernest Iiyama, Chizu Iiyama, Yoshido "Chico" Uyeda, Jim Kajiwara, Noriko Bridges, Susan Hayase, Dale Minami, Janice Sakamoto, Lorraine Bannai, Donald Tamaki, Minoru Tamaki, Amy Eto

FOXTRAP (Snizzlefritz) Producer/Director/Story, Fred Williamson; Executive Producers, Linda Radovan, Marcello & Pier Luigi Ciriaci; Screenplay, Aubrey K. Rattan; Photography, John Stephens, Steve Shaw; Editor, Giorgio Venturoli; Music, Patrizio Fariselli; Sound, Clark Will, Olivier Schwos, Giuseppe Testa; A Realta Cinematografica presentation of a Po' Boy production; Italian/U.S.; Luciano Vittori Color; Rated R; 88 minutes; February release. CAST: Fred Williamson (Thomas Fox), Chris Connelly (John Thomas), Arlene Golonka (Emily), Donna Owen (Susan), Beatrice Palme (Mariana), Cleo Sebastian (Josie), Lela Rochon (Lindy)

THE CRAZY FAMILY (New Yorker) Producers, Kazuhiko Hasegawa, Toyoji Yamane, Shiro Sasaki; Director, Sogo Ishii; Screenplay, Yoshinori Kobayashi (from his story), Fumio Kohnami, Sogo Ishii; Photography, Masaki Tamura; Sound, Shin Fukuda; Art Director, Terumi Hosoishi; Editor, Junnichi Kikuchi; Music, 1984; In color; Japanese with English subtitles; 106 minutes; February release. CAST: Katsuya Kobayashi (Father), Mitsuko Baisho (Saeko the Mother), Yoshiki Arizono (Masaki the Son), Yuki Kudo (Erika the Daughter), Hitoshi Ueki (Hisakuni the Grandfather)

TOBY McTEAGUE (Spectrafilm) Producer, Nicolas Clermont; Director, Jean-Claude Lord; Screenplay, Jeff Maguire, Djordje Milicevic, Jamie Brown; Story, Jeff MaGuire, Djordje Milicevic, Jamie Brown; Executive Producers, Pieter Kroonenburg, David Patterson; Photography, Rene Verzier; Editor, Yves Langlois; Designer, Jocelyn Joly; Production Manager, Wendy Grean; Assistant Director, David Hood; Sound, Patrick Rousseau; Assistant Designer, Raymond DuPuis; Stunts, Jerome Tiberghien; Special Effects, Bill Orr; Costumes, Michele Hamel; Music, Claude Demrs; Soundtrack Producer, Kevin Hunter; Songs, Peter Pringle, Kevin Hunter; Produced with the participation of Telefilm Canada, the Societe Generale Du Cineman, CBC, Radio Canada; Canadian; Colour; Rated PG; 95 minutes; February release. CAST: Winston Rekert (Tom McTeague), Yannick Bisson (Toby McTeague), Timothy Webber (Edison Crowe), Stephanie Morgenstern (Sara), Andrew Bednarski (Sam McTeague), Liliane Clune (Jenny Lessard), George Clutesi (Chief George Wild Dog), Evan Adams (Jacob), Hamish McEwan (Mike Lynn), Anthony Levinson (Peter), Mark Kulik (Ben), JoAnne Vanicola (Girl Punker), Tom Rack (Faulkner), Dick McGrath, Doug Price (Announcers), Ian Findlay (TV Reporter)

Yoshiki Arizono, Hitoshi Ueki, Katsuya Kobayashi,
Mitsuko Baisho, Yuki Kudo in "The Crazy Family"
© *New Yorker*

"Toby McTeague"
© *International Spectrafilm* **205**

"Kindergarten"
© *International Film Exchange*

"The Courtesans of Bombay"
© *New Yorker*

SCREAMTIME (Rugged Films) Producer/Director, Al Beresford; Screenplay, Michael Armstrong; Photography, Don Lord, Alan Pudney, Mike Spera; Editor, uncredited; Music, KPM; Sound, Gene Defever, Stan Phillips, David Stevenson; Art Directors, Adrian Atkinson, Martin Atkinson, Brian Savegar; Assistant Directors, Tony Dyer, Rex Piano, Paul Tivers; Production Managers, Brian Bilgorri, Hugh O'Donnell; Special Makeup Effects, Nick Maley; A Manson Intl. presentation; British; Rank Color; Rated R; 89 minutes; February release. CAST: Robin Bailey (Jack Grimshaw), Ann Lynn (Lena), Ian Saynor (Tony), Yvonne Nicholson (Susan), David Van Day (Gavin), Dora Bryan (Emma), Jean Anderson (Mildred), and Vincent Russo, Michael Gordon, Marie Scinto, Jonathan Morris, Dione Inman, Bosco Hogan, Lally Bowers, Veronica Doran, Matthew Peters, Phillip Bloomfield, Gary Linley

L'AFRICAIN aka *The African* (AMFL) Producer, Claude Berri; Director, Philippe de Broca; Screenplay, Philippe de Broca, Gerard Brach; Photography, Jean Penzer; Art Director, Francois de Lamothe; Sound, Jean Labussiere; Makeup, Jackie Reynal; Costumes, Sylvie Gautrelet; Editor, Henri Lanoe; Music, Georges Delerue; Stunts, Daniel Verite; A Renn Productions picture; French; Color; Not rated; 101 minutes; February release. CAST: Catherine Deneuve (Charlotte), Philippe Noiret (Victor), Jean-Francois Balmer (Planchet), Joseph Momo (Bako), Vivian Reed (Josephine), Jacques Francois (Patterson), Jean Benguigui (Poulakis)

THE KINDERGARTEN (International Film Exchange Ltd.) Producer, Mosfilm; Director/Screenplay, Yevgeny Yevtushenko; Photography, Vladimir Palyan; Music, Gleb May; U.S.S.R., 1984; Russian with subtitles; Not Rated; 143 minutes; February release. CAST: Klaus Maria Brandauer, Sergej Gusak, Svalna Evstratova, Galina Stachanova, Sergej Bobrovskiy, and others

FRENCH LESSON (Warner Bros.) formerly *The Frog Prince*; Producer, Iain Smith; Director/Adaptation, Brian Gilbert; Original Screenplay, Posy Simmonds; Editor, Jim Clark; Executive Producer, David Puttnam; Music Arrangements/Additional Material, Richard

Myhill; Music, Enya Ni Bhraonain; Photography, Clive Tickner; Designer, Anton Furst; Story Editor, Susan Richards; Production Manager, Dominic Fulford; Sound, Ken Weston; Costumes, Judy Moorcroft; Soundtrack on Island Visual Arts Records and Tapes; Presented by Warner Bros, Inc and Goldcrest Films and Television Ltd; French; 1984; Color by Eastman Kodak; Rated PG; 90 minutes; February release. CAST: Jane Snowden (Jenny), Alexandre Sterling (Jean Philippe), Diana Blackburn (Ros), Oystein Wiik (Niels), Jacqueline Doyen (Mme. Peroche), Raoul Delfosse (M. Peroche), Francoise Brion (Mme. Bourneuf), Pierre Vernier (M. Bourneuf), Fabienne Tricotte (Annie Bourneuf), Marc Andre Brunet (Didier), Jeanne Herviale (Mme. Duclos), Martine Ferriere (Tante Billy), Catherine Berrian (Chantal), Olivier Achard (Claude), Michele Gleizer (Lucienne), Brigitte Chamarande (Dominique), Paul Yvon Colpin (Serge), Andre Dumas (M. Pevost), Arabella Weir (Zar), Lucy Durham-Matthew (Prissie), Jean-Marc Barr (James), Hugette Faget (M. Comte), and Bernard Rosselli, Serge Uzan, Gilles Laurent, Louis Leonet, Laurenc Merchet, Manuel Collas, Rene Urtreger, Alby Cullaz, Jean-Loui Chautemps, Eric Dervieu

BAHIA (Atlantic) Director, Marcel Camus; Screenplay, Marcel Camus, Jorge Amado; From the novel by Jorge Amado; Photography Andre Domage; Editor, Andree Felix; Music, Antonio Carlos Jobim, Walter Queiroz; Brazil, 1976; Not rated; 90 minutes; March release. CAST: Mira Fonseca, Zen Pereira, Maria Viana, Antonio Pitanga, Paco Sanches, Massu, Jolie Soares, Grande Otelo

CARE BEARS MOVIE II: A NEW GENERATION (Columbia) Producers, Michael Hirsh, Patrick Loubert, Clive A. Smith; Director, Dale Schott; Executive Producers, John Bohach, Jack Chojnacki, Harvey Levin, Carole MacGillvray, Paul Pressler; Animation Director, Charles Bonifacio; Assistant Director, Laura Shepherd; Supervising Producer, Lenora Hume; Character Development, Ralph Shaffer, Linda Edwards, Tom Schneider; Music, Patricia Cullen; Songs, Dean Parks, Carol Parks; Vocals, Stephen Bishop, Debbie Allen; Screenplay, Peter Sauder; Story, Nelvana; Voice Directors, Rob Kirkpatrick, Susan Phillips; Casting, Arlene Berman, Deborah Patz; Line Producers, Peter Hudecki, Heather Walker; Production Supervisors, Rob Kirkpatrick, Dale Cox; Editor, Evan Landis; Production Manager, Karyn Booth Chadwick; Art Director, Wayne Gilbert; Design Coordinator, Cathy Parkes; In association with Wang Film Productions Co Ltd.; A Nelvana Production; An LBS Communications Inc. Presentation; Canadian; Animated; Color; Rated G; 77 minutes; March

Alexandre Sterling, Jane Snowden
in "French Lesson" © *Warner Bros.*

"Care Bears II"
© *Columbia*

206

Steve Bisley, Rod Zuanic
in "Fast Talking" © *Cinecom*

Billy Zoom, Exene Cervenka, D. J. Bonebrake,
John Doe in "The Unheard Music"
© *Skouras/Michael Hyatt*

release. VOICE CAST: Hadley Kay (Dark Heart/The Boy), Chris Wiggins (Great Wishing Star), Cree Summer Francks (Christy), Alyson Court (Dawn), Michael Fantini (John), Sunny Besen Thrasher (Camp Champ), Maxine Miller (True Heart Bear), Pam Hyatt (Noble Heart Horse), Dan Hennessey (Brave Heart Lion), Billie Mae Richards (Tender Heart Bear), Eva Almos (Friend Bear), Bob Dermer (Grumpy Bear), Patrice Black (Share/Funshine Bear), Jim Henshaw (Bright Heart Raccoon), Melleny Brown (Cheer Bear), Janet-Laine Green (Wish Bear), Marla Lukofsky (Playful Heart Monkey), Gloria Figura (Bestime Bear)

ANTONIO GAUDI (Film Forum) Producer/Director/Editor, Hiroshi Teshigahara; Photography, Junichi Segawa, Yoshikazu Yanagida, Ryu Segawa; Sound, Koji Asari; Music, Toru Takemitsu, Kurodo Mori, Shinji Hori; Color; Japan, 1984; Documentary; Not Rated; 72 minutes; March release. With: Isidro Puig Boada

THE COURTESANS OF BOMBAY (New Yorker Films) Producer/Director, Ismail Merchant for Channel 4, England; A film by Ismail Merchant, Ruth Prawer, Jhabvala & James Ivory; Documentary/Narrative; England, 1982; Color; Not Rated; 73 minutes; March release. CAST: Saeed Jaffrey (The Actor), Zohra Segal (The Retired Courtesan), Kareem Samar (The Rent Collector) (No other credits submitted)

QUILOMBO (New Yorker) Producer, Augusto Arraes; Direction/Screenplay, Carlos Diegues; Executive Producer, Marco Altberg; Photography, Lauro Escorel Filho; Editor, Mair Tavares; Scenery and Costumes, Luiz Carlos Ripper; Musical Direction, Gilberto Gil; Songs, Gilberto Gil, Walid Salomao; Brazil; Portugese with English subtitles; In color; Not rated; 119 minutes; March release. CAST: Antonio Pompeo (Zumbi), Zeze Motta (Dandara), Toni Tornado (Ganga Zumba), Vera Fischer (Ana de Ferro), Antonio Pitanga (Acaiuba), Mauricio do Valle (Domingos Jorge Velho), Grande Otelo (Baba), Daniel Filho (Carrilho), Joao Nogueira (Rufino), Jorge Coutinho (Sale), Jofre Soares (Caninde)

THE ALCHEMIST (Empire) Producer, Lawrence Appelbaum; Director, James Amante; Screenplay, Alan J. Adler; Executive Producer, Billy Fine; Color; Rated R; 84 minutes; March release. CAST: Robert Ginty, Lucinda Dooling, John Sanderford, Viola Kate Stimpson, Robert Glaudini (no other credits submitted)

THE UNHEARD MUSIC (Skouras Pictures) Producer, Christopher Blakely; Director/Screenplay, W. T. Morgan; Co-Producer, Everett Greaton; Associate Producers/Animation, Elizabeth Foley, W. T. Morgan; Photography, Karem John Monsour; Designer, Alizabeth Foley; Music, X; Songs, John Doe, Exene Cervenka; Editors, Charlie Mullin, Kent Beyda, Curtiss Clayton, W. T. Morgan; Additional Photography, Marino Colmano; Home Movies, John Doe, Billy Zoom, Denise Zoom, Mr. & Mrs. Zoom, Sr.; Sound, Craig Smith, John Huck, Everett Greaton; An Angel City Production; Documentary; Color; Rated R; 86 minutes; March release. CAST: John Doe, Exene Cervenka, Billy Zoom, D. J. Bonebrake, Ray Manzarek, Rodney Bingenheimer, Brendan Mullen, Frank Gargani, Alizabeth Foley, Denis Zoom, Dinky Bonebrake, Rob Biggs, Al Bergamo, Joe Smith, Robert Hilburn, Jello Biafra, Tom Hadges

FAST TALKING (Cinecom) Producer, Ross Matthews; Director/Screenplay, Ken Cameron; Photography, David Gribble; Music, Sharon Calcraft; Featuring Music from Eurogliders; Designer, Neil Angwin; Sound, Tim Lloyd; Editor, David Huggett; A Merchant Ivory Productions Presentation; Australia; Dolby Stereo; Color; Not Rated; 93 minutes; April release. CAST: Rod Zuanic (Steve Carson), Toni Allaylis (Vicki), Chris Truswell (Moose), Gail Sweeny (Narelle), Steve Bisley (Redback), Peter Hehir (Ralph Carson), Tracy Mann (Sharon Hart), Denis Moore (Yates)

HIDDEN PLEASURES (Azteca Films) *Los Placeres Ocultos;* Producers, Alborada P. C., Oscar Guarido; Director, Eloy de la Iglesia; Story/Screenplay, Rafael Sanchez Campoy, Eloy de la Iglesia, Gonzalo Goicoecha; Photography, Carlos Suarez; Editor, Jose Luis Matesanz; Music, Carmelo A. Bernaola; Art Director, Justo Pastor; Associate Producer, Angel Huete; Assistant Director, Loren Alejo; Costumes, Antonio Munoz; Songs, Juan Martinez Abades, Raquel Meller, Lola Flores, Rafael de Leon, Juan Solano, Paco Espana; Spanish, 1977; Not Rated; 97 minutes; April release. CAST: Simon Andreu (Eduardo), Charo Lopez (Rosa), Tony Fuentes (Miguel), Beatriz Rossat (Carmen), Angel Pardo (Miguel's Friend), German Cobos (Raul), Carmen Platero (Eduardo's Mother), Queta Claver (Maria), Antonio Corencia, Antonio Gamero, Pilar Vela, Carmen Lujan, Amparo Climent, Fabian Conde, Victor Lara, Antonio Ramis, Antonio Retuerto, Juan Carlos Alvarez, Antonio Fernandez, Jose S. Triguero, Antonio Iranzo, Ana Farra, Felix Rotaeta, Antonio Vigo, Rafael Vaquero, Sandra Ribes, Jesus Angel Huerta, Manuel Pena, Ignacio Rodrigo, Alfonso Luque, Antonio Bentacour, Josele Roman, Paco Espana

Zeze Motta in "Quilombo"
© *New Yorker*

Tony Fuentes (c) in "Hidden Pleasures"
© *Azteca Films*

FUNNY DIRTY LITTLE WAR (Cinevista) Producers, Fernando Ayala, Luis Osvaldo Repetto; Director, Hector Olivera; Screenplay, Roberto Cossa, Hector Olivera; Based on a novel by Osvaldo Sorino; Photography, Leonardo Rodriguez Solis; Editor, Eduardo Lopez; Music, Oscar Cardozo Ocampo; Spanish with subtitles; Argentina; Not rated; 80 minutes; April release. CAST: Federico Luppi (Ignacio Fuentes), Hector Bidonde (Suprino), Victor Laplace Commissar (Reinaldo), Rodolfo Ranni (Llanos), Miguel Angel Sola (Juan), Julio de Grazia (Garcia), Lautaro Murua Felisa (Guglielmi), Graciela Dufau (Fuentes), Ulisses Dumont (Cervino), Raul Rizzo (Inspector Rossi), Arturo Maly (Toto)

SEPARATE VACATIONS (RSK Entertainment) Producers, Robert Lantos, Stephen J. Roth; Associate Producers, Andras Hamori, Julian Marks; Director, Michael Anderson; Screenplay, Robert Kaufman; Photography, Francois Protat; Editor, Ron Wisman; Sound, Doug Ganton; Designer, Csaba Kertesz; Set Decorator, Murray Sumner; Costumes, Laurie Drew; Casting, Clare Walker; Produced with Playbody Enterprises; Canadian; Color; Rated R; 82 minutes; April release. CAST: David Naughton (Richard Moore), Jennifer Dale (Sarah Moore), Mark Keyloun (Jeff Ferguson), Laurie Holden (Karen), Blanca Guerra (Alicia), Suzie Almgren (Helen Gilbert), Lally Cadeau (Shelle), Jackie Mahon (Annie Moore), Lee-Max Walton (Donald Moore), Jay Woodcroft (Bobby Moore), Tony Rosato (Harry Blender), Colleen Embree (Robyn)

TRACKS IN THE SNOW directed by Orlow Seunke; Dutch film; Not rated 95 minutes; April release. CAST: Bram van der Vlugt, Gerard Thoolen. No other credits submitted.

HOME OF THE BRAVE (Cinecom) Producer, Paula Mazur; Director/Screenplay/Visuals, Laurie Anderson; Executive Producer, Elliot Abbott; Photography, John Lindley; Editor, Lisa Day; Artistic Director, Perry Hoberman; Soundtrack Co-producers, Roma Baran, Laurie Anderson; Sound, Leanne Ungar; Designer, David Gropman; Electronics, Bob Bielecki; Costumes, Susan Hilferty; Soundtrack on Warner Bros. Records; Dolby Stereo; Panavision; Color; Not Rated; 90 minutes; April release. CAST: Laurie Anderson, Joy Askew, Adrian Belew, Richard Landry, Dollette McDonald, Janice Pendarvis, Sang Won Park, David Van Tieghem, Bobby Butler, Sam Butler, Jimmy Carter, Jane Ira Bloom, Bill Obrecht, Isidro Bobadillo, Daniel Ponce, George Fendrich, Michael Kostroff, Paula Mazur, William S. Burroughs

RONJA ROBBERSDAUGHTER (1900 Film Corporation) Producer/Director, Tage Danielsson; Screenplay, Astrid Lindgren; Photography, Rune Ericson, Mischa Gavrjusjov; Editor, Jan Persson; Music, Bjorn Isfalt; Swedish with subtitles; Sweden; Color; Not rated; 124 minutes; May release. CAST: Hanna Zetterberg (Ronja), Dan Hafstrom (Birk), Borje Ahlstedt (Matt), Lena Nyman (Lovis), Per Oscarsson (Borka), Med Reventberg (Undis), Allan Edwall (Noddle-Pete)

IN NOME DEL PAPA RE (Kino International) Producer, Franco Commifteri; Director/Story/Screenplay, Luigi Magni; Photography, Danilo Desideri; Editor, Ruggero Mastroianni; Music, Armando Trovaioli; Production Company, Juppiter Cinematograficia; Italian; Not rated; 105 minutes; May release. CAST: Nino Manfredi (Don Colom-

bo), Danilo Mattei (Cesare Costa), Carmen Scarpitta (Countess Flaminia), Giovannella Grifed (Teresa), Carlo Bagno (Housekeeper), Gabriella Glacobbe (Marita Tognetti), Ettore Magni (Count Ditavio), Camillo Milli (Don Marino), Rosalino Cellamare (Gaetano Tognetti), Giovanni Rovini (Presiding Judge), Renata Zamengo (Lucia Monti), Salvo Randone (Black Pope), Luigi Basagaluppi (Giuseppe Monti)

DEATH OF A SOLDIER (Scotti Bros. Pictures) Producers, David Hannay, William Nagle; Executive Producers, Oscar Scherl, Richard Tanner; Director, Philippe Mora; Screenplay, William Nagle; Photography, Louis Irving; Editor, John Scott; Music, Alan Zavod; Coproducer, Lance Reynolds; Associate Producers, Honnan Page, Richard Jabara; Art Director, Geoff Richardson; Costumes, Alexandr Tynan; Production Supervisor, Charles Hannah; A Suatu Film Management production; Australian; Color; Panavision; Rated R; 93 minutes; May release. CAST: James Coburn (Maj. Patrick Dannenberg), Reb Brown (Edward J. Leonski), Bill Hunter (Det. Sgt. Adams), Maurie Fields (Det. Sgt. Martin), Belinda Davey (Margot Saunders), Max Fairchild (Maj. William Fricks), Jon Sidney (Gen. MacArthur), Michael Pate (Maj. Gen Sutherland), Randall Berger (Gallo), and John Cottone, Nell Johnson, Mary Charleston, Jeanette Leigh, Rowena Mohr, Duke Bannister, John Murphy, Brian Adams, Arthur Sherman, Terry Donovan, Ken Wayne, Ron Pinnell

CUT AND RUN (New World) Producer, Alessandro Fracassi; Director, Ruggero Deadato; Screenplay, Cesare Frugoni, Dardano Sacchetti; Photography, Alberto Spagnoli; Editor, Mario Morra; Music, Claudio Simonetti; Sound, Piero Fondi; Art Director, Claudio Cinini; Production Manager, Maurizio Anticoli; A Racing Pictures Production; Italian: Telecolor; Rated R; 87 minutes; May release. CAST: Lisa Blount (Fran Hudson), Leonard Mann (Mark), Willie Aames (Tommy), Richard Lynch (Col. Brian Horne), Richard Bright (Bob), Karen Black (Karin), Valentina Forte (Ana), Michael Berryman (Quecho), John Steiner (Vlado), Gabriele Tinti (Manuel)

THE BOY IN BLUE (20th Century Fox) Producer, John Kemeny; Director, Charles Jarrott; Executive Producer, Steve North; Screenplay, Douglas Bowie; Photography, Pierre Mignot; Editor, Rit Wallis; Music, Roger Webb; Designer, William Beeton; Production Manager, Stephane Reichel; Costumes, John Hay; Assistant Director, Jacque Methe; An ICC-Denis Heroux-John Kemeny production; Canadian; Color; Rated R; 93 minutes; May release. CAST: Nicolas Cage (Ned), Cynthia Dale (Margaret), Christopher Plummer (Knox), David Naughton (Bill), Sean Sullivan (Walter), Melody Anderson (Dulcie), James B. Douglas (Collins), Walter Massey (Mayor), Austin Willi (Bainbridge), Philip Craig (Kinnear), Robert McCormick (Trickett)

DEMONS (Ascot Entertainment Group) Producer, Dario Argento for Dacfilm; Director, Lamberto Bava; Italian; Color; Not rated; 8 minutes; May release. No other credits available.

DARK NIGHT (Goodyear Movie Company) Producer, Hsu Li-Hwa; Executive Producer, Lo Wai; Direction and Apstein, Fred Tan; Based on novel by Sue Li-Eng; Photography, Yang Wei-Han; Editor, Chen Po-Wen; Music, Peter Chang; Sound, Duh Duu-Jy; Art/Costume Design, Yu Wei-Yen; In color; Taiwanese/Hong Kong; In Chinese with subtitles; Not Rated; 115 minutes; June release. CAST: Sue Ming-Ming (Li Ling), Hsu Ming (Yeh Yeun), Chang Kuo-Chu (Hwong), Emily Y Chang (Mrs. Niu)

BLOOD LINK (Zadar Films) Producer, Robert Palaggi; Director, Alberto de Martino; Screenplay, Theodore Apstein; Story, Max di Rita, Alberto de Martino; Photography, Romano Albani; Editor, Russell Lloyd; Music, Ennio Morricone; Associate Producer, Robert Gordon Edwards; Art Director, Uberto Bertacca; Italian; Technicolor; Rated R; 94 minutes; June release. CAST: Michael Moriarty (Dr. Craig Mannings/Keith Mannings), Penelope Milford (Dr. Julie Warren), Cameron Mitchell (Bud Waldo), Sarah Langenfeld (Christine Waldo), Martha Smith (Hedwig), Geraldine Fitzgerald (Mrs. Thomason), Virginia McKenna (Ballroom victim), Reinhold K. Olszewski (Insp Hersinger)

THE THRONE OF FIRE (Cannon Group) Producer, Ettore Spagnuolo; Director, Franco Prosperi; Screenplay, Nino Marino; Story, Nino Marino, Giuseppe Buricchi; Photography, Guglielmo Mancori; Editor, Alessandro Lucidi; Music, Carlo Rustichelli, Paolo Rustichelli; Art Director, Franco Cuppini; Costumes, Silvio Laurenzi; Special Effects, Paolo Ricci; Associate Producer, Umberto Innocenzi; A Visione Cinematografica production; Italian; Technicolor; Not rated; 89 minutes; June release. CAST: Sabrina Siani (Princess Valkari), Peter McCoy (Siegfried), Harrison Muller (Morak), and Benny Carduso, Peter Caine, Dan Collins, Stefano Abbati

208

Graciela Dufau, Federico Luppi
in "Funny Dirty Little War"
© Cinevista

Laurie Anderson in "Home of the Brave"
© Cinecom

Kristina Soderbaum, Kathe Gold, Helmut Kautner
in "Karl May" © Film Forum

SPRING SYMPHONY (Warner/Columbia/Greentree) Director/Screenplay, Peter Schamoni; Screenplay Assistance, Hans A. Neunzig; Photography, Gerard Vandenberg; Editor, Elfi Tillack; Sound, Gerard Rueff; Sets/Art Director, Alfred Hirschmeier; Costumes, Christiane Dorst; Assistant Directors, Harold Fischer, Guenter Kraeae; Production Managers, Horst Hartwig, Lilo Pleimes; Music, Robert Schumann; An Allianz Film and Peter Schamoni Film in coproduction with Second German Television (ZDF) and DEFA Filmproduktion; West Germany/East Germany; Color; Rated PG-13; 103 minutes; June release. CAST: Natassia Kinski (Clara Wieck), Rolf Hoppe (Friedrich Wieck), Herbert Groenemeyer (Robert Schumann), Anja-Christine Preussler (Clara as child), Edda Seippel (Mutter Schumann), Andre Heller (Felix Mendelssohn-Bartholdy), Gideon Kremer (Nicolo Paganini), Bernhard Wicki (Baron von Fricken), Gisela Rimpler (Baronin von Fricken), Sonja Tuchmann (Ernestine von Fricken), Margit Geissler (Christel), Uwe Mueller (Becker), Gunter Kraeae (Karl Banck), Inge Marschall (Clemenza Wieck), Helmust Oskamp (Alwein Wieck).

DEATH SENTENCE (Sphinx Films) Produced by Film Polski, Silesia Film Productions; Direction/Screenplay, Witold Orzechowski; Photography, Kazimierz Konrad; Music, Andrzej Korzynski; In Polish with subtitles; In color; Not rated; 104 minutes; June release. CAST: Doris Kuntsmann (Christine), Wojciech Wysocki (Smukley), Jerzy Bonczak (Nurek), Stanislaw Igar (Voh Dehl), Stawromira Lozinska (Zyta), Erich Thiede (Heinrich Himmler), Holger Mahlich (Hans Frank)

TEA IN THE HAREM (Cinecom) Executive Producer, Michele Ray-Gavras; Director/Screenplay, Mehdi Charef, based on his novel "Le Thé au Harem d'Archi Ahmen"; Music, Karim Kacel; Photography, Dominique Chapuis; Assistant Director, Jacques Fontanier; Sets/Costumes, Thierry Flamand; Sound, Jean-Paul Mugel; Dubbing, Claude Villand; Editor, Kenout Peltier; Production Manager, Jean-Loup Monthieux; A K.G. Production with the participation of the French Ministries of Culture and Exterior Relations; An M & R Films Release; French; Color; Not Rated; 110 minutes; June release. CAST: Kader Boukhanef (Madjid), Remi Martin (Pat), Laure Duthilleul (Josette), Saida Bekkouche (Malika), Nicole Hiss (Solange), Brahim Ghenaiem (Majid's father), Nathalie Jadot (Chantal), Frederic Ayivi (Bengston), Pascal Dewaeme (Thierry), Sandrine Dumas (Anita), Bourlem Guerdjou (Bibiche), Jean-Pierre Sobeaux (Jean-Marc), Nicolas Wostrikoff (Stephane), Alicha Bekkaye (Amara), Corine Blue (Josephine), Patrick Bonnel (Mallard), Naima Boukhanef (Malika's daughter), Charly Chemouny (Balou), Marie Collins (Mme. Leves-

que), Albert Delpy (Pelletier), Vincent Fernoit (Gros-Luc), Anne-Marie Jabraud (Isa), Pierre Julien (Levesque), Rita Maiden (Maguy), and Laurence Maravelle Owens, Vincent Martin, Didier Pain, Veronique Sudry, The Zaoui Boys

KARL MAY (Film Forum) Producer/Director/Screenplay, Hans-Jurgen Syberberg; Photography, Dietrich Lohmann; Editor, Ingrid Brozat; Music, Mahler, Chopin, Liszt; Presented in association with Goethe House, New York; West Germany, 1974; German with subtitles; Color; Not Rated; 187 minutes; June release. CAST: Helmut Kautner (Karl May), Kathe Gold (Klara), Kristina Soderbaum (Emma), Mady Rahl (Pauline Munchmeyer), Lil Dagover (Berta v. Suttner)

NOT QUITE PARADISE (New World) Producer/Director, Lewis Gilbert; Screenplay, Paul Kember; Co-Producer, William P. Cartlidge; Music, Rondo Veneziano, Gian Reverberi; Photography, Tony Imi; Designer, John Stoll; Editor, Alan Strachan; Executive Producer, Herbert Oakes; Production Supervisor, Zvi Spielman; Assistant Directors, Michel Cheyko, Avner Orshalimi, Peter Cotton, Mike Katzin; Production Managers, Patricia Carr, Gady Levy; Sound, Daniel Brisseau; Production Coordinators, Gail Samuelson, Ronit Chayun; Special Effects, Richard Richtsfeld, Helmut Klee, Pini Klavir; Costumes, Candy Paterson; An Acorn Pictures Production; Israel; Dolby Stereo; Rated R; 106 minutes; June release. CAST: Sam Robards (Mike), Todd Graff (Rothwell T. Schwartz), Kevin McNally (Pete), Bernard Strother (Dave), Selina Cadell (Carrie), Ewan Stewart (Angus), Sawally Srinonton (Yoshiko), Kate Ingram (Grace), Gary Cady (Steve), Naomi & Schuli Rosenberg (Finnish Twins), Joanna Pacula (Gila), Zafrir Kochanovsky (Menachem), Poli Reshef (Ami), Yaacov Ben Sira (Dobush), Shlomo Tarshish (Reuven), Esti Katz (Rivka), Aharon Greener (Asher), Peter Freistadt (Father), Sara Aman (Mother), Irit Frank (Nurse), Libby Morris (Mrs. Schwartz), Bernard Spear (Mr. Schwartz), Juliano Mer (Hassan), David Menachem (Aziz), Rita Shukroon (Faiza), Menachem Bar'am (Gen. Ashman), Zeev Shimshoni (Sgt.), Avi Keidar (M.P.)

LAMB (Film Forum) Producer, Neil Zeiger; Director, Colin Gregg; Screenplay, Bernard MacLaverty, based on his novel "Lamb"; Photography, Mike Garfath; Sets, Austen Spriggs; Editor, Peter Delfgou; Music, Van Morrison; A Films Four Intl./Flickers-Limehouse release; British; Color; Not Rated; 109 minutes; July release. CAST: Liam Neeson (Michael Lamb), Ian Bannen (Owen Kane), Frances Tomelty, Dudley Sutton, Hugh O'Connor

Kader Boukhaneff, Remi Martin
in "Tea in the Harem" © Cinecom

Todd Graff, Sawally Srinonton
in "Not Quite Paradise"
© New World

209

**Sarah Miles, Ian McKellen
in "Loving Walter"** © *Film Forum*

**Cris Campion, Walter Matthau
in "Pirates"** © *Cannon*

THUNDER RUN A Lynn-Davis production in association with Panache Prods.; Producer, Carol Lynn; Executive Producer, Peter Strauss; Coproducer, Lawrence Applebaum; Director, Gary Hudson; Screenplay, Charles Davis, Carol Heyer; Story, Clifford Wenger Sr., Carol Lynn; Photography, Harvey Genkins; Editor, Burton Lee Harry; Music, Matthew McCauley, Jay Levy; Stunts, Rod Amateau; Special Action Unit, Alan Gibbs; Special Effects, Clifford Wenger Sr.; Associate Producers, Clifford Wenger Sr., Charles Davis; Production Manager, Steve Traxler; Assistant Director, Rob Roda; Art Director, Carol Heyer; Australian; DeLuxe Color; Rated PG-13; 91 minutes; July release. CAST: Forrest Tucker (Charlie Morrison), John Ireland (George Adams), John Sheperd (Chris), Jill Whitlow (Kim), Wally Ward (Paul), Cheryl M. Lynn (Jilly), Marilyn O'Connor (Maggie Morrison), Graham Ludlow (Mike), Alan Rachins (Carlos), Tom Dugan (Wolf)

WALTER AND JUNE aka LOVING WALTER (Film Forum) Producer, Richard Creasey; Director, Stephen Frears; Screenplay, David Cook, from his book *Winter Doves;* Photography, Chris Menges; Editor, Mick Audsley; Art Director, Michael Minas; Music, George Fenton; Sound, Tony Jackson; British; Color; Not rated; 110 minutes; July release. CAST features Ian McKellen, Sarah Miles (no other credits available)

SACRED HEARTS (Film Forum) Producer, Dee Dee Glass; Director/Screenplay, Barbara Rennie; Photography, Diane Tammes; A Reality Films Production for Film Four International; Color; British; Not Rated; 95 minutes; July release. CAST: Anna Massey (Sister Thomas), Katrin Cartlidge (Doris), Oona Kirsch (Maggie) Fiona Shaw (Sister Felicity), Anne Dyson (Sister Perpetua)

HEAVEN, MAN, EARTH (Film Forum) Producers, Laurens C. Postma, Phillip Bartlett; Director, Laurens C. Postma; Screenplay, Jonathan Frost; Photography, David Scott, Billy Wo; Editor, Hussein Younis; Sound, Miranda Watts, Stanley Ko; Music, David Hewson; Graphics, David J. Linggard; Voice, Saul Reichling; YoYo Film Video & Theatre Productions for Channel Four; Documentary; Great Britain, 1984; Not rated; 78 minutes; July release

ZINA (Film Forum) Executive Producers, Andrew Lee, Penny Corke, Adrian Munsey, Paul Levinson; Producer/Director, Ken McMullen; Screenplay, Ken McMullen, Terry James; Photography, Bryan Loftus; Editor, Robert Hargreaves; Designer, Paul Cheetham; Line Producer, Kim Nygaard; Music, David Cunningham, Barry Guard, Simon Heyworth; A TSI/Looseyard Production; British; Color/B&W; Not Rated; 92 minutes; July release. CAST: Domiziana Giordano, Ian

McKellen, Philip Madoc, Rom Anderson, Micha Bergese, Gabrielle Dellal, Paul Geoffreys, William Hootkins, Leonic Mellinger, Maureen O'Brien, Dominique Pinon, Tusse Silberg, George Yiasoumi

PIRATES (Cannon) Producer, Tarak Ben Ammar; Director, Roman Polanski; Screenplay, Gerard Brach, Roman Polanski; Music, Philippe Sarde; Executive Producers, Thom Mount, Mark Lombardo, Umberto Sambuco; Screenplay Collaboration, John Brownjohn; Fight Staging, William Hobbs; Editors, Herve De Luze, William Reynolds; Sound, Jean-Pierre Ruh; Photography, Witold Sobocinski; Costumes, Anthony Powell; Designer, Pierre Guffroy; Assistant Director, Thierry Chabert; Production Supervisors, Roy Stevens, Mohamed Ali Cherif, Carlo Lastricati, Andre Pergament; Production Managers, Alain Depardieu, Hamid Elleutch; Special Make-up, Tom Smith; Special Effects, John Evans, Antonio Corridori, Paul Trielli, Mario Cassar, Marcello Martinelli, Enzo Massari, Franco Ragusa, Augusta Salvati, Gilberto Carbonaro; Choreography, Wanda Szczuka; Sound, Laurent Quaglio; Original Soundtrack on Varese Sarabande Records; Panavision; Color; Rated PG-13; 124 minutes; July release. CAST: Walter Matthau (Capt. Red), Cris Campion (The Frog), Damien Thomas (Don Alfonso), Olu Jacobs (Boomako), Ferdy Mayne (Capt. Linares), David Kelly (Surgeon), and Anthony Peck, Anthony Dawson, Richard Dieux, Jacques Maury, Jose Santamaria, Robert Dorning, Luc Jamati, Emilio Fernandez, Wladyslaw Komar, Georges Trillat, Richard Pearson, Charlotte Lewis, Georges Montillier, John Gill, David Foxxe, Brian Maxine, Raouf Ben Amor, Eugengiusz Priwieziencew, Roger Ashton-Griffiths, Ian Dury, Bill Stewart, Sydney Bromley, Cardew Robinson, Roy Kinnear, Daniel Emilfork, Carole Fredericks, Allen Hoist, Denis Fontayne, Michael Elphick, Angelo Casadei, Bill Fraser, Antonio Spoletini, Bill MacCabe, Smilja Mihailovitch, Bernard Musson, Josine Comelas

THE GIRL IN THE PICTURE (Samuel Goldwyn) Producer, Paddy Higson; Director/Screenplay, Cary Parker; Production Supervisor, Alan J. Wands; Photography, Dick Pope; Sound, Louis Kramer; Editor, Bert Eeles; Designer, Gemma Jackson; Costumes, Mary-Jane Reyner; Production Co-ordinator, Alison Campbell; First Assistant, Catherine McFarlane; Continuity, Margaret Waldie; Scottish; Color; Rated PG-13; 90 minutes; July release. CAST: John Gordon-Sinclair (Alan), Irina Brook (Mary), David McKay (Ken), Gregor Fisher (Bill), Caroline Guthrie (Annie), Paul Young (Smiley), Rikki Fulton (Minister), Simone Lahbib (Girl), Helen Pike (Susannah), Joyce Deans (Stephanie)

Domiziana Giordano in "Zina"
© *Film Forum*

**John Gordon-Sinclair, Irina Brook
in "The Girl in the Picture"**
© *Samuel Goldwyn*

"Pigs and Battleships"
© East-West Classics

Gary Oldman, Tim Roth
in "Meantime" © Film Forum

PIGS AND BATTLESHIPS (East-West Classics) Producer, Nikkatsu Corp; Director, Shohei Imamura; Screenplay, Hisashi Yamauchi; Photography, Shinsaku Himeda; Music, Toshiro Mayazumi; Japan, 1961; Japanese with subtitles; Color; Not Rated; 108 minutes; July release. CAST: Hiroyuki Nagato (Kinta), Jitsuko Yoshimura (Haruko), Tetsuro Tanba (Tetsu)

MEANTIME (Film Forum) Producer, Graham Benson; Devised and Directed by Mike Leigh; Photography, Roger Pratt; Music, Andrew Dickson; Editor, Lesley Walker; Production Company, Central Productions Ltd/Mostpoint Ltd/Channel Four; Color; 100 minutes; July release. CAST: Marion Bailey (Barbara), Tim Roth (Colin), Jeff Robert (Frank), Gary Oldman (Coxy), Phil Daniels (Mark), Pam Ferris (Mavis), Alfred Molina (John), Tilly Vosburgh (Hayley)

50/50 (New Line Cinema) Director/Screenplay, Uwe Brandner; Photography, Juergen Juerges; Editor, Helga Beyer; Music, Peer Rabin, J. J. Cale, Munich Factory; German with subtitles; West Germany; Color; Not rated; 105 minutes; August release. CAST: Hans Peter Hallwachs (Bert Maschkara), Bernd Tauber (Thomas Berger), Agnes Duenneisen (Katrin Adams), Masch Gonska (Eva Hauff), Kai Fischer (Heidi Brunner), Ivan Desny (Baron Wurlitzer), Gerhard Olschewski (Walter Brunner)

CHILD OF THE PALENQUE/Hijo del Palenque (Peliculas Mexicanas) Direction/Screenplay, Ruben Galindo; Music, Gustavo Carrion; Mexican; In Color; Not rated; 88 minutes; August release. CAST: Valentin Trujillo (Damian Corona), Patricia Maria (Flor Corona), Pedro Infante, Jr. (Anatasio)

HANDS OF STEEL (Almi Pictures) Director/Story, "Martin Dolman" (Sergio Martino); Screenplay, "Martin Dolman," Elizabeth Parker, Saul Sasha, John Crowther; Additional Dialog, Lewis Clanelli; Photography, "John McFerrand" (Giancarlo Ferrando); Editor, Alan Devgen; Music, Claudio Simonetti; Special Makeup Effects, Sergio Stivaletti; Special Effects, Robert Callmard, Paul Callmard, Elio Terry; A National Cinematografica/Dania Film/Medusa Distribuzione production; Italian; Color; Rated R; 94 minutes; August release. CAST: Daniel Greene (Paco Querak), Janet Agren (Linda), John Saxon (Francis Turner), George Eastman (Raoul Fernandez), Amy Werba (Dr. Peckinpaugh), and Claudio Cassinelli, Robert Ben, Pat Monti, Andrew Louis Coppola, Donald O'Brien

BLACK JOY (Oakwood Entertainment) Producers, Elliott Kastner, Arnon Milchan; Director, Anthony Simmons; Screenplay, Jamal Ali, Anthony Simmons; From the play by Jamal Ali; Photography, Philip Meheux; Editor, Terry Tom Noble; British; Eastmancolor; Rated R; 110 minutes; August release. CAST: Norman Beaton (Dave), Trevor Thomas (Ben), Dawn Hope (Saffra), Floella Benjamin (Miriam), Oscar James (Jomo), Paul Medford (Devon)

STEAMING (New World) Executive Producer, Richard F. Dalton; Producer, Paul Mills; Director, Joseph Losey; Screenplay, Patricia Losey; From the play by Nell Dunn; Photography, Christopher Challis; Editor, Reginald Beck; Music, Richard Harvey; Art Director, Michael Pickwoad; Sound, Malcolm Davis; A World Film Services production; British; Color; Rated R; 95 minutes; August release. CAST: Vanessa Redgrave (Nancy), Sarah Miles (Sarah), Diana Dors (Violet), Patti Love (Josie), Brenda Bruce (Mrs. Meadows), Felicity Dean (Dawn Meadows), Sally Sagoe (Celia) (no other credits available)

CARAVAGGIO (Cinevista) Producer, Sarah Radclyffe; Executive Producer, Colin MacCabe; Director/Screenplay, Derek Jarman; Photography, Gabriel Beristain; Editor, George Akers; Music, Simon Fisher Turner, assisted by Mary Phillips; Designer, Christopher Hobbs; Costumes, Sandy Powell; Assistant Director, Glynn Purcell; Production Manager, Sarah Wilson; Sound, Billy McCarthy; A British Film Institute production, in association with Channel 4 and Nicholas Ward-Jackson; Technicolor; British; Not rated; 89 minutes; August release. CAST: Nigel Terry (Caravaggio), Sean Bean (Ranuccio Thomasoni), Garry Cooper (Davide), Spencer Leigh (Jerusaleme), Tilda Swinton (Lena), Michael Gough (Cardinal Del Monte), Nigel Davenport (Marchese Giustiniani), Robbie Coltrane (Cardinal Borghese), Jonathon Hyde (Baglione), Dexter Fletcher (Young Caravaggio), Noam Almaz (Boy Caravaggio), Jack Birkett (The Pope)

DO YOU REMEMBER DOLLY BELL? (International Home Cinema Inc.) Producer, Sutjeska Film Sarajevo and TV Sarajevo; Director, Emir Kusturica; Screenplay, Abdulah Sidran; Photography, Vilko Filac; Music, Zoran Simjanovic; Yugoslavia; Color; Not rated; 106 minutes; August release. CAST: Slavko Stimac (Dino), Slobodan Aligrudic (Father), Ljiljana Blagojevic (Dolly Bell), Mira Banjac (Mother), Pavle Vujisic (Uncle), Nada Pani (Aunt), Boro Stjepanovic (Pog)

Daniel Greene, John Saxon
in "Hands of Steel" © ALMI

Nigel Terry, Sean Bean
in "Caravaggio"
© Cinevista/Mike Laye

"The Liberation of Auschwitz"
© *Film Forum*

Jonathan Crombie, Bernie Coulson
in "Bullies" © *Universal*

IN 'N' OUT/Gringo Mojado (Peliculas Mexicanas) Producer, Michael James Egan; Director, Ricardo Franco; Screenplay, Eleen Kesend, Ricardo Franco; Photography, Juan Ruiz Anchias; Music, T-Bone Burnett; U.S./Mexican in English; In color; Not rated; 106 minutes; August release. CAST: Sam Bottoms (Murray Lewis, Jr.), Rafael Inclan (Nieves Blanco), Rebecca Jones (Lupita Blanco), Isela Vega (Mona Mur)

A NIGHT ON THE TOWN/Noche de Juerga (Videocine) Director, Manuel M. Delgado; Screenplay, Jose Maria Fernandez Unsain; Photography, Miguel Arena; Music, Nacho Mendez; Mexican; In color; Not rated; 91 minutes; August release. CAST: Juan Ferrara (Ricardo Bermudes), Helena Rojo (Dolores Vertiz), Victor Junco (Police Lieutenant), Norma Herrera (Alicia Bermudes)

HEIMAT (Edgar Reitz) Producer/Director, Edgar Reitz; Screenplay, Edgar Reitz, Peter Steinbach; Photography, Gernot Roll; Editor, Heidi Handorf; Music, Nikos Mamangakis; In color, black and white; Not rated; In German; Not rated; 940 minutes; August release. CAST: Willi Burger (Mathias Simon), Gertrud Bredel (Katharina Simon), Rudiger Weigang (Eduward Simon), Karin Rasenack (Lucie Simon), Dieter Schaad (Paul Simon), Marita Breuer (Maria Simon), Eva Maria Bayerwaites (Pauline Krober), Arno Lang (Robert Krober), Mathias Kniesbeck (Anton Simon), Sabine Wagner (Martha Simon), Michael Kausch (Ernst Simon)

THE LIBERATION OF AUSCHWITZ (National Center for Jewish Films, Brandeis University) Producer, Bengt von zur Muhlen; Director, Irmgard von zur Muhlen; Documentary; West Germany, 1986; In English; Not Rated; 60 minutes; August release

DEAD END DRIVE-IN (New World) Producer, Andrew Williams; Director, Brian Trenchard-Smith; Co-Producer, Damien Parer; Screenplay, Peter Smalley; Editors, Alan Lake, Lee Smith; Music, Frank Strangio; Costumes, Anthony Jones; Designer, Larry Eastwood; Photography, Paul Murphy; Production Manager, Anne Bruning; Production Coordinator, Judith Ditter; Assistant Directors, Adrian Pickersgill, John Titley, Lisa Harrison; Sound, Leo Sullivan, Martin Oswin; Art Director, Nick McCallum; Assistant Art Director, Rob Robinson; Special Effects, Chris Murray, Alan Maxwell, Peter Evans; Songs by various artists; Presented by Springvale Productions Pty. Ltd. in association with The New South Wales Film Corporation; Documentary; Rated R; 92 minutes; August release. CAST: Ned Manning

(Crabs), Natalie McCurry (Carmen), Peter Whitford (Thompson), Wilbur Wilde (Hazza), Dave Gibson (Dave), Sandie Lillingston (Beth), Ollie Hall (Frank), Lyn Collingwood (Fay), Nikki McWaters (Shirl), Melissa Davis (Narelle), Margi Di Ferranti (Jill), Desiree Smith (Jill), Murray Fahey (Tracey), Jeremy Shadlow (Mickey), Brett Climo (Jeff), Brett Climo (Don), Bernadette Foster (Momma), Ron Sinclair (Reporter), Ghandi McIntyre (Indian), David Jones (Newsreader), Alan McQueen, Ken Snodgrass, Bill Lyle, Garry Who (Cops)

BULLIES (Universal) Producer, Peter Simpson; Director, Paul Lynch; Production Executive, Ray Sager; Screenplay, John Sheppard, Bryan McCann; Executive Producers, Peter Simpson, Peter Haley; Associate Producer, Ilana Frank; Photography, Rene Verzier; Editor, Nick Rotundo; Music, Paul Zaza; Designer, Jack McAdam; Production Manager, Robert Wertheimer; Casting, Lucinda Sill; Assistant Directors, David Robertson, Woody Sidarous, Frank Siracusa; Production Coordinator, Sandy Webb; Sound, Clark McCarron; Special Effects, Bob Shelley, Bob Shelley, Jr.; Set Decorator, Linda Allen; Costumes, Maya Mani; Song, Peter Simpson, Paul Zaza; Produced in association with Allarcom, British Columbia TV, CFCN Communications Ltd.; Color; Rated R; 95 minutes; August release. CAST: Jonathan Crombie (Matt Morris), Janet Laine Green (Jenny Morris), Stephen B. Hunter (Clay Morris), Dehl Berti (Will Crow), Olivia D'Abo (Becky), Bill Croft (Ben), Bernie Coulson (Jimmy), Adrien Dorval (Judd), William Nunn (Jonah), Thick Wilson (Sam), Shay Garner (Maggie Sullivan), Wayne Robson (Vern), Ed Milaney (Frank), Brock Simpson (Arnie), LeRoy Shultz (Murray), Ernie Prentice (Fred), Beth Amos (Martha), and Christianne Hirt, Larry McLean, Brent Meyer, Shane Cardwell, Stacey Kennedy

ISAAC IN AMERICA: A Journey with Isaac Bashevis Singer (Direct Cinema LTD) Producer, Kirk Simon; Director, Amram Nowak; Narrated by Judd Hirsch; Executive Producer, Manya Starr; Photography, Jerry Pantzer, Greg Andracke, Brian Kellman, David Lerner, Kirk Simon, Burleigh Wartes; Music, Ross Levinson; Clarinets, Jack Bashkow; Editors, Riva Freifeld, Toby Shimin, Win Hoover; Sound Editor, Rhetta Barron; Sound, Dan Kinoy, Larry Lowinger, Paul Coombe; Art Director, Marlene Marta; "A Day in Coney Island" from *A Crown of Feathers;* In Association with WNET/13 and The ASDA Foundation; ASDA Consulting Producer, Muriel Peters; Documentary; Not rated; 58 minutes; September release

Isaac Bashevis Singer
in "A Journey with Isaac Bashevis Singer"
© *Direct Cinema*

Maria Pakulnis in "No End"
© *New Yorker*

"Farewell"
© *International Film Exchange*

"Fraggi Deprived of Happiness"
© *International Film Exchange*

SCENE OF THE CRIME Director, Andre Techine; Screenplay, Andre Techine, Pascal Bonitzer, Oliver Assayas; Photography, Pascal Marti; Editor, Martine Giordano; Music, Philippe Sarde; French with subtitles; France; Color; Not rated; 90 minutes; September release. CAST: Catherine Deneuve (Lili), Danielle Darrieux (Grandmother), Wadeck Stanczak (Martin), Nicolas Giraudi (Thomas), Victor Lanoux (Maurice), Jean Bousquet (Grandfather), Claire Nebout (Alice), Jacques Nolot (Father Sorbier)

THE PROMISED LAND/La Tierra Prometida (Peliculas Mexicanas) Producer-Director, Roberto G. Rivera; Screenplay, Ricardo Gariby; Photography, Raul Dominguez; Editor, Enrique Puente Portillo; Music, Rafael Carrion; Mexican; In color; Not rated; 101 minutes; September release. CAST: Roberto Guzman (Serafin), Manuel Ibanez (Pascual), Pedro Weber (Con Man), Claudia Guzman (Serviana), Alejandro Guce (Tolin), Alejandra Meyer (Mother), Lilia Prado (Madame)

CODENAME: WILDGEESE (New World) Producer, Erwin C. Dietrich; Director, Anthony M. Dawson (Antonio Margheriti); Screenplay, Michael Lester; Photography, Peter Baumgartner; Music, Jan Nemec; An Ascot Film/Gico Cinematografica coproduction; West German/Italian; Dolby Stereo; Rated R; 101 minutes; September release. CAST: Lewis Collins (Capt. Wesley), Lee Van Cleef (China), Ernest Borgnine (Fletcher), Mimsy Farmer (Kathy Robson), Klaus Kinski (Charlton), Alan Collins (Priest)

THE QUEST (Miramax) Producer, Barbi Taylor; Director, Brian Trenchard-Smith; Screenplay, Everett DeRoche; Music, Brian May; Executive Producer, David Thomas; Editor, Brian Kavanagh; A Middle Reef Production; Color; Rated PG; September release. CAST features Henry Thomas, Tony Barry (no other credits available)

NO END (New Yorker) Director, Krzysztof Kieslowski; Screenplay, Krzysztof Keislowski, Krzysztof Piesiewicz; Photography, Jacek Petrycki; Editor, Krystyna Rutkowska; Production Manager, Ryszard Chutkowski; Sound, Michal Zarnecki; Music, Zbigniew Preisner; Designer, Allan Starski; Polish with English subtitles; 1984; In color; Not rated; 108 minutes; September release. Grazyna Szapolowska (Ulla Zyro), Jerzy Radziwilowicz (Antoni "Antek" Zyro), Maria Pakulnis (Joanna), Aleksander Bardini (Labrador), Krzysztof Irzeminski (Jacek Zyro), Artur Barcis (Darius), Marek Kondrat (Tom)

THE BLIND DIRECTOR (Spectrafilm) Director/Screenplay, Alexander Kluge; Photography, Thomas Mauch, Werner Luring, Hermann Fahr, Judith Kaufmann; Editor, Jane Seitz; A Kairos-Film in cooperation with ZDF and Stadtisch Buhne Frankfurt am Main/Opera Production; German with subtitles; German; Not rated; 113 minutes; September release. CAST: Jutta Hoffmann (Gertrud Meinecke), Armin Mueller-Stahl (Blind Director), Michael Rehberg (Herr von Gerlach), Peter Roggisch (Big Boss), Rosel Zech (Superfluous Person), Maria Slatinaru (Tosca), Gunther Reich (Scarpia), Piero Visconti (Cavaradossi)

THE CHILDREN ARE WATCHING US Director, Vittorio De Sica; Screenplay, Vittorio De Sica, Cesare Zavattini, Cesare Giulio Viola, Adolfo Franci, Margherita Maglione; Based on the novel "Prico" by Cesare Giulio Viola; Photography, Giuseppe Caracciolo; Music, Renzo Rossellini; Italian with subtitles; Italy; Not Rated; 84 minutes; September release. CAST: Luciano De Ambrosis (Prico), Isa Pola (Mother), Emilio Cigoli (Father), Adriano Rimoldi (Lover)

FAREWELL (IFEX) Director, Elem Klimov; Production Company, Mosfilm Studios; Screenplay, Larissa Shepitko, Rudolf Turin, German Klimov; From the novel "Farewell to Matyora" by Valentin Rasputin; Photography, Alexei Rodionov, Yuri Skhirtladze, with the participation of Sergei Taraskin; Russian with subtitles; Russia, 1982; 128 minutes October release. CAST: Stefania Stanyuta, Lev Durov, Alexei Petrenko, Vadim Yakovenko

FRAGGI DEPRIVED OF HAPPINESS (IFEX) Director, Hodjakuli Narliyev; Production Company, Turkmenfilm Studio; Screenplay, Bulat Mansurov, Moris Simashko, Hodjakuli Narliyev; Based on K. Kulijev's novel "Makhtumkuli"; Photography, Usman Saparov, Ovez Velmuradov; Music, Redjep Redjepov; Art Director, Hussein Husseinov; Turkmenia, 1985/Russia; Turkmenian with subtitles; 138 minutes; October release. CAST: Annasaid Annamuradov, Sona Penaeva, Baba Annanov, Maigozel Aimedova, Hodjadurda Narliyev

HERE YOU WON'T SEE PARADISE (IFEX) Director, Tofik Ismailov; Production Company, Azerbaidjanfilm Studio; Screenplay, Oktai Mamedov; Photography, Sharif Sharifov, Vladimir Sapozhnikov; Music Tofik Kuliyev; Art Directors, Elbek Rzakuliyev, Tofik Nasirov; Azerbaidjan, 1982/Russia; Azerbaidjan with subtitles; 77 minutes; October release. CAST: Otkam Izkanderov, Elyshad Kaziyev, Viktor Demirtash, Sonahanum Aliyeva

**Krzysztof Krzeminski, Grazyna Szapolowska
in "No End"** © *New Yorker*

"Here You Won't See Paradise"
© *International Film Exchange*

"Come and See"
© *International Film Exchange*

"My Home in the Green Hills"
© *International Film Exchange*

KNIGHTS AND EMERALDS (Warner Bros.) Producers, Susan Richards, Raymond Day; Executive Producer, David Puttnam; Direction/Screenplay, Ian Emes; Photography, Richard Greatrex; Editor, John Victor-Smith; Choreographer, Quinny Sacks; Crusaders' Theme/Music Coordinator, Colin Towns; Costumes, Ann Hollowood; Casting, Marilyn Johnson, Avril Jones; Art Director, Deborah Gillingham; Production Manager, Mo Coppitters; Production Coordinator, Joyce Turner; Assistant Directors, Jake Wright, Paul Frift, Peter Corbett; Music by various artists; An Enigma Production in Panavision and Dolby Stereo; PG13; 94 minutes; British; October release. CAST: Christopher Wild (Kevin), Beverley Hills (Melissa), Warren Mitchell (Kirkpatrick), Bill Leadbitter (Enoch), Rachel Davies (Mrs. Fontain), Tracie Bennett (Tina), Nadim Sawalha (Bindu), Tony Milner (Ted), David Cann (Albert), Annette Badland (Daisy), Rodney Litchfield (Kevin's Dad), Mary Ordish (Kevin's Mum), David Neilson (Ashby), Gordon Coulson (Compere), Ingram Hood (Indian Doctor), The Windyvale Band, the Marching Emeralds

KARAYUKI: THE MAKING OF A PROSTITUTE (Kino International) Produced by Imamura Productions; Director, Shohei Imamura; Photography, Masao Tochizawa; Sound, Senichi Benitani; Japanese 1975; In color; Not rated; 70 minutes. No further credits submitted.

COME AND SEE (IFEX) Director, Elem Klimov; Production Company, Byelarusfilm/Mosfilm Studios; Screenplay, Elem Klimov, Ales Adamovich; Based on *"The Story of Khatyn"* and other stories by Ales Adamovich; Photography, Alexei Rodionov; Music, Oleg Yanchenko; Art Director, Viktor Petrov; Byelorussia 1985/Russia; Byelorussian with subtitles; 142 minutes; October release. CAST: Alexei Kravchenko (Florya), Ooga Mironova, Lubomiras Lauciavicus, Vladas Bagdonas, Viktor Lorents

DESCENDANT OF THE SNOW LEOPARD (IFEX) Director, Tolomush Okeev; Production Company, Kirghizfilm Studio; Screenplay, Mar Baidjiev, Tolomush Okeev; Photography, Nurtai Borbiev; Music, Murad Begaliev; Art Director, Alexei Makarov; Kirghizia, 1984/Russia; Kirghizian with subtitles; Russia; 137 minutes; October release. CAST: Dogdurbek Kydyraliev (Kozhozhash), Aliman Djankorozova (Ssaikal), Doskhan Zholzhadsynov (Mundusbai), Gulnara Alimbaeva (Aike)

THE LAUTARS (IFEX) Director/Screenplay, Emil Lotyanu; Production Company, Moldovafilm Studio; Photography, V. Kalashnikov; Music, E. Doga; Art Direction, G. Dmitriu; Moldavia, 1972/Russia; Moldavian with subtitles; 140 minutes; October release. CAST: Sergei Lunkevich (Toma Alistar as Old Man), Olga Kympyanu (Lyanka at 16), Galina Vodyanitskaya (Lyanka as Old Woman), Dimitru Khebeshescu (Toma Alistar as Young Man), G. Grigoriu, S. Toma, Ilye Meskeya, V. Kubcha

THE LEGEND OF SURAM FORTRESS (IFEX) Director, Sergei Paradjanov, Dodo Abashidze; Production Company, Gruziafilm Studio; Screenplay, Vazha Ghigashvili; Based on a novel by Daniel Chonkadze; Photography, Yury Klimenko; Music, Djansug Kakhidze; Georgia, 1985/Russia; Georgian with subtitles; 89 minutes; October release. CAST: Levan Outchanechvili (Zorab), Zourab Kipchidze, Lela Alibegashvili, Dodo Abashidze, Veriko Andjaparidze, Sofiko Chiaureli

MY HOME IN THE GREEN HILLS (IFEX) Director, Assya Suleyeva; Screenplay, Sergei Bodrov, Assya Suleyeva; Photography, Aubakir Sulejev, Bolat Sulejev; Music, Tles Kazhgaliev; Art Director, Alexandr Derighanov; Kazakhstan, 1986/Russia; In Kazakh with subtitles; 67 minutes; October release. CAST: Sanzhar Jaksylykov, Dimasch Akhimov, Murat Mukashev, Zauresh Abutalieva

MEETING IN THE MILKY WAY (IFEX) Director, Ian Streitch; Production Company, Riga Film Studio; Screenplay, Ingrida Sokolova; Photography, Valdis Eglitis; Music, Martina Brauns; Art Director, Viktor Shildknecht; Latvia, 1985/Russia; In Latvian with subtitles; 91 minutes; October release. CAST: Inara Sloutsky (Astra), Nina Ilyna, Elena Skorokhodova, Elena Kazarinova

THE NUT-BREAD (IFEX) Director, Arunas Zhebrunas; Production Company, Lithuanian Film Studio; Screenplay, Saulus Shaltanis; Photography, Algimantas Motzkus; Lithuania, 1977/Russia; Russian with subtitles; 70 minutes; October release. CAST: Leonid Obolensky (Andrus), Saulus Sipaitis (Liuka), Antanas Shurna, Elvira Pishkinaite

THE REVOLT OF THE DAUGHTERS-IN-LAW (IFEX) Director, Elis Abzalov; Production Company, Uzbekfilm; Screenplay, Edward Akopov; Photography, Nadjim Gulyamov; Music, Mirkalil Makhmudov; Art Director, Emmanuel Kalantarov; Uzbekistan, 1985/Russia; Uzbek with subtitles; 77 minutes; October release. CAST: Dilorom Egamberdieva (Nigora), Tursuna Djafarova (Forman-bibi), Dilbar Ikramova, Clara Djalilova

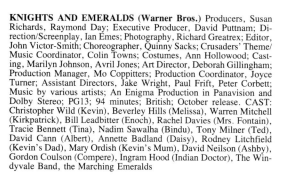

"The Legend of Suram Fortress"
© *International Film Exchange*

"The Revolt of the Daughters-in-law"
© *International Film Exchange*

"The Blue Mountains"
© International Film Exchange

Scott McGinnis, Jeff Osterhage
in "Sky Bandits" © Galaxy International

BLUE MOUNTAINS (International Film Exchange) Director, Eldar Shengelaya; Production Company, Gruziafilm Studio; Screenplay, Revaz Chishvili, Eldar Shengelaya; Photography, Levan Paatashvili; Music, Guia Kancheli; Art Director, Boris Tskhakaia; Georgia, 1984/Russia; Georgian with subtitles; 97 minutes; October release. CAST: Ramaz Giorgobiani, Vasili Kakhnishvili, Teymuraz Chirgadze, Ivan Sakvarelidze, Daredjan Sumbatashvili

THE BULLFIGHT/Corrida (IFEX) Director/Screenplay, Olev Neuland; Production Company, Tallinfilm Studios; Photography, Arvo Iho; Music, Sven Grunberg; Art Direction, Heiki Halla; Estonia, 1982/Russia; Estonian with subtitles; 81 minutes; October release. CAST: Rein Aren, Rita Paawe, Sulev Luik, Veino Wahing

CLOCKWISE (Universal) Producer, Michael Codron; Director, Christopher Morahan; Screenplay, Michael Frayn; Associate Producer, Gregory Dark; Designer, Roger Murray-Leach; Editor, Peter Boyle; Photography, John Coquillon; Music, George Fenton; Executive Producers, Verity Lambert, Nat Cohen; Production Executive, Graham Easton; Production Associate, Bob Mercer; Costumes, Judy Moorcroft; Sound, Chris Munro; Assistant Directors, Tony Hopkins, Crispin Reece, Tim Coddington; Production Coordinator, Julie Baines; Art Director, Diana Charnley; British; Color; Rated PG; 105 minutes; October release. CAST: John Cleese (Brian Stimpson), Alison Steadman (Gwenda Stimpson), Penny Leatherbarrow (Teacher), Howard Lloyd-Lewis (Ted), Jonathan Bowater (Clint), Stephen Moore (Mr. Jolly), Mark Bunting (Studious Boy), Robert Wilkinson (Streaker), John Bardon (Ticket Collector), Mark Burdis (Glen), Nadia Carina (Mandy), Dickie Arnold (Man at station), Angus MacKay (Man on train), Peter Needham (Porter), Peter Lorenzelli (Taxi Driver), Chip Sweeney (Paul), Sharon Maiden (Laura), Joan Hickson (Mrs. Trellis), Constance Chapman (Mrs. Wheel), Ann Way (Mrs. Way), Ann-Marie Gwatkin (Cashier), Mohammed Ashiq (Manager), Pat Keen (Mrs. Wisely), Geoffrey Hutchings (Mr. Wisely), and Geoffrey Greenhill, Richard Ridings, Geoffrey Davion, Charles Bartholomew, Sheila Keith, Penelope Wilton, Christian Regan, Alan Parnaby, Tony Haybarth, Michael Aldridge, Ronald Sowton, Alan Granton, Susan Field, Leslie Scofield, Mike Glynn, Benjamin Whitrow, Geoffrey Palmer, Nicholas Le Prevost, Peter Cellier, David Conville, Patrick Godfrey, Rupert Massey, John Rowe, Philip Voss, Jeffrey Wickham, Nick Stringer, Graeme Green, Sidney Livingstone, Michael Percival, Peter Jonfield, Brian Portsmouth

SKY BANDITS (Galaxy International) Producer, Richard Herland; Director, Zoran Perisic; Screenplay, Thom Keyes; In charge of production, Stephen Lanning; Production Managers, Loretta Ordewer, Robert Fennell; Designer, Tony Woollard; Production Associate, Graham Ford; Photography, David Watkin; Art Director, Charles Bishop; Art Directors, Malcolm Stone, John Siddall, Gavin Bocquet; Costumes, Betsy Hermann, Karen Lansdown; Production Coordinator, Moyra Simpson; Stunts, Marc Boyle; Editor, Peter Tanner; Special Effects, Ian Wingrove, Trevor Neighbour, Dave Beavis; Music, Alfie Kabiljo, Roland Shaw; Assistant Directors, Michael Murray, Jan Hickinbotham, Peter Heslop, Martin Lee; Sound, David Hildyard; Choreographer, Domini Winter; British; Color; Rated PG; 93 minutes; October release. CAST: Scott McGinnis (Barney), Jeff Osterhage (Luke), Ronald Lacey (Fritz), Miles Anderson (Bannock), Valerie Steffen (Yvette), Ingrid Held (Mitsou), Keith Buckley (Commander von Schlussel), Terrence Harvey (Col. Canning), Ten Maynard (Big Jake), Bill Bailey (Sheriff), John Cassady (Deputy Rezin), Bill Reimbold (Bank Manager), Michael Jenn (Nicky), Simon Harrison (Aldiss), Nicholas Lyndhurst (Chalky), David English (Hamilton), Conrad Asquith (Hawkins), Nicholas Frankau (Ffolkes), Slim Gaillard (Piano Player)

LINK (Cannon) Producer/Director, Richard Franklin; Screenplay, Everett De Roche; Based on a Story by Lee Zlotoff and Tom Ackerman; Co-Producer, Rick McCallum; Executive Producer, Verity Lambert; Music, Jerry Goldsmith; Ape Trainer, Ray Berwick; Designer, Norman Garwood; Photography, Mike Malloy; Editor, Andrew London; Production Executive, Graham Easton; Production Associate, Bob Mercer; Production Supervisor, Selwyn Roberts; Assistant Directors, Chris Rose, John Dodds, Chris Hall; Production Coordinator, Clare St. John; Art Director, Keith Pain; Sound, David Stephenson, Steve O'Brien, Mike Harris; Orchestrations, Arthur Morton; Costumes, Terry Smith; Special Effects, John Gant, Chris Corbould; Stunts, Tony Smart, Tracey Eddon; Special Character Design, Lyle Conway; Animatronics Designers, Nick Rayburn, David White, Lesja Liber; Song, The Kinks, Ray Davies; British; Technicolor; Dolby Stereo; Rated R; 103 minutes; October release. CAST: Terence Stamp (Dr. Steven Phillip), Elisabeth Shue (Jane Chase), Steven Pinner (David), Richard Garnett (Dennis), David O'Haro (Tom), Kevin Lloyd (Bailey), Joe Belcher (Taxi Driver), and Apes: Locke (Link), Carrie (Voodoo), Jed (Imp)

Penelope Wilton, John Cleese
in "Clockwise" © Universal

Elisabeth Shue, Link in "Link"
© Cannon

Neil Munro, Martha Henry
in "Dancing in the Dark"
© *New World*

"Sheherazade's 1002nd Night"
© *International Film Exchange*

EMPTY QUARTER (Nicole Jouve Interama) Producers, Francois Margolin, Pascale Dauman (Pari Films and Copyright Films); Director/Photography, Raymond Depardon; Screenplay, Francois Weyermans, Raymond Depardon; French; Not rated; 87 minutes; October release. CAST: Francoise Prenant (no other credits available)

LOOPHOLE (Almi Pictures) Producers, David Korda, Julian Holloway; Director, John Quested; Screenplay, Jonathan Hales; Based on the novel by Robert Pollock; Music, Lalo Schifrin; Editor, Ralph Sheldon; English 1983; Color; Not rated; 96 minutes; October release. CAST: Albert Finney (Mike Daniels), Martin Sheen (Stephen Booker), Susannah York (Jenny Booker), Colin Blakely (Gardner), Jonathan Pryce (Taylor), Robert Morley (Bodfrey)

DANCING IN THE DARK (New World) Executive Producer, Don Haig; Producer, Anthony Kramreither; Director/Story, Leon Marr; Based on the novel by Joan Barfoot; Photography, Vic Sarin; Editor, Tom Berner; Coproducer, John Ryan; A Brightstar Films/Film Arts/Film House Group production, in association with the Canadian Broadcasting Corp.; Canadian; Color; Rated PG-13; 98 minutes; October release. CAST: Martha Henry (Edna), Neil Munro (Henry), Rosemary Dunsmore (Nurse), Richard Monette (Doctor), Elena Kudaba (Edna's roomate), Brenda Bazinet (Susan)

RAGE (Gel Intl.) Producer, Paolo Ferrara; Director, "Anthony Richmond" (Tonino Ricci); Screenplay, Jaime Comas Gil, Eugenio Benito; Photography, Gianni Bergamini; Editor, Vincenzo Tomazzi; Music, Stelvio Cipriani; Production Manager, Maurizio Mattei; Assistant Director, Giancarlo Bastianori; Stunts, Roland Zamperla; Set Designer, Javier Fernandez; A Tiber Intl./Arco Fil coproduction; Italian/Spanish; Color; Not rated; 91 minutes; October release. CAST: Conrad Nichols (Rage), and Stelio Candelli, Werner Pochat, Taida Urruzola, Chris Huerta

FORMULA FOR MURDER (Fulvia Intl. Films) Director, "Martin Herbert" (Alberto De Martino); Screenplay, Hank Walker, "Martin Herbert" (Alberto De Martino); Photography, Lawrence Barkey; Editor, "Vincent P. Thomas" (Vincenzo Tomassi); Music, Francesco De Masi; Sound, Steve Connely; Art Director, Julian Wilson; Stunts, Arthur Mulkey; Dubbing, Nick Alexander; Italian; Luciano Vittori Color; Not rated; 88 minutes; October release. CAST: Christina Nagy (Joanna), David Warbeck (Craig), Carroll Blumenberg (Ruth), Rossano Brazzi (Dr. Sernich), and Andrea Bosic, Loris Loddi, Adriana Giuffre, Daniela De Carolis, Arthur Webber Jr.

SHEHERAZADE'S 1002nd NIGHT (IFEX) Director, Takhir Sabirov; Production Company, Tadjikfilm Studio; Screenplay, Valery Karen, with the participation of Takhir Sabirov; Based on *"The Arabian Nights"* and tales by W. Hauff; Photography, Vladimir Klimov; Music, Gannady Alexandrov; Art Director, Vladimir Ptitsyn; Tadjikstan, 1984/Russia; Tadjikstanian with subtitles; 82 minutes; October release. CAST: Al-Khadad Adel, Larisa Belogurova, Yelena Tonunts, Takhir Sabirov

TANGO OF OUR CHILDHOOD (IFEX) Director/Screenplay, Albert Mkrtchian; Production Company, Armenfilm Studio; Photography, Rudolf Vatinian; Music, Tigran Mansurian; Art Directors, Rafael Babayan, Gagik Babayan; Armenia, 1985/Russia; Armenian with subtitles; 91 minutes; October release. CAST: Galia Noventz (Siranush), Mgher Mkrtchian (Ruben)

TRIAL ON THE ROAD/CHECKPOINT (IFEX) Director, Alexei German; Production Company, Lenfilm Seudios; Screenplay, Eduard Volodarsky; Based on the war novels of Yury German; Photography, Yasha Sklansky; Music, Isaak Shwartz; Art Director, Valery Yurkevitch; 1971, released in 1985, Russia; Russian with subtitles; 99 minutes; October release. CAST: Rolan Bykov, Vladimir Zamansky, Anatoly Solonitsyn, Oleg Borisov, Anda Zaitzs

THE UNMARKED LOAD (IFEX) Director, Vladimir Popkov; Production Company, A. Dovzhenko Kiev Film Studios; Screenplay, Vladimir Mazur; Photography, Valery Anisimov; Music, Oleg Kiva; Art Director, Vyacheslav Ershov; Ukraine, 1985/Russia; Ukrainian with subtitles; 92 minutes; October release. CAST: Alexei Gorbunov (Stenjko), Tynu Kark, Yury Grigoriev

MONSTER SHARK aka *Red Ocean* **(Cinema Shares)** Producer, Mino Loy (uncredited); Director "John Old Jr." (Lamberto Bava); Screenplay, Gianfranco Clerici, others; Story, "Lewis Coates" (Luigi Cozzi), Don Lewis, "Martin Dolman" (Sergio Martino); Photography, "John McFerrand" (Giancarlo Ferrando); Editor, Bob Wheeler; Music, Anthony Barrymore; Assistant Directors, Gilbert Roussel, Fredy Unger; Special Effects, Germano Natali; Designer, A. M. Geleng; Monster Shark Creator, Ovidio Talto; A Filmes Intl.-Nuovo Dania-National Cinematografica/Les Filmes du Griffon coproduction; Telecolor; Not rated; 92 minutes; November release. CAST: Michael Sopkiw (Peter), Valentina Monnier, "John" (Gianni) Garko (Sheriff Gordon), William Berger (Dr. West), Ira Peynard, Lawrence Morgant, Dagmar Lysander (Sonja)

"Tango of Our Childhood"
© *International Film Exchange*

"Trial on the Road"
© *IFEX*

**Jean-Hugues Anglade, Beatrice Dalle
in "Betty Blue"** © *Alive Films*

Marshall Islanders in "Half Life"
© *Kino International*

THE SCORPION/La Alacrana (Peliculas Mexicanas) Executive Producer, Eddie Rodriguez; Producer, Roberto Rodriguez E.; Director, Jose Luis Urquieta; Screenplay, Jorge Patino; Based on an argument by Roberto Rodriguez R.; Photography, Alberto Arellanos; Editor, Rogelio Zuniga; In color; Not rated; Mexican; 86 minutes; November release. CAST: Maribel Guardia (Eugenia/La Alacrana), Carlos Ancira (Don Eliseo Mendieta), Juan Delaez (Fernando), Naciso Busquets (Colonel), Claudia Guzman (Raquel), Susy Rodriguez (Irene), and Barbara Gil, Gina Morett, Sandra Boyd, Maria Luisa Alcala, Carlos Pouliot, Rojo Grau

ZONING (CineInternational) Director, Ulrich Krenkler; Screenplay, Ulrich Krenkler, Angelika Hacker; Photography, Nikolaus Starkmeth; Editor, Ute Albrecht-Lovell; Music, Tangerine Dream; Sound, Christian Baudisson; Art Director, Thomas V. Klier, P. Ranody; West German; In color; Not rated; 89 minutes; November release. CAST: Norbert Lamla, Hubertus Gertzen, Vernika Wolff, Rainer Frieb, Dieter Meier, Eleonore Weisgerber

BETTY BLUE (Alive Films) Producers, Claudie Ossard, Jean-Jacques Beineix; Director/Screenplay, Jean-Jacques Beineix; Based on the book "372 Le Matin" by Philippe Djian; Production Manager, Claudie Ossard; Assistant Directors, Jean-Francois Chaintron, Laurent Duquesnoy; Casting, Dominique Besnehard; Photography, Jean-Francois Robin; Sound, Pierre Befve, Pierre Excoffier; Art Director, Carlos Conti; Designer, Kim Doan; Special Effects, Jean-Francois Cousson; Costumes, Elisabeth Tavernier; Editor, Monique Prim; Sound Effects, Jean-Pierre Lelong; Music, Gabriel Yared; A Gaumont Presentation; French with subtitles; Color; Not rated; 120 minutes; November release. CAST: Beatrice Dalle (Betty), Jean-Hugues Anglade (Zorg), Consuelo de Haviland (Lisa), Gerard Darmon (Eddy), Clementine Celarie (Annie), Jacques Mathou (Bob), Claude Confortes (Owner), Philippe Laudenbach (Gyneco Publisher), Vincent Lindon (Policeman Richard), Raoul Billeray (Old Policeman), Claude Aufaure (Doctor), Andre Julien (Old Georges), Nathalie Dalyan (Maria), Louis Bellanti (Mario), Bernard Robin (Renter #2), Nicolas Jalowyj (Little Nicolas)

HAPPILY EVER AFTER (European Classics) Producers, Lucy Barreto, Antonio Calmon; Director, Bruno Barreto; Screenplay, Antonio Calmon; Photography, Affonso Beato; Editor, Vera Freire; Music, Cesar Camargo Mariano; Portuguese with subtitles; Brazil; Not rated; 110 minutes; November release. CAST: Regina Duarte (Fernanda), Paulo Castelli (Miguel), Patricio Bisso (Bombom), Flavio Galvao (Roberto), and Felipe Martins, Flavio Sao Thiago, Ivan Setta

TRICHEURS (Les Films Galatee) Director, Barbet Schroeder; Screenplay, Pascal Bonitzer, Steve Baes, Barbet Schroeder; Story, Steve Baes; Photography, Robby Muller; Editor, Denise de Casabianca; Music, Peer Raben; A Coproduction of Les Films du Losange and Bloskop Film; French with subtitles; France; Not rated; 94 minutes; November release. CAST: Jacques Dutronc (Elric), Bulle Ogier (Suzie), Kurt Raab (Jorg), Virgilio Teixeira (Toni), Steve Baes (Casino Director), Claus-Dieter Reents (Aldo), Karl Wallenstein (Boudha), Robby Muller (Engineer), Leandro Vale (Derelict)

HALF LIFE (Kino International) Producer/Director/Screenplay/ Photography, Dennis O'Rourke; Music, Bob Brozman; Archival Film Research, David Thaxton, Kevin Green; Australia 1985; Documentary; Not rated; 86 minutes; December release. Winner of 1986 Berlin Film Festival International Jury Prize, 1986 U.S. Film Festival Director's Award for Extraordinary Achievement

MISS MARY (New World) Executive Producer, Lita Stantic; Director, Maria Luisa Bemberg; Original Idea, Maria Luisa Bemberg, Beda Docampo Feijoo, Juan Bautista Stagnaro; Screenplay, Jorge Goldenberg, Maria Luisa Bemberg; Production, Marta Parga; Associate Producers, Joan Baribeault, Carlos Gaustein; Production Administrator, Jose Strier; Photography, Miguel Rodriguez; Editor, Cesar D'Angiolillo; Music, Luis Maria Serra; Music Coordinators, Luis Maria Serra, Jorge Andres; Assistant Director, Victor Dinenzon, Norberto Cesca; Sound, Jorge Stavropoulos; Hair Designs, Osvaldo Speron; Argentina; Color; Rated R; 100 minutes; December release. CAST: Julie Christie (Miss Mary), Nacha Guevara (Mecha), Luisina Brando (Perla), Tato Pavlovsky (Alfredo), Gerardo Romano (Ernesto), Iris Marga (Abuelo), Guillermo Battaglia (Abuelo), Sofia Viruboff (Carolina), Donald McIntyre (Johnny), Barbara Bunge (Teresa), and Alberto Busaid, Ricardo Hanglin, Laura Moss, Carlos Pamplona, Georgina Parpacnoli, Nora Zinsky, Regina Lam, Anne Henry, Sandra Ballesteros, Anita Larronde, Alfredo Quesada, Osvaldo Flores, Tessie Gilligan, Carlos Usay, Oscar Lopez, Susana Veron, Albeto Marty, Beatriz Thibaudin, Laura Feal, Lidia Cortinez, Juan Palomino, Facundo Zuviria, Lila Di Palma, Mercedes Van Gelderen, Paula Muschietti, Julio Cesar Srur

TYPHOON CLUB (A.T.G.) Producer, Susumu Miyasaka; Director, Shinji Somai; Screenplay, Yuji Katoh; Photography, Akihiro Itoh; Design, Norivoshi Ikeya; Editor, Isao Tomita; Color; Not rated; 115 minutes; Japan 1985; December release (no other credits submitted)

"The Unmarked Load"
© *International Film Exchange*

Julie Christie as "Miss Mary"
© *New World*

217

Karen
Akers

Edward
Albert

Suzy
Amis

Alec
Baldwin

Lisa
Banes

Ruben
Blades

BIOGRAPHICAL DATA

(Name, real name, place and date of birth, school attended)

AAMES, WILLIE (William Upton): 1961.

ABBOTT, DIAHNNE: NYC, 1945.

ABBOTT, JOHN: London, June 5, 1905.

ABRAHAM, F. MURRAY: Pittsburgh, PA, Oct. 24, 1939. UTx.

ADAMS, BROOKE: NYC, 1949. Dalton.

ADAMS, DON: NYC, Apr. 13, 1926.

ADAMS, EDIE (Elizabeth Edith Enke): Kingston, PA, Apr. 16, 1929. Juilliard, Columbia.

ADAMS, JULIE (Betty May): Waterloo, Iowa, Oct. 17, 1928. Little Rock Jr. College.

ADAMS, MAUD (Maud Wikstrom): Lulea, Sweden.

ADDY, WESLEY: Omaha, NB, Aug. 4, 1913. UCLA.

ADJANI, ISABELLE: Germany, June 27, 1955.

ADRIAN, IRIS (Iris Adrian Hostetter): Los Angeles, May 29, 1913.

AGAR, JOHN: Chicago, Jan. 31, 1921.

AGUTTER, JENNY: Taunton, Eng, 1952.

AIELLO, DANNY: June 20, 1935, NYC.

AIMEE, ANOUK (Dreyfus): Paris, Apr. 27, 1934. Bauer-Therond.

AKERS, KAREN: NYC, Oct. 13, 1945, Hunter Col.

AKINS, CLAUDE: Nelson, GA, May 25, 1936. Northwestern U.

ALBERGHETTI, ANNA MARIA: Pesaro, Italy, May 15, 1936.

ALBERT, EDDIE (Eddie Albert Heimberger): Rock Island, IL, Apr. 22, 1908. U. of Minn.

ALBERT, EDWARD: Los Angeles, Feb. 20, 1951. UCLA.

ALBRIGHT, LOLA: Akron, OH, July 20, 1925.

ALDA, ALAN: NYC, Jan. 28, 1936. Fordham.

ALDERSON, BROOKE: Dallas, Tx.

ALEJANDRO, MIGUEL: NYC, Feb. 21, 1958.

ALEXANDER, JANE (Quigley): Boston, MA, Oct. 28, 1939. Sarah Lawrence.

ALLEN, JOAN: Rochelle, IL, Aug. 20, 1956, EastIllU.

ALLEN, KAREN: Carrollton, IL. Oct. 5, 1951. UMd.

ALLEN, NANCY: NYC June 24, 1950.

ALLEN, REX: Wilcox, AZ, Dec. 31, 1922.

ALLEN, STEVE: New York City, Dec. 26, 1921.

ALLEN, WOODY (Allen Stewart Konigsberg): Brooklyn, Dec. 1, 1935.

ALLYSON, JUNE (Ella Geisman): Westchester, NY, Oct. 7, 1917.

ALONSO, MARIA CONCHITA: Cuba 1957.

ALVARADO, TRINI: NYC, 1967.

AMECHE, DON (Dominic Amichi): Kenosha, WI, May 31, 1908.

AMES, ED: Boston July 9, 1929.

AMES, LEON (Leon Wycoff): Portland, IN, Jan. 20, 1903.

AMIS, SUZY: Oklahoma City, Ok., Jan. 5, 1958. Actors Studio.

AMOS, JOHN: Newark, NJ, Dec. 27, 1940. Colo. U.

ANDERSON, JUDITH: Adelaide, Australia, Feb. 10, 1898.

ANDERSON, LONI: St. Paul, Mn., Aug. 5, 1946.

ANDERSON, LYNN: Grand Forkes, ND; Sept. 26, 1947. UCLA.

ANDERSON, MELODY: Canada 1955, Carlton U.

ANDERSON, MICHAEL, JR.: London, Eng., 1943.

ANDERSON, RICHARD DEAN: Minneapolis, Mn, 1951.

ANDERSSON, BIBI: Stockholm, Nov. 11, 1935. Royal Dramatic Sch.

ANDES, KEITH: Ocean City, NJ, July 12, 1920. Temple U., Oxford.

ANDRESS, URSULA: Switz., Mar. 19, 1936.

ANDREWS, ANTHONY: London, 1948.

ANDREWS, DANA: Collins, MS, Jan. 1, 1909. Sam Houston Col.

ANDREWS, HARRY: Tonbridge, Kent, Eng., Nov. 10, 1911.

ANDREWS, JULIE (Julia Elizabeth Wells): Surrey, Eng., Oct. 1, 1935.

ANNABELLA (Suzanne Georgette Charpentier): Paris, France, July 14, 1912/1909.

ANN-MARGRET (Olsson): Valsjobyn, Sweden, Apr. 28, 1941. Northwestern U.

ANSARA, MICHAEL: Lowell, MA, Apr. 15, 1922. Pasadena Playhouse.

ANTHONY, TONY: Clarksburg, WV, Oct. 16, 1937. Carnegie Tech.

ANTON, SUSAN: Yucaipa, CA. Oct. 12, 1950. Bernardino Col.

ANTONELLI, LAURA: Pola, Italy.

ARANHA, RAY: Miami, Fl, May 1, 1939. FlaA&M, AADA.

ARCHER, JOHN (Ralph Bowman): Osceola, NB, May 8, 1915. USC.

ARDEN, EVE (Eunice Quedens): Mill Valley, CA, Apr. 30, 1912.

ARKIN, ALAN: NYC, Mar. 26, 1934. LACC.

ARNAZ, DESI, JR.: Los Angeles, Jan. 19, 1953.

ARNAZ, LUCIE: Hollywood, July 17, 1951.

ARNESS, JAMES (Aurness): Minneapolis, MN, May 26, 1923. Beloit College.

ARTHUR, BEATRICE (Frankel): NYC, May 13, 1926. New School.

ARTHUR, JEAN: NYC, Oct. 17, 1905.

ASHLEY, ELIZABETH (Elizabeth Ann Cole): Ocala, FL, Aug. 30, 1939.

ASSANTE, ARMAND: NYC, Oct. 4, 1949. AADA.

ASTAIRE, FRED (Fred Austerlitz): Omaha, NB, May 10, 1899.

ASTIN, JOHN: Baltimore, MD, Mar. 30, 1930. U. Minn.

ASTIN, PATTY DUKE: (see Patty Duke)

ASTOR, MARY (Lucile V. Langhanke): Quincy, IL, May 3, 1906. Kenwood-Loring School.

ATHERTON, WILLIAM: Orange, CT, July 30, 1947. Carnegie Tech.

ATKINS, CHRISTOPHER: Rye, NY, Feb. 21, 1961.

ATTENBOROUGH, RICHARD: Cambridge, Eng., Aug. 29, 1923. RADA.

AUBERJONOIS, RENE: NYC, June 1, 1940. Carnegie Tech.

AUDRAN, STEPHANE: Versailles, Fr., 1933.

AUGER, CLAUDINE: Paris, Apr. 26, 1942. Dramatic Cons.

AULIN, EWA: Stockholm, Sweden, Feb. 14, 1950.

AUMONT, JEAN PIERRE: Paris, Jan. 5, 1909. French Nat'l School of Drama.

AUTRY, GENE: Tioga, TX, Sept. 29, 1907.

AVALON, FRANKIE (Francis Thomas Avallone): Philadelphia, Sept. 18, 1940.

AYKROYD, DAN: Ottawa, Can., July 1, 1952.

YRES, LEW: Minneapolis, MN, Dec. 28, 1908.

ZNAVOUR, CHARLES (Varenagh Aznourian): Paris, May 22, 1924.

ACALL, LAUREN (Betty Perske): NYC, Sept. 16, 1924. AADA.

ACH, BARBARA: Aug. 27, 1946.

ACKER, BRIAN: NYC, Dec. 5, 1956. Neighborhood Playhouse.

ACKUS, JIM: Cleveland, Ohio, Feb. 25, 1913. AADA.

ACON, KEVIN: Philadelphia, PA., July 8, 1958.

AILEY, PEARL: Newport News, VA, March 29, 1918.

AIN, BARBARA: Chicago, Sept. 13, 1934. U. ILL.

AIO, SCOTT: Brooklyn, NY, Sept. 22, 1961.

AKER, BLANCHE: NYC, Dec. 20, 1956.

AKER, CARROLL: Johnstown, PA, May 28, 1931. St. Petersburg Jr. College.

AKER, DIANE: Hollywood, CA, Feb. 25, 1938. USC.

AKER, KATHY WHITTON: Midland, TX., June 8, 1950. UCBerkley.

ALABAN, ROBERT (Bob); Chicago, Aug. 16, 1945. Colgate.

ALDWIN, ADAM: Chicago, IL. 1962.

ALDWIN, ALEC: Massapequa, NY, Apr. 3, 1958. NYU.

ALIN, INA: Brooklyn, Nov. 12, 1937. NYU.

ALL, LUCILLE: Celaron, NY, Aug. 6, 1910. Chatauqua Musical Inst.

ALSAM, MARTIN: NYC, Nov. 4, 1919. Actors Studio.

ANCROFT, ANNE (Anna Maria Italiano): Bronx, NY, Sept. 17, 1931. AADA.

ANES, LISA: Chagrin Falls, Oh, July 9, 1955, Juilliard.

ANNEN, IAN: Airdrie, Scot., June 29, 1928.

ARANSKI, CHRISTINE: Buffalo, NY, May 2, 1952, Juilliard.

ARBEAU, ADRIENNE: Sacramento, CA. June 11, 1945. Foothill Col.

ARDOT, BRIGITTE: Paris, Sept. 28, 1934.

ARKIN, ELLEN: Bronx, NY, 1959. Hunter Col.

ARNES, BINNIE (Gitelle Enoyce Barnes): London, Mar. 25, 1906

ARRAULT, JEAN-LOUIS: Vesinet, France, Sept. 8, 1910.

ARRAULT, MARIE-CHRISTINE: Paris, 1946.

ARRETT, MAJEL (Hudec): Columbus, OH, Feb. 23. Western Reserve U.

ARRON, KEITH: Mexborough, Eng., Aug. 8, 1936. Sheffield Playhouse.

ARRY, GENE (Eugene Klass): NYC, June 14, 1921.

ARRY, NEILL: NYC, Nov. 29, 1965.

ARRYMORE, DREW: Los Angeles, Feb. 22, 1975.

ARRYMORE, JOHN BLYTH: Beverly Hills, CA, June 4, 1932. St. John's Military Academy.

ARTHOLOMEW, FREDDIE: London, Mar. 28, 1924.

ARYSHNIKOV, MIKHAIL: Riga, Latvia, Jan. 27, 1948.

BASINGER, KIM: Athens, GA. 1954. Neighborhood Playhouse.

BATEMAN, JUSTINE: Woodland Hills, Ca., 1966.

BATES, ALAN: Allestree, Derbyshire, Eng., Feb. 17, 1934. RADA.

BAUER, STEVEN: (Steven Rocky Echevarria): Havana, Cuba, Dec. 2, 1956. UMiami.

BAXTER, KEITH: South Wales, Apr. 29, 1933. RADA.

BEAL, JOHN (J. Alexander Bliedung): Joplin, MO, Aug. 13, 1909. PA. U.

BEATTY, NED: Louisville, KY. 1937.

BEATTY, ROBERT: Hamilton, Ont., Can., Oct. 19, 1909. U. of Toronto.

BEATTY, WARREN: Richmond, VA, March 30, 1937.

BECK, MICHAEL: Horseshoe Lake, AR, 1948.

BEDELIA, BONNIE: NYC, Mar. 25, 1952. Hunter Col.

BEDI, KABIR: India, 1945.

BEERY, NOAH, JR.: NYC, Aug. 10, 1916. Harvard Military Academy.

BEGLEY, ED, JR.: NYC, Sept. 16.

BELAFONTE, HARRY: NYC, Mar. 1, 1927.

BELASCO, LEON: Odessa, Russia, Oct. 11, 1902.

BEL GEDDES, BARBARA: NYC, Oct. 31, 1922.

BELL, TOM: Liverpool, Eng., 1932.

BELLAMY, RALPH: Chicago, June 17, 1904.

BELLER, KATHLEEN: NYC, 1957.

BELLWOOD, PAMELA (King): Scarsdale, NY

BELMONDO, JEAN PAUL: Paris, Apr. 9, 1933.

BENEDICT, DIRK (Niewoehner): White Sulphur Springs, MT. March 1, 1945. Whitman Col.

BENJAMIN, RICHARD: NYC, May 22, 1938. Northwestern U.

BENNENT, DAVID: Lausanne, Sept. 9, 1966.

BENNETT, BRUCE (Herman Brix): Tacoma, WA, May 19, 1909. U. Wash.

BENNETT, JILL: Penang, Malay, Dec. 24, 1931.

BENNETT, JOAN: Palisades, NJ, Feb. 27, 1910. St. Margaret's School.

BENSON, ROBBY: Dallas, TX, Jan 21, 1957.

BERENSON, MARISSA: NYC, Feb. 15, 1947.

BERGEN, CANDICE: Los Angeles, May 9, 1946. U. PA.

BERGEN, POLLY: Knoxville, TN, July 14, 1930. Compton Jr. College.

BERGER, HELMUT: Salzburg, Aus., 1942.

BERGER, SENTA: Vienna, May 13, 1941. Vienna Sch. of Acting.

BERGER, WILLIAM: Austria, Jan. 20, 1928. Columbia.

BERGERAC, JACQUES: Biarritz, France, May 26, 1927. Paris U.

BERLE, MILTON (Berlinger): NYC, July 12, 1908.

BERLIN, JEANNIE: Los Angeles, Nov. 1, 1949.

BERLINGER, WARREN: Brooklyn, Aug. 31, 1937. Columbia.

BERNHARD, SANDRA: Arizona 1956.

BERRI, CLAUDE (Langmann): Paris, July 1, 1934.

BERRIDGE, ELIZABETH: Westchester, NY, May 2, 1962. Strasberg Inst.

BERTO, JULIET: Grenoble, France, Jan. 1947.

BEST, JAMES: Corydon, IN, July 26, 1926.

BETTGER, LYLE: Philadelphia, Feb. 13, 1915. AADA.

BEYMER, RICHARD: Avoca, IA, Feb. 21, 1939.

BIEHN, MICHAEL: Ala. 1957.

BIKEL, THEODORE: Vienna, May 2, 1924. RADA.

BIRNEY, DAVID: Washington, DC, Apr. 23, 1939. Dartmouth, UCLA.

BIRNEY, REED: Alexandria, VA., Sept. 11, 1954. Boston U.

BISHOP, JOEY (Joseph Abraham Gottlieb): Bronx, NY, Feb. 3, 1918.

BISHOP, JULIE (formerly Jacqueline Wells): Denver, CO, Aug. 30, 1917. Westlake School.

BISSET, JACQUELINE: Waybridge, Eng., Sept. 13, 1944.

BIXBY, BILL: San Francisco, Jan. 22, 1934. U. CAL.

BLACK, KAREN (Ziegler): Park Ridge, IL, July 1, 1942. Northwestern.

BLADES, RUBEN: Panama 1948, Harvard.

BLAINE, VIVIAN (Vivian Stapleton): Newark, NJ, Nov. 21, 1923.

BLAIR, BETSY (Betsy Boger): NYC, Dec. 11, 1923.

BLAIR, JANET (Martha Jane Lafferty): Blair, PA, Apr. 23, 1921.

BLAIR, LINDA: Westport, CT, Jan. 22, 1959.

BLAKE, AMANDA (Beverly Louise Neill): Buffalo, NY, Feb. 20, 1921.

BLAKE, ROBERT (Michael Gubitosi): Nutley, NJ, Sept. 18, 1933.

BLAKELY, SUSAN: Frankfurt, Germany 1950. U. TEX.

BLAKLEY, RONEE: Stanley, ID, 1946. Stanford U.

BLOOM, CLAIRE: London, Feb. 15, 1931. Badminton School.

BLYTH, ANN: Mt. Kisco, NY, Aug. 16, 1928. New Wayburn Dramatic School.

BOCHNER, HART: Toronto, 1956. U. San Diego.

BOGARDE, DIRK: London, Mar. 28, 1918. Glasgow & Univ. College.

BOLKAN, FLORINDA (Florinda Soares Bulcao): Ceara, Brazil, Feb. 15, 1941.

BOND, DEREK: Glasgow, Scot., Jan. 26, 1920. Askes School.

BONO, SONNY (Salvatore): Feb. 16, 1935.

BOONE, PAT: Jacksonville, FL, June 1, 1934. Columbia U.

BOOTH, SHIRLEY (Thelma Ford): NYC, Aug. 30, 1907.

BORGNINE, ERNEST (Borgnino): Hamden, CT, Jan. 24, 1918. Randall School.

BOSCO, PHILIP: Jersey City, NJ, Sept. 26, 1930, CatholicU.

BOSTWICK, BARRY: San Mateo, CA., Feb. 24, 1945. NYU.

BOTTOMS, JOSEPH: Santa Barbara, CA, Aug. 30, 1954.

BOTTOMS, TIMOTHY: Santa Barbara, CA, Aug. 30, 1951.

BOULTING, INGRID: Transvaal, So. Africa, 1947.

BOVEE, LESLIE: Bend, OR, 1952.

BOWIE, DAVID: (David Robert Jones) Brixton, South London, Eng. Jan. 8, 1947.

BOWKER, JUDI: Shawford, Eng., Apr. 6, 1954.

BOXLEITNER, BRUCE: Elgin, IL., May 12, 1950.

BOYLE, PETER: Philadelphia, PA, 1933. LaSalle Col.

BRACKEN, EDDIE: NYC, Feb. 7, 1920. Professional Children's School.

BRAEDEN, ERIC: (Hans Gudegast): Braeden, Germany.

BRAGA, SONIA: Maringa, Brazil, 1951.

BRAND, NEVILLE: Kewanee, IL, Aug. 13, 1920.

BRANDO, JOCELYN: San Francisco, Nov. 18, 1919. Lake Forest College, AADA.

BRANDO, MARLON: Omaha, NB, Apr. 3, 1924. New School.

BRANDON, CLARK: NYC 1959.

BRANDON, HENRY: Berlin, Ger., June 18, 1912. Stanford.

BRANDON, MICHAEL (Feldman): Brooklyn, NY.

BRANTLEY, BETSY: Rutherfordton, NC, 1955. London Central Sch. of Drama.

BRAZZI, ROSSANO: Bologna, Italy, Sept. 18, 1916. U. Florence.

BRENNAN, EILEEN: Los Angeles, CA., Sept. 3, 1935. AADA.

BRIALY, JEAN-CLAUDE: Aumale, Algeria, 1933. Strasbourg Cons.

BRIAN, DAVID: NYC, Aug. 5, 1914. CCNY.

BRIDGES, BEAU: Los Angeles, Dec. 9, 1941. UCLA.

BRIDGES, JEFF: Los Angeles, Dec. 4, 1949.

BRIDGES, LLOYD: San Leandro, CA, Jan. 15, 1913.

BRINKLEY, CHRISTIE: Malibu, CA., Feb. 2, 1954.

BRISEBOIS, DANIELLE: Brooklyn, June 28, 1969.

BRITT, MAY (Maybritt Wilkins): Sweden, Mar. 22, 1936.

BRITTANY, MORGAN: (Suzanne Caputo): Los Angeles, 1950.

BRITTON, TONY: Birmingham, Eng., June 9, 1924.

BRODERICK, MATTHEW: NYC, Mar. 21, 1963.

BRODIE, STEVE (Johnny Stevens): Eldorado, KS, Nov. 25, 1919.

BROLIN, JAMES: Los Angeles, July 18, 1940. UCLA.

BROMFIELD, JOHN (Farron Bromfield): South Bend, IN, June 11, 1922. St. Mary's College.

BRONSON, CHARLES (Buchinsky): Ehrenfield, PA, Nov. 3, 1920.

BROOKES, JACQUELINE: Montclair, NJ, July 24, 1930, RADA.

BROOKS, MEL (Melvyn Kaminski): Brooklyn, 1926.

BROSNAN, PIERCE: County Meath, Ireland, May 16, 1952.

BROWN, BLAIR: Washington, DC, 1948; Pine Manor.

BROWN, BRYAN: Panania, Aust., 1947.

BROWN, GARY (Christian Brando): Hollywood, Ca., 1958.

BROWN, GEORG STANFORD: Havana, Cuba, June 24, 1943. AMDA.

BROWN, JAMES: Desdemona, TX, Mar. 22, 1920. Baylor U.

BROWN, JIM: St. Simons Island, NY, Feb. 17, 1935. Syracuse U.

BROWNE, CORAL: Melbourne, Aust., July 23, 1913.

BROWNE, LESLIE: NYC, 1958.

BUCHHOLZ, HORST: Berlin, Ger., Dec. 4, 1933. Ludwig Dramatic School.

BUCKLEY, BETTY: Big Spring, Tx., July 3, 1947. TxCU.

BUETEL, JACK: Dallas, TX, Sept. 5, 1917.

BUJOLD, GENEVIEVE: Montreal, Can., July 1, 1942.

BURKE, DELTA: Orlando, FL, July 30, 1956, LAMDA.

BURKE, PAUL: New Orleans, July 21, 1926. Pasadena Playhouse.

BURNETT, CAROL: San Antonio, TX, Apr. 26, 1933. UCLA.

BURNS, CATHERINE: NYC, Sept. 25, 1945. AADA.

BURNS, GEORGE (Nathan Birnbaum): NYC, Jan. 20, 1896.

BURR, RAYMOND: New Westminster, B.C., Can., May 21, 1917. Stanford, U. CAL., Columbia.

BURSTYN, ELLEN (Edna Rae Gillooly): Detroit, MI, Dec. 7, 1932.

BURTON, LeVAR: Los Angeles, CA. Feb. 16, 1958. UCLA.

BUSEY, GARY: Goose Creek, Tx, June 29, 1944.

BUTTONS, RED (Aaron Chwatt): NYC, Feb. 5, 1919.

BUZZI, RUTH: Wequetequock, RI, July 24, 1936. Pasadena Playhouse.

BYGRAVES, MAX: London, Oct. 16, 1922. St. Joseph's School.

BYRNES, EDD: NYC, July 30, 1933. Haaren High.

CAAN, JAMES: Bronx, NY, Mar. 26, 1939.

CAESAR, SID: Yonkers, NY, Sept. 8, 1922.

CAINE, MICHAEL (Maurice Michelwhite): London, Mar. 14, 1933.

CAINE, SHAKIRA (Baksh): Guyana, Feb. 23, 1947. Indian Trust Col.

CALHOUN, RORY (Francis Timothy Durgin): Los Angeles, Aug. 8, 1922.

CALLAN, MICHAEL (Martin Calinieff): Philadelphia, Nov. 22, 1935.

CALVERT, PHYLLIS: London, Feb. 18, 1917. Margaret Morris School.

CALVET, CORRINE (Corrine Dibos): Paris, Apr. 30, 1925. U. Paris.

CAMERON, KIRK: Panorama City, CA, 1970.

CAMP, COLLEEN: San Francisco, 1953.

CAMPBELL, BILL: Virginia 1960.

CAMPBELL, GLEN: Delight, AR, Apr. 22, 1935.

CANALE, GIANNA MARIA: Reggio Calabria, Italy, Sept. 12.

CANNON, DYAN (Samille Diane Friesen): Tacoma, WA, Jan. 4, 1937.

CANTU, DOLORES: 1957, San Antonio, TX.

CAPERS, VIRGINIA: Sumter, SC, 1925. Juilliard.

CAPSHAW, KATE: Ft. Worth, TX. 1953. UMo.

CAPUCINE (Germaine Lefebvre): Toulon, France, Jan. 6, 1935.

CARA, IRENE: NYC, Mar. 18, 1958.

CARDINALE, CLAUDIA: Tunis, N. Africa, Apr. 15, 1939. College Paul Cambon.

CAREY, HARRY, JR.: Saugus, CA, May 16, 1921. Black Fox Military Academy.

CAREY, MACDONALD: Sioux City, IA, Mar. 15, 1913. U. of Wisc., U. Iowa.

CAREY, PHILIP: Hackensack, NJ, July 15, 1925. U. Miami.

CARMEN, JULIE: Mt. Vernon, NY, Apr. 4, 1954.

CARMICHAEL, IAN: Hull, Eng., June 18, 1920. Scarborough Col.

CARNE, JUDY (Joyce Botterill): Northampton, Eng., 1939. Bush-Davis Theatre School.

CARNEY, ART: Mt. Vernon, NY, Nov. 4, 1918.

CARON, LESLIE: Paris, July 1, 1931. Nat'l Conservatory, Paris.

CARPENTER, CARLETON: Bennington, VT, July 10, 1926. Northwestern.

CARR, VIKKI (Florence Cardona): July 19, 1942. San Fernando Col.

CARRADINE, DAVID: Hollywood, Dec. 8, 1936. San Francisco State.

CARRADINE, JOHN: NYC, Feb. 5, 1906.

CARRADINE, KEITH: San Mateo, CA, Aug. 8, 1950. Colo. State U.

CARRADINE, ROBERT: San Mateo, CA, Mar. 24, 1954.

CARREL, DANY: Tourane, Indochina, Sept. 20, 1936. Marseilles Cons.

CARRIERE, MATHIEU: West Germany 1950.

CARROLL, DIAHANN (Johnson): NYC, July 17, 1935. NYU.

CARROLL, MADELEINE: West Bromwich, Eng., Feb. 26, 1902. Birmingham U.

CARROLL, PAT: Shreveport, LA, May 5, 1927. Catholic U.

CARSON, JOHN DAVID: 1951, Calif. Valley Col.

CARSON, JOHNNY: Corning, IA, Oct. 23, 1925. U. of Neb.

CARSTEN, PETER (Ransenthaler): Weissenberg, Bavaria, Apr. 30, 1929. Munich Akademie.

CARTER, NELL: Birmingham, AL., Dec. 13.

CASH, ROSALIND: Atlantic City, NJ, Dec. 31, 1938. CCNY.

CASON, BARBARA: Memphis, TN, Nov. 15, 1933. U. Iowa.

CASS, PEGGY (Mary Margaret): Boston, May 21, 1925.

CASSAVETES, JOHN: NYC, Dec. 9, 1929. Colgate College, AADA.

CASSAVETES, NICK: NYC 1959, Syracuse U, AADA.

CASSEL, JEAN-PIERRE: Paris, Oct. 27, 1932.

CASSIDY, DAVID: NYC, Apr. 12, 1950.

CASSIDY, JOANNA: Camden, NJ, 1944. Syracuse U.

CASSIDY, PATRICK: Los Angeles, CA, Jan. 4, 1961.

CASSIDY, SHAUN: Los Angeles, CA., Sept. 27, 1958.

CASTELLANO, RICHARD: Bronx, NY, Sept. 3, 1934.

CATTRALL, KIM: England, Aug. 21, 1956, AADA.

CAULFIELD, JOAN: Orange, NJ, June 1, 1922. Columbia U.

CAULFIELD, MAXWELL: Glasgow, Scot., Nov. 23, 1959.

CAVANI, LILIANA: Bologna, Italy, Jan. 12, 1937. U. Bologna.

CHAKIRIS, GEORGE: Norwood, OH, Sept. 16, 1933.

| Gary Busey | Kate Capshaw | Maxwell Caulfield | Irene Cara | Richard Chaves | Jane Curtin |

CHAMBERLAIN, RICHARD: Beverly Hills, CA, March 31, 1935. Pomona.

CHAMPION, MARGE: Los Angeles, Sept. 2, 1923.

CHANNING, CAROL: Seattle, Jan. 31, 1921. Bennington.

CHANNING, STOCKARD (Susan Stockard): NYC, 1944. Radcliffe.

CHAPIN, MILES: NYC, Dec. 6, 1954. HB Studio.

CHAPLIN, GERALDINE: Santa Monica, CA, July 31, 1944. Royal Ballet.

CHAPLIN, SYDNEY: Los Angeles, Mar. 31, 1926. Lawrenceville.

CHARISSE, CYD (Tula Ellice Finklea): Amarillo, TX, Mar. 3, 1922. Hollywood Professional School.

CHASE, CHEVY (Cornelius Crane Chase): NYC, Oct. 8, 1943.

CHAVES, RICHARD: Jacksonville, FL, Oct. 9, 1951, Occidental Col.

CHER (Cherlin Sarkesian): May 20, 1946, El Centro, CA.

CHIARI, WALTER: Verona, Italy, 1930.

CHONG, RAE DAWN: Vancouver, Can., 1962.

CHRISTIAN, LINDA (Blanca Rosa Welter): Tampico, Mex., Nov. 13, 1923.

CHRISTIE, JULIE: Chukua, Assam, India, Apr. 14, 1941.

CHRISTOPHER, DENNIS (Carelli): Philadelphia, PA, 1955. Temple U.

CHRISTOPHER, JORDAN: Youngstown, OH, Oct. 23, 1940. Kent State.

CILENTO, DIANE: Queensland, Australia, Oct. 5, 1933. AADA.

CLAPTON, ERIC: London, Mar. 30, 1945.

CLARK, DANE: NYC, Feb. 18, 1915. Cornell, Johns Hopkins U.

CLARK, DICK: Mt. Vernon, NY, Nov. 30, 1929. Syracuse U.

CLARK, MAE: Philadelphia, Aug. 16, 1910.

CLARK, PETULA: Epsom, England, Nov. 15, 1932.

CLARK, SUSAN: Sarnid, Ont., Can., Mar. 8, 1940. RADA.

CLAYBURGH, JILL: NYC, Apr. 30, 1944. Sarah Lawrence.

CLERY, CORRINNE: Italy, 1950.

CLOONEY, ROSEMARY: Maysville, KY, May 23, 1928.

CLOSE, GLENN: Greenwich, CT., Mar. 19, 1947. William & Mary Col.

COBURN, JAMES: Laurel, NB, Aug. 31, 1928. LACC.

COCA, IMOGENE: Philadelphia, Nov. 18, 1908.

CODY, KATHLEEN: Bronx, NY, Oct. 30, 1953.

COLBERT, CLAUDETTE (Lily Chauchoin): Paris, Sept. 15, 1903. Art Students League.

COLE, GEORGE: London, Apr. 22, 1925.

COLEMAN, GARY: Zion, IL., Feb. 8, 1968.

COLEMAN, JACK: Easton, PA., 1958. Duke U.

COLLETT, CHRISTOPHER: NYC, Mar. 13, 1968. Strasberg Inst.

COLLINS, JOAN: London, May 21, 1933. Francis Holland School.

COLLINS, STEPHEN: Des Moines, IA, Oct. 1, 1947. Amherst.

COLON, MIRIAM: Ponce, PR., 1945. UPR.

COMER, ANJANETTE: Dawson, TX, Aug. 7, 1942. Baylor, Tex. U.

CONANT, OLIVER: NYC, Nov. 15, 1955. Dalton.

CONAWAY, JEFF: NYC, Oct. 5, 1950. NYC.

CONDE, RITA (Elizabeth Eleanor): Cuba.

CONNERY, SEAN: Edinburgh, Scot., Aug. 25, 1930.

CONNERY, JASON: London 1962.

CONNORS, CHUCK (Kevin Joseph Connors): Brooklyn, Apr. 10, 1921. Seton Hall College.

CONNORS, MIKE (Krekor Ohanian): Fresno, CA, Aug. 15, 1925. UCLA.

CONRAD, WILLIAM: Louisville, KY, Sept. 27, 1920.

CONVERSE, FRANK: St. Louis, MO, May 22, 1938. Carnegie Tech.

CONVY, BERT: St. Louis, MO, July 23, 1935. UCLA.

CONWAY, KEVIN: NYC, May 29, 1942.

CONWAY, TIM (Thomas Daniel): Willoughby, OH, Dec. 15, 1933. Bowling Green State.

COOK, ELISHA, JR.: San Francisco, Dec. 26, 1907. St. Albans.

COOPER, BEN: Hartford, CT, Sept. 30, 1932. Columbia U.

COOPER, JACKIE: Los Angeles, Sept. 15, 1921.

CORBETT, GRETCHEN: Portland, OR, Aug. 13, 1947. Carnegie Tech.

CORBY, ELLEN (Hansen): Racine, WI, June 13, 1913.

CORCORAN, DONNA: Quincy, MA, Sept. 29, 1942.

CORD, ALEX (Viespi): Floral Park, NY, Aug. 3, 1931. NYU, Actors Studio.

CORDAY, MARA (Marilyn Watts): Santa Monica, CA, Jan. 3, 1932.

COREY, JEFF: NYC, Aug. 10, 1914. Fagin School.

CORLAN, ANTHONY: Cork City, Ire., May 9, 1947. Birmingham School of Dramatic Arts.

CORLEY, AL: Missouri, 1956. Actors Studio.

CORNTHWAITE, ROBERT: St. Helens, OR. Apr. 28, 1917. USC.

CORRI, ADRIENNE: Glasgow, Scot., Nov. 13, 1933. RADA.

CORTESA, VALENTINA: Milan, Italy, Jan. 1, 1925.

COSBY, BILL: Philadelphia, July 12, 1937. Temple U.

COSTER, NICOLAS: London, Dec. 3, 1934. Neighborhood Playhouse.

COTTEN, JOSEPH: Petersburg, VA, May 13, 1905.

COURTENAY, TOM: Hull, Eng., Feb. 25, 1937. RADA.

COURTLAND, JEROME: Knoxville, TN, Dec. 27, 1926.

CRAIG, MICHAEL: India, Jan. 27, 1929.

CRAIN, JEANNE: Barstow, CA, May 25, 1925.

CREMER, BRUNO: Paris, 1929.

CRENNA, RICHARD: Los Angeles, Nov. 30, 1926. USC.

CRISTAL, LINDA (Victoria Moya): Buenos Aires, Feb. 25, 1934.

CROSBY, HARRY: Los Angeles, CA, Aug. 8, 1958.

CROSBY, KATHRYN GRANT: (see Kathryn Grant)

CROSBY, MARY FRANCES: Calif., Sept. 14, 1959.

CROSS, BEN: London, 1948. RADA.

CROSS, MURPHY (Mary Jane): Laurelton, MD, June 22, 1950.

CROUSE, LINDSAY ANN: NYC, May 12, 1948. Radcliffe.

CROWLEY, PAT: Olyphant, PA, Sept. 17, 1932.

CRUISE, TOM: Syracuse, NY, 1962.

CRYER, JON: NYC, Apr. 16, 1965, RADA.

CRYSTAL, BILLY: Long Beach, NY, Mar. 14, 1947. Marshall U.

CULLUM, JOHN: Knoxville, TN, Mar. 2, 1930. U. Tenn.

CULP, ROBERT: Oakland, CA., Aug. 16, 1930. U. Wash.

CULVER, CALVIN: Canandaigua, NY, 1943.

CUMMINGS, CONSTANCE: Seattle, WA, May 15, 1910.

CUMMINGS, QUINN: Hollywood, Aug. 13, 1967.

CUMMINGS, ROBERT: Joplin, MO, June 9, 1910. Carnegie Tech.

CUMMINS, PEGGY: Prestatyn, N. Wales, Dec. 18, 1926. Alexandra School.

CURTIN, JANE: Cambridge, MA; Sept. 6, 1947.

CURTIS, JAMIE LEE: Los Angeles, CA., Nov. 21, 1958.

CURTIS, KEENE: Salt Lake City, UT, Feb. 15, 1925. U. Utah.

CURTIS, TONY (Bernard Schwartz): NYC, June 3, 1924.

CUSACK, CYRIL: Durban, S. Africa, Nov. 26, 1910. Univ. Col.

CUSHING, PETER: Kenley, Surrey, Eng., May 26, 1913.

DAHL, ARLENE: Minneapolis, Aug. 11, 1928. U. Minn.

DALLESANDRO, JOE: Pensacola, FL, Dec. 31, 1948.

DALTON, TIMOTHY: Wales, Mar. 21, 1946, RADA.

DALTREY, ROGER: London, Mar. 1, 1945.

DALY, TYNE: NYC, 1946. AMDA.

DAMONE, VIC (Vito Farinola): Brooklyn, June 12, 1928.

DANCE, CHARLES: Plymouth, Eng., 1946.

D'ANGELO, BEVERLY: Columbus, OH., Nov. 15, 1953.

DANGERFIELD, RODNEY (Jacob Cohen): Babylon, NY, 1922.

DANIELS, JEFF: Georgia, 1955. EastMichState.

DANIELS, WILLIAM: Bklyn, Mar. 31, 1927. Northwestern.

DANNER, BLYTHE: Philadelphia, PA. 1944. Bard Col.

DANO, ROYAL: NYC, Nov. 16, 1922. NYU.

DANSON, TED: Flagstaff, AZ, Dec. 29, 1947. Stanford, Carnegie Tech.

DANTE, MICHAEL (Ralph Vitti): Stamford, CT, 1935. U. Miami.

DANTON, RAY: NYC, Sept. 19, 1931. Carnegie Tech.

DANZA, TONY: Brooklyn, NY., Apr. 21, 1951. UDubuque.

DARBY, KIM: (Deborah Zerby): North Hollywood, CA, July 8, 1948.

DARCEL, DENISE (Denise Billecard): Paris, Sept. 8, 1925. U. Dijon.

DARREN, JAMES: Philadelphia, June 8, 1936. Stella Adler School.

DARRIEUX, DANIELLE: Bordeaux, France, May 1, 1917. Lycee LaTour.

DAVIDSON, JOHN: Pittsburgh, Dec. 13, 1941. Denison U.

DAVIS, BETTE: Lowell, MA, Apr. 5, 1908. John Murray Anderson Dramatic School.

DAVIS, BRAD: Fla., Nov. 6, 1949. AADA.

DAVIS, MAC: Lubbock, TX, Jan. 21, 1942.

DAVIS, NANCY (Anne Frances Robbins): NYC July 8, 1921, Smith Col.

DAVIS, OSSIE: Cogdell, GA, Dec. 18, 1917. Howard U.

DAVIS, SAMMY, JR.: NYC, Dec. 8, 1925.

DAVIS, SKEETER (Mary Frances Penick): Dry Ridge, KY. Dec. 30, 1931.

DAY, DENNIS (Eugene Dennis McNulty): NYC, May 21, 1917. Manhattan College.

DAY, DORIS (Doris Kappelhoff); Cincinnati, Apr. 3, 1924.

DAY, LARAINE (Johnson): Roosevelt, UT, Oct. 13, 1917.

DAYAN, ASSEF: Israel, 1945. U. Jerusalem.

DEAKINS, LUCY: NYC 1971.

DEAN, JIMMY: Plainview, TX, Aug. 10, 1928.

DeCARLO, YVONNE (Peggy Yvonne Middleton): Vancouver, B.C., Can., Sept. 1, 1922. Vancouver School of Drama.

DEE, FRANCES: Los Angeles, Nov. 26, 1907. Chicago U.

DEE, JOEY (Joseph Di Nicola): Passaic, NJ, June 11, 1940. Patterson State College.

DEE, RUBY: Cleveland, OH, Oct. 27, 1924. Hunter Col.

DEE, SANDRA (Alexandra Zuck): Bayonne, NJ, Apr. 23, 1942.

DeFORE, DON: Cedar Rapids, IA, Aug. 25, 1917. U. Iowa.

DeHAVEN, GLORIA: Los Angeles, July 23, 1923.

DeHAVILLAND, OLIVIA: Tokyo, Japan, July 1, 1916. Notre Dame Convent School.

DELAIR, SUZY: Paris, Dec. 31, 1916.

DELL, GABRIEL: Barbados, BWI, Oct. 7, 1930.

DELON, ALAIN: Sceaux, Fr., Nov. 8, 1935.

DELORME, DANIELE: Paris, Oct. 9, 1927. Sorbonne.

DeLUISE, DOM: Brooklyn, Aug. 1, 1933. Tufts Col.

DEMONGEOT, MYLENE: Nice, France, Sept. 29, 1938.

DeMORNAY, REBECCA: Los Angeles, Ca., 1962. Strasberg Inst.

DeMUNN, JEFFREY: Buffalo, NY, Apr. 25, 1947. Union Col.

DENEUVE, CATHERINE: Paris, Oct. 22, 1943.

DeNIRO, ROBERT: NYC, Aug. 17, 1943, Stella Adler.

DENISON, MICHAEL: Doncaster, York, Eng., Nov. 1, 1915. Oxford.

DENNEHY, BRIAN: Bridgeport, CT, 1939.

DENNER, CHARLES: Tarnow, Poland, May 29, 1926.

DENNIS, SANDY: Hastings, NB, Apr. 27, 1937. Actors Studio.

DEPARDIEU, GERARD: Chateauroux, Fr., Dec. 27, 1948.

DEREK, BO (Mary Cathleen Collins): Long Beach, CA, Nov. 20, 1956.

DEREK, JOHN: Hollywood, Aug. 12, 1926.

DERN, BRUCE: Chicago, June 4, 1936. U PA.

DERN, LAURA: California, 1966.

DeSALVO, ANNE: Philadelphia, PA., Apr. 3.

DEVINE, COLLEEN: San Gabriel, CA, June 22, 1960.

DEWHURST, COLLEEN: Montreal June 3, 1926. Lawrence U.

DEXTER, ANTHONY (Walter Reinhold Alfred Fleischmann): Talmadge, NB, Jan. 19, 1919. U. Iowa.

DEY, SUSAN: Pekin, Il, 1953.

DeYOUNG, CLIFF: Los Angeles, CA, Feb. 12, 1945. Cal State.

DHIEGH, KHIGH: New Jersey, 1910.

DIAMOND, NEIL: NYC, Jan. 24, 1941. NYU.

DICKINSON, ANGIE: Kulm, ND, Sept. 30, 1932. Glendale College.

DIETRICH, MARLENE (Maria Magdalene von Losch): Berlin, Ger., Dec. 27, 1901. Berlin Music Academy.

DILLER, PHYLLIS (Driver): Lima, OH, July 17, 1917. Bluffton College.

DILLMAN, BRADFORD: San Francisco, Apr. 14, 1930. Yale.

DILLON, KEVIN: Mamaroneck, NY, 1965.

DILLON, MATT: Larchmont, NY., Feb. 18, 1964. AADA.

DILLON, MELINDA: Hope, AR, Oct. 13, 1939. Goodman Theatre School.

DIVINE (Glenn) Baltimore, MD, 1945.

DOBSON, TAMARA: Baltimore, MD, 1947. MD. Inst. of Art.

DOMERGUE, FAITH: New Orleans, June 16, 1925.

DONAHUE, TROY (Merle Johnson): NYC, Jan. 27, 1937. Columbia U.

DONAT, PETER: Nova Scotia, Jan. 20, 1928. Yale.

DONNELL, JEFF (Jean Donnell): South Windham, ME, July 10 1921. Yale Drama School.

DOOHAN, JAMES: Vancouver, BC, Mar. 3, Neighborhood Playhouse.

DOOLEY, PAUL: Parkersburg, WV, Feb. 22, 1928. U. WV.

DOUGLAS, DONNA (Dorothy Bourgeois): Baton Rouge, LA, 1935.

DOUGLAS, KIRK (Issur Danielovitch): Amsterdam, NY, Dec. 9, 1916. St. Lawrence U.

DOUGLAS, MICHAEL: New Brunswick, NJ, Sept. 25, 1944. U Cal.

DOUGLASS, ROBYN: Sendai, Japan; June 21, 1953. UCDavis.

DOURIF, BRAD: Huntington, WV Mar. 18, 1950. Marshall U.

DOVE, BILLIE: NYC, May 14, 1904.

DOWN, LESLEY-ANN: London, Mar. 17, 1954.

DRAKE, BETSY: Paris, Sept. 11, 1923.

DRAKE, CHARLES (Charles Rupert): NYC, Oct. 2, 1914 Nichols College.

DREW, ELLEN (formerly Terry Ray): Kansas City, MO, Nov. 23 1915.

DREYFUSS, RICHARD: Brooklyn NY, Oct. 19, 1947.

DRILLINGER, BRIAN: Brooklyn NY, June 27, 1960, SUNY Purchase.

DRU, JOANNE (Joanne LaCock) Logan, WV, Jan. 31, 1923. John Robert Powers School.

DUBBINS, DON: Brooklyn, NY June 28.

DUFF, HOWARD: Bremerton, WA Nov. 24, 1917.

DUFFY, PATRICK: Townsend, Mt Mar. 17, 1949. U. Wash.

DUKE, PATTY (Anna Marie): NYC Dec. 14, 1946.

DUKES, DAVID: San Francisco June 6, 1945.

DULLEA, KEIR: Cleveland, NJ May 30, 1936. SF State Col.

DUNAWAY, FAYE: Bascom, FL Jan. 14, 1941, Fla. U.

DUNCAN, SANDY: Henderson, TX Feb. 20, 1946. Len Morris Col.

DUNNE, GRIFFIN: NYC June 8 1955, Neighborhood Playhouse.

DUNNE, IRENE: Louisville, KY Dec. 20, 1898. Chicago College of Music.

DUNNOCK, MILDRED: Baltimore Jan. 25, 1900. Johns Hopkins and Columbia U.

DUPEREY, ANNY: Paris, 1947.

DURBIN, DEANNA (Edna): Winnipeg, Can., Dec. 4, 1921.

DURNING, CHARLES: Highland Falls, NY, Feb. 28, 1933. NYU.

DUSSOLLIER, ANDRE: Annecy France, Feb. 17, 1946.

DUVALL, ROBERT: San Diego CA, 1930. Principia Col.

Troy Donahue

Yvonne de Carlo

Giancarlo Esposito

Linda Evans

James Farentino

Tovah Feldshuh

DUVALL, SHELLEY: Houston, TX, July 7, 1949.

EASTON, ROBERT: Milwaukee, Nov. 23, 1930. U. Texas.

EASTWOOD, CLINT: San Francisco, May 31, 1930. LACC.

EATON, SHIRLEY: London, 1937. Aida Foster School.

EBSEN, BUDDY (Christian, Jr.): Belleville, IL, Apr. 2, 1910. U. Fla.

ECKEMYR, AGNETA: Karlsborg, Swed., July 2. Actors Studio.

EDEN, BARBARA (Moorhead): Tucson, AZ, Aug. 23, 1934.

EDWARDS, VINCE: NYC, July 9, 1928. AADA.

EGAN, RICHARD: San Francisco, July 29, 1923. Stanford U.

EGGAR, SAMANTHA: London, Mar. 5, 1939.

EICHHORN, LISA: Reading, PA, 1952. Queens Ont. U. RADA.

EILBER, JANET: Detroit, MI, July 27, 1951. Juilliard.

EKBERG, ANITA: Malmo, Sweden, Sept. 29, 1931.

EKLAND, BRITT: Stockholm, Swed., 1942.

ELIZONDO, HECTOR: NYC, Dec. 22, 1936.

ELLIOTT, DENHOLM: London, May 31, 1922. Malvern College.

ELLIOTT, PATRICIA: Gunnison, Co, July 21, 1942, UCol.

ELLIOTT, SAM: Sacramento, CA, Aug. 9, 1944. U. Ore.

ELY, RON (Ronald Pierce): Hereford, TX, June 21, 1938.

ERDMAN, RICHARD: Enid, OK, June 1, 1925.

ERICSON, JOHN: Dusseldorf, Ger., Sept. 25, 1926. AADA.

ESMOND, CARL: Vienna, June 14, 1906. U. Vienna.

ESTEVEZ, EMILIO: NYC 1962.

ESPOSITO, GIANCARLO: Copenhagen, Den., Apr. 26, 1958.

ESTRADA, ERIK: NYC, Mar. 16, 1949.

EVANS, DALE (Francis Smith): Uvalde, TX, Oct. 31, 1912.

EVANS, GENE: Holbrook, AZ, July 11, 1922.

EVANS, LINDA (Evanstad): Hartford, CT., Nov. 18, 1942.

EVANS, MAURICE: Dorchester, Eng., June 3, 1901.

EVERETT, CHAD (Ray Cramton): South Bend, IN, June 11, 1936.

EVERETT, RUPERT: Norfolk, Eng., 1959.

EWELL, TOM (Yewell Tompkins): Owensboro, KY, Apr. 29, 1909. U. Wisc.

FABARES, SHELLEY: Los Angeles, Jan. 19, 1944.

FABIAN (Fabian Forte): Philadelphia, Feb. 6, 1943.

FABRAY, NANETTE (Ruby Nanette Fabares): San Diego, Oct. 27, 1920.

FAIRBANKS, DOUGLAS JR.: NYC, Dec. 9, 1907. Collegiate School.

FAIRCHILD, MORGAN: (Patsy McClenny) Dallas, TX., Feb. 3, 1950. UCLA.

FALK, PETER: NYC, Sept. 16, 1927. New School.

FARENTINO, JAMES: Brooklyn, Feb. 24, 1938. AADA.

FARINA, SANDY (Sandra Feldman): Newark, NJ, 1955.

FARR, FELICIA: Westchester, NY, Oct. 4, 1932. Penn State Col.

FARRELL, CHARLES: Onset Bay, MA, Aug. 9, 1901. Boston U.

FARROW, MIA: Los Angeles, Feb. 9, 1945.

FAULKNER, GRAHAM: London, Sept. 26, 1947. Webber-Douglas.

FAWCETT, FARRAH: Corpus Christie, TX. Feb. 2, 1947. TexU.

FAYE, ALICE (Ann Leppert): NYC, May 5, 1912.

FEINSTEIN, ALAN: NYC, Sept. 8, 1941.

FELDON, BARBARA (Hall): Pittsburgh, Mar. 12, 1941. Carnegie Tech.

FELDSHUH, TOVAH: NYC, Dec. 27, 1953, Sarah Lawrence Col.

FELLOWS, EDITH: Boston, May 20, 1923.

FERRELL, CONCHATA: Charleston, WV, Mar. 28, 1943. Marshall U.

FERRER, JOSE: Santurce, P.R., Jan. 8, 1909. Princeton U.

FERRER, MEL: Elberon, NJ, Aug. 25, 1917. Princeton U.

FERRIS, BARBARA: London, 1943.

FERZETTI, GABRIELE: Italy, 1927. Rome Acad. of Drama.

FIEDLER, JOHN: Plateville, Wi, Feb. 3, 1925.

FIELD, SALLY: Pasadena, CA, Nov. 6, 1946.

FIGUEROA, RUBEN: NYC 1958.

FINNEY, ALBERT: Salford, Lancashire, Eng., May 9, 1936. RADA.

FIRESTONE, ROCHELLE: Kansas City, MO., June 14, 1949. NYU.

FIRTH, PETER: Bradford, Eng., Oct. 27, 1953.

FISHER, CARRIE: Los Angeles, CA, Oct. 21, 1956. London Central School of Drama.

FISHER, EDDIE: Philadelphia, Aug. 10, 1928.

FITZGERALD, BRIAN: Philadelphia, Pa, 1960, West Chester U.

FITZGERALD, GERALDINE: Dublin, Ire., Nov. 24, 1914. Dublin Art School.

FLANNERY, SUSAN: Jersey City, NJ, July 31, 1943.

FLEMING, RHONDA (Marilyn Louis): Los Angeles, Aug. 10, 1922.

FLEMYNG, ROBERT: Liverpool, Eng., Jan. 3, 1912. Haileybury Col.

FLETCHER, LOUISE: Birmingham, AL, July 1934.

FOCH, NINA: Leyden, Holland, Apr. 20, 1924.

FOLDI, ERZSEBET: Queens, NY, 1967.

FONDA, JANE: NYC, Dec. 21, 1937. Vassar.

FONDA, PETER: NYC, Feb. 23, 1939. U. Omaha.

FONTAINE, JOAN: Tokyo, Japan, Oct. 22, 1917.

FOOTE, HALLIE: NYC 1953. UNH.

FORD, GLENN (Gwyllyn Samuel Newton Ford): Quebec, Can., May 1, 1916.

FORD, HARRISON: Chicago, IL, July 13, 1942. Ripon Col.

FOREST, MARK (Lou Degni): Brooklyn, Jan. 1933.

FORREST, STEVE: Huntsville, TX, Sept. 29, 1924. UCLA.

FORSLUND, CONNIE: San Diego, CA, June 19, 1950, NYU.

FORSTER, ROBERT (Foster, Jr.): Rochester, NY, July 13, 1941. Rochester U.

FORSYTHE, JOHN (Freund): Penn's Grove, NJ, Jan. 29, 1918.

FOSTER, JODIE (Ariane Munker): Bronx, NY, Nov. 19, 1962. Yale.

FOX, EDWARD: London, 1937, RADA.

FOX, MICHAEL J.: Vancouver, BC, June 9, 1961.

FOX, JAMES: London, 1939.

FOXWORTH, ROBERT: Houston, TX, Nov. 1, 1941. Carnegie Tech.

FOXX, REDD: St. Louis, MO, Dec. 9, 1922.

FRANCIOSA, ANTHONY (Papaleo): NYC, Oct. 25, 1928.

FRANCIS, ANNE: Ossining, NY, Sept. 16, 1932.

FRANCIS, ARLENE (Arlene Kazanjian): Boston, Oct. 20, 1908. Finch School.

FRANCIS, CONNIE (Constance Franconero): Newark, NJ, Dec. 12, 1938.

FRANCISCUS, JAMES: Clayton, MO, Jan. 31, 1934. Yale.

FRANCKS, DON: Vancouver, Can., Feb. 28, 1932.

FRANK, JEFFREY: Jackson Heights, NY, 1965.

FRANKLIN, PAMELA: Tokyo, Feb. 4, 1950.

FRANZ, ARTHUR: Perth Amboy, NJ, Feb. 29, 1920. Blue Ridge College.

FRAZIER, SHEILA: NYC, Nov. 13, 1948.

FREEMAN, AL, JR.: San Antonio, TX, 1934. CCLA.

FREEMAN, MONA: Baltimore, MD, June 9, 1926.

FREEMAN, MORGAN: Memphis, Tn, June 1, 1937, LACC.

FREWER, MATT: Washington, DC, 1968, Old Vic.

FREY, LEONARD: Brooklyn, Sept. 4, 1938. Neighborhood Playhouse.

FULLER, PENNY: Durham, NC, 1940. Northwestern U.

FURNEAUX, YVONNE: Lille, France, 1928. Oxford U.

FYODOROVA, VICTORIA: Russia 1946.

GABOR, EVA: Budapest, Hungary, Feb. 11, 1920.

GABOR, ZSA ZSA (Sari Gabor): Budapest, Hungary, Feb. 6, 1918.

GAINES, BOYD: Atlanta, GA., May 11, 1953. Juilliard.

GALLAGHER, PETER: Armonk, NY, Aug. 19, 1955, Tufts U.

GALLIGAN, ZACH: NYC, 1963. ColumbiaU.

GAM, RITA: Pittsburgh, PA, Apr. 2, 1928.

GARBER, VICTOR: Montreal, Can., Mar. 16, 1949.

GARBO, GRETA (Greta Gustafson): Stockholm, Sweden, Sept. 18, 1905.

GARDENIA, VINCENT: Naples, Italy, Jan. 7, 1922.

GARDNER, AVA: Smithfield, NC, Dec. 24, 1922. Atlantic Christian College.

GARFIELD, ALLEN: Newark, NJ, Nov. 22, 1939. Actors Studio.

GARLAND, BEVERLY: Santa Cruz, CA, Oct. 17, 1930. Glendale Col.

GARNER, JAMES (James Baumgarner): Norman, OK, Apr. 7, 1928. Okla. U.

GARR, TERI: Lakewood, OH, 1952.

GARRETT, BETTY: St. Joseph, MO, May 23, 1919. Annie Wright Seminary.

GARRISON, SEAN: NYC, Oct. 19, 1937.

GARSON, GREER: Ireland, Sept. 29, 1906.

GASSMAN, VITTORIO: Genoa, Italy, Sept. 1, 1922. Rome Academy of Dramatic Art.

GAVIN, JOHN: Los Angeles, Apr. 8, 1935. Stanford U.

GAYLORD, MITCH: Van Nuys, CA, 1961, UCLA.

GAYNOR, MITZI (Francesca Marlene Von Gerber): Chicago, Sept. 4, 1930.

GAZZARA, BEN: NYC, Aug. 28, 1930. Actors Studio.

GEARY, ANTHONY: Utah, 1948.

GEESON, JUDY: Arundel, Eng., Sept. 10, 1948. Corona.

GEOFFREYS, STEPHEN: Cincinnati, Oh., Nov. 22, 1964. NYU.

GEORGE, BOY (George O'Dowd): London 1962.

GEORGE, SUSAN: West London, Eng. July 26, 1950.

GERARD, GIL: Little Rock, AR, Jan. 23, 1940.

GERE, RICHARD: Philadelphia, PA, Aug. 29, 1949. U. Mass.

GERROLL, DANIEL: London, Oct. 16, 1951. Central.

GETTY, ESTELLE: NYC, July 25, 1923, New School.

GHOLSON, JULIE: Birmingham, AL, June 4, 1958.

GHOSTLEY, ALICE: Eve, MO, Aug. 14, 1926. Okla U.

GIANNINI, CHERYL: Monessen, PA., June 15.

GIANNINI, GIANCARLO: Spezia, Italy, Aug. 1, 1942. Rome Acad. of Drama.

GIBSON, MEL: Oneonta, NY., Jan. 1951. NIDA.

GIELGUD, JOHN: London, Apr. 14, 1904. RADA.

GILES, NANCY: NYC, July 17, 1960. Oberlin Col.

GILFORD, JACK: NYC, July 25, 1907.

GILLIS, ANNE (Alma O'Connor): Little Rock, AR, Feb. 12, 1927.

GINTY, ROBERT: NYC, Nov. 14, 1948, Yale.

GIRARDOT, ANNIE: Paris, Oct. 25, 1931.

GIROLAMI, STEFANIA: Rome, Italy, 1963.

GISH, LILLIAN: Springfield, OH, Oct. 14, 1896.

GLASER, PAUL MICHAEL: Boston, MA, Mar. 25, 1943. Boston U.

GLASS, RON: Evansville, IN, 1946.

GLEASON, JACKIE: Brooklyn, Feb. 26, 1916.

GLEASON, JOANNA: Winnipeg, Can, June 2, 1950, UCLA.

GLENN, SCOTT: Pittsburgh, PA, Jan. 26, 1942; William and Mary Col.

GLOVER, DANNY: San Francisco, Ca., July 22, 1947, SFStateCol.

GLOVER, JOHN: Kingston, NY, Aug. 7, 1944.

GLYNN,CARLIN: Cleveland, Oh, Feb. 19, 1940, Actors Studio.

GODDARD, PAULETTE (Levy): Great Neck, NY, June 3, 1911.

GODUNOV, ALEKSANDR: Sakhalin, 1949.

GOLDBERG, WHOOPI (Caryn Johnson): NYC, Nov. 13, 1949.

GOLDBLUM, JEFF: Pittsburgh, PA, Oct. 22, 1952. Neighborhood Playhouse.

GOLDEN, ANNIE: NYC, 1952.

GOLDSTEIN, JENETTE: Beverley Hills, CA, 1960.

GONZALES-GONZALEZ, PEDRO: Aguilares, TX, Dec. 21, 1926.

GOODMAN, DODY: Columbus, OH, Oct. 28, 1915.

GORDON, GALE (Aldrich): NYC, Feb. 2, 1906.

GORDON, KEITH: NYC, Feb. 3, 1961.

GORING, MARIUS: Newport Isle of Wight, 1912. Cambridge, Old Vic.

GORMAN, CLIFF: Jamaica, NY, Oct. 13, 1936. NYU.

GORSHIN, FRANK: Apr. 5, 1933.

GORTNER, MARJOE: Long Beach, CA, 1944.

GOSSETT, LOUIS: Brooklyn, May 27, 1936. NYU.

GOULD, ELLIOTT (Goldstein): Brooklyn, Aug. 29, 1938. Columbia U.

GOULD, HAROLD: Schenectady, NY, Dec. 10, 1923. Cornell.

GOULET, ROBERT: Lawrence, MA, Nov. 26, 1933. Edmonton.

GRAF, DAVID: Lancaster, OH, Apr. 16, 1950. OhStateU.

GRAF, TODD: NYC, Oct. 22, 1959, SUNY/Purchase.

GRANGER, FARLEY: San Jose, CA, July 1, 1925.

GRANGER, STEWART (James Stewart): London, May 6, 1913. Webber-Douglas School of Acting.

GRANT, DAVID MARSHALL: Westport, CT, 1955. Yale.

GRANT, KATHRYN (Olive Grandstaff): Houston, TX, Nov. 25, 1933. UCLA.

GRANT, LEE: NYC, Oct. 31, 1930. Juilliard.

GRANVILLE, BONITA: NYC, Feb. 2, 1923.

GRAVES, PETER (Aurness): Minneapolis, Mar. 18, 1926. U. Minn.

GRAY, CHARLES: Bournemouth, Eng., 1928.

GRAY, COLEEN (Doris Jensen): Staplehurst, NB, Oct. 23, 1922. Hamline U.

GRAY, LINDA: Santa Monica, CA, Sept. 12, 1940.

GRAYSON, KATHRYN (Zelma Hedrick): Winston-Salem, NC, Feb. 9, 1922.

GREEN, KERRI: Fort Lee, NJ, 1967. Vassar.

GREENE, ELLEN: NYC, Feb. 22, Ryder Col.

GREENE, LORNE: Ottawa, CAN., Feb. 12, 1915. Queens U.

GREER, JANE: Washington, DC, Sept. 9, 1924.

GREER, MICHAEL: Galesburg, IL, Apr. 20, 1943.

GREGORY, MARK: Rome, Italy. 1965.

GREY, JENNIFER: NYC 1960.

GREY, JOEL (Katz): Cleveland, OH, Apr. 11, 1932.

GREY, VIRGINIA: Los Angeles, Mar. 22, 1917.

GRIEM, HELMUT: Hamburg, Ger. U. Hamburg.

GRIFFITH, ANDY: Mt. Airy, NC, June 1, 1926. UNC.

GRIFFITH, MELANIE: NYC, Aug. 9, 1957 Pierce Col.

GRIMES, GARY: San Francisco, June 2, 1955.

GRIMES, TAMMY: Lynn, MA, Jan. 30, 1934. Stephens Col.

GRIZZARD, GEORGE: Roanoke Rapids, NC, Apr. 1, 1928. UNC.

GRODIN, CHARLES: Pittsburgh, PA, Apr. 21, 1935.

GROH, DAVID: NYC, May 21, 1939. Brown U., LAMDA.

GUARDINO, HARRY: Brooklyn, Dec. 23, 1925. Haaren High.

GUINNESS, ALEX: London, Apr. 2, 1914. Pembroke Lodge School.

GUNN, MOSES: St. Louis, MO, Oct. 2, 1929. Tenn. State U.

GUTTENBERG, STEVEN: Brooklyn, NY, Aug. 1958. UCLA.

GWILLIM, DAVID: Plymouth, Eng., Dec. 15, 1948. RADA.

HACKETT, BUDDY (Leonard Hacker): Brooklyn, Aug. 31, 1924.

HACKMAN, GENE: San Bernardino, CA, Jan. 30, 1931.

HADDON, DALE: Montreal, CAN., May 26, 1949. Neighborhood Playhouse.

HAGERTY, JULIE: Cincinnati, OH, June 15, 1955. Juilliard.

HAGMAN, LARRY: (Hageman): Weatherford, TX., Sept. 21, 1931. Bard.

Morgan Freeman	Estelle Getty	George Grizzard	Julie Hagerty	Dorian Harewood	Celeste Holm

HAIM, COREY: Toronto, Can, 1972.

HALE, BARBARA: DeKalb, IL, Apr. 18, 1922. Chicago Academy of Fine Arts.

HALEY, JACKIE EARLE: Northridge, CA, 1963.

HALL, ALBERT: Boothton, AL, Nov. 10, 1937. Columbia.

HALL, ANTHONY MICHAEL: NYC, 1968.

HALL, KEVIN PETER: Pittsburgh, Pa, GeoWashU.

HAMILL, MARK: Oakland, CA, Sept. 25, 1952. LACC.

HAMILTON, GEORGE: Memphis, TN, Aug. 12, 1939. Hackley.

HAMLIN, HARRY: Pasadena, CA, Oct. 30, 1951. Yale.

HAMPSHIRE, SUSAN: London, May 12, 1941.

HANKS, TOM: Oakland, CA., 1957. CalStateU.

HANNAH, DARYL: Chicago, IL., 1960, UCLA.

HANNAH, PAGE: Chicago, IL., 1964.

HARDIN, TY (Orison Whipple Hungerford II): NYC, June 1, 1930.

HAREWOOD, DORIAN: Dayton, OH, Aug. 6. U. Cinn.

HARMON, MARK: Los Angeles, CA, 1951; UCLA.

HARPER, VALERIE: Suffern, NY, Aug. 22, 1940.

HARRELSON, WOODY: Lebanon, OH, 1962.

HARRINGTON, PAT: NYC, Aug. 13, 1929. Fordham U.

HARRIS, BARBARA (Sandra Markowitz): Evanston, IL, 1935.

HARRIS, ED: Tenafly, NJ, Nov. 28, 1950. Columbia.

HARRIS, JULIE: Grosse Point, MI, Dec. 2, 1925. Yale Drama School.

HARRIS, RICHARD: Limerick, Ire., Oct. 1, 1930. London Acad.

HARRIS, ROSEMARY: Ashby, Eng., Sept. 19, 1930. RADA.

HARRISON, GREG: Catalina Island, CA, May 31, 1950; Actors Studio.

HARRISON, NOEL: London, Jan. 29, 1936.

HARRISON, REX: Huyton, Cheshire, Eng., Mar. 5, 1908.

HARROLD, KATHRYN: Tazewell, VA. 1950. Mills Col.

HART, ROXANNE: Trenton, NJ, 1952. Princeton.

HARTLEY, MARIETTE: NYC, June 21, 1941.

HARTMAN, DAVID: Pawtucket, RI, May 19, 1935. Duke U.

HASSETT, MARILYN: Los Angeles, CA, 1949.

HAUER, RUTGER: Amsterdam, Hol. Jan. 23, 1944.

HAVER, JUNE: Rock Island, IL, June 10, 1926.

HAWN, GOLDIE: Washington, DC, Nov. 21, 1945.

HAYDEN, LINDA: Stanmore, Eng. Aida Foster School.

HAYES, HELEN: (Helen Brown): Washington, DC, Oct. 10, 1900. Sacred Heart Convent.

HAYS, ROBERT: Bethesda, MD., 1948; SD State Col.

HEADLY, GLENNE: New London, Ct, Mar. 13, 1955. AmCol.

HEALD, ANTHONY: New Rochelle, NY, Aug. 25, 1944, MiStateU.

HEARD, JOHN: Washington, DC, Mar. 7, 1946. Clark U.

HEATHERTON, JOEY: NYC, Sept. 14, 1944.

HECKART, EILEEN: Columbus, OH, Mar. 29, 1919. Ohio State U.

HEDISON, DAVID: Providence, RI, May 20, 1929. Brown U.

HEGYES, ROBERT: NJ, May 7, 1951.

HEMINGWAY, MARIEL: Nov. 22, 1961.

HEMMINGS, DAVID: Guilford, Eng. Nov. 18, 1938.

HENDERSON, FLORENCE: Feb. 14, 1934.

HENDERSON, MARCIA: Andover, MA, July 22, 1932. AADA.

HENDRY, GLORIA: Jacksonville, FL. 1949.

HENNER, MARILU: Chicago, IL. Apr. 4, 1952.

HENREID, PAUL: Trieste, Jan. 10, 1908.

HENRY, BUCK (Zuckerman): NYC, 1931. Dartmouth.

HENRY, JUSTIN: Rye, NY, 1971.

HEPBURN, AUDREY: Brussels, Belgium, May 4, 1929.

HEPBURN, KATHARINE: Hartford, CT, Nov. 8, 1907. Bryn Mawr.

HERRMANN, EDWARD: Washington, DC, July 21, 1943. Bucknell, LAMDA.

HERSHEY, BARBARA: see Seagull, Barbara Hershey.

HESTON, CHARLTON: Evanston, IL, Oct. 4, 1922. Northwestern U.

HEWITT, MARTIN: Claremont, CA, 1960; AADA.

HEYWOOD, ANNE (Violet Pretty): Birmingham, Eng., Dec. 11, 1932.

HICKEY, WILLIAM: Brooklyn, NY, 1928.

HICKMAN, DARRYL: Hollywood, CA, July 28, 1933. Loyola U.

HICKMAN, DWAYNE: Los Angeles, May 18, 1934. Loyola U.

HIGGINS, MICHAEL: Brooklyn, NY, Jan. 20, 1926, AmThWing.

HILL, ARTHUR: Saskatchewan, CAN., Aug. 1, 1922. U. Brit. Col.

HILL, STEVEN: Seattle, WA, Feb. 24, 1922. U. Wash.

HILL, TERENCE (Mario Girotti): Venice, Italy, Mar. 29, 1941. U. Rome.

HILLER, WENDY: Bramhall, Cheshire, Eng., Aug. 15, 1912. Winceby House School.

HILLIARD, HARRIET: (See Harriet Hilliard Nelson)

HINGLE, PAT: Denver, CO, July 19, 1923. Tex. U.

HIRSCH, JUDD: NYC, Mar. 15, 1935. AADA.

HOBEL, MARA: NYC, June 18, 1971.

HODGE, PATRICIA: Lincolnshire, Eng., 1946. LAMDA.

HOFFMAN, DUSTIN: Los Angeles, Aug. 8, 1937. Pasadena Playhouse.

HOGAN, PAUL: Australia, 1941.

HOLBROOK, HAL (Harold): Cleveland, OH, Feb. 17, 1925. Denison.

HOLLIMAN, EARL: Tennessee Swamp, Delhi, LA, Sept. 11, 1928. UCLA.

HOLM, CELESTE: NYC, Apr. 29, 1919.

HOMEIER, SKIP (George Vincent Homeier): Chicago, Oct. 5, 1930. UCLA.

HOOKS, ROBERT: Washington, DC, Apr. 18, 1937. Temple.

HOPE, BOB (Leslie Townes Hope): London, May 26, 1903.

HOPPER, DENNIS: Dodge City, KS, May 17, 1936.

HORNADAY, JEFFREY: San Jose, Ca., 1956.

HORNE, LENA: Brooklyn, June 30, 1917.

HORSLEY, LEE: May 15, 1955.

HORTON, ROBERT: Los Angeles, July 29, 1924. UCLA.

HOSKINS, BOB: Bury St. Edmunds, Eng., Oct. 26, 1942.

HOUGHTON, KATHARINE: Hartford, CT, Mar. 10, 1945. Sarah Lawrence.

HOUSEMAN, JOHN: Bucharest, Sept. 22, 1902.

HOUSER, JERRY: Los Angeles, July 14, 1952. Valley Jr. Col.

HOUSTON, DONALD: Tonypandy, Wales, 1924.

HOVEY, TIM: Los Angeles, June 19, 1945.

HOWARD, KEN: El Centro, CA, Mar. 28, 1944. Yale.

HOWARD, RON: Duncan, OK, Mar. 1, 1954. USC.

HOWARD, RONALD: Norwood, Eng., Apr. 7, 1918. Jesus College.

HOWARD, TREVOR: Kent, Eng., Sept. 29, 1916. RADA.

HOWELLS, C. THOMAS: 1967.

HOWELLS, URSULA: London, Sept. 17, 1922.

HOWES, SALLY ANN: London, July 20, 1930.

HUDDLESTON, MICHAEL: Roanoke, VA., AADA.

HUGHES, BARNARD: Bedford Hills, NY, July 16, 1915. Manhattan Col.

HUGHES, KATHLEEN (Betty von Gerkan): Hollywood, CA, Nov. 14, 1928. UCLA.

HULCE, THOMAS: Plymouth, MI, Dec. 6, 1953. N.C.Sch. of Arts.

HUNNICUT, GAYLE: Ft. Worth, TX, Feb. 6, 1943. UCLA.

HUNT, LINDA: Morristown, NJ, Apr. 2, 1945. Goodman Theatre.

HUNT, MARSHA: Chicago, Oct. 17, 1917.

HUNTER, HOLLY: Atlanta, Ga, Mar. 20, 1958, Carnegie-Mellon.

HUNTER, KIM (Janet Cole): Detroit, Nov. 12, 1922.

HUNTER, TAB (Arthur Gelien) NYC, July 11, 1931.

HUPPERT, ISABELLE: Paris, Fr., Mar. 16, 1955.

HURT, MARY BETH (Supinger): Marshalltown, IA., 1948. NYU.

HURT, WILLIAM: Washington, D.C., Mar. 20, 1950. Tufts, Juilliard.

HUSSEY, RUTH: Providence, RI, Oct. 30, 1917. U. Mich.

HUSTON, JOHN: Nevada, MO, Aug. 5, 1906.

HUTTON, BETTY (Betty Thornberg): Battle Creek, MI, Feb. 26, 1921.

HUTTON, LAUREN (Mary): Charleston, SC, Nov. 17, 1943. Newcomb Col.

HUTTON, ROBERT (Winne): Kingston, NY, June 11, 1920. Blair Academy.

HUTTON, TIMOTHY: Malibu, CA, Aug. 16, 1960.

HYDE-WHITE, WILFRID: Gloucestershire, Eng., May 13, 1903. RADA.

HYER, MARTHA: Fort Worth, TX, Aug. 10, 1924. Northwestern U.

IGLESIAS, JULIO: Madrid, Spain, Sept. 23, 1943.

INGELS, MARTY: Brooklyn, NY, Mar. 9, 1936.

IRELAND, JOHN: Vancouver, B.C., CAN., Jan. 30, 1914.

IRONS, JEREMY: Cowes, Eng. Sept. 19, 1948. Old Vic.

IVANEK, ZELJKO: Ljubljana, Yugo., Aug. 15, 1957. Yale, LAMDA.

IVES, BURL: Hunt Township, IL, June 14, 1909. Charleston ILL. Teachers College.

IVEY, JUDITH: El Paso, Tx, Sept. 4, 1951.

JACKSON, ANNE: Alleghany, PA, Sept. 3, 1926. Neighborhood Playhouse.

JACKSON, GLENDA: Hoylake, Cheshire, Eng., May 9, 1936. RADA.

JACKSON, KATE: Birmingham, AL. Oct. 29, 1948. AADA.

JACKSON, MICHAEL: Gary, Ind., Aug. 29, 1958.

JACOBI, DEREK: Leytonstone, London, Eng. Oct. 22, 1938. Cambridge.

JACOBI, LOU: Toronto, CAN., Dec. 28, 1913.

JACOBS, LAWRENCE-HILTON: Virgin Islands, 1954.

JACOBY, SCOTT: Chicago, Nov. 19, 1956.

JAECKEL, RICHARD: Long Beach, NY, Oct. 10, 1926.

JAGGER, DEAN: Lima, OH, Nov. 7, 1903. Wabash College.

JAGGER, MICK: July 26, 1943.

JAMES, CLIFTON: NYC, May 29, 1921. Ore. U.

JAMES, JOHN (Anderson): Apr. 1956, New Canaan, Ct., AADA.

JARMAN, CLAUDE, JR.: Nashville, TN, Sept. 27, 1934.

JASON, RICK: NYC, May 21, 1926. AADA.

JEAN, GLORIA (Gloria Jean Schoonover): Buffalo, NY, Apr. 14, 1927.

JEFFREYS, ANNE (Carmichael): Goldsboro, NC, Jan. 26, 1923. Anderson College.

JEFFRIES, LIONEL: London, 1927, RADA.

JERGENS, ADELE: Brooklyn, Nov. 26, 1922.

JETT, ROGER (Baker): Cumberland, MD., Oct. 2, 1946. AADA.

JILLIAN, ANN (Nauseda): Massachusetts, Jan. 29, 1951.

JOHN, ELTON: (Reginald Dwight) Middlesex, Eng., Mar. 25, 1947. RAM.

JOHNS, GLYNIS: Durban, S. Africa, Oct. 5, 1923.

JOHNSON, BEN: Pawhuska, Ok, June 13, 1918.

JOHNSON, DON: Galena, Mo., Dec. 15, 1950. UKan.

JOHNSON, PAGE: Welch, WV, Aug. 25, 1930. Ithaca.

JOHNSON, RAFER: Hillsboro, TX, Aug. 18, 1935. UCLA.

JOHNSON, RICHARD: Essex, Eng., 1927. RADA.

JOHNSON, ROBIN: Brooklyn, NY: May 29, 1964.

JOHNSON, VAN: Newport, RI, Aug. 28, 1916.

JONES, CHRISTOPHER: Jackson, TN, Aug. 18, 1941. Actors Studio.

JONES, DEAN: Morgan County, AL, Jan. 25, 1936. Actors Studio.

JONES, JACK: Bel-Air, CA, Jan. 14, 1938.

JONES, JAMES EARL: Arkabutla, MS, Jan. 17, 1931. U. Mich.

JONES, JENNIFER (Phyllis Isley): Tulsa, OK, Mar. 2, 1919. AADA.

JONES, SAM J.: Chicago, IL, 1954.

JONES, SHIRLEY: Smithton, PA, March 31, 1934.

JONES, TOM (Thomas Jones Woodward): Pontypridd, Wales, June 7, 1940.

JONES, TOMMY LEE: San Saba, TX, Sept. 15, 1946. Harvard.

JORDAN, RICHARD: NYC, July 19, 1938. Harvard.

JOURDAN, LOUIS: Marseilles, France, June 18, 1920.

JOY, ROBERT: Montreal, Can, Aug. 17, 1951, Oxford.

JULIA, RAUL: San Juan, PR, Mar. 9, 1940. U PR.

JURADO, KATY (Maria Christina Jurado Garcia): Guadalajara, Mex., 1927.

KAHN, MADELINE: Boston, MA, Sept. 29, 1942. Hofstra U.

KANE, CAROL: Cleveland, OH, 1952.

KAPLAN, JONATHAN: Paris, Nov. 25, 1947. NYU.

KAPLAN, MARVIN: Brooklyn, Jan. 24, 1924.

KAPOOR, SHASHI: Bombay 1940.

KAPRISKY, VALERIE: Paris, 1963.

KATT, WILLIAM: Los Angeles, CA, 1955.

KAUFMANN, CHRISTINE: Lansdorf, Graz, Austria, Jan. 11, 1945.

KAVNER, JULIE: Burbank, CA, 1951, UCLA.

KAYE, STUBBY: NYC, Nov. 11, 1918.

KEACH, STACY: Savannah, GA, June 2, 1941. U. Cal., Yale.

KEATON, MICHAEL: Coraopolis, Pa., 1951. KentStateU.

KEATON, DIANE (Hall): Los Angeles, CA, Jan. 5, 1946. Neighborhood Playhouse.

KEATS, STEVEN: Bronx, NY, 1945.

KEDROVA, LILA: Leningrad, 1918.

KEEL, HOWARD (Harold Leek): Gillespie, IL, Apr. 13, 1919.

KEELER, RUBY (Ethel): Halifax, N.S., Aug. 25, 1909.

KEITH, BRIAN: Bayonne, NJ, Nov. 15, 1921.

KEITH, DAVID: Knoxville, Tn., 1954. UTN.

KELLER, MARTHE: Basel, Switz., 1945. Munich Stanislavsky Sch.

KELLERMAN, SALLY: Long Beach, CA, June 2, 1938. Actors Studio West.

KELLEY, DeFOREST: Atlanta, GA, Jan. 20, 1920.

KELLY, GENE: Pittsburgh, Aug. 23, 1912. U. Pittsburgh.

KELLY, JACK: Astoria, NY, Sept. 16, 1927. UCLA.

KELLY, NANCY: Lowell, MA, Mar. 25, 1921. Bentley School.

KEMP, JEREMY: (Wacker) Chesterfield, Eng., Feb. 3, 1935, Central Sch.

KENNEDY, ARTHUR: Worcester, MA, Feb. 17, 1914. Carnegie Tech.

KENNEDY, GEORGE: NYC, Feb. 18, 1925.

KENNEDY, LEON ISAAC: Cleveland, OH., 1949.

KERR, DEBORAH: Helensburg, Scot., Sept. 30, 1921. Smale Ballet School.

KERR, JOHN: NYC, Nov. 15, 1931. Harvard, Columbia.

KHAMBATTA, PERSIS: Bombay, Oct. 2, 1950.

KIDDER, MARGOT: Yellow Knife, CAN., Oct. 17, 1948. UBC.

KIER, UDO: Germany, Oct. 14, 1944.

KILEY, RICHARD: Chicago, Mar. 31, 1922. Loyola.

KILMER, VAL: 1960, Juilliard.

KINCAID, ARON (Norman Neale Williams III): Los Angeles, June 15, 1943. UCLA.

KING, ALAN (Irwin Kniberg): Brooklyn, Dec. 26, 1927.

Thomas Hulce	Judith Ivey	Page Johnson	Carol Kane	Aron Kincaid	Charlotte Lewis

KING, PERRY: Alliance, OH, Apr. 30, 1948. Yale.

KINGSLEY, BEN (Krishna Bhanji): Snaiton, Yorkshire, Eng., Dec. 31, 1943.

KINSKI, CLAUS: (Claus Gunther Nakszynski) Sopot, Poland, 1926.

KINSKI, NASTASSJA: Germany, Jan. 24, 1960.

KITT, EARTHA: North, SC, Jan. 26, 1928.

KLEMPERER, WERNER: Cologne, Mar. 22, 1920.

KLINE, KEVIN: St. Louis, Mo, Oct. 24, 1947, Juilliard.

KLUGMAN, JACK: Philadelphia, PA, Apr. 27, 1925. Carnegie Tech.

KNIGHT, SHIRLEY: Goessel, KS, July 5, 1937. Wichita U.

KNOWLES, PATRIC (Reginald Lawrence Knowles): Horsforth, Eng., Nov. 11, 1911.

KNOX, ALEXANDER: Strathroy, Ont., CAN., Jan. 16, 1907.

KNOX, ELYSE: Hartford, CT, Dec. 14, 1917. Traphagen School.

KOENIG, WALTER: Chicago, IL, Sept. 14. UCLA.

KOHNER, SUSAN: Los Angeles, Nov. 11, 1936. U. Calif.

KORMAN, HARVEY: Chicago, IL, Feb. 15, 1927. Goodman.

KORVIN, CHARLES (Geza Korvin Karpathi): Czechoslovakia, Nov. 21. Sorbonne.

KOSLECK, MARTIN: Barkotzen, Ger., Mar. 24, 1907. Max Reinhardt School.

KOTTO, YAPHET: NYC, Nov. 15, 1937.

KRABBE, JEROEN: Holland 1944.

KREUGER, KURT: St. Moritz, Switz., July 23, 1917. U. London.

KRISTEL, SYLVIA: Amsterdam, Hol., Sept. 28, 1952.

KRISTOFFERSON, KRIS: Brownsville, TX, June 22, 1936, Pomona Col.

KRUGER, HARDY: Berlin Ger., April 12, 1928.

KULP, NANCY: Harrisburg, PA, 1921.

KUNTSMANN, DORIS: Hamburg, 1944.

KWAN, NANCY: Hong Kong, May 19, 1939. Royal Ballet.

LaBELLE, PATTI: Philadelphia, Pa., May 24, 1944.

LACY, JERRY: Sioux City, IA, Mar. 27, 1936. LACC.

LADD, CHERYL: (Stoppelmoor): Huron, SD, July 12, 1951.

LADD, DIANE: (Ladnier): Meridian, MS, Nov. 29, 1932. Tulane U.

LaGRECA, PAUL: Bronx, NY, June 23, 1962. AADA.

LAHTI, CHRISTINE: Detroit, MI, Apr. 4, 1950; U. Mich.

LAMARR, HEDY (Hedwig Kiesler): Vienna, Sept. 11, 1913.

LAMAS, LORENZO: Los Angeles, Jan. 28, 1958.

LAMB, GIL: Minneapolis, June 14, 1906. U. Minn.

LAMBERT, CHRISTOPHER: NYC, 1958.

LAMOUR, DOROTHY (Mary Dorothy Slaton): New Orleans, LA.; Dec. 10, 1914. Spence School.

LANCASTER, BURT: NYC, Nov. 2, 1913. NYU.

LANDAU, MARTIN: Brooklyn, NY, June 20, 1931. Actors Studio.

LANDON, MICHAEL (Eugene Orowitz): Collingswood, NJ, Oct. 31, 1936. USC.

LANDRUM, TERI: Enid, OK., 1960.

LANE, ABBE: Brooklyn, Dec. 14, 1935.

LANE, DIANE: NYC, Jan. 1963.

LANGAN, GLENN: Denver, CO, July 8, 1917.

LANGE, HOPE: Redding Ridge, CT, Nov. 28, 1933. Reed Col.

LANGE, JESSICA: Cloquet, Mn, Apr. 20, 1949. U. Minn.

LANSBURY, ANGELA: London, Oct. 16, 1925. London Academy of Music.

LANGELLA, FRANK: Bayonne, NJ, Jan. 1, 1940, SyracuseU.

LANSING, ROBERT (Brown): San Diego, CA, June 5, 1929.

LAUPER, CYNTHIA: Astoria, Queens, NYC. June 20, 1953.

LAURE, CAROLE: Montreal, Can., 1951.

LAURIE, PIPER (Rosetta Jacobs): Detroit, MI, Jan. 22, 1932.

LAW, JOHN PHILLIP: Hollywood, Sept. 7, 1937. Neighborhood Playhouse, U. Hawaii.

LAWRENCE, BARBARA: Carnegie, OK, Feb. 24, 1930. UCLA.

LAWRENCE, CAROL (Laraia): Melrose Park, IL, Sept. 5, 1935.

LAWRENCE, VICKI: Inglewood, CA, Mar. 26, 1949.

LAWSON, LEIGH: Atherston, Eng., July 21, 1945. RADA.

LEACHMAN, CLORIS: Des Moines, IA, Apr. 30, 1930. Northwestern U.

LEAUD, JEAN-PIERRE: Paris, 1944.

LEDERER, FRANCIS: Karlin, Prague, Czech., Nov. 6, 1906.

LEE, BRANDON: Feb. 1, 1965. EmersonCol.

LEE, CHRISTOPHER: London, May 27, 1922. Wellington College.

LEE, PEGGY (Norma Delores Egstrom): Jamestown, ND, May 26, 1920.

LEE, MARK: Australia, 1958.

LEE, MICHELE (Dusiak): Los Angeles, June 24, 1942. LACC.

LEIBMAN, RON: NYC, Oct. 11, 1937. Ohio Wesleyan.

LEIGH, JANET (Jeanette Helen Morrison): Merced, CA, July 6, 1926. College of Pacific.

LEMMON, JACK: Boston, Feb. 8, 1925. Harvard.

LENZ, RICK: Springfield, IL, Nov. 21, 1939. U. Mich.

LEONARD, SHELDON (Bershad): NYC, Feb. 22, 1907, Syracuse U.

LEROY, PHILIPPE: Paris, Oct. 15, 1930. U. Paris.

LESLIE, BETHEL: NYC, Aug. 3, 1929. Brearley School.

LESLIE, JOAN (Joan Brodell): Detroit, Jan. 26, 1925. St. Benedict's.

LESTER, MARK: Oxford, Eng., July 11, 1958.

LEVELS, CALVIN: Cleveland, OH., Sept. 30, 1954. CCC.

LEWIS, CHARLOTTE: London, 1968.

LEWIS, DANIEL DAY: London, 1958, Bristol Old Vic.

LEWIS, EMMANUEL: Brooklyn, NY, March 9, 1971.

LEWIS, JERRY: Newark, NJ, Mar. 16, 1926.

LIGON, TOM: New Orleans, LA, Sept. 10, 1945.

LILLIE, BEATRICE: Toronto, Can., May 29, 1898.

LINCOLN, ABBEY (Anna Marie Woolridge): Chicago, Aug. 6, 1930.

LINDFORS, VIVECA: Uppsala, Sweden, Dec. 29, 1920. Stockholm Royal Dramatic School.

LINN-BAKER, MARK: St. Louis, Mo, Yale.

LISI, VIRNA: Rome, Nov. 8, 1937.

LITHGOW, JOHN: Rochester, NY, Oct. 19, 1945. Harvard.

LITTLE, CLEAVON: Chickasha, OK, June 1, 1939. San Diego State.

LOCKE, SONDRA: Shelbyville, TN, 1947.

LOCKHART, JUNE: NYC, June 25, 1925. Westlake School.

LOCKWOOD, GARY: Van Nuys, CA, Feb. 21, 1937.

LOCKWOOD, MARGARET: Karachi, Pakistan, Sept. 15, 1916. RADA.

LOGGIA, ROBERT: Staten Island, NY., Jan. 3, 1930. UMo.

LOLLOBRIGIDA, GINA: Subiaco, Italy, July 4, 1927. Rome Academy of Fine Arts.

LOM, HERBERT: Prague, Czechoslovakia, 1917. Prague U.

LOMEZ, CELINE: Montreal, Can., 1953.

LONDON, JULIE (Julie Peck): Santa Rosa, CA, Sept. 26, 1926.

LONE, JOHN: China, 1961, AADA.

LONG, SHELLEY: Indiana, 1950. Northwestern U.

LONOW, MARK: Brooklyn, NY.

LOPEZ, PERRY: NYC, July 22, 1931. NYU.

LORD, JACK (John Joseph Ryan): NYC, Dec. 30, 1928. NYU.

LOREN, SOPHIA (Sofia Scicolone): Rome, Italy, Sept. 20, 1934.

LOUISE, TINA (Blacker): NYC, Feb. 11, 1934, Miami U.

LOVELACE, LINDA: Bryan, TX, 1952.

LOWE, CHAD: NYC, Jan, 15, 1968.

LOWE, ROB: Ohio, 1964.

LOWITSCH, KLAUS: Berlin, Apr. 8, 1936. Vienna Academy.

LOY, MYRNA (Myrna Williams): Helena, MT, Aug. 2, 1905. Westlake School.

LUCAS, LISA: Arizona, 1961.

LULU: Glasglow, Scot., 1948.

LUNA, BARBARA: NYC, Mar. 2, 1939.

LUND, JOHN: Rochester, NY, Feb. 6, 1913.

LUNDGREN, DOLPH: Stockholm, Sw., 1959. Royal Inst.

LUPINO, IDA: London, Feb. 4, 1916. RADA.

LuPONE, PATTI: Northport, NY, Apr. 21, 1949, Juilliard.

LYDON, JAMES: Harrington Park, NJ, May 30, 1923.

LYNLEY, CAROL (Jones): NYC, Feb. 13, 1942.

LYNN, JEFFREY: Auburn, MA, 1909. Bates College.

LYON, SUE: Davenport, IA, July 10, 1946.

LYONS, ROBERT F.: Albany, NY. AADA.

MacARTHUR, JAMES: Los Angeles, Dec. 8, 1937. Harvard.

MACCHIO, RALPH: Huntington, NY., 1962.

MacGINNIS, NIALL: Dublin, Ire., Mar. 29, 1913. Dublin U.

MacGRAW, ALI: NYC, Apr. 1, 1938. Wellesley.

MacLAINE, SHIRLEY (Beatty): Richmond, VA, Apr. 24, 1934.

MacLEOD, GAVIN: Mt. Kisco, NY, Feb. 28, 1931.

MacMAHON, ALINE: McKeesport, PA, May 3, 1899. Barnard College.

MacMURRAY, FRED: Kankakee, IL, Aug. 30, 1908. Carroll Col.

MACNAUGHTON, ROBERT: NYC, Dec. 19, 1966.

MACNEE, PATRICK: London, Feb. 1922.

MacNICOL, PETER: Dallas, TX, Apr. 10, UMN.

MADISON, GUY (Robert Moseley): Bakersfield, CA, Jan. 19, 1922. Bakersfield Jr. College.

MADONNA (Madonna Louise Veronica Cicone): Pontiac, Mi., 1961 UMi.

MAHARIS, GEORGE: Astoria, NY, Sept. 1, 1928. Actors Studio.

MAHONEY, JOCK (Jacques O'Mahoney): Chicago, Feb. 7, 1919. U. of Iowa.

MAHONEY, JOHN: Manchester, Eng., June 20, 1940, WUIll.

MAJORS, LEE: Wyandotte, MI, Apr. 23, 1940. E. Ky. State Col.

MAKEPEACE, CHRIS: Toronto, Can., 1964.

MALDEN, KARL. (Mladen Sekulovich): Gary, IN, Mar. 22, 1914.

MALET, PIERRE: St. Tropez, Fr., 1955.

MALKOVICH, JOHN: Christopher, IL, Dec. 9, 1953, IllStateU.

MALONE, DOROTHY: Chicago, Jan. 30, 1925. S. Methodist U.

MANN, KURT: Roslyn, NY, July 18, 1947.

MANOFF, DINAH: NYC, Jan. 25, 1958. CalArts.

MANTEGNA, JOE: Chicago, IL, Nov. 13, 1947, Goodman Theatre.

MANZ, LINDA: NYC, 1961.

MARAIS, JEAN: Cherbourg, France, Dec. 11, 1913. St. Germain.

MARGOLIN, JANET: NYC, July 25, 1943. Walden School.

MARIN, JACQUES: Paris, Sept. 9, 1919. Conservatoire National.

MARINARO, ED: NYC, 1951. Cornell.

MARSHALL, BRENDA (Ardis Anderson Gaines): Isle of Negros, P.I., Sept. 29, 1915. Texas State College.

MARSHALL, E. G.: Owatonna, MN, June 18, 1910. U. Minn.

MARSHALL, KEN: NYC, 1953. Juilliard.

MARSHALL, PENNY: Bronx, NY, Oct. 15, 1942. U. N. Mex.

MARSHALL, WILLIAM: Gary, IN, Aug. 19, 1924. NYU.

MARTIN, DEAN (Dino Crocetti): Steubenville, OH, June 17, 1917.

MARTIN, GEORGE N.: NYC, Aug. 15, 1929.

MARTIN, MARY: Weatherford, TX, Dec. 1, 1914. Ward-Belmont School.

MARTIN, STEVE: Waco, TX, 1945. UCLA.

MARTIN, TONY (Alfred Norris): Oakland, CA, Dec. 25, 1913. St. Mary's College.

MARVIN, LEE: NYC, Feb. 19, 1924.

MASON, MARSHA: St. Louis, MO, Apr. 3, 1942. Webster Col.

MASON, PAMELA (Pamela Kellino): Westgate, Eng., Mar. 10, 1918.

MASSEN, OSA: Copenhagen, Den., Jan. 13, 1916.

MASSEY, DANIEL: London, Oct. 10, 1933. Eton and King's Col.

MASTERS, BEN: Corvallis, Or, May 6, 1947, UOr.

MASTERSON, MARY STUART: NYC, 1967, NYU.

MASTERSON, PETER: Angleton, TX, June 1, 1934. Rice U.

MASTRANTONIO, MARY ELIZABETH: Chicago, Il., Nov. 17, 1958. UIll.

MASTROIANNI, MARCELLO: Fontana Liri, Italy, Sept. 28, 1924.

MATHESON, TIM: Glendale, CA, Dec. 31, 1947. CalState.

MATHIS, JOHNNY: San Francisco, Ca., Sept. 30, 1935. SanFranStateCol.

MATLIN, MARLEE: Morton Grove, IL., 1965.

MATTHAU, WALTER (Matuschanskayasky): NYC, Oct. 1, 1920.

MATTHEWS, BRIAN: Philadelphia, PA, Jan. 24, 1953. St. Olaf.

MATURE, VICTOR: Louisville, KY, Jan. 29, 1915.

MAY, ELAINE (Berlin): Philadelphia, Apr. 21, 1932.

MAYEHOFF, EDDIE: Baltimore, July 7. Yale.

MAYO, VIRGINIA (Virginia Clara Jones): St. Louis, MO, Nov. 30, 1920.

McCALLUM, DAVID: Scotland, Sept. 19, 1933. Chapman Col.

McCAMBRIDGE, MERCEDES: Jolliet, IL, Mar. 17, 1918. Mundelein College.

McCARTHY, ANDREW: NYC, 1963, NYU.

McCARTHY, KEVIN: Seattle, WA, Feb. 15, 1914. Minn. U.

McCLANAHAN, RUE: Healdton, OK, Feb. 21, 1935.

McCLORY, SEAN: Dublin, Ire., Mar. 8, 1924. U. Galway.

McCLURE, DOUG: Glendale, CA, May 11, 1935. UCLA.

McCOWEN, ALEC: Tunbridge Wells, Eng., May 26, 1925. RADA.

McCREA, JOEL: Los Angeles, Nov. 5, 1905. Pomona College.

McDOWALL, RODDY: London, Sept. 17, 1928. St. Joseph's.

McDOWELL, MALCOLM (Taylor): Leeds, Eng., June 15, 1943. LAMDA.

McENERY, PETER: Walsall, Eng., Feb. 21, 1940.

McFARLAND, SPANKY: Dallas, TX, 1936.

McGAVIN, DARREN: Spokane, WA, May 7, 1922. College of Pacific.

McGILLIS, KELLY: Newport Beach, CA, 1958. Juilliard.

McGOVERN, ELIZABETH: Evanston, IL, July 18, 1961. Juilliard.

McGUIRE, BIFF: New Haven, CT, Oct. 25, 1926. Mass. State Col.

McGUIRE, DOROTHY: Omaha, NE, June 14, 1918.

McHATTIE, STEPHEN: Antigonish, NS, Feb. 3. AcadiaU, AADA.

McKAY, GARDNER: NYC, June 10, 1932. Cornell.

McKEE, LONETTE: Detroit, MI, 1954.

McKELLEN, IAN: Burnley, Eng., May 25, 1939.

McKENNA, VIRGINIA: London, June 7, 1931.

McKEON, DOUG: New Jersey, 1966.

McKUEN, ROD: Oakland, CA, Apr. 29, 1933.

McLERIE, ALLYN ANN: Grand Mere, Can., Dec. 1, 1926.

McNAIR, BARBARA: Chicago, Mar. 4, 1939. UCLA.

McNALLY, STEPHEN (Horace McNally): NYC, July 29, 1913. Fordham U.

McNICHOL, KRISTY: Los Angeles, CA, Sept. 11, 1962.

Sophia
Loren

Rob
Lowe

Shirley
MacLaine

John
Mahoney

Elizabeth
McGovern

James
Naughton

McQUEEN, ARMELIA: North Carolina, Jan. 6, 1952. Bklyn Consv.

McQUEEN, BUTTERFLY: Tampa, FL, Jan. 8, 1911. UCLA.

McQUEEN, CHAD: Los Angeles, CA, 1961. Actors Studio.

MEADOWS, AUDREY: Wuchang, China, 1919. St. Margaret's.

MEADOWS, JAYNE (formerly, Jayne Cotter): Wuchang, China, Sept. 27, 1920. St. Margaret's.

MEARA, ANNE: Brooklyn, NY, Sept. 20, 1929.

MEDWIN, MICHAEL: London, 1925. Instut Fischer.

MEEKER, RALPH (Ralph Rathgeber): Minneapolis, Nov. 21, 1920. Northwestern U.

MEISNER, GUNTER: Bremen, Ger., Apr. 18, 1926. Municipal Drama School.

MEKKA, EDDIE: Worcester, MA, 1932. Boston Cons.

MELATO, MARIANGELA: Milan, Italy, 1941. Milan Theatre Acad.

MELL, MARISA: Vienna, Austria, Feb. 25, 1939.

MERCADO, HECTOR JAIME: NYC, 1949. HB Studio.

MERCOURI, MELINA: Athens, Greece, Oct. 18, 1915.

MEREDITH, BURGESS: Cleveland, OH, Nov. 16, 1908. Amherst.

MEREDITH, LEE (Judi Lee Sauls): Oct., 1947. AADA.

MERRILL, DINA (Nedinia Hutton): NYC, Dec. 9, 1925. AADA.

MERRILL, GARY: Hartford, CT, Aug. 2, 1915. Bowdoin, Trinity.

METZLER, JIM: Oneonda, NY. Dartmouth Col.

MICHELL, KEITH: Adelaide, Aus., Dec. 1, 1926.

MIDLER, BETTE: Honolulu, HI., Dec. 1, 1945.

MIFUNE, TOSHIRO: Tsingtao, China, Apr. 1, 1920.

MILANO, ALYSSA: Brooklyn, NY, 1975.

MILES, JOANNA: Nice, France, Mar. 6, 1940.

MILES, SARAH: Ingatestone, Eng., Dec. 31, 1941. RADA.

MILES, SYLVIA: NYC, Sept. 9, 1932. Actors Studio.

MILES, VERA (Ralston): Boise City, OK, Aug. 23, 1929. UCLA.

MILFORD, PENELOPE: Winnetka, IL.

MILLER, ANN (Lucille Ann Collier): Chireno, TX, Apr. 12, 1919. Lawler Professional School.

MILLER, BARRY: Los Angeles, Ca., Feb. 6, 1958

MILLER, JASON: Long Island City, NY, Apr. 22, 1939. Catholic U.

MILLER, LINDA: NYC, Sept. 16, 1942. Catholic U.

MILLS, HAYLEY: London, Apr. 18, 1946. Elmhurst School.

MILLS, JOHN: Suffolk, Eng., Feb. 22, 1908.

MILNER, MARTIN: Detroit, MI, Dec. 28, 1931.

MIMIEUX, YVETTE: Los Angeles, Jan. 8, 1941. Hollywood High.

MINNELLI, LIZA: Los Angeles, Mar. 12, 1946.

MIOU-MIOU: Paris, Feb. 22, 1950.

MITCHELL, CAMERON (Mizell): Dallastown, PA, Nov. 4, 1918. N.Y. Theatre School.

MITCHELL, JAMES: Sacramento, CA, Feb. 29, 1920. LACC.

MITCHUM, JAMES: Los Angeles, CA, May 8, 1941.

MITCHUM, ROBERT: Bridgeport, CT, Aug. 6, 1917.

MONTALBAN, RICARDO: Mexico City, Nov. 25, 1920.

MONTAND, YVES (Yves Montand Livi): Mansummano, Tuscany, Oct. 13, 1921.

MONTGOMERY, BELINDA: Winnipeg, Can., July 23, 1950.

MONTGOMERY, ELIZABETH: Los Angeles, Apr. 15, 1933. AADA.

MONTGOMERY, GEORGE (George Letz): Brady, MT, Aug. 29, 1916. U. Mont.

MOOR, BILL: Toledo, OH, July 13, 1931. Northwestern.

MOORE, CONSTANCE: Sioux City, IA, Jan. 18, 1919.

MOORE, DEMI (Guines): Roswell, NMx. Nov. 11, 1962.

MOORE, DICK: Los Angeles, Sept. 12, 1925.

MOORE, DUDLEY: London, Apr. 19, 1935.

MOORE, FRANK: Bay-de-Verde, Newfoundland, 1946.

MOORE, KIERON: County Cork, Ire., 1925. St. Mary's College.

MOORE, MARY TYLER: Brooklyn, Dec. 29, 1936.

MOORE, ROGER: London, Oct. 14, 1927. RADA.

MOORE, TERRY (Helen Koford): Los Angeles, Jan. 7, 1929.

MORALES, ESAI: Brooklyn, 1963.

MOREAU, JEANNE: Paris, Jan. 23, 1928.

MORENO, RITA (Rosita Alverio): Humacao, P.R., Dec. 11, 1931.

MORGAN, DENNIS (Stanley Morner): Prentice, WI, Dec. 10, 1910. Carroll College.

MORGAN, HARRY (HENRY) (Harry Bratsburg): Detroit, Apr. 10, 1915. U. Chicago.

MORGAN, MICHELE (Simone Roussel): Paris, Feb. 29, 1920. Paris Dramatic School.

MORIARTY, CATHY: Bronx, NY, 1961.

MORIARTY, MICHAEL: Detroit, MI, Apr. 5, 1941. Dartmouth.

MORISON, PATRICIA: NYC, 1915.

MORLEY, ROBERT: Wiltshire, Eng., May 26, 1908. RADA.

MORRIS, ANITA: Durham, NC, 1932.

MORRIS, GREG: Cleveland, OH, Sept. 27, 1934. Ohio State.

MORRIS, HOWARD: NYC, Sept. 4, 1919. NYU.

MORSE, DAVID: Hamilton, MA, 1953.

MORSE, ROBERT: Newton, MA, May 18, 1931.

MORTON, JOE: NYC, Oct. 18, 1947. HofstraU.

MOSS, ARNOLD: NYC, Jan. 28, 1910. CCNY.

MOUCHET, CATHERINE: Paris, 1959, Ntl. Consv.

MOYA, EDDY: El Paso, TX, Apr. 11, 1963. LACC.

MULL, MARTIN: N. Ridgefield, Oh., 1941. RISch. of Design.

MULLIGAN, RICHARD: NYC, Nov. 13, 1932.

MURPHY, EDDIE: Brooklyn, NY, Apr. 3, 1961.

MURPHY, GEORGE: New Haven, CT, July 4, 1902. Yale.

MURPHY, MICHAEL: Los Angeles, CA, May 5, 1938, UAz.

MURRAY, BILL: Evanston, IL, Sept. 21, 1950. Regis Col.

MURRAY, DON: Hollywood, July 31, 1929. AADA.

MURRAY, KEN (Don Court): NYC, July 14, 1903.

MUSANTE, TONY: Bridgeport, CT, June 30, 1936. Oberlin Col.

NABORS, JIM: Sylacauga, GA, June 12, 1932.

NADER, GEORGE: Pasadena, CA, Oct. 19, 1921. Occidental College.

NADER, MICHAEL: Los Angeles, CA, 1945.

NAMATH, JOE: Beaver Falls, Pa, May 31, 1943. UAla.

NAPIER, ALAN: Birmingham, Eng., Jan. 7, 1903. Birmingham University.

NATWICK, MILDRED: Baltimore, June 19, 1908. Bryn Mawr.

NAUGHTON, DAVID: 1955

NAUGHTON, JAMES: Middletown, CT, Dec. 6, 1945. Yale.

NAVIN, JOHN P., JR.: Philadelphia, PA, 1968.

NEAL, PATRICIA: Packard, KY, Jan. 20, 1926. Northwestern U.

NEFF, HILDEGARDE (Hildegard Knef): Ulm, Ger., Dec. 28, 1925. Berlin Art Academy.

NELL, NATHALIE: Paris, Oct. 1950.

NELLIGAN, KATE: London, Ont., Can., Mar. 16, 1951. U Toronto.

NELSON, BARRY (Robert Nielsen): Oakland, CA, 1920.

NELSON, DAVID: NYC, Oct. 24, 1936. USC.

NELSON, GENE (Gene Berg): Seattle, WA, Mar. 24, 1920.

NELSON, HARRIET HILLIARD (Peggy Lou Snyder): Des Moines, IA, July 18, 1914.

NELSON, JUDD: Maine, 1959, Haverford Col.

NELSON, LORI (Dixie Kay Nelson): Santa Fe, NM, Aug. 15, 1933.

NELSON, WILLIE: Texas, Apr. 30, 1933.

NETTLETON, LOIS: Oak Park, IL. Actors Studio.

NEWHART, BOB: Chicago, IL, Sept. 5, 1929. Loyola U.

NEWLEY, ANTHONY: Hackney, London, Sept. 21, 1931.

NEWMAN, BARRY: Boston, MA, Mar. 26, 1938. Brandeis U.

NEWMAN, PAUL: Cleveland, OH, Jan. 26, 1925. Yale.

NEWMAR, JULIE (Newmeyer): Los Angeles, Aug. 16, 1935.

NEWTON-JOHN, OLIVIA: Cambridge, Eng., Sept. 26, 1948.

NICHOLAS, PAUL: London, 1945.

NICHOLS, MIKE (Michael Igor Peschkowsky): Berlin, Nov. 6, 1931. U. Chicago.

NICHOLSON, JACK: Neptune, NJ, Apr. 22, 1937.

NICKERSON, DENISE: NYC, 1959.

NICOL, ALEX: Ossining, NY, Jan. 20, 1919. Actors Studio.

NIELSEN, LESLIE: Regina, Saskatchewan, Can., Feb. 11, 1926. Neighborhood Playhouse.

NIMOY, LEONARD: Boston, MA, Mar. 26, 1931. Boston Col., Antioch Col.

NIXON, CYNTHIA: NYC, Apr. 9, 1966.

NOBLE, JAMES: Dallas, TX, Mar. 5, 1922, SMU.

NOLAN, KATHLEEN: St. Louis, MO, Sept. 27, 1933. Neighborhood Playhouse.

NOLTE, NICK: Omaha, NE, 1941. Pasadena City Col.

NORRIS, CHRISTOPHER: NYC, Oct. 7, 1943. Lincoln Square Acad.

NORRIS, CHUCK (Carlos Ray): Ryan, OK, 1939.

NORTH, HEATHER: Pasadena, CA, Dec. 13, 1950. Actors Workshop.

NORTH, SHEREE (Dawn Bethel): Los Angeles, Jan. 17, 1933. Hollywood High.

NORTON, KEN: Aug. 9, 1945.

NOURI, MICHAEL: Washington, DC, Dec. 9, 1945.

NOVAK, KIM (Marilyn Novak): Chicago, Feb. 18, 1933. LACC.

NUREYEV, RUDOLF: Russia, Mar. 17, 1938.

NUTE, DON: Connellsville, PA, Mar. 13, Denver U.

NUYEN, FRANCE (Vannga): Marseilles, France, July 31, 1939. Beaux Arts School.

O'BRIAN, HUGH (Hugh J. Krampe): Rochester, NY, Apr. 19, 1928. Cincinnati U.

O'BRIEN, CLAY: Ray, AZ, May 6, 1961.

O'BRIEN, MARGARET (Angela Maxine O'Brien): Los Angeles, Jan. 15, 1937.

O'CONNOR, CARROLL: Bronx, NY, Aug. 2, 1925. Dublin National Univ.

O'CONNOR, DONALD: Chicago, Aug. 28, 1925.

O'CONNOR, GLYNNIS: NYC, Nov. 19, 1956. NYSU.

O'CONNOR, KEVIN: Honolulu, HI, May 7, 1938. U. Hi.

O'HANLON, GEORGE: Brooklyn, NY, Nov. 23, 1917.

O'HARA, MAUREEN (Maureen FitzSimons): Dublin, Ire., Aug. 17, 1920. Abbey School.

O'HERLIHY, DAN: Wexford, Ire., May 1, 1919. National U.

O'KEEFE, MICHAEL: Paulland, NJ, Apr. 24, 1971, NYU, AADA.

OLIVIER, LAURENCE: Dorking, Eng., May 22, 1907. Oxford.

O'LOUGHLIN, GERALD S.: NYC, Dec. 23, 1921. U. Rochester.

OLSON, NANCY: Milwaukee, WI, July 14, 1928. UCLA.

O'NEAL, GRIFFIN: Los Angeles, 1965.

O'NEAL, PATRICK: Ocala, FL, Sept. 26, 1927. U. Fla.

O'NEAL, RON: Utica, NY, Sept. 1, 1937. Ohio State.

O'NEAL, RYAN: Los Angeles, Apr. 20, 1941.

O'NEAL, TATUM: Los Angeles, Nov. 5, 1963.

O'NEIL, TRICIA: Shreveport, LA, Mar. 11, 1945. Baylor U.

O'NEILL, JENNIFER: Rio de Janeiro, Feb. 20, 1949. Neighborhood Playhouse.

O'SULLIVAN, MAUREEN: Byle, Ire., May 17, 1911. Sacred Heart Convent.

O'TOOLE, ANNETTE (Toole): Houston, TX, Apr. 1, 1952. UCLA.

O'TOOLE, PETER: Connemara, Ire., Aug. 2, 1932. RADA.

PACINO, AL: NYC, Apr. 25, 1940.

PAGE, GERALDINE: Kirksville, MO, Nov. 22, 1924. Goodman School.

PAGE, TONY (Anthony Vitiello): Bronx, NY, 1940.

PAGET, DEBRA (Debralee Griffin): Denver, Aug. 19, 1933.

PAIGE, JANIS (Donna Mae Jaden): Tacoma, WA, Sept. 16, 1922.

PALANCE, JACK (Walter Palanuik): Lattimer, PA, Feb. 18, 1920. UNC.

PALMER, BETSY: East Chicago, IN, Nov. 1, 1929. DePaul U.

PALMER, GREGG (Palmer Lee): San Francisco, Jan. 25, 1927. U. Utah.

PAMPANINI, SILVANA: Rome, Sept. 25, 1925.

PANTALIANO, JOEY: Hoboken, NJ. 1952.

PAPAS, IRENE: Chiliomodion, Greece, Mar. 9, 1929.

PARE, MICHAEL: Brooklyn, NY, 1959.

PARKER, ELEANOR: Cedarville, OH, June 26, 1922. Pasadena Playhouse.

PARKER, FESS: Fort Worth, TX, Aug. 16, 1927. USC.

PARKER, JAMESON: 1947. Beloit Col.

PARKER, JEAN (Mae Green): Deer Lodge, MT, Aug. 11, 1912.

PARKER, SUZY (Cecelia Parker): San Antonio, TX, Oct. 28, 1933.

PARKER, WILLARD (Worster Van Eps): NYC, Feb. 5, 1912.

PARKINS, BARBARA: Vancouver, Can., May 22, 1943.

PARSONS, ESTELLE: Lynn, MA, Nov. 20, 1927. Boston U.

PARTON, DOLLY: Sevierville, TN, Jan. 19, 1946.

PATINKIN, MANDY: Chicago, IL, Nov. 30, 1952. Juilliard.

PATRICK, DENNIS: Philadelphia, Mar. 14, 1918.

PATTERSON, LEE: Vancouver, Can., Mar. 31, 1929. Ontario Col.

PATTON, WILL: Charleston, SC, June 14, 1954.

PAVAN, MARISA (Marisa Pierangeli): Cagliari, Sardinia, June 19, 1932. Torquado Tasso College.

PAYNE, JOHN: Roanoke, Va., March 23, 1912.

PEACH, MARY: Durban, S. Africa, 1934.

PEARL, MINNIE (Sarah Cannon): Centerville, TN, Oct. 25, 1912.

PEARSON, BEATRICE: Denison, TX, July 27, 1920.

PECK, GREGORY: La Jolla, CA, Apr. 5, 1916. U. Calif.

PELIKAN, LISA: Paris, July 12. Juilliard.

PENHALL, BRUCE: Balboa, CA, 1958.

PENN, SEAN: California, Aug. 17, 1960.

PENNY, JOE: London, 1957.

PEPPARD, GEORGE: Detroit, Oct. 1, 1928. Carnegie Tech.

PEREZ, JOSE: NYC 1940.

PERKINS, ANTHONY: NYC, Apr. 14, 1932. Rollins College.

PERKINS, ELIZABETH: Queens, NY, Nov. 18, 1960. Goodman School.

PERREAU, GIGI (Ghislaine): Los Angeles, Feb. 6, 1941.

PERRINE, VALERIE: Galveston, TX, Sept. 3, 1944. U. Ariz.

PESCOW, DONNA: Brooklyn, NY, 1954.

PETERS, BERNADETTE (Lazzara): Jamaica, NY, Feb. 28, 1948.

PETERS, BROCK: NYC, July 2, 1927. CCNY.

PETERS, JEAN (Elizabeth): Canton, OH, Oct. 15, 1926. Ohio State U.

PETERS, MICHAEL: Brooklyn, NY, 1948.

PETTET, JOANNA: London, Nov. 16, 1944. Neighborhood Playhouse.

PFEIFFER, MICHELLE: Santa Ana, CA, 1957.

PHILLIPS, MacKENZIE: Hollywood, CA, 1960.

PHILLIPS, MICHELLE (Holly Gilliam): NJ, June 4, 1944.

PHOENIX, RIVER: Madras, Ore., 1970.

PICERNI, PAUL: NYC, Dec. 1, 1922. Loyola U.

PINCHOT, BRONSON: NYC May 20, 1959, Yale.

PINE, PHILLIP: Hanford, CA, July 16, 1925. Actors' Lab.

PISIER, MARIE-FRANCE: Vietnam, May 10, 1944. U. Paris.

PLACE, MARY KAY: Port Arthur, TX, Sept., 1947. U. Tulsa.

PLAYTEN, ALICE: NYC, Aug. 28, 1947. NYU.

PLEASENCE, DONALD: Workshop, Eng., Oct. 5, 1919. Sheffield School.

PLESHETTE, SUZANNE: NYC, Jan. 31, 1937. Syracuse U.

| **Don** | **Jennifer** | **Jameson** | **Alice** | **Dennis** | **Molly** |
| **Nute** | **O'Neill** | **Parker** | **Playten** | **Quaid** | **Ringwald** |

PLOWRIGHT, JOAN: Scunthorpe, Brigg, Lincolnshire, Eng., Oct. 28, 1929. Old Vic.

PLUMB, EVE: Burbank, Ca, Apr. 29, 1958.

PLUMMER, AMANDA: NYC, Mar. 23, 1957. Middlebury Col.

PLUMMER, CHRISTOPHER: Toronto, Can., Dec. 13, 1927.

PODESTA, ROSSANA: Tripoli, June 20, 1934.

POITIER, SIDNEY: Miami, FL, Feb. 27, 1924.

POLITO, LINA: Naples, Italy, Aug. 11, 1954.

POLLARD, MICHAEL J.: Pacific, NJ, May 30, 1939.

PORTER, ERIC: London, Apr. 8, 1928. Wimbledon Col.

POWELL, JANE (Suzanne Burce): Portland, OR, Apr. 1, 1928.

POWELL, ROBERT: Salford, Eng., June 1, 1944. Manchester U.

POWER, TARYN: Los Angeles, CA, 1954.

POWER, TYRONE IV: Los Angeles, CA, Jan. 1959.

POWERS, MALA (Mary Ellen): San Francisco, Dec. 29, 1921. UCLA.

POWERS, STEFANIE (Federkiewicz): Hollywood, CA, Oct. 12, 1942.

PRENTISS, PAULA (Paula Ragusa): San Antonio, TX, Mar. 4, 1939. Northwestern U.

PRESLE, MICHELINE (Micheline Chassagne): Paris, Aug. 22, 1922. Rouleau Drama School.

PRESNELL, HARVE: Modesto, CA, Sept. 14, 1933. USC.

PRESTON, WILLIAM: Columbia, Pa., Aug. 26, 1921. PaStateU.

PRICE, LONNY: NYC, Mar. 9, 1959. Juilliard.

PRICE, VINCENT: St. Louis, May 27, 1911. Yale.

PRIMUS, BARRY: NYC, Feb. 16, 1938. CCNY.

PRINCE (Rogers Nelson): Minneapolis, MN, 1960.

PRINCE, WILLIAM: Nicholas, NY, Jan. 26, 1913. Cornell U.

PRINCIPAL, VICTORIA: Fukuoka, Japan, Mar. 3, 1945. Dade Jr. Col.

PROCHNOW, JURGEN: Germany, 1941.

PROVAL, DAVID: Brooklyn, NY, 1943.

PROVINE, DOROTHY: Deadwood, SD, Jan. 20, 1937. U. Wash.

PROWSE, JULIET: Bombay, India, Sept. 25, 1936.

PRYCE, JONATHAN: Wales, UK, June 1, 1947. RADA.

PRYOR, RICHARD: Peoria, IL, Dec. 1, 1940.

PULLMAN, BILL: Delhi, NY, 1954, SUNY/Oneonta, UMass.

PURCELL, LEE: Cherry Point, NC, June 15, 1947. Stephens.

PURDOM, EDMUND: Welwyn Garden City, Eng., Dec. 19, 1924. St. Ignatius College.

PYLE, DENVER: Bethune, CO, 1920.

QUAID, DENNIS: Houston, TX, Apr. 9, 1954.

QUAID, RANDY: Houston, TX, 1950, UHouston.

QUAYLE, ANTHONY: Lancashire, Eng., Sept. 7, 1913. Old Vic School.

QUINE, RICHARD: Detroit, MI, Nov. 12, 1920.

QUINLAN, KATHLEEN: Mill Valley, CA, Nov. 19, 1954.

QUINN, AIDAN: Chicago, IL, Mar. 8, 1959.

QUINN, ANTHONY: Chihuahua, Mex., Apr. 21, 1915.

RADNER, GILDA: Detroit, MI, June 28, 1946.

RAFFERTY, FRANCES: Sioux City, IA, June 16, 1922. UCLA.

RAFFIN, DEBORAH: Los Angeles, Mar. 13, 1953. Valley Col.

RAINER, LUISE: Vienna, Aust., 1912.

RAINES, ELLA (Ella Wallace): Snoqualmie Falls, WA, Aug. 6, 1921. U. Wash.

RALSTON, VERA: (Vera Helena Hruba) Prague, Czech., July 12, 1919.

RAMPLING, CHARLOTTE: Surmer, Eng., Feb. 5, 1946. U. Madrid.

RAMSEY, LOGAN: Long Beach, CA, Mar. 21, 1921. St. Joseph.

RANDALL, TONY (Leonard Rosenberg): Tulsa, OK, Feb. 26, 1920. Northwestern U.

RANDELL, RON: Sydney, Australia, Oct. 8, 1920. St. Mary's Col.

RASULALA, THALMUS (Jack Crowder): Miami, FL, Nov. 15, 1939. U. Redlands.

RAY, ALDO (Aldo DeRe): Pen Argyl, PA, Sept. 25, 1926. UCLA.

RAYE, MARTHA (Margie Yvonne Reed): Butte, MT, Aug. 27, 1916.

RAYMOND, GENE (Raymond Guion): NYC, Aug. 13, 1908.

REAGAN, RONALD: Tampico, IL, Feb. 6, 1911. Eureka College.

REASON, REX: Berlin, Ger., Nov. 30, 1928. Pasadena Playhouse.

REDDY, HELEN: Australia, Oct. 25, 1942.

REDFORD, ROBERT: Santa Monica, CA, Aug. 18, 1937. AADA.

REDGRAVE, CORIN: London, July 16, 1939.

REDGRAVE, LYNN: London, Mar. 8, 1943.

REDGRAVE, VANESSA: London, Jan. 30, 1937.

REDMAN, JOYCE: County Mayo, Ire., 1919. RADA.

REED, OLIVER: Wimbledon, Eng., Feb. 13, 1938.

REED, REX: Ft. Worth, TX, Oct. 2, 1939. LSU.

REEMS, HARRY (Herbert Streicher): Bronx, NY, 1947. U. Pittsburgh.

REEVE, CHRISTOPHER: NJ, Sept. 25, 1952. Cornell, Juilliard.

REEVES, STEVE: Glasgow, MT, Jan. 21, 1926.

REGEHR, DUNCAN: Lethbridge, Can., 1954.

REID, ELLIOTT: NYC, Jan. 16, 1920.

REINER, CARL: NYC, Mar. 20, 1922. Georgetown.

REINER, ROB: NYC, 1945. UCLA.

REINHOLD, JUDGE (Edward Ernest, Jr.): Wilmington, DE, 1957. NCSchool of Arts.

REINKING, ANN: Seattle, WA, Nov. 10, 1949.

REMAR, JAMES: Boston, Ma., Dec. 31, 1953. Neighborhood Playhouse.

REMICK, LEE: Quincy, MA. Dec. 14, 1935. Barnard College.

RETTIG, TOMMY: Jackson Heights, NY, Dec. 10, 1941.

REVILL, CLIVE: Wellington, NZ, Apr. 18, 1930.

REY, FERNANDO: La Coruna, Spain, Sept. 20, 1917.

REYNOLDS, BURT: Waycross, GA, Feb. 11, 1935. Fla. State U.

REYNOLDS, DEBBIE (Mary Frances Reynolds): El Paso, TX, Apr. 1, 1932.

REYNOLDS, MARJORIE: Buhl, ID, Aug. 12, 1921.

RHOADES, BARBARA: Poughkeepsie, NY, 1947.

RICH, IRENE: Buffalo, NY, Oct. 13, 1891. St. Margaret's School.

RICHARDS, JEFF (Richard Mansfield Taylor): Portland, OR, Nov. 1. USC.

RICKLES, DON: NYC, May 8, 1926. AADA.

RIEGERT, PETER: NYC, Apr. 11, 1947. U Buffalo.

RIGG, DIANA: Doncaster, Eng., July 20, 1938. RADA.

RINGWALD, MOLLY: Sacramento, CA, 1968.

RITTER, JOHN: Burbank, CA, Sept. 17, 1948. U.S. Cal.

RIVERS, JOAN (Molinsky): Brooklyn, NY, June 8, 1933.

ROBARDS, JASON: Chicago, July 26, 1922. AADA.

ROBERTS, ERIC: Biloxi, MS, Apr. 18, 1956. RADA.

ROBERTS, RALPH: Salisbury, NC, Aug. 17, 1922. UNC.

ROBERTS, TANYA (Leigh): NYC, 1955.

ROBERTS, TONY: NYC, Oct. 22, 1939. Northwestern U.

ROBERTSON, CLIFF: La Jolla, CA, Sept. 9, 1925. Antioch Col.

ROBERTSON, DALE: Oklahoma City, July 14, 1923.

ROBINSON, CHRIS: Nov. 5, 1938, West Palm Beach, FL. LACC.

ROBINSON, JAY: NYC, Apr. 14, 1930.

ROBINSON, ROGER: Seattle, WA, May 2, 1941. USC.

ROCHEFORT, JEAN: Paris, 1930.

ROCK-SAVAGE, STEVEN: Melville, LA, Dec. 14, 1958. USC.

ROGERS, CHARLES "BUDDY": Olathe, KS, Aug. 13, 1904. U. Kan.

ROGERS, GINGER (Virginia Katherine McMath): Independence, MO, July 16, 1911.

ROGERS, ROY (Leonard Slye): Cincinnati, Nov. 5, 1912.

ROGERS, WAYNE: Birmingham, AL, Apr. 7, 1933. Princeton.

ROLAND, GILBERT (Luis Antonio Damaso De Alonso): Juarez, Mex., Dec. 11, 1905.

ROLLINS, HOWARD E., JR.: 1951, Baltimore, MD.

ROMAN, RUTH: Boston, Dec. 23, 1922. Bishop Lee Dramatic School.

ROMANCE, VIVIANE (Pauline Ronacher Ortmanns): Vienna, Aust. 1912.

ROME, SIDNE: Akron, OH. Carnegie-Mellon.

ROMERO, CESAR: NYC, Feb. 15, 1907. Collegiate School.

RONSTADT, LINDA: Tucson, AZ, July 15, 1946.

ROONEY, MICKEY (Joe Yule, Jr.): Brooklyn, Sept. 23, 1920.

ROSE, REVA: Chicago, IL, July 30, 1940. Goodman.

ROSS, DIANA: Detroit, MI, Mar. 26, 1944.

ROSS, JUSTIN: Brooklyn, NY, Dec. 15, 1954.

ROSS, KATHARINE: Hollywood, Jan. 29, 1943. Santa Rosa Col.

ROSSELLINI, ISABELLA: Rome, June 18, 1952.

ROUNDTREE, RICHARD: New Rochelle, NY, Sept. 7, 1942. Southern Ill.

ROURKE, MICKEY: Miami, FL, 1950.

ROWE, NICHOLAS: London, Nov. 22, 1966. Eton.

ROWLANDS, GENA: Cambria, WI, June 19, 1934.

RUBIN, ANDREW: New Bedford, MA, June 22, 1946. AADA.

RUBINSTEIN, JOHN: Los Angeles, Ca, Dec. 8, 1946, UCLA.

RUCKER, BO: Tampa, Fl, Aug. 17, 1948.

RUDD, PAUL: Boston, MA, May 15, 1940.

RULE, JANICE: Cincinnati, OH, Aug. 15, 1931.

RUPERT, MICHAEL: Denver, CO, Oct. 23, 1951. Pasadena Playhouse.

RUSH, BARBARA: Denver, CO, Jan. 4, 1929. U. Calif.

RUSSELL, JANE: Bemidji, MI, June 21, 1921. Max Reinhardt School.

RUSSELL, JOHN: Los Angeles, Jan. 3, 1921. U. Calif.

RUSSELL, KURT: Springfield, MA, Mar. 17, 1951.

RUSSO, JAMES: NYC, Apr. 23, 1953.

RUTHERFORD, ANN: Toronto, Can., Nov. 2, 1917.

RUYMEN, AYN: Brooklyn, July 18, 1947. HB Studio.

SACCHI, ROBERT: Bronx, NY, 1941. NYU.

SAINT, EVA MARIE: Newark, NJ, July 4, 1924. Bowling Green State U.

ST. JACQUES, RAYMOND (James Arthur Johnson):CT.

ST. JAMES, SUSAN (Suzie Jane Miller): Los Angeles, Aug. 14, 1946. Conn. Col.

ST. JOHN, BETTA: Hawthorne, CA, Nov. 26, 1929.

ST. JOHN, JILL (Jill Oppenheim): Los Angeles, Aug. 19, 1940.

SALDANA, THERESA: Brooklyn, NY, 1955.

SALINGER, MATT: New Hampshire, 1960. Princeton, Columbia.

SALMI, ALBERT: Coney Island, NY, 1925. Actors Studio.

SALT, JENNIFER: Los Angeles, Sept. 4, 1944. Sarah Lawrence Col.

SANDS, TOMMY: Chicago, Aug. 27, 1937.

SAN JUAN, OLGA: NYC, Mar. 16, 1927.

SARANDON, CHRIS: Beckley, WV, July 24, 1942. U. WVa., Catholic U.

SARANDON, SUSAN (Tomalin): NYC, Oct. 4, 1946. Catholic U.

SARGENT, RICHARD (Richard Cox): Carmel, CA, 1933. Stanford.

SARRAZIN, MICHAEL: Quebec City, Can., May 22, 1940.

SAVAGE, JOHN (Youngs): Long Island, NY, Aug. 25, 1949. AADA.

SAVALAS, TELLY (Aristotle): Garden City, NY, Jan. 21, 1925. Columbia.

SAVIOLA, CAMILLE: Bronx, NY, July 16, 1950.

SAVOY, TERESA ANN: London, July 18, 1955.

SAXON, JOHN (Carmen Orrico): Brooklyn, Aug. 5, 1935.

SCALIA, JACK: Brooklyn, NY, 1951.

SCARPELLI, GLEN: Staten Island, NY, July 1966.

SCARWID, DIANA: Savannah, GA. AADA, Pace U.

SCHEIDER, ROY: Orange, NJ, Nov. 10, 1932. Franklin-Marshall.

SCHEINE, RAYNOR: Emporia, Va., Nov. 10th. VaCommonwealthU.

SCHELL, MARIA: Vienna, Jan. 15, 1926.

SCHELL, MAXIMILIAN: Vienna, Dec. 8, 1930.

SCHNEIDER, MARIA: Paris, Mar. 27, 1952.

SCHRODER, RICKY: Staten Island, NY, Apr. 13, 1970.

SCHWARZENEGGER, ARNOLD: Austria, July 30, 1947.

SCHYGULLA, HANNA: Katlowitz, Poland. 1943.

SCOFIELD, PAUL: Hurstpierpoint, Eng., Jan. 21, 1922. London Mask Theatre School.

SCOTT, DEBRALEE: Elizabeth, NJ, Apr. 2.

SCOTT, GEORGE C.: Wise, VA, Oct. 18, 1927. U. Mo.

SCOTT, GORDON (Gordon M. Werschkul): Portland, OR, Aug. 3, 1927. Oregon U.

SCOTT, LIZABETH (Emma Matso): Scranton, Pa., Sept. 29, 1922.

SCOTT, MARTHA: Jamesport, MO, Sept. 22, 1914. U. Mich.

SCOTT-TAYLOR, JONATHAN: Brazil, 1962.

SEAGULL, BARBARA HERSHEY (Herzstein): Hollywood, Feb. 5, 1948.

SEARS, HEATHER: London, Sept. 28, 1935.

SECOMBE, HARRY: Swansea, Wales, Sept. 8, 1921.

SEGAL, GEORGE: NYC, Feb. 13, 1934. Columbia.

SELLARS, ELIZABETH: Glasgow, Scot., May 6, 1923.

SELLECK, TOM: Detroit, MI, Jan. 29, 1945.

SELWART, TONIO: Watenberg, Ger., June 9, 1906. Munich U.

SERNAS, JACQUES: Lithuania, July 30, 1925.

SERRAULT, MICHEL: Brunoy, France, 1928, Paris Consv.

SETH, ROSHAN: New Delhi, India, 1942.

SEYLER, ATHENE (Athene Hannen): London, May 31, 1889.

SEYMOUR, ANNE: NYC, Sept. 11, 1909. American Laboratory Theatre.

SEYMOUR, JANE (Joyce Frankenberg): Hillingdon, Eng., Feb. 15, 1951.

SEYRIG, DELPHINE: Beirut, 1932.

SHANDLING, GARRY: Tucson, Az, 1951, UAz.

SHARIF, OMAR (Michel Shalhoub): Alexandria, Egypt, Apr. 10, 1932. Victoria Col.

SHARKEY, RAY: Brooklyn, NY, 1952. HB Studio.

SHATNER, WILLIAM: Montreal, Can., Mar. 22, 1931. McGill U.

SHAVER, HELEN: St. Thomas, Ontario, Can., 1951.

SHAW, SEBASTIAN: Holt, Eng., May 29, 1905. Gresham School.

SHAW, STAN: Chicago, IL, 1952.

SHAWLEE, JOAN: Forest Hills, NY, Mar. 5, 1929.

SHAWN, DICK (Richard Shulefand): Buffalo, NY, Dec. 1, 1929. U. Miami.

SHEA, JOHN V.: North Conway, NH, Apr. 14, 1949. Bates, Yale.

SHEARER, MOIRA: Dunfermline, Scot., Jan. 17, 1926. London Theatre School.

SHEEDY, ALLY: NYC, June 13, 1962. USC.

SHEEN, CHARLIE (Carlos Irwin Estevez): Los Angeles, Ca., 1966.

SHEEN, MARTIN (Ramon Estevez): Dayton, OH, Aug. 3, 1940.

SHEFFIELD, JOHN: Pasadena, CA, Apr. 11, 1931. UCLA.

SHEPARD, SAM (Rogers): Ft. Sheridan, IL, Nov. 5, 1943.

SHEPHERD, CYBIL: Memphis, TN, Feb. 18, 1950. Hunter, NYU.

SHIELDS, BROOKE: NYC, May 31, 1965.

SHIRE, TALIA: Lake Success, NY, Apr. 25, 1946, Yale.

SHORE, DINAH (Frances Rose Shore): Winchester, TN, Mar. 1, 1917. Vanderbilt U.

SHORT, MARTIN: Toronto, Can, 1950, McMasterU.

SHOWALTER, MAX (formerly Casey Adams): Caldwell, KS, June 2, 1917. Pasadena Playhouse.

SIDNEY, SYLVIA: NYC, Aug. 8, 1910. Theatre Guild School.

Cliff Robertson

Diana Ross

James Russo

Ally Sheedy

Terence Stamp

Stella Stevens

SILVER, RON: NYC, July 2, 1946. SUNY.

SILVERMAN, JONATHAN: Los Angeles, Ca, Aug. 5, 1966, USCal.

SIMMONS, JEAN: London, Jan. 31, 1929. Aida Foster School.

SIMON, SIMONE: Marseilles, France, Apr. 23, 1910.

SIMPSON, O. J. (Orenthal James): San Francisco, CA, July 9, 1947. UCLA.

SINATRA, FRANK: Hoboken, NJ, Dec. 12, 1915.

SINCLAIR, JOHN (Gianluigi Loffredo): Rome, Italy, 1946.

SINDEN, DONALD: Plymouth, Eng., Oct. 9, 1923. Webber-Douglas.

SINGER, LORI: NYC, 1962, Juilliard.

SKALA, LILIA: Vienna. U. Dresden.

SKELTON, RED (Richard): Vincennes, IN, July 18, 1910.

SKERRITT, TOM: Detroit, MI, 1935. Wayne State U.

SLATER, HELEN: NYC, Dec. 15, 1965.

SMITH, ALEXIS: Penticton, Can., June 8, 1921. LACC.

SMITH, CHARLES MARTIN: Los Angeles, CA, 1954. CalState U.

SMITH, JACLYN: Houston, TX, Oct. 26, 1947.

SMITH, JOHN (Robert E. Van Orden): Los Angeles, Mar. 6, 1931. UCLA.

SMITH, LEWIS: Chattanooga, Tn, 1958. Actors Studio.

SMITH, LOIS: Topeka, KS, Nov. 3, 1930. U. Wash.

SMITH, MAGGIE: Ilford, Eng., Dec. 28, 1934.

SMITH, ROGER: South Gate, CA, Dec. 18, 1932. U. Ariz.

SMITHERS, WILLIAM: Richmond, VA, July 10, 1927. Catholic U.

SNODGRESS, CARRIE: Chicago, Oct. 27, 1946. UNI.

SOLOMON, BRUCE: NYC, 1944. U. Miami, Wayne State U.

SOMERS, SUZANNE (Mahoney): San Bruno, CA, Oct. 16, 1946. Lone Mt. Col.

SOMMER, ELKE (Schletz): Berlin, Nov. 5, 1940.

SORDI, ALBERTO: Rome, Italy, June 15, 1919.

SORVINO, PAUL: NYC, 1939. AMDA.

SOTHERN, ANN (Harriet Lake): Valley City, ND, Jan. 22, 1907. Washington U.

SOUL, DAVID: Aug. 28, 1943.

SPACEK, SISSY: Quitman, TX, Dec. 25, 1949. Actors Studio.

SPANO, VINCENT: Brooklyn, NY, Oct. 18, 1962.

SPENSER, JEREMY: Ceylon, 1937.

SPRINGER, GARY: NYC, July 29, 1954. Hunter Col.

SPRINGFIELD, RICK (Richard Springthorpe): Sydney, Aust. Aug. 23, 1949.

STACK, ROBERT: Los Angeles, Jan. 13, 1919. USC.

STADLEN, LEWIS J.: Brooklyn, Mar. 7, 1947. Neighborhood Playhouse.

STAFFORD, NANCY: Ft. Lauderdale, FL.

STALLONE, FRANK: NYC, July 30, 1950.

STALLONE, SYLVESTER: NYC, July 6, 1946. U. Miami.

STAMP, TERENCE: London, July 23, 1939.

STANDER, LIONEL: NYC, Jan. 11, 1908. UNC.

STANG, ARNOLD: Chelsea, MA, Sept. 28, 1925.

STANLEY, KIM (Patricia Reid): Tularosa, NM, Feb. 11, 1925. U. Tex.

STANWYCK, BARBARA (Ruby Stevens): Brooklyn, July 16, 1907.

STAPLETON, JEAN: NYC, Jan. 19, 1923.

STAPLETON, MAUREEN: Troy, NY, June 21, 1925.

STEEL, ANTHONY: London, May 21, 1920. Cambridge.

STEELE, TOMMY: London, Dec. 17, 1936.

STEENBURGEN, MARY: Newport, AR, 1953. Neighborhood Playhouse.

STEIGER, ROD: Westhampton, NY, Apr. 14, 1925.

STERLING, JAN (Jane Sterling Adriance): NYC, Apr. 3, 1923. Fay Compton School.

STERLING, ROBERT (William Sterling Hart): Newcastle, PA, Nov. 13, 1917. U. Pittsburgh.

STERN, DANIEL: Bethesda, MD, 1957.

STEVENS, ANDREW: Memphis, TN, June 10, 1955.

STEVENS, CONNIE (Concetta Ann Ingolia): Brooklyn, Aug. 8, 1938. Hollywood Professional School.

STEVENS, FISHER: Chicago, IL, Nov. 27, 1963. NYU.

STEVENS, KAYE (Catherine): Pittsburgh, July 21, 1933.

STEVENS, MARK (Richard): Cleveland, OH, Dec. 13, 1920.

STEVENS, STELLA (Estelle Eggleston): Hot Coffee, MS, Oct. 1, 1936.

STEVENSON, PARKER: CT, June 4, 1953, Princeton.

STEWART, ALEXANDRIA: Montreal, Can., June 10, 1939. Louvre.

STEWART, ELAINE: Montclair, NJ, May 31, 1929.

STEWART, JAMES: Indiana, PA, May 20, 1908. Princeton.

STEWART, MARTHA (Martha Haworth): Bardwell, KY, Oct. 7, 1922.

STIMSON, SARA: Helotes, TX, 1973.

STING (Gordon Matthew Sumner): Wallsend, Eng., 1951.

STOCKWELL, DEAN: Hollywood, Mar. 5, 1935.

STOCKWELL, JOHN: Texas, 1961. Harvard.

STOLER, SHIRLEY: Brooklyn, NY, Mar. 30, 1929.

STOLTZ, ERIC: California, 1961, USC.

STORM, GALE (Josephine Cottle): Bloomington, TX, Apr. 5, 1922.

STRAIGHT, BEATRICE: Old Westbury, NY, Aug. 2, 1916. Dartington Hall.

STRASBERG, SUSAN: NYC, May 22, 1938.

STRASSMAN, MARCIA: New Jersey, 1949.

STRAUSS, PETER: NY, 1947.

STREEP, MERYL (Mary Louise): Summit, NJ, June 22, 1949., Vassar, Yale.

STREISAND, BARBRA: Brooklyn, Apr. 24, 1942.

STRITCH, ELAINE: Detroit, MI, Feb. 2, 1925. Drama Workshop.

STRODE, WOODY: Los Angeles, 1914.

STROUD, DON: Hawaii, 1937.

STRUTHERS, SALLY: Portland, OR, July 28, 1948. Pasadena Playhouse.

SULLIVAN, BARRY (Patrick Barry): NYC, Aug. 29, 1912. NYU.

SUMMER, DONNA (LaDonna Gaines): Boston, MA, Dec. 31, 1948.

SUTHERLAND, DONALD: St. John, New Brunswick, Can., July 17, 1934. U. Toronto.

SVENSON, BO: Goteborg, Swed., Feb. 13, 1941. UCLA.

SWINBURNE, NORA: Bath, Eng., July 24, 1902. RADA.

SWIT, LORETTA: Passaic, NJ, Nov. 4. AADA.

SYLVESTER, WILLIAM: Oakland, CA, Jan. 31, 1922. RADA.

SYMONDS, ROBERT: Bistow, AK, Dec. 1, 1926. TexU.

SYMS, SYLVIA: London, June 1, 1934. Convent School.

SZARABAJKA, KEITH: Oak Park, IL, Dec. 2, 1952, UChicago.

T, MR. (Lawrence Tero): Chicago, 1952.

TABORI, KRISTOFFER (Siegel): Los Angeles, Aug. 4, 1952.

TAKEI, GEORGE: Los Angeles, CA, Apr. 20. UCLA.

TALBOT, LYLE (Lysle Hollywood): Pittsburgh, Feb. 8, 1904.

TALBOT, NITA: NYC, Aug. 8, 1930. Irvine Studio School.

TAMBLYN, RUSS: Los Angeles, Dec. 30, 1934.

TANDY, JESSICA: London, June 7, 1909. Dame Owens' School.

TAYLOR, DON: Freeport, PA, Dec. 13, 1920. Penn State U.

TAYLOR, ELIZABETH: London, Feb. 27, 1932. Byron House School.

TAYLOR, ROD (Robert): Sydney, Aust., Jan. 11, 1929.

TAYLOR-YOUNG, LEIGH: Wash., DC, Jan. 25, 1945. Northwestern.

TEAGUE, ANTHONY SKOOTER: Jacksboro, TX, Jan. 4, 1940.

TEAGUE, MARSHALL: Newport, Tn.

TEEFY, MAUREEN: Minneapolis, MN, 1954; Juilliard.

TEMPLE, SHIRLEY: Santa Monica, CA, Apr. 23, 1927.

TERRY-THOMAS (Thomas Terry Hoar Stevens): Finchley, London, July 14, 1911. Ardingly College.

TERZIEFF, LAURENT: Paris, June 25, 1935.

THACKER, RUSS: Washington, DC, June 23, 1946, Montgomery Col.

THAXTER, PHYLLIS: Portland, ME, Nov. 20, 1921. St. Genevieve.

THELEN, JODI: St. Cloud, MN., 1963.

THOMAS, DANNY (Amos Jacobs): Deerfield, MI, Jan. 6, 1914.

THOMAS, MARLO (Margaret): Detroit, Nov. 21, 1938. USC.

THOMAS, PHILIP MICHAEL: Columbus, OH, May 26, 1949. Oakwood Col.

THOMAS, RICHARD: NYC, June 13, 1951. Columbia.

THOMPSON, JACK (John Payne): Sydney, Aus., 1940. U. Brisbane.

THOMPSON, MARSHALL: Peoria, IL, Nov. 27, 1925. Occidental.

THOMPSON, REX: NYC, Dec. 14, 1942.

THOMPSON, SADA: Des Moines, IA, Sept. 27, 1929. Carnegie Tech.

THOMSON, GORDON: Ottawa, Can., 1945.

THULIN, INGRID: Solleftea, Sweden, Jan. 27, 1929. Royal Drama Theatre.

TICOTIN, RACHEL: Bronx, NY, 1958.

TIERNEY, GENE: Brooklyn, Nov. 20, 1920. Miss Farmer's School.

TIERNEY, LAWRENCE: Brooklyn, Mar. 15, 1919. Manhattan College.

TIFFIN, PAMELA (Wonso): Oklahoma City, Oct. 13, 1942.

TILLY, MEG: Texada, Can., 1960.

TODD, ANN: Hartford, Eng., Jan. 24, 1909.

TODD, RICHARD: Dublin, Ire., June 11, 1919. Shrewsbury School.

TOGNAZZI, UGO: Cremona, Italy, 1922.

TOLO, MARILU: Rome, Italy, 1944.

TOMEI, MARISA: Brooklyn, NY, Dec. 4, 1964, NYU.

TOMLIN, LILY: Detroit, MI, Sept. 1, 1939. Wayne State U.

TOPOL (Chaim Topol): Tel-Aviv, Israel, Sept. 9, 1935.

TORN, RIP: Temple, TX, Feb. 6, 1931. U. Tex.

TORRES, LIZ: NYC, 1947. NYU.

TOTTER, AUDREY: Joliet, IL, Dec. 20, 1918.

TOWSEND, ROBERT: Chicago, 1966.

TRAVERS, BILL: Newcastle-on-Tyne, Engl, Jan. 3, 1922.

TRAVIS, RICHARD (William Justice): Carlsbad, NM, Apr. 17, 1913.

TRAVOLTA, JOEY: Englewood, NJ, 1952.

TRAVOLTA, JOHN: Englewood, NJ, Feb. 18, 1954.

TREMAYNE, LES: London, Apr. 16, 1913. Northwestern, Columbia, UCLA.

TREVOR, CLAIRE (Wemlinger): NYC, March 8, 1909.

TRINTIGNANT, JEAN-LOUIS: Pont-St. Esprit, France, Dec. 11, 1930. Dullin-Balachova Drama School.

TRYON, TOM: Hartford, CT, Jan. 14, 1926. Yale.

TSOPEI, CORINNA: Athens, Greece, June 21, 1944.

TUBB, BARRY: 1963, Snyder, Tx., AmConsv.Th.

TURNER, KATHLEEN: Springfield, MO, June 19, 1954. UMd.

TURNER, LANA (Julia Jean Mildred Frances Turner): Wallace, ID, Feb. 8, 1921.

TURNER, TINA: (Anna Mae Bullock) Nutbush, Tn, Nov. 25, 1939.

TURTURRO, John: Brooklyn, NY, Feb. 28, 1957, Yale.

TUSHINGHAM, RITA: Liverpool, Eng., 1940.

TUTIN, DOROTHY: London, Apr. 8, 1930.

TWIGGY (Lesley Hornby): London, Sept. 19, 1949.

TWOMEY, ANNE: Boston, Ma, June 7, 1951, Temple U.

TYLER, BEVERLY (Beverly Jean Saul): Scranton, PA, July 5, 1928.

TYRRELL, SUSAN: San Francisco, 1946.

TYSON, CATHY: Liverpool, Eng., 1966, RoyalShakeCo.

TYSON, CICELY: NYC, Dec. 19, 1933, NYU.

UGGAMS, LESLIE: NYC, May 25, 1943, Juilliard.

ULLMANN, LIV: Tokyo, Dec. 10, 1938. Webber-Douglas Acad.

USTINOV, PETER: London, Apr. 16, 1921. Westminster School.

VACCARO, BRENDA: Brooklyn, Nov. 18, 1939. Neighborhood Playhouse.

VALANDREY, CHARLOTTE: (Anne-Charlotte Pascal) Paris, 1968.

VALLI, ALIDA: Pola, Italy, May 31, 1921. Rome Academy of Drama.

VALLONE, RAF: Riogio, Italy, Feb. 17, 1916. Turin U.

VAN CLEEF, LEE: Somerville, NJ, Jan. 9, 1925.

VAN DE VEN, MONIQUE: Holland, 1957.

VAN DEVERE, TRISH (Patricia Dressel): Englewood Cliffs, NJ, Mar. 9, 1945. Ohio Wesleyan.

VAN DOREN, MAMIE (Joan Lucile Olander): Rowena, SD, Feb. 6, 1933.

VAN DYKE, DICK: West Plains, MO, Dec. 13, 1925.

VAN FLEET, JO: Oakland, CA, Dec. 30, 1919.

VAN PATTEN, DICK: NYC, Dec. 9, 1928.

VAN PATTEN, JOYCE: NYC, Mar. 9, 1934.

VAUGHN, ROBERT: NYC, Nov. 22, 1932. USC.

VEGA, ISELA: Mexico, 1940.

VENNERA, CHICK: Herkimer, NY, Mar. 27, 1952. Pasadena Playhouse.

VENORA, DIANE: Hartford, Ct., 1952. Juilliard.

VENTURA, LINO: Parma, Italy, July 14, 1919.

VENUTA, BENAY: San Francisco, Jan. 27, 1911.

VERDON, GWEN: Culver City, CA, Jan. 13, 1925.

VEREEN, BEN: Miami, FL, Oct. 10, 1946.

VICTOR, JAMES (Lincoln Rafael Peralta Diaz): Santiago, D.R., July 27, 1939. Haaren HS/NYC.

VILLECHAIZE, HERVE: Paris, Apr. 23, 1943.

VINCENT, JAN-MICHAEL: Denver, CO, July 15, 1944. Ventura.

VIOLET, ULTRA (Isabelle Collin-Dufresne): Grenoble, France.

VITALE, MILLY: Rome, Italy, July 16, 1938. Lycee Chateaubriand.

VOHS, JOAN: St. Albans, NY, July 30, 1931.

VOIGHT, JON: Yonkers, NY, Dec. 29, 1938. Catholic U.

VOLONTE, GIAN MARIA: Milan, Italy, Apr. 9, 1933.

VON DOHLEN, LENNY: Augusta, Ga., Dec. 22, 1958, UTex.

VON SYDOW, MAX: Lund, Swed., July 10, 1929. Royal Drama Theatre.

WAGNER, LINDSAY: Los Angeles, June 22, 1949.

WAGNER, ROBERT: Detroit, Feb. 10, 1930.

WAHL, KEN: Chicago, IL, 1957.

WAITE, GENEVIEVE: South Africa, 1949.

WALKEN, CHRISTOPHER: Astoria, NY, Mar. 31, 1943. Hofstra.

WALKER, CLINT: Hartfold, IL, May 30, 1927. USC.

WALKER, NANCY (Ann Myrtle Swoyer): Philadelphia, May 10, 1921.

WALLACH, ELI: Brooklyn, Dec. 7, 1915. CCNY, U. Tex.

WALLACH, ROBERTA: NYC, Aug. 2, 1955.

WALLIS, SHANI: London, Apr. 5, 1941.

WALSH, M. EMMET: Ogdensburg, NY, Mar. 22, 1935, Clarkson Col., AADA.

WALSTON, RAY: New Orleans, Nov. 22, 1917. Cleveland Playhouse.

WALTER, JESSICA: Brooklyn, NY, Jan. 31, 1940. Neighborhood Playhouse.

WALTON, EMMA: London, Nov. 1962, Brown U.

WANAMAKER, SAM: Chicago, June 14, 1919. Drake.

WARD, BURT (Gervis): Los Angeles, July 6, 1945.

WARD, FRED: San Diego, Ca.

WARD, RACHEL: London, 1957.

WARD, SIMON: London, 1941.

WARDEN, JACK: Newark, NJ, Sept. 18, 1920.

WARNER, DAVID: Manchester, Eng., 1941. RADA.

Rachel Ticotin	Peter Ustinov	Brenda Vaccaro	Paul Winfield	Susannah York	Efrem Zimbalist, Jr.

WARREN, JENNIFER: NYC, Aug. 12, 1941. U. Wisc.

WARREN, LESLEY ANN: NYC, Aug. 16, 1946.

WARREN, MICHAEL: South Bend, IN, 1946. UCLA.

WARRICK, RUTH: St. Joseph, MO, June 29, 1915. U. Mo.

WASHBOURNE, MONA: Birmingham, Eng., Nov. 27, 1903.

WASHINGTON, DENZEL: Mt. Vernon, NY, Dec. 28, 1954. Fordham.

WASSON, CRAIG: Ontario, OR, Mar. 15, 1954. UOre.

WATERSTON, SAM: Cambridge, MA, Nov. 15, 1940. Yale.

WATLING, JACK: London, Jan. 13, 1923. Italia Conti School.

WATSON, DOUGLASS: Jackson, GA, Feb. 24, 1921. UNC.

WAYNE, DAVID (Wayne McKeehan): Travers City, MI, Jan. 30, 1914. Western Michigan State U.

WAYNE, PATRICK: Los Angeles, July 15, 1939. Loyola.

WEATHERS, CARL: New Orleans, LA, 1948. Long Beach CC.

WEAVER, DENNIS: Joplin, MO, June 4, 1924. U. Okla.

WEAVER, MARJORIE: Crossville, TN, Mar. 2, 1913. Indiana U.

WEAVER, SIGOURNEY (Susan): NYC, 1949. Stanford, Yale.

WEBBER, ROBERT: Santa Ana, CA, Sept. 14, 1925. Compton Jr. Col.

WEDGEWORTH, ANN: Abilene, TX, Jan. 21, 1935. U. Tex.

WELCH, RAQUEL (Tejada): Chicago, Sept. 5, 1940.

WELD, TUESDAY (Susan): NYC, Aug. 27, 1943. Hollywood Professional School.

WELDON, JOAN: San Francisco, Aug. 5, 1933. San Francisco Conservatory.

WELLER, PETER: Stevens Point, Ws., June 24, 1947. AmThWing.

WELLES, GWEN: NYC, Mar. 4.

WESTON, JACK (Morris Weinstein): Cleveland, OH, Aug. 21, 1915.

WHITAKER, JOHNNY: Van Nuys, CA, Dec. 13, 1959.

WHITE, BETTY: Oak Park, IL, Jan. 17, 1922.

WHITE, CAROL: London, Apr. 1, 1944.

WHITE, CHARLES: Perth Amboy, NJ, Aug. 29, 1920. Rutgers U.

WHITE, JESSE: Buffalo, NY, Jan. 3, 1919.

WHITMAN, STUART: San Francisco, Feb. 1, 1929. CCLA

WHITMORE, JAMES: White Plains, NY, Oct. 1, 1921. Yale.

WHITNEY, GRACE LEE: Detroit, MI, Apr. 1, 1930.

WHITTON, MARGARET: Philadelphia, PA., Nov. 30.

WIDDOES, KATHLEEN: Wilmington, DE, Mar. 21, 1939.

WIDMARK, RICHARD: Sunrise, MN, Dec. 26, 1914. Lake Forest.

WIEST, DIANNE: Kansas City, MO, Mar. 28, 1948. UMd.

WILCOX, COLIN: Highlands, NC, Feb. 4, 1937. U. Tenn.

WILDE, CORNEL: NYC, Oct. 13, 1915. CCNY, Columbia.

WILDER, GENE (Jerome Silberman): Milwaukee, Ws., June 11, 1935. UIowa.

WILLIAMS, BILLY DEE: NYC, Apr. 6, 1937.

WILLIAMS, CINDY: Van Nuys, CA, Aug. 22, 1947. LACC.

WILLIAMS, DICK A.: Chicago, IL, Aug. 9, 1938.

WILLIAMS, EMLYN: Mostyn, Wales, Nov. 26, 1905. Oxford.

WILLIAMS, ESTHER: Los Angeles, Aug. 8, 1921.

WILLIAMS, JOBETH: Houston, Tx. BrownU.

WILLIAMS, ROBIN: Chicago, IL, July 21, 1952. Juilliard.

WILLIAMS, TREAT (Richard): Rowayton, CT. Jan. 1952.

WILLIAMSON, FRED: Gary, IN, Mar. 5, 1938. Northwestern.

WILLIAMSON, NICOL: Hamilton, Scot; Sept. 14, 1938.

WILLIS, BRUCE: Penns Grove, NJ, Mar. 18, 1956.

WILLISON, WALTER: Monterey Park, CA., June 24, 1947. LACC.

WILSON, DEMOND: NYC, Oct. 13, 1946. Hunter Col.

WILSON, FLIP (Clerow Wilson): Jersey City, NJ, Dec. 8, 1933.

WILSON, LAMBERT: Paris, 1959.

WILSON, NANCY: Chillicothe, OH, Feb. 20, 1937.

WILSON, SCOTT: Atlanta, GA, 1942.

WINCOTT, JEFF: Toronto, Can., 1957, Juilliard.

WINDE, BEATRICE: Chicago, Jan. 6.

WINDOM, WILLIAM: NYC, Sept. 28, 1923. Williams Col.

WINDSOR, MARIE (Emily Marie Bertelson): Marysvale, UT, Dec. 11, 1924. Brigham Young U.

WINFIELD, PAUL: Los Angeles, 1940. UCLA.

WINFREY, OPRAH: Kosciusko, Ms., 1953. TnStateU.

WINGER, DEBRA: Cleveland, OH, May 17, 1955. Cal State.

WINKLER, HENRY: NYC, Oct. 30, 1945. Yale.

WINN, KITTY: Wash., D.C., 1944. Boston U.

WINTERS, JONATHAN: Dayton, OH, Nov. 11, 1925. Kenyon Col.

WINTERS, ROLAND: Boston, Nov. 22, 1904.

WINTERS, SHELLEY (Shirley Schrift): St. Louis, Aug. 18, 1922. Wayne U.

WITHERS, GOOGIE: Karachi, India, Mar. 12, 1917. Italia Conti.

WITHERS, JANE: Atlanta, GA, Apr. 12, 1926.

WOODLAWN, HOLLY (Harold Ajzenberg): Juana Diaz, PR, 1947.

WOODS, JAMES: Vernal, UT, Apr. 18, 1947. MIT.

WOODWARD, EDWARD: England, 1930

WOODWARD, JOANNE: Thomasville, GA, Feb. 27, 1930. Neighborhood Playhouse.

WOOLAND, NORMAN: Dusseldorf, Ger., Mar. 16, 1910. Edward VI School.

WOPAT, TOM: Lodi, WI, Sept. 9, 1951, UWis.

WORONOV, MARY: Brooklyn, Dec. 8, 1946. Cornell.

WORTH, IRENE: (Hattie Abrams) June 23, 1916. Neb. UCLA.

WRAY, FAY: Alberta, Can., Sept. 15, 1907.

WRIGHT, MAX: Detroit, MI, Aug. 2, 1943, WayneStateU.

WRIGHT, TERESA: NYC, Oct. 27, 1918.

WYATT, JANE: Campgaw, NJ, Aug. 10, 1911. Barnard College.

WYMAN, JANE (Sarah Jane Fulks): St. Joseph, MO, Jan. 4, 1914.

WYMORE, PATRICE: Miltonvale, KS, Dec. 17, 1926.

WYNN, MAY (Donna Lee Hickey): NYC, Jan. 8, 1930.

WYNTER, DANA (Dagmar): London, June 8, 1927. Rhodes U.

YORK, DICK: Fort Wayne, IN, Sept. 4, 1928. De Paul U.

YORK, MICHAEL: Fulmer, Eng., Mar. 27, 1942. Oxford.

YORK, SUSANNAH: London, Jan. 9, 1941. RADA.

YOUNG, ALAN (Angus): North Shield, Eng., Nov. 19, 1919.

YOUNG, BURT: Queens, NY, Apr. 30, 1940.

YOUNG, LORETTA (Gretchen): Salt Lake City, Jan. 6, 1912. Immaculate Heart College.

YOUNG, ROBERT: Chicago, Feb. 22, 1907.

ZACHARIAS, ANN: Stockholm, Sw., 1956.

ZADORA, PIA: Forest Hills, NY. 1954.

ZETTERLING, MAI: Sweden, May 27, 1925. Ordtuery Theatre School.

ZIMBALIST, EFREM, JR.: NYC, Nov. 30, 1918. Yale.

Brian Aherne

Robert Alda

Heather Angel

Desi Arnaz

Edith Atwater

Hermione Baddeley

1986 OBITUARIES

BRIAN AHERNE, 83, British-born actor who played the classic handsome leading man in films and on stage, died of heart failure on Feb. 10, 1986 in Venice, Fla. He made his acting debut at age 8 in his native England in a pantomime with Noel Coward. He appeared on stage most frequently with Katharine Cornell, and made 37 films, including *The Eleventh Commandment, Shooting Stars, I Was a Spy, Song of Songs, What Every Woman Knows, The Constant Nymph, Sylvia Scarlett, Beloved Enemy, The Great Garrick, Merrily We Live, Juarez, My Son My Son, The Lady in Question, Skylark, My Sister Eileen, I Confess, The Swan, The Best of Everything,* and *Lancelot and Guinevere.* He is survived by his wife whom he married in 1946.

ROBERT ALDA, 72, Manhattan-born actor, died May 3, 1986 at his home in Los Angeles as a result of a stroke he suffered two years prior. His films include *Rhapsody in Blue, Cinderella Jones, Cloak and Dagger, The Man I Love, April Showers, Tarzan and the Slave Girl, Imitation of Life, Cleopatra's Daughter,* and *The Girl Who Knew Too Much,* and for his Broadway debut in *Guys and Dolls* in 1950, he won the Tony, Drama Critics Circle and Donaldson Awards. He is survived by his second wife, two sons, actors Alan and Antony Alda, a brother, and sister.

HEATHER ANGEL, 77, British-born film, stage, and TV actress died Dec. 13, 1986 of cancer in Santa Barbara, CA. She appeared in more than 60 films, most notably *Pilgrimage, Berkeley Square, The Mystery of Edwin Drood, The Informer, Pride and Prejudice, That Hamilton Woman, Suspicion,* and *Lifeboat.* Also, *Hound of the Baskervilles, The Three Musketeers, The Orient Express, Springtime for Henry, Last of the Mohicans, Cry Havoc,* the *Bulldog Drummond* series, and *Premature Burial* in 1962. She is survived by her son and sister.

HAROLD ARLEN, 81, one of America's greatest songwriters, died on April 23, 1986 in his New York apartment. The Buffalo-born composer penned more than 500 songs for stage and screen in collaboration with lyricists E. Y. Harburg, Johnny Mercer, and Ira Gershwin. He contributed scores for 24 films, including *Let's Fall in Love, Star-Spangled Rhythm, The Sky's the Limit, Here Come the Waves, Rio Rita, Take a Chance, The Singing Kid, Blues in the Night, Cabin in the Sky, Out Of This World, Casbah, My Blue Heaven, Mr. Imperium, The Country Girl, A Star Is Born* (Judy Garland version), and *The Wizard of Oz* featuring "Over the Rainbow," for which he and collaborator Yip Harburg received an Oscar in 1939. He is survived by a son and a brother.

DESI ARNAZ, 69, Cuban-born film-stage-TV actor, bandleader, and pioneer TV Producer, died on Dec. 2, 1986 in the arms of his daughter, actress Lucie Arnaz, at his home in Del Mar, CA. He is forever identified with his role of Ricky Ricardo, opposite his then-wife Lucille Ball in the *I Love Lucy* TV series of the 1950's, He is credited by many, including Ball, as being the genius behind the series success. He eventually spearheaded their Desilu Productions, a high-powered Hollywood studio between 1957 and 1967 (now Paramount Television). As an actor, Arnaz's film credits include *Too Many Girls, Four Jacks and a Jill, Father Takes a Wife, The Navy Comes Through, Bataan, Cuban Pete, Holiday in Havana,* and, with Ball, *The Long, Long Trailer* and *Forever Darling.* He is survived by his daughter, son, actor Desi Arnaz Jr., and three grandchildren.

ROBERT ARTHUR, 77, New York-born veteran film producer and screenwriter died Oct. 28, 1986 in Beverly Hills, CA after a long illness. His film credits as writer include *New Moon* and *Chip off the Old Block,* and he produced such films as the *Francis* series, *The Story of Will Rogers, The Big Heat, The Long Gray Line, A Time to Love and A Time to Die, Operation Petticoat, Lover Come Back, That Touch of Mink, Buck Privates Come Home, Abbott & Costello Meet Frankenstein, Mexican Hayride, Louisa, The Man of a Thousand Faces, The Great Imposter, Come September, Father Goose, Shenandoah, A Man Could Get Killed, Sweet Charity,* and *One More Train to Rob.* Survivors include his widow and brother.

EDITH ATWATER, 74, film, stage, and TV actress, died of cancer on March 14, 1986 at Cedars Sinai in Los Angeles, CA. The original Maggie Cutler in *The Man Who Came to Dinner* on Broadway, her film credits include *We Went to College, The Gorgeous Hussey, The Body Snatcher, C-Man, Teresa, Sweet Smell of Success, Sweet Bird of Youth, Take Me to the Fair, It Happened at the World's Fair, Straight-Jacket, Strange Bedfellows, True Grit, Norwood, Pieces of Dreams, Zabriskie Point, The Love Machine, Our Time, Mackintosh & T.J.,* and *Family Plot.* She was the widow of actor Kent Smith, who died last year.

HERMIONE BADDELEY, 77, England-born film, stage, and TV actress and comedienne, died Aug. 19, 1986 in Los Angeles, CA of complications from a stroke. Although perhaps best remembered for her role as Mrs. Naugatuck on the TV series *Maude,* she appeared in 22 films including *The Guns of Loos, Caste, Kipps, Brighton Rock, Passport to Pimlico, Quartet, Hell is Sold Out, A Christmas Carol, The Pickwick Papers, The Belles of St. Trinian's, Room at the Top* (for which she received an Academy Award Nomination), *Midnight Lace, The Unsinkable Molly Brown, Mary Poppins, Harlow, Marriage on the Rocks, Do Not Disturb, Casino Royale, The Adventures of Bullwhip Griffin, The Happiest Millionaire, The Black Windmill,* and *C.H.O.M.P.S.* She is survived by her daughter, a son and a sister.

ELISABETH BERGNER, 85, Vienna-born international screen and stage star, died May 12, 1986 in London after a long illness. Her films include *Der Evangelimann, Der Traumende Mund, Catherine the Great* (banned, along with her other films, by the Nazis in the 30's), *Paris Calling* (her only U.S. film), *Dreaming Lips, Stolen Life, Die Glucklichen Jahre der Thorwalds, Cry of the Banshee, The Pedestrian,* and *Escape,* directed by her husband Dr. Paul Czinner, for which she was nominated for an Academy Award in 1935. There are no survivors.

HERSCHEL BERNARDI, 62, New York-born film, stage, and TV actor, died in his sleep of a heart attack on May 9, 1986 at his home in Los Angeles, CA. A product of Yiddish theatre and Yiddish movies, he is perhaps best remembered for his long starring role in *Fiddler on the Roof,* on Broadway and on tour. His films include *Green Fields, Miss Susie Slagle's, Stakeout on Dope Street, Irma La Douce, Murder by Contract, A Cold Wind in August, The George Raft Story, Love with the Proper Stranger, The Honey Pot, The Savage Eye, Anyone for Venice . . .?, Almonds and Raisins,* and *The Front.* Bernardi is also familiar as the voice of the Jolly Green Giant and, for some 20 years, Charlie Tuna on the TV commercials. He is survived by his wife and their infant son, a son and daughter by a previous marriage, and two brothers, including actor Jack Bernardi.

| Gunnar Bjornstrand | Elisabeth Bergner | Adolph Caesar | James Cagney | Adolfo Celli | Jerry Colonna |

GUNNAR BJORNSTRAND, 76, distinguished Swedish character actor of screen and stage, died May 24, 1986 in Stockholm after a prolonged illness. He appeared in Ingmar Bergman films including *It Rains on Our Love, Sawdust and Tinsel, Smiles of a Summer Night, The Seventh Seal, Wild Strawberries, The Magician, Through a Glass Darkly, Persona, Shame, Autumn Sonata,* and *Fanny and Alexander.* He appeared in more than 140 other films, including *The False Millionaire, Panic, An Adventurer, Torment, The Pawnshop, Seventh Heaven, Pleasure Garden, My Love Is a Rose, Loving Couples, My Sister, My Love, Here's Your Life, The Sadist, Hagbard and Signe (The Red Mantle), Stimulantia,* and *Tabu.* He is survived by his wife and three children.

LEE BONNELL, 67, Indiana-born former film actor and husband of actress Gale Storm, died May 12, 1986 of a heart attack in Santa Monica, CA. His films include *Stranger on the Third Floor, The Saint in Palm Springs, Men Against the Sky, Let's Make Music, Lady Scarface, The Gay Falcon, Look Who's Laughing, Parachute Battalion, Father Takes a Wife, The Navy Comes Through, Army Surgeon, Jiggs and Maggie in Society,* and *Smart Woman.* He retired from the screen to establish an insurance agency which grew to become one of the largest in Southern CA. He is survived by his wife, three sons, and a daughter.

ALLEN BORETZ, 85, New York City-born screenwriter and playwright, died of cancer on May 21, 1986 in Branford, Ct. He was co-author with John Murray of the Broadway play *Room Service* which he adapted for the film starring the Marx Bros., and also as the musical film *Step Lively.* Among his other screenplays are *Copacabana, Where There's Life, Up in Arms, My Girl Tisa, Two Guys from Texas, It Had To Be You,* and *The Girl from Jones Beach.* He continued to write scripts and novels in the 50's despite being on the Hollywood "blacklist." Survived by his wife, two sons, a daughter, two stepsons and a sister.

HARRY BROWN, 69, Portland, ME-born novelist, poet, and Academy Award winning screenwriter, died of emphysema on Nov. 2, 1986 in Cedars-Sinai Medical Center in Los Angeles, CA. He wrote or co-wrote such films as *Arch of Triumph, Only the Valiant, The Virgin Queen, D-Day the Sixth of June, Many Rivers to Cross, Wake of the Red Witch, Sands of Iwo Jima, Kiss Tomorrow Goodbye, The Man on the Eiffel Tower, Ocean's 11,* and *A Place in the Sun,* for which he received his Oscar. He is survived by his wife and a son.

SUSAN CABOT-ROMAN, 59, Boston-born film actress, was beaten to death in the master bedroom of the Encino, CA home she shared with her son, 22 year-old Timothy Scott Roman. He was arrested and charged with the murder, on Dec. 10, 1986. She acted in numerous films including *Machine Gun Kelly, The Enforcer, Son of Ali Baba, Gunsmoke, Ride Clear of Diablo, The Wasp Woman, The Battle of Apache Pass, Flame of Araby, Tomahawk,* and *On the Isle of Samoa.* No other survivors reported.

ADOLPH CAESAR, 52, Harlem-born film and stage actor, died of an apparent heart attack on the set of the film *Tough Guys,* in Los Angeles, CA on March 6, 1986, after completing one day's filming. His films include *Che, The Hitter, Club Paradise, The Color Purple,* and *A Soldier's Story* for which he received an Academy Award nomination. Survived by his wife, three children, and a brother.

JAMES CAGNEY, 86, New York City-born actor, dancer, and quintessential tough guy who became one of Hollywood's greatest stars died March 30, 1986 at his Duchess County farm in Stanfordville, N.Y. He had been in declining health for several years, suffering from diabetes, heart and lung problems, and a circulatory ailment. Forever remembered as America's *Yankee Doodle Dandy* (winning an Oscar for his portrayal of George M. Cohan), his 65 films include *Sinner's Holiday, The Public Enemy, Blonde Crazy,*

Taxi!, The Crowd Roars, Winner Take All, Hard to Handle, Footlight Parade, Lady Killer, Jimmy the Gent, He Was Her Man, The St. Louis Kid, G-Men, A Midsummer Night's Dream, Frisco Kid, Boy Meets Girl, Angels with Dirty Faces (Oscar nomination), *Each Dawn I Die, The Roaring Twenties, The Fighting 69th, The Strawberry Blonde, The Bride Came C.O.D., Johnny Come Lately, Blood on the Sun, 13 Rue Madeleine, The Time of Your Life, White Heat, The West Point Story, What Price Glory, A Lion Is in the Streets, Love Me or Leave Me* (Oscar nomination), *Mister Roberts, The Seven Little Foys* (as Cohan again), *Tribute to a Bad Man, Man of a Thousand Faces,* and *Shake Hands with the Devil.* In 1960 Cagney retired from the screen for 20 years, returning in 1981 for *Ragtime,* and his last appearance in the 1984 TV film *Terrible Joe Moran.* His honors include a Kennedy Center Lifetime Achievement Award and he was the second recipient of the American Film Institute's Life Achievement Award. The Cagneys' adopted son, James Jr., died in 1985. He is survived by his wife, adopted daughter, brother and sister.

YAKIMA CANUTT, 90, Colfax, Wash.-born rodeo rider who became an actor, stuntman, and director in films, died May 24, 1986 of natural causes. Awarded a special oscar in 1966 "for creating the profession of stuntman" and the creation of safety devices used by stuntmen. A cowboy star in the 20's, his films include *Romance and Rustlers, Ridin' Mad, Westward Ho!, The Great Train Robbery, In Old Oklahoma, Stagecoach,* and *Gone With The Wind.* He directed such films as *Sheriff of Cimarron* and *Oklahoma Badlands,* and staged stunts for films including the spectacular chariot race in *Ben Hur.* Survived by his wife, son, brother and a sister.

ADOLFO CELI, 64, Italian actor and director, died on Feb. 19, 1986, two days after suffering a heart attack. His more than three dozen films include *Thunderball, The Agony and the Ecstasy, King of Hearts, That Man From Rio, Von Ryan's Express, Grand Prix, The Alibi* (co-director/co-author), *Murders in the Rue Morgue* (1971), *And Then There Were None, Amici Miei,* and he directed and acted in *The St. Petersburg Mysteries,* which premiered a few hours after his fatal heart attack. No reported survivors.

MAMO CLARK, 72, Honolulu-born actress who played opposite Clark Gable in *Mutiny On The Bounty,* died of cancer in Panorama City, CA on Dec. 18, 1986. She appeared in some 20 films, including *The Hurricane, Hawaii Calls, Air Devils, Booloo, Mutiny on the Blackhawk, One Million B.C.,* and *Girl from God's Country.* Survived by her husband, actor-teacher James Rawley, and a son.

WILLIAM (BUSTER) COLLIER, JR., 86, leading romantic film actor of the 20's whose New Year's Eve marriage to Ziegfeld girl Marie Stevens (with William Randolph Hearst as best man) made headlines, died Feb. 6, 1986 of cardiac arrest in San Francisco, CA. His films include *The Bugle Call, The Wanderer, Devil's Cargo, Lion and the Mouse, Donovan Affair, Bachelor Girl, Cimarron, Street Scene, Secret Witness, Little Caesar,* and *The People's Enemy.* He retired from the screen in 1935 and became an agent at the William Morris Agency. He is survived by his daughter and two grandchildren.

JERRY COLONNA, 82, Boston-born comic actor, died of kidney failure on Nov. 21, 1986 at the Motion Picture and Television Country House and Hospital in Woodland Hills, CA. Known for his trademark wide, rolling eyes, walrus mustache, and bellowing voice, his film appearances include *52nd Street, College Swing, Little Miss Broadway, Naughty But Nice, Comin' Round the Mountain, Sis Hopkins, Ice Capades, True to the Army, Priorities on Parade, Road to Singapore, Atlantic City, It's in the Bag, Kentucky Jubilee, Star-Spangled Rhythm, Road to Rio, Meet Me in Las Vegas, Andy Hardy Comes Home, Road to Hong Kong,* and *The Bob Hope Vietnam Christmas Show* (originally made for TV, released to theatres in 1966). Survived by his widow and son.

COLUCHE, 41, Paris-born comic actor, died in a motorcycle accident in the south of France on June 19, 1986. His films include *Le Pistonne, Inspecteur la Bavure, L'Aile ou la Cuisse, Le Maitre d'Ecole, Banzai, Vous n'Aurez pas l'Alsace et Lorraine* (director), *Les Veces Etaient Ferms de l'Interieur, My Best Friend's Girl, Le Vengeance du Serpent a Plumes, Dagobert, Le War Fool, Les Rois du Gag,* and *Tchao Pantin* for which he won a Cesar Award in 1983. Survived by his wife and two sons.

EDNA MAE COOPER, 85, silent screen actress who became well known as a pilot in the 30's and set the women's world refueling record, died June 27, 1986 in Woodland Hills, CA. Her films include, *The Folly of Vanity, Beauty and the Bad Man, Grounds for Divorce, Sally, Irene and Mary,* DeMille's *The King of Kings, Say It with Sables, Code of the Air,* and *George Washington Cohen.* She is survived by her husband, writer-director-cameraman Karl Brown.

HELEN CRAIG, 74, San Antonio-born film, stage, TV and radio actress, died of cardiac arrest on July 20, 1986. Film roles include *The Snake Pit, They Live by Night, The Sporting Club, Heroes, War and Peace* (dubbing the role of the countess for the U.S. release of the Russian film). Survived by her husband, actor John Beal, two daughters, a brother, and a sister.

BRODERICK CRAWFORD, 74, Philadelphia-born actor who won an Academy Award for *All The King's Men* in 1949, died April 26, 1986 in Rancho Mirage, CA. as a result of complications from a stroke. Known for his starring role in the TV series *Highway Patrol,* his films include *Beau Geste, Slightly Honorable, Butch Minds the Baby, Broadway, Sin Town, Black Angel, The Time of Your Life, Sealed Verdict, Anna Lucasta, Born Yesterday, The Mob, Down Three Dark Streets, Fellini's Il Bidone (The Swindle), New York Confidential, A House is Not a Home, The Oscar, Terror in the Wax Museum, The Private Files of J. Edgar Hoover, A Little Romance, Harlequin, There Goes the Bride, The Uppercrust,* and *Liar's Moon.* He is survived by his fourth wife and two sons.

SCATMAN CROTHERS (born Benjamin Sherman Crothers), 76, Indiana-born film, stage, and TV actor and musician, died of cancer on Nov. 22, 1986 at his home in Van Nuys, CA. His film credits include *Meet Me at the Fair, One Flew over the Cuckoo's Nest, The Shootist, Hello, Dolly!, Bronco Billy, The Shining,* and *Twilight Zone:The Movie.* Survived by his wife of 49 years and a daughter.

HOWARD DA SILVA, 76, Cleveland-born film, stage, and TV actor, director, producer and author, died on Feb. 16, 1986 of lymphoma at his home in Ossining, NY. Perhaps best known for his role of Benjamin Franklin in both the Broadway and film versions of the musical *1776,* his more than 40 film appearances include *Lost Weekend* and *Two Years before the Mast* (both winning him Academy Award nominations), *David and Lisa, Unconquered, They Live by Night, The Great Gatsby, Mommie Dearest,* and *Garbo Talks.* He won an Emmy Award in 1978 for his performance in the TV-film *Verna:U.S.O. Girl.* Survived by his wife, two sons, and three daughters.

CARMEN DeRUE, 78, silent screen actress and child star, died of a heart attack on Sept. 28, 1986 in North Hollywood, CA. Known as Baby DeRue, at age 5 she was cast in Cecil B. DeMille's 1913 *The Squaw Man,* the first feature shot in Hollywood. She appeared in roughly 200 films including the Franklin's Triangle Kiddies and Fox Kiddies series, *Masterminds, Carmen's Race for Life, Carmen's Wild Ride, Wash Day, Flirt, Broken Doll, Babes in the Woods,* and *The Girl with the Champagne Eyes.* She is survived by her son.

ROBERT DRIVAS, 50, Florida-born film, stage, and TV actor and director, died June 29, 1986 at the Memorial Sloan-Kettering Cancer Center in New York City. His films include *Cool Hand Luke, The Illustrated Man, Where It's At, Road Movie,* and *Crazy American Girl.* He is survived by his mother, a sister and two brothers.

VIVIAN DUNCAN, 84, who with her sister Rosetta performed as the Duncan Sisters, died Sept. 19, 1986 in Los Angeles, CA, after suffering from Alzheimer's disease for several years. The sisters reprised their famous stage roles in the 1927 film version of *Topsy and Eva,* and also appeared in *It's a Great Life.* She is survived by her daughter, a brother, And several grandchildren.

LEIF ERICKSON, 74, Alameda, CA-born film, stage and TV actor, died of cancer on Jan. 29, 1986 in Pensacola, FL. Perhaps best known as Big John Cannon in the 1967–71 *High Chaparral* TV series, his more than 75 films include *Conquest* (opposite Greta Garbo), *Big Broadcast of 1938, Nothing but the Truth, College Holiday, The Fleet's In, Pardon My Sarong, The Gay Intruders, Sorry, Wrong Number, Miss Tatlock's Millions, Joan of Arc, The Snake Pit, Johnny Stool Pigeon, Eagle Squadron, Show Boat, With a Song in My Heart, Carbine Williams, Invaders from Mars, On the Waterfront, Tea and Sympathy* (recreating his Broadway role), *The Young Lions, A Gathering of Eagles, The Carpetbaggers, Straight-Jacket, Mirage, Winterhawk,* and *Twilight's Last Gleaming.* He is survived by his wife and daughter.

EMILIO FERNANDEZ, 82, Coahuila, Mexico-born director writer, who was famous for having shot a film critic in a dispute, died of a heart attack Aug. 6, 1986 in Mexico City. He directed 42 films, winning international prizes for 16 of them, including *Maria Candelaria, Rio Escondido, Enamorado* (remade in 1950 as *The Torch* starring Paulette Goddard), and John Steinbeck's *The Pearl.* He acted in dozens of films, including *The Appaloosa, Return of the Seven, Lucky Lady,* and *Under the Volcano.* He is survived by his wife, actress Columba Dominquez.

MARTIN GABEL, 73, Philadelphia-born film and stage actor, producer, and director, died of a heart attack on May 22, 1986 in New York City. His films include *M, The Thief, Deadline U.S.A., Tip On a Dead Jockey, Marnie, Divorce American Style, Lord Love a Duck, Lady in Cement, Fourteen Hours, There Was a Crooked Mile, The Front Page* (remake), *The First Deadly Sin,* and he directed *The Lost Moment.* Survived by his wife, actress Arlene Francis, and a son.

VIRGINIA GILMORE, 66, El Monte, CA.-born film, stage, and TV actress, died March 28, 1986 of complications from emphysema in Santa Barbara, CA. Her more than 40 films include *Winter Carnival, Swamp Water, Wonder Man, Pride of the Yankees, Western Union, Manhattan Heartbeat, Orchestra Wives, Close-Up,* and *Walk East on Beacon.* She is survived by a son, Rock Brynner, by her former husband, actor Yul Brynner.

BENNY GOODMAN, 77, the King of Swing in the Big Band era, died of an apparent heart attack on June 13, 1986 at his NYC apartment. The famed clarinet playing bandleader appeared in films including *The Big Broadcast of 1937,* and *Hollywood Hotel,* and *The Benny Goodman Story,* a biographical film in which Steve Allen played Goodman, was made in 1955. He is survived by two daughters, four brothers, two sisters, and three stepdaughters.

CARY GRANT, 82, British-born actor and consummate leading man of the screen, died of a stroke on Nov. 29, 1986 in Davenport, Iowa where he had been scheduled to appear in his one-man show of film clips and reminiscences. One of the screens greatest stars, he appeared in 72 films including *This Is the Night, The Devil and the Deep, Blonde Venus, Madame Butterfly, She Done Him Wrong, The Eagle and the Hawk, I'm No Angel, Alice in Wonderland, Born to Be Bad, Enter Madam, Wings in the Dark, Sylvia Scarlett, Topper, Toast of New York, The Awful Truth, Bringing Up Baby, Holiday Gunga Din, Only Angels Have Wings, In Name Only, His Girl Friday, My Favorite Wife, The Howards of Virginia, The Philadelphia Story, Penny Serenade* (Academy Award nomination), *Suspicion, Talk of the Town, Mr. Lucky, Destination Tokyo, Once Upon a Time, None But the Lonely Heart* (Academy Award nomination), *Suspicion, Talk of the Town, Mr. Lucky, Destination Tokyo, Once Upon a Time, None But the Lonely Heart* (Academy Award nomination), *Arsenic and Old Lace, Night and Day, Notorious. The Bachelor and the Bobby-Soxer, The Bishop's Wife, Mr. Blandings Builds His Dream House, I Was a Male War Bride, Monkey Business, To Catch a Thief, An Affair To Remember, Kiss Them for Me, Indiscreet, Houseboat, North by Northwest, Operation Petticoat, That Touch of Mink, Charade, Father Goose,* and *Walk, Don't Run.* In 1970 he received a special Oscar, inscribed "to Cary Grant, for his unique mastery of the art of film acting". He is survived by his fifth wife, Barbara Harris, and his daughter, Jennifer, by a previous marriage.

VIRGINIA GREGG, 69, Harrisburg, Ill.-born film, radio, and TV actress, died of lung cancer on Sept. 15, 1986 in Encino, CA. Her films include *Body and Soul, Dragnet, Journey to Nowhere, Spencer's Mountain, I'll Cry Tomorrow, Operation Petticoat, Casbah, Love Is a Many Splendored Thing,* and she was the off-screen voice of Norman Bates' "mother" in *Psycho.* She is survived by her three sons.

| Broderick Crawford | Robert Drivas | Leif Erickson | Cary Grant | Elsa Lanchester | Bessie Love |

MURRAY HAMILTON, 63, film, stage, and TV actor, died of cancer on Sept. 1, 1986 in his native Washington, N.C. His films include *Bright Victory, The Whistle at Eaton Falls, Toward the Unknown, The Spirit of St. Louis, Jeanne Eagels, Darby's Rangers, Too Much, Too Soon, No Time for Sergeants, Houseboat, Anatomy of a Murder, The FBI Story, Tall Story, The Hustler, Papa's Delicate Condition, The Cardinal, An American Dream, Seconds, The Graduate, No Way to Treat a Lady, The Brotherhood, The Boston Strangler, If It's Tuesday, This Must Be Belgium, The Way We Were, Jaws, Jaws II, Casey's Shadow, The Amityville Horror, 1941, Brubaker, Hysterical,* and *Too Scared to Scream.* He won a Tony Award for his performance on Broadway in *Absence of a Cello* in 1964. Surviving are his wife, Terry, who was one of the DeMarco sisters, and son, actor David Hamilton.

STERLING HAYDEN, 70, Montclair, N.J.-born film actor and adventurer, died in his sleep, surrounded by his wife and children, at his home in Sausalito, CA. on May 23, 1986, after suffering from prostate cancer for over two years. His more than 50 films include *Virginia, Bahama Passage, The Asphalt Jungle, Flat Top, The Star, So Big, Johnny Guitar, Crime Wave, Prince Valiant, The Last Command, Crime of Passion, Zero Hour, The Killing, Dr. Strangelove, Loving, The Godfather, The Long Goodbye, 1900, King of the Gypsies, Winter Kills, The Outsider, Nine to Five, Venom,* and *Gas.* He was the subject of the acclaimed documentary *Pharos of Chaos* in 1983. Surviving are his wife and five children.

ROBERT HELPMANN, 77, Australian-born dancer who became an international ballet star and choreographer as well as a film actor and director, died on Sept. 28, 1986 in Sydney after a long illness. Best known for 1948's *The Red Shoes,* his other films include *Tales of Hoffmann, Chitty Chitty Bang Bang, One of Our Aircraft is Missing,* Olivier's *Henry V, Caravan, 55 Days at Peking, The Iron Petticoat, The Quiller Memorandum, The Big Money, The Soldier's Tale, Alice's Adventures in Wonderland, The Mango Tree, Patrick,* and he and Rudolf Nureyev both directed and starred in the film version of the ballet *Don Quixote.* He was knighted in 1968. No reported survivors.

TIM HERBERT, 71, film, stage, and TV actor-comedian, died of a heart attack on June 20, 1986 in Los Angeles, CA. His films include *A Guide for the Married Man, The Boston Strangler, Soylent Green, They Shoot Horses, Don't They?, Earthquake,* and *The Jazz Singer.* Survived by his wife, three sons and a brother.

DAVID HUFFMAN, 40, Illinois-born screen, TV and stage actor, was stabbed to death with a screwdriver on Feb. 27, 1985 in San Diego's Balboa Park where he was appearing at the Old Globe Theatre in the play "Of Mice and Men." His films include *F.I.S.T., Ice Castles, Honor Guard, The Onion Field, Leo and Loree, Blood Beach, St. Helens, Firefox,* and for TV *Pueblo, F. Scott Fitzgerald and the Last of the Belles, Gibbsville, Sandburg's Lincoln, Eleanor and Franklin, Captains and the Kings, Amelia Earhart, Testimony of Two Men, In the Matter of Karen Ann Quinlan, The Winds of Kitty Hawk, Sidney Shorr, Jane Doe, Sparkling Cyanide, When She Says No, Children in the Crossfire.* Surviving are his widow and two sons.

CHRISTOPHER ISHERWOOD, 81, Bisley, England-born author best known for his *Goodbye to Berlin* stories which served as the basis for the play and film *I Am a Camera* and the musical *Cabaret,* died of cancer on Jan. 4, 1986 at his home in Santa Monica, CA. He wrote many novels and short stories, as well as for stage and TV. His films include *The Sailor from Gibralter, The Loved One, Diane, I Am a Camera, The Great Sinner, Adventures in Baltimore, Forever and a Day,* and *Rage in Heaven.* He became a naturalized US citizen in 1946. He is survived by his longtime companion, artist Don Bachardy.

CLAIRE JAMES, 65, Minneapolis-born film and TV actress and first runnerup in the 1938 Miss America pageant who was crowned "the real Miss America" by Judge Earl Carroll, died Jan. 18, 1986 following a short illness in Woodland Hills, CA. Her films include *Forty Little Mothers, Gone With the Wind, The Ziegfeld Girl, Road to Singapore, Road to Utopia, I Wake Up Screaming, Coney Island, Good Sam* (billed as Carol Stevens), *Only the Valiant, Caprice,* and *The Sunshine Boys.* She is survived by a son, actor Blake James, and a brother, stuntman Roger James.

ELSA LANCHESTER, 84, British-born stage, film, and TV actress best known for her eccentric and comic roles died of bronchiopneumonia on Dec. 26, 1986 in Woodland Hills, CA. Frequently appearing opposite her husband, the late Charles Laughton, on stage and in her early films, her screen appearances include *Bluebottles, Day Dreams, The Cure, One of the Best, The Constant Nymph, The Private Life of Henry VIII, Naughty Marietta, David Copperfield, The Ghost Goes West, The Beachcomber, Ladies in Retirement, Tales of Manhattan, Forever and a Day, Lassie Come Home, The Spiral Staircase, The Bride of Frankenstein, The Razor's Edge, The Bishop's Wife, The Big Clock, The Inspector General, Les Miserables, Androcles and the Lion, The Glass Slipper, Bell, Book and Candle, Honeymoon Hotel, That Darn Cat, Me Natalie, Willard, Terror in the Wax Museum, Arnold, Mary Poppins, Blackbeard's Ghost, Murder by Death,* and *Die Laughing.* She was nominated for Academy Awards for *Come to the Stable* (1949) and *Witness for the Prosecution* (1958). There are no survivors.

ALAN JAY LERNER, 67, New York City-born lyricist, playwright, and screenwriter who formed with composer Frederick (Fritz) Loewe one of the legendary partnerships of the American musical theatre, died of lung cancer on June 14, 1986 in New York City. His screen credits include the successful film translation of Lerner & Loewe's stage hits *My Fair Lady, Camelot, Brigadoon, Paint Your Wagon,* and (written for the screen) *Gigi* (nine Academy Awards), as well as *On a Clear Day You Can See Forever* (with composer Burton Lane), and the screenplays for *Royal Wedding* and *An American in Paris.* He is survived by his wife, actress Liz Robertson, a son, and three daughters.

BESSIE LOVE, 87, Midland, TX-born film, stage, and TV actress, died April 26, 1986 in London of undisclosed causes. The silent screen star's some 120 film appearances include *Intolerance, The Good Bad Man, The Flying Torpedo, The Aryan, Nina the Flower Girl, The Enchanted Barn, Pegeen, The Swamp, Forget-Me-Not, Human Wreckage, The Eternal Three, St. Elmo, Slave of Desire, The Lost World, The King of Main Street, The Song and Dance Man, Dress Parade, Sally of the Scandals, Anybody Here Seen Kelly?, Matinee Idol, The Broadway Melody* (1929 Oscar nomination), *The Hollywood Revue of 1929, The Idle Rich, Chasing Rainbows, Good News, The Barefoot Contessa, Touch and Go, The Story of Esther Costello, The Roman Spring of Mrs. Stone, Children of the Damned, Promise Her Anything, Isadora, Sunday Bloody Sunday, The Ritz, Lady Chatterley's Lover, Ragtime, Reds,* and *The Hunger.* She is survived by her daughter.

HELEN MACK, 72, Rock Island, ILL-born film and stage actress who evolved from a child star in silents to a leading lady in talkies, died of cancer on Aug. 13, 1986 at the home of a friend, Aleen Leslie, with whom she lived in Beverly Hills, CA. Her films include *Zaza, Pied Piper Malone, Strange Holiday, My Girl Friday* (as Molly Malone), *Not So Long Ago, All of Me, Up the Ladder, Melody Cruise, The Last Train from Madrid, Gambling Ship,* and *Son of Kong.* She is survived by two sons.

| Gordon MacRae | Tim McIntire | Siobhan McKenna | Una Merkel | Ray Milland | Vincente Minnelli |

GORDON MacRAE, 64, East Orange, NJ-born film, stage, radio and TV actor and singer, immortalized by his screen portrayals of Curly in *Oklahoma* and Billy Bigelow in *Carousel*, died Jan 24, 1986 in Lincoln, Neb. He had been hospitalized since November with cancer of the mouth and jaw as well as pneumonia. His other film appearances include *The Big Punch, Look for the Silver Lining, Blackfire, The Daughter of Rosie O'Grady, Return of the Frontier-man, Tea for Two, The West Point Story, On Moonlight Bay, Starlift, About Face, By the Light of the Silvery Moon, Desert Song, Three Sailors and a Girl, The Best Things in Life Are Free,* and *The Pilot.* He is survived by his wife, their daughter, Amanda, and from his first marriage to actress Sheila MacRae two sons, actors-musicians Garr and Bruce, and two daughters, actresses Meredith and Heather.

HERBERT MAGIDSON, 79, Braddock, PA-born lyricist who shared the first Academy Award for best song with composer Con Conrad ("The Continental" from *The Gay Divorcee*), died Jan. 2, 1986 in Beverly Hills, CA. Also Oscar nominated for "Say a Prayer for the Boys Over There" (from *Hers to Hold*) and "I'll Buy That Dream" (from *Sing Your Way Home*), he was inducted into the Songwriters Hall of Fame in 1980. He is survived by his wife.

FRANK McCARTHY, 74, film producer and retired brigadier general whose 1970 film *Patton* won 7 Academy Awards, died Dec. 1, 1986 in Los Angeles, CA. He was technical advisor on *Brother Rat,* and he produced such films as *MacArthur, Decision Before Dawn, Sailor of the King, A Guide for the Married Man,* and *Fireball Forward.* His World War II honors include the Distinguished Service Medal and Legion of Merit, and Officer of the Most Excellent Order of the British Empire. Survived by two brothers.

TIM McINTIRE, 42, film and TV actor, musician, and composer, died of congestive heart failure April 15, 1986 at his home in Los Angeles, CA. His films include *American Hot Wax, The Gumball Rally, The Choirboys, Brubaker, Sacred Ground, Jeremiah Johnson* (for which he co-wrote and performed the songs), and *A Boy and His Dog* (as the voice of Blood the dog). He is survived by his wife, his parents (actor John McIntire and actress Jeanette Nolan), and a sister, Holly Wright.

SIOBHAN McKENNA, 63 or 64, Belfast-born film and stage actress, once described as "the greatest of Ireland's colleens," died Nov. 16, 1986 in Dublin of a heart attack following surgery for lung cancer. She was acclaimed for her New York portrayal of *Saint Joan* in 1956. Her films include *Hungry Hill, King of Kings, Of Human Bondage* (1964 remake), *Playboy of the Western World,* and *Doctor Zhivago.* Her husband of 22 years, actor Denis O'Dea, died in 1978. She is survived by their son, Donnacha O'Dea, and a sister.

IDA MAE McKENZIE, age unreported, film, stage, and TV actress, died June 29, 1986 in Los Angeles,CA. She and her sister Ella appeared as child actors in over 100 films with Charlie Chaplin, Ben Turpin, Bronco Billy, and Edna Purviance. As an adult she was in *International Squadron.* Surviving are two sisters, including Ella.

UNA MERKEL, 82, Covington, KY-born film and stage actress who appeared in more than 100 films and numerous plays, died Jan. 2, 1986 at her home in Los Angeles, CA. A 1953 Tony Award winner for *The Ponder Heart,* her many films include *The Fifth Horseman, Abraham Lincoln, The Bat Whispers, Command Performance, Maltese Falcon, Daddy Long Legs, Private Lives, Red-Headed Women, 42nd Street, Reunion in Vienna, Bombshell, The Merry Widow, Evelyn Prentice, Biography of a Bachelor Girl, Baby Face Harrington, Broadway Melody of 1936, It's in the Air, Riff-raff, Born to Dance, Saratoga, Test Pilot, Four Girls in White, Destry Rides Again, The Bank Dick, Road to Zanzibar, Mad Doctor of Market Street, This is the Army, With a Song in My Heart, I Love Melvin,* and *Summer and Smoke* (Academy Award nomination). There are no immediate survivors.

RAY MILLAND, 81, Wales-born film, stage, and TV actor died of cancer on March 10, 1986 in Torrance, CA. He won an Academy Award in 1945 for his memorable alcoholic in *The Lost Weekend* (as well as winning Best Actor honors from the New York Film Critics, Cannes Film Festival, and Foreign Language Press Film Critics of New York), Among his more than 170 films (he also directed several pictures) are *The Informer, The Flying Scotsman, The Bachelor Father, Just a Gigolo, Bought, Blonde Crazy, Polly of the Circus, Payment Deferred, Bolero, We're Not Dressing, Three Smart Girls, The Big Broadcast of 1937, Bulldog Drummond Escapes, Ebb Tide, Men With Wings, Hotel Imperial, Beau Geste, Everything Happens at Night, Irene, I Wanted Wings, Reap the Wild Wind, Are Husbands Necessary, The Major and the Minor, The Crystal Ball, Forever and a Day, Till We Meet Again, The Uninvited, Kitty, Golden Earrings, It Happens Every Spring, A Life of Her Own, Circle of Danger, Jamaica Run, Dial M for Murder, The Girl in the Red Velvet Swing, Panic in the Year Zero, Hostile Witness* (directing himself), *The River's Edge, Premature Burial, Terror in the Wax Museum, Love Story, Gold, Escape to Witch Mountain, The Last Tycoon, Oil, Oliver's Story, Battlestar Galactica, Survival Run,* and *The Sea Serpent.* He is survived by his wife, and a daughter.

VINCENTE MINNELLI, 83, Chicago-born Academy Award winning film and stage director and designer, died July 25, 1986 in his sleep at home in Beverly Hills, CA. One of the foremost cinematic stylists of his era, he began his career on Broadway as a set and costume designer, then director, before moving to films. During his almost 26 years under contract to MGM his films include *Cabin in the Sky* (from his Broadway success), *I Dood It, Meet Me In St.Louis, The Clock, Ziegfeld Follies, Till the Clouds Roll By* (Garland sequence), *The Pirate, Yolanda and the Thief, Undercurrent, Father of the Bride, Father's Little Dividend, An American in Paris, The Bad and the Beautiful, The Band Wagon, The Long, Long Trailer, Brigadoon, The Cobweb, Kismet, Lust for Life, Tea and Sympathy, Designing Woman, The Seventh Sin, Gigi* (9 Oscars including Best Picture and Best Director), *The Reluctant Debutante, Some Came Running, Home from the Hill, Bells are Ringing, The Four Horsemen of the Apocalypse, Two Weeks in Another Town, The Courtship of Eddie's Father, Goodbye Charlie, The Sandpiper, On a Clear Day You Can See Forever,* and *A Matter of Time* starring daughter Liza Minnelli (by former wife Judy Garland). Surviving are his fourth wife, and his two daughters, Liza and Christiana Nina Minnelli, from his second marriage.

DAME ANNA NEAGLE, 81, British-born film and stage actress, and first lady of the English screen from the late 30's through the early 50's, died June 3, 1986 at a nursing home in Surrey. She made 32 films with her husband, the late director-producer Herbert Wilcox, representing one of the longest continuing collaborations in screen history. Those films include *The Little Damozel, Bitter Sweet, The Queen's Affair, Nell Gwyn, Peg of Old Drury, Limelight, The Three Maxims, London Melody, Victoria the Great, Sixty Glorious Years, Nurse Edith Cavell, Irene, No, No, Nannette, Sunny, They Flew Alone, Forever and a Day, The Yellow Canary, I Live in Grosvenor Square, Piccadilly Incident, The Courtneys of Curzon Street, Spring in Park Lane* (the most successful British film ever made), *Elizabeth of Ladymean, Maytime in Mayfair, Odette, The Lady With a Lamp,* and *The Lady Is a Square.* She also produced *These Dangerous Years, Wonderful Things,* and *The Heart of a Man.* There are no survivors.

Anna
Neagle

Lilli
Palmer

Otto
Preminger

Donna
Reed

Kate
Smith

Charles
Starrett

LILLI PALMER, 71, Posen, Germany-born film, stage, and TV actress and author, died of cancer Jan 27, 1986 at her home in Los Angeles, Ca. Her films include *Crime Unlimited, First Offense, Secret Agent, Sunset in Vienna, Command Performance, Crackerjack, Montparnasse 19, But Not for Me, Conspiracy of Hearts, The Pleasure of His Company, The Counterfeit Traitor, And So to Bed, Miracle of the White Stallions, Operation Crossbow, Notorious Gentleman (The Rake's Progress), Cloak and Dagger, Body and Soul, The Four Poster* (Best Actress Award 1953 Venice Film Festival), *The Amorous Adventures of Moll Flanders, Sebastian, Oedipus the King, Hard Contract, DeSade, The House that Screamed, Murders in the Rue Morgue, Lotte in Weimar, The Boys from Brazil, The Holcroft Covenant,* and her final role as the mother of *Peter the Great* in the NBC-TV miniseries. She is survived by her husband, Carlos Thompson, an Argentine author and actor, a son, and two sisters.

JERRY PARIS, 60, film and TV director, producer, and actor who won an Emmy as director for *The Dick Van Dyke Show*, died of complications from a brain tumor on March 31, 1986 in Los Angeles, CA. He appeared in the films *Outrage, Cyrano de Bergerac, Call Me Mister, The Wild One, The Caine Mutiny, Marty, The View from Pompey's Head, Good Morning, Miss Dove, D-Day, The Sixth of June, Zero Hour, The Lady Takes a Flyer, The Naked and the Dead,* and *The Great Imposter.* He co-wrote/associate produced *The Caretakers,* directed *Don't Raise the Bridge-Lower the River!, Never a Dull Moment, How Sweet It Is!, Viva Max!, The Grasshopper,* and *Star Spangled Girl.* He directed and acted in *Leo and Loree,* and directed *Police Academy 2-Their First Assignment,* and *Police Academy 3-Back in Training.* He is survived by two sons, a daughter and two sisters.

OTTO PREMINGER, 79 or 80, Austrian-born film and stage director, producer, and actor, and controversial film genius who fought censorship all the way to the Supreme Court, died of cancer April 23, 1986 at his apartment in New York City. One of the best known and most recognizable directors of his time, his films include *Die Grosse Liebe, Under Your Spell, Danger-Love at Work, Laura* (considered his masterpiece and for which he received an Oscar nomination), *Fallen Angel, Whirlpool, Where the Sidewalk Ends, The Thirteenth Letter, A Royal Scandal, That Lady in Ermine, Centennial Summer, Daisy Kenyon, The Fan, Forever Amber, Angel Face, The Moon is Blue, River of No Return, The Court-Martial of Billy Mitchell, The Man With the Golden Arm, Saint Joan, Bonjour Tristesse, Porgy and Bess, Anatomy of a Murder* (Oscar nomination), *Exodus, Advise and Consent, The Cardinal* (Oscar nomination), *In Harm's Way, Bunny Lake Is Missing, Hurry Sundown, Skidoo, Tell Me That You Love Me, Junie Moon, Such Good Friends, Rosebud,* and his last film,*The Human Factor.* He also acted in *The Pied Piper, They Got Me Covered, Margin for Error,* and *Stalag 17.* He is survived by his wife, their twin son and daughter, another son, Erik (by the late Gypsy Rose Lee), and brother Ingo, a producer.

DONNA REED, 64, Denison, Iowa-born film and TV actress who won an Academy Award for *From Here to Eternity* in 1953, died Jan. 14, 1986 from complications from pancreatic cancer at her home in Beverly Hills, CA. She was perhaps best known as the quintessential mother and wife of middle America on TV's *Donna Reed Show* in the 50's and 60's. Among her more than 40 films are (billed as Donna Adams in her earlier films) *The Get-Away, Shadow of the Thin Man, Babes on Broadway, The Courtship of Andy Hardy, The Human Comedy, Calling Dr. Gillespie, Eyes in the Night, Thousands Cheer, See Here, Private Hargrove, Mrs. Parkington, The Picture of Dorian Gray, They Were Expendable, It's a Wonderful Life, Green Dolphin Street, Beyond Glory, Chicago Deadline,*

Saturday's Hero, Scandal Sheet, Hangman's Knot, Raiders of the Seven Seas, Trouble Along the Way, The Caddy, Gun Fury, The Last Time I Saw Paris, They Rode West, The Far Horizons, Ransom!, The Benny Goodman Story, Backlash, Beyond Mombasa, The Whole Truth, and *Pepe.* Her last role was Miss Ellie on TV's *Dallas,* temporarily replacing Barbara Bel Geddes. She is survived by her husband, two daughters and two sons.

HARRY RITZ, 78, the youngest and last surviving member of the Ritz Brothers comedy team of film and stage, died of pneumonia March 29, 1986 at his home in San Diego, CA. He appeared with his brothers in 15 films, including *Sing, Baby, Sing, One in a Million, The Three Musketeers, Kentucky Moonshine, The Goldwyn Follies,* and he appeared without them in his last film, *Silent Movie.* He is survived by his wife, six children, and a sister.

KATE SMITH, 79, Greenville, VA-born singer, film, radio, and TV personality, best known for her powerful rendition of *God Bless America,* died June 17, 1986 at her home in Raleigh, NC. She virtually dominated radio of the 30's and 40's and had more than 700 of her 2,200 recording make the Hit Parade. She became a success on TV with the first major daytime TV program on a network. Her films include *Hello, Everybody!* and *This is the Army.* She is survived by her sister and two nieces.

CHARLES STARRETT, 82, Athol, Mass-born cowboy film star, best known for his role as The Durango Kid in 66 films, died March 22, 1986 of cancer in Borrego Springs, CA. One of the 17 founders of SAG, his films include *The Quarterback, Fast and Loose, The Royal Family of Broadway, Damaged Love, Touchdown, The Mask of Fu Manchu, Mr. Skitch, Our Betters, One in a Million, Shooting Showdown, Two-Gun Law, Spoilers of the Range, Two-Fisted Rangers, Thundering Frontier, The Medico of Painted Springs, Bad Men of the Hills, Overland to Deadwood, Fighting Buckaroo, Pardon my Gun,* and *Rough Tough West.* He is survived by his wife and two sons.

ROBERT STEVENSON, 81, England-born director died April 30 after a long illness in Santa Barbara, CA. According to *Variety* in 1977 he was "the most commercially successful director of all time" having a record 17 films (all for Disney) on the all-time b.o. hit list. His films include *Happy Ever After, Falling for You, Jack of All Trades, Nine Days a Queen* (also screenwriter), *The Man Who Lived Again (The Man Who Changed His Mind), King Solomon's Mines, Non-Stop New York, Return to Yesterday, Tom Brown's Schooldays, Back Street, Joan of Paris, Forever and a Day, Jane Eyre, Dishonored Lady, To the Ends of the Earth, I Married a Communist (The Woman on Pier 13), The Las Vegas Story, Johnny Tremain, Old Yeller, Darby O'Gill and the Little People, Kidnapped, The Absent-Minded Professor, In Search of the Castaways, The Misadventures of Merlin Jones, Mary Poppins* (Oscar nomination, winner of 5 Academy Awards), *The Monkey's Uncle, That Darn Cat, The Gnome-Mobile, Blackbeard's Ghost, The Love Bug, Bedknobs and Broomsticks, Herbie Rides Again, The Island at the Top of the World, One of Our Dinosaurs is Missing,* and *The Shaggy D.A..* He is survived by his third wife, a son and daughter.

PAUL STEWART, 77, New York City-born film, stage, radio, and TV actor, died of heart failure Feb. 17, 1986 in Los Angeles, CA. A member of Orson Welles' Mercury Theatre Group in 1938, his more than 50 films include *Citizen Kane, Mr. Lucky, Twelve O'Clock High, The Greatest Story Ever Told, In Cold Blood, Opening Night, Revenge of the Pink Panther,* and *A Child is Waiting.* He also appeared in or directed some 5,000 radio and TV shows. He is survived by his wife, former singer Peg LaCentra.

| Blanche Sweet | Forrest Tucker | Lurene Tuttle | Rudy Vallee | Hal B. Wallace | Keenan Wynn |

NIGEL STOCK, 66, Malta-born veteran character actor of films, stage, radio, and TV, died June 23, 1986 in London, apparently of a heart attack. His more than 40 films include *The Lion in Winter*, *Cromwell*, *Seven Men at Daybreak*, *Dam Busters*, *Brighton Rock*, *The Lost Continent*, *The Nelson Affair*, *Russian Roulette*, *Eye Witness*, and *Young Sherlock Holmes*. He is perhaps best known for his role of Dr. Watson in the BBC-TV series *Sherlock Holmes*. He is survived by his wife and three children.

BLANCHE SWEET, 90, Chicago-born silent screen star, who rose to fame in D. W. Griffith films died Sept. 6, 1986 of a stroke at her home in NYC. After her debut at age 12, she made 124 movies, including *The Man with Three Wives*, *A Corner in Wheat*, *The Lonedale Operator*, *The Goddess of Sagebrush Gulch*, *The Painted Lady*, *Judith of Bethulia*, *Anna Christie*, *Tess of the D'Urbervilles*, *Always Together*, *The Woman Racket*, and *The Silver Horde*. She left films for the theatre for 29 years, returning in 1959's *The Five Pennies*, and two documentaries: *Portrait of Blanche* and *Before the Nickelodeon*. She is survived by her brother-in-law.

FORREST TUCKER, 67, Plainfield, IND-born film, stage, and TV actor, died of cancer Oct. 25, 1986 in Woodland Hills, CA. Probably best known for his role as Sgt. Morgan O'Rourke in the 60's TV series *F Troop*, his more than 50 films include *The Westerner*, *Emergency Landing*, *New Wine*, *Keeper of the Flame*, *Renegades*, *The Yearling*, *The Sands of Iwo Jima*, *Oh Susanna!*, *Fighting Coast Guard*, *Warpath*, *The Wild Blue Yonder*, *Hoodlum Empire*, *Montana Belle*, *Pony Express*, *Laughing Anne*, *Jubilee Trail*, *Stagecoach to Fury*, *The Abominable Snowman*, *Three Violent People*, *Auntie Mame*, *Fort Massacre*, *Counterplot*, *The Night They Raided Minsky's*, *Chisum*, *Barquero*, *Cancel My Reservation*, *The Wild McCullochs*, *The Wackiest Wagon Train in the West*, *Final Chapter-Walking Tall*, *Carnauba (A Rare Breed)*, *Thunder Run*, and *Outtakes*. He is survived by his third wife, two daughters, a son, a sister, and his mother.

LORENZO TUCKER, 79, Philadelphia-born film and stage actor known as "the colored Valentino" in all-black films of the 20's and 30's, died Aug. 19, 1986 of cancer in Hollywood, CA. His some 20 films, through 1948, include *Wages of Sin*, *When Men Betray*, *A Daughter of the Congo*, *Harlem After Midnight*, *The Black King*, *Harlem Big Show*, *Temptation*, *Veiled Aristocrats*, *Reet, Petite and Gone*, and *The Emperor Jones*. He is survived by his widow.

LURENE TUTTLE, 79, film, stage, radio, and TV actress, died May 28, 1986 of an undisclosed illness in Encino, CA. Best known as "the first lady of radio" from the 30's through the 50's, her films include *Heaven Only Knows*, *Macbeth*, *Mr. Blandings Builds His Dream House*, *Don't Bother to Knock*, *Niagara*, *The Affairs of Dobie Gillis*, *Goodbye, My Fancy*, *Sweet Smell of Success*, *Psycho*, *The Fortune Cookie*, *Ma Barker's Killer Brood*, *Testament*, and all three installments in the *Walking Tall* series. She is survived by her grandchildren Jennifer Gruska, a story editor, Mark Williams, a drummer and actor, and Joseph Williams, a composer and singer.

RUDY VALLEE, 84, Island Point, VT-born film, stage, radio, TV and recording crooner of the 30's and 40's, famed for his handheld megaphone, died July 3, 1986 of a heart attack at his home in North Hollywood, CA. while watching the Statue of Liberty centennial salute on TV. The *"My Time is Your Time"* singer's films include *The Vagabond Lover*, *Sweet Music*, *The Palm Beach Story*, *Happy Go Lucky*, *Man Alive*, *It's in the Bag*, *People Are Funny*, *My Dear Secretary*, *The Fabulous Suzanne*, *The Bachelor and the Bobby Soxer*, *I Remember Mama*, *Father Was a Fullback*, *The Beautiful Blonde from Bashful Bend*, *Mother Is a Freshman*, *The Admiral Was a Lady*, *Ricochet Romance*, *Gentlemen Marry Brunettes*, *The Helen

Morgan Story, *Glorifying the American Girl*, *International House*, *George White's Scandals* (1934), *Gold Diggers in Paris*, *Time Out for Rhythm*, *Too Many Blondes*, *Mad Wednesday*, *So This Is New York*, *Second Fiddle*, *Unfaithfully Yours*, *Live a Little Love a Little*, *The Night They Raided Minsky's*, *The Phynx*, *Sunburst*, *Won Ton Ton*, *The Dog Who Saved Hollywood*, *The Perfect Woman*, and the 1984 music video *"Girls Talk."* He is perhaps best known for his role as J. B. Biggley in *How To Succeed in Business Without Really Trying*, both on stage and screen. Married four times, but had no children. His fourth wife survives.

HERBERT VIGRAN, 76, veteran character actor of films, stage, and TV, died in Los Angeles, Ca., of cancer on Nov. 29, 1986. His films include *Bedtime for Bonzo*, *It All Came True*, *Murder by Invitation*, *Night into Morning*, *Just for You*, *Susan Slept Here*, *The Midnight Story*, *Cancel My Reservation*, *First Monday in October*, and *The Shaggy D.A.* No reported survivors.

HAL WALLIS, 88, Chicago-born producer, co-producer, or production supervisor of more than 400 films, died in his sleep Oct. 5, 1986 at his home in Rancho Mirage, CA. He was the executive and/or producer for such films as *Little Caesar*, *I Am a Fugitive from a Chain Gang*, *Gold Diggers of 1933*, *Captain Blood*, *The Charge of the Light Brigade*, *Jezebel*, *The Adventures of Robin Hood*, *The Roaring Twenties*, *High Sierra*, *Sergeant York*, *Yankee Doodle Dandy*, *Air Force*, *Casablanca*, *Gunfight at the O.K. Corral*, *The Dawn Patrol*, *Five Star Final*, *Sally*, *Mystery of the Wax Museum*, *Dangerous*, *A Midsummer Night's Dream*, *The Story of Louis Pasteur*, *Anthony Adverse*, *Footlight Parade*, *G-Men*, *Green Pastures*, *Kid Galahad*, *The Life of Emile Zola*, *Tovarich*, *Four Daughters*, *The Private Lives of Elizabeth and Essex*, *The Old Maid*, *The Story of Dr. Ehrlich's Magic Bullet*, *All This and Heaven Too*, *The Sea Hawk*, *They Drive by Night*, *The Sea Wolf*, *The Letter*, *The Strawberry Blonde*, *The Bride Came C.O.D.*, *The Maltese Falcon*, *They Died with Their Boots On*, *The Man Who Came to Dinner*, *King's Row*, *The Male Animal*, *Watch on the Rhine*, *Love Letters*, *The Strange Love of Martha Ivers*, *I Walk Alone*, *So Evil My Love*, *Sorry, Wrong Number*, *September Affair*, *My Friend Irma*, *Come Back Little Sheba*, *The Rose Tattoo*, *About Mrs. Leslie*, *The Rainmaker*, *Loving You*, *Summer and Smoke*, *Boeing Boeing*, *The Sons of Katie Elder*, *Barefoot in the Park*, *True Grit*, *Anne of the Thousand Days*, *Red Sky at Morning*, *Mary, Queen of Scots*, *The Public Eye*, *The Nelson Affair*, and *Rooster Cogburn*. 130 of his films earned Academy Award nominations, and 32 of them won Oscars. He was twice awarded the Irving Thalberg Award, in '38 and '43. He is survived by his wife, actress Martha Hyer, and a son, Brent.

KEENAN WYNN, 70, New York City-born film, stage, and TV actor, died of cancer Oct. 14, 1986 at his home in Brentwood, CA. One of Hollywood's most versatile supporting actors, he appeared in more than 220 films, 250 TV shows, and 100 stage productions. His films include *Northwest Rangers*, *See Here Private Hargrove*, *For Me and My Gal*, *Lost Angel*, *Since You Went Away*, *The Clock*, *Ziegfeld Follies*, *Son of the Thin Man*, *The Three Musketeers*, *Neptune's Daughter*, *Annie Get Your Gun*, *Royal Wedding*, *Kiss Me Kate*, *The Long Long Trailer*, *All the Brothers Were Valiant*, *The Man in the Gray Flannel Suit*, *The Great Man*, *Some Came Running*, *Hole in the Head*, *King of the Roaring Twenties*, *The Absent-Minded Professor*, *Dr. Strangelove*, *The Patsy*, *The Americanization of Emily*, *Stagecoach*, *Point Blank*, *Finian's Rainbow*, *Once Upon a Time in the West*, *Loving*, *The Mechanic*, *Herbie Rides Again*, *Nashville*, *The Shaggy D.A.*, *Best Friends*, *Hyper Sapien:People from Another Star*, and *Black Moon Rising*. He is survived by his second wife, two sons, two daughters and four grandchildren, including actor Aidan Keenan.

244

245

249

251

256

257

259

260

261

267

269

von Manteuffel, Felix, 204
von Martius, Katharina, 204
Von Sass, Benita, 122
von Sydow, Max, 16, 234
von Verschuer, Leopold, 204
Von Wernherr, Otto, 132
Von Wright, Victor, 139
von zur Muhlen, Bengt, 212
von zur Muhlen, Irmgard, 212
Vonnegut, Kurt, Jr., 42
Vorgan, Gig, 74
Vorstman, Frans, 142
Vosburgh, Tilly, 211
Vosgitel, Ethel, 141
Voss, Phillip, 162, 215
Votel, Jeanette, 177
Votel, Wendy, 177
Votsou, Stella, 142
Vujisic, Pavle, 211
Vuollo, Marjo, 134
Vuosalmi, Piita, 134
Wach, Volker, 182
Wachs, Robert D., 112
Wachsberger, Patrick, 142
Wachtel, Brooks, 29
Waddington, Rona, 137
Wade, Brian, 90, 134
Wager, Dianne, 36, 127
Wagerman, Heath, 55
Wagner, Bruce, 135
Wagner, Chuck, 126
Wagner, David, 139
Wagner, Jerald F., 179
Wagner, Kathy, 40, 115
Wagner, Lindsay, 234
Wagner, Richard, 48
Wagner, Robert, 234
Wagner, Roy, 116
Wagner, Sabine, 212
Wagrowski, Gregory, 12, 119
Wahing, Veino, 215
Wahl, Ken, 234
Wai, Lo, 208
Waite, Genevieve, 234
Waite, Ric, 36
Waites, Thomas G., 114
Waits, Tom, 76
Wakefield, Rebecca, 98
Wakefield, Stan M., 143
Wakeling, John, 141
Walas, Chris, 65
Walcutt, John, 117
Wald, Robby, 121
Wald, Robert, 61
Wald, Stephen L., 32
Waldeitner, Luggi, 204
Waldie, Margaret, 210
Waldman, Harvey, 84
Waldrip, Tim, 117
Waldron, De, 143
Waletzky, Josh, 138
Walken, Christopher, 128, 234
Walker, Amanda, 172
Walker, Ann, 86
Walker, Christopher, 27
Walker, Chuck, 126
Walker, Clare, 208
Walker, Clint, 234
Walker, Giles, 192
Walker, Graham (Grace), 190
Walker, Greg, 50, 118
Walker, Hank, 216
Walker, Heather, 206
Walker, Jimmie, 125, 138
Walker, John Thomas, 27
Walker, Junior, 104
Walker, Kerry, 168
Walker, Lesley, 168, 177, 180, 211
Walker, Michelle, 92
Walker, Nancy, 234
Walker, Paul, 116
Walker, Roy, 101
Walker, Sari, 78
Walker, Scott, 128
Walker, Shirley, 74, 119
Walker, Sullivan, 190
Wall, James E., 143
Wall, Richard, 66
Wall, Robert, 93
Wall, The, 181
Wallace, Bill, 122, 138
Wallace, Dee, 80, 146
Wallace, Edgar, 110
Wallace, George D., 23
Wallace, Hal B., 242
Wallace, Loraine, 97
Wallace, Phyllis, 85
Wallace, Rosalie, 145
Wallace, Royce, 15
Wallace, Tim, 120
Wallace, Tommy, 89
Wallace, William, 19, 126
Wallace-Stone, Dee, 80
Wallach, Eli, 87, 234
Wallach, Roberta, 138, 234
Wallenstein, Karl, 217
Waller, David, 162
Wallis, Hal, 242
Wallis, Rit, 208
Wallis, Shani, 60, 234
Wallner, Jack, 143
Walmsley, Craig, 203
Walsh, Christopher, 205
Walsh, Eileen, 186
Walsh, J. T., 12, 16, 129
Walsh, M. Emmet, 8, 15, 42, 125, 234
Walsh, Mandy, 177
Walsh, Richard, 134
Walsh, Rob, 131
Walsh, Thomas A., 117
Walston, Ray, 122, 234
Walter and June aka *Loving Walter*, 210
Walter, Harriet, 165
Walter, Jessica, 234
Walter, Laurel, 144
Walter, Richard, 33
Walter, Rita, 122
Walter, Tracey, 83, 128
Walters, Julie, 183
Walters, Martin, 127, 133, 134
Walters, Rupert, 192
Waltezky, Josh, 138
Walthall, Wade, 98
Waltman, Alan (Norg), 115
Walton, Cedar, 189
Walton, Chutney, 71
Walton, Emma, 71, 133, 234
Walton, Fred, 120
Walton, Lee-Max, 208
Walton, Tony, 59
Walton, Willie J., 15
Waltz, Lisa, 102
Walzer, Irene, 145
Wanamaker, Sam, 50, 234
Wands, Alan J., 210
Wang, Peter, 36
Wang, Ronald Z., 128
Wanger, Leslie, 119
Warbeck, David, 216
Ward, B. J., 121
Ward, Burt, 234
Ward, David S., 133
Ward, David, 115
Ward, Fred, 234
Ward, Geoffrey C., 119
Ward, Jeff, 144
Ward, Kirby, 121
Ward, Lyman, 38
Ward, Mary B., 142
Ward, Olivia, 51
Ward, Rachel, 234
Ward, Sela, 54
Ward, Simon, 234
Ward, Stan, 119
Ward, Tom, 27, 111
Ward, Wally, 86, 210
Ward, Wayne, 146
Ward-Jackson, Nicholas, 211
Wardell, Fred, 132
Warden, Jack, 234
Wardlow, John, 114, 120
Wardlow, Keith, 114
Ware, Ralph, 141
Warfield, Marlene, 127
Warfield, Marsha, 133
Warhit, Doug, 142
Warlock, Richard, 119
Warnecke, Gordon, 170, 171
Warner, Brian, 109
Warner, David, 234
Warner, Mark, 64
Warner, Martin Charles, 134
Warner, Pamela B., 121
Warren, Jason, 116
Warren, Jennifer, 235
Warren, Joyce, 129
Warren, Lesley Ann, 235
Warren, Linda, 135
Warren, Marcia, 175
Warren, Michael, 235
Warren, Tom, 102
Warren, Tony, 22
Warrick, Ruth, 235
Warschilka, Edward, 31, 64
Wartes, Burleigh, 212
Washbourne, Mona, 235
Washington, Dennis, 53
Washington, Denzel, 12, 235
Washington, John, 128
Washington, Ludie C., 127
Wasley, Charlie, 116
Wass, Ted, 115
Wasson, Craig, 74, 77, 235
Wasyliw, Mitzi, 116
Watanabe, Gedde, 56
Watanabe, George, 121
Watchurst, Neville, 192
Water, 125
Waterbury, Laura, 135
Waters, Andre, 124
Waters, Chuck, 112
Waters, John, 83
Waters, Lila, 136
Waterston, Sam, 16, 23, 235
Watkins, David, 136, 137, 214
Watkins, Johnny L., 30
Watkins, Leonard, 69
Watkins, Marcia, 22
Watkins, Robin, 136
Watkins, William, 128
Watling, Jack, 235
Watson, Donald, 135
Watson, Douglass, 26, 235
Watson, Loraine, 142
Watson, Woody, 130
Watters, George, II, 130
Watts, Miranda, 210
Watts, Roy, 146
Waugh, Fred, 128
Waver, Bernard, 131
Waxman, Al, 137
Waxman, Michael, 135
Way It Is, The, 126
Way, Ann, 60, 215
Wayne, David, 235
Wayne, Ken, 208
Wayne, Patrick, 235
We Were So Beloved, 136
Weagle, Cynthia, 114
Weagle, Stephen, 114
Weatherhead, Chris, 122
Weatherly, Shawn, 22
Weathers, Carl, 235
Weaver, Courtland, 98
Weaver, Deane, 124
Weaver, Dennis, 235
Weaver, Fritz, 12
Weaver, Kathie, 131, 137
Weaver, Kenneth, 123
Weaver, Lee, 15
Weaver, Malcolm, 62
Weaver, Marjorie, 235
Weaver, Sigourney, 6, 62, 63, 94, 235
Webb, Chloe, 195
Webb, Chris, 62
Webb, David, 120
Webb, Gordon A., 15, 112
Webb, Jim, 10, 51
Webb, Leigh, 14
Webb, Robert, 138
Webb, Roger, 208
Webb, Sandy, 212
Webber, Arthur, Jr., 216
Webber, Deborah, 15
Webber, Robert, 204, 235
Webber, Timothy, 205
Weber, Billy, 34
Weber, Charles J., 121
Weber, Jacques, 185
Weber, Pedro, 213
Webster, Daniel, 128
Webster, Harry, 186
Webster, Lynn, 24
Webster, Paul Francis, 105
Wedding, The, 167
Weddle, Vernon, 36
Wedgeworth, Ann, 74, 77, 235
Weekend Warriors, 140
Weeks, Alan, 102
Weeks, Christopher, 117
Weeks, Doug, 124
Weeks, Jimmy Ray, 52, 110
Weeks, Michelle, 101
Wegener, Sabine, 182
Wei-Han, Yang, 208
Wei-Hui, Mao, 169
Wei-Yen, Yu, 208
Weigang, Rudiger, 212
Weigel, Herman, 73
Weil, Cynthia, 100
Weil, Samuel, 146
Wein, Dean, 127
Weinbren, Grahame, 36
Weincke, Jan, 186
Weindler, Helge, 182
Weiner, Hal, 118
Weiner, Marilyn, 118
Weinlein, Thad, 100
Weinstein, Bob, 142
Weinstein, David Z., 64
Weinstein, Harvey, 142
Weinstein, Henry T., 92
Weinstein, Vickie, 142
Weinstock, Gerry, 19
Weintraub, Bruce, 23
Weintraub, Carl, 145
Weintraub, Jerry, 44
Weir, Arabella, 206
Weir, Peter, 96
Weiser, Norbert, 139
Weiser, Shari, 43
Weisgerber, Eleonore, 217
Weiskopf, Hermann, 174
Weisman, Neal, 85
Weisman, Orit, 145
Weiss, Chuck, 117
Weiss, Dannielle J., 48
Weiss, Fredda, 8
Weiss, JoAnne, 150
Weiss, Joel, 119
Weiss, Julie, 20
Weist, Dwight, 18, 73
Welbeck, Peter, 133
Welch, Bo, 31
Welch, Eric, 56
Welch, Fred, 202
Welch, James, 138
Welch, Julie, 164
Welch, Kevin, 128
Welch, Lynetta, 130
Welch, Raquel, 235
Welcome to 18, 145
Weld, Tuesday, 235
Weldon, Joan, 235
Welker, Calvert L., 84
Welker, Frank, 47, 112, 121, 136
Weller, Elly, 142
Weller, Peter, 235
Welles, Gwen, 25, 74, 97, 235
Welles, Mel, 120
Welles, Orson, 136
Welles, T. G., 137
Wells, Adrian, 47
Wells, Cheri, 127
Wells, David, 134
Wells, Mary, 135
Wells, Patrick, 116
Welsh, Kenneth, 59
Weltman, Stu, 139
Welz, Peter, 73
Wen, E. N., 36
Wendt, George, 114, 121
Wener, Michael, 137
Wenger, Cliff, 15, 22, 112
Wenger, Clifford, Sr., 210
Wenk, Richard, 56
Werba, Amy, 211
Wertheim, Allan, 55
Wertheimer, Robert, 212
Wescott, Anne, 98
Wesley, Billy, 133
Wesley, John, 82
Wesley, Richard, 146
Weslow, William, 52
West, Adam, 126
West, Brian, 94
West, Charles, 24
West, Donald, 22
West, Kit, 95
West, Leslie, 26
West, Paul, 24
West, Wendy, 146
Westbrook, Darrin, 124
Westcott, Carol, 132
Westerdale, Donald J., 120
Westfall, Mathew, 150
Westhead, Victoria, 66
Westley, Bill, 124, 198
Westley, Kevin, 175
Westlund, Chris, 52
Westmore, Michael, 57, 114
Weston, Bill, 62
Weston, Jack, 115, 122, 235
Weston, Ken, 96, 206
Weston, Paul, 62
Weston, Stan, 124
Westover, Richard E., 117, 139
Westover, Rick, 143
Wetherell, Dean, 159
Wexler, Haskell, 119
Wexler, Howard, 136
Wexler, Jeff, 27
Wexler, Jerry, 127
Wexler, Milton, 71
Wexler, Norman, 50
Wexley, John, 158
Weyermans, Francois, 216
Whaley, George, 168
Whalley, Joanne, 186
Wharton, Richard, 46
Wharton, Wally, 126
What Comes Around, 128
What Happened to Kerouac?, 120
Whatever It Takes, 122
Wheat, Belle Maria, 146
Wheater, Mac, 95
Wheatley, Ken, 176
Wheaton, Wil, 53
Wheeler, Bob, 216
Wheeler, Charles F., 8
Wheeler, Ira, 16
Wheeler, John W., 47
Whelan, Gil, 62
Whelpton, Gerry, 122
Where Are the Children, 146
Where the River Runs Black, 81
Whinery, Webster, 18
Whinnery, Barbara, 114
Whipp, Joseph, 146
Whipple, Kay H., 46
Whipple, Sam, 130
Whipple, Shonda, 132
Whitaker, Albie, 61
Whitaker, Christina, 122
Whitaker, Forest, 150
Whitaker, Harvey, 146
Whitaker, Johnny, 235
Whitcher, Patricia, 120
Whitchurch, Philip, 94
White, Al, 9, 33
White, Amy, 92
White, Andrew, 52
White, Betty, 235
White, Carol, 235
White, Carole Ita, 122
White, Cary, 136, 141
White, Charles, 235
White, David, 215
White, Dennis, 115
White, Diz, 131
White, Douglas J., 144
White, Ed, 58, 108, 140, 144
White, Edward, 120
White, Erik, 146
White, Gerry, 186
White, Jason, 62
White, Jesse, 116, 235
White, Joniruth, 137
White, Karla, 137
White, Kerryann, 170
White, King, 135
White, Lauren, 132
White, Maurice, 134
White, Michael, 43, 132
White, Scott, 122, 133, 140
White, Stephanie, 116
White, Sylvia, 98
White, Terry, 47
White, Timothy, 182
Whitecloud, John P., 40
Whitehead, Michael, 137
Whitehead, Paxton, 42, 88
Whitehouse, Max, 92
Whitford, Peter, 212
Whiting, Richard, 41
Whitlock, Tom, 34
Whitlow, Jill, 133, 210
Whitman, Elizabeth, 146
Whitman, John, 116
Whitman, Peter, 101
Whitman, Stuart, 235
Whitmire, Steve, 43
Whitmore, James, 14, 235
Whitney, Grace Lee, 90, 235
Whitrow, Benjamin, 163, 215
Whittaker, Forrest, 151
Whittaker, Ian, 56, 122
Whittle, Miranda, 38
Whittle, Peter, 133
Whitton, Margaret, 8, 18, 235
Whitworth, Dean, 110
Who, Garry, 212
Whoopee Boys, The, 133
Whyhowski, Hugo Luczyc, 170
Whyle, James, 203
Wibom, Anna-Lena, 201
Wicket, W. W., 47
Wickham, Jeffrey, 215
Wicki, Bernhard, 209
Wicking, Christopher, 176
Wickman, Karl, 36
Widdoes, Kathleen, 235
Widen, Gregory, 122
Widmark, Richard, 235
Wiebe, Linda, 166
Wiebe, Lisa, 166
Wiedlin, Jane, 90
Wieland, Ute, 182
Wiener, Charles, 141
Wiener, Jack, 20
Wiertz, Lex, 142
Wiessenhaan, Harry, 142
Wiest, Dianne, 16, 17, 155, 235
Wigand, Thomas, 205
Wiggins, Chris, 206
Wiggins, Jimmy, 110
Wiggins, Les, 95
Wiik, Oystein, 206
Wilber, Bob, 102
Wilborn, Chuck, 52
Wilbur, George, 40, 50
Wilcots, Joe, 127
Wilcox, Colin, 235
Wilcox, Peter M., 138
Wilcox, Shannon, 51, 139
Wild Geese II, 204
Wild Kingdom, The, 124
Wild, Christopher, 214
Wild, Susan, 202
Wildcats, 15
Wilde, Cornel, 235
Wilde, Wilbur, 212
Wilder, David, 119
Wilder, Gene, 60, 235
Wilder, Scott, 26
Wildes, Warren Skip, 126
Wildman, John, 166
Wildman, Valerie, 21, 133
Wildsmith, Dawn, 139
Wiley, Edward, 60, 101, 122
Wiley, Ethan, 114
Wilfong, Christina, 119
Wilhite, Thomas L., 98
Wilhoite, Benji, 143
Wilhoite, Kathleen, 29, 111
Wilkens, Gary, 168
Wilkerson, Don, 120
Wilkes, Elaine, 117, 131, 133
Wilkes, Jack, 144
Wilkey, Jim, 36
Wilkins, Eric, 67
Wilkins, Gary, 190
Wilkins, Jeremy, 109
Wilkinson, Elizabeth, 124
Wilkinson, Geoff, 120
Wilkinson, June, 132, 139
Wilkinson, Robert, 215
Wilkinson, Tom, 163
Wilkus, Patti, 121
Will, Clark, 205
Willaidom, Gerald, 146
Willard, Jean, 106
Willard, Ralph, 141
Willette, Jo Ann, 145
Williams, Allen, 146
Williams, Andrew, 212
Williams, Anthony, 126
Williams, Barbara, 127
Williams, Bernard, 108, 135
Williams, Bert, 29, 36
Williams, Billy Dee, 235
Williams, Billy, 52
Williams, Caroline, 130, 136
Williams, Chino "Fats", 15, 88, 115
Williams, Cindy, 235
Williams, Clarence, III, 92
Williams, David S., Jr., 140
Williams, Dean, 186
Williams, Diana, 143
Williams, Dick A., 235
Williams, Doris Sherman, 150
Williams, Dwight, 143
Williams, Ed, 142
Williams, Emlyn, 235
Williams, Eric Austin, 141
Williams, Esther, 235
Williams, Ian Patrick, 118
Williams, Jason, 10
Williams, JoBeth, 30, 40, 235
Williams, John, 47
Williams, Kevin, 13
Williams, Larry, 46, 47
Williams, Matt, 53
Williams, Michael, 127
Williams, Pat, 135
Williams, Patrick, 23, 31
Williams, Peter, 94, 204
Williams, R. J., 52
Williams, Ray, 176
Williams, Robin, 8, 132, 235